JIMMY SWAGGART
BIBLE
COMMENTARY

I John
II John
III John
Jude

JIMMY SWAGGART BIBLE COMMENTARY

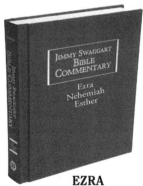

Jimmy Swaggart Bible Commentary

I John
II John
III John
Jude

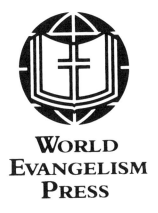

WORLD
EVANGELISM
PRESS

ISBN 978-1-934655-20-7
11-089 • COPYRIGHT © 2002 World Evangelism Press®
P.O. Box 262550 • Baton Rouge, Louisiana 70826-2550
Website: www.jsm.org • Email: info@jsm.org • (225) 768-7000
15 16 17 18 19 20 21 22 23 24 25 26 / RRD / 17 16 15 14 13 12 11 10 9 8 7 6 5 4 3

Jimmy Swaggart
Bible
Commentary

I John
II John
III John
Jude

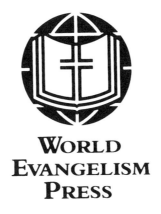

World
Evangelism
Press

ISBN 978-1-934655-20-7
11-089 • COPYRIGHT © 2002 World Evangelism Press®
P.O. Box 262550 • Baton Rouge, Louisiana 70826-2550
Website: www.jsm.org • Email: info@jsm.org • (225) 768-7000
15 16 17 18 19 20 21 22 23 24 25 26 / RRD / 17 16 15 14 13 12 11 10 9 8 7 6 5 4 3

TABLE OF CONTENTS

■

THE
BOOK OF I JOHN

◼

THE INTRODUCTION TO THE FIRST EPISTLE OF JOHN THE APOSTLE

John was the Son of Zebedee, probably the younger son, for except in Luke and Acts he is mentioned after his brother James. Luke gives the order Peter, John, and James, probably because in the early days of the Church John was closely associated with Peter (Lk. 8:51; 9:28; Acts 1:13).

That John's mother's name was Salome is an inference from Mark 16:1 and Matthew 27:56; for the third woman who is said to have accompanied the two Mary's to the tomb is designated Salome by Mark, and *"the mother of Zebedee's children"* by Matthew. Salome is usually regarded as the sister of Mary the Mother of Jesus, because in John 19:25 four women are said to have stood near the Cross, the two Mary's mentioned in Mark and Matthew, the Mother of Jesus, and His Mother's sister. If this identification is correct, John was a cousin of Jesus on his Mother's side.

His parents would appear to have been well-to-do, for his father, a fisherman, had *"hired servants"* (Mk. 1:20); and Salome was one of the women who *"provided for Jesus out of their means"* (Lk. 8:3; Mk. 15:40).

After their subsequent call by Jesus to leave their father and their fishing (Mk. 1:19-20), James and John were nicknamed by Him *"Boanerges,"* which means *"sons of thunder"* (Mk. 3:17), probably because they were high-spirited, impetuous Galileans, whose zeal was undisciplined and sometimes misdirected (Lk. 9:49).

On three important occasions in the earthly Ministry of Jesus, John is mentioned in company with his brother James and Simon

Peter, to the exclusion of the other Apostles: at the raising of Jairus' daughter (Mk. 5:37), at the Transfiguration (Mk. 9:2), and in the Garden of Gethsemane (Mk. 14:33); and, according to Luke, Peter, and John were the two Disciples sent by Jesus to make preparations for the final Passover meal (Lk. 22:8).

John is not mentioned by name in the Fourth Gospel (though the sons of Zebedee are referred to in Jn. 21:2), but he is almost certainly the Disciple called *"the Disciple whom Jesus loved,"* who lay close to the breast of Jesus at the Last Supper (Jn. 13:23); who was entrusted with the care of His Mother at the time of the Death of Christ (Jn. 19:26-27); who ran with Peter to the tomb on the first Easter morning and was the first to see the full significance of the undisturbed grave clothes with no body inside them (Jn. 20:2, 8); and who was present when the risen Christ revealed Himself to the seven of His Disciples by the Sea of Tiberius.

THE DEATH OF JOHN

Polycrates, who was the Pastor of the Church at Ephesus in A.D. 190, said that John *"who reclined on the Lord's breast,"* after being *"a witness and a teacher"* (note the order of the words), *"fell asleep at Ephesus."*

According to Irenaeus, it was at Ephesus that John *"gave out"* the Gospel, and confuted the heretics, refusing to remain under the same roof as Cerinthus, *"the enemy of truth"*; at Ephesus that he lingered on *"till the days of Trajan,"* who reigned in A.D. 98-117.

Jerome also repeats the tradition that John tarried at Ephesus to extreme old age, and records that, when John had to be carried to the Christian meetings, he used to

1

repeat again and again *"little children, love one another."*

THE PURPOSE OF I JOHN

This Epistle, it seems was called forth by the activities of false teachers who had seceded from the Church (or Churches) to which John is writing and who were attempting to seduce the faithful (I Jn. 2:18, 26). They formed a particular group, believing that they had superior knowledge to the ordinary Christians (I Jn. 2:20, 27; II Jn. vs. 9) and as well, showing little love.

They were the forerunners of the later heretics generally known as *"Gnostics,"* and claimed a special knowledge of God and of theology.

On the basis of their new doctrine they appear to have denied that Jesus was the Christ (I Jn. 2:22), the preexistent (I Jn. 1:1) Son of God (I Jn. 4:15; 5:5, 10), in the flesh (I Jn. 4:2; II Jn. vs. 7) to provide Salvation for men (I Jn. 4:9, 14). But the precise form from which this heresy took is uncertain.

The false teachers further claimed that they were *"sinless"* (I Jn. 1:8, 10) and possibly also that they did not need Redemption through the Death of Jesus Christ, while they were in fact morally indifferent, following the ways of the world (I Jn. 2:15), ignoring the Commandments of Christ (I Jn. 2:4), and freely doing what they pleased (without, however, indulging it seems, in gross sin).

They did not seem to realize that sin is a moral category, i.e., *"lawlessness"* (I Jn. 3:4, 7), and consequently they felt quite consistent in claiming sinlessness while indulging in selfishness and lack of love.

THE DATE OF THIS EPISTLE

The fact that the First Epistle of John was written by the Apostle John and by no one else is beyond serious question. This Letter is an Epistle that is intended for the congregations that were under John's special care; it was occasioned by the anti-Christian teachings of Cerinthus and of his following.

It is obvious that the same pen that wrote this Letter wrote the Fourth Gospel as well. Before the year 66, John and other Apostles were forced to leave Jerusalem because of the war that ended with the destruction of

Jerusalem and the Jewish nation. John made Ephesus his headquarters and worked from this as a center until he died at an advanced age about the year 100. He was buried at Ephesus.

Although no date is certain, some believe that John wrote this First Epistle at about the year 90. He writes as an old man. He does not indicate that he is the founder of the congregations addressed in his letter but that he has been known to them for many years and that a tender bond of affection exists between him and all his many readers. Sometimes he referred to them as *"little children,"* twice he addresses them as *"children,"* six times as *"beloved."* This is the voice of a father.

As well, it is almost certain that he wrote from Ephesus.

As is known, Paul established the Church at Ephesus; consequently, the Gospel that John preached and stood for, was actually the same as that of Paul.

THE CROSS

As in our previous Volume on James, I Peter, and II Peter, I will take every opportunity to open up the meaning of the Cross. How can I do less! Even though the meaning of the New Covenant wasn't given to John but rather to Paul, still, everything that John wrote complemented what the great Apostle said. Inasmuch as all he wrote was inspired by the Holy Spirit, it could be no other way.

It is February 19, 2001, as I begin work on this particular Commentary as it regards the First Epistle of the Apostle John. If the Lord helps us, and which I know that He shall, then it will be a blessing to you.

"Thy Word is a lamp unto my feet, and a light unto my path" (Ps. 119:105).

"Born among cattle, in poverty sore,
"Living in meekness by Galilee's shore,
"Dying in shame as the wicked one
    swore:
"Jesus wonderful Lord!"

"Weary yet He is the world's only rest,
"Hungry and thirsty with plenty has
    blest,
"Tempted He promises grace for each
    test:
"Jesus, wonderful Lord!"

*"Friend of the friendless betrayed and
    denied,*
"Help of the weak in Gethsemane cried,
*"Light of the world in gross darkness
    He died:*
"Jesus, wonderful Lord!"

CHAPTER 1

(1) "THAT WHICH WAS FROM THE BE-
GINNING, WHICH WE HAVE HEARD,
WHICH WE HAVE SEEN WITH OUR EYES,
WHICH WE HAVE LOOKED UPON, AND
OUR HANDS HAVE HANDLED, OF THE
WORD OF LIFE;"

The composite is:

1. John speaks of Jesus Christ, and He is
from everlasting.

2. He had the privilege of hearing Him
for some three and one half years; consequently, his information is firsthand.

3. Not only did he hear Him, but also he
saw Him with his eyes, and looked upon His
Person, regarding all that He did.

4. Not only did he hear Him, see Him, but
as well, he touched Him, and did so many times.

5. The One He heard, looked upon, and
handled, was the *"Word of Life,"* i.e., *"Living Word."*

FROM THE BEGINNING

The phrase, *"That which was from the beginning,"* relates exclusively to the Lord Jesus
Christ. Jesus Christ is God, and as God, He
had no beginning, so John refers to the beginning of created things. That is, when all
creation came into existence, our Lord was
in existence. Since He antedated all creation,
He must be uncreated. Since He is uncreated,
He must be without beginning and, therefore, Deity.

In His Gospel, John reaches back into the
eternity before the universe was brought into
existence to speak of the Lord Jesus as in fellowship with the Father, and as the Light that
shone through the darkness of sin through
His creative acts (Jn. 1:1-10).

In this, his first Epistle, he goes back only
to the time when the created universe came
into existence, and speaks of that which was

NOTES

true concerning Him since that time and
until His Incarnation (*"that which was in the
beginning,"* which would include the things
true of Him mentioned in John 1:1-10), and
then in the words *"which we have heard,
which we have looked upon, and as our hands
have handled,"* he speaks of His Incarnation,
as he does also in John 1:11-14 and on
through the entire Gospel (Wuest).

As we read these words of John, we must
read historically with the eyes of the first Readers. We will then see the full significance of
every line as it appears before us. Every repetition is freighted with power. All the phrases
combine in a mighty basic unit that is im-
pressive, convincing, uplifting, encouraging
the Readers to stand solid in the Divine fellowship against any little antichrists who may
have appeared (I Jn. 2:18).

The voice is that of John; it is the same
voice that testifies in the Fourth Gospel. The
simplest words convey the deepest, the loftiest thoughts.

As John writes, we learn that Jesus Christ
cannot be separated from what He was and
is for us. Both belong together like the Sun
and its glorious light. The theme of this Letter is the same as that of the Gospel: the
Eternal Son Incarnate for our life and Salvation to the confounding of all pretenders.

When John uses the word *"beginning,"* as
in his Gospel, he begins with the grandeur
of an indefiniteness beyond which no eye can
pierce: At the beginning of all that concerns
us, be it world or universe or all creation,
there was — that which we are announcing.
It is not merely the Person of Christ which
he is going to declare, but also His Being,
all that relates to Him, His Gospel, the treasures of wisdom that lay in Him, His Truth,
all that could be known about Him by humanity (Ellicott).

FALSE DOCTRINE

Westcott said that John wrote his Gospel
to prove the Deity of our Lord, assuming His
humanity, whereas he wrote his first Epistle
to prove His humanity, assuming His Deity.
In the words, *"which we have heard, which
we have seen with our eyes, which we have
looked upon, and our hands have handled,"*
he is maintaining the real humanity of our

Lord against its denial by a certain group in the Church at that time. These were the Gnostics. There were two groups among them, each with a different take on the Person of our Lord. Without going into detail, both denied the physical Person of Christ, claiming that had He actually had a physical body, He could not have been God. They taught that all matter was evil. Consequently, they denied the Incarnation, *"God becoming man,"* and as such, they denied the Cross as well as having any validity.

As someone has well said, *"man has a tendency to make too little of Christ and too much of man."*

One of the leaders of this false way was a man by the name of Cerinthus who lived at Ephesus. John strenuously controverted this man's error.

Irenaeus and Eusebius quote a story of Polycarp's that the Apostle once visited the public baths, and seeing Cerinthus within, sprang out of the building. *"Let us flee,"* he cried, *"lest the building fall, since Cerinthus, the foe of Truth, is within it."* And to be sure, all through this Epistle, he has this heresy in view.

The modern *"Word of Faith"* teaching is not totally unlike the error which John refuted. While this modern teaching does not deny the Incarnation of Christ, it in effect, does deny the Cross. It teaches that the Cross was merely incidental, with one of its bright lights openly stating that the *"Blood of Jesus Christ didn't atone for anything,"* or words to that effect (Kenneth Copeland).

They teach that the Death of Christ on the Cross was insignificant. They actually claim that any *"born again"* Believer could die on a Cross and accomplish the same thing as did Christ. This can be construed as none other than blasphemy.

They claim that Jesus on the Cross took upon Himself the nature of Satan. In other words, He did not merely suffer as a *"Sin-Offering,"* but actually became a sinner. As a sinner, they teach, He went to Hell, as all sinners do upon death.

In Hell, He suffered the pangs and horror of one without God, and at the end of three days and nights, God then said, *"It is enough."* At that point, they teach, Jesus was then

NOTES

"born again," just as any sinner is Born-Again, and was raised from the dead.

In fact, they really do not have much point of contact as it regards Faith in anything that Christ did regarding the Atonement, but if there is any point of contact, it would be faith, as they teach it, in His three days and nights of suffering in Hell and then being Born-Again and raised from the dead. As stated, they place no significance whatsoever in the Cross, referring to it as *"the greatest defeat in human history."*

Their teaching on faith, which they do constantly, is more *"faith in faith,"* than anything else. They claim it's *"faith in the Word,"* but it's more a perverted Word, which means it's the Word as they want it to be, instead of as it actually is.

This false gospel, and false it is, has done more to hurt the modern Pentecostal and Charismatic Church than anything else. It has almost *"gutted"* the Charismatic Church, with the *"Word of Faith"* being its basic doctrine. Of course, there are exceptions to that, but for the most part I think, the Charismatic world is strongly influenced by this false message.

As John was bitterly opposed to the Gnostics of his time, we must as well be bitterly opposed to any message presently which falsifies in any way, the Person of our Lord and His atoning Work on the Cross.

WE HAVE HEARD

The phrase, *"Which we have heard,"* proclaims the fact that John was with the Savior through the whole of His Ministry, and he has recorded more of what the Savior said than either of the other Evangelists. It is on what He said of Himself that he grounds much of the evidence that He was the Son of God. So in effect, John is saying that one can believe what he heard Christ say, plus Who Christ was, which was proven by the tremendous miracles which He accomplished and carried out, or one could believe these doubters with their self-instituted doctrines.

THE TRUE AND THE FALSE

Going back to the First Century, how could anyone of that particular time hear John the Beloved, who was with the Lord for some three and one half years, and at the same time, prefer one of these false teachers?

The answer to that question is no doubt many and varied. Many people accept things, as they are impressed to accept them. In other words, many people are impressed by outward appearances, by what is popular or unpopular, by the crowd, etc., and they thereby, accept that upon perception alone.

And as well, all false doctrine is empowered by demon spirits. Paul referred to them as *"seducing spirits, and doctrines of devils"* (I Tim. 4:1).

Peter referred to the same as, *"damnable heresies"* (II Pet. 2:1).

It is my contention that if the modern Believer, which would go as well for all Believers for all time, doesn't properly understand the Cross, he is an open target for false doctrine. In fact, if a Believer doesn't properly understand the Cross, he is already into false doctrine of some nature. That's the reason so many accept the *"Word of Faith"* philosophy, because they do not understand the Cross. The same could go for any other type of false doctrine.

HAVE SEEN WITH OUR EYES

The phrase, *"Which we have seen with our eyes,"* means that John saw what Christ was as a man; how He appeared on Earth; and he is in effect saying, *"I have seen whatever there was in His works to indicate His character and origin."* John professes here to have seen enough in this respect as to furnish evidence that Christ was the Son of God. It is not hearsay on which he relies, but rather the testimony of his own eyes in the case.

John in effect is saying, *"we beheld His Glory as of the Only-Begotten from the Father, full of Grace and Truth"* (Jn. 1:14).

WE HAVE LOOKED UPON

The phrase, *"Which we have looked upon,"* means that which he saw was more than a passing glance. It was a *"gazing with a purpose."* It was a *"seeing with desire."* In other words, he looked hard, and he looked hard to see. He looked at the miracles; he looked at the healings; he looked at all the astounding things that were done. And in this *"looking"* he could find nothing wrong,

nothing amiss, and nothing out of the way. It is like someone putting something under a microscope in order to inspect it minutely.

OUR HANDS HAVE HANDLED

The phrase, *"And our hands have handled,"* refers to the fact that Christ was human. John touched His hands, His feet, His physical body, His Person, and there was no doubt that Jesus Christ was human.

In effect, John is saying that this false teacher by the name of Cerinthus and his supporters are not witnesses. They have not heard, seen, beheld, or touched anything as it pertains to Christ. All they have are their made up stories, with which they can use flowery words, attempting to contradict what the Apostles had seen with their own eyes, and felt with their own hands.

How foolish were these followers of this false teacher. And to be sure, such a teacher had to have many followers, or he would not have rated the attention of John the Beloved, and more specifically, the Holy Spirit.

THE WORD OF LIFE

The phrase, *"Of the Word of Life,"* actually says in the Greek, *"The Word of the Life."* It is not just any general idea of life here, but the particular life that God is and which was revealed in concrete form in the humanity of our Lord. This is the Second Person of the Godhead Who is called *"The Word"* because He is the complete and final Revelator of the will and the thought of God. He is called *"Faithful and True"* (Rev. 19:11). *"And His Name is called 'The Word* (logos) *of God'"* (Rev. 19:13). He is also called the *"Amen, the Faithful and True Witness"* (Rev. 3:14).

As John declares Jesus to be the *"Word"* (Jn. 1:1), he also says that this *"Word was made flesh, and dwelt among us"* (Jn. 1:14).

And then he records the words of John the Baptist concerning Christ: *"Behold the Lamb of God, which taketh away the sin of the world"* (Jn. 1:29).

In other words, this eternal Logos came to this world specifically for one purpose, and that was to go to the Cross in order that man might be redeemed.

Considering what John has said in this First Verse, can Cerinthus or can any of the antichrists (I Jn. 2:18) offer counterwitness? What have they heard, seen, beheld, handled? Nothing. They have absolutely nothing to offer but their own imaginations and delusions. That is true to this day with regard to all who deny the Deity of Jesus, the efficacy of His shed Blood for our sins, etc.

The case is plain even for people who have only common sense and ordinary judgment: on the one side, competent witnesses in solid array — on the other, no witnesses at all, nothing but perverted men who with brazen boldness contradict the most complete testimony. John gives them the right name. He calls them *"liars,"* and *"antichrists"* (I Jn. 2:22).

LIFE

John uses the word *"Life,"* as it refers to Christ, because Christ is the Source of all life. Jesus said of Himself: *"I am the Way, the Truth, and the Life: no man cometh unto the Father, but by Me"* (Jn. 14:6).

This means that Christ not only has *"Life,"* but in reality *"is Life."* As stated, He is the Source of all Life, and by that we speak of *"spiritual life,"* which is in a sense, from which all other life flows.

We know that He has and is *"Life,"* but the great question is, *"how does He impart this Life to us, who within ourselves, have no life?"*

THE CROSS, THE MANNER IN WHICH LIFE IS IMPARTED

The idea as John makes his statements is, the Incarnation, God becoming man, i.e., *"flesh,"* in no way negated or abbreviated the Life which He has as God. This *"Life"* was just as present in Him as the human Jesus, as it was before His Incarnation.

The very purpose and reason for the Incarnation, was that this Life might be imparted to mankind. Due to man's terrible crime and sin against God, God could not by fiat or decree, issue life to man, who is spiritually dead. Life must be issued on the basis of justice satisfied, and the only way that justice could be satisfied, was for God to become man, and thereby pay the debt which man owed but could not pay, and do so by offering up Himself as a Sacrifice on the Cross. By the pouring out of His Life's Blood, which

incidentally was Perfect, which means it was not stained by Adam's Fall, all due to the Virgin birth, and the fact that Jesus never sinned, He thereby paid the price.

So, the only manner and way in which the Life which Christ is and which Christ has, can be imparted to believing sinners, is through the Cross. The Cross must ever stand at the apex of God's dealings with humanity. Except by the Cross, a thrice-Holy God could not have even looked at man, much less have fellowship with him. Except for the Cross, man has no access to God whatsoever, and if he attempts to come any other way, he is judged by God as a *"thief and robber"* (Jn. 10:1).

LOGOS

The word *"Logos* (Word)*"* was already in use among the Greeks before John used it. It was used to denote the principle which maintains order in the world.

In connection with the Greek word for *"seed"* in its adjective form, it was used to express the generative principle or creative force in nature. The term was familiar to Greek philosophy. Thus, the word being already in use, among the Hebrews in a Biblical way, and among the Greeks in a speculative and rather hazy, undefined way, John now proceeds to unfold the true nature of the *"Logos,"* Jesus Christ.

Godet said: *"To those Hellenists and Hellenistic Jews, on the one hand, who were vainly philosophizing on the relations of the finite and infinite; to those investigators of the letter of the Scriptures, on the other, who speculated about the theocratic revelations, John said, by giving this name 'Logos' to Jesus: 'The unknown Mediator between God and the world, the knowledge of Whom you are striving after, we have seen, heard, and touched. Your philosophical speculations and your scriptural subtleties will never raise you to Him. Believe as we do in Jesus, and you will possess in Him that Divine Revealer Who engages your thoughts'."*

Vincent says: *"As 'Logos' has the double meaning of 'thought' and 'speech,' so Christ is related to God as the word to the idea, the word being not merely a 'name' for the idea, but the idea itself expressed."*

Austin said: *"The name 'Word' is most excellently given to our Savior; for it expresses His nature in one, more than any others. Therefore John, when he names the Person in the Trinity (I Jn. 5:7), chooses rather to call Him 'Word' than 'Son;' for 'Word' is a phrase more communicable than 'Son.' 'Son' has only reference to the 'Father' Who begot Him; but 'Word' may refer to Him Who 'conceives' it; to Him Who 'speaks' it; to that which is spoken by it; to the voice that it is clad in; and to the effects it raises in Him who hears it."*

So Christ, as He is *"The Word,"* not only refers to His Father Who begot Him, and from Whom He comes forth, but to all the creatures that were made by Him; to the flesh that He took to clothe Him; and to the Doctrine He brought and taught, and which lives yet in the hearts of all them who obediently do hear it.

He is *"This Word"*; and any other, Prophet or Preacher, is but a voice (Lk. 3:4).

"Word" is an inward conception of the mind; and *"voice"* is but a sign of intention. John was but a sign, a voice; not worthy to untie the shoes of this *"Word."* Christ is the inner conception *"in the bosom of His Father"*; and that is properly *"The Word."*

And yet the *"Word"* is the intention uttered forth, as well as conceived within; for Christ was no less *"The Word"* in the womb of the Virgin, or in the cradle of the manger, or on the Altar of the Cross, than He was in the beginning, *"in the bosom of His Father."*

For as the intention departs not from the mind when the word is uttered, so Christ, proceeding from the Father by eternal generation, and after here by Birth and Incarnation, remains still in Him and with Him in essence; as the intention, which is conceived and born in the mind, remains still with it and in it, though the word be spoken. He is, therefore, rightly called *"The Word,"* both by His coming from, and yet remaining still in, the Father (Wuest).

(2) "(FOR THE LIFE WAS MANIFESTED, AND WE HAVE SEEN IT, AND BEAR WITNESS, AND SHOW UNTO YOU THAT ETERNAL LIFE, WHICH WAS WITH THE FATHER, AND WAS MANIFESTED UNTO US;)"

The structure is:

1. This *"Life"* which Christ is, was not hidden, but rather manifested.

2. It was made visible to the human race through the humanity of our Lord, and John says, *"We have seen it."*

3. John further says, we can testify to this fact, i.e., *"bear witness."*

4. This *"Life"* which Christ is and has, is *"eternal."*

5. This *"Life,"* i.e., *"the Logos,"* was *"with the Father,"* which means that the same essence which the Father is, the Son is as well. Since this life is *"eternal,"* which means, *"without beginning,"* it, therefore, must be uncreated, thus, Deity in its essence.

6. This glorious wonderful life was made visible to us, and as well, given to us.

THE MANIFESTATION OF LIFE

The phrase, *"For the Life was manifested,"* means that this Life was made visible to the human race through the humanity of our Lord. This is as simple as Christ appearing among men so that they could see Him and hear Him. Though originally with God, and dwelling with Him, yet He came forth and appeared among men. He is the great Source of all Life, He appeared on the Earth, and we had an opportunity of seeing and knowing What and Who He was.

This *"Life"* was manifested in and through His Person. It was not a mere philosophy, but rather what true Spiritual Life was actually all about. Men talked about it, but Jesus manifested or portrayed this Life.

He did so by walking perfect, living perfect, acting perfect, thinking perfect, and in fact, being Perfect. In other words, this *"Life"* was constantly throbbing, pulsating, flowing in, and through Him. As stated, it manifested itself in His Perfect Life.

It bloomed forth as well in His healings and miracles and all that He did, even to the raising of the dead.

Do you realize that there is no record that anyone ever died in the Presence of Christ? And that He never met a funeral procession which He did not break up by raising the corpse from the dead, at least of which we are aware. Death could not stay in His Presence, and because He was not only the personification of life, but in reality, was Life.

As well, He manifested this Life, not merely on an occasional basis, but constantly.

It resulted in perfection, healings, miracles, all done through the Person, Office, Agency, and Power of the Holy Spirit. One might say that the Holy Spirit superintended and directed the manifestation of this *"Life."*

In John 1:14, the Apostle said, *"The Word became flesh."* This contemplates simply the historic fact of the Incarnation. *"The life was manifested,"* sets forth the unfolding of that fact in the various operations of life and living. The first denotes the process by which the Incarnation happened, with the latter proclaiming the result of that process as related to human capacity of receiving and understanding it. Thus, the Incarnation of the Son of God was the making visible to human understanding, the life which God is.

A WITNESS

The phrase, *"And we have seen it, and bear witness,"* in effect says, *"What I have said, I have seen."* All of which means that the life referred to here is a Person, for it requires a person to have fellowship. A mere abstraction can have no fellowship.

Among other reasons, the Apostles were selected by our Lord that they may do this very thing, be a witness to Whom and What He actually was.

John saw and heard our Lord so much, which was about three and one half years, even along with all the other Disciples, that he would never forget what he had seen and heard.

About 60 years had lapsed between the impression he had received and the time of the recording of the events in the Gospel which he wrote, the date of which is about the same as that of this first Epistle. Sixty years is a long time to remember the discourses of an individual. John was an unlettered man. He was not trained in the Greek schools of the time, as was the Apostle Paul.

However, there are several things which account for John's memory of the events in the life of our Lord. One is that in the First Century books were few and men trained themselves to remember much, whereas today books are plentiful and men remember little.

Another is that in the case of unlettered ancient people, a vast amount of their literature was remembered and repeated letter perfect through generation after generation.

NOTES

Still another is that our Lord's wonderful personality and discourses made an indelible impression upon those who were His constant companions for over three years.

Finally, His words to His Disciples, *"He (the Holy Spirit) shall teach you all things, and bring to your remembrance, whatsoever I have said unto you"* (Jn. 14:26), account for any facts which was necessary for John to know in order to write the Gospel which bears his name, and which he may have forgotten.

As John thought over those eventful years, which he no doubt did over and over again, often the Holy Spirit would, during those 60 years, bring back to his memory things that had slipped his mind. Thus, John gives his Readers the assurance that he is well-equipped to write his Gospel, for he was a competent witness of the events recorded, and as well, remembered them accurately, all of this from the human standpoint. Of course, from the Doctrine of verbal inspiration, and that division of it which we call the inspiration of superintendence, we are assured that the Holy Spirit superintended the recording of the historical facts so as to guarantee an infallible record of our Lord's life. John said in his Greek: *"And we have seen it, and bear witness."*

WHAT JOHN SAW

By the use of the phrase, *"We have seen it,"* the Apostle uses a distinctive Greek word for *"seeing"* which is *"horao."* It refers to the physical act of seeing, giving prominence to the discerning mind, to mental perception, and to mental activity. By the use of this particular Greek word for the act of seeing, John assures his Readers that he not only had the sensory impressions on his retinae, but he understood what he was looking at. He was a correct interpreter of the events in our Lord's life for the reader. He says he saw the events in the Lord's life *"with his eyes."*

How else can one see anything except by the aid of his eyes? While this is a self-evident thing, yet John felt it necessary to mention it in order to be absolutely sure that his Readers understood him to be referring to sensory impressions from our Lord's actual human body. They were actual, discerning impressions, not an optical illusion or an hallucination (Wuest).

THAT ETERNAL LIFE

The phrase, *"And show unto you that Eternal Life,"* goes back to the first words of the First Verse, *"that which was."* It doesn't say that which *"began to be,"* but rather *"was,"* which means it was always in existence. The *"Life"* which He had before the Incarnation, was no less after the Incarnation. It was *"eternal"* which means it had no beginning, and will have no end.

THE REASON FOR HIS COMING

In fact, the very reason for His coming to this Earth was that He might give this *"eternal life,"* which He possessed, and was actually the Source, to humanity which was dead in trespasses and sins. Adam's Fall had rendered the entirety of the human population *"spiritually dead."* For when their federal head fell, the entirety of humanity which in essence were in his loins, fell as well!

As a result, unredeemed man has no life. He is totally depraved, meaning that he doesn't know God, cannot know God, at least from his own initiative. In fact, he cannot initiate anything toward his Salvation, or knowing God in any capacity. The Lord had told Adam and Eve: *"Of every tree of the garden you may freely eat:*

"But of the tree of the knowledge of good and evil, you shall not eat of it: for in the day that you eat thereof you shall surely die" (Gen. 2:16-17).

And that's exactly what happened! Upon disobedience, both Adam and Eve died instantly, and we refer to *"spiritual death,"* which is *"separation from God."*

So if man is to be redeemed from this awful condition, God will have to initiate the Redemption in totality. In effect, God would become man, i.e., *"The Last Adam,"* i.e., *"The Second Man,"* and would thereby purchase back what the original Adam had lost (I Cor. 15:45-47).

As we've said in previous Commentary, the Cross made it possible for the *"Eternal Life"* possessed by Christ, to be given to believing sinners. As our Substitute, Christ took our place. He did for us what we couldn't do for ourselves, and the only thing that is required of us is to simply *"believe"* in what He has done at the Cross (Jn. 3:16). Faith in that

Finished Work, will instantly grant the believing sinner *"Eternal Life,"* which is the *"born again"* experience (Jn. 3:3).

The moment this happens, the believing sinner has *"Eternal Life,"* which means that it's not something in the future, but something which is possessed at present.

It all comes by Faith, and by that, we speak of Faith in Christ and more particularly, what Christ did for us at the Cross (Eph. 2:8-9).

WITH THE FATHER

The phrase, *"Which was with the Father,"* in essence proclaims the fact that such fellowship guarantees Deity on the part of Christ. It cannot be otherwise!

The Life, the Lord Jesus, is of such a nature as to have been in fellowship with God the Father, very God, of very God Himself, possessing coeternally with God the Father and God the Spirit, the Divine essence. This life, a Person, the Lord Jesus, is described by John as, *"without beginning and without end, that which always has been and always will be, eternal."* Since this life is without beginning, as we've already stated, it must be uncreated, thus, Deity in its essence.

The particular word for *"Life"* here is *"Zoe,"* here used as *"the absolute fullness of life, both essential and ethical, which belongs to God."* Thus, this life that God is, is not to be defined as merely animation, but as definitely ethical in its content.

God is not the mere reason for the universe, as the Greeks thought, but a Person with the characteristics and qualities of a Divine Person. In fact, the ethical and spiritual qualities of this life which God is, are communicated to the sinner when the latter places his Faith in the Lord Jesus as Savior, and this becomes the new, animating, energizing, motivating principle which transforms the experience of that individual, and the Saint thus lives a Christian life.

The Message of John is that since the Believer is a partaker of this life, it is an absolute necessity that he show the ethical and spiritual qualities that are part of the essential nature of God, in his own life. If these are absent, John says that person is devoid of the life of God, and is unsaved. The ethical and spiritual qualities of this life were exhibited to the human race in the earthly life of the Lord Jesus. His life thus becomes the pattern of what our lives should be in holiness, self-sacrifice, humility, and love (Thayer).

As we've already stated, this life is imparted to us through what Jesus did at the Cross, and our Faith in that Finished Work. In this manner the Holy Spirit works, and in this manner alone, and I continue to speak of our Faith in the Cross.

COMPLICATED?

While all of this sounds complicated, and in fact is very complicated; still, it can all be defined in one word, and that word is *"the Cross of Christ."* For us to understand God, there is only so far as we can go in that exercise. In fact, the only way that anyone can properly understand God is to accept, know, and understand the Lord Jesus Christ. He is the essence of the Father, and in fact, He told Philip: *"He that hath seen Me hath seen the Father"* (Jn. 14:9). But more particularly, it's what Jesus did at the Cross which makes all of this possible.

MANIFESTED UNTO US

The phrase, *"And was manifested unto us,"* proclaims the second time this has been said:

1. The Being here referred to was forever with God.

2. That it was proper before the Incarnation that the word *"Life"* should be given to Him as descriptive of His nature.

3. That there was a manifestation of Him Who was thus called *"Life,"* on Earth; that He appeared among men; that He had a real existence here, and not a merely assumed appearance.

4. That the true characteristics of this Incarnate Being could be borne testimony to by those who had seen Him, and who had been long with Him.

(3) "THAT WHICH WE HAVE SEEN AND HEARD DECLARE WE UNTO YOU, THAT YE ALSO MAY HAVE FELLOWSHIP WITH US: AND TRULY OUR FELLOWSHIP IS WITH THE FATHER, AND WITH HIS SON JESUS CHRIST."

The composite is:

1. John takes up the thought here of Verse 1, which was interrupted by the contents of Verse 2.

2. He is declaring to his Readers that which he had seen and heard, as it regarded Christ.

3. *"Fellowship"* carries the idea of one person having a joint-participation with another in something possessed in common by both.

4. This *"fellowship"* is with the Father and with His Son Jesus Christ.

DECLARATION

The phrase, *"That which we have seen and heard declare we unto you,"* proclaims the Apostle writing this Epistle, as well as his Gospel, so that his Readers who were not eyewitnesses of the life of our Lord might enjoy joint-participation with him in his firsthand knowledge of the Lord as gained through the senses of sight, hearing, and touch. When his Readers studied the Gospel under the guidance of the Spirit, they would be looking at the Lord Jesus as He appeared on Earth through John's eyes; they would be hearing Him speak through John's ears, and would be touching Him with John's hands. That's the general idea!

Thus, having a supernatural, Holy Spirit energized, first-hand knowledge of the Lord Jesus, they, therefore, would be able to have a real, practical, actual, and more intimate companionship with Him.

What if John had not written his Gospel and his Epistles? We could find the way of Salvation through the Pauline Epistles and could be saved. We could have some mystical companionship with our Lord, but not such an intelligent, practical fellowship as we do have, since His Portrait, painted by the Holy Spirit in the Gospels would be lacking.

One cannot have very intelligent fellowship with a person whom we have never seen, even though reams of paper would be used in an effort to describe Him. But as the Child of God ponders the life of our Lord through Spirit-ground lenses, he sees Him in his spiritual mind's eye so that an intelligent fellowship can be enjoyed by the Saint. Thus, a joint-participation on the part of the Christian in John's first-hand knowledge of the Lord Jesus, will issue in a real, practical, intelligent fellowship (companionship) with the Lord Jesus (Wuest).

FELLOWSHIP

The phrase, *"That ye also may have fellowship with us,"* presents at least one of the reasons for this Epistle.

John takes up the thought here of Verse 1, which was interrupted by the contents of Verse 2. The purpose for which he wrote the Gospel which bears his name and which contains the things which he had seen our Lord do and heard our Lord speak, was that his Readers might have fellowship with Him.

This word *"fellowship"* is one of the important words in this Letter.

First, the word is used in two different senses in this Epistle, and second, because the English word as it is normally used today has a different meaning from that in which it was used in A.D. 1611 when the King James edition was translated. The Greek word is *"koinonia,"* and means *"belonging in common to, and having a joint-participation with another in something possessed in common by both."*

A very touching use of the verbal form of this word was found in a Fourth Century inscription; a doctor of medicine had put up an inscription to his wife who had also studied medicine, and who had died. It read, *"As with you alone I shared my life."* How beautiful it is when a person saved by Grace comes to the sunset of life and can say to the Lord Jesus, *"as with You Alone I have shared my life."*

So John in essence is saying, *"That which we have seen with discernment and at present have in our mind's eye, and have heard and at present is ringing in our ears, we are reporting also to you in order that as for you also, a joint-participation you may be having in common with us."*

The word *"fellowship"* today means usually *"companionship, social intercourse."* In this sense of the word, it was impossible for John to have had fellowship with many of his Readers, for this is a general letter sent to the Church at large, and John would never have had opportunity to see them all personally and thus have fellowship with them. Consequently, the word *"fellowship"* cannot be understood here in its commonly

accepted usage. How are we to understand John here then?

As John related in his Gospel, and in this particular Epistle, he is describing the events which took place as it regards Christ and his own particular participation, in such a way, that his Readers, including us presently, can share with him the intimacy of our Lord. We were not there, while John was; so, the Holy Spirit through John makes it so real as to Who Christ was, and What Christ did, and does so through the eyes, ears, and hands of the Apostle, that it's like we were there as well.

THE FATHER AND THE SON

The phrase, *"And truly our fellowship is with the Father, and with His Son Jesus Christ,"* proclaims the intention of the Holy Spirit through John. The idea is that through John's description, we can know the Father better, and as well, know His Son Jesus Christ. That's the idea of the fellowship!

As we follow the gist of John's discourse, we will have fellowship with the Lord Jesus in the sense of companionship, with common likes and dislikes. We must love what He loves, namely, Righteousness, and hate what He hates, namely, sin. If such are not present in the Child of God, then there can be no fellowship.

FELLOWSHIP AND THE CROSS

Putting the Epistles of Paul together with those of John, we know that fellowship with Christ and with the Father, can only come through the Cross of Christ (Rom. 6:3-14; I Cor. 1:17-18, 21, 23; 2:2, 5). In fact, it is the Cross alone that opened up the way to the very heart of God, i.e., *"the Throne of God"* (Heb. 1:3; 4:16; 7:25; 9:8, 12). If we attempt to have fellowship with God the Father or Christ the Son in any other manner than by our Faith and trust in the Cross, we are plainly told in the Word that the Holy Spirit will block all access (Eph. 2:16-18).

The eternal Deity of Jesus of Nazareth is here affirmed; and the unity of the Father and the Son is declared in the statement that fellowship with either means fellowship with both.

(4) "AND THESE THINGS WRITE WE UNTO YOU, THAT YOUR JOY MAY BE FULL."

The exegesis is:

1. In effect, John is saying that what he is writing is Truth.

2. *"Your joy may be full,"* should have been translated *"our joy may be full,"* because the best texts, it is said, contain the word *"our"* not *"your."*

3. Error brings trouble, while truth brings joy.

THESE THINGS

The phrase, *"And these things write we unto you,"* fills our hearts with gladness, especially considering that through the eyes, hands, and ears of John, we have such an intimate portrait of our Lord and Savior, Jesus Christ.

It is believed that John was in his late 80's, and possibly even in his early 90's when this Epistle was written, along with his Gospel which bears his name, and the other two very short Epistles along with the Book of Revelation.

I personally think the Lord delayed John writing these great accounts for a particular purpose and reason. The Holy Spirit knew of course that many would rise up about this time, attempting to project fanciful doctrines about Christ which were grossly wrong. John would set the record straight by his accounts, thereby giving the Church several more decades of straight Doctrine.

We should understand that error generally has its beginning by misunderstanding, whether intentionally or not, the Person and Work of Christ. To miss it there is to miss it altogether! This was the problem of the Gnostics in John's day, and it is the problem presently with many in the modern Church. As we've said previously, the general direction of false teachers has always been to make Jesus too human, and man too Divine.

JOY

The phrase, *"That your joy may be full,"* should have been translated, as stated, *"our joy may be full."* This expression is used by John four times (Jn. 15:11; 16:24; I Jn. 1:4; II Jn. vs. 12) and only once elsewhere (Acts 2:28).

The phrase *"may be full,"* refers to something, here namely the Saint, who was completely filled with joy in times past, and that

it is meant to continue in this capacity. In other words, the *"more abundant life"* is definitely not to wear off. If anything, the idea is that this *"full condition"* not only continue, but also expand as the capacity for such expands in the heart and life of the Child of God.

This is almost the same language that the Savior used when addressing His disciples as He was about to leave them (Jn. 15:11) and there can be little doubt that John had that declaration in remembrance when he uttered this remark.

Is every Christian guaranteed this *"fullness of joy"*? Yes, but only if we go God's way. The truth is, many, if not most, Christians do not experience this of which John states. That being the case, how can this problem be remedied?

If the Christian doesn't experience this of which John proclaims, this means that such a Christian doesn't understand the Message of the Cross.

If the Christian doesn't understand the Cross as it pertains to his everyday walk before God, this means the Christian is trying to live for the Lord by means other than Faith in the Cross, which means that in some way he is failing. As a result, his *"joy cannot be full,"* as should be obvious. And as stated, that's the present position of most Christians.

Whenever the individual is totally trusting Christ and what Christ did at the Cross, which means he's not trusting in himself, victory is the result, because such a Christian has the help of the Holy Spirit Who is God, and Who can do anything. The joy of such a Christian is definitely full, and will remain that way, which is the *"more abundant life"* of which Jesus spoke (Jn. 10:10).

WHAT DOES IT MEAN TO PLACE ONE'S FAITH TOTALLY IN THE CROSS?

I will give the following teaching quite a few times in this Volume, seeking to do so a little differently each time, in order that we be certain that you the Reader understand what is being said. Satan will fight the Cross as he fights nothing else. He will do everything within his power to hinder the Believer from understanding what we are about to teach you.

I will give it here in capsule form, and enlarge upon it as we go forward throughout this Volume.

THE CROSS

The Believer is to understand, that every single thing he needs, the answer to every question, the solution to every problem, is found totally and entirely in what Jesus did for us at the Cross. And of course when we use the term *"Cross,"* even as Paul, we are not speaking of a wooden beam, but rather what Jesus did there (I Cor. 1:17-18, 21, 23; 2:2, 5).

On the Cross, He addressed every need of the human race, every sin it had committed, every disobedience and rebellion, in fact, everything that man lost in the Fall was addressed at the Cross. Admittedly, we do not have as of yet the benefits of all that He did there, in fact having only a down-payment; however, when the Trump sounds, we will then definitely have all at that time for which Jesus paid (Rom. 8:17-23).

OUR FAITH

Understanding that the Cross of Christ holds the answer to everything we need, then the Cross must ever be the object of our Faith. Now this is very, very important!

Satan will try to push your faith off to other things. And he really doesn't care what the other things are, because he knows that if your faith is not properly placed, which means to be placed in the Cross and the Cross exclusively, then the Holy Spirit will not help you. So, your Faith must ever rest in the Cross of Christ (Rom. 6:3-14; I Cor. 1:17-18, 21, 23; 2:2, 5).

THE HOLY SPIRIT

Everything that's done in our lives for the Lord must be done through the Person, Agency, Office, and Power of the Holy Spirit. We cannot make ourselves righteous or holy. In fact, we cannot even overcome sin within our lives. All that's done, and without exception, is a work of the Spirit within us.

As well, we must understand that what He does is not automatic. While He definitely dwells in the hearts and lives of all Believers, it should be obvious that many Believers are failing. That being the case, the question must be asked as to why they are failing, especially considering that they have the Holy Spirit.

They are failing, even as we've said, because the object of their faith is elsewhere other than the Cross, which denies them the help of the Holy Spirit.

The Spirit of God works exclusively within the parameters of the Finished Work of Christ, which means He will not deviate from these parameters. He doesn't ask much of us, but He does ask that we evidence Faith in the Sacrifice of Christ. When we do that, to be sure, He will begin to work within our lives, performing great and mighty things, bringing us to the place of Righteousness, Holiness, and Christlikeness (Rom. 8:1-2, 11).

So, in abbreviated form, we have given to you God's prescribed order of victory. As stated, we will enlarge upon this as we go along through this Volume, and because the Message of the Cross actually incorporates the entirety of the meaning of the New Covenant, in other words, this for which Jesus died.

(5) "THIS THEN IS THE MESSAGE WHICH WE HAVE HEARD OF HIM, AND DECLARE UNTO YOU, THAT GOD IS LIGHT, AND IN HIM IS NO DARKNESS AT ALL."

The diagram is:

1. John proclaims the correct message concerning the Lord.

2. God as to His nature, essence, and character, is Light.

3. Darkness in Him does not exist, not even one bit.

THE MESSAGE

The phrase, *"This then is the Message which we have heard of Him,"* presents the true Message, by comparison with the false. Then as now, Satan was laboriously attempting to dilute the Message.

One of those false messages then was that sin did not matter that much. It was the heresy called *"Antinomianism."* The word means literally *"against law."* In other words, nothing is wrong. It is disregard for any moral tone on the part of the one who professes to be a Christian.

This teaching followed out to its logical conclusion results in the two things John is opposing in Verses 5 and 6. The first is there is evil in God. The second is that the person who lives in sin may still have fellowship with Him.

This heresy was rampant among the Churches of Asia Minor in John's day (Rev. 2:6, 14-15), and he deals with it in this Epistle.

The modern counterpart of this false message is found in the thinking of some so-called modern Christians, even entire Denominations, that we can't help but sin a little bit every day, and that the only difference between the Believer and the unbeliever, is the Blood of Jesus. In other words they are claiming that if they have faith in Christ, then this covers all of their constant sinning.

They evidently ignore the teaching given by Paul as to how we are to overcome sin within our lives, which is by Faith in Christ and what He did at the Cross. The Lord didn't save us in sin, but rather from sin. Any idea that says that God condones sin, or that it doesn't matter very much about a Christian sinning, just as long as he has faith, is unbiblical and will lead to spiritual destruction.

GOD IS LIGHT

The phrase, *"And declare unto you, that God is Light,"* in effect presents the fact that there can be no evil about God, that He cannot condone sin, that He cannot condone sin in any capacity.

The manner in which John is saying this in the Greek concerning God being Light is, *"God as to His nature, essence, and character, is Light."* The light of which John speaks is not physical light, for John in the context is speaking of spiritual things. The light of which he speaks is ethical, spiritual, and moral.

To the heathen, Deity had meant angry, malevolent beings, worshipped best by the secrecy of outrageous vice; to the Greeks and Romans, forces of nature transformed into superhuman men and women, powerful and impure; to the philosophers, an abstraction either moral or physical; to the Gnostics it was a remote idea, equal and contending forces of good and evil, recognizable only through less and less perfect deputies.

All this John, summing up what the Old Testament and our Lord had said about the Almighty Father, sweeps away in one simple

declaration of truth. Light is God's garment (Ps. 104:2). To Ezekiel the appearance of the likeness of the Glory of the Lord was brightness (Ezek. 1:4); to Habakkuk, His brightness was as the light (Hab. 3:3); Christ had called the sons of God children of the light (Jn. 12:36), and announced Himself as the Light of the world (Jn. 8:12); in Hebrews, Christ is the refracted ray of the Father's Glory, *"the express Image of His Person"* (Heb. 1:3); to James, the Almighty was the Father of all lights (James 1:17); to Paul, He dwells *"in the light that no man can approach unto"* (I Tim. 6:16); to Peter, the Christian state is an admission *"into His marvellous Light"* (I Pet. 2:9). These ideas John comprehends: God is Light.

Regarding light, His Perfection shows that the difference between good and evil is not merely a question of degree, but fundamental and final. In fact, the Life of Christ, which John highlights, had exhibited that contrast sharply: once for all.

Thus, on this declaration, *"God is Light"* depends the whole Doctrine of sin: sin is not merely imperfection; it is enmity to God. There can be no shades of progression, uniting good and evil: in Him is no darkness at all. Good and evil may be mixed in an individual, but even in that case, they are contrary. But in God there can be no mixture of good and evil, only good prevails (Ellicott).

NO DARKNESS

The phrase, *"And in Him is no darkness at all,"* presents in the total phrase a statement of the absolute nature of God.

When the Holy Spirit through John said, *"God is Light,"* and it means *"Light in His very nature,"* we must understand that the expression is not a metaphor. All that we are accustomed to term *"Light"* in the domain of the creature, whether with a physical or metaphysical meaning, is only an effluence of that one and only primitive Light which appears in the nature of God.

To attempt to define *"darkness"* as it refers to God, we might say that it is *"an absence of light."* To understand that there is no such thing as an absence of Light as it regards God, we then understand that in Him there can be no darkness. To properly understand *"Light"* as it refers to God is to properly understand that there can be no darkness in Him. Physically, light represents *"glory"*; intellectually, it represents *"Truth"*; morally, it represents *"Holiness."*

In understanding it in an immaterial sense, it corresponds to God as *"Spirit"*; as to what He is, Light refers to God as *"Love"*; as the condition of life, Light to God is *"Life."*

In the Old Testament, light is often the medium of God's visible revelations to men. It was the first manifestation of God in creation. As well, the burning lamp passed between the pieces of the parted victim in God's Covenant with Abraham.

God went before Israel in a pillar of fire (Light), descended in fire at Sinai, and appeared in a luminous cloud which rested on the Mercy Seat in the Most Holy Place.

So in the words of Wuest we can say, *"God as to His nature is Light, and darkness in Him does not exist, not even one bit."*

(6) "IF WE SAY THAT WE HAVE FELLOWSHIP WITH HIM, AND WALK IN DARKNESS, WE LIE, AND DO NOT THE TRUTH:"

The exegesis is:

1. Millions claim Salvation when in reality, there is no Salvation.

2. To claim Salvation while at the same time *"walking in darkness,"* automatically dismisses our claims.

3. Such a life is a *"lie,"* and is not *"Truth."*

FELLOWSHIP WITH HIM

The phrase, *"If we say that we have fellowship with Him,"* proclaims by John a hypothetical situation. The claims of this individual are that he is having fellowship with God, while at the same time living in sin and compromising with it.

In this scenario regarding *"sin"* and the Christian, or the professed Christian, there are two types of people at whom we must look.

THE PROFESSING CHRISTIAN BUT NOT ACTUALLY SAVED

First of all, John is dealing with this type of individual. In John's day there were some, if not many, who were living in darkness, while at the same time professing Salvation. They were the victims of false doctrine.

NOTES

Unfortunately, the far greater majority of the modern Church makes up this particular category. In other words, most of the people presently who claim Salvation aren't actually saved. There is no change in their lives, with them continuing to walk in sin as they always have, only professing Salvation. Most of these people, have adopted a philosophy of Christianity, but not actually the true Christ of Christianity, Who is the Christ of the Cross. These individuals belong to Churches, consider themselves to be religious, and also consider themselves to adhere to the *"golden rule."* But as far as a personal experience with Christ, this they have never had. In short, they are unsaved despite their claims.

THE BELIEVER WHO IS TRULY A CHRISTIAN BUT DOESN'T KNOW GOD'S PRESCRIBED ORDER OF VICTORY

Of the people who are truly saved, regrettably this makes up the majority. They do not know and understand the Message of the Cross, so they do not know God's prescribed order of victory, so they live a life of *"sinning and repenting,"* *"sinning and repenting,"* etc.

They do not condone sin, and do not compromise with it; however, despite all of their efforts, and to be sure, they try very hard, the end result is still that the sin nature dominates their lives in some way. It may be in the realm of the vices, or it may not, but in some way, *"works of the flesh"* manifest themselves in their lives (Gal. 5:19-21).

John is not primarily dealing with this type of Christian here, but rather with those who have believed false doctrine, and are thereby spelling out for themselves a false Salvation.

While we are addressing the subject, however, please allow me to make the following statements:

GOD'S PRESCRIBED ORDER OF VICTORY

The only way for the Believer to have victory over sin is for him to understand that all victory is found in the Cross, and that our Faith must ever rest in the great Sacrifice of Christ. Then the Holy Spirit will work mightily on our behalf, guaranteeing the victory for which Jesus paid such a price. Now, having said that, let me make the following statement very boldly:

It doesn't matter who the person is, even if he is the Pastor of the largest Church in the country, or the Evangelist drawing the largest crowds, if he doesn't understand the Message of the Cross, realizing that in the Cross all victory is found, and realizing that outside of the Cross no victory is found, whomever he might be, and ever how many accolades the Church may pour out upon him, he is not living a victorious life.

The sadness is, most modern Christians, and of course I speak of those who truly know the Lord, know and understand the Cross as it relates to the initial Salvation experience, but they have no understanding whatsoever as it regards the part the Cross plays in our everyday Walk before God. They do not understand primarily how the Holy Spirit relates to the Cross, and the Cross to the Holy Spirit.

Unfortunately, many Preachers are guilty of specializing in things that matter little. Listen to what Paul said:

"For Christ sent me not to baptize, but to preach the Gospel: not with wisdom of words, lest the Cross of Christ should be made of none effect" (I Cor. 1:17).

The Holy Spirit through Paul is saying here that our emphasis must not be on anything except the Cross. Unfortunately, little knowing and understanding the Cross, the emphasis of most Preachers is on *"Water Baptism," "faith,"* but not the right kind of faith, *"manifestations," "Church membership," "affiliation with a particular Denomination,"* etc.

Unfortunately again, if the Preacher specializes in anything other than the Cross, in actuality, he is not *"preaching the Gospel."* In fact, Paul said that he was preaching *"another gospel"* (II Cor. 11:4).

And then, if the Preacher is not specializing in something other than the Cross, too oftentimes, he leans too heavily toward intellectualism. The idea is this:

The Preacher of the Gospel must specialize in *"The Cross of Christ."* In other words, he must preach the Cross as the answer for hurting, dying humanity. He must preach the Cross as well, for Christians in order that they might live a holy life.

NOTES

Paul also said: *"And my speech and my preaching was not with enticing words of man's wisdom, but in demonstration of the Spirit and of power"* (I Cor. 2:4). Paul *"preached the Cross"* (I Cor. 1:23), and whenever we preach the Cross, the Holy Spirit will always demonstrate His power.

There are millions of Christians at this very moment who are struggling with sin in their lives, with some of them having been struggling in this manner for many years. If they could but understand that every answer for which they seek is found in the Cross, and thereby place their Faith, they would see a demonstration of the Holy Spirit within their lives, with an exhibition of power that would overcome their problem. What is impossible for you and me is nothing at all for the Holy Spirit, for He is God. He waits to demonstrate His power on our behalf, but He will not do so unless we place our faith totally and completely in what Jesus did for us at the Cross. The Scripture plainly says:

"For the Law (the Holy Spirit works within this Law) *of the Spirit* (Holy Spirit) *of life* (He guarantees the life made possible by what Christ did at the Cross) *in Christ Jesus* (meaning that this 'Law' is in what Christ did at the Cross on our behalf) *has made me free from the law of sin and death"* (Rom. 8:2).

"The law of sin and death" is so powerful that only what Jesus did at the Cross can offset this thing, which is done by the Power and Person of the Holy Spirit.

WALKING IN DARKNESS

The phrase, *"And walk in darkness,"* proclaims the fact that the person is not saved. This person is sinning habitually, even continuously, which shows that he is an unsaved person. No Child of God sins habitually to the exclusion of righteous acts.

The word *"walk"* refers to the manner in which he orders his behavior, conducts himself, which is in the sphere of the darkness of sin. His actions and words are ensphered by sin. Nothing of God's Righteousness or Goodness ever enters that circle of sin which surrounds such a person. The individual making this claim of fellowship with God, while at the same time ordering his behavior within this sphere of sin, is an unsaved person. As we have said and will continue to say, the Lord does not save in sin, but rather from sin.

THE LIE AND THE TRUTH

The phrase, *"We lie, and do not the truth,"* proclaims our Salvation as false.

Some of the modern claims considering the spirit, the soul, and the body, are very similar to that which John was addressing.

The Gnostics who were in their beginning stages in John's day, claimed that all matter, including human flesh, is inherently evil. Hence, according to them the human body serves as a mere container in which the human spirit resides. This would mean, therefore, that what the material part of a human does has no bearing whatever on the immaterial portion of his being. To their way of thinking, how one lived did not matter; it was only this esoteric knowledge which really counted.

This unbiblical approach made it possible to justify any sin which they were practicing, and at the same time to claim a personal and abiding relationship with God. This is the worst kind of darkness because it involves knowing but not doing.

Their modern counterparts, who are mostly in the *"Word of Faith"* camp, claim pretty much the same thing.

They claim that when a person comes to Christ, their spirit is made perfect, and whatever the physical body does, has no bearing on the spirit. In other words, the perfect spirit of the converted man is unsullied and untouched by the actions of the sinful, physical body. They also teach that the soul is being brought into line with the spirit. What does the Bible say?

Paul said: *"Having therefore these Promises, dearly beloved, let us cleanse ourselves from all filthiness of the flesh and spirit, perfecting holiness in the fear of God"* (II Cor. 7:1).

This Passage plainly tells us that the spirit of a redeemed person can be *"filthy"* the same as the flesh.

Paul also said: *"And the very God of peace sanctify you wholly; and I pray God your whole spirit and soul and body be preserved blameless unto the coming of our Lord Jesus Christ"* (I Thess. 5:23).

NOTES

Both these Passages tell us that the spirit, soul, and body of Believers, are all affected the same. In other words, if we sin, we sin spirit, soul, and body. And when we are sanctified (set apart unto God) we are as well, sanctified *"spirit, soul, and body."*

The Bible in no way separates the spirit and the soul of man from the body, or its actions, until death, when the spirit and soul are separated from the physical body, which then goes back to dust.

Our *"Word of Faith"* friends, seek to minimize sin by relegating it only to the physical body, but succeed only in deceiving themselves.

(7) "BUT IF WE WALK IN THE LIGHT, AS HE IS IN THE LIGHT, WE HAVE FELLOWSHIP ONE WITH ANOTHER, AND THE BLOOD OF JESUS CHRIST HIS SON CLEANSETH US FROM ALL SIN."

The diagram is:

1. If we claim fellowship with Him, we will at the same time, have to walk in the light, which is the sphere of His walk.

2. Only then can the Believer have fellowship with God.

3. Our Faith being in the Cross, the shed Blood of Jesus Christ constantly cleanses us from all sin.

WALKING IN THE LIGHT

The phrase, *"But if we walk in the light,"* proclaims by the word *"walk"* a sphere of action. In other words, this is what we do.

How can we walk in the light? And more particularly, how can we guarantee ourselves that we are in fact, walking in the light? All the hundreds of millions of professing Christians, but who aren't really saved, claim to be walking in the light. So how can we be certain of this single most important aspect of our life and living?

We will find the answer in the last phrase of this Verse.

HE IS IN THE LIGHT

The phrase, *"As He is in the light,"* refers to the fact that *"He is Light."*

This means that we're walking in the same kind of Light that He has and is. The measure of light that we have is not the same in degree, but it is of the same kind. In other words, the true Christian in his character and feelings resembles God.

The idea given here as well proclaims that which the light exposes. The Biblical approach is to keep on walking totally exposed to *"the Light,"* or to the Truth of God expressed in Scripture.

Light is Righteousness, sin is darkness. To live a sinful life and at the same time to profess to have fellowship with God, is to act a lie. That fellowship can only be enjoyed as a man walks in the light as God is in the light.

The reference in Verse 7 is to Aaron, as representative of Israel, having fellowship with God in the Most Holy Place. There was the Light, the sinner, and the blood. The Light flashing from between the Cherubim above the blood-sprinkled Mercy Seat revealed the sinfulness of Aaron, and at the same time revealed the preciousness of the blood sprinkled upon and before the Mercy Seat. That blood was all the time he was there cleansing him in type, from all sin; that is, it had an ever-present efficacy (Williams).

FELLOWSHIP

The phrase, *"We have fellowship one with another,"* in effect has a twofold meaning, but its heavier emphasis is the fellowship which we as Believers have with God and God with us.

Wonder of wonders, not only do we have fellowship with God, but He reciprocates in having fellowship with us! This fellowship is not a one-sided affair like that of a couple, only one of which is in love with the other. God condescends to have fellowship with worms of the dust, Believers saved by grace, creatures of His handiwork (Wuest).

In effect, he is telling us that we cannot have fellowship with Him, while at the same time having fellowship with sin.

At the same time, we as Believers cannot have fellowship with others who claim to be Believers, but are rather espousing false doctrine concerning the Person of Christ and His Work on the Cross. That's why the Holy Spirit said through Paul:

"Be ye not unequally yoked together with unbelievers: for what fellowship has righteousness with unrighteousness? And what communion has light with darkness?

"Wherefore come out from among them, and be ye separate, saith the Lord, and touch not the unclean thing; and I will receive you" (II Cor. 6:14, 17).

THE BLOOD OF JESUS CHRIST

The phrase, *"And the Blood of Jesus Christ His son cleanseth us from all sin,"* proclaims Sacrifice.

The Believer can guarantee himself that he is *"walking in the Light,"* when his Faith and trust are totally and completely in the Sacrifice of Christ. This means that he perfectly trusted in Christ and what Christ did at the Cross when he was saved, and it also means, that he continues to trust the Sacrifice of Christ as it regards his daily walk.

If it is to be noticed, the force of the word *"cleanseth"* is in the present tense. It doesn't say *"has cleansed,"* or *"will cleanse."* This means that it has no reference to time but rather to efficacy (effectiveness), as when it is said that a medicine cures a disease.

The fellowship *"one with another"* means fellowship of the Believer with God in the Light, just as Aaron had fellowship with God in the Light. It is only in the Light, and in virtue of the efficacy of the atoning Blood of Christ, that fellowship with God can be enjoyed. All who declare that they have fellowship with God and yet deny the Deity and the Atonement of Christ are self-deceived and are liars, exactly as John says in Verse 6, for they are walking in darkness (Williams).

THE OBJECT OF OUR FAITH

Even though the idea of the Blood of Jesus constantly cleansing from all sin is enjoined here, that, I think, is not the major thrust of this statement as given by John.

The Holy Spirit through John is expressing the fact of the Sacrifice of Christ. *"The blood"* denotes sacrifice. It is always the blood that is shed. The Lamb of God shed His Blood in expiation. He is the expiation for our sins, moreover not for ours only, but also for the whole world (I Jn. 2:2). It is the Blood *"of Jesus, His Son,"* of Jesus as a man Who had a human nature and thus also blood and Who is *"God's Son,"* the Logos of the Life, the Second Person of the Deity, Who became flesh (Jn. 1:14), Whose Blood, when shed, has the power to cleanse us from all sin. Consequently, several things are being stated here:

1. The very fact of His shed Blood cleansing us from all sin precludes the idea that we are to continue sinning.

2. As well, the idea that if His Blood cleanses us from all sin, then it doesn't really matter how much we sin, makes a mockery of the Sacrifice of Christ. The *"cleansing from sin"* lays claim to the fact that we are to walk free from sin.

3. The idea is we cannot have victory over sin, unless the Sacrifice of Christ is the total and complete object of our Faith. If the object of our faith is something else, sin will most definitely be the result, which speaks of the bondage of sin.

4. The only way that the sinner can be cleansed from sin is through Faith in Christ and what Christ did at the Cross on our behalf. The only way the Believer can stay free from sin is by continuing to evidence Faith in the Finished Work of Christ. God has no remedy for sin other than the Sacrifice of Christ.

5. As stated, there can be no fellowship with God, unless our Faith is totally and completely in the Sacrifice of Christ. In fact, the Holy Spirit bars the entrance of any who attempt to worship God, or to have fellowship with God, outside of this sphere (Eph. 2:16, 18).

(8) "IF WE SAY THAT WE HAVE NO SIN, WE DECEIVE OURSELVES, AND THE TRUTH IS NOT IN US."

The structure is:

1. *"Sin"* is in the singular, and actually refers to the sin nature, and not acts of sin.

2. If we claim as Christians that we do not have a sin nature, then we are deceiving ourselves.

3. The emphatic position of the pronoun *"ourselves"* proclaims the fact that a Christian who believes his evil nature has been completely eradicated is deceiving himself.

4. John says that the truth is not in such a person.

THE SIN NATURE

The phrase, *"If we say that we have no sin,"* refers to *"the sin nature."* As stated, *"sin"* is in the singular, so does not speak of acts of sin, but rather *"the sin nature."*

Here we have the denial of the indwelling, totally depraved nature passed down the race from Adam.

Whenever the believing sinner comes to Christ, most definitely he then becomes a *"new creature,"* with old things having passed away and all things having become new (II Cor. 5:17). But due to the fact that we are not yet glorified, the *"sin nature"* remains in the Child of God. In fact, Paul spent more time on this than possibly anything else.

In Romans, Chapter 6 he mentions *"sin"* some 17 times. With the exception of three times (vss. 14-16), the definite article is used with the word sin, which in effect says *"the sin,"* which refers to *"the sin nature."* Actually, in Verses 14 and 16, *"the sin"* is implied.

When the Holy Spirit through Paul speaks of *"the sin,"* He isn't speaking of acts of sin, but rather that from which acts of sin proceed, *"the sin nature."* In fact, one might be able to say that acts of sin are merely a symptom of the real problem.

The real sin is rebellion against God's prescribed order of victory, which is Faith exclusively in the Sacrifice of Christ. Once that sin is committed, then acts of sin are guaranteed.

THE *"NATURES"* OF THE CHRISTIAN

Every true Christian has three natures:

1. Human nature: even Christ, as would be obvious, had a human nature.

2. Divine nature: The moment the believing sinner comes to Christ, he is then *"born again,"* which refers to being regenerated by the Holy Spirit, with him then gaining the *"Divine Nature"* (Jn. 3:3; II Pet. 1:4).

3. Sin nature: This nature need not be any trouble or difficulty for the Believer, providing the Believer keeps his faith totally and completely in the Sacrifice of Christ, which enables the Holy Spirit to function on our behalf. When Jesus died on the Cross, He died not only to save us from *"sin,"* but as well, from *"self."* *"Self-will"* and the *"sin nature,"* go hand in hand. To be sure, when the person comes to Christ, they do not cease to be a self, for that's what we actually are; however, the idea is, that *"self"* be placed in Christ, which it is at conversion (Rom. 6:3), and to remain in Christ, and can do so only

by constant faith expressed in the Sacrifice of Christ.

THE UNDERSTANDING OF SIN

Most Christians do not understand sin. At this very moment, millions of Christians are attempting to overcome sin within their lives, and mostly what they are doing is addressing themselves to symptoms instead of the real problem. In fact, much of the Christian world has adopted humanistic psychology as the answer for sin. As a result, we are admonished to *"forgive God,"* or *"forgive ourselves,"* or to take out our hostility on some inanimate object such as a pillow, by beating it, which is supposed to relieve frustration, etc.

All of that is foolishness, to say the least!

I think one can say without fear of contradiction, that all acts of sin in one way or the other are symptoms of the real problem instead of the actual problem itself. Now what do we mean by that?

The real sin is rebelling against God's prescribed order of victory, which is the Cross of Christ, and our Faith in that Finished Work, which gives the Holy Spirit latitude to work within our lives (I Cor. 1:17-18). If our faith as it concerns our daily walk before God, is not exclusively in the Cross, believing that Jesus there met every need, then our faith is in ourselves or other things, which is always woefully insufficient for the task. In other words, faith in the incorrect object, will always and without exception, result in failure, which fuels the *"sin nature,"* and if it's not stopped, will ultimately control the Believer exactly as it did before the Believer came to Christ.

Paul said: *"Let not sin* (the sin nature) *therefore reign* (rule) *in your mortal body, that you should obey it in the lusts thereof"* (Rom. 6:12).

Now if it wasn't possible for such to be, then the Apostle was wasting his words. But of course, we know that he wasn't wasting words, and we also know that the Holy Spirit actually said these words through him.

At this very moment, in the hearts and lives of millions of Christians, the sin nature is ruling some way in their lives, exactly as it was before they were saved. Now please understand, I'm not speaking of hypocrites, but

NOTES

rather Christians who truly love God. In fact, they are fighting this thing with all of their strength, but with no success. In fact, this thing is getting worse within their lives instead of better, and that despite all their efforts otherwise.

WHAT IS WRONG?

To put it in a nutshell, the object of their faith is wrong. Their faith is not in the Cross, where it ought to be, but rather in other things. And it doesn't really matter what the other things are, how holy they may be in their own right, how correct they may be in their own right. If one's faith is not in the Finished Work of Christ, then one is denying oneself the help of the Holy Spirit, without Whom we cannot succeed (Rom. 8:1-2, 11).

Considering the price that Jesus paid at the Cross, it's a shame for us not to know and understand how to avail ourselves of all that He did. And please understand that everything He did on that memorable day was done totally and completely for you and me. His great Sacrifice was not done for Himself, Angels, or anything that pertains to Heaven, but strictly for you and me. Among other things, this shows us how awful, how terrible that sin really is. In fact, it is so terrible that there is no way man within his own strength and ability can overcome this monster. It could only be done by what Christ did at the Cross, which demands our constant faith in that Finished Work.

The major problem is, the Church has had so little teaching and preaching on the Cross in the last several decades, that for all practical purposes, the modern Church is Cross illiterate, which carries with it all types of negative fallout.

The non-Pentecostal branch of the Church for years attempted to preach the Cross without the Holy Spirit. They have now been reduced for the most part, to preaching neither one. The Pentecostal sector of the Church, has attempted to preach the Holy Spirit without the Cross. Until now it has by and large been reduced to chasing *"spirits,"* thinking it's the Holy Spirit.

The Holy Spirit and the Cross cannot be separated. They are indivisible. Every single thing the Holy Spirit does is always and without exception predicated on what Jesus did at the Cross (Eph. 2:13-18). In fact, the Holy Spirit was so close to Christ at the Cross that Christ couldn't actually die until the Holy Spirit allowed Him to do so. Paul said:

"How much more shall the Blood of Christ, Who through the Eternal Spirit offered Himself without spot to God, purge your conscience from dead works to serve the living God?" (Heb. 9:14).

In other words, the Holy Spirit superintended every single thing that Christ did, but especially the Sacrifice of Himself on the Cross. Listen again to what Paul said:

"But if the Spirit (Holy Spirit) *of Him* (God the Father) *Who raised up Jesus from the dead dwell in you, He Who raised up Christ from the dead shall also quicken your mortal bodies by His Spirit Who dwelleth in you"* (Rom. 8:11).

In Hebrews we have the Holy Spirit superintending the Death of Christ, and now we have Him superintending the Resurrection of Christ. And we are as well told that if our Faith is properly placed (Rom. 8:2), the Holy Spirit, Who raised Christ from the dead, will *"also quicken our mortal bodies,"* which refers to giving us power and strength to live this life as it ought to be lived. Please understand that Paul is not speaking here of the coming Resurrection, but rather, of our daily lives and living before God. In other words, in the Holy Spirit, we have the same power within us that raised Christ from the dead; consequently, we are speaking here of unlimited power, which means that anything Satan may bring our way can be totally and completely thrown aside. In other words, *"sin shall not have dominion over us,"* as long as the Holy Spirit is allowed to function as He desires to do so (Rom. 6:14). And because it's so important, please allow me to say it again:

The Holy Spirit doesn't require much of us, but He does require that we exhibit Faith in the Finished Work of Christ at all times, understanding that it was there that all victory was won, and it is there that all victory is maintained (Rom. 8:2).

DECEPTION

The phrase, *"We deceive ourselves,"* refers as is obvious, to *"self deception."* Here we

have the heresy (and it is heresy) of the eradication of the totally depraved nature during the earthly life of the Christian. In other words, the Bible doesn't teach such a thing.

Until we die, or until the Trump of God sounds, the Christian has to be on guard against the *"sin nature"* which continues to dwell within him. Now please read the following very carefully:

Before we were saved, the *"sin nature"* dwelt in us, and as well, ruled and reigned. Now that we are Christians, while the sin nature continues to dwell within us, even as Romans, Chapter 6 graphically brings out, it is not to rule or reign; however, it will definitely rule within our lives, if our Faith is in anything other than the Finished Work of Christ.

For the Christian to claim that he no longer has a sin nature, presents the ignoring of two basic fundamentals:

1. First of all, the actions of such a Christian, and all Christians for that matter, prove that the *"sin nature"* continues to dwell in one's life, and regrettably and sadly, rules and reigns in many, if not most, Christians. That is because they do not understand Paul's teaching on this subject as given in Romans, Chapter 6.

2. As we've already mentioned, in Romans, Chapter 6 alone, *"sin"* is mentioned some 17 times. With the exception of three of these times, it is always preceded in the Greek by what is known as the *"definite article,"* which actually reads *"the sin."* This means that it's not speaking of a particular act of sin, but rather the *"sinful nature,"* or *"evil nature,"* etc. In other words, to deny that we as Believers have a sin nature is to deny the plain and clear teaching of the Word of God.

Again as we've already stated, but because of its vast significance please allow me to say it again: *"Sin"* as used here by John in Verse 8, is singular in number and is used without the definite article, all pointing to the fact that the nature is referred to, not acts of sin. Here we have the denial of the indwelling, totally depraved nature passed down the race from Adam. John says, therefore, *"If we say that sin we are not having, ourselves we are deceiving."* Notice, if you will, the emphatic position of the pronoun *"ourselves."* The

Christian, who believes his evil nature has been completely eradicated, and he'll never have to worry about it again, is deceiving himself, nobody else. All others, as we've just stated, can see this depraved nature coming out at times in his life. And to be sure, whatever that person believes, such sin must come from the indwelling sinful nature.

ONLY ONE WAY TO ADDRESS SIN

Since John's time sin has been addressed in various ways. With some, the sinfulness of sin is denied. Others claim perfection, and lay aside the Lord's Prayer with its petition: *"Forgive us our trespasses."* They claim that they have no sins to be cleansed away.

The *"Word of Faith"* people claim that sin is not to be mentioned, and because if it is mentioned, it creates, they say, a *"sin consciousness"* in the Believer, which causes the person to sin.

In the first place, if the mere act of not mentioning sin will solve this problem, then I wonder why the Holy Spirit through Paul, and John as well as the other writers didn't think of that? As well, it must be remembered that both Paul and John were speaking to Believers and not unbelievers. As well, the *"Word of Faith"* people claim they have no sin nature, which means they are deceiving themselves, even as John says here.

Others claim that once we are now a Believer, God doesn't look at sin in our lives as He did before conversion. In other words, sin, they say, is not something to be concerned about, because the Blood of Jesus Christ is constantly cleansing us.

Once again, were that the case, why did Paul give all of his teaching concerning God's way of overcoming sin, as recorded in Romans, Chapter 6?

To be sure, sin is just as deadly in the heart and life of a Christian, as it is in a non-Christian.

In Verse 6 John says: *"We are lying and are not doing the truth"*; he now states it in stronger terms: *"We are deceiving our own selves,"* i.e., are making our own selves the victims of our lying, are not only not doing the truth but are wholly devoid of it.

The only answer for sin, and I mean the only answer, is the Cross. And when I say *"the only answer,"* I'm speaking of original sin as well as acts of sin within our hearts and lives.

The entirety of the Book of Hebrews is given over to God's remedy for sin, which is the Cross. This means the following:

There is no way the sinner can be saved, unless he believes in Christ and what Christ did at the Cross. To be sure, he doesn't know anything about this great Truth, but he must believe, or else he cannot be saved (Jn. 3:16).

Also, the only way the Christian can live above sin, which refers to keeping the sin nature at bay, is to continue to have faith in Christ and what Christ did at the Cross, even on a daily basis. That's why Jesus told us to deny ourselves, and take up our Cross daily and follow Him (Lk. 9:23-24; Rom. 6:3-5, 11, 14; 8:1-2, 11, 13).

THE TRUTH

The phrase, *"And the Truth is not in us,"* must be interpreted correctly.

In the case of the Gnostics in John's day, that statement must be taken in an absolute sense. They were unsaved. In the case of a misinformed and mistaken present-day Christian, the statement will have to be qualified to mean that the truth of the indwelling sinful nature is not in him. The context would require this interpretation. However, if this particular Truth concerning the sin nature is not believed and understood by any Christian, while that individual certainly is saved, still, such erroneous thinking will fall out to great difficulties in that particular heart and life.

If the Christian denies that he has a *"sin nature,"* then he will also not properly equip himself to address this thing, according to what Paul taught in Romans, Chapter 6.

When *"the truth"* in any capacity, is not in us, we are not by any means empty but are full of fictions, fables, myths, self-made fancies, and notions that are not so. Already those early heretics call these things *"gnosis,"* which speaks of knowledge. In other words, they were claiming they had a superior knowledge, and that this superior knowledge gave them a place and position above all sin. To be frank, their greatest sin was not properly understanding the Cross, or else ignoring it altogether.

Paul opposed such *"gnosis"* which paraded as *"wisdom."* *"Professing themselves to be wise,"* he said, *"they became fools"* (Rom. 1:22). The greatest fools are those who deceive their own selves, even as John states here.

As by now should be obvious, the Bible does not teach sinless perfection, but it does teach, that is if we properly adhere to the Word of God, that *"sin shall not have dominion over us"* (Rom. 6:14). However, the only way that we can live a life that is pleasing to God, which means that sin is not dominating us in any way, is by understanding how all of this comes about, which is through the Cross. It was there that Jesus atoned for all sin, past, present, and future. It was there that Satan's legal claim upon humanity was broken. Sin is his claim, and with all sin atoned, he is left without any claim.

But yet he continues to hold sway over untold millions, even billions. That being the case, that his claim was broken at Calvary, how do we explain the untold millions who are presently in bondage?

As it regards the unsaved, they continue to be under the sway of Satan, because they have not availed themselves of what Jesus did at the Cross. In other words, they have refused to believe and, therefore, Satan, due to their faithlessness, can hold them in bondage, which he does (Jn. 3:3, 16).

Sadder still, are the many Christians whom Satan continues to hold in bondage, despite the price that Jesus paid. How can this be?

If a Christian is in bondage to sin in any fashion, it is because of spiritual and scriptural ignorance.

Romans, Chapters 6, 7, and 8, present the foundation of Paul's teaching as it regards the Believer living a holy, upright life, and how this is to be brought about. Some 15 times in these three Chapters, he uses the word *"know,"* or *"knowing,"* etc.

For instance, he begins this teaching by saying, *"Know ye not that so many of us as were baptized into Jesus Christ were baptized into His Death?"* (Rom. 6:3).

The sad truth is, most modern Christians simply don't *"know."* They don't *"know"* that their victory is totally and completely in the Cross! They don't *"know"* that they must

evidence Faith constantly in that Finished Work of Christ! They don't *"know"* that this is the way in which the Holy Spirit works, which is always in the parameters of the Sacrifice of Christ.

With many, if not most, it's not a matter of willful rebellion, but rather, as stated, a matter of spiritual and Scriptural ignorance.

A PERSONAL TESTIMONY

I empathize with that position very readily. In fact, not *"knowing"* this great Truth, which is God's prescribed order of victory, and God's only prescribed order of victory, I suffered terrible failure and humiliation. But the sad part is, I didn't know any other Preacher who at the time knew this foundational Truth.

And please understand, we're not teaching something new here, actually that which the Lord gave to Paul, and the great Apostle gave to us (Gal. 1:11-12).

I believe I can say in all honesty before God, that during those years of not knowing the Victory of the Cross, I personally tried so very, very hard to live this life exactly as it ought to be lived. To be sure, my efforts were in the realm of good things. Those good things included prayer, fasting, constant study of the Word, winning souls to Christ, etc. Now please understand, these things within themselves, are definitely that which good Christians will always do; however, while these things certainly aren't wrong within themselves, but rather right, making them the object of our faith, is wrong, and terribly so!

For instance, if I could pray my way through to victory, which I tried to do, then Jesus didn't need to come down here and die on a Cross. My problem was, exactly as is the problem of most modern Christians, I was frustrating the Grace of God (Gal. 2:21).

What kind of prayer life do I now have after having come to the knowledge of the Cross of Christ?

The truth is, I have a greater prayer life today than ever before. The reason is simple, my purpose for constant communion with the Lord as it regards prayer, is entirely different than before. Now it's for communion and fellowship, as well as petition; however, in those days before the knowledge of the

Cross, I'm afraid that I turned prayer into *"works,"* which God cannot honor. Let me say it in a more complete way:

If the Believer emphasizes anything within his heart and life other than the Cross, he in effect, is sinning, which means that he is rebelling against God's way, whether he realizes it or not. Our emphasis, which includes our knowledge, must always be in the Cross; otherwise, we will make the Cross of Christ of none effect, which means we nullify all that Jesus did there (I Cor. 1:17).

The Gnostics of John's day, were claiming a superior knowledge; however, what made it wrong, it wasn't knowledge in the Cross of Christ, but rather something else, which means that it wasn't in the Word of God at all. Let the Reader read these words carefully:

If our knowledge concerning the Cross is skewed, this means that our knowledge regarding the entirety of the Word of God will be skewed in some manner.

To be sure, there is a true, Biblical knowledge, which all Believers must have as it regards victorious living. That *"knowledge"* is found in Romans, Chapter 6, which refers to the knowledge of the Cross. Any other type of knowledge breeds self-superiority, self-righteousness, and arrogance. Proper knowledge, which is knowledge of the Cross, breeds the very opposite, which is humility. In fact, the Cross of Christ was the greatest object of humility that man has ever known, and in fact, will ever know. There can be no true humility without a proper knowledge of the Cross.

(9) "IF WE CONFESS OUR SINS, HE IS FAITHFUL AND JUST TO FORGIVE US OUR SINS, AND TO CLEANSE US FROM ALL UNRIGHTEOUSNESS."

The composite is:

1. Now John instructs the Saints what to do about sins in their lives.

2. The sinner is to believe (Jn. 3:16). The Saint is to confess.

3. God will always be faithful, and without exception, to forgive confessed sins.

4. He will not only forgive, but will cleanse us from the defilement of sins.

CONFESSION

The phrase, *"If we confess our sins,"* pertains to acts of sin, whatever they might be.

NOTES

No Christian has to sin; however, the sad truth is, every single Christian does at times sin.

"Confess" in the Greek is *"homologeo,"* and means *"to say the same thing as another,"* or, *"to agree with another."* Confession of sin on the part of the Saint means, therefore, to say the same thing that God does about that sin, to agree with God as to all the implication of that sin as it relates to the Christian who commits it and to a Holy God against Whom it is committed (Wuest).

All of this includes the Saint's hatred of that sin, his sense of guilt because of it, his contrition because of it, the determination to put it out of his life, which can be done only by understanding that all victory is in the Cross, and that our Faith must ever be in that Finished Work. In fact, the very reason that we sin is because we get our eyes off the Cross (Lk. 9:23-24), onto other things.

The English word *"confess"* means *"to admit the truth of an accusation, to own up to the fact that one is guilty of having committed the sin."* But the Greek word means far more than that, as we have addressed above.

The Greek word teaches that the constant attitude of the Saint towards sin should be one of a contrite heart, ever eager to have the Holy Spirit to point out all wrong, and to put it out of the life by the power of that same Holy Spirit.

To whom are we to confess our sins?

We are to confess them to the One Who is going to forgive us, namely the Lord. Also, if we have harmed someone else, we should confess our wrong to that person as well.

In fact, the very moment that we do something wrong, the Holy Spirit without fail, will convict us (Jn. 16:8). At that moment we should confess our sin to the Lord, whatever it might be, and wherever we might be. This is a matter of the heart, so it does not need ceremony of any kind.

BUT WHAT IF THE CHRISTIAN DOES NOT CONFESS HIS SIN?

Failing to confess his sin to God means that the Lord at the same time, cannot forgive such a sin, which leaves the Believer in a precarious situation. Forgiveness by God, in the context of which the Holy Spirit here speaks, is not automatic. It requires confession of our sin to Him and for many and varied reasons.

The Believer is to never take sin lightly. In fact, there is really nothing anyone can do to make amends for sin. All we can do is to acknowledge our guilt and turn to God for forgiveness. As well, there is really nothing we can do to make up for the hurt we cause others, other than mutually extending and accepting forgiveness. However, if we have harmed someone else in any way, and refuse to confess our wrongdoing to that person, John plainly says that such a person *"walks in darkness"* (I Jn. 2:11). Jesus said: *"Therefore your sin remaineth"* (Jn. 9:41).

Any Christian who sins, and refuses to confess that sin to the Lord, or sins against a Brother or Sister and refuses to confess the wrongdoing to the individual, asking forgiveness, is in serious spiritual trouble indeed! If that person continues on in such a state, it is impossible but that spiritual deterioration must be the case. As it regards the Salvation of such a person, I'll have to leave that to the Lord; however, it should be well understood that we are speaking here of very serious things.

FAITHFUL AND JUST

The phrase, *"He is faithful and just to forgive us our sins,"* proclaims one of the greatest Promises in the entirety of the Word of God.

"Faithful" in the Greek is *"pistos,"* and means *"true to His Own nature and Promises; keeping faith with Himself and with man."* The word is applied to God as fulfilling His Own Promises (Heb. 10:23; 11:11); as fulfilling the purpose for which He called men (I Cor. 1:9; I Thess. 5:24); as responding with guardianship to the trust reposed in Him by men (I Cor. 10:13; I Pet. 4:19). *"He abideth faithful. He cannot deny Himself"* (II Tim. 2:13). The same term is again applied to Christ (II Thess. 3:3; Heb. 2:17; 3:2).

God's faithfulness is spoken of here not only as essential to His Own Being, but as faithfulness toward us; fidelity to that nature of truth and light related to His Own essence, which rules in us as far as we confess our sins (Ebrard).

These sins for which confession is required are infrequent, isolated instances in the well-ordered life of a Believer; however, if the Believer doesn't understand the Cross, to be sure, sins will not be infrequent, but rather very frequent, even habitual. Irrespective, if we as Believers confess our sins to the Lord, He will always be faithful and just to forgive us those sins. But just because this is the case, let not the Believer think that sin is inconsequential. Just because there is a serum that will save the life of a person who has been bitten by a rattlesnake, doesn't mean that such a bite is without consequences. While we dare not minimize the cleansing of the Precious Blood of Christ and all its effects, at the same time, we must not trivialize or minimize sin as well. Sin in some way, some form, even though God cleanses and forgives, still has its side effects, so to speak. Let not the Christian ever take sin lightly!

FAITHFUL

The faithfulness of God in forgiving sin that is confessed knows no bounds nor has no parameters. God never says in His Word that He will forgive a sin so many times, but after that there is no more forgiveness. There is no limit to the *"faithfulness of God."* But once again, let not the Believer ever take God's faithfulness for granted. In other words, that sin doesn't matter, because God will always instantly forgive.

God is faithful to forgive us our confessed sins, because of what Jesus did for us at the Cross. On the basis of justice satisfied, which Christ did at the Cross, God can be faithful to always forgive sins. But let not the Reader ever forget that His faithfulness is made possible by the great Sacrifice of Christ. Let us say it another way:

God can forgive sins only on the basis of Christ's atoning work at the Cross. The Scripture plainly says: *"And without shedding of blood is no remission"* (Heb. 9:22).

Because of what Jesus did at the Cross, we can *"come boldly unto the Throne of Grace, that we may obtain mercy, and find grace to help in time of need"* (Heb. 4:16). So, His faithfulness to forgive sins is predicated solely and completely on Christ and what Christ did at the Cross, and by no other means.

JUST

Even though God is *"faithful,"* at the same time, He must always be *"just."* In other words, He cannot forgive sins, unless the failing Christian has placed his faith and confidence in Christ and what Christ did at the Cross.

At the Cross, Jesus satisfied the demands of the broken law. In other words, He died as a Sacrifice, in order that the price be paid, which it was paid to the full. All sin being atoned at the Cross, which it was, refers to the fact that the justice of God was totally and completely satisfied. As we've said before, we'll say again, sin can only be forgiven on the basis of justice satisfied. That justice was satisfied at the Cross and only at the Cross.

That's the reason that God could accept Abel's sacrifice, but could not accept that of Cain. Abel offered up a lamb which was a type of the coming Redeemer Who would give Himself on the Cross, and do so by the shedding of His Blood.

Cain offered up the fruit of his own hands, which God could not accept. The offering being rejected, of necessity, the offerer was rejected as well! Let the Reader always understand that.

The justice of God was forever satisfied at the Cross; therefore, God can be *"just"* in forgiving sins, that is if they are properly confessed, and can do so only on the basis of the price paid at Calvary (Jn. 3:16; Rom. 4:25; 5:1-2; Eph. 2:13-18; Col. 2:14-15).

John will go into more detail on this in the First and Second Verses of the next Chapter.

TO CLEANSE FROM ALL UNRIGHTEOUSNESS

The phrase, *"And to cleanse us from all unrighteousness,"* is based as well on what Jesus did at the Cross.

All sin was remitted, paid for, put away on the basis of the satisfaction offered for the demands of God's Holy Law which sinners broke, when the Lord Jesus died on the Cross. In other words, the Law was satisfied. All the sins the Believer commits, past, those in his unsaved condition, and future, those in his saved state, were put away on a legal basis at the Cross, and are in that sense forgiven the Believer the moment he places his faith in the Lord Jesus.

NOTES

But the forgiveness spoken of here by John has to do, not primarily with the breaking of God's Law, for that was taken care of at the Cross and recognized as such at the time the sinner placed his faith in the Savior. Therefore, sin in a Christian's life is a matter, not between a lawbreaker and a judge, but between a child and his father. It is a matter of grieving the Father's heart when a Child of God sins.

The putting away of the Believer's sin upon confession is, therefore, a forgiveness granted by the Father and a restoration to the fellowship that was broken by that sin. When the Saint confesses immediately after the commission of that sin, fellowship is not broken except for that time in which the sin was committed.

Not only does God forgive the Believer, but He also cleanses him from the defilement which he incurred in committing that act of sin (Wuest).

The verb *"to cleanse"* speaks of a single act of cleansing, which pertains to the *"sin"* committed. All the previous sins of the Believer, and no matter how many they previously were, were handled at the Cross, and are held against the Believer no longer. In other words, in God's Books, the account has been cleared, and because of what Jesus did at the Cross.

So the act of cleansing pertains only to the one sin committed, and because everything else has been cleansed.

When a Christian has been cleansed from all unrighteousness, it means exactly what it says — *"all unrighteousness."* This should be obvious, because the least unrighteousness would compel the *"Righteousness of God"* to pronounce the verdict of damnation upon us.

To be cleansed so completely of all unrighteousness is to be declared righteous by the righteous Judge, and is to be admitted to fellowship with God Who is Light. In other words, fellowship and communion with the Lord is instantly restored.

DOES GOD REQUIRE MORE THAN CONFESSION ON THE PART OF THE FAILING BELIEVER?

No, He doesn't! And if anyone else requires anything else other than proper confession of our sin to the Lord, those who are demanding such, and whatever it might be, and whomever they might be, are sinning against the price paid by Christ at the Cross, which as should be obvious, is a very serious offense.

Unfortunately, much of the modern Church world no longer accepts God's way of restoration. It has a tendency to add its own foolishness, which is a terrible sin against the Grace of God. To add anything to this which the Bible declares alone is necessary, is in effect stating that what Jesus did at the Cross is not enough, and needs other things added. In fact, such could only be concluded as blasphemy. Such direction presents a vote of *"no confidence"* as it regards the Cross. But let the Reader understand the following:

Either what Jesus did at the Cross is enough as it regards sin and sinners, or else it isn't enough, and we must turn to the likes of humanistic psychology, etc. I happen to believe that what Jesus did at the Cross is in truth not only enough, but more than enough. In fact, John will say this very same thing in Verse 2 of the next Chapter.

Everything and always without exception, in some way comes back to the Cross. If it's sin, it means that we as Believers are failing to interpret the Cross correctly. If it's blessing, it's because of what Jesus did at the Cross, and solely because of what Jesus did at the Cross.

(10) "IF WE SAY THAT WE HAVE NOT SINNED, WE MAKE HIM A LIAR, AND HIS WORD IS NOT IN US."

The exegesis is:

1. John is here denouncing the claims of sinless perfection.

2. In effect, John is going back to Verse 8, speaking of Christians who claim they have no sin nature.

3. The person who makes such a claim, John says, makes God a liar, and because the Word says the opposite.

4. If we properly know the Word, we will properly know that perfection is not in us at present, and will not be, until the Trump sounds.

THE DENIAL OF SIN

The phrase, *"If we say that we have not sinned,"* presents the claim of sinless perfection, and the denial of specific acts of sin. In other

words, the Gnostics of John's day were claiming they had no *"sin nature"* and at the same time, were denying all acts of sin. In other words, they were claiming spiritual perfection.

How could they do that, and even their modern counterparts, when the evidence is so conclusive otherwise?

They explained it away by claiming that the physical body was evil and, therefore, whatever it did was not concluded to be sin. They claimed their spirits and souls to be perfect, thereby untouched by whatever sins their bodies committed. As stated, their modern counterparts in the *"Word of Faith"* camp do the same.

Since their so-called conversion the Gnostics were denying any acts of sin committed in past time with the implication that none are able to be committed at present. This presents the claims of sinless perfection to the degree of the absurd.

IS GOD A LIAR?

The phrase, *"We make Him a liar,"* speaks of the persons who make such claims.

Wuest translated this: *"If we say that we have not sinned and are not now in such a state that we could sin, a liar we are making Him, and His Word is not in us."*

The emphasis is on the words *"a liar"* which in the Greek is placed forward in the sentence. We are doing more than just lying, more than deceiving our own selves by our lying. These two statements are incomplete. The worst that we are doing by our false claim is really blasphemous: we are making *"God a liar!"*

If you and I philosophize or theologize our sins away and think that they do not need the Blood of Jesus, God's Son, we are making God Himself a liar! No less. Let us face this fact! Let it frighten us away from such foolish claims!

HIS WORD

The phrase, *"And His Word is not in us,"* presents *"the truth"* of Verses 6 and 8. This Truth and this Light are the contents of *"His Word,"* and they come to us in *"His Word."*

The whole Word of God declares that we were sinners, and at times, even as Christians, that we still sin. So in a sense that makes us

NOTES

"sinners," even at the present, and even though converted. From beginning to end the Word of God deals with us as with sinners. Its history, its law, its Gospel presents sinners: lost sinners, ransomed sinners, saved sinners, damned sinners, glorified sinners.

To have God's Word "in us" is to have received it in the heart, to hold it in faith, to be governed by it and by all it says to us, as we attempt to live this life for the Lord. It is not in us when we close our hearts to it and believe something else, holding to something else, following something else. This is making God a liar.

The fact of sin is such that God had to become man, and die on a Cross, in order that sin may be properly addressed. If we properly understand His Word, we will properly understand the Cross. We will then know how bad that sin is, and as well, the only way of victory over sin that it not rule and reign in our lives.

Even if we know these great Truths, and especially if we do know these great Truths, we will know our frailty, our tendency toward wrongdoing, and how that we must ever deny ourselves, thereby taking up the Cross daily to follow Christ. In this way only, can the domination of sin in our lives be defeated. But even then, it doesn't teach sinless perfection, as should be obvious.

"Oh, now I see the cleansing wave!
"The fountain deep and wide;
"Jesus, my Lord, mighty to save,
"Points to His wounded side."

"I rise to walk in Heaven's own light
"Above the world of sin,
"With heart made pure and garments
     white,
"With Christ enthroned within."

"Amazing Grace! 'Tis Heaven below
"To feel the Blood applied,
"And Jesus, only Jesus know,
"My Jesus crucified."

CHAPTER 2

(1) "MY LITTLE CHILDREN, THESE THINGS WRITE I UNTO YOU, THAT YE SIN NOT. AND IF ANY MAN SIN, WE HAVE AN ADVOCATE WITH THE FATHER, JESUS CHRIST THE RIGHTEOUS:"

The composite is:

1. The phrase, *"My little children,"* was a phrase used by Christ (Jn. 13:33). John had caught the phrase and its spirit.

2. The Holy Spirit here through John tells us *"sin not."* Were that not possible, the Holy Spirit would not have said such a thing. In other words, no Believer has to sin.

3. The phrase, *"And if any man sin"* shows that John regarded sin in the Believer's life, not as habitual, but as extraordinary, as infrequent.

4. *"Advocate"* in the Greek is *"parakletos,"* and means, *"one called to your side."*

5. This advocate is the Lord Jesus Christ, Who is Righteous, and Who pleads our case on the basis of His Righteousness, and our Faith therein.

LITTLE CHILDREN

The phrase, *"My little children,"* presents evidence, I think, that John had reached an advanced period of life when he wrote this Epistle. Such terminology as *"my little children,"* could only come from one who was of advanced years. In fact, six times in this Letter occurs this tender and caressing phrase (I Jn. 2:1, 12, 28; 3:18; 4:4; 5:21).

John was now aged and he felt a fatherly care for those over whom he had influenced. In a sense, he was their spiritual progenitor.

John was the last of the original Twelve to die. It is said as he grew increasingly older, knowing that he would soon leave this mortal coil, he made the statement quite often, *"When I'm gone, there will be no one left who saw Him, who heard Him, who walked with Him, who knew Him."*

SIN NOT

The phrase, *"These things write I unto you, that ye sin not,"* presents the fact that the Lord saves us from sin and not in sin. Two facts are presented in this Verse:

1. The fact that we as Believers do not have to sin.

2. But if we sin, we have Christ as our Advocate, to forgive, cleanse, and restore.

Even though John emphatically tells us to *"sin not,"* he doesn't really tell us how to carry this out, leaving that to Paul.

There is only one way the Believer can live free from sin, which refers to the fact of sin not having dominion over him. That is the way of the Cross. And if the Believer doesn't know and understand this particular way, which is God's only prescribed order of victory, then the sin nature will dominate the Believer just as surely as it did before his conversion.

In this prescribed order of victory for the Child of God, there are three principles to which one must look, to which I will continue to champion throughout this Volume. They are as follows:

THE CROSS OF CHRIST

Paul said: *"Know you not, that so many of us as were baptized into Jesus Christ were baptized into His Death?"*

"Therefore we are buried with Him by baptism into death: that like as Christ was raised up from the dead by the Glory of the Father, even so we also should walk in newness of life.

"For if we have been planted together in the likeness of His Death, we shall be also in the likeness of His Resurrection" (Rom. 6:3-5).

Please understand that the Apostle here is not speaking of Water Baptism, but rather the Crucifixion of Christ. He uses the word *"Baptism,"* because it comes closer to explaining that which really happens than any other word.

Whenever you as a believing sinner evidence Faith in Christ, and we speak of the time that you were initially saved, in the Mind of God, you were literally baptized into the Death of Christ, buried with Him, and raised with Him in newness of life.

Of course, you were not at the Cross when Jesus died, but in the Mind of God your Faith put you there. The Believer must understand, that Jesus died for us. His Death was not an accident or an incident or an execution. He freely breathed out His Own Life, offering up Himself as a Sacrifice, all for us, in order that we might be *"delivered from this present evil world"* (Gal. 1:4).

NOTES

Whenever this took place something happened to us, something so glorious that it defies description. Listen again to what Paul said:

"Knowing this, that our old man is crucified with Him, that the body of sin might be destroyed, that henceforth we should not serve sin" (Rom. 6:6).

This means that when Jesus died, you dying with Him destroyed the power of sin within your life. Your *"old man"* was crucified with Him, meaning that everything you were before Salvation, all the evil, iniquity, bondage of darkness, etc., all and without exception were totally and completely destroyed at that time.

The actual meaning is, the power of the sin nature was destroyed in your life at that time. As we've said in previous Commentary, the sin nature controlled you before Salvation, now its power is broken. Paul plainly said:

"For he that is dead is freed from sin" (Rom. 6:7).

This is not speaking of physical death, but rather when your *"old man"* died with Christ at His Crucifixion.

These Scriptures we've just quoted from Romans, are your foundation. You must ever understand that the reason for your victory is because of what Christ did at the Cross. You must never leave this Finished Work, understanding that all of your victory is found in what Jesus did at the Cross.

YOUR FAITH IN HIS FINISHED WORK

Paul said: *"Now if we be dead with Christ, we believe that we shall also live with Him"* (Rom. 6:8).

The idea here is that we died with Christ when He died on the Cross. Our Faith in Him put us literally into His Crucifixion, as well as His Burial and Resurrection.

Understanding that our Faith is to ever be anchored in what He did there, believing that as we died with Him, *"we shall also live with Him."*

Now this is not speaking of the coming Resurrection when all of us will be changed, but rather our present life and living. This is what Paul was speaking of when he said:

"I am crucified with Christ: nevertheless I live; yet not I, but Christ liveth in me: and

the life which I now live in the flesh I live by the Faith of the Son of God, Who loved me, and gave Himself for me" (Gal. 2:20).

Our Faith is to ever be anchored in what Jesus did for us at the Cross, knowing that it is by this and this alone that we can walk in victory. It is all because of Christ. Listen again to Paul:

"Knowing that Christ being raised from the dead dieth no more; death has no more dominion over Him" (Rom. 6:9).

When Jesus died on the Cross, He atoned for all sin, past, present, and future. The wages of sin is death, but if there is no more sin, at least no more sin unatoned, then death couldn't hold Christ. In other words, His Resurrection was a foregone conclusion. Having atoned for all sin, death has no more dominion over Him. And if it has no more dominion over Him, it has no more dominion over us who have placed our Faith and trust in Him.

The Believer must understand that sin and death go hand in hand. To pull sin to the breast is to pull death to the breast as well. Conversely, to defeat sin, which Jesus did, is also to defeat death.

When the Believer places his Faith exclusively in Christ and what Christ did at the Cross, he now begins to travel a road of life, victory, and power. It is all dependent on our faith, but more particularly, our Faith in what Jesus did for us at the Cross. Through what He did, we are no longer dominated by sin and death. Listen again to Paul:

"For in that He died, He died unto sin once: but in that He liveth, He liveth unto God" (Rom. 6:10).

Him dying unto sin once, means that His Death was so effective in paying the price for sin that it will never have to be done again. His work is a Finished Work, with Him now literally seated *"on the right hand of the Majesty on High"* (Heb. 1:3).

At the Cross all sin was atoned, which means that Satan lost his legal hold on humanity, at least for those who will believe, which also means that every demon was defeated, and man can go free. The price has been fully paid, and the Believer must place his Faith exclusively in that Finished Work (Col. 2:14-15).

NOTES

In that Jesus now lives, and He definitely does, having overcome sin and death, this means that due to the fact that we are *"in Christ,"* we as well, *"live,"* and furthermore, we *"live unto God."* This means that our life is anchored in the Lord and all that He has done for us. Let's go again to Paul:

"Likewise reckon ye also yourselves to be dead indeed unto sin, but alive unto God through Jesus Christ our Lord" (Rom. 6:11).

Understanding all of this, that Calvary was totally and completely for you, and that you are now raised in newness of life, you are to *"reckon yourselves to be dead indeed unto sin,"* which actually says *"dead indeed unto the sin."* This again speaks of your Faith.

You are to believe that what Jesus did for you at the Cross was totally and completely sufficient. Now notice what this text says:

It doesn't say that *"the sin"* or *"the sin nature"* is dead, but it does say that we are *"dead indeed unto the sin nature."* And we must continue to understand that we are dead unto this sin nature, because of what Jesus did at the Cross, and our Faith in His great Sacrifice.

At the same time, while I conclude myself by my faith to be *"dead indeed unto sin,"* which speaks of my *"old man being crucified with Him,"* on the other side of the coin so to speak, I am now *"alive unto God through Jesus Christ my Lord,"* which refers to what Jesus did at the Cross.

Any time the phrase is used *"through Jesus Christ,"* or *"in Jesus Christ,"* etc., always and without exception, it is speaking of what Christ did at the Cross. Our Faith must be anchored in that Finished Work, and we must never allow it to be moved to other things.

THE POWER OF THE HOLY SPIRIT

Once our faith is properly placed, the Holy Spirit will grandly and gloriously help me. Listen again to Paul:

"There is therefore now no condemnation to them which are in Christ Jesus, who walk not after the flesh, but after the Spirit" (Rom. 8:1).

In a moment I'm going to deal with *"walking after the flesh"* and *"walking after the Spirit."* But first of all, let us understand that with the Holy Spirit now helping us, which

He definitely will do, once we understand the Cross, and there place our faith, we can now easily do what Paul told us we must do:

"Let not sin therefore reign in your mortal body, that you should obey it in the lust thereof" (Rom. 6:12).

While the sin nature continues to dwell within our mortal bodies, even as we have addressed some pages back, it is not to rule or reign in our lives. With our Faith properly placed in the Cross, which guarantees the help of the Holy Spirit, we can now do exactly what Paul said to do, just simply not allow the sin nature to reign. But the Believer must understand that we can only do this in this fashion, providing our faith is placed securely in the Cross of Christ, which means that we're depending totally on what Jesus did there for us, which guarantees the help of the Holy Spirit.

To be frank, without the help of the Spirit, there is no way that the Believer can keep the sin nature from reigning in his life. But with the help of the Holy Spirit, Who will always help us according to our Faith in Christ, victory comes easily. We can then do exactly which John said do, *"sin not."*

Paul said, *"let no"* and John said, *"sin not."* They both refer to the same thing, but can only be brought about by Faith and confidence exclusively placed in the Finished Work of Christ.

Paul also said:

"Neither yield ye your members as instruments of unrighteousness unto sin (the sin) *but yield yourselves unto God, as those that are alive from the dead, and your members as instruments of Righteousness unto God"* (Rom. 6:13).

As should be understandable, with the Believer's Faith properly placed, which guarantees the help of the Holy Spirit, yielding the members of our physical bodies as instruments of righteousness is an easy thing to do. This speaks of our tongue, eyes, ears, feet, hands, sexual organs, etc. However, if we try to obey this in any other manner, we simply will not be able to do here what Paul says we must do. Notice again what Paul said:

"For sin shall not have dominion over you: for you are not under the Law, but under Grace" (Rom. 6:14).

NOTES

If we understand the veracity of the Cross, and there place our Faith and there leave our Faith, which guarantees the help of the Spirit, we have the assurance of the Word of God, which definitely cannot lie, that *"sin shall not have dominion over us."* This is God's prescribed order of victory. And it is His only prescribed order of victory. This we must never forget!

WALKING AFTER THE FLESH

In Romans 8:1, we are told not to walk after the flesh. So what does walking after the flesh actually mean?

Most Christians think that it refers to watching too much television, or being too interested in sports, etc. No, that's not the idea at all!

"Walking after the flesh" is trying to live this life and I speak of this Christian life, by means other than *"walking after the Spirit."* Let us be more specific:

"Walking after the flesh" is depending on self, or other things, other than the Cross and what Jesus did there. In fact, the *"other things"* in which we place our faith and trust, may in fact be good things. And oftentimes, because these things are *"good,"* it makes us think that what we are doing is spiritual.

Let the Reader understand, if it's not Faith exclusively in what Jesus did at the Cross, then irrespective as to what it is we might be doing, we are actually *"walking after the flesh."* The Scripture is very blunt as to what the Lord thinks of this.

The Holy Spirit though Paul bluntly says: *"So then they that are in the flesh cannot please God"* (Rom. 8:8).

When Paul uses the word *"flesh,"* most of the time he is speaking of our own strength and ability minus the help of the Holy Spirit. By the use of this word *"flesh,"* he is bluntly telling us that we simply cannot be what we ought to be in the Lord by our own efforts. No matter how consecrated these efforts may be, no matter how dedicated they may be, if our faith and trust is in these efforts, the Holy Spirit constitutes it as *"flesh,"* which God can never bless.

We can be what we ought to be only by trusting in what Jesus did at the Cross on our behalf.

In fact, *"walking after the flesh,"* is the same thing as being *"carnally minded"* (Rom. 8:6).

WALKING AFTER THE SPIRIT

Many Christians have the idea that their doing spiritual things constitutes *"walking after the Spirit."* It doesn't! And that's what confuses most Christians.

Were we to ask what constitutes walking after the Spirit, most would answer according to the following:

They would think that reading one's Bible, or a dedicated prayer life, or witnessing to souls, or giving money to the Work of the Lord, or other similar things, constitutes walking after the Spirit. While these things are definitely good, and while every true Christian will definitely engage himself in these things, that is not what Paul is talking about.

"Walking after the Spirit" is understanding the Cross, and placing one's Faith in that Finished Work of Christ, understanding that He had to do for us what we couldn't do for ourselves.

The Spirit of God works exclusively within the parameters of the Finished Work of Christ. In fact, He works so closely within these parameters that it is referred to as *"the Law of the Spirit of Life in Christ Jesus"* (Rom. 8:2). In other words, what Christ did at the Cross was a legal work, and is referred to as a *"Law,"* and of course, a Law made by God. The Holy Spirit works exclusively within this *"Law,"* from which He will not deviate. That's the reason we continue to say that the object of our Faith must always, and without exception be, *"in Christ Jesus,"* which refers to what He did at the Cross.

The Holy Spirit fastidiously adheres to this *"Law,"* and He demands that we as well hold fast to this Law, and our doing so guarantees us *"freedom from the law of sin and death."*

This is the only way we can obey the admonition given by John the Beloved, that *"ye sin not."*

OUR ADVOCATE

The phrase, *"And if any man sin, we have an Advocate with the Father, Jesus Christ the Righteous,"* speaks volumes to us.

As we've said several times, the Bible does not teach sinless perfection. And those who would claim they have reached that place need only look closer at themselves. As well, if someone questions our loved ones, and those who are around us constantly, it will quickly become obvious that we haven't reached the place of sinless perfection. In fact, such a thought borders on the ludicrous.

Even if the Believer fully understands the Cross, and has his Faith properly placed there, still, the struggle between the flesh and the Spirit is always so constant that the Believer will slip up at times. It shouldn't happen, but it does! However, this is far different than sin dominating an individual, which it does with any and every Christian who doesn't understand the Cross.

Even though there is no limit placed on the Advocacy of Christ, and because there can be no limit, still, the Holy Spirit is assuming here that the sin or sins of which He speaks are infrequent.

The word *"Advocate"* is the same as *"lawyer,"* which refers to *"one who undertakes and champions our cause."* As someone has well said, if we have to have an advocate (lawyer), and of course we're speaking in the spiritual sense, it doesn't hurt to have One Whose Father is the Judge.

Christ as our Advocate does not plead that we are innocent or adduce extenuating circumstances. In fact, He acknowledges our guilt and presents His vicarious work as the ground of our acquittal. He stands in the Court of Heaven *"a Lamb as it had been slain"* (Rev. 5:6), and the marks of His sore passion are a mute but eloquent appeal.

The Scripture says, *"We have an advocate with the Father."* *"With"* in the Greek is *"pros,"* and means, *"facing the Father."*

Actually, this is what Paul was speaking of when He said: *"Wherefore He is able also to save them to the uttermost who come unto God by Him, seeing He ever liveth to make intercession for them"* (Heb. 7:25).

"Intercession" is what the *"Advocate"* does! So what does it all mean?

INTERCESSION

As it regards *"intercession,"* exactly what does Christ do on our behalf, whenever we sin?

In fact, He really doesn't do anything. His work has already been done, and was done at the Cross. His very Presence before God guarantees this of which we speak. That's what the Holy Spirit means by Jesus *"Facing the Father."*

His very Presence at the Throne of God proclaims the fact that the Father has accepted the Sacrifice made, which, therefore, guarantees all that Calvary has accomplished.

If it is to be noticed, Christ is referred to as *"Jesus Christ the Righteous."* God can accept Christ, because Christ is perfectly Righteous. Our Faith in Christ, guarantees us the Righteousness of Christ.

The Holy Spirit mentions the Righteousness of Christ, because it would be unjust to punish sin a second time — the penalty of the Believers' sins having been already borne at Calvary. In fact, the Spirit reveals these truths in order that the Believer may not sin; but if we do sin, we have an Advocate Who is the Righteous One and at the same time the Mercy Seat. His Work, His Person, and His Action all unite in maintaining the Believer in the enjoyment of conscious fellowship with God. As a Priest He deals with the guilt of sin; as an Advocate, with the restoration of the soul. Sin interrupts communion; the Advocate restores it.

The efficacy of His action is guaranteed by the Righteousness of His Person and the value of His propitiation, and these are unchangeable.

Before Peter sinned Christ prayed for him; when he sinned He looked on him; and when he repented He restored him — and restored him so effectually that Peter was able to strengthen his brother Apostles.

So effective is that Mercy Seat as a propitiation for sins that if all men would approach Him for forgiveness of sins, then all men would be pardoned. The atoning Sacrifice of Christ furnishes an ample provision for the Redemption of all men, but its benefit is only appropriated by those who believe.

THE PUNISHING OF SIN

Whenever the Church attempts to punish a fellow Christian for sin, in effect it is saying that Christ wasn't punished enough, and something needs to be added. As should be obvious, such action presents a monstrous sin against God.

If a Christian is sinning, and refuses to quit, according to I Corinthians, Chapter 5 that individual has to be disfellowshipped. But if the individual repents, and it's not hard at all to ascertain the sincerity of such a person, the Brother or Sister is to be instantly restored. They are to be told why they have failed the Lord, which means they have departed from total trust in the Cross of Christ, in fact placing their faith elsewhere, which caused the problem to begin with. The failing person is to be brought back to the Cross, his Faith once again anchored securely therein, which will guarantee his victory. This is proper restoration (Gal. 6:1).

But the idea that we are to punish the individual is completely foreign to the Word of God, and in fact, and as stated, is an insult to Christ and what He did at the Cross. For we as Believers to do anything that would insinuate that His Work was not sufficient, is a monstrous sin within itself.

Let the Reader understand that we have only one Advocate Who can do us some good, and that is Christ Jesus. We must be very careful we do not lean on the frail arm of man. But the tragedy is, most modern Churches demand that we lean on that frail arm. But let the Reader also understand that if we do such, we are abrogating the advocacy of Christ, for one cannot have two advocates. There is only one Advocate who the Father will recognize, and that is *"Jesus Christ the Righteous."*

(2) "AND HE IS THE PROPITIATION FOR OUR SINS: AND NOT FOR OURS ONLY, BUT ALSO FOR THE SINS OF THE WHOLE WORLD."

The structure is:

1. Christ is the satisfaction for our sins.

2. This *"satisfaction"* is of such magnitude that it includes the sins of the entirety of the world, if they will only believe.

3. Considering this, the heart must not deceive itself by thinking *"the Lord died for Peter, John, and Paul, but not for me."*

PROPITIATION

The phrase, *"And He is the propitiation for our sins,"* could be translated, *"He is the satisfaction for our sins."*

In the Biblical usage of the word *"propitiation,"* the thought is not that of placating the anger of a vengeful God, but that of satisfying the righteous demands of His justice so that His Government might be maintained, and that Mercy might be shown on the basis of justice duly satisfied (Wuest).

To properly understand *"propitiation,"* we must first of all understand that God is not of Himself alienated from man. God is as to His nature, love, and He loves the sinner. Witness the statement in John 3:16.

His feelings with respect to the human race have not changed and in fact, will not change. So let us say it again, *"God loves the human race."*

But the sin of man placed an obstacle in God's way when He in His infinite love desired to bless man with Salvation, and that obstacle was the broken Law and the guilt of man. The former cried out for justice to be satisfied, and the latter needed to be cleansed away.

Thus, in order that it might not be necessary for Him to demand that the penalty be meted out upon guilty mankind so that He might lavish His Mercy upon man upon the basis of justice satisfied, He Himself became the expiation demanded by His holiness and justice. There is no thought here of God placating Himself, or of rendering Himself conciliatory to Himself, or of appeasing His Own anger. The thought would be ridiculous. It is purely a legal operation.

The Judge takes upon Himself the penalty of the one whom He has adjudged guilty, and thus can show mercy. The judgment seat then becomes a Mercy Seat.

When the publican asked God to be merciful to him the sinner (Lk. 18:13), he really asked Him to offer that sacrifice for his sin which would put that sin away and thus allow a Holy and a Righteous God to bless him with Salvation. In fact, one might say that he was looking ahead to the accomplishment of the Work of Salvation at the Cross. His faith stretched out to that event and laid hold of it (Wuest).

Propitiation goes strictly to the Cross, where our Lord assumed the guilt and paid the penalty in His Own Blood, and thus removed the cause of alienation. Now a Holy and Righteous God can bestow mercy upon a believing sinner on the basis of justice satisfied.

FOR THE SINS OF THE WHOLE WORLD

The phrase, *"And not for ours only, but also for the sins of the whole world,"* regards the fact that the propitiation is as wide as the sin. If men do not experience its benefit, the fault is not in its efficacy, but in man himself.

The phrase of our study is one of the expressions occurring in the New Testament which demonstrate that the Atonement was made for all men, and which cannot be reconciled with any other opinion. If Jesus had died only for a part of the race, this language could not have been used. The phrase, *"the whole world,"* is one which naturally embraces all men; is such as would be used if it be supposed that the Apostle meant to teach that Christ died for all men; and is such as cannot be explained on any other supposition.

If He died only for the elect, it is not true that He is the *"propitiation for the sins of the whole world"* in any proper sense, nor would it be possible then to assign a sense in which it could be true. This Passage, interpreted in its plain and obvious meaning, teaches the following things:

1. That the Atonement in its own nature is adapted to all men, or that it is as much fitted to one individual, or one class, as another.

2. That it is sufficient in merit for all; that is, that if any more should be saved than actually will be, there would be no need of any additional suffering in order to save them.

3. That it has no special adaptedness to one person or class more than another; that is, that in its own nature it did not render the Salvation of one more easing than that of another.

4. What Jesus did on the Cross, so magnified the Law, so honored God, so fully expressed the Divine sense of the evil of sin in respect to all men, that the offer of Salvation might be made as freely to one as to another, and that any and all might take shelter under it and be safe.

Let the Reader understand that every major word in the realm of Christianity, whether it be Redemption, Salvation, propitiation,

Faith, Grace, Peace, Atonement, forgiveness, Mercy, etc., are all, and without exception, tied fully and totally to the Cross. In other words, the *"word"* in question, is either what was done at the Cross, or was made possible by the Cross.

(3) "AND HEREBY WE DO KNOW THAT WE KNOW HIM, IF WE KEEP HIS COMMANDMENTS."

The exegesis is:

1. The Apostle foresees the question which may be raised: how can I be assured that Christ is all this to me — my Propitiation, my Advocate?

2. We attain to personal and conscious acquaintance with Christ by observance of His Commandments.

3. The word *"Commandments"* as used here is not *"Law,"* which John never uses for the rule of Christian obedience. In the Greek it is *"entole,"* which means *"an order, command, charge, precept."* These precepts (Commandments) are those given by our Lord either Personally while on Earth or through His Apostles in the New Testament Books. Consequently, it refers to what Paul taught on the Cross as well as what John taught, etc.

WE KNOW

The phrase, *"And hereby we do know that we know Him,"* refers to a *"know so Salvation."*

In this instance, John using the word *"know,"* which speaks of knowledge, the language probably is a response to the opponents for whom knowledge was a key term.

The following is an example of Gnostic thought:

"Not yet are we able to open the eyes of the mind and to behold the beauty, the imperishable, inconceivable beauty, of the Good. For you will see it when you cannot say anything about it. For the knowledge of it is divine silence and annihilation of all senses . . . Irradiating the whole mind, it shines upon the soul and draws it up from the body, and changes it all into divine essence."

Irrespective of the long string of words, nothing is actually said here. As well, such thinking is clearly devoid of interest in moral conduct and unconcerned about human behavior. For the Hebrew or Christian mind, however, knowledge of God is not separable

from the experience of Righteousness. Consequently there is no greater claim one can make in knowing God than to obey Him. For John, therefore, the test of true knowledge of God is moral conduct. It is keeping God's Commandments. Let's say it another way:

If our claims of Christ do not fall out to the changing of our lives, and changed for the better, then our claims are hollow. True knowledge of Christ, changes one totally and completely, which is obvious to all.

COMMANDMENTS

The phrase, *"If we keep His Commandments,"* presents a different meaning than appears on the surface.

The word *"Commandments"* is not here *"nomos,"* which is translated *"law."* It is rather *"entole,"* which refers to *"a charge or a precept."* Consequently, it refers not only to that which Christ said while on Earth, but as well, the entirety of the New Testament.

Inasmuch as the theme of John's discourse is *"victory over sin,"* I would have to take this word *"Commandments"* to Romans, Chapter 6, where the Holy Spirit through Paul gives us God's prescribed order of victory. In fact, Paul bluntly stated that this Gospel which he preached *"is not after man."*

"For I neither received it of man, neither was I taught it, but by the Revelation of Jesus Christ" (Gal. 1:11-12).

The idea is, we will *"know that we know Him,"* if we place our faith and trust in Him and what He did at the Cross on our behalf. This way alone leads to victory over sin, and as the song says, *"purity within."*

Sadly, *"His Commandments"* are little known in the modern Church.

This morning while taping television programs for our daily telecast, *"A Study In The Word"*, I made mention to our audience that a study of the Cross was a study of the entirety of the New Covenant. And yet, most modern Christians know almost nothing about the Cross as it refers to our everyday walk before God. They understand it somewhat as it regards the initial Salvation experience, but that's about as far as it goes.

It's not a question of the modern Church refusing these Commandments, but rather, that they simply know nothing about these

Commandments. This is tragic, because it leaves the Believer without knowledge as to how to live for God; consequently, he tries to walk holy before the Lord by his own strength and ability, thinking all the time he's trusting Christ, which always falls out to defeat in one way or the other. In fact, attempting to live for God in this manner, due to constant failure, will plant seeds of doubt in the minds of such Christians, wondering if they really do know Him?

(4) "HE THAT SAITH, I KNOW HIM, AND KEEPETH NOT HIS COMMANDMENTS, IS A LIAR, AND THE TRUTH IS NOT IN HIM."

The diagram is:

1. It is easy to say, *"I know Him."*

2. If our claims do not correspond with keeping His Commandments, then we really don't know Him.

3. The Holy Spirit says that such a person is a *"liar,"* and the *"Truth"* is not in him.

HE THAT SAITH

The phrase, *"He that saith, I know Him, and keepeth not His Commandments,"* presents the fact that a true knowledge of Christ will always portray itself in Christlike living. If it doesn't, this is a sure sign that the claims are false.

There are tens of millions of professing Christians who presently fall into this category. They claim to know Christ, but there is no change within their lives. The Word of God plainly tells us that in such a case, these people are merely professing but do not possess.

According to Romans, Chapter 7, we know that the Holy Spirit through John is not speaking here of true Christians who really do not understand the precepts of the Cross, and are thereby failing, even though they are trying hard not to. These people are truly saved, with many of them even being used by God, and some being used in a great sense. Concerning these individuals, the Holy Spirit is constantly moving upon them, attempting to bring them to the place of victory, which is the place of the Cross.

The people of whom John speaks, concerns those who make great claims, but really aren't even trying to live for God. As someone has said, they try to cover up the

barrenness of their profession, by the loudness of their confession.

A LIAR

The phrase, *"Is a liar, and the truth is not in him,"* presents the Apostle mincing no words.

Whoever professes to know Him and yet does not subject his heart and mind to the Bible, i.e., *"His Commandments"* — is a liar and self-deceived. He who is governed by the Bible in him is the love of God perfected; that is, His love aims at the Believer being saved and knowing it, and living a life of victory over sin and of conscious communion. That love plans and provides this life of assurance, enjoyment, and holiness, and is perfected where these aims are realized.

The main thrust of this statement as given by John, is directed to self-called teachers, who claim to be teaching the Word of God. They were teaching error, and the Holy Spirit through the Apostle calls them *"a liar."* It has not changed to the present.

Every Preacher who preaches and teaches error is preaching and teaching a lie. To preach and teach a lie makes the one doing such, a liar as well.

The doctrine which has made greater inroads into the Pentecostal and Charismatic communities at the present time is the *"Word of Faith"* philosophy. To be blunt, this doctrine is not true and, therefore, that means that it is a lie. And as well, those who propagate this error are *"liars."* To lie about anything is bad, but to lie about the Gospel is something else altogether.

In John's day, those who believed error were led to perdition, which refers to the total wreckage of their souls. Presently, those who follow the error we have just mentioned will be led to destruction also. To be sure, this of which we speak is not the only error, but it is one of the most prominent.

There are many lies, while there is only one Truth. In effect, the Truth is *"Christ"* (Jn. 14:6).

Most all false doctrines in Christendom claim to preach Jesus, just as much as those who are teaching the truth. So what is the difference?

The difference is, those who claim to know Christ and who claim to preach Christ, but in reality are preaching error, are in effect serving *"another Jesus."* And that's the problem in the modern Church:

It's *"another Jesus,"* which is proclaimed by *"another spirit,"* which means it's *"another gospel"* (II Cor. 11:4).

Satan counterfeits his *"lies,"* by making them seem to be right, claiming Biblical foundation, and at times actually presenting some truth. In fact, error rides into the Church on the back of truth. This is one of Satan's greatest ploys. He presents some truth, but only to serve as bait, that he might project his *"lie,"* which will destroy the individual who follows such teaching.

(5) "BUT WHOSO KEEPETH HIS WORD, IN HIM VERILY IS THE LOVE OF GOD PERFECTED: HEREBY KNOW WE THAT WE ARE IN HIM."

The exegesis is:

1. We are to keep the Word of God, and can do so, if our Faith is solidly placed in the Cross.

2. Only then can the Love of God be perfected in one's heart.

3. Keeping the Word of God which perfects the Love of God within our hearts, are the two signs that *"we are in Him."*

KEEPING HIS WORD

The phrase, *"But whoso keepeth His Word,"* actually proclaims both the Old and the New Testaments. Of course, much of the Old Testament has been fulfilled by Christ. Nevertheless, it definitely provides a foundation for the New.

As we've already said several times in this Volume, the story of the Word of God in its entirety is the story of the Cross. At the same time, one might well say that the story of the Cross is the story of the Word of God. The entirety of the Word, be it Old or New Testaments, point toward one Figure, Who is Jesus Christ. More particularly, it points to what He did on our behalf by going to the Cross, in order that man might be redeemed. Again, allow me to make another statement which I've already made several times:

If one doesn't understand the Cross of Christ, that it is actually the center and circumference of all things, then one cannot really understand the Bible. In other words,

one's knowledge will be skewed in some way. In effect, John says this in his Gospel. Read carefully his words:

"In the beginning was the Word, and the Word was with God, and the Word was God" (Jn. 1:1). Here we have Jesus and the Word spoken of as one and the same. Jesus is the Living Word, which in effect states, that the entirety of the Word of God points exclusively to Him.

And then John said: *"And the Word was made flesh, and dwelt among us"* (Jn. 1:14). God became man, and for one purpose. John now tells us in the words of John the Baptist what that purpose was:

"Behold the Lamb of God, which taketh away the sin of the world" (Jn. 1:29).

So in these three Verses we are given the entirety of the Plan of God as it regards the human race. Furthermore, John said this:

"And I beheld, and, lo, in the midst of the Throne and of the four beasts, and in the midst of the Elders, stood a Lamb as it had been slain, having seven horns and seven eyes, which are the seven Spirits of God sent forth into all the earth" (Rev. 5:6).

This one Verse tells us what the Mission of Christ accomplished on this Earth. Christ represents us before the Throne of God, and does so as the *"slain Lamb."* Furthermore, we also see here the Holy Spirit, Who is so intertwined with Christ, one might say, that They are inseparable.

This proclaims the fact that the Holy Spirit works exclusively with us, for us, and in us, within the parameters of the Finished Work of Christ. In other words, the Cross made it possible for the Holy Spirit to do all the great things He does within our hearts and lives.

WHOSO

If it is to be noticed, John used the word *"whoso,"* or *"whoever,"* which includes all, and at the same time, destroys the religious exclusiveness of those who claim such.

The Gnostics, who were just beginning in John's day, claimed an intellectual superiority, and that only a few had this superior knowledge, which was actually one of their drawing cards. John shows here that a personal experiential knowledge of the Lord Jesus is open to all true Believers.

In fact, *"whosoever will,"* is the story of the Bible, which includes all, which means that Jesus died for all (Mat. 11:28-30; Jn. 3:16; Rev. 22:17).

We can only *"keep the Word,"* by understanding that every single thing we receive from the Lord comes exclusively through the Cross of Christ, and thereby placing our Faith. Then the Holy Spirit will help us do the things that need to be done, i.e., *"keep His Word,"* actually as is outlined in Romans, Chapter 8. It cannot be done any other way.

THE LOVE OF GOD

The phrase, *"In Him verily is the Love of God perfected,"* refers to the fruit of one who *"keeps His Word."*

God is love; He wants to perfect His love in the hearts of all Saints. In fact, this is the greatest thing of all. It's greater than signs and wonders; it's greater than earthly riches; it's the greatest thing that God can do for a human being — to perfect His love within the heart and life of a person.

The idea of Divine Love is thus complex. Love, in its very essence, is reciprocal. Its perfect ideal requires two parties. It is not enough to tell us, as a bare, abstract truth that God is love. The truth must be rounded and filled out for us by the appreciable exertion of Divine Love upon an object, and by the response of the object. The Love of God is perfected or completed by the perfect establishment of the relation of love between God and man. When man loves perfectly, his love is the Love of God shed abroad in his heart. His love owes its origin and its nature to the Love of God.

To sum up the matter, we would say that the Love of God here is the love that God is in His nature, produced in the Believer yielded to the Holy Spirit by the same Holy Spirit, which love causes him to have a solicitous watchful care of His precepts. This love is brought to its completion or perfection in the sense that it accomplishes that for which it is intended, namely, to cause the Saint to obey God's Word, not because he should, not because it is right to do so, not in order to escape chastisement should he disobey it, all of which motives may enter into the subconscious reasons he may have

for obeying it and which in themselves are proper motives, but he obeys the Word because he loves the Lord Jesus.

Paul, in Galatians 5:1-26, teaches that the Saint is not under Law, and has been put under a superior restraint to evil and a compelling urge to do right, namely, Divine Love produced in the heart by the Holy Spirit.

WE KNOW

The phrase, *"Hereby know we that we are in Him,"* actually refers to Romans 6:3. Paul there said:

"Know ye not, that so many of us as were baptized into Jesus Christ were baptized into His Death?"

We are *"in Him,"* by virtue of Faith placed in His Atoning Work on the Cross, which the Father recognizes in the sense of Jesus being our Substitute.

If we are truly *"in Him,"* we will *"keep His Word,"* wherein the *"Love of God"* will be perfected in us.

Many Believers do not know or understand what it actually means to be *"in Him."* In fact, Paul used the term *"in Christ,"* or *"in Him,"* about 170 times in his fourteen Epistles. Every time and without exception, it refers to what Christ did at the Cross, and our Faith in that Finished Work, which in the Mind of God literally placed us *"in Him."* It has to do with His Death, Burial, and Resurrection. He did all of this as our Substitute, which means He did it for us. Faith in Him, places us *"in Him."*

(6) "HE THAT SAITH HE ABIDETH IN HIM OUGHT HIMSELF ALSO SO TO WALK, EVEN AS HE WALKED."

The structure is:

1. To *"abide"* in Christ is to abide permanently, and denotes position and relationship.

2. Our walk is to be straight, which means the order of our behavior.

3. Christ is our example.

TO ABIDE

The phrase, *"He that saith he abideth in Him,"* pertains to a claim being made. Millions claim to abide in Christ, when in reality only a few actually do.

"Abide" in the Greek is *"meno,"* and means, *"to abide, to remain, to sojourn, tarry."* The

word refers, in a connection like this, to more than merely a position. It is used very often of persons abiding in a home, which implies more than mere position, but rather fellowship, communion, dependence, harmony, and friendship.

Therefore, to abide in the Lord Jesus implies not only position, but also relationship. There are three Greek words that give us the three aspects of a Believer's life.

1. The verb of being *"eimi,"* refers to the Saint's position in Christ. He has been placed into vital union with Him by the act of the Holy Spirit baptizing (placing) him in Christ, which is outlined to us in Romans 6:3-5.

2. After being placed into Christ, the Saint there abides (meno), which refers to fellowship with and dependence upon Christ, which speaks of communion and closeness of intercourse.

3. With the Saint now in Christ, and there abiding, he is to *"order his behavior (peripateo),"* to be like Christ, which speaks of the Saint's manner of life (Wuest).

When John used the word *"abideth,"* he was no doubt speaking of the dissertation he had given in the Fifteenth Chapter of the Gospel which bears his name.

He quotes the words of Christ: *"Abide in Me* (Christ), *and I in you. As the branch cannot bear fruit of itself, except it abide in the vine; no more can you, except you abide in Me"* (Jn. 15:4).

OUR WALK

The phrase, *"Ought himself also so to walk, even as He* (Christ) *walked,"* pertains to the manner in which we order our behavior. The Christlike life here admonished must be the continuous, habitual, moment-by-moment experience of the Believer, which means that it is no spasmodic infrequent sort of thing.

How are we to do that?

If it is to be noticed, the Holy Spirit through John placed Christ as our example.

There is a way it can be done, at least as far as a poor human being can do so, but it must be done God's way.

That way is, actually as we've already said several times, the way of the Cross. The Believer must know and understand that every single thing we receive from God has been

made possible by what Jesus did at the Cross. This must be the bedrock of our Faith, actually the foundation of all faith. In fact, the Cross can be termed *"the faith."*

Understanding this, our Faith is to be anchored into this solid rock of the Cross, which speaks of its benefits, and is never to be moved. I'm sure the Reader understands, however, when we speak of the *"Cross,"* we're not speaking of a wooden beam. In fact, the Cross is something which took place now nearly 2,000 years ago. The Sacrifice was done so effectively that it will never have to be done again.

But what took place at the Cross has continuing benefits, and it's the benefits of which we speak. These benefits continue, and in fact will never be discontinued.

As well, we should understand that it's the Holy Spirit Who Alone can help us to *"walk"* before God as we should. We must know and understand this. Within ourselves we can do nothing. Please allow me again to quote the Passage which we quoted some paragraphs back:

Jesus said: *"Abide in Me, and I in you. As the branch cannot bear fruit of itself, except it abide in the vine, no more can you, except you abide in Me"* (Jn. 15:4).

How can we abide in Him?

To fully understand this we must go to Romans 6:3. Paul said there: *"Know ye not, that so many of us as were baptized into Jesus Christ were baptized into His Death?"*

We are now *"in Christ,"* or rather *"into Christ,"* by virtue of what Jesus did at the Cross, and only by virtue of what He did at the Cross. We *"abide"* in Him, by continuing to make the Cross the object of our Faith.

This portrays the fact that we know and understand that within ourselves we cannot *"walk"* as we should, much less as Christ walked. Therefore, if it is to be done, the Holy Spirit must carry out this task, which He gladly will do. It is all predicated, however, on what Christ did at the Cross, and our continuing Faith in that great Sacrifice.

Faith in the Cross says several things:

First of all, as stated, it says that we know and understand that within ourselves we cannot *"walk"* as we ought to walk. It also says that Christ did for us what we couldn't do for ourselves. The Cross strikes at the very heart of man's problem.

In the Garden of Eden, Adam and Eve made the decision to *"go it alone,"* which means to do so without God. That has been man's problem ever since, even Christian man.

ERRONEOUS DIRECTION

Just today over our daily Telecast, *"A Study In The Word"*, Frances was reading parts of a letter written to me by a particular Preacher, with whom I'm not acquainted.

In essence, he was stating in the letter that he had found the key to all victory. And what is that key which he is proclaiming?

In essence, it was that we should go to particular meetings which specialize in deliverance. And the way of deliverance is that we write our problems down on a piece of paper, read them aloud to a friend in the meeting, tear the paper into pieces and throw the pieces on the floor, and then walk on the pieces, which is supposed to be symbolic of our victory.

It just so happens that there is absolutely nothing in the Word of God about such foolishness. This is just another one of man's foolish efforts which is similar to a thousand and one others of like kind, all and without exception, very wrong.

The tragedy about this, is that this came from a Brother who claims to be Spirit-filled; however, it goes along with what I've been saying, that if someone doesn't understand the Cross, two things become apropos in such a life:

1. Such a person doesn't really understand the Word of God.

2. The person is an open target for all types of false doctrine. Until man comes back to the Cross, he cannot understand himself, he cannot understand Christ, and he cannot understand what Christ has done for him. The key is the Cross and the Cross alone! (I Cor. 1:17).

(7) "BRETHREN, I WRITE NO NEW COMMANDMENT UNTO YOU, BUT AN OLD COMMANDMENT WHICH YE HAD FROM THE BEGINNING. THE OLD COMMANDMENT IS THE WORD WHICH YE HAVE HEARD FROM THE BEGINNING."

The composite is:

1. To love the Brethren is not a new Commandment.

2. To love the Brethren has been the foundation and the keynote of the Plan of God from the very beginning.

3. Since the old Commandment of love has been ever before the Believer, there is no excuse not to walk after this direction.

NO NEW COMMANDMENT

The phrase, *"Brethren, I write no new Commandment unto you,"* is once again not in the sense of law, but rather as an exhortation to the Christian.

The Believer is to walk as Christ walked. He is sanctified unto the obedience of Jesus Christ. He obeys on the same principles as those on which Jesus obeyed. It is the obedience of a life to which it is natural and delightful to do the Will of God.

A child submits to the will of the parent, but Christ did not obey in that particular way. He actually came to do the Will of God. Obedience was His mode of being and the law of His nature. This great inward principle, that is, the Divine nature operating in the Believer, motivates and characterizes his life. Only those who possess that new nature can understand this principle of obedience. All who are destitute of a spiritual birth are outside of, and ignorant of, this realm of love and light. And yet it is a common life — but common only to Christ and to the Believer.

The Old Commandment and the New Commandment are the One Commandment, and the word *"love"* is the Commandment (Jn. 13:34).

AN OLD COMMANDMENT

The phrase, *"But an Old Commandment which ye had from the beginning,"* proclaims John assuring his readers that the Commandment or Precept he is giving them is nothing new in quality, but on the other hand, old.

"Had" in the Greek speaks of continuous state or action in past time. The beginning here is the beginning of the Christian experience of the Readers. They had this Commandment before them and with them constantly during their lives as saved individuals.

FROM THE BEGINNING

The phrase, *"The Old Commandment is the word which ye have heard from the beginning,"* presents John putting an old truth in a new form or aspect in order to make it emphatic, and to prevent the possibility of misapprehension. The sense here is:

"All that I am saying to you is in fact an Old Commandment or one which you have always had. There is nothing new in what I am enjoining on you."

(8) "AGAIN, A NEW COMMANDMENT I WRITE UNTO YOU, WHICH THING IS TRUE IN HIM AND IN YOU: BECAUSE THE DARKNESS IS PAST, AND THE TRUE LIGHT NOW SHINETH."

The exegesis is:

1. The Commandment of love is both old and new.

2. Old, because John's readers have had it from the beginning of their Christian experience. New, because, in the unfolding of Christian experience, it has developed new power, meaning, and obligation, and close correspondence with the facts of Christ's life, with the crowning mystery of His passion, which translates into the Christian life.

3. Which fact is true in Him and in you.

4. The *"darkness"* pertains to the time before Christ.

5. The *"true light"* is Christ, and pertains to the time since Christ has come, which light will shine forever.

A NEW COMMANDMENT

The phrase, *"Again, a new commandment I write unto you,"* is actually the old commandment renewed and made complete in meaning by Jesus Christ (Lev. 19:18; Jn. 13:34).

The idea is that which had been given under the Old Covenant could not be brought to fruition, until the coming of Christ. When He came, He made it real, because in essence, He was and is the Commandment. Of course, we speak of the commandment of love.

The word *"again"* as John uses it, in effect says, *"in another sense, from another point of view, not in itself but in our recognition of it, it is a new commandment."* The next phrase tells us why.

IN HIM AND IN YOU

The phrase, *"Which thing is true in Him and in you,"* refers to the fact that Jesus has

NOTES

made everything real, or one might say, *"everything new."*

This commandment of love is as old as the story of Cain and Abel, but it really could not be put into practice until Jesus came. It was all *"in Him,"* and now it can be *"in you."*

I think one could safely say that in Old Testament times, all that which the Lord gave to Israel as it regards the Law and in fact, every precept, could only be said to be *"with them."* Now it is *"in them,"* exactly as Jesus told His Disciples that it would be. He said, and speaking of the Holy Spirit Who would make it all possible, and according to what He did at the Cross:

"Even the Spirit of Truth; Whom the world cannot receive, because it seeth Him not, neither knoweth Him: but you know Him; for He dwelleth with you, and shall be in you" (Jn. 14:17).

Before the Cross the Holy Spirit could help the Saints, and even enter into some of them for short periods of time. But it was not until the Cross, when the sin debt was paid, that the Spirit could come in to the heart and life of all Believers to abide, and in fact, to abide forever (Jn. 14:16).

Everything we receive from the Lord is a work of the Holy Spirit within our lives. In other words, He Alone is the One Who can bring about the Fruit of the Spirit or any and all of the Gifts for that matter. But the other point I wish to stress is that He is able to do this only because of what Jesus did at the Cross. It's the Cross that made all of this possible, and this we must never forget (Mat. 3:11-12).

DARKNESS IS PAST

The phrase, *"Because the darkness is past,"* refers to the fact that Jesus is now come, and because He has now come, ultimately all the darkness of sin and unbelief will pass as a parade goes by on the street. All parades have an end. So will end someday the parade of Satan's hosts. All of this is because of what Jesus did at the Cross.

THE TRUE LIGHT

The phrase, *"And the true light now shineth,"* refers exclusively to Christ, as the *"Light of the world."*

The word *"true"* refers to the fact that there are many fake luminaries in the world. They claim to be the true light, but they fall woefully short. I speak of Mohammad, Buddha, Confucius, plus a host of others which come and go.

Christ Who is this Light, has illuminated the hearts and lives of untold millions, and continues to do so even unto this hour. When He comes in, the darkness is dispelled, and we speak of the darkness of superstition, ignorance, fear, and unbelief. And if I didn't say the following I would be remiss:

Christ as the *"Light,"* was made possible by the Cross and by the Cross alone! The uncrucified Christ could not have delivered anyone. The crucified Christ can deliver everyone. So He is the Light, not only because of Who He is, which within itself is extremely important, but as well, and most of all, because of What He has done. That's the reason that Paul said: *"We preach Christ crucified"* (I Cor. 1:23).

(9) "HE THAT SAITH HE IS IN THE LIGHT, AND HATETH HIS BROTHER, IS IN DARKNESS EVEN UNTIL NOW."

The diagram is:

1. We can claim Salvation all day long, but if we hate our Brother, our claims are false.

2. How can we claim to have love, and at the same time hate our Brother?

3. If there is hate in our heart, then we are in darkness, which means that we're not walking in light.

FALSE CLAIMS

The phrase, *"He that saith he is in the Light,"* presents the fact that Christians fall into two classes:

1. Those who are in fellowship with God and, therefore, walk in light and love.

2. Those who are not in fellowship with God and, therefore, walk in darkness and hatred. Where love is not there is hatred. To be sure, the heart is not empty (Jn. 3:20; 7:7; 15:18; 17:14).

HATE

The phrase, *"And hateth his Brother,"* presents that which cannot be, that is, if we are truly in the light.

NOTES

Due to the frequency of the emotion of hate, let us look closer at the word.

In both Testaments the word for hatred describes an emotional response or attitude toward persons or things. The hated thing is decisively rejected; it is detested, and the individual wants no contact or relationship with it.

The fact that both God and human beings hate brings up a series of theological questions.

THE OBJECTS OF GOD'S HATRED

It is not surprising to read that God hates wickedness and will have no relationship with the evildoer. God, Who loves justice, rightly hates robbery and iniquity (Isa. 61:8). The Bible tells us that God also hates hypocritical worship offered by those whose lifestyles show that His moral standards have been ignored (Isa. 1:13-15; Amos 5:21). God's hatred of idolatry is also well established.

Usually we human beings are fearful of hatred. Both in ourselves and in others it becomes a dominating emotion that robs one of judgment and of compassion. But God's hatred is different. His hatred is always appropriate, focused on evil and the evildoer. And God's hatred is always balanced by His attributes of love and compassion.

Because God is the moral Judge of the universe, He must make distinctions between good and evil. Because God is wholly committed to good, He must react to wickedness and act passionately but wisely to punish. As the Psalmist says: *"You are not a God Who takes pleasure in evil; with you the wicked cannot dwell. The arrogant cannot stand in Your Presence; You hate all who do wrong. You destroy those who tell lies; bloodthirsty and deceitful men the LORD abhors"* (Ps. 5:4-6).

HATRED'S EFFECT ON HUMAN BEINGS

Old Testament occurrences of the word *"hatred"* usually depict this emotion in human beings as directed against other people. While the Psalmist can say he hates those who hate the Lord (Ps. 139:21), hatred generally is recognized as a destructive emotion. Hatred is associated with violence (Prov. 29:10), with interpersonal strife (Prov. 10:12), and with lies (Prov. 10:18).

The Old Testament specifically commands that God's people are not to hate their Brothers, as we read in Leviticus 19:17. The Passage goes on:

"Do not seek revenge or bear a grudge against one of your people, but love your neighbor as yourself" (Lev. 19:18).

Believers are, however, called on to join God in His hatred of evil ways. This is to be expressed by a decisive rejection of that which is wrong.

When a moral issue is involved, as in the statement, *"I hate every wrong path"* (Ps. 119:128), we can best understand hatred not so much as an emotion but as a value judgment expressed in a choice to have nothing to do with what is *"hated"* (Ps. 119:163; Prov. 8:13; 13:5).

HATRED OF GOD

In a few instances the Old Testament speaks of man's hatred for God (Deut. 7:9-11; II Chron. 19:2). This aversion for the Lord is expressed in Israel's history by idolatry and by rejection of the holy way of life regulated by the Mosaic Law.

Speaking of the final judgment against Judah in the Babylonian captivity, Jeremiah reports God's description of His people's antagonism and the tragic results of their rejection of God:

"Again and again I sent My servants the Prophets, who said, 'Do not do this detestable thing that I hate!' But they did not listen or pay attention; they did not turn from their wickedness or stop burning incense to other gods. Therefore, My fierce anger was poured out; it raged against the towns of Judah and the streets of Jerusalem and made them the desolate ruins they are today" (Jer. 44:4-6).

THE DYNAMICS OF HATRED

In human beings, hatred is a dangerous emotion. It is listed in Galatians 5:20 among the works flowing from the old sin nature. It describes the antagonisms that are so deeply rooted in human society (Titus 3:3).

The New Testament is clear that when Christ enters our life, we are to control hatred. As John points out twice in his first Epistle, our lives are to be marked by love

NOTES

for our Brothers (I Jn. 2:9-11; 3:14-15). These Passages show that the experience of hatred transformed to love is one of the evidences that Christ has entered our life! In fact, Divine renewal of our capacity to love even frees us to love our enemies, something that went against the common wisdom of the religious leaders of Jesus' day, who said, *"Love your neighbor and hate your enemy"* (Mat. 5:43-48).

VALUE JUDGMENTS

The transformed attitude toward people does not, however, mean that Believers are freed from making value judgments. We are still called on to *"hate what is evil"* (Rom. 12:9).

At times, even more difficult choices are called for. We best understand Jesus' call to *"hate . . . father and mother, wife and children, brothers and sisters — yes, even our own life"* (Lk. 14:26) in this context of choice. Where there is conflict between the Disciples' commitment to Jesus and other commitments, Jesus has prior and total claim on our lives.

Finally, John shifts our attention back to the raw emotional reaction of despising, which is part of the concept of hatred. He reports Jesus' warning that the unregenerate world is deeply antagonistic to Him (Jn. 15:25). John has earlier explained that *"everyone who does evil hates the light"* (Jn. 3:20). It should be no surprise that if we follow Jesus closely and live His kind of holy life, the world will hate us as well (Jn. 15:18-25).

Hatred, as an emotional reaction to persons, and particularly as a reaction that spills over into antagonistic acts, is wrong for Believers. Hatred, as a value judgment that guides us to have no contact with that which is wrong, is another matter entirely.

THE MEANING OF
"ESAU HAVE I HATED"

Many have been troubled by the quote in Romans 9:13 of Malachi 1:2-3: *"I have loved Jacob, but Esau I have hated."*

It is important here to note both the historical and logical context of each quote. In the original incident, God chose Jacob, rather than his older twin, Esau, to inherit the

Covenant Promises given to Abraham. This choice was made before the birth of the children (Gen. 25:19-23).

Malachi the Prophet answers the skeptical query of a spiritually wandering Israel, which says in response to God's affirmation of love, *"How have you loved us?"* (Mal. 1:2). The Prophet's answer is to point to the evidence of history. Jacob (Israel) and Esau were brothers. But God chose to give Jacob's children the land they were then enjoying, while Esau's ancient land became a desert.

In the Book of Romans, Paul is arguing that God exercises sovereign choice. He points to history for several illustrations. God chose Jacob (Israel) over Esau before the twins were born. Thus, His choice could not rest on any action or moral superiority of one of the twins. The choice was free, not based on any human works.

But yet, we know that God through foreknowledge knew what Jacob would be and as well what Esau would be. Also, we are to always understand that God's sovereignty will never violate His justice or nature. Whatever God does is right, and it's not right simply because He does it, but it's right because in fact, it is right.

There is no unrighteousness with God if, through foreknowledge, He sees the dispositions of two boys and chooses on the basis of what He can foresee in each one. So it is with God's present dealings with Israel and the Gentiles.

If He sees that Jews will be continually rebelling against Him and the Gentiles will not, can He not act accordingly without unrighteousness? God is not responsible for the acts of Esau or Jacob; Jews or Gentiles. He had to make the choice of Jacob over Esau due to the dispositions and lives of the boys, which he saw, as stated, by foreknowledge.

Concerning Israel, He as well, had to set aside Israel, due to her ever increasing rebellion of over 1,800 years. The only thing left for Him to do is to use the Gentiles if they will carry out His program.

DARKNESS

The phrase, *"Is in darkness even until now,"* presents the fact that the absence of love is the absence of Salvation. It is not

possible to *"walk in darkness"* and at the same time be saved.

Love and hatred cannot dominate the heart at the same time.

Hatred means not merely the absence of love, but the presence, in ever so small a degree, of dislike or any of the feelings already described, or those kindred to them. He who truly loves will harbor no ill will, or resentment, nor will he bear a grudge of any nature.

A PERSONAL EXPERIENCE

Some time back an investigative reporter who worked for CNN, which incidentally goes into about 150 countries of the world, set about to do a program on us which would be aired over that Network, which he said would put us out of business. In fact, this man had been our enemy for some years and had made one effort after the other to cause us great problems. His other efforts had been carried out over a local station, actually in Baton Rouge; however, this was to be over one of the world's largest Networks, so in his mind, he felt he could administer the death blow.

The truth was, he had nothing to air, so he had to rehash things which were 10 years old, and then make up lies concerning the balance of the program.

The morning after the program aired the night before, I was in prayer meeting. I was trying to pray for the man, but to be honest I was having a very difficult time doing so.

I finally gave up on my efforts, saying to the Lord, *"Please show me how to pray for this man."*

The Lord very sweetly and beautifully spoke to my heart saying, *"Ask Me to show Grace to him as I have shown Grace to you."*

I'll never forget that moment. All of a sudden, my entire thinking patterns about the man changed. I saw him in an entirely different light, and began to pray for him with an honest heart.

I realized how that the Lord had been so merciful and gracious to me, realizing that, it was easy to ask the Lord to then do the same for him.

To be sure, what the Lord did that morning in my heart, was more so for me than it was for anyone else. Despite the great harm this man had attempted to do, I must not allow anything negative to get in my heart toward him, and at the same time, must love him. And when the Lord showed me how as well as why, the task became much easier.

Incidentally, I learned a short time later that he was terminated from his employment. I have no idea as to why, but I know the Lord had a hand in the situation.

It's easy to love those who love you, but it's something else again to love those who have dedicated themselves to your hurt. But yet Christ is our great example, having died on the Cross for a world which in effect hated Him.

(10) "HE THAT LOVETH HIS BROTHER ABIDETH IN THE LIGHT, AND THERE IS NONE OCCASION OF STUMBLING IN HIM."

The structure is:

1. The type of love addressed here, is the God kind of love.

2. The fact that this Christian habitually loves his Brother-Christian with a God kind of love is indicative of his close fellowship with and dependence upon the Lord Jesus.

3. Love will remove the *"stumbling-blocks."*

THE GOD KIND OF LOVE

The phrase, *"He that loveth his Brother abideth in the light,"* presents as is obvious, the opposite of hate.

The word *"loveth"* as it is used here, is *"agapao,"* which is the *"God kind of love."* In other words, this love is not possible to come by except from the Lord, and it is given only to Believers. The world actually knows nothing of this type of love, and in fact, cannot have this type of love.

The meaning of the word, at least as it is used here, is that of a self-sacrificial love that gives of itself for the happiness and well-being of a fellow-Christian (Wuest).

The *"Light"* mentioned here, is Christ Himself. The idea is that such a Brother *"abides in Christ."*

STUMBLING

The phrase, *"And there is none occasion of stumbling in him,"* actually has two meanings:

A. It means that such a person will not cause anyone else to stumble; and, B. There is nothing in him that will cause himself to

stumble. He who loves dwells in the light and is not a moral stumbling-block to others. To walk in the light is to be governed by love; to walk in the darkness is to be governed by hatred.

(11) "BUT HE THAT HATETH HIS BROTHER IS IN DARKNESS, AND WALKETH IN DARKNESS, AND KNOWETH NOT WHITHER HE GOETH, BECAUSE THAT DARKNESS HATH BLINDED HIS EYES."

The composite is:

1. He that has hatred in his heart is not merely going toward darkness, but in fact, *"is in darkness."*

2. Observe the climax: *"In the darkness is, and in the darkness walketh."*

3. The penalty of living in the darkness is not merely that one does not see, but that one goes blind.

HATES HIS BROTHER

The phrase, *"But he that hateth his Brother is in darkness,"* refers here to Christians, which shoots down the unscriptural doctrine of unconditional eternal security. One cannot have a Brother in the Lord, unless one is a fellow Christian. So, this is an individual who has given his heart to Christ, but has allowed something to come into his heart as it regards another Brother. As a result he hates this Brother, and as a further result, *"is in darkness."*

The idea as presented here, pertains to the fact that it doesn't matter what the Brother has done. We must not allow hate to fester in our heart, no matter the infraction of the other Christian toward us.

WALKS IN DARKNESS

The phrase, *"And walketh in darkness,"* proclaims a fulfilled condition. This is an individual who has once known the Lord, but is losing his way with God, simply because of hatred in his heart for a fellow Christian. Consequently, he walks in darkness.

Once again, the word *"walketh"* portrays the manner in which one orders one's behavior. This individual has purposely and deliberately chosen to go in this direction — the direction of grudge, ill-will, contention, i.e., *"hatred."* Why?

When a Believer ceases to look to the Cross, he begins to look to himself and not at all to the Lord. In fact, unless one properly understands the Cross, thereby placing his Faith, he doesn't really understand how to properly depend on the Lord. Consequently, he is depending on *"self,"* and because of that he gets offended very easily, etc.

While John mentions the Cross at least in the sense of the Blood of Christ, he doesn't go into detail. The reason is, it was to Paul that the great Truth was given as it regards the Cross. To be sure, everything that John said complemented exactly that which Paul taught, just as did Peter and the other writers; however, none of these writers went into any detail with the exception of Paul, and simply because this great Truth was not given directly to them.

BLIND

The phrase, *"And knoweth not whither he goeth, because that darkness hath blinded his eyes,"* presents the penalty of such a position, which is blindness. The penalty of living in the darkness is not merely that one does not see, but that one goes blind. The neglected faculty is atrophied.

Because of the position of hatred that one has taken, such indicates a definite, decisive act. In other words, one has purposely placed himself in the position of *"darkness,"* with the result being *"spiritual blindness."*

(12) "I WRITE UNTO YOU, LITTLE CHILDREN, BECAUSE YOUR SINS ARE FORGIVEN YOU FOR HIS NAME'S SAKE."

The composite is:

1. *"Little children"* refers to those who have been saved only a short time.

2. Our sins were put away at the Cross, with the result that they are never more remembered against us.

3. The permanent putting away of sin was *"for His Name's sake."*

LITTLE CHILDREN

The phrase, *"I write unto you, little children,"* in the Greek is *"teknion,"* and means *"little born ones,"* or those who have been recently saved. In fact, in this and the following statements, John will categorize Believers. The categories are as follows:

1. The Greek word is *"teknia,"* and means, *"infants, newborn"* (vs. 12).

2. The Greek is *"paidia,"* and means, *"little children, those able to walk and talk"* (vs. 13).

3. The Greek is *"neaniskoi,"* and means, *"young men, those grown to the prime of life and no longer tossed about like little children"* (vss. 13-14).

4. The Greek is *"pateres,"* and means, *"fathers, those who are matured in the Lord"* (vss. 13-14).

Of course, all of this is speaking in the spiritual sense, as would be obvious.

FORGIVEN SINS

The phrase, *"Because your sins are forgiven you,"* refers to the greatest blessing that any human being could ever know or understand. God's forgiveness includes the putting away of our sins, their guilt, defilement, and penalty, which was done at the Cross. Our sins were put away at the Cross, with the result that they are never more remembered against us. Our Lord cried on the Cross, *"It is finished."*

The Atonement, to which He had reference, was effected at the Cross and became forever the all-sufficient payment for sin. Actually, the translation should read, *"It stands finished"* (Wuest). God forgives sin not because of any merit in the sinner, but because of the infinite merit of the Savior.

HIS NAME'S SAKE

The phrase, *"For His Name's sake,"* pertains to what He did at the Cross. The words *"the Name,"* are an Old Testament term expressing the sum of the qualities which mark the nature or character of a person, in this case, the Person of God. It refers to all that is true of God in His glory, majesty, and might.

The expression here as used by John, refers to our Lord, and includes all that He is in His Glorious Person. Paul in Philippians 2:9-11 tells us that in view of the self-emptying of our Lord as He chose the Cross rather than remain in Glory (*"Who instead of the joy then present with Him, endured the Cross."* Heb. 12:2), God the Father exalted Him and gave Him *"The Name"*; placed upon the shoulders of the Man Christ Jesus, all the majesty, glory, and splendor of Deity, which He was. Because of what our Lord was in His Person as Very God of Very God, God the Father put away our sins, recognizing and accepting the Atonement He offered on the Cross (Wuest).

(13) "I WRITE UNTO YOU, FATHERS, BECAUSE YE HAVE KNOWN HIM THAT IS FROM THE BEGINNING. I WRITE UNTO YOU, YOUNG MEN, BECAUSE YE HAVE OVERCOME THE WICKED ONE. I WRITE UNTO YOU, LITTLE CHILDREN, BECAUSE YE HAVE KNOWN THE FATHER."

The exegesis is:

1. John writes to the *"fathers,"* those mature in the Lord.

2. He writes to the *"young men,"* which refers to those who are mature enough in the Lord to have *"overcome the wicked one."*

3. He writes to the *"little children,"* referring to those who have been saved for a period of time, and ought to know how to walk before the Lord.

FATHERS

The phrase, *"I write unto you, fathers, because you have known Him that is from the beginning,"* refers to those who were mature in the Christian life, having lived in fellowship with the Lord Jesus for many years, and thus having gained much personal knowledge of Him by experience.

While the youth provide energy for the Church, it is those who are older in the Lord, who are really the foundation of the Church. They have come through the stages of development, and as such have grown in the Lord, and as such are mature. While prayer intercessors certainly aren't limited to this group, still, I think that one for the most part, will find the majority of intercessors in this capacity.

While the designation has something to do with age, it is not limited to that. There are some who are aged in years, but very immature in the Lord, and some who are not very aged in years, who are in fact, very mature in the Lord. So, the designation has to do with spiritual maturity and not the number of years.

YOUNG MEN

The phrase, *"I write unto you, young men, because you have overcome the wicked one,"*

refers to Believers who have now come to the place where they were living in the power of the Spirit where their victory over Satan was a consistent one.

This is the Christian who has come to understand the Cross and what it all means, and has thereby placed his Faith. As a consequence, he is now witnessing the Holy Spirit working within his life, bringing forth victory after victory.

There was a time this wasn't the case. Not understanding the Cross, at least as it refers to Believers living an overcoming life, they tried to overcome by means of the flesh, which led to one defeat after the other. But now they've come to the knowledge of the Cross, just as had the *"fathers,"* and everything is changing. In fact, it should be the business of the *"fathers"* to tell the *"young men,"* what the Cross means as it regards our everyday lives and living.

The problem in the modern Church is, there aren't many *"fathers."* We have many who have been living for God for a long time, but they have little or no understanding of God's prescribed order of victory, so they cannot even help themselves much less someone else. This is a tragedy, but in the modern Church it just happens to be true. The idea is, we have people who have been living for God for many, many years, but yet as far as spiritual maturity is concerned, they are put in the category of *"little children."*

There is only one way to *"overcome the wicked one,"* and I mean that literally, just *"one!"* Listen to what Paul said:

"But God forbid that I should glory (boast), *save in the Cross of our Lord Jesus Christ, by Whom the world is crucified unto me, and I unto the world"* (Gal. 6:14).

Plainly, purely, and simply, the Holy Spirit through Paul tells us here that the only way to *"overcome the wicked one,"* i.e., *"the world,"* is by placing our Faith and trust *"in the Cross of our Lord Jesus Christ,"* which refers to what He did there.

WHY THE CROSS?

At the Cross, Jesus did two things:

1. He *"blotted out the handwriting of ordinances that was against us, which was*

contrary to us, and took it out of the way, nailing it to His Cross" (Col. 2:14).

Before the Law of God, which is oftentimes referred to as the *"Law of Moses,"* and I especially speak of the moral part, i.e., *"The Ten Commandments,"* man was found guilty. And the wages of that crime was death (Rom. 6:23).

On the Cross Jesus offered up Himself in Sacrifice, which paid that debt owed by man, and paid it totally and completely. For all who will believe, there is no more sin debt owing, and we speak of a sin debt owed to God. Jesus paid it all!

2. He *"spoiled principalities and powers (Satan and demon spirits), and made a show of them openly, triumphing over them in it"* (Col. 2:15).

How did He do that?

Sin was Satan's legal claim on humanity. In other words, due to the fact that man had sinned, i.e., *"broken the Law of God,"* this gave Satan a legal right to hold man in bondage and captivity. But when Jesus paid the debt, in effect, atoning for all sin, this removed Satan's legal right to hold man captive. So, the death of Christ on the Cross left Satan with no authority. And if he exercises authority presently, it is a pseudo-authority. In other words, he holds people in captivity by their consent. And how does he do that?

Regarding the unsaved, he continues to hold them in captivity because they will not accept what Christ has done for them.

Regarding Christians, regrettably and sadly, he holds millions of Christians in captivity in some way, because they do not know God's prescribed order of victory, which is the Cross of Christ. Just as we've said, his authority is a pseudo-authority, which means it's authority he shouldn't have.

But once the Christian begins to learn and understand that his victory is in the Cross, just as Paul said, then Satan is stripped of this pseudo-authority, and the Believer then *"overcomes the wicked one."*

LITTLE CHILDREN

The phrase, *"I write unto you, little children, because you have known the Father,"* refers to Believers who haven't been saved very long. The Greek word used here is *"paidion,"* and refers to a child in training.

It is the business of the *"fathers"* and the *"young men"* to help train this one in the ways of the Lord, which refers to the ways of the Cross (Rom. 6:3-14).

(14) "I HAVE WRITTEN UNTO YOU, FATHERS, BECAUSE YOU HAVE KNOWN HIM THAT IS FROM THE BEGINNING. I HAVE WRITTEN UNTO YOU, YOUNG MEN, BECAUSE YOU ARE STRONG, AND THE WORD OF GOD ABIDETH IN YOU, AND YOU HAVE OVERCOME THE WICKED ONE."

The diagram is:

1. The Holy Spirit uses the same phrase again as in Verse 13, and for purpose.

2. The answer is found in the Word (Rom. 6:3-14).

3. The Believer can overcome Satan (Rom. 6:14; 8:1-2, 11).

I HAVE WRITTEN UNTO YOU

The phrase, *"I have written unto you, fathers, because you have known Him that is from the beginning,"* presents the same that was given in the previous Verse.

The Holy Spirit through John repeats what was said for a particular reason. Of course, anytime the Lord says something once it is of great importance; however, when He says it twice, it is of double importance.

John is repeating himself here in order that the *"fathers"* may know and understand that God's prescribed order of victory has gotten them to this place — a place of overcoming strength — and they must not allow false doctrine to come in and destroy that. In other words, don't forsake the Cross!

From this we learn of the seducing power of false doctrine. That's why Paul referred to such in the following manner:

"Now the Spirit speaketh expressly, that in the latter time some shall depart from the Faith, giving heed to seducing spirits, and doctrines of Devils" (I Tim. 4:1). So the Apostle is warning the fathers that even though they've been living for God a long, long time, they must be on guard against these doctrines which on the surface seem so right, but in reality are so wrong.

THE WORD OF GOD

The phrase, *"I have written unto you, young men, because you are strong, and the*

Word of God abideth in you, and you have overcome the wicked one," presents the same warning to them. They are *"strong"* and have *"overcome the wicked one,"* only because *"the Word of God abides in them."* However, they are just as susceptible to false doctrine as the *"fathers."*

The idea is, if they start looking to that which is not actually the *"Word of God,"* and in reality is false, they will be brought to the place that they cannot overcome the wicked one. In other words, their spiritual strength will dissipate.

The Believer is *"strong,"* because he realizes that he personally is weak, and, therefore, has to rely totally and completely on Christ and what Christ did at the Cross. He must not forget that.

Most false doctrines teach the very opposite. Instead of building up Christ, they build up the individual. Think about the following for a moment:

False doctrine draws people to a Preacher. The True Gospel draws people to Christ. Let's say it another way:

The Message of the Cross draws people to Christ, while all other messages, draw people to Preachers, etc.

(15) "LOVE NOT THE WORLD, NEITHER THE THINGS THAT ARE IN THE WORLD. IF ANY MAN LOVE THE WORLD, THE LOVE OF THE FATHER IS NOT IN HIM."

The structure is:

1. The *"world"* as spoken here by John, pertains to the ordered system of which Satan is the head.

2. The things that are in the world pertain to its allurement.

3. It is the love of the heart and its object, which is at stake.

4. If the love of the Saint ceases to be for God, but rather the world, that individual has then lost his way.

LOVE OF THE WORLD

The phrase, *"Love not the world,"* speaks of the system of this world.

The word *"love"* as here used, is *"agapo,"* and speaks of the *"God kind of love."* It is the word used of God's love for a lost race of sinners, and which is self-sacrificial in its essence (Jn. 3:16), the love which He is by

nature (I Jn. 4:8), and the love which is produced in the heart of the yielded Saint by the Holy Spirit (Gal. 5:22).

Consequently, the question confronts us now as to how Believers can love the sinful world with a love produced in their hearts by the Holy Spirit. In other words, how can this God kind of love, which comes exclusively from God, be taken away from God as its object, and rather have the world as its object?

It is the same as when Jesus said: *"Take heed therefore that the light which is in you be not darkness"* (Lk. 11:35). How can this love which comes from God Alone, be changed as to its object? How can this *"light"* which is altogether from the Lord, be turned to darkness?

Some Greek Scholars claim that the Bible writers when taking certain Greek words over into the Bible, poured an additional content of meaning into them, as in this case, but at times used the word, not in its newly-acquired New Testament meaning, but in its purely classical connotation.

However, I personally don't think this is the case.

Before the Fall in the Garden of Eden, everything about Adam and Eve was of God. But due to free moral agency, they had the capabilities of taking that which was all of God and using it for selfish purposes, which they did. So if it could be done then, it can continue to be done, and in fact does continue to be done, even as John here bears out. Whatever God gives a person, be it love or particular gifts, which means it's all of God, can in fact, be turned to that which is evil. This is the warp and woof of the human being. This is why the Believer has to stay in a literal state of consecration, and to come to the bottom line, this is why Jesus said that one must *"deny oneself, and take up the Cross daily,"* that is, if they were to follow Him (Lk. 9:23-24).

THE WORLD

What did John refer to when he spoke of loving the world?

The word *"world"* as used here by the Holy Spirit through John, refers to the world system, wicked and alienated from God yet cultured, educated, powerful, outwardly moral at times, the system of which Satan is the head, the fallen Angels and the demons are his servants, and all mankind other than the saved, are his subjects.

This includes those people, pursuits, pleasures, purposes, and places where God is not wanted (Mat. 4:8; Jn. 12:31; I Jn. 2:15-16, being examples).

It refers also to the human race, fallen, totally depraved (Jn. 3:16). As such, it has its enticements and allurements. In fact, it is at least one of the greatest temptations to the Child of God.

The temptation is always present to borrow its systems or a part of its systems, and bring it over into the Church. We seem to forget that every single part of the world system is ungodly, unholy, and without merit of any nature.

The Holy Spirit has a way of doing things, and it does not include the things of the world. For instance, He has His Government for the Church, and it does not include any part of the manner and way in which the world operates its government. Also, He has a way and manner of attracting people to Christ, which is by the Word preached or sung or witnessed in some manner, anointed by the Spirit, and if we attempt to put the ways of the world into this mix, the Holy Spirit withdraws completely (Mk. 16:15).

So the *"love of the world,"* as it regards the Christian, can come about in various different ways. It attracts by its enticements, and it also seeks to become a part of the Church, of which the Holy Spirit will have no part.

THINGS

The phrase, *"Neither the things that are in the world,"* is referred to in the next Verse as *"the lust of the flesh, the lust of the eyes, and the pride of life."*

He does not say that we are in no sense to love anything that is in the material world; that we are to feel no interest in flowers, streams, forests, and fountains; that we are to have no admiration for what God has done as the Creator of all things; that we are to cherish no love for any or the inhabitants of the world, our friends and kindred; or that we are to pursue none of the objects of this

NOTES

life in making provision for our family; but that we are not to love the things which are sought merely to pamper the appetite, to please the eye, or to promote pride in living. These are the objects sought by the people of the world; these are not the objects to be sought by the Christian (Barnes).

In respect to *"things"* the Bible teaches separation, but it doesn't teach isolation. We are in the world, but we are not to be of the world. Our affections are to be on the things of the Lord. We are to use the things of this world, but not to abuse them, which refers to the understanding that our use is temporal.

THE LOVE OF THE FATHER

The phrase, *"If any man love the world, the love of the Father is not in him,"* records the fact that one or the other must go. God the Father will not share the love that must go exclusively to Him, with the world.

This one statement as given by John, puts a great part of the modern Church in serious jeopardy.

Regarding you the Reader, how much interest does the world and its carryings on hold for you? Naturally, in this age of information, we are aware as Christians of most everything that goes on. And as Christians we have an interest in what happens; however, that interest must be limited as to information only, and then only in a limited way.

The world system is very seductive. If we are not careful, our interests will go beyond the ordinary and can become enamored with what is taking place.

This is not a matter of rules and regulations, but rather, a matter of the love of the heart. If the *"love of the Father"* is as it ought to be, the world will hold no interest beyond a passing glance. In fact, the things of the world, no matter how highly touted by the world, will look tawdry to the Child of God. He sees through and beyond its allurements and enticements, and they hold no interest for him. As stated, we are in the world but not of the world.

(16) "FOR ALL THAT IS IN THE WORLD, THE LUST OF THE FLESH, AND THE LUST OF THE EYES, AND THE PRIDE OF LIFE, IS NOT OF THE FATHER, BUT IS OF THE WORLD."

The structure is:

1. There is nothing in this world's system that is of God.

2. The *"lust of the flesh"* is the passionate desire or the craving that comes from the evil nature.

3. The *"lust of the eyes"* also coming from the evil nature, craves that which it sees.

4. The *"pride of life"* is that which trusts in its own power and resources and shamefully despises and violates Divine laws and human rights.

5. These things have the world's system as its source, and not the Heavenly Father.

ALL THAT IS IN THE WORLD

The phrase, *"For all that is in the world,"* speaks of the world's system, and the fact that there is absolutely nothing of God in that system. That should settle the question.

Not only is that the case, to the contrary of that which is Righteous, everything in the system of this world in one way or the other is evil. Sometimes it comes from the evil side of the tree and sometimes from the good side; however, it is all from the same tree (Gen. 2:17). And because there are some good things from this particular tree, it deceives many people, and even many in the Church. While we as Christians are in the world, and as such we use certain things in the world as would be obvious; however, our sights, affections, and ambitions, must always and without exception, be directed toward the things of God.

THE LUST OF THE FLESH

The phrase, *"The lust of the flesh,"* refers to a craving, passionate desire, good or evil, according to the context. Here it refers to evil cravings.

"Flesh" in the Greek is *"sarx"* which here refers to the totally depraved nature as governing the individual's reason, will, and emotions. Thus, the lust of the flesh is the passionate desire or the craving that comes from the evil nature.

The word *"flesh"* here has no reference to the physical body except as that body is controlled or energized by the evil nature. The physical body and its members in themselves have no evil desires except as controlled by the totally depraved nature. To say that the physical body of itself has evil desires is Gnosticism, the heresy that matter is inherently evil.

To be frank, the human body and its members, are neutral. It is either controlled by the Holy Spirit, or it is controlled by the sin nature.

Of course, we know and understand that all unsaved people are controlled by the sin nature; however, the sadness is, many Christians are as well. How? Why?

Paul said: *"Let not sin* (the sin nature) *therefore reign* (rule) *in your mortal body, that you should obey it in the lusts thereof.*

"Neither yield ye your members as instruments of unrighteousness unto sin (unto the sin nature), *but yield yourselves unto God, as those who are alive from the dead, and your members as instruments of righteousness unto God"* (Rom. 6:12-13).

What did Paul mean by the statement, *"as those who are alive from the dead"*?

He is meaning that when we initially came to Christ, we were in the Mind of God, *"baptized into His Death"* (Rom. 6:3). Of course, this speaks of the Crucifixion of Christ. In essence we died with Him and in fact, *"in Him."* This was necessary because there was nothing in the *"old man"* that was salvageable. It was totally depraved and had to die. The way it came about is according to the following:

Jesus Christ was our Substitute, He died for us, or in our place. Our Faith in Him identifies ourselves with Him; therefore, in the Mind of God, it is reckoned unto us whatever it is that He did.

We died with Him, were buried with Him, and were raised with Him in newness of life (Rom. 6:3-5). That's what Paul meant by us being *"alive from the dead."*

We are to ever understand the means by which we were saved (baptized into His Death), understanding that all that we receive from God from henceforth will be because of what Jesus did for us at the Cross. We are to keep our Faith anchored in that Finished Work. This being done, the Holy Spirit, Who works within the confines of the Sacrifice of Christ, will then grandly help us. Now the Holy Spirit is controlling us, which means that we are *"walking after the Spirit"* (Rom. 8:1). This is so important that I must say it again:

For the Holy Spirit to reign supreme within our hearts and lives, the object of our Faith must ever be the Cross. This is absolutely essential (Rom. 8:2).

This being the case, there will be no *"lust of the flesh,"* which means that the sin nature will have no control. We can then yield the members of our bodies to Righteousness.

LUST OF THE EYES

The phrase, *"And the lust of the eyes,"* presents that which will definitely take place, if the *"lust of the flesh"* is predominant. If the Holy Spirit is in control, there will be no *"lust of the flesh,"* and there will be no *"lust of the eyes."* Now let the Reader peruse these words carefully, because they are very, very important.

There are millions of Christians trying not to look at that which is wrong, trying not to *"see"* that which is wrong, but rather fighting a losing battle, with their eyes being drawn to the ungodly. And let the Reader also understand that it really doesn't matter what measures that one takes in this particular state, they will not be able to control the *"lust of the eyes."* Whatever they do will be in the sense of opposing symptoms instead of the real cause of the problem.

WHAT IS THE CAUSE OF THE PROBLEM?

The *"lust of the eyes"* is caused by the *"lust of the flesh,"* so we have to know what is causing this initial lust.

It is the Christian's business to *"live for God."* This refers to being a good Christian, to being close to the Lord, etc. The great question is how do we do that?

The only thing the Christian can actually furnish as it regards what he does in order to live a holy life is to *"furnish a willing mind and an obedient heart."* While all the other things he does might be good, it's not going to draw him closer to the Lord.

In the first place every single thing we receive from the Lord, everything we are in the Lord, all and without exception, comes through the Person, Work, Ministry, and Office of the Holy Spirit. In other words, He Alone can make us what we ought to be in

Christ. It's all a work of the Spirit, and if we try to do it any other way, it simply won't work. In fact, the Holy Spirit actually refers to us in such a case as a *"spiritual adulterer"* (Rom. 7:3).

For the Holy Spirit to work within our lives, He demands only one thing, and that is for us to exhibit Faith totally and completely in the great Sacrifice of Christ. Faith in the Finished Work will always guarantee the help of the Spirit (Rom. 8:1-2, 11, 13). Let's say it another way:

The only way to defeat the *"lust of the flesh,"* the *"lust of the eyes,"* and the *"pride of life,"* is for the Christian to exclusively place their Faith in the Sacrifice of Christ, ever making that the object of our Faith. Otherwise, we've got a problem on our hands.

As it regards the Child of God, every single thing centers up in the Cross. We must never forget that. It's *"The Cross!" "The Cross!" "The Cross!"*

FAITH

Listen to Paul: *"For whatsoever is not of faith is sin"* (Rom. 14:23).

What did Paul mean by this statement?

When Paul speaks of faith, always and without exception, he is speaking of Faith in Christ, but more particularly, he's speaking of Faith in what Christ did at the Cross on behalf of lost humanity.

When Jesus died on the Cross, He died to not only save us from *"sin,"* but as well from *"self."* The *"sin"* pertains to our initial Salvation experience, while *"self"* pertains to our Sanctification. So we are to have Faith in Christ not only for our Salvation, but as well, for our Sanctification, i.e., *"our walk with God."* If we try to live this life by any other means other than by Faith in the Cross, God constitutes it as *"sin."* How is it sin?

It is sin because we are actually rebelling against God's prescribed order of victory. In other words, we are attempting to devise a way of victory by our own machinations, ability, and strength. We may not think of ourselves as doing this, but if we are not trusting in what Christ did at the Cross, and doing so exclusively as it regards our everyday walk, then whether we realize it or not, we are devising other ways, which is sin.

THE PRIDE OF LIFE

The phrase, *"And the pride of life,"* hits at the very core of man's problem.

It must be understood that John is speaking here to Believers. Strangely enough, when the Believer attempts to live for God outside of Faith in the Cross, which means he's trying to do so by his own strength and ability, even though such an effort always produces the *"lust of the flesh,"* and the *"lust of the eyes"*; still, even though such a direction brings on failure, the *"pride of life,"* is the result. In other words, faith in anything other than the Cross breeds self-righteousness.

THE FATHER AND WORLD

The phrase, *"Is not of the Father, but is of the world,"* refers to the source.

The idea is this: It is understandable as to what the system of this world is; however, the Holy Spirit through John is informing us that the things of the world can inculcate themselves in the heart and life of the Christian. There is only one way to overcome the world and all its allurements, and that is for the Christian to keep his eyes on Christ, and more particularly, on what Christ did at the Cross. Out of the Father proceeds all of the things of Heaven, while out of the world proceeds all the things of the world, which doesn't comprise a very pleasant scene. The beginning stages of the world may seem to be satisfactory; however, the end result will always be death. Satan is the God of this present world, and his method is to *"steal, kill, and destroy"* (Jn. 10:10).

The only true life and living there is, that which really satisfies the soul, is that which comes from the Father.

(17) "AND THE WORLD PASSETH AWAY, AND THE LUST THEREOF: BUT HE THAT DOETH THE WILL OF GOD ABIDETH FOREVER."

The composite is:

1. Whatever the allurements of the world, they soon fade.

2. The one who keeps on habitually doing the Will of God abides forever.

3. The Christian has a choice, the *"world"* or *"the Will of God."* One cannot have both!

THE WORLD AND ITS LUSTS

The phrase, *"And the world passeth away, and the lust thereof,"* refers to the fact that whatever the system of this world is, and whatever it promises, it cannot fulfill. And furthermore, the whole system of the world will one day come to an end.

The human race is a fallen race. This means that the world, too, is presented as alienated from God, especially by Paul and John. Paul in I Corinthians uses a whole series of contrasts to make it plain beyond all possibility of doubt that there is this alienation.

The wisdom of this world contrasts with the wisdom of God, and the spirit of the world contrasts with the Spirit of God. An even darker picture is painted in Romans.

Since sin has entered the world, the whole world is guilty, and it is judged and condemned by God (Rom. 3:6, 19; I Cor. 6:2). The ultimate and definitive nature of this sin is manifested in the fact that the rulers of this world crucified the Lord of Glory. Yet it is more, for angelic powers rule the sinful world (I Cor. 2:6; Eph. 2:2). This explains why God is not called Lord of the world, and also why there is no world to come.

So fully is the world identified with sin and the Fall that it can only be condemned and destroyed, or rather changed, in the coming judgment. This world of evil is in irreconcilable conflict with the world of God.

CHRIST AND THE WORLD

John uses different language, but the thought is materially the same. Christ is not of the world; He has come to it from God. He is in the world but the world does not know Him (Jn. 1:10). Nor does it believe in Him (Jn. 7:7). Though He comes to save, not to condemn, His coming does in fact bring judgment on the sinful, unbelieving world.

The prince of this world is judged first (Jn. 12:31). The first Epistle of John has contrasts reminiscent of Paul: He that is in you and he that is in the world (I Jn. 4:4), and those who are of the world and those who are of God (I Jn. 4:5-6), we who are in Christ and the world which is in wickedness or the wicked one (I Jn. 5:19).

Here again is the final conflict. The world has not escaped God's control, but it is in revolt against Him. By a new birth from God men may be saved. The world itself, as a sinful world, cannot be saved.

THE OBJECT OF SALVATION

This evil world is condemned and lost. Yet the world is still the theatre of God's saving action and the object of His saving love. Paul and John are again as one in stating this fundamental truth.

Thus, Paul says plainly that Christ Jesus came into the world to save sinners (I Tim. 1:15). The world is not just that from which sinners are saved; it is the place where they are saved. John made the same point with even greater cogency.

Christ has not merely come into the world. He has come as the Savior of the world (Jn. 4:42) or the light of the world (Jn. 8:12). He has come into the world in order that in it, as the abode of men, He might be the Savior of men.

The impulse behind this mission is that the world is the object of God's reconciling love. Two of the most basic and comprehensive Verses in the whole of the New Testament state this fact: John 3:16: *"God so loved the world . . ."* and II Corinthians 5:19: *"God was in Christ, reconciling the world . . ."* (Rom. 11:15). Predominantly the world here is, of course, mankind, but there are hints that it might have a wider reference, namely, to the world as God's creation.

Though the world is thus the sphere and object of God's gracious work, it is still true that there is no world to come. The reconciled world is the kingdom of God, the future creation, in effect, a new creation.

Though the world is reconciled, Believers are saved out of the world. A deep ambivalence lies over the word. *"When the world is redeemed, it ceases to be the world."*

CHRISTIANS AND THE WORLD

The theological understanding of the world determines the relation of Christians to it. This may be summed up in three statements:
1. Christians continue to live in the world.
2. We are not of the world.
3. We are sent in order to be a witness to the world.

The world is still the setting forth of human life and also of Christian life and ministry. As Paul says, Christians cannot leave it (I Cor. 5:10). We have to care for its affairs (I Cor. 7:32). As well, we cannot avoid dealing with it (I Cor. 7:31).

John gives the same teaching. Christians are in the world as Christ was (Jn. 17:11). We cannot try to remove ourselves from it. It is here that we war and conquer (Jn. 16:33).

We are in the world, but not of it. Paul puts this in many ways. Christians are dead with Christ from the rudiments of the world (Col. 2:20). The world is crucified to us and we to the world (Gal. 6:14). We are not to be conformed to it (Rom. 12:2). James adds a similar testimony. Love of the world is enmity against God (James 4:4).

As Christians, we must keep ourselves from the world. John is no less explicit. Believers are chosen from the world (Jn. 15:19). By the new birth we belong to God (Jn. 1:12). The world hates us, and we are not to love the world or the things in it (Jn. 15:18; I Jn. 2:15). This is why the world is a place of affliction (Jn. 16:33).

But we may be of good courage, for Christ has overcome the world, and in Him we have our own victory, even our Faith. Faith enables us to see beyond the world's enticements and sufferings to the new world to come so to speak (I Cor. 7:33; I Jn. 2:17).

Finally, and in more ways than one, Christians are to preach to the world. As God loved the world and Christ came into it, so Christians are to go into the world as the Ambassadors of reconciliation. The great commission enjoins this.

Paul states it in his own way (II Cor., Chpt. 5). Christ says plainly that He sends His Disciples into the world (Jn. 17:18). The world is to see in us the love of the Father (Jn. 17:21, 23). While the Church is not of the world (the evil world), it is set in the world (the theater of history) to minister to the world (humanity). In this sense it is true that, though the Church is not of the world, its life here is for the sake of the world.

If Believers know that to gain the world and lose the soul is folly, we have also to remember that saving the soul is an unavoidable commitment to the winning of the world.

(Bibliography: G. E. Ladd *"Age"*; E. F. Harrison *"World"*; C. R. North.)

THE WILL OF GOD

The phrase, *"But he that doeth the Will of God abideth forever,"* refers to eternal life.

There is no permanence but that of defeat and failure in what is in rebellion to the Supreme Author and Ruler of all things. Everything that is good is a part of Him, and can no more fade than He can. It is by being in harmony with this undeviating tendency of Righteousness to victory that real happiness and joy discovers its own secret.

(18) "LITTLE CHILDREN, IT IS THE LAST TIME: AND AS YE HAVE HEARD THAT ANTICHRIST SHALL COME, EVEN NOW ARE THERE MANY ANTICHRISTS; WHEREBY WE KNOW THAT IT IS THE LAST TIME."

The exegesis is:

1. All the period, from the First to the Second Advents may, in this sense, truly be called *"the last Time."*

2. The first time John uses the term *"antichrist,"* he is speaking of the coming man of sin, who will make his debut after the Rapture of the Church.

3. All during the Church age, there have been, and there are *"many antichrists."*

4. Because of these *"antichrists,"* we know this is the last dispensation before the Second Coming of the Lord.

THE LAST TIME

The phrase, *"Little children, it is the last time,"* actually says in the Greek, *"It is a last hour."* This means that the emphasis is not, therefore, upon the fact of a particular, definite time, but upon the character of that particular, definite time.

While it refers to the entirety of the Church age in a sense, the greater emphasis is on the last of the last days, in fact, the time in which we now live, which is immediately preceding the fulfillment of Endtime events. I speak of the Rapture of the Church, the rise of the Antichrist, the great tribulation, the Battle of Armageddon, and the Second Coming of the Lord, which will commence the coming Kingdom Age.

ANTICHRIST

The phrase, *"And as ye have heard that antichrist shall come,"* refers to the *"man of sin,"* the one referred to by Paul as *"the son of perdition,"* who will arise after the Rapture of the Church. Israel will think that he is actually the Messiah. In fact, this is the one of whom Jesus spoke when He said: *"I am come in My Father's Name, and you receive Me not: if another shall come in his own name, him you will receive"* (Jn. 5:43). The *"another"* addressed here, is the Antichrist.

The manner in which John uses the title *"antichrist"* in the Greek, shows that it is a proper name; consequently, it is the one who will arise in the last of the last days.

There is a difference in the two words used here by John in this Verse as it regards *"antichrist"* and *"antichrists."*

The first use of the word *"antichrist"* places him as against Christ, not pretending to be Christ, but proposing to do the work of Christ.

Trench says of Antichrist, *"To me John's word seemed decisive, that resistance to Christ, and defiance of Him, this, and not any treacherous assumption of his character and offices, is the essential mark of the Antichrist; is that which, therefore, we should expect to find embodied in his name . . . one who shall not pay so much homage to God's Word as to assert its fulfillment in himself, for he shall deny that Word altogether; hating even erroneous worship, because it is worship at all, and everything that is called 'God'* (II Thess. 2:4), *but hating most of all the Church's worship in spirit and in truth* (Dan. 8:11); *who, on the destruction of every religion, every acknowledgment that man is submitted to higher powers than his own, shall seek to establish his throne; and, for God's great truth that in Christ God is man, to substitute his own lie, that in him man is God."*

The meaning of the word *"antichrists"* is in the next phrase:

MANY ANTICHRISTS

The phrase, *"Even now are there many antichrists,"* presents a problem which has plagued the Church from its infancy unto the present.

"Antichrists" in the Greek is *"pseudochristos,"* and refers to one who claims to be Christ, or one might say, *"claims to be of Christ."*

Both alike make war against the Christ of God, and would set themselves, though under different pretenses, on the throne of His Glory. And yet, while the words *"Antichrist"* and *"Antichrists"* have this broad distinction between them, while they represent two different manifestations of the kingdom of wickedness, there is a sense in which the final *"Antichrist"* will be a *"pseudochrist"* as well; even as it will be the very character of that last revelation of Hell to gather up into itself, and to reconcile for one last assault against truth, all anterior and subordinate forms of error.

While it is true that the Antichrist will not call himself the Christ, for he will be filled with deadliest hatred against the Name and Offices, as against the whole spirit and temper of Jesus of Nazareth, the exalted King of Glory. But, inasmuch as no one can resist the truth by a mere negation, he must offer and oppose something positive in the room of that faith which he will assail and endeavor to utterly abolish.

And thus we may certainly conclude that the final Antichrist will reveal himself to the world — for he too will have his revelation (II Thess. 2:3, 8), his advent (II Thess. 2:9) — as, in a sense, the Messiah of God, but still as the world's savior; as the one who will make the blessedness of as many as obey him, giving them the full enjoyment of a present material Earth, instead of a distant, shadowy, and uncertain Heaven. This is the personal Antichrist to which John has referenced.

Now what about the Antichrists, i.e., *"pseudochristos"*?

In His Olivet discourse, Jesus mentioned this when He said: *"For many shall come in My Name, saying, I am Christ; and shall deceive many"* (Mat. 24:5). This could probably be better translated, *"I am of Christ...."* These *"false prophets"* shall come in the Name of the Lord saying that they are of Christ, and will in fact, *"deceive many."*

CHRIST AND THE CROSS

If the Preacher is preaching and proclaiming any Jesus other than *"Jesus Christ and Him Crucified,"* pure and simple, he is proclaiming *"another Jesus"* (II Cor. 11:4).

What Jesus did at the Cross is the answer for hurting humanity, and in fact, the only answer. If the Church promotes something else, in other words a solution other than the Cross, no matter how much it mouths the Name of Jesus, the one being promoted is not the Jesus of the Bible. Unfortunately, there are more Preachers promoting this *"pseudochristos"* than those truly preaching Christ. And the sadness is, most of the modern Church little knows the difference in Christ and *"pseudochristos."*

As well, the *"pseudochristos"* are promoted by *"another spirit,"* which produces *"another gospel"* (II Cor. 11:4). This all comes under the heading of *"an angel of light"* (II Cor. 11:14). And those who promote this *"pseudochristos"* are *"Satan's ministers"* (II Cor. 11:15).

MODERN EXAMPLES

Last night (March 2, 2001) I watched for a few minutes a so-called Christian Television Network. They were promoting a movie they had made, which incidentally they claimed, was going to change Hollywood, and would be the answer for world evangelism as well. The sadness about this farce, this bringing of the world into the Church, is that this movie was paid for by Pentecostal and Charismatic people, allegedly Spirit-filled.

Well of course they aren't Spirit-filled and neither are they Spirit-led. They are spirit-led, but it's not the Holy Spirit, but rather evil spirits.

In 1988, whether realized or not, the Pentecostal and Charismatic worlds in effect said, *"We don't want the Cross!"* They opted for other things, and the other things they have received.

As a result, at the present time, some 13 years later, for all practical purposes, there is no Pentecostal Church left. I'm told that only about a third of those who are associated with Assemblies of God and Churches of God, the two largest Pentecostal Denominations, even claim to be baptized with the Holy Spirit. And if the truth be known, the number is probably even far less than that. This means that if less than half of their people even claim to be Spirit-filled, they cannot even legitimately any more claim to be Pentecostal.

The Assemblies of God was once one of the strongest Missions Denominations in the world; however, for the last two decades, instead of sending out Missionaries, for the most part, they've been sending out amateur psychologists. Consequently, a Missions program which once touched the world little touches anything at present. In fact, the two Denominations mentioned, have opted 100 percent for humanistic psychology, which means that they have disavowed the Cross.

The Church world is rapidly being divided by the Holy Spirit I think, into two divisions, those who accept the Cross of Christ as the answer for hurting humanity, and those who reject the Cross. The former is the True Church while the latter is the Apostate Church. At the present time, the de facto head of the Apostate Church is T.B.N. The head of the True Church is the Holy Spirit. This Apostate Church is promoting the *"pseudochristos."* He is called *"Christ,"* but he is not the Christ of the Cross. As stated, the Holy Spirit is making the Cross the dividing line. In fact, it has always been that way.

Martin Luther stated that as one looked at the Cross, one as well looked at the Reformation. In other words, if they were opposed to the Cross, they were opposed to the Reformation, etc.

WE KNOW IT IS THE LAST TIME

The phrase, *"Whereby we know that it is the last time,"* tells us in effect, that we are now living in the last great apostasy, the last of the last days.

(19) "THEY WENT OUT FROM US, BUT THEY WERE NOT OF US: FOR IF THEY HAD BEEN OF US, THEY WOULD NO DOUBT HAVE CONTINUED WITH US: BUT THEY WENT OUT, THAT THEY MIGHT BE MADE MANIFEST THAT THEY WERE NOT AT ALL OF US."

The diagram is:

1. This crowd of whom John speaks, claims to be of the True Church, but John says, *"they were not of us."*

2. Had they been of the True Church, they would not have succumbed to false doctrine.

3. Them *"going out"* means they turned their backs on the Christ of the Cross.

THE APOSTATE CHURCH

The phrase, *"They went out from us, but they were not of us,"* refers to the fact, that those of whom John speaks, claimed Christ exactly as did those in the True Church. In effect, they denied the Cross, exactly as John will portray in Verses 22 and 23.

TO CONTINUE

The phrase, *"For if they had been of us, they would no doubt have continued with us,"* in effect says the same thing that Christ said.

He said: *"If you continue in My Word, then are you My Disciples indeed;*

"And you shall know the truth, and the truth shall make you free" (Jn. 8:31-32).

Had these people ever truly known the Lord?

I think the terminology proclaims the fact that definitely they had once known the Lord; however, they did not continue in the Word of God, but rather began to devise their own word so to speak.

MADE MANIFEST

The phrase, *"But they went out, that they might be made manifest that they were not at all of us,"* refers to the fact that the dividing line was ultimately brought about.

If the Holy Spirit is followed, He will ultimately *"make manifest"* that which is right and that which is wrong. But yet, as it regards many Christians, despite that which is done by the Holy Spirit, they can little see. That's why Jesus said: *"Anoint thine eyes with eyesalve, that you may see"* (Rev. 3:18). The idea is this:

Every Believer should constantly ask the Lord to show him what is right and what is wrong, in other words, what is of God and what isn't of God. The Devil's wares are made to look like God and to sound like God. Of course, they are done that way for a reason. These are *"seducing spirits and doctrines of Devils"* (I Tim. 4:1).

These *"seducing spirits"* function in the capacity of making that which isn't of God, seem as if it is; and that which is of God, to seem as if it isn't. But as stated, if the Believer will earnestly ask the Lord for leading and guidance, to be sure, such leading and guidance will definitely be accorded.

THE CROSS AND DECEPTION

Even though the following statement has already been made in this Volume, it is so important that I must address it again.

I personally feel that the only protection against *"seducing spirits,"* is for the Believer to have a proper understanding of the Finished Work of Christ. Without such understanding, the Believer is an open target for doctrines of Devils.

To understand the Cross, is to understand Christ, at least as far as we can actually understand Him. As well, to understand the Cross is to understand ourselves. And on top of that, to understand the Cross, is to properly understand the Word of God. And as I've said repeatedly, I do not feel it's possible to properly understand the Bible unless one first understands the Cross, or at least evidences Faith in that great Sacrifice.

The story of the Cross is the story of the Word of God and vice versa. Everything from Genesis 1:1 through Revelation 22:21, points to the Cross of Christ. It is the very center of the Word of God, that around which everything revolves.

And of course, when we speak of the Cross, we are rather speaking of Christ, and what He did there.

So the only protection against false doctrine is a proper understanding of the Sacrifice of Christ. That and that alone will keep the Believer in the place he ought to be.

(20) "BUT YOU HAVE AN UNCTION FROM THE HOLY ONE, AND YOU KNOW ALL THINGS."

The structure is:

1. Every true Believer has the *"Anointing."*

2. This Anointing is from the Holy Spirit.

3. *"You know all things,"* should have been translated *"you all know."*

THE ANOINTING

The phrase, *"But you have an unction,"* actually refers to the *"Anointing."* The two words meaning *"to anoint"* in the New Testament, *"aleipho"* and *"chrio,"* refer to the act of applying something to something else for a certain purpose.

Thus, the Anointing with the Holy Spirit refers to the act of God the Father sending the Spirit in answer to the prayer of God the Son to take up His permanent residence in the Believer.

James 4:5 reads in the Greek text, *"Do you think the Scripture says in vain, The Spirit Who has been caused to take up His permanent residence in us has a passionate longing to the point of envy?"*

This refers to the initial coming of the Spirit into the heart of the believing sinner at the moment he places his Faith in the Saviour. This Anointing is never repeated.

The Old Testament Priests were anointed with oil just once, when they were inducted into their office. The New Testament Priest so to speak (the Believer) is anointed with the Spirit just once, when he is Baptized with the Holy Spirit. However, this anointing is only potential. That is, in itself it offers no help to the Believer.

The help the Saint receives from the Spirit is through the fullness or control of the Spirit, which control is consequent upon his yieldability and trust. The Anointing, one might say, is for the purpose of placing the Holy Spirit in a position where He can be of service to the Believer, namely, in the Saint's inner being. From His position in the Believer, the Spirit performs all His office work for him.

HOW THE HOLY SPIRIT WORKS

While the Holy Spirit definitely comes into the heart and life of the believing sinner at conversion, we believe and teach as well that such a Believer should go on and be Baptized with the Holy Spirit, which only Believers can receive, and which is always accompanied by the speaking with other tongues as the Spirit of God gives the utterance (Jn. 14:17; Acts 2:4).

We believe this was typified by the Old Testament Priests being anointed with oil when they were inducted into their office, as we have previously mentioned. Concerning this, Jesus said:

"And, being assembled together with them, commanded them that they should not depart from Jerusalem, but wait for the Promise of the Father, which, said He, you have heard of Me.

"For John truly baptized with water; but you shall be baptized with the Holy Spirit not many days hence" (Acts 1:4-5).

First of all, Jesus was speaking here to Believers. In other words, they had already been saved, but were now to be Baptized with the Spirit.

As well, this which He said to them is constituted a *"command,"* and not a suggestion.

The Baptism with the Holy Spirit, which is not received at conversion, is an experience separate and apart from Salvation. It is always received after Salvation. In fact, even again as we've already stated, it's not possible for a believing sinner to be baptized with the Spirit. They first must be saved, hence Jesus saying, *"Even the Spirit of truth; Whom the world cannot receive"* (Jn. 14:17).

However, does the Baptism with the Holy Spirit guarantee a victorious, overcoming, Christian life?

No it doesn't! As stated, the potential is definitely there, but only the potential. In fact, at this very moment, there are millions of Spirit-filled Believers who aren't living victorious lives. Why?

The main reason is, they do not really know and understand exactly how the Spirit works.

As stated, the Spirit wants to control us, but He will only do so as we give Him such control. He will never take the control by force. He is always a perfect gentleman.

So how do we give Him control?

Everything the Holy Spirit does through us and for us, is done in totality within the parameters of the Finished Work of Christ. In other words, the Cross made it possible for the Holy Spirit to come in and to abide forever, and because the sin debt was paid there, and as well, makes possible everything else that He does for us. Consequently, He demands of us that our Faith ever be in the Cross of Christ. Paul said:

"And that He (Christ) *might reconcile both* (Jews and Gentiles) *unto God in one body by the Cross, having slain the enmity thereby."*

And then He said: *"For through Him* (Christ and what He did at the Cross) *we both* (Jews and Gentiles) *have access by one Spirit* (the Holy Spirit) *unto the Father"* (Eph. 2:16, 18).

In other words, what Jesus did at the Cross, made it possible for us to be *"an habitation of God through the Spirit"* (Eph. 2:22).

Once the Believer's Faith is in the Cross, which is constituted as *"walking after the Spirit,"* then the Anointing of the Spirit will definitely take place in our lives, as the Holy Spirit then *"helps us"* (Jn. 14:16).

While every Believer has this *"unction,"* sadly and regrettably, because of not understanding the Cross, in most hearts and lives this *"unction"* doesn't *"function."* It's definitely not automatic, but always predicated on our Faith in what Jesus has done for us at the Cross.

If you the Reader, holding this book in your hands, will place your Faith conclusively in the Cross of Christ, ever making that great Sacrifice the object of your Faith, and do so continuously, even taking up the Cross daily in your following of Christ (Lk. 9:23), you will find the Holy Spirit beginning to do great things for you, in a manner in which you have never known before (Rom. 8:2, 11, 13). Things you have struggled with for years, and have been unable to dislodge, will suddenly fall away. To be sure that which is impossible with us, is in fact, very easy with God, and the Holy Spirit is God.

THE ONE PASSAGE THAT HELPED CHANGE MY LIFE

In answer to some five years of prayer, literally seeking the face of the Lord day and night, the Lord first of all (1996), showed me that the answer for which I sought was found in the Cross. In other words, everything we need from the Lord comes to us strictly and totally through what Jesus did at the Cross on our behalf. To be sure, the Cross at least at the present, took place nearly 2,000 years ago; however, it was done so perfectly and so effectively that this act of Sacrifice by Christ will never have to be repeated. As well, benefits and results come from the Cross on a continuing basis, and in fact will never be discontinued. It is these *"benefits"* and *"results"* of which we speak (Rom. 4:25; 5:1-2; 6:3-14; Eph. 2:13-18; Col. 2:14-15).

The Lord then showed me that inasmuch as the Cross was the answer to all my questions, then my Faith must ever be anchored in this great Finished Work (Gal. 2:20).

And then the Lord showed me how the Holy Spirit works. He took me to Romans 8:2: *"For the Law of the Spirit of Life in Christ Jesus has made me free from the law of sin and death."*

From this Passage He showed me that all that the Holy Spirit does within us, and for us, is all made possible by what Jesus did at the Cross, hence the phrase, *"in Christ Jesus."* He showed me this was the manner in which the *"unction,"* i.e., *"Anointing,"* actually works within our hearts and lives. When we place our Faith exclusively in the great Sacrifice of Christ, the Holy Spirit Who always works within the confines of that Sacrifice, will then do great and mighty things for us.

THE HOLY ONE

The phrase, *"From the Holy One,"* refers here to the Holy Spirit.

Every single thing carried out in the Believer's life which is from the Lord, is always and without exception, done by and through the Office, Ministry, and Person of the Holy Spirit. He carries out everything on Earth ordained by the Godhead (Gen. 1:2).

The information we've just given you respecting how He works within our lives, which is predicated on our Faith in the Cross of Christ, is of such value that it can literally change your life. There is nothing the Holy Spirit cannot do. And for us to have an understanding as to how He works gives us access to all of His Graces. In fact, the Christian could have no greater knowledge than that.

KNOW ALL THINGS?

The phrase, *"And you know all things,"* should have been translated *"you all know."* The idea is this:

As a result of the indwelling of the Holy Spirit, the Saints are given the ability to know God's truth. The particular word for *"know"* here is not *"ginosko,"* which means, *"to know by experience,"* but rather *"oida,"* which means, *"to know absolutely and finally."*

If the Saint truly wants to know the Word of God, and truly wants to know what is of God and is not of God, the Holy Spirit will see to it that such knowledge comes about. So there is no excuse for the Christian believing error.

NOTES

(21) "I HAVE NOT WRITTEN UNTO YOU BECAUSE YOU KNOW NOT THE TRUTH, BUT BECAUSE YOU KNOW IT, AND THAT NO LIE IS OF THE TRUTH."

The composite is:

1. What he has written in this Epistle only reinforces what they have already known.

2. The Saints know the Truth by the power of the Holy Spirit, which is reinforced by Apostles, Prophets, Evangelists, Pastors, and Teachers.

3. The truth will never produce a lie, and a lie can never produce the truth.

THE TRUTH

The phrase, *"I have not written unto you because you know not the truth,"* reaches back up to the previous Verse with its closing remark, *"you all know."* These Believers had been taught the truth, and the Holy Spirit had verified it.

In effect, John is saying to his Readers, *"don't depart from the truth you know."*

The Devil will do everything within his power to keep the Child of God from knowing the truth. And then when the Saint knows the truth, he will try to lead the Saint astray. It is a constant battle for the Saint to stay in the Word, and thereby, to stay on the Word. But if the heart is honest, and the desire is for truth, the Holy Spirit Who always leads into all truth, will definitely satisfy that hunger and thirst (Jn. 16:13).

THE LIE

The phrase, *"But because you know it, and that no lie is of the truth,"* presents the fact that the two, the *"lie"* and the *"truth"* cannot mix.

First of all, let us say that the Believer cannot know or understand the Truth, i.e., *"the Bible,"* without the leading and help of the Holy Spirit. So one of the reasons that so many Christians believe *"lies,"* is because the Holy Spirit has been pushed aside so long that He can no longer be heard. To be sure, He will always lead into all truth.

John is dealing with the fact that these false teachers presented some truth; however, they did this only in order to buttress their *"lie."* Therefore, John is actually saying that the *"truth,"* in the mouth of a liar, becomes a *"lie."* This is the one thing that Christians have to watch very carefully.

Just because a Preacher is preaching some truth, doesn't mean that his message is right. First of all, it has to be ascertained as to where his emphasis is. Is he emphasizing the truth, or is he emphasizing something else?

For instance, the Word of Faith people teach and believe that the Blood of Jesus does not avail or atone for anything. In actuality, they teach that the Cross was the greatest defeat in human history. They teach that Salvation comes by Jesus dying as a sinner on the Cross, actually taking upon Himself the Satanic nature, and then going to Hell as sinners do. And when we speak of *"Hell,"* we're speaking of the burning side of the pit.

They teach that Jesus suffered the agonies of the burning side of Hell for three days and nights, until God said, *"It is enough,"* and at that time, He was *"born again,"* thereby becoming the firstborn of many Brethren, and then was raised from the dead.

The faith they teach is not in the Cross, but rather in the supposed suffering of Christ in Hell and His Resurrection.

The trouble with all of this is, it's pure fiction. It's not in the Bible, and because it never happened.

When Jesus died on the Cross, He shed His Life's Blood, which atoned for all sin. And at the moment He cried, *"It is finished, Father, into Thy hands I commend My Spirit"* (Jn. 19:30; Lk. 23:46), *"The Veil of the Temple was rent in twain from the top to the bottom; and the earth did quake, and the rocks rent"* (Mat. 27:51).

This signified that the way to the Holy of Holies, i.e., *"the very Throne of God,"* was now open to all who would come, and made possible by what Jesus did at the Cross. It should be understood that the Lord didn't wait until the Resurrection to do this, but did it the moment that Jesus died, which proves that it is the Cross which paid the price (Gal. 6:14).

EMPHASIS

Now the Word of Faith people do not emphasize their false teaching concerning the Cross, even though this error is what they

believe — and a gross error it is. So many of their followers do not even really know this is what they believe and teach, and because the emphasis is on other things, namely money. While I'm on the subject, however, please note the following:

If the emphasis of the Preacher is not *"Jesus Christ and Him Crucified,"* then in some way that particular Preacher is into error; therefore, there are two problems with the ministry:

1. False doctrine, just as we have mentioned as it regards the Word of Faith people.

2. The wrong emphasis.

This particular problem of wrong emphasis is rampant even among Preachers who truly love the Lord, and are truly trying to preach the Gospel. Most Preachers not knowing and understanding the part the Cross plays in our everyday living for God, place the emphasis of their Message on things other than the Cross. While they preach some good things, some true things, the fact of their emphasis being in the wrong direction, pulls their Message into territory that will little help the Believer.

All Preachers who are true to the Word, or at least attempting to be faithful to the Word, understand the part the Cross plays in one's initial Salvation experience; however, most have absolutely no idea as to the part the Cross plays in the Sanctification process. Consequently, they can little tell people how they actually should live. Paul emphatically told us that the emphasis must not be on other things, *"Lest the Cross of Christ be made of none effect"* (I Cor. 1:17).

(22) "WHO IS A LIAR BUT HE THAT DENIETH THAT JESUS IS THE CHRIST? HE IS ANTICHRIST, THAT DENIETH THE FATHER AND THE SON."

The structure is:

1. Anyone who denies Who Jesus is, and What He has done to redeem humanity, and does so in any fashion, is a *"liar."*

2. The actual Greek says *"the liar,"* referring to the greatest lie of all.

3. In effect, we might say, he is antichrist who denies the Trinity. God the Father, and God the Son are represented here, and it is the Holy Spirit Who inspires the Text, so we have here the Trinity.

THE LIAR

The question, *"Who is a liar but he that denieth that Jesus is the Christ?"*, proclaims Who Christ is and What Christ has done.

First of all, the definite article appears in the Greek text before the word *"liar,"* making it read, *"who is the liar?"* By the definite article *"the liar,"* the lie is set forth in its concrete personality, in other words, that this is the greatest lie of all.

Anyone who denies Who Christ is, and What He has done as it regards the Atonement, represents every form of hostility and opposition to Christ.

These words as given by John, were directed in particular at the heresy of Cerinthus, a man of Jewish descent and educated at Alexandria. He denied the miraculous conception of Jesus (the Virgin Birth), and taught that after the Baptism of Christ, that Messiahship descended upon Him in the form of a dove, and that He then announced the unknown Father and wrought miracles; but that, towards the end of His Ministry, the Christ or the Messiahship departed from Jesus, and that Jesus then suffered and rose from the dead, which means that He did not die as the Anointed One, the Messiah, etc.

As stated, this denial of Who Jesus actually was and What He actually did, and we refer to what He did on the Cross, was being denied by some in the Early Church. In other words, heresy was already rearing its ugly head, hence this Epistle as written by John. I think one can say without fear of contradiction that all false doctrine in some way, centers up on Who Jesus really is, and What He really did. If His Person and His Function, which were the Cross, are in any way denied, or misunderstood, the least that can happen is a lack of victory in one's life, and the worst is, the loss of the soul.

THE NAMES *"JESUS"* AND *"CHRIST"*

What is involved in the names *"Jesus"* and *"Christ"*? They are more than mere designations of the identity of a certain individual Who lived in the First Century.

The English name *"Jesus"* is the transliteration (spelling) of the Greek name *"Iesous,"* which in turn is the transliteration of the Hebrew word which in English is spelled *"Jehoshua,"* and which means *"Jehovah saves."* Thus, in the name *"Jesus"* there is contained the Doctrines of the Deity, humanity, and vicarious (substitutionary) Atonement of the Person Who bears that Name. Only Jehovah could offer a sacrifice which would satisfy the demands of His holy law which the human race broke. But that Sacrifice had to include within itself human nature without its sin, for Deity in itself could not die, and Deity acting as Priest for the sinner must partake of the nature of the individual on whose behalf He officiates.

Therefore, God had to become man, that is if this Sacrifice was to be offered up.

The name *"Christ"* is the transliteration of *"Christos,"* a Greek word meaning *"The Anointed One,"* and this is the translation of the Hebrew word from which we get the name *"Messiah."*

The denial, therefore, is that the Person called Jesus was neither God nor man, and that on the Cross He did not offer an Atonement for sin. As regrettably stated, the Word of Faith people fall into this category by denying the substitutionary Atonement that Christ offered on the Cross. Consequently, the *"Word of Faith"* teaching and teachers, are branded here by John as *"the liars."*

This would go not only for the group mentioned, but also for anyone who falls into this category. As we have stated and will continue to state, as Believers, we must not be confused about the Person of Christ, or the function of Christ.

DENIAL

The phrase, *"He is antichrist, that denieth the Father and the Son,"* presents John, or rather the Holy Spirit through John, mincing no words.

The Jews denied the Son, hence our Lord asking the Pharisees: *"What do you think concerning the Christ* (Messiah)? *Whose Son is He?"*

They answered, *"The Son of David."*

Our Lord then asks, *"How then does David in* (the) *Spirit call Him Lord?* (*'Kurios,' 'Lord,'* the Greek word used to translate the august title of God, *'Jehovah.'*) *If David therefore calls Him Lord, how is He his son?"*

Our Lord was pinning down these false teachers to an admission of the two Persons of the Trinity, and in effect, three Persons, because He referred to the Holy Spirit as it regarded David (Mat. 22:42-43). However, His greater emphasis was on the reality of *"God the Father and God the Son."*

The Pharisees believed in the One God Who manifested Himself as the Jehovah of the Old Testament, but they refused to believe in the Deity of Jesus of Nazareth and His relation to their God as Son of God.

The idea was and is, correct views of the Father could not be held without correct views of the Son; correct views of the Son could not be held without correct views of the Father. The Doctrines respecting the Father and the Son were and are so connected that one could not be held without holding the other, and one could not be denied without denying the other. No man can have correct views of God the Father who has not right apprehensions of the Son. As a matter of fact in the world, men have right apprehensions of God only when they have correct views of the character of the Lord Jesus Christ.

Inasmuch as this is so very, very important, let us look closer at the word *"denial."*

DENIAL OF THE FAITH

Many Passages in the Bible which use the word *"deny"* may puzzle or concern us. What about those warnings against denying Jesus? What do they mean? And how about denying ourselves?

What is it that Jesus demands from those who want to follow Him? And what of Jesus' statement that He will deny in Heaven those who deny Him on Earth?

DENIAL AS REJECTION OF JESUS AND THE GOSPEL

John writes of those who deny *"that Jesus is the Christ,"* which is actually the subject of our study. He calls them *"antichrists,"* and says that no one who denies the Son has the Father (I Jn. 2:22-23).

Here *"denial"* stands in contrast with *"confess (acknowledge)."* These persons refuse to acknowledge that Jesus is the Christ, the Son of God.

The same sense of rejection is found in Jude, Verse 4. Certain individuals who claimed to be Believers were distorting the message of Grace, twisting it into a license for immorality. They also denied Christ as sovereign Lord. Even though they claimed to be Believers, in fact, they were not Believers: they had rejected Jesus as He is presented in the Gospel.

It is likely that a similar rejection of Jesus in the saving sense is meant when Christ warned the crowds, *"Whoever disowns Me before men, I will disown him before My Father in Heaven"* (Mat. 10:33; Lk. 12:9).

DENIAL AS A FALL FROM FELLOWSHIP

Peter's denial of Jesus in the High Priest's courtyard (Mat., Chpt. 26, Mk., Chpt. 14, Lk., Chpt. 22, Jn., Chpt. 18) was not a rejection of his Lord. But it was a definite step back from the commitment Peter had made to die for Jesus if necessary, and that he would never, never disown Him (Mat. 26:33-35). Later Jesus gently restored Peter, leading his repentant Disciple to reaffirm the love that Peter always had for Christ, even though fear had gained momentary control. Each of us, no matter how firm our personal commitment to Jesus is, is just as vulnerable to the momentary lapse.

In the context of the Church's early creedal statement in II Timothy 2:11-13, Paul is speaking of Believers, eager that each might experience the full meaning of the Salvation we have in Christ. Here he repeats this trustworthy saying of the Early Church:

"If we died with Him (Rom. 6:3), *we will also live with Him* (Rom. 6:4-5); *if we endure, we will also reign with Him. If we disown Him, He will also disown us; if we are faithless, He will remain faithful, for He cannot disown Himself."*

If we remain in fellowship (endure), we will experience His ruling authority. But if we abandon fellowship with Jesus (deny Him or disown Him), then He will withdraw from fellowship with us. Yet even should we prove unfaithful, He remains faithful in His commitment to us, for relationship with God does not depend on our own fallible character but on the flawless and faithful nature of the Son of God, in Whom we have placed our Faith;

however, if Faith is discontinued, commitment by Christ will be discontinued as well.

Peter experienced all this when he disowned Jesus in a moment of fear. However, Peter's Faith didn't fail; therefore, Jesus continued committed to Peter. Christ not only restored Peter to fellowship but also restored him to his place of leadership in the Early Church.

SELF-DENIAL AS THE PATH OF DISCIPLESHIP

Matthew, Chapter 16 reports Jesus' first announcement to His Disciples that He must die and be raised again. It also contains an instruction that is repeated in each of the synoptics (Matthew, Mark, and Luke): *"If anyone would come after Me, he must deny himself and take up his Cross and follow Me"* (Mat. 16:24; Mk. 8:34; Lk. 9:23). If it is to be noticed, Luke inserts *"daily"* after *"Cross."*

The thought reflects the New Testament teaching on transformation. Jesus brings each of us new life, which we obtain by being *"born again,"* and which He can give us, by virtue of what He did at the Cross on our behalf, and our Faith in that Finished Work.

He makes possible an inner transformation that enables us to grow in Christlikeness (II Cor. 3:18). As Jesus works within us, we learn to reject the desires and motives that swell up from our old nature. We do this, by having constant Faith in the Cross, which made all of this possible (Rom. 6:3-14; 8:1-2, 11). We turn from these evil desires and motives and commit ourselves to live by the Will of God, even as Jesus did. In taking daily steps of obedience, we deny ourselves, which refers to denying our own strength and ability, and as well our own self-will, and choose instead the Will of God. And in doing so we find ourselves being transformed.

(23) "WHOSOEVER DENIETH THE SON, THE SAME HATH NOT THE FATHER: (BUT) HE THAT ACKNOWLEDGETH THE SON HATH THE FATHER ALSO."

The composite is:

1. No matter the claims, if the Son is denied, so is the Father.

2. If the Son is accepted, the Father is as well, for the Son is the only way to the Father.

3. Sadly, the nation of Israel as a whole fell into this category, for they denied the Son.

THE FATHER AND THE SON

The phrase, *"Whosoever denieth the Son, the same hath not the Father,"* in essence proclaims the fact that there is no way to the Father except through the Son. Actually, Jesus said this very thing:

"I am the Way, the Truth, and the Life: no man cometh unto the Father, but by Me" (Jn. 14:6).

So this means that every religion in the world such as Buddhism, Islam, Hinduism, etc., has no validity as far as God is concerned. The only way to the Father is through the Son, Who is the Lord Jesus Christ. This as well, means that Jesus is Deity. It is only by the Son of God that the Father is made known to men (Mat. 11:27; Heb., Chpts. 1-3) and it is only through Him that we can become reconciled to God, and obtain evidence of His favor, which is all done through the Cross.

We must always remember that when we speak of the *"Son,"* i.e., *"the Lord Jesus Christ,"* that we have access to the Father through Him, but not just because He is the Son. It is what the Son did, which refers to the Cross, which makes access to the Father possible. In fact, the Cross is the very reason that God became man. Regrettably, the Church tends to forget this Truth.

Not only have we denied the Father if we deny the Son, but at the same time, if we deny the Cross we have denied the Son. When we think of the *"Son,"* it must ever be in connection with the Cross. If it's not that way, we will find ourselves serving *"another Jesus"* (II Cor. 11:4), which regrettably, is where much of the modern Church presently is.

CONFESSION

The phrase, *"But he that acknowledgeth the Son has the Father also,"* refers to confessing the Son.

The word *"confess"* in the Greek is *"homologeo,"* and means, *"to speak the same thing that another does,"* hence, *"to agree with that person."* Thus, the word refers here to the act of a person agreeing with what the Bible teaches regarding the unique Sonship of Jesus of Nazareth with respect to God as His Father.

The unique sonship of Jesus of Nazareth is clearly brought out in John 5:18 where the First Century false teachers accuse Him of claiming to be the unique Son of God. The Text says:

"Therefore the Jews sought the more to kill Him, because He not only had broken the Sabbath, but said also that God was His Father, making Himself equal with God" (Jn. 5:18).

The word *"His"* in this Text is the translation of the Greek word *"idios"* which means *"one's own private, personal, unique possession."* In other words, Jesus was using the term *"Father"* as it refers to God, in such a way that the Jews knew that He was saying God was His Father in such a manner, as He was not the Father to anyone else. They saw that if that were true, it would make Him equal with God. Sadly and regrettably, the Jews rejected His claim.

If it is to be noticed, this Passage, is printed in italics, as if it were not in the original, but was supplied by the translators. It is true that it is not found in all the Manuscripts and versions; but it is found in a large number of Manuscripts and also in the Vulgate, the Syriac, the Aethiopic, the Coptic, the Armenian, and the Arabic versions, and in the critical editions of several others. It is probable, therefore, that it should be regarded as a genuine portion of the Sacred Text.

This great Truth can never be too clearly stated, or too often inculcated that it is only by a knowledge of the Lord Jesus Christ that we can have any true acquaintance with God, and that all who have just views of the Savior are in fact acquainted with the True God, and are heirs of eternal life (Barnes).

To confess is the opposite of to deny. Both are open, public statements. The confession voices Faith and states what is in the heart; the denial voices unbelief, hostility, and reveals that these are as well in the heart. There is no avenue to the Father for any sinner save through the Son and through His expiating Blood.

(24) "LET THAT THEREFORE ABIDE IN YOU, WHICH YE HAVE HEARD FROM THE BEGINNING. IF THAT WHICH YE

HAVE HEARD FROM THE BEGINNING SHALL REMAIN IN YOU, YE ALSO SHALL CONTINUE IN THE SON, AND IN THE FATHER."

The exegesis is:

1. We must not deviate from the True Gospel which originally brought us to Christ.

2. We are to continue to hold it fast.

3. We must not allow ourselves to become entangled in false doctrine, whatever such doctrine might be.

4. It is the responsibility of the Believer to nurture the stability and growth of correct Doctrines by a holy life and a determination to cling to them and remain true to them.

ABIDE

The phrase, *"Let that therefore abide in you, which ye have heard from the beginning,"* concerns the True Way.

From the moment the believing sinner comes to Christ, Satan sets about to lead the person astray. Even though he does this in many and varied ways, perhaps his greatest effort is found in his moving the Church away from the Cross.

When the sinner comes to Christ, which actually doesn't take much understanding, he is saved because of his Faith in Christ and what Christ did for him at the Cross. As stated, at the initial Salvation experience, the believing sinner knows almost nothing about these things of which we have said. He just simply believes and calls upon the Lord. In fact, the Scripture plainly says:

"For whosoever shall call upon the Name of the Lord shall be saved" (Rom. 10:13).

But after the believing sinner comes to Christ, which means that he is now *"born again,"* which also means that he now has the Divine nature within him, the Lord expects him to instantly begin to study the Word, etc. In fact, there will be placed in the heart of the young convert a love for the Word, which falls out to a desire to understand its meaning.

However, to properly understand what he is studying, he needs the help of the five-fold ministry, *"Apostles, Prophets, Evangelists, Pastors, and Teachers"* (Eph. 4:11-12).

But the trouble is presently, Satan has been so successful at pushing the Church away from the Cross that most Ministers have little knowledge of the part the Cross plays in our everyday living and walk before God. In fact, the situation is far worse than merely lacking in understanding. In some circles, especially among some Charismatics, the Cross is openly repudiated. As well, the Leadership of the major Pentecostal Denominations, as well as every Denomination in fact of which I am aware, has opted for humanistic psychology, which is a vote of no confidence as it regards the Cross. So this leaves the Church as a whole, in a most precarious situation.

If the Preachers little know and understand the veracity of the Cross, at least as it regards our everyday living, they can little teach this great Truth to the people. So in a sense, what Believers *"heard from the beginning,"* can little continue to *"abide"* in them. The result is, a modern Church which doesn't know God's prescribed order of victory can, therefore, little walk in victory.

Now most Preachers would be loathe to admit that they do not understand the Cross, but the truth is they don't. As a result, the Church is grasping for every proverbial straw it can find, attempting to find answers to questions and solutions to problems.

There is only one solution, which means there is only one answer to the question, and that is the Cross of Christ. This is what Paul gave us in Romans, Chapter 6, and which we must know and understand, that is if we are to walk victorious before the Lord. The Lord doesn't have several ways of victory, only one, and that is the Cross.

REMAIN

The phrase, *"If that which ye have heard from the beginning shall remain in you,"* verifies what I've just said.

The words *"abide"* and *"remain,"* carry a much greater meaning than it appears on the surface. The exhortation includes more than that the Saint should allow the basic teaching concerning the Person of our Lord to remain in Him. He should have that attitude towards it that it will also feel at home in him, have ready access to every part of his life. In other words, it is the responsibility of the Believer to nurture the stability and

growth of these foundational Doctrines by a holy life and a determination to cling to them and remain true to them. To be frank, the word *"doctrine"* can be summed up in the word *"Cross."* Listen to what Paul said:

FORM OF DOCTRINE

"But God be thanked, that you were the servants of sin (the sin) *but you have obeyed from the heart that form of doctrine which was delivered you"* (Rom. 6:17).

The Greek word for *"form"* is *"tupos,"* and means *"a die as something struck, a statue, a model."*

"Doctrine" is *"didache,"* which means *"to instruct or to teach."*

The *"form of doctrine"* which Paul had taught, and which his Readers had heard and believed, was in effect, *"the Cross."* In fact, this is what the entirety of Romans, Chapter 6 is all about.

Romans, Chapter 6 tells the Saint how to live for God, which refers to walking in victory, and not only victory, but also perpetual victory.

The foundation is laid in Romans 6:3-5. The Believer is there told as to how we are *"in Christ,"* which refers to the Death, Burial, and Resurrection of our Lord. He suffered as our Substitute, and our Faith in Him and what He did, literally, at least in the Mind of God, places us *"in Him."*

We are to thereafter continue to understand that all of our victory, in fact everything that comes to us from the Lord, which is carried out by the Holy Spirit within our lives, has all been made possible, and without exception, by and through the Cross of Christ. If we understand that, thereby continuing to express Faith in the Cross, which Jesus referred to as *"taking up the Cross daily,"* we will then walk in victory all the days of our lives (Lk. 9:23). In fact, unless the Believer understands Romans, Chapter 6, which brief synopsis we have already given in this Volume, he literally cannot live for God as he should. But we have two problems here:

1. As we have stated, Satan will try to keep the Believer from understanding this *"form of doctrine,"* in which he has been very successful. Let me make a blunt statement:

If the Believer doesn't understand the *"form of doctrine"* as Paul outlines in Romans, Chapter 6, there is no way that Believer can walk in victory. It simply cannot be done. And the tragedy is, the modern Church as a whole little knows and understands the *"form of doctrine"* that Paul mentions here.

2. Even after the Saint hears and understands this *"form of doctrine,"* Satan will try to push him away from the victory of the Cross to other things. That's why Paul wrote the Epistle to the Galatians.

These Galatians had been brought in right. In fact, all of them had either been saved under Paul, or someone who preached exactly that which Paul preached. So their foundation was correct; however, false teachers had come into the Churches in Galatia, telling the people that they must embrace the Law as well as Grace. In other words, if they wanted to be a total Christian, they must not only accept Christ and what He did at the Cross, but as well they must also take upon themselves the Law of Moses.

In effect, Paul in his Epistle to these people told them that if they went in that direction, they would be *"entangled again with the yoke of bondage"* (Gal. 5:1). In fact, he further told them that if they accepted anything, other than the Cross, *"Christ would become of no effect unto them"* (Gal. 5:4).

So the Saint must work diligently that not only must this *"form of doctrine"* remain, but as well, that it might grow and expand. In fact, it is impossible to exhaust the potential of the Cross, hence Paul referring to it as *"the everlasting Covenant"* (Heb. 13:20).

CONTINUE

The phrase, *"You also shall continue in the Son, and in the Father,"* tells us several things:

1. The terminology tells us that it's quite possible for a person to come to Christ, thereby becoming a true Believer, and then fail to continue in the Son, and because they departed from the original Faith.

2. The Child of God must ever seek to improve his standing in the Lord, and do so by learning more and more about the Finished Work of Christ. That's at least one of the reasons I plead with people to get these Commentaries.

NOTES

3. The idea of the Text also is, as great as the loss will be if one departs from the Faith, as great will the blessings be as one continues in the Faith.

(25) "AND THIS IS THE PROMISE THAT HE HATH PROMISED US, EVEN ETERNAL LIFE."

The diagram is:

1. God has made many Promises in His Word, and He's never failed on even one.

2. The greatest Promise of all is *"Eternal Life,"* which comes through Jesus Christ, and what He did for us at the Cross.

3. Christ is actually referred to as *"Eternal Life"* (I Jn. 1:1-2).

THE PROMISE

The phrase, *"And this is the Promise that He hath promised us,"* tells us several things:

1. First of all, God Alone is able to keep every Promise that He makes.

2. All of God's Promises are to all people, *"whosoever will,"* unless they are limited to a certain group, such as to Israel.

3. Even though the Promises of God may take some time to come to fulfillment, one can be absolutely certain, however, that God will honor every Promise.

ETERNAL LIFE

The phrase, *"Even Eternal Life,"* refers to a Promise of astounding proportions.

Before Christ, man was eternally dead. Due to the Fall in the Garden of Eden, everything was lost. In fact, at the moment of disobedience, man spiritually died, which means that he was eternally separated from God.

In order to rectify the situation, God would have to become man and pay the penalty for man's crime, which He did at the Cross.

Every single thing that Jesus did in His earthly life, including the Cross, was all for sinners. In other words, He did nothing for Himself, for Angels, or for Heaven in any capacity. It was all for sinners.

When He died on the Cross, the debt was paid in full, and that means for the entirety of the human race, at least for all who will believe (Jn. 3:16).

Eternal Life is a gift. All one has to do to receive this greatest of all benefits, is simply to place their Faith and trust in Jesus Christ and what He did at the Cross.

WHAT IS ETERNAL LIFE?

Eternal life is not the physical life of the body for we have this life only as long as the soul and spirit remain in the body. Death in Scripture means separation from the purpose for which a creature was created. Physical death is the separation of the inner man from the body. When this takes place one loses physical life (James 2:26). Eternal life is not the natural immortality or consciousness of the soul and spirit, for both the saved and unsaved exist forever and are fully conscience after physical death (Mat. 10:28; 17:3; Lk. 16:19-31; 20:38; 23:43; Jn. 11:24-25; 14:19; II Cor. 5:8; Phil. 1:21-23; Heb. 12:23; I Pet. 3:4; Rev. 6:9-11).

The soul exists and is conscience even though it is dead (Mat. 8:22; Eph. 2:1-10; I Tim. 5:6). Spiritual death is the separation of the inner man from God because of sin (Isa. 59:2; Eph., Chpt. 2). Eternal life, therefore, could not be the natural eternal life or consciousness of the inner man either in or out of the body. Eternal life could not be the eternal existence or consciousness of eternal souls in eternal Hell, for only the righteous have eternal life by abiding in Christ (Jn. 3:15-18, 36; 5:24; 15:1-7; I Jn. 2:24-25; 5:11). Eternal death is the eternal *"separation"* from God (Isa. 66:22-24; Mat. 10:28; 25:41, 46; Rev. 2:11; 14:9-11; 20:11-15; 21:8). Eternal life is the opposite of eternal death — eternal union with God (Jn. 17:3; I Cor. 6:17; I Jn. 2:24-25; 5:11-12).

Eternal life was given to Adam upon condition that he would remain in union with God and not sin, and it was said that if he did sin he would die or be separated from God and lose that life (Gen. 2:17). Sin was the only thing that could take away his eternal life (Rom. 5:12-21; I Cor. 15:21-22). Since Adam could have lived forever if he had not sinned, then he had eternal life. If he had eternal life he lost it by sin. If he could lose it by sin, then all other men who regain it can also lose it again by sin. What kind of life was it that he lost the day he sinned if it was not eternal life? The penalty for sin was eternal death, thus he had to lose the opposite of eternal death, or eternal life.

Just because a man is once saved from sin and Hell is no sign that he cannot go back into sin, lose his Faith in Christ, and be lost again and finally go to Hell. No Scripture has yet been found that says he cannot lose eternal life and no one will ever be able to produce a Scripture that says such a thing, so it will take more than statements of men to prove this claim.

Men gain eternal life, as stated, by exhibiting simple Faith in Christ, and they keep eternal life by continued Faith in Christ (Rom. 10:9-10, 13; Eph. 2:8-9; Rev. 22:17).

(26) "THESE THINGS HAVE I WRITTEN UNTO YOU CONCERNING THEM THAT SEDUCE YOU."

The structure is:

1. The Saints must be warned about false apostles and false doctrine.

2. All false doctrine in one way or the other comes under the heading of *"seducing spirits,"* and is, therefore, labeled *"doctrines of Devils"* (I Tim. 4:1).

3. Under the guise of *"unity"* the modern Church little addresses this most important subject.

THE WRITTEN WORD OF GOD

The phrase, *"These things have I written unto you,"* concerns that which the Holy Spirit desired that John would write. While it dealt with several subjects, the main thrust of I John is to expose false apostles and as well, false doctrine.

We must understand that the Spirit of God wanted this done, and that everything that John wrote, was that which the Holy Spirit desired. To be sure, if false apostles and false doctrine were a problem then, they are a problem now. Taking our cue from John, and Paul as well, in fact all of the Bible writers, if we are to be true to the Gospel, we must as well warn the Church of that which is wrong. The Word of God is our example, and if the Word is not a proper example, then what is!

SEDUCTION

The phrase, *"Concerning them that seduce you,"* refers first of all to the individuals, and then to what they were promoting.

All false doctrine has its foundation in *"seducing spirits,"* which gives it its power. It produces doctrines that are smooth in their make-up, but which always appeal in some way to a base motive, and in actuality are *"doctrines of Devils."*

John had identified the heretical beliefs of those who had deserted the community of Believers. He had properly labeled these false apostles as *"antichrists,"* and had described them as *"those trying to lead you astray"* (I Jn. 4:6; II Jn. vs. 7). This description is the most significant because it reveals the actual intent of those who have deserted the Scriptural way. Not only have they forsaken the true Faith, but also they intend to lead the faithful astray. Their aim is to assume leadership. They are enemies who are not content to spread new teaching, but *"invaders"* and *"deceivers"* who seek to win the entirety of the Body of Christ over to their position.

"Seduce" in the Greek is *"pianao,"* and means *"to stray from; wander, go astray, be out of the way, to be deceived, to err from the truth."* If they went astray from the right and straight way, this shows they had once been in the way. It's pointless trying to seduce someone who has never known the True Way of God. The facts are, Believers can be led astray from the truth, until they no longer believe, and that being the case, they will ultimately lose their souls, that is if they remain in this erroneous direction. In fact, that is Satan's design.

It wasn't pleasant or easy for John to point out those who were leading the people astray. This no doubt gathered much animosity against him, not only from those who were guilty, but as well, from those who had bought into these *"lies."* However, John's position was not that of popularity, but rather, to do the Will of God. The Holy Spirit had the Apostle to write these words, even to calling these false apostles *"antichrists"* and *"liars."*

Some people get upset with me, as well as with others in this Ministry for pointing out error, and at times even calling names. But let me remind all concerned:

There will never be a reprimand from the Lord as it regards Preachers being too clear and plain in the presentation of Truth; however, there will be many reprimands, regarding Preachers who compromise the Message. The Word is very clear on the subject:

The Lord told the Prophet Ezekiel: *"Son of man, I have made thee a watchman unto the house of Israel: therefore hear the word at My mouth, and give them warning from Me."*

He then said: *"If you do not warn the wicked, the same wicked man shall die in his iniquity; but his blood will I require at thine hand"* (Ezek. 3:17-18).

Let the Reader understand that we aren't speaking here of mundane matters, but rather the issues of life and death! That should put an entirely different complexion on the whole of the matter.

When I say to you that I believe the Lord has spoken to my heart that the Cross is the dividing line between the True Church and the Apostate Church, if in fact that is the case, then what we're saying is of utmost importance. In truth, He definitely has spoken that to my heart. So for the Believer to ignore this statement is to do so at his own peril. It also means if Preachers aren't preaching the Cross, then they aren't preaching the Word (I Cor. 1:17-18, 21, 23; 2:2, 5).

Now what is the difference in that which John wrote and this which I have just written, and Preachers such as myself?

What John wrote was the *"Word of the Lord,"* which means that it is infallible. What I have written is a *"Word from the Lord,"* which is different, and is meant to subscribe to that which John wrote as well as other Bible writers. The Word of God as it regards the Bible must not be added to or taken from. And everything else given which purports to be from the Lord must always coincide with the written Word, and in every manner. While the Canon of Scripture concluded with Revelation 22:21, which means that God is not going to give anything else as it regards His Word, in fact, He is still giving His Word, and doing so constantly; however, that which He gives since the Canon of Scripture closed, will always match up perfectly with that which He has already given, that is if it's truly the Lord giving such a Word.

So what I'm giving you is a Word from the Lord, but it matches up perfectly with that which has already been written.

(27) "BUT THE ANOINTING WHICH YOU HAVE RECEIVED OF HIM ABIDETH

IN YOU, AND YOU NEED NOT THAT ANY MAN TEACH YOU: BUT AS THE SAME ANOINTING TEACHETH YOU OF ALL THINGS, AND IS TRUTH, AND IS NO LIE, AND EVEN AS IT HAS TAUGHT YOU, YOU SHALL ABIDE IN HIM."

The composite is:

1. The Anointing of the Holy Spirit abides in the Christian permanently, to help him ascertain if what he is hearing is Scriptural or not!

2. No Believer needs anything that's not already found written in the Word.

3. The Holy Spirit constantly helps the Saint through His Anointing, and does so by leading the Believer to the Word.

4. The Word always *"is truth,"* which means that it is *"no lie."*

5. The Believer is to abide in what the Spirit has taught him through the Word.

THE ANOINTING

The phrase, *"But the anointing which you have received of Him abideth in you,"* refers to that which is constant, and thereby permanent.

There are two Greek words, *"aleipho"* and *"chrio,"* used in the New Testament, translated by the one English word *"anoint."* The two words refer to the act of applying something to a person for a certain purpose, and to meet a certain condition.

We will look at Peter's words, *"God anointed Jesus of Nazareth with the Holy Spirit and with power"* (Acts 10:38). The subject here is *"God,"* Who does the acting. He is the One Who anoints Christ with the Holy Spirit and with Power.

This means that the Holy Spirit did not do the anointing. He is that with which Jesus was anointed. We saw that both Greek words meaning, *"to anoint,"* refer to the application of something to a person. Thus, the act of God in anointing Jesus with the Holy Spirit, referred to His act of sending the Holy Spirit to rest upon Him for the Ministry which He as the Man Christ Jesus was to accomplish on Earth. So let us say it again:

The Holy Spirit does not anoint. He is the anointing Himself. Thus, in the case of our Lord, the anointing with the Spirit refers to the Person of the Holy Spirit coming

upon Him, this position of the Holy Spirit providing the potential equipment for Ministry of which our Lord was to avail Himself. The anointing with the Holy Spirit would only become a factor in our Lord's life resulting in the impartation of power for service as He depended upon the Spirit for His Ministry to and through Him.

THE ANOINTING OF THE BELIEVER WITH THE SPIRIT

We come now to the anointing of the Believer with the Holy Spirit and this Age of Grace. Paul says in II Corinthians 1:21-22, *"Now He which stablisheth us with you in Christ, and has anointed us, is God, Who has also sealed us, and given the earnest of the Spirit in our hearts."* In I John 2:27, the Passage of our study, we have the words *"But the anointing which you have received of Him abideth in you, and you need not that any man teach you: but as His anointing teaches you of all things, and is truth, and is no lie, and even as it has taught you, you shall abide in Him."* John also said in Verse 20, *"But you have an unction from the Holy One, and you all know."*

The ministry of the Holy Spirit to the Believer today is not only for service as was the case in Old Testament times, but also for Sanctification. But His indwelling is only potential so far as His ministry is concerned. His indwelling does not at all mean that His ministry is performed in its fullest manifestation and in an automatic way. And this confuses most Christians, and especially, Spirit-filled Believers. For most in this category think that being baptized with the Holy Spirit (Acts 2:4) automatically means that the Spirit is automatically helping.

While He definitely does help all He can, we know from Romans 8:2 that He requires of us that we evidence Faith at all times in Christ, and more particularly, what Christ did at the Cross. With our Faith properly placed, the Holy Spirit will then do great and mighty things, even to the full potential of His Ministry on our behalf.

JOHN SAID TWO THINGS

Concerning that which John gave in this Chapter, two of the Spirit's Ministries are given here. Those two are: A. His work of teaching the Believer the Word; and, B. His work of giving the Believer an innate ability to know in an intuitive way, things spiritual. The Greek word for *"know"* given in Verse 20 gives us this latter truth.

TEACHING GIVEN BY FALSE APOSTLES

The phrase, *"And you need not that any man teach you,"* does not mean as some think that God-called Teachers aren't needed. In fact they are needed very much (Eph. 4:11-12). The idea here as given by John pertains to the fact that whatever teaching is given, even by God-called Teachers, must be backed up 100 percent by the Word of God. No Teacher, even a God-appointed one is the only and ultimate source of the Saint's instruction. He has the Holy Spirit and the Word, and to be sure, the Holy Spirit will always see to it that correct teaching is always backed up by the Word. In other words, the Word is always the final authority.

If in fact the Holy Spirit is teaching the Believer the Word, which He most certainly does, and as well, if He is giving the Believer an innate ability to know in an intuitive way, things spiritual, how is it that Believers go astray by listening to these *"seducers"*?

The Believer tends to forget that all that the Spirit can do, and in fact, desires to do, is potential. In other words, He has the potential to do these things, but His actually doing them, depends upon our cooperation.

As I've said several times already in this Volume, the Believer must constantly pray that the Holy Spirit will lead him into all truth. He must let the Spirit know that he needs, wants, and desires His help, and if we have a tendency to go astray that we desire Him to pull us back to the right way. To be sure, He will definitely answer such a prayer, but if we tend to think that we can get by without Him, He will let us go on our own, which no sane Christian desires to do.

IN CHRIST

As well, considering the fact that Paul used the term *"in Christ,"* or *"in Him,"* or one of its derivatives, some 170 times in his 14 Epistles, I think the understanding of the following is absolutely necessary, that

is if we are to have the proper help of the Holy Spirit.

Every single thing the Believer has from the Lord can be summed up in the words *"in Christ."* Without exception, this refers to what He did for us at the Cross, and the means by which the Holy Spirit works. The idea is, the Believer must without exception and must without fail, place his Faith exclusively in the great Sacrifice of Christ. The Holy Spirit demands this (Rom. 8:2, 11). Without proper Faith in the Cross, which means continued Faith in the Cross, I do not feel that the potential of the Holy Spirit can be realized within our lives.

In fact, proper Faith in the Cross guarantees protection against false doctrine, or one might say the potential for protection against false doctrine. If our faith is improperly placed, or rather has something else as its object rather than the Cross, such a position seriously curtails the work and operation of the Holy Spirit within our lives (Rom., Chpt. 8).

THE TEACHING OF THE ANOINTING

The phrase, *"But as the same anointing teacheth you of all things, and is truth, and is no lie,"* in effect, presupposes a Person. This means that this anointing, therefore, is a Person, the Holy Spirit Himself. The idea here is:

If the Believer's Faith is anchored firmly in Christ and what He did for us at the Cross, and the Believer sincerely wants and desires the leading and the operation of the Holy Spirit within his heart and life regarding all things, the Spirit, to be sure, will let us know as to what we are hearing, if it's right or wrong.

Each and every Believer should know the Word to the extent that he can spot that which is right or wrong immediately; however, even then, the Holy Spirit is greatly needed in any and all cases. To be frank, the presentation of false doctrine is always done so cleverly and skillfully that it's difficult at the outset for many to spot the wrong direction. A part of the seduction used by *"seducing spirits,"* is to make whatever is being offered sound and seem to be as close to the Word of God as is possible. In fact, there is always much truth given along with error; however, that which is strictly according to the Word, and is, therefore, sanctioned by the Holy Spirit, is not part truth and part lie, but in reality, 100 percent truth. The Holy Spirit leads the seeking Believer into all Truth, and He will not stop until all truth is reached (Jn. 16:13).

TEACHING AND ABIDING

The phrase, *"And even as it has taught you, you shall abide in Him,"* refers to the fact that what we are taught as it refers to the Word of God, helps us to abide in Christ.

The idea is the minds of the Saints led by the Spirit of God are visibly alive to spiritual insight. As well, this insight is from God, a living power, witnessed to by the Life of Christ and all that pertains to Christianity. It is no mere human theory like the speculation of false teachers, demonstrably at variance with Christ; and, lastly, that it had already brought home to their inmost souls the priceless lessons of which they were aware. Let's say it in this manner:

The Gospel of Jesus Christ, which was bought and paid for by what Christ did at the Cross, is, to use some street terminology, set in concrete. There is no room for deviation or variance. That Gospel is:

1. Jesus saves.
2. Jesus baptizes with the Holy Spirit.
3. Jesus heals.
4. Jesus is coming again.

If the Church drifts from either one or more of this four-cornered stanchion of the Faith, it becomes overly obvious, at least to those who know the Word of God. All four corners of the Doctrine of Christ pin themselves to the Cross, which made everything possible. We are saved because of what Christ did at the Cross. As well, we can be baptized with the Holy Spirit due to the fact that Jesus paid the totality of the sin debt at the Cross. Also, *"by His stripes we are healed,"* and He couldn't come the second time, if He had not come the first time.

(28) "AND NOW, LITTLE CHILDREN, ABIDE IN HIM; THAT, WHEN HE SHALL APPEAR, WE MAY HAVE CONFIDENCE, AND NOT BE ASHAMED BEFORE HIM AT HIS COMING."

The exegesis is:

1. The Believer must live in close fellowship with his Lord that he may be ready for that coming.

2. The invisible Lord Jesus will some day be made visible as He comes from Heaven into the atmosphere of this Earth to catch out His people, the Church.

3. *"Confidence"* speaks of the heart's attitude of the Saint who lives so close to the Lord Jesus that there is nothing between him and his Lord. Such a person is ready for the coming. How many Christians will be ashamed *"at His Coming"*? Were it not possible for this to be, then the Holy Spirit would not have said such through John.

ABIDE IN HIM

The phrase, *"And now, little children, abide in Him,"* presents the condition of fruit-bearing (Jn. 15:4, 7), and as well is the condition of being ready when He does come. What we were in the Lord six months ago will not suffice for today. That's why Jesus spoke of *"denying ourselves, and taking up the Cross daily"* (Lk. 9:23).

As we've said in previous Commentary, the phrase *"in Him,"* describes Christianity best of all. It speaks of our initial Salvation experience, when we were literally *"baptized into His Death"* (Rom. 6:3). As a result we died with Him, or more particularly, *"in Him,"* and were buried in Him, and rose in Him in newness of life (Rom. 6:3-5).

Our *"abiding in Him,"* means that we are to understand that all we have in Christ, is strictly because of our being *"in Him,"* and more particularly, as to how we are *"in Him."* The *"how"* of course refers to the Cross. Consequently, we *"abide in Him,"* meaning that we maintain this place and position and all of its benefits, by continuing to have Faith in that which He did for us. This stops self-will cold, and places total confidence in Christ and what Christ has done. The Holy Spirit can then work within our lives, and because we know and understand the purpose and reason for our Salvation.

Let the Believer understand that everything is in the Cross. This means that we couldn't be saved were it not for the Cross. We couldn't be baptized with the Holy Spirit were it not for the Cross. In fact, we couldn't receive anything from the Lord, were it not for the Cross. So what is our problem?

THE PROBLEM OF THE SAINT

The problem is, we forget these things which I've just mentioned. We shift our Faith from the Cross to other things, and to be sure, Satan doesn't too much care what those other things are. He knows if our faith is not in the Cross, we're not going to get anything done. So he encourages other directions which means, that these other directions do not garner his opposition.

A proper evaluation of the Cross, means that the Saint has a proper evaluation of himself, which means that he knows that he cannot perform as demanded, and in fact, that Jesus has already done for us what we couldn't do for ourselves. When self is properly placed in Christ, which it can only be as the Believer properly understands the Cross, then the Holy Spirit can function as He so desires (Rom. 8:1-2, 11, 13).

THE RAPTURE

The phrase, *"That, when He shall appear,"* doesn't present a question as to the fact of our Lord's coming for His Church, but as to the *"time"* of that coming. One could translate, *"whenever He shall appear."* In fact, the exhortation, *"Be constantly abiding in Him"* is given in view of the uncertainty of the time of His coming. The Believer must live in close fellowship with His Lord that he may be ready for that coming.

"Appear" in the Greek is *"phaneroo,"* and means, *"to be made manifest or visible."* The invisible Lord Jesus will some day be made visible as He comes from Heaven into the atmosphere of this Earth to catch out His Church (Wuest).

It is tragic, much of the modern Church anymore little believes in the Rapture; consequently, there is as well, precious little *"abiding in Him."* The two *"abiding in Him,"* and *"the Rapture"* go hand in hand.

If it is to be noticed, professing Christians who little respect the Cross, are at the same time, little looking for the Rapture of the Church. In fact, I think one can say without any fear of contradiction that most all who

NOTES

denigrate the Cross, at the same time, denigrate the Rapture.

CONFIDENCE

The phrase, *"We may have confidence,"* speaks of the heart attitude of the Saint who lives so close to the Lord Jesus that there is nothing between him and his Lord. There is nothing of known sin in his life when the Rapture occurs. He is truly *"abiding in Christ."* Such a Saint maintains a constant yieldedness to and dependence upon the Holy Spirit to show him sin in his life and give him the grace to judge it and put it out (Wuest).

It is said that *"confidence"* is too weak a word to translate the Greek, but that there is no suitable alternative.

When one is truly following Christ, and is truly subscribing to Sound Doctrine, such a place and position produces a holy boldness in the heart and life of such a Christian. This means there is no doubt or unbelief. He is ready should the Lord choose to come today.

SHAME

The phrase, *"And be not ashamed before Him at His Coming,"* presents the fact, that some certainly will be ashamed.

We are speaking here of Believers, and that being the case, what will happen to these particular individuals when the Lord does come?

If these individuals are truly Believers, they are saved. So that means they won't lose their souls; however, they will definitely lose reward (I Cor. 4:15). And we must remember, the loss of this reward is an eternal loss, which means that it is incalculable as far as the potential is concerned.

If our being what we ought to be in Christ is predicated on our Faith in the Cross, which demands some knowledge of the Cross, and considering that the modern Church is almost Cross illiterate, where does that leave the present Body of Christ? The immediate answer is, the modern Church is in a very precarious condition; however, the Holy Spirit is in the process of remedying this situation. In other words, He is in the process of making this foundation known to the Church. As the Church is now in the last great apostasy, it is also in the last great outpouring of the Spirit (Acts 2:18). That outpouring says:

"That whosoever shall call on the Name of the Lord shall be saved" (Acts 2:21).

Knowing and understanding that one cannot be saved unless one places Faith and trust in Christ Jesus and what He has done at the Cross, we learn that this great outpouring is intended to pull the Church toward the Cross.

(29) "IF YOU KNOW THAT HE IS RIGHTEOUS, YOU KNOW THAT EVERYONE WHO DOES RIGHTEOUSNESS IS BORN OF HIM."

The diagram is:

1. Jesus Christ is righteous.

2. All who are truly Born-Again, *"does righteousness."*

3. If we truly *"abide in Him"* Righteousness will definitely be the result.

HE IS RIGHTEOUS

The phrase, *"If you know that He is righteous,"* could be translated, *"Since you know that He is righteous."* In fact, the Righteousness of Christ is what Christianity is all about. As God, Christ is perfectly righteous, and in fact, has always been; however, whenever the Righteousness of Christ is addressed, it is not actually speaking of His Righteousness as Deity, but rather as the Man, Jesus Christ. The idea is this:

When God became Man, He did so as the Last Adam and to carry out a particular purpose (I Cor. 15:45-47). He must gain back the righteousness which the original Adam lost in the Fall in the Garden of Eden.

About 1,500 years before Christ, God had given the Law to Moses. This Law was His Standard of Righteousness, and man was demanded to keep it in every respect. The upshot was, man could not keep the Law of God and in fact, every single man failed.

Jesus had to address this Law and keep it in every respect. The Scripture says:

"But when the fullness of the time was come, God sent forth His Son, made of a woman, made under the Law" (Gal. 4:4).

In fact, the Law contained Righteousness, but for this Righteousness to be had, man would have to keep the Law perfectly, which as stated, none ever did. But Christ did keep it perfectly, thereby gaining its Righteousness, and doing so on behalf of fallen man.

However, there was another matter of the Law to be addressed, referred to as *"the curse of the broken law"* (Gal. 3:13). As stated, every single human being had broken the Law of God, thereby bringing upon themselves its penalty, which is death. On behalf of mankind, Jesus suffered the curse of the broken law by going to the Cross, and dying in the place of man. In other words, He became the Substitute of man. So He not only gained a Perfect Righteousness by perfectly keeping the Law, but He also addressed the curse of the broken Law, thereby settling its claims, and doing so once and for all.

For every single soul who accepts Christ, and what He did on behalf of fallen man, and did so specifically at the Cross, the Perfect Righteousness which belongs to Christ is thereby granted to the believing sinner. God can only accept a Perfect Righteousness, and the only Perfect Righteousness there is, is that which is of Christ, Who will freely give such righteousness to all who will believe, irrespective of what their past life has been (Jn. 3:16; Rom. 10:9-10, 13; Rev. 22:17).

DOING RIGHTEOUSNESS

The phrase, *"You know that everyone that does Righteousness is born of Him,"* proclaims the fact, that if one is truly Born-Again, such a one is righteous, because he has the Righteousness of Christ, and as such, will *"do Righteousness."*

Three things are here said:

1. That Christ is righteous.

2. That every Born-Again one is righteous.

3. That doing righteousness is proof of the new birth.

HOW DOES ONE DO RIGHTEOUSNESS?

The truth is, even though the Believer is now a new creation in Christ Jesus, and as well has the Holy Spirit, still, within his own capabilities he still cannot *"do Righteousness."* This in effect, is the great battleground of the Christian. Every Christian instinctively knows that since he is now a Child of God, he must *"do Righteousness,"* i.e., *"be Righteous."*

Many, if not most, Christians think that now because they belong to Christ that it's a simple matter for them to *"do Righteousness."* As one man said to me just the other day, *"Now that I'm a Christian, I have the power to say 'No' or the power to say 'Yes'!"*

Is that correct?

In a limited sense it is, but only in a limited sense. Let me explain it:

The Believer can say *"Yes"* or *"No"* to Christ. Beyond that, he will soon find his power of choice very, very limited. In other words, if he does not address this thing Scripturally, he will find Satan literally overriding his will, which is a precarious position indeed (Rom. 7:18).

To *"do Righteousness,"* the Believer must understand that every single thing he receives from the Lord comes totally and completely through the Cross of Christ. He is to say, *"Yes"* to the Cross, understanding that the Cross has made everything possible. That's why Paul said: *"But God forbid that I should glory, save in the Cross of our Lord Jesus Christ, by Whom the world is crucified unto me, and I unto the world"* (Gal. 6:14).

Understanding that everything comes to the Believer through the Cross, this means that the Cross must ever be the object of our Faith. Now this is very, very important! We must not allow our Faith to be moved to other things, which Satan will constantly attempt to do.

Inasmuch as our Faith is properly placed, which means we have said *"Yes"* to Jesus Christ, the Holy Spirit Who works exclusively within the parameters of the Finished Work of Christ, will then work mightily on our behalf, helping us in every way to *"do Righteousness."* In fact, this is the only way that Righteousness can be done. Paul told us exactly how it is done in Romans, Chapter 6.

If the Believer ignores the Cross, thereby placing his faith in other things, as regrettably does most of the modern Church, the result will not be the *"doing of Righteousness,"* but rather the *"doing of unrighteousness."* It cannot be any other way. Paul said:

"This I say then, walk in the Spirit, and you shall not fulfill the lust of the flesh" (Gal. 5:16).

"Walking in the Spirit" is trusting completely in what Christ has done at the Cross, for this is the manner in which the Spirit

always leads (Rom. 8:1-2, 11). If that is not done, the only other alternative is *"the lust of the flesh,"* which always corresponds into *"the works of the flesh"* (Gal. 5:19-21).

"I heard an old, old story, how a Savior came from glory,
"How He gave His life on Calvary to save a wretch like me;
"I heard about His groaning, of His precious blood's atoning,
"Then I repented of my sins and won the victory."

"I heard about His healing, of His cleansing power revealing,
"How He made the lame to walk again and caused the blind to see;
"And then I cried 'dear Jesus, come and heal my broken spirit,'
"And somehow Jesus came and brought to me the victory."

"I heard about a mansion He has built for me in glory,
"And I heard about the streets of gold beyond the crystal Sea;
"About the Angels singing, and the old redemption story,
"And some sweet day I'll sing up there the song of victory."

CHAPTER 3

(1) "BEHOLD, WHAT MANNER OF LOVE THE FATHER HATH BESTOWED UPON US, THAT WE SHOULD BE CALLED THE SONS OF GOD: THEREFORE THE WORLD KNOWETH US NOT, BECAUSE IT KNEW HIM NOT."

The exegesis is:

1. The love of God is foreign to the human race. It is not found naturally in humanity.

2. This love is freely given upon Faith in Christ and what He has done for us at the Cross.

3. God has placed His love upon the Saints in the sense that we have become the permanent objects of His love.

4. We are *"sons of God"* by virtue of adoption into the Family of God, derived through

the Born-Again experience. The world doesn't understand Christians, because the world does not understand Christ.

LOVE

The phrase, *"Behold, what manner of love the Father hath bestowed upon us,"* presents that which is foreign to this present world, and in fact, which comes from another world.

"Behold" carries the idea that the love of God is something extraordinary, which should be looked at with wonder and amazement.

John is speaking here of love in *"kind"* and in *"degree."* In *"kind"* the most tender and the most ennobling, in adopting us into His family, and in permitting us to address Him as our Father; in *"degree"* the most exalted, since there is no higher love that can be shown than in adopting a poor and friendless orphan, and giving him a parent and a home. Even God could bestow upon us no more valuable token of affection than that we should be adopted into His family, and permitted to regard Him as our Father.

When we remember how insignificant we are as creatures, and how ungrateful, rebellious, and vile we have been as sinners, we may well be amazed at the love which would adopt us into the holy family of God, so that we may be regarded and treated as the children of the Most High (Barnes).

"Has bestowed," means simply *"to give something to someone."* God has placed His love upon the Saints in the sense that we have become the permanent objects of His love. Let the Reader understand that God is love. This means that He is much more than merely having love, but as it regards *"degree,"* He actually is love. In fact, He has always been love. But it took the Cross, which was the greatest display of love that man has ever known, to make it possible for the Love of God to be shed abroad in the hearts of undeserving sinners.

Before the Cross, God could not readily bestow His love as freely as He now can. What Jesus did at the Cross made it possible for God to draw nigh unto believing sinners, and for believing sinners to draw nigh unto Him. On our part, it is accomplished by faith, and by using that term, we are speaking of having Faith in what Jesus did at the Cross,

which is the same thing as having Faith in the Word.

SONS OF GOD

The phrase, *"That we should be called the sons of God,"* refers to the family of God, which is gained by adoption (Rom. 8:15; Gal. 4:5; Eph. 1:5), and not by begetting as in the case of Christ, Who is the only Begotten Son of God (Jn. 1:14, 18; 3:16, 18).

The phrase, *"Born of Him* (God)*"* which the Apostle mentions in the last Verse of the previous Chapter, causes him to marvel at the wonder of God's redemptive activity. See how great the gift of His love really is! Why He has identified us as being His very Own children! And this is exactly what we have become through His acts. We have really been born of Him.

THE WORLD

The phrase, *"Therefore the world knoweth us not, because it knew Him not,"* refers to the fact that the world does not recognize nor acknowledge Believers as sons of God; just as they did not recognize nor acknowledge Christ to be the Son of God.

In fact, it is impossible for the world to understand who and what the Christian actually is, since unsaved people never have had a saving relationship with and knowledge of God. Intimate understanding and knowledge of another person is based upon fellowship with Him. Since the people of the world have nothing in common with the Children of God, they have no fellowship with us, therefore, have no intelligent appreciation and understanding of us.

The foreign kind of love (and that's what it is) produced in us by the Holy Spirit constitutes us a foreign kind of person to the people of this world, and since they do not understand foreigners, people of a different race from themselves, they simply do not understand Christians. Children of God could just as well have come to earth from a strange planet so far as the people of the world are concerned. We are strangers to them (Wuest).

In fact, during Romans times, Christians were referred to as *"the third race."* Romans were referred to as one race, with everyone else in the world who were not Romans referred to as the second race.

The world did not understand Christ when He was on the Earth. They mistook Him for an enthusiast or an imposter; and it is no wonder that having wholly mistaken His character, they should mistake ours.

And not only did the world not understand Him when He was on this Earth, they still don't understand Him.

The world is proud of its knowledge, but the real things worth knowing it does not know. The mystery of Regeneration is foolishness in its eyes; those who are Children of God in Christ it considers deluded. Its own idea of a universal fatherhood of men without Redemption and Regeneration it regards as the height of wisdom.

Therefore, let no true spiritual Child of God count on recognition from the world. The names of God's greatest Saints are not engraved on the tablets of the world's temple of fame. This cannot be otherwise; if it were, the world would not be the world, and we should not be God's children.

Grieve not that the world does not know you; this is one proof that you are God's child. If the world knows you, you should grieve, for then there is proof that you are not God's child.

The phrase, *"It knew Him not,"* states the fact historically; since it never knew Him it does not now know you.

The world has only fictional, false conceptions regarding our Heavenly Father, His Son the Lord Jesus Christ, and regarding us, His children. That will not change, because it cannot change!

(2) "BELOVED, NOW ARE WE THE SONS OF GOD, AND IT DOTH NOT YET APPEAR WHAT WE SHALL BE: BUT WE KNOW THAT, WHEN HE SHALL APPEAR, WE SHALL BE LIKE HIM; FOR WE SHALL SEE HIM AS HE IS."

The structure is:

1. We are just as much a *"son of God"* now, as we will be after the Resurrection.

2. However, our present state as a *"son of God,"* is not at all like that which we shall be in the coming Resurrection.

3. The words *"When He shall appear,"* refer to the coming Rapture.

4. *"We shall be like Him,"* refers more to a physical likeness than a spiritual one. It speaks of being glorified.

5. Only at the Rapture will we be able to see our Lord as He is now, for physical lives in a mortal body could not look upon that glory, only eyes in a glorified body.

SONS OF GOD NOW

The phrase, *"Beloved, now are we the sons of God,"* presents the fact that even though there will be a tremendous change in the Resurrection, still, we are just as much *"sons of God"* presently, as we will be then. In other words, the change will not make us any more *"sons of God"* then, than we are presently. The reason is the Cross.

The effected work which Faith in the Cross carries out presently, cannot be improved upon, simply because the Sacrifice of Christ is total and complete within itself. Even though all the results of the Finished Work of Christ have not yet accrued to the Believer, that coming in the Resurrection, still, as far as the legal rudiments of Salvation are concerned, that is total and complete.

WHAT WE SHALL BE?

The phrase, *"And it does not yet appear what we shall be,"* in effect says, *"It has not yet been made manifest or visible."*

Concerning the word *"what"* Bengel comments: *"This word suggests something beyond comprehension, which pertains to the likeness of God."*

The idea is, it is not yet fully revealed what we shall be like as it regards the glorified body. Perhaps the Holy Spirit has not given us further revelation, simply because in our present state, we could little comprehend His meaning. And then again, if He told us exactly what the coming glorified state will exactly be like, and gave us full comprehension now as to understand all that it means, perhaps we might be too anxious to reach that coming world, with no desire at all to remain here. In other words, the Work of God would little get done on Earth in such a climate.

If it is to be noticed, the Holy Spirit through John encourages no speculation in these matters. He just makes the statement as it regards that coming time, leaving it mostly in mystery. Not yet has God made a public display of the glory that belongs to His children, of the inheritance incorruptible, unstained, unfading, reserved for us in Heaven (I Pet. 1:4). Not yet do we wear the white robes of Heaven; not yet does the crown of glory sparkle on our brow. The robe of Christ's Righteousness, our crown of hope, the diamond of faith, the pearls of love, are invisible to physical eyes. We still wrestle with the flesh; in a sinful world and with a mortal nature we plod on, at times very wearily.

A Child of God is here and now, indeed, like a diamond that is crystal white within but is still uncut and shows no brilliant flashes from reflecting facets (Lenski).

WHEN HE SHALL APPEAR

The phrase, *"But we know that, when He shall appear, we shall be like Him,"* refers here as John makes the statement, moreso to physical likeness than anything else.

Saints are already spiritually like the Lord Jesus in a relative sense, and through the sanctifying work of the Holy Spirit, we are being conformed more and more to His spiritual likeness. So John is speaking more so of physical likeness. As well, he is speaking here of the Rapture.

Paul in Philippians 3:20 says: *"For the commonwealth of which we are citizens has its fixed abode in Heaven, out from which also the Savior, we with our attention withdrawn from all else, are eagerly waiting to welcome, the Lord Jesus Christ, and to receive Him to ourselves; Who shall change the outward appearance of the body of humiliation so as to conform it to an outward expression like to the body of His glory."*

The word *"change"* used here by Paul in the Greek is *"metaschematizo,"* and means *"to change the outward expression by assuming one put on from the outside."*

The words *"be fashioned like,"* are in the Greek *"summorphon,"* and means *"an outward expression which comes from within, and is truly representative of one's inner character."* Both words refer to an outward, not an inward change.

The Rapture has to do with the glorification of the physical body of the Believer, not with a change of our inner Spiritual Life. In

NOTES

fact, when the Saint enters Heaven in a sinless state, he is not catapulted ahead to absolute spiritual maturity in an instant of time. He grows in likeness to the Lord Jesus spiritually through the sanctifying work of the Holy Spirit all through eternity, always approaching that likeness but never equaling it, for finiteness (which we humans are) can never equal infinity (what Jesus is). The change which will come at the Rapture is, therefore, a physical one. We shall be like our Lord as to His physical, glorified body.

The Greek word *"summorphon,"* which we have just mentioned, which means, *"be fashioned like,"* speaks of that outer enswathement of glory that now covers the body of the Lord Jesus, and which will at the Rapture cover ours (Wuest).

AS HE TRULY IS

The phrase, *"For we shall see Him as He is,"* refers to the fact that only at the Rapture will we be able to see our Lord as He is now, for physical lives in a mortal body could not look on that glory, only eyes in glorified bodies. And that is at least one of the reasons we shall be like Him, for only in that state can we see Him just as He is (Wuest).

The world has never seen Him as He actually is. And in fact, we as Believers at the present can actually only see Him as He truly is by faith. But at the Rapture, we will look upon Him in all of His glory, and due to being glorified ourselves, will then have the capacity to do so.

To be sure, the world will in fact see Him in all of His glory at the Second Coming, and the Scripture says regarding Israel, *"In that day there shall be a great mourning in Jerusalem . . . and the land shall mourn, every family apart"* (Zech. 12:11-12).

Israel will then realize the One they thought was merely a Peasant, even an imposter, was in fact, their Messiah, the Lord of Glory, the King of kings.

In the midst of His Glory they *"shall say unto Him, what are these wounds in Thine hands?"* For in the midst of the glory there will be the wounds, in fact, there will always be the wounds, signifying the price He paid at Calvary's Cross for the Redemption of lost humanity (Zech. 13:6).

(3) "AND EVERY MAN THAT HATH THIS HOPE IN HIM PURIFIETH HIMSELF, EVEN AS HE IS PURE."

The diagram is:

1. *"Every man"* refers to all who are truly saved, which will fall into the category mentioned here.

2. This *"hope"* is the Resurrection.

3. *"Him"* refers to the Lord Jesus Christ, and what He has done for us at the Cross.

4. Purifying oneself refers to the Christian supplying a willing mind and an obedient heart.

5. The idea is to be pure like Christ.

THIS HOPE

The phrase, *"And every man that hath this hope,"* refers to the coming Resurrection.

The world is full of men who have a certain kind of hope, but see on what it rests — not on Christ, on His Blood and expiation, on His promise. They invent their own foundation for the hope they have. It is sand, and is swept away when the great flood comes as it always does (Mat. 7:24-27).

ON HIM

The short phrase, *"In Him,"* speaks of Christ, and should have been translated *"on Him."*

Most every time Christ is mentioned by any of the Bible writers in this fashion, always and without exception, it refers to what He did for humanity in the sacrifice of Himself on the Cross. Even though the weight of the Text, even as here, may point to something else, such as the coming Resurrection in this case; still, the coming Resurrection and everything else in fact, are made possible by what Jesus did at the Cross. When studying the Word of God the Reader must always understand that. Christ is to never be separated from the Cross, as the Cross is to never be separated from Christ. The Cross was the intended destination of His coming to this Earth. In fact, the Cross was a planned principal even before the foundation of the world (I Pet. 1:18-20).

PURIFIETH HIMSELF

The phrase, *"Purifieth himself,"* is not meant to be taken in the sense that it is possible for a human being within himself to purify himself. *"Apart from Me,"* says our Lord, *"you can do nothing"* (Jn. 15:5). This statement implies a will to purify oneself. As we've already stated, all the Believer can actually do in this matter, is to provide a willing mind and an obedient heart. And to be sure, these two factors must be present in the heart and life of the Believer before the Holy Spirit can bring about this intended result (Rev. 22:17).

Purification is a work of the Holy Spirit within our lives (Gal. 5:16, 22-23). However, the Holy Spirit works strictly on the principle of what Christ did at the Cross. In other words, He makes possible all the benefits of the Finished Work of Christ. All that is demanded is that we as Believers have faith and in fact, maintain faith, in the Cross of Christ, understanding that the Cross is the means by which all things are made possible to the Believer.

The following is a short diagram that will help you to understand what we are here saying:

GOD'S PRESCRIBED ORDER

1. FOCUS: The Cross (I Cor. 1:17-18, 21, 23; 2:2, 5).

2. THE OBJECT OF FAITH: The Cross (Rom. 6:3-14).

3. THE POWER SOURCE: The Holy Spirit (Rom. 8:1-2, 11, 13).

4. THE RESULTS: Victory (Gal. 2:20; 6:14).

The focus of the Child of God must ever be the Cross, understanding, as stated, that this is the means by which all things come to the Believer. Understanding that, we will always make the Cross the object of our Faith. This is very, very important!

The power source is always the Holy Spirit (Acts 1:8; I Cor. 1:18); however, He always and without exception, works within the parameters of the Finished Work of Christ (Rom. 8:2). To be sure, with the Holy Spirit working within our hearts and lives, anything can be done, which then translates into *"victory"* on all accounts.

If man attempts to purify himself by his own efforts, ability, strength, and machinations, he will function in the following, which will always lead one to spiritual disaster. The description is as follows:

MAN'S PRESCRIBED ORDER

1. FOCUS: The Law (Gal. 2:15-16).
2. THE OBJECT OF FAITH: Works (Gal. 3:10).
3. POWER SOURCE: Self (Gal. 5:16).
4. RESULTS: Failure (Gal. 5:19-21).

If the Christian is not functioning in Grace, the Christian is then functioning in Law (Rom. 6:14). Now the tragedy is, most Christians don't know anything about the Cross as it refers to their life and living, so this means, and without exception, that whether they realize it or not, they are functioning in Law. There is no other place to go, there being only two rooms in this house so to speak.

What do we mean by functioning in Law?

We're not speaking of the Law of Moses, but rather laws we make up ourselves, or laws made up by our Church or others. And because it's so important, let me state the case again:

If the Believer doesn't understand the rudiments of the Cross as it regards victorious, overcoming, Christian living, then without fail, such a Believer will resort to Law, because there is no place else to go. And the tragedy is, most Christians not understanding the Cross, are functioning in Law, while they think they are functioning in Grace. So how can we know for sure as to how we are trying to live this life?

The results are very telling. If you are walking in victory, then you are functioning in the Grace of God; otherwise, you are functioning in Law.

To function in Grace (Rom. 6:14), one must know and understand that everything he receives from the Lord comes through and by the Cross of Christ. In other words, it is the Cross that has made everything possible. Understanding that, and as we have repeatedly stated, we must make the Cross the object of our Faith.

When we do this, the Holy Spirit Who is actually the result of the Grace of God, begins to function in our lives, carrying out His work, which helps us to be that which we ought to be. As stated, the result of this course is *"victory."*

FRUSTRATING THE GRACE OF GOD

Paul said: *"I do not frustrate the Grace of God: for if righteousness come by the Law, then Christ is dead in vain"* (Gal. 2:21).

The Apostle is telling us several things in this one Verse:

1. First of all he is telling us that it is possible for the Christian to frustrate the Grace of God, which means that we stop the Grace of God from working within our lives, which spells disaster.

2. He also tells us that Righteousness cannot come by works of the law, in other words, things that we do. Righteousness is always a work of the Holy Spirit, always made possible by what Jesus did at the Cross, and by this way alone. In other words, to obtain Righteousness, one must make the Cross of Christ the object of one's faith. Then Righteousness will be the result. If we try to come by Righteousness in any other manner, which means we're trying to do it by *"law,"* whether we realize it or not, we only seek in frustrating the Grace of God.

3. If in fact, Righteousness could be obtained by the Law, then Christ did not need to come down here and die on a Cross. The Believer should understand that.

If we can obtain anything from the Lord by means other than Faith in Christ and what Christ did at the Cross on our behalf, then Jesus died needlessly. Of course, we know that He didn't die needlessly, which means that it's not possible for us to receive anything from the Lord, unless it comes by and through the Cross, which demands and necessitates our Faith in that Finished Work.

Any time the Christian seeks to obtain anything from the Lord by any means other than simple Faith in Jesus Christ and Him Crucified, we then instantly stop the Grace of God, which as stated, spells disaster for the Christian. For us to properly live for God, we must have a constant, uninterrupted flow of the Grace of God. And this is guaranteed by our focus always being on the Cross, and ever making the Cross the object of our Faith.

Now what I've told you in these last few paragraphs can literally change your life; consequently, you ought to read these paragraphs several times until the Holy Spirit makes the teaching given literal and real in your heart.

HE IS PURE

The phrase, *"Even as He is pure,"* places Christ as our example.

"Pure" in the Greek is *"hagnos,"* and means *"without sin of any description."* This purity denotes such with effort and fearfulness amid defilements and allurements, especially carnal.

God is called *"hagios* (holy)*"* but never *"hagnos."* Christ is *"hagnos"* because of His human experience. God the Father has not had, as should be obvious, except through His Son, a human experience.

(4) "WHOSOEVER COMMITTETH SIN TRANSGRESSETH ALSO THE LAW: FOR SIN IS THE TRANSGRESSION OF THE LAW."

The structure is:

1. John shows here the incompatibility of being a Child of God and yet continuing in sin.

2. The *"transgression of the law"* refers to the moral law, referred to as the Ten Commandments.

3. *"Sin"* and *"lawlessness"* are identified here as identical.

THE SIN

The phrase, *"Whosoever committeth sin,"* should have been translated, *"Whosoever committeth the sin."*

The idea here definitely includes acts of sin; however, the broader meaning refers to what we have just described for you in the above diagram concerning the Law. The focus of such a Believer is on the law, whether he realizes it or not, which refers to particular laws he has made up or others. The object of his faith becomes *"works,"* with the source of his power being *"self."* The end result will always be *"failure."* This presents the Believer attempting to live for God by means other than Faith in the Finished Work of Christ. In fact, this is the highest form of rebellion against God, hence it is called *"the sin."*

TRANSGRESSION OF THE LAW

The phrase, *"Transgresseth also the Law,"* literally says in the Greek, *"doeth lawlessness."* In fact, the words *"the transgression of the Law"* are in the Greek text one word, *"anomia,"* which means *"lawlessness."*

The *"Law"* as John uses the word here, actually refers to the moral Law of God,

which is the Ten Commandments. For all of this to be properly understood, several things need to be said:

First of all, we have just quoted Paul as saying: *"For if Righteousness come by the Law, then Christ is dead in vain."*

In fact, Paul talks about the Law constantly, even much more than John. In fact, he spoke of it in a negative sense so much that he had to explain himself by saying, *"Is the Law sin?"* His answer was instant, *"God forbid"* (Rom. 7:7). The idea is this:

The *"Law"* was all satisfied in Christ. He kept it perfectly in every respect, and then satisfied its penalty by dying on the Cross (Gal. 3:13-14).

The Law of God is God's Standard of Righteousness, which He demands of man. Man could not live up to that Standard, so God became man, i.e., *"Jesus Christ,"* and kept the Law on our behalf. As a result, the Scripture says that Christians are *"dead to the Law"* (Rom. 7:4). Now notice, it didn't say that the Law is dead, but that we are dead to the Law. This means we have no more connection with it in any manner, and because of what Jesus has done on our behalf.

ARE WE AS CHRISTIANS SUPPOSED TO KEEP THE TEN COMMANDMENTS?

In fact, the Ten Commandments as well as every other part of the Law have already been kept and kept perfectly by Christ. He did for us what we could not do ourselves.

Most definitely, we as Christians are supposed to keep the Ten Commandments; however, it's the manner in which they are kept which is in question.

If we set out to keep the Ten Commandments, we will fail and because we aren't giving Christ His due. As a Christian I don't have to worry about the Ten Commandments in any fashion, because Jesus has already kept them for me, plus suffered the penalty of the broken Law, all on my behalf, and if I am *"in Him,"* which means trusting in what He has already done, all of this has already been done. I am dead to the Commandments and because I am in Christ.

So the Commandments are kept, but they are kept in Christ, which means they are something that I'm not bothered with.

But if I set out as a Christian to try to keep them, in effect, I will be attempting to do what no other human being has ever done. As well, I will be insulting Christ, because He's already kept them for me.

In Christ it is all done, and in Christ I reside, and in Christ I am victorious, which means that my Faith is totally and completely *"in Him,"* and more particularly, what He has done for me at the Cross. This being the case, the Holy Spirit guarantees all the work of Christ to be realized within my life. As long as my Faith is properly placed, which means that the Cross is its object, I walk in perpetual victory (Rom. 6:14). If I try to live for God other than by Faith in the Cross of Christ, this means that I'm attempting to do so by keeping the Law by my own strength and ability, which will never work. That's the reason we say that the Christian has one of two choices, *"Grace"* or *"Law."* The problem is, he doesn't understand either one too very well.

THE DISPENSATION OF GRACE

Many Christians have it in their minds that because this present age is the Dispensation of Grace, which it is, that this means they are automatically living in and under Grace. The truth is, it doesn't mean any such thing. The facts are, most Christians, even though this is the age of Grace, are in fact, living under *"Law."* Let me say again what I've been saying all long:

If the Believer doesn't understand the Cross, and by that I speak of the part the Cross plays in our every day living for God, then without exception that Christian is going to function in Law whether he realizes it or not. If the Believer doesn't understand the Cross, and I am referring to the Sanctification process, then it's impossible for the Believer to rightly function in Grace. The two *"Grace"* and *"the Cross,"* go hand in hand. In fact, the Grace of God comes exclusively through what Jesus did at the Cross.

TRANSGRESSION

The phrase, *"For sin is the transgression of the Law,"* tells us what sin actually is. In some way sin is disobedience as it regards the moral law of God, which is the Ten Commandments.

In the Greek it has before the word *"sin,"* the definite article, which actually says *"the sin."* This means that John is not specifically speaking of acts of sin, but rather the sin nature of the Believer. The act of sin on the part of the Believer in a sense activates the sin nature, which then activates many more acts of sin.

While it is definitely true that sin is the transgression of the moral Law of God, to go into detail, I think John is also saying the following:

Inasmuch as he uses the definite article before the word *"sin"* both times (the sin) in this Verse, the *"Law"* of which he speaks, could very well be *"The Law of the Spirit of Life in Christ Jesus"* (Rom. 8:2). This is in fact, the Law by which every Christian should live. We could say that this is the *"good law."* Of course, every Law given by God is good, but this law, *"The Law of the Spirit of Life in Christ Jesus"* is the only law which *"has made me free from the law of sin and death."*

This *"Law"* is *"in Christ Jesus,"* which means that it is predicated on what Jesus did at the Cross. That's the reason I keep saying that our Faith must rest within the Cross.

By John using the term *"the sin,"* he is speaking of rebellion against God's prescribed order, which is Faith in the Cross. When that happens, *"the law of sin and death,"* is going to take over in one's life, and because *"The Law of the Spirit of Life in Christ Jesus"* has been abandoned in favor of self-effort. There is no victory outside of the Cross, and the quicker the Saint learns this Truth the quicker he will walk in victory.

(5) "AND YOU KNOW THAT HE WAS MANIFESTED TO TAKE AWAY OUR SINS; AND IN HIM IS NO SIN."

The composite is:

1. Sin is lawlessness.

2. Jesus appeared in history in order to remove sin.

3. Jesus lived a sinless life. Consequently, He was able to offer Himself as a Perfect Sacrifice which would take away sin.

4. Jesus' sinlessness reveals what kind of lifestyle is proper for those who abide in Him.

HE WAS MANIFESTED

The phrase, *"And you know that He was manifested,"* speaks of His Incarnation.

He became Incarnate, for the very purpose of putting an end to sin (Mat. 1:21). This argument is a clear one, and is perhaps the strongest that can be made to bear on the mind of a true Christian, that the Lord Jesus saw sin to be so great an evil, that He came into our world, and gave Himself to the bitter sorrows of death on the Cross, to redeem us from it.

The term *"manifested"* occurs three times in the Greek text (I Jn. 3:5, 2, 8) and responds to three cries of the heart:

1. Verse 5: The cry for liberation from sins and their eternal doom. The answer to that cry is that He was manifested to take away sins, and as He could not possibly fail in what He came to do the Believer learns with wonder and joy that his sins are taken away forever.

2. Verse 2: This Verse tells us of the cry of the renewed heart to be sinless. This cry will be satisfied when He shall be manifested, for His people shall be like Him.

3. Verse 8: The cry of anguish and perplexity of the heart awakened to the misery, injustice, cruelty, and suffering in the world. The cause of this as we shall see in Verse 8 is, *"the works of the Devil."* The Son of God was manifested to destroy them, and will do so in totality.

TAKE AWAY SINS

The phrase, *"To take away our sins,"* was carried out at the Cross. The Christian cannot practice what Christ came to take away and to destroy.

The essential argument here is that the whole work of Christ was designed to deliver us from the dominion of sin, not to furnish us the means of indulgence in it; and that, therefore, we should be deterred from it by all that Christ has done and suffered for us. He perverts the whole design of the coming of the Saviour who supposes that His work was in any degree designed to procure for His followers the indulgences of sin, or who so interprets the methods of His Grace as to suppose that it is now lawful for him to indulge his guilty passions. The argument essentially is this:

1. That we profess to be followers of Christ, and should carry out His ends and views in coming into the world.

NOTES

2. That the great and leading purpose of His coming was to set us free from the bondage of transgression.

3. That in doing this He gave Himself up to a life of poverty, shame, sorrow, and to a most bitter death on the Cross.

4. That we should not indulge in that from which He came to deliver us, and which cost Him so much toil and such a death. Still more, how can we be so ungrateful and hardhearted as to indulge in that which crushed our Redeemer in death?

This statement as given beautifully by John the Beloved, was also stated very succinctly by John the Baptist when he introduced Christ: *"Behold the Lamb of God, which taketh away the sin of the world"* (Jn. 1:29). This was His great mission, and He carried it out.

HOW HE TOOK THE SINS AWAY

He did this by the expiatory power of His Blood. John the Beloved said:

"The Blood of Jesus Christ His Son cleanses us from all sin" (I Jn. 1:7). The Cross where Jesus gave Himself in Sacrifice was absolutely necessary, if this tremendous deed should be done. Paul plainly said: *"For it is not possible that the blood of bulls and goats should take away sins"* (Heb. 10:4). Inasmuch as sins before the Cross were not taken away, but only covered, this means that the sin debt remained.

This is the reason that the work of the Holy Spirit was limited in what He could do before the Cross. Until the sin debt was settled, which means that all sins were taken away, which in fact happened at the Cross, the Holy Spirit could not come in to the hearts and lives of even the greatest of Believers to abide permanently.

As well, before the sin debt was settled, Believers during Old Testament times upon the advent of death, did not go to Heaven, but were rather taken down into Paradise in the heart of the Earth, which was really a part of Hell. They were actually held captive there by Satan, and this includes all the Old Testament greats.

When Jesus died on the Cross, thereby atoning for all sin and settling the sin debt, and doing so for all who will believe, He then *"descended first into the lower parts of the earth,"* where *"He led captivity captive (all the Old Testament Saints), and gave gifts unto men"* (Eph. 4:9, 8). Now when Saints die, they instantly go to Heaven and because the sin debt had been removed (Phil. 1:23).

If it is to be noticed, we are told that He was *"manifested to take away our sins,"* which means that He wasn't manifested to do a lot of other things.

One foolish Preacher said that Jesus died on the Cross in order to glorify His self-esteem. No He didn't, but rather to *"take away our sins."*

Another foolish Preacher said that Jesus went to the Cross in order to make all of us financially rich. No He didn't, but to take away our sins.

The idea of Sacrificial substitution was uppermost in I John 2:2. Here it is rather that of Sanctification; but the former is not excluded. The two, Salvation and Sanctification, are always connected in John's mind. The purpose of Christ's coming was not so much to teach a new doctrine as to produce a new life; the first (Salvation) was the means to the second (Sanctification).

IN HIM NO SIN

The phrase, *"And in Him is no sin,"* presents the fact that He was able to be the Sacrifice to take away the sins of others.

As well, the idea is, as He was perfectly pure and spotless, so should all His followers aim to be; and none can truly pretend to be His who do not desire and design to become like Him. The very fact that Christ is perfectly sinless is dwelt on because He is the vital element of the Christian's being, and if present in Him must produce a result like Himself (Ellicott).

THE JESUS DIED SPIRITUALLY DOCTRINE

This doctrine as taught by many of the Word of Faith people, claim that Jesus became a sinner on the Cross, literally taking upon Himself the nature of Satan. They claim He died as a sinner and went to Hell, even as all sinners do. Consequently, they also teach that the Cross was the worst defeat in human history, and that the Blood

of Jesus did not atone for anything, much less sin.

They teach that He agonized in Hell for three days and nights, when the Father then said, *"It is enough,"* and Christ was then *"born again."* They derive this latter statement from the Passage which states: *"For whom He did foreknow, He also did predestinate to be conformed to the Image of His Son, that He might be the firstborn among many Brethren"* (Rom. 8:29).

They evidently completely misunderstand the phrase *"firstborn among many Brethren,"* claiming that it means that Jesus was Born-Again.

The word *"firstborn"* as used here means no such thing. In the Greek the word is *"prototokos,"* and means *"protos (first)," and "tikto (to beget)."* It means that Christ is the One Who has founded or instituted the Church. In other words, what He did, made it possible for men to be *"born again,"* and, thereby, to become a part of the Body of Christ.

They then teach after Christ was *"born again,"* that He was then raised from the dead. Consequently, Salvation as they see it, pertains to faith in His sufferings in Hell and in His Resurrection. As stated, the Cross in their thinking doesn't enter at all into the Salvation process.

In fact, they teach that once a person is *"born again,"* that his spirit thereby becomes perfect, and he is now in the *"God-class,"* and as such, could die on the Cross the same as did Christ.

Every bit of this so-called teaching is pure fiction. You won't find it in the Bible, because it's not there. It is made up out of whole cloth, and in fact is blasphemy.

To have a misconception concerning anything in the Bible is always hurtful; however, to have a misconception about the Atonement is disastrous.

Peter plainly said concerning the death of Christ on the Cross: *"For Christ also has once suffered for sins . . . being put to death in the flesh, but quickened by the Spirit"* (I Pet. 3:18).

This plainly tells us that Jesus died physically; He did not die spiritually.

Peter also said: *"Forasmuch then as Christ has suffered for us in the flesh"* (I Pet. 4:1).

Once again, this tells us that Jesus died physically and not spiritually.

Paul said: *"Having therefore, Brethren, boldness to enter into the holiest by the Blood of Jesus,*

"By a new and living way, which He has consecrated for us, through the veil, that is to say His flesh" (Heb. 10:19-20).

Once again we are told, and plainly so, that He died physically and not spiritually. And then on top of that, John plainly says, *"In Him is no sin."*

Paul said: *"For such an High Priest became us, Who is holy, harmless, undefiled, separate from sinners, and made higher than the heavens"* (Heb. 7:26).

Had He become a sinner on the Cross as the Word of Faith people contend, this would mean that He was unfit to serve as a Sacrifice. Concerning the Old Testament Sacrifices which were a type, the Scripture plainly says, *"Your lamb shall be without blemish"* (Ex. 12:5).

How in the world could One Who was manifested to take away sin, do so by becoming a sinner Himself? No, He didn't become a sinner on the Cross, but rather a Sin-Offering (Isa. 53:10).

(6) "WHOSOEVER ABIDETH IN HIM SINNETH NOT: WHOSOEVER SINNETH HATH NOT SEEN HIM, NEITHER KNOWN HIM."

The structure is:

1. The words *"abideth"* and *"sinneth"* are used here to designate a certain class of individual.

2. *"Everyone who habitually is abiding in Him,"* is a saved person, and, *"everyone who habitually is sinning,"* is an unsaved person.

3. Sin in the life of the Christian is an exception, not the rule.

ABIDETH

The phrase, *"Whosoever abideth in Him sinneth not,"* must be understood according to the original Greek language.

John does not teach that Believers do not sin, but is speaking of a character, a habit. He does not deny that a Christian sins at times. Indeed he admits the possibility of sin in the Christian's life in I John 1:9, and

forbids sin in I John 2:1. What John denies here is that a Christian sins habitually.

To properly understand what is being said here, as stated, we have to go to the original Greek language. The tense of the verbs is present, pertaining to the kind of action which is continuous and habitual. Thus, *"everyone who habitually is abiding in Him,"* is a saved person, which at the same time, means that this person is not habitually sinning. If one is habitually sinning, he is an unsaved person.

A Christian as a habit of life is abiding in fellowship with the Lord Jesus. Sin may at times enter his life, but sin is the exception, not the rule.

By contrast, the unsaved person as a habit of life sins continually. *"Sinneth"* is present in tense, continuous action being indicated. The person who is abiding in Christ is not habitually sinning. The Child of God as a habit of life, does Righteousness, and sin is not a habit with him.

John is not teaching sinless perfection here, for the Bible does not teach such a doctrine. But it does teach that sin is to not have dominion over the Believer (Rom. 6:14).

THE CROSS: THE ONLY ANSWER FOR SIN

As should be by now overly obvious, both Paul and John deal with sin extensively. John tells us what is to be and what is not, while Paul tells us how to arrive at the position of which John speaks. John wrote his Epistles quite a number of years after Paul, so would have seen no need to duplicate that which Paul had already given. Because it's so important, let me say it again:

The Cross is the only answer for sin, whether in the lives of unbelievers or in the lives of Believers. So what does that mean?

It means the only way to obtain victory over sin is to have Faith in Christ and what He did at the Cross. This means that as Scriptural as laying on of hands is, sin cannot be eradicated in this manner. It means as holy as true manifestations of the Spirit actually are, sin cannot be eradicated in this manner. In fact, there is absolutely nothing that man can do, which can eradicate sin within his life. It is beyond the pale of human endeavor. But there is a remedy!

The remedy, which in fact is the only remedy, is *"Jesus Christ and Him Crucified"* (I Cor. 2:2).

Most Christians will readily agree with this statement as it regards the sinner initially coming to Christ; however, most Christians have little knowledge of the Cross as it regards the Sanctification experience.

If the Church really knew and understood the part the Cross plays in the Sanctification process, which speaks of ridding one of all sin, and as well believed what the Bible says on this subject, they wouldn't recommend humanistic psychology.

For the most part, the Church little understanding the Cross as it refers to the life of the Believer, addresses the problem of sin in about every fashion that one could imagine. However, whatever way it suggests, and whatever method it proposes, if it's not Faith exclusively in the Cross of Christ, which gives the Holy Spirit latitude to work within our lives (Rom. 8:1-2, 11, 13), there will be no favorable results. But if the weakest Christian, whomever he or she might be, who is saddled with all types of problems, will but turn his Faith toward the Sacrifice of Christ, understanding that in that Sacrifice every victory was won, and there maintain his faith, he will find himself getting stronger and stronger in the Lord, with defeats turning into victories.

TO KNOW JESUS

The phrase, *"Whosoever sinneth hath not seen Him, neither known Him,"* could be translated, *"Whosoever habitually sinneth. . . !"*

Some have tried to force the unscriptural doctrine of *"sinless perfection"* into these particular Scriptures, or that the Christian may live entirely without sin. And some have held that the Apostle meant to teach that this is always the characteristic of the true Christian.

Against such an interpretation, however, which supposes that it teaches that the Christian is absolutely perfect, and lives wholly without sin, there are objections:

First of all, if it teaches that doctrine at all, it teaches that *"all"* Christians are perfect; *"whosoever abideth in Him," "whosoever is born of God," "he cannot sin,"* (vs. 9).

This is not true, and cannot be held to be true by those who have any just views of what the Children of God have been and are. Who can maintain that Abraham, Isaac, or Jacob; that Moses, David, or Job; that Peter, John, or Paul, were absolutely perfect, and were never, after their Regeneration, guilty of an act of sin? Certainly they never affirmed it of themselves, nor did the sacred record attribute to them any such perfection.

Are we to come to the painful conclusion that all who are not absolutely perfect in thought, word, and deed, are destitute of Salvation, and are to be set down as hypocrites or self-deceivers? If that is to be done, then there will be no one left standing.

No, the Bible, nor does John teach sinless perfection. As previously stated, to properly understand these texts, we have to resort to the original language. Let us say it again:

"Everyone who habitually is abiding in Him," is a saved person, and, *"everyone who is habitually sinning, is not habitually abiding in Him, and in fact is not saved."*

(7) "LITTLE CHILDREN, LET NO MAN DECEIVE YOU: HE THAT DOETH RIGHTEOUSNESS IS RIGHTEOUS, EVEN AS HE IS RIGHTEOUS."

The exegesis is:

1. It is Satan's business to endeavor to deceive the Child of God.

2. This Verse, and in reality the entirety of the Epistle, is a warning against antinomianism. Basically, this is a teaching which claims that sin doesn't matter, because Grace covers it.

3. One is Righteous only as one does Righteousness.

4. If we are *"sons of God,"* we will be Righteous as He is Righteous.

DECEPTION

The phrase, *"Little children, let no man deceive you,"* proclaims the fact that deception certainly is possible. It is a mistake to think that the fact of being a Christian is proof against cunning deceivers. Deception is one of Satan's most powerful weapons, and the proof of this is in the millions of Christians who lose their way.

Regarding deception we would like to think that most all Preachers are Godly, with only an exception here and there; however, the truth is the opposite. There is only one true Preacher here and there. The far, far greater majority, are not truly preaching the Gospel, but rather something else altogether. In fact, the Church offers presently a tidbit for every base desire held in the unconsecrated heart of the Christian. Good Churches aren't easy to find, and if one is to be found, the Believer must ardently seek the Lord asking to be led by the Spirit in this all important task. The primary reason for the existence of a Church is twofold:

1. Where the Word of God is preached without fear or compromise, which is at the same time saying that the Cross is preached.

2. Where the Holy Spirit can move and operate and have His way.

But unfortunately, these two things just mentioned, are not exactly high on the list of things sought by most modern Christians. They have other fish to fry so to speak; therefore, they look for other things, and as stated, there are Churches galore who will provide those things. Truly blessed is the Believer who has a Church where the Word of God is preeminent along with the Moving and Operation of the Holy Spirit.

To be deceived is to be led astray, and to be more particular, it is to be led away from the Cross. And let the Reader understand the following:

I am linking Christ, the Cross, and the Word as one and the same. They cannot be divided (Jn. 1:1, 14, 29). In effect, when we say one, we have said the other. And if the Believer doesn't understand these three names in this capacity, then the Believer really doesn't understand Christ. Christ came to this world to fulfill the Word, which was to die on a Cross.

WHO HE IS OR WHAT HE DID?

Someone asked me once as to what is the most important, Who Christ is, or What Christ has done, as it refers to the Cross?

I don't think it's proper to make a division in this manner; however, for the sake of clarification, I will state the following:

If one would be allowed to put it in this fashion, What Christ did is the most important. But yet, What He did, had to be done by Who He was.

NOTES

When we speak of Who He was, we are speaking of His Deity. While Christ was Very Man, He was also Very God. And to be sure, it took the God-Man Jesus Christ to carry out this great task of Redemption.

But yet, the mere fact of Christ being God did not really save anyone. If the fact of His Deity alone would have redeemed mankind, then Jesus died on the Cross needlessly. So, Who He was, as important as that was and is, did not really save anyone. As stated, this was absolutely necessary, and I continue to refer to Who He was, but within itself contained no saving grace.

To bring about the Redemption of fallen humanity, Christ would have to go to the Cross, offer Himself up as Sacrifice, which necessitated the pouring out of His Precious Blood, which alone would atone for the sins of man. Therefore, while Who He was is of utmost significance, it was What He did, which refers to the Cross, which brought about the Redemption of mankind.

FAITH

From the mid 1900's to the turn of the century, the Church has had more teaching on faith, than possibly all the balance of its history put together. However, this teaching has not been Faith in Jesus Christ and Him Crucified, but rather in something else altogether. In other words, the object of faith, which mostly came from the Word of Faith people, centered up on self more so than anything else.

While it claims to be faith in the Word, it is not the Word of God as it pertains to the Cross, but something else altogether. Actually, it is faith in a perverted word.

In these circles, the Cross is actually denigrated. It is referred to as *"past miseries,"* and called *"the greatest defeat in human history."* In fact, Kenneth Copeland, one of the bright lights of this false way, actually says that *"the Blood of Jesus Christ didn't atone for anything."*

This teaching has done more to hinder the Work of God than possibly any error that's been promoted in the last century. Millions in the Church have bought into this façade, and because it promises instant gratification for the lust of the flesh. At the present time, its greatest emphasis is *"money."* Most every message is designed to tell Christians how to use their faith in order to get rich. It's a heady doctrine, simply because there seems to be an ample amount of greed in the hearts of all of us. Of course, the only ones who get rich are the Preachers promoting this false doctrine.

This is a false doctrine which makes Jesus too human and man too divine.

Let the Reader understand, whenever the Bible speaks of *"Faith"* or *"believing,"* at least as it refers to God and His Word, without exception, the root meaning of these words is actually Faith in the Cross of Christ. And if the faith you have in your heart is not faith in the Cross, while it may continue to be faith, it is not faith that God will recognize. He honors the Faith which has the Cross as its object. The Believer must never forget that.

Paul said: *"Whom God has set forth to be a propitiation through faith in His Blood, to declare His Righteousness for the remission of sins that are past, through the forbearance of God"* (Rom. 3:25).

Paul also said: *"One Lord, one faith, one baptism"* (Eph. 4:5). What did he mean by that?

He meant there is only one Lord Jesus Christ, Who has given Himself as a Sacrifice on the Cross of Calvary, in order that we might be saved.

In view of that, there is only *"one Faith,"* which refers to what Jesus did on the Cross. Any other type of faith is that which God will not recognize and will not honor. If it's not Faith in *"Jesus Christ and Him Crucified,"* then it's not Faith.

"One Baptism," refers to the Crucifixion of Christ, and our *"Baptism into His Death"* (Rom. 6:3). It has nothing to do with Water Baptism. This *"Baptism into the Death of Christ,"* is that in which we are to anchor our Faith, or that which must ever be the object of our Faith.

There are untold millions of Christians trying to increase their faith, when that's not their need. They need to change the object of their faith from other things, to the Cross of Christ.

The Disciples once said unto the Lord, *"Increase our faith."*

NOTES

The Lord then told them that if they had Faith as a grain of mustard seed, which of course is a very small seed, they *"might say unto this sycamine tree, be thou plucked up by the root, and be thou planted in the sea; and it should obey you"* (Lk. 17:5-6).

In other words, Jesus was telling His Disciples that it wasn't really an increase of faith which they needed, but rather that their Faith be planted in the right object.

He did not at that time tell them as to exactly what that object should be, and because they could not have then received it. That information would be given by Christ to Paul, when the Master explained to him the meaning of the New Covenant, which in effect, was the meaning of the Cross. That explanation is found in Romans, Chapter 6. The Cross of Christ is to ever be the object of our Faith. That's what Jesus came to do, and that's what Jesus did. The answer for which the human race seeks, whether it knows it or not, is found only in the Cross. The Cross opened up the way to God, which is outlined to us in graphic detail throughout the entirety of the Book of Hebrews.

RIGHTEOUSNESS

The phrase, *"He that doeth righteousness is righteous,"* could be turned around in this manner, *"He is righteous who does righteousness."* As well, in this statement, we are told that proper Faith will always produce Righteousness. However, let us turn it around and say it in another way:

Trying to do Righteousness will never produce proper faith. And regrettably, that's where most of the modern Church presently is. If one's Faith is properly placed in the Cross of Christ, ever making that its focus, without fail, such Faith will produce Righteousness. In fact, that's the very purpose of such Faith, which means that was the purpose of the Cross. With Faith properly placed, the Holy Spirit will bring about and guarantee Righteousness in one's life.

John was addressing himself to the false teachers who claimed that it didn't really matter what type of sin or sins they committed, inasmuch as their spirit had been perfected. The Holy Spirit through John completely refutes this erroneous doctrine by saying that it is only the one who does Righteousness who in fact, is Righteous. In other words, if a person sins, them claiming that it is only their physical body that did this and not their spirit is foolishness indeed! *"Righteousness"* carries through to the entirety of the whole man, *"spirit, soul, and body"* (I Thess. 5:23). And if Righteousness carries forth in this manner, and it definitely does, so does sin.

In fact, Paul said: *"Neither yield ye your members as instruments of unrighteousness unto sin: but yield yourselves unto God, as those who are alive from the dead* (every Believer has in effect died in Christ, and has been raised in newness of life), *and your members as instruments of righteousness unto God"* (Rom. 6:13).

HE IS RIGHTEOUS

The phrase, *"Even as He is righteous,"* is meant to claim for the true Christian a likeness of nature to Christ. Although there is no allusion to it here, the teaching of the Epistle to the Romans shows that the eternal Righteousness of Christ which is made possible by the Cross, may ever be the object of Faith.

God's verdict of approval ever rested upon Jesus. Jesus is our model, yet He is more than our model because of our union with Him, our remaining in Him, from which comes all that we are (Rom. 6:3-5).

(8) "HE THAT COMMITTETH SIN IS OF THE DEVIL; FOR THE DEVIL SINNETH FROM THE BEGINNING. FOR THIS PURPOSE THE SON OF GOD WAS MANIFESTED, THAT HE MIGHT DESTROY THE WORKS OF THE DEVIL."

The diagram is:

1. *"Committeth"* refers to one *"who is continually doing sin."*

2. He who continually does sin is out of the Devil as a source.

3. The word *"beginning"* shows that the Devil is not only the ultimate source of sin, but actually its originator.

4. The very purpose for which Christ was manifested was that He might destroy the works of the Devil, which He most definitely did do, and did so at the Cross.

5. The argument here is that as the Son of God came to destroy all of the works of

the Devil, he cannot be his true follower who lives in sin.

SIN IS OF THE DEVIL

The phrase, *"He that committeth sin is of the Devil,"* presents the fact that whoever is truly born of God does not live a life of habitual sinning. This statement harks back to I Jn. 1:6: *"If we say that we have fellowship with Him, and walk in darkness, we lie, and do not the truth."*

There is clearly a progression in the author's thought on sin in this section. He begins with the *"sinfulness of sin,"* by saying in effect, *"It is lawlessness,"* which is rebellion against God (I Jn. 3:4). Next he shows its incompatibility with Christ: *"He appeared so that He might take away our sins"* (I Jn. 3:5). Then he shows its incompatibility for anyone who lives in Christ: *"No one who lives in Him keeps on sinning"* (I Jn. 3:6). Now he shows the diabolic nature of sin — its source is the Devil who *"has been sinning from the beginning."*

THE WORDS OF JOHN

"Committeth" in the Greek is *"poiao,"* and means *"he who is continually doing sin."* *"He that makes sin his business or practice."*

He who continually does sin is out of the Devil as a source. That is, his sinful propensities, issuing from his totally depraved nature inherited from Adam, find their ultimate source in the Devil who brought about the downfall of our first parents. This person who is constantly sinning is as well, constantly of the Devil. It does not refer to a Christian who occasionally sins, as bad as that is, for the Bible doesn't teach sinless perfection.

John is saying that people who practice sin are not of God, which means they aren't saved. In fact, they are *"of the Devil."*

Unfortunately, John's statements given here impact untold millions of professing Christians. They claim to have faith in Christ, but in fact, live a life of constant sinning. There is no witness of the Spirit within their hearts and lives, simply because the Holy Spirit isn't there, and because they aren't saved.

These people, who number into the millions, are in fact very religious, at least after a fashion; however, they are deceived by the doing of religion, which is the greatest narcotic there is. So let no professing Believer who is continually practicing sin, think that he is saved, for he isn't!

FROM THE BEGINNING

The phrase, *"For the Devil sinneth from the beginning,"* does not mean that he sinned from the beginning of his existence, for he was originally made holy like the other Angels. The meaning is that he at a point rebelled against God, which introduced sin into the universe, and which he has continued to practice ever since. The word *"sinneth"* here implies continued and habitual sin. He did not commit one act of sin and then reform; but he has continued, and still continues, his course of sin.

TO DESTROY THE WORKS OF THE DEVIL

The phrase, *"For this purpose the Son of God was manifested, that He might destroy the works of the Devil,"* proclaims what was done at the Cross. By the Blood of His Cross He has paid for sin, made a way of escape from the arch enemy of men's souls, defeated the purposes of the Devil, and will finally bring about his complete downfall.

John sees the enmity of God against the Devil as absolute. No quarter is asked and no quarter is given. It lies at the heart of God's commitment to rescue man from the Devil's clutches. The Lord will destroy the Devil and all his works, including those children of the Devil who accept sinning as a way of life. In other words, all who follow Satan are going down with him.

The *"works of the Devil"* include all that which *"steal, kill, and destroy"* (Jn. 10:10).

HOW DID JESUS DESTROY THE WORKS OF THE DEVIL?

John tells us in I John 4:10. He said: *"God . . . sent His Son to be the propitiation for our sins."*

Jesus destroyed the works of the Devil at the Cross. But He did it in a most unusual way.

Let not the Reader think that Jesus went to the Cross because a ransom was owed to the Devil. God owed Satan nothing and neither did man. There was in fact a monstrous

NOTES

debt owed, but it was to God. Man had sinned grievously against God, so the Cross was a necessity, in order that this debt may be paid. So how did this affect Satan?

Satan has a legal right to hold man in bondage because of sin. And so, almost all of humanity is in bondage to the Evil One. But when Jesus went to the Cross and shed His Life's Blood, He then atoned for all sin, which means that He paid the debt to God which man rightly owed, but could not pay. When He atoned for all sin, which He did, Satan now had no more hold on humanity, except a pseudo-hold he could effect, because of man refusing to take advantage of what Christ has done. So the atoning work of Christ at the Cross effectively destroyed the *"works of the Devil."* This is portrayed in Colossians 2:14-15.

What Jesus did at the Cross has also made possible the future domain of Christ.

At the Second Coming Satan along with all his fallen Angels and demon spirits, will be locked away in the bottomless pit (Rev. 20:1-3). The world will then know a thousand years of peace, prosperity, and plenty such as it has never known before. Jesus Christ will reign personally from Jerusalem, in effect being the King of kings and Lord of lords of the entirety of the Earth. The world will then know Righteousness as it has not known previously, and because the Kingdom of Christ is now supreme. Once again, all of this has been made possible and will be made possible, by the Cross.

(9) "WHOSOEVER IS BORN OF GOD DOTH NOT COMMIT SIN; FOR HIS SEED REMAINETH IN HIM: AND HE CANNOT SIN, BECAUSE HE IS BORN OF GOD."

The exegesis is:

1. Being *"born of God"* speaks of the completed act of Regeneration, with the impartation of the Divine nature.

2. Whosoever is born of God does not practice sin.

3. *"His seed"* refers to the Word of God in the Believer.

4. It is this principle of Divine life through the Word that makes it impossible for a Christian to live habitually in sin, for the Divine nature causes the Child of God to hate sin and love Righteousness.

5. *"Cannot sin"* means *"he is not able to habitually sin."*

BORN OF GOD

The phrase, *"Whosoever is born of God does not commit sin,"* could be translated, *"Does not habitually practice sin."* According to Wuest the translation actually reads, *"Every one who has been born out of God, with the present result that he is a born-one of God, does not habitually do sin."* The Greek Text bears this out.

To ascertain from this Passage that everyone who is a true Christian is absolutely perfect, and never commits any sin, is not borne out by the Text. Neither is it borne out by experience. While no Christian has to sin, and in fact we are told to *"sin not"*; still, John also went on to say, *"And if any man sin, we have an advocate with the Father, Jesus Christ the righteous"* (I Jn. 2:1).

When Jesus went to the Cross, He there destroyed the Devil's works (Col. 2:14-15). Therefore, Satan has no more hold on the Child of God; however, if the Believer doesn't understand the Cross as it relates to the Sanctification process, he definitely will find himself habitually committing sin. In other words, unless he places his Faith exclusively in the Cross of Christ, which is the only answer for sin, he will find the sin nature once again ruling within his heart and life. That's why Paul said:

"Let not sin (the sin nature) *therefore reign in your mortal body, that you should obey it in the lusts thereof"* (Rom. 6:12).

Were it not possible for this to happen, the Apostle would not have even broached the subject, much less given us instruction pertaining to the entirety of Romans, Chapter 6.

When it comes to sin the Reader must understand, there is only one Sacrifice for sin, and that is the Cross. In other words, if the Believer attempts to overcome sin in any way, shape, form, or manner, other than by expressing simple Faith in the Cross of Christ, he in fact, will not overcome sin. That's why Paul also said:

"But God forbid that I should glory (boast), *save in the Cross of our Lord Jesus Christ, by Whom the world is crucified unto me, and I unto the world"* (Gal. 6:14).

NOTES

This is how he could say: *"For sin shall not have dominion over you: for you are not under the law, but under Grace"* (Rom. 6:14).

HOW IS ONE BORN OF GOD?

The answer to that should be very simple. One is born of God simply by trusting in Jesus Christ, which means to trust in what He did at the Cross on our behalf, thereby making Him the Saviour and Lord of one's life (Jn. 3:3, 16). When the believing sinner accepts Christ as Saviour, the power of sin is then broken in that person's life, all because of the Cross.

Inasmuch as the power of sin was broken due to Faith in Christ and what He did at the Cross, it stands to reason that victory is maintained in this way as well. But the problem is this:

The True Church believes in Christ and the Cross as it refers to the initial Salvation experience; however, it has almost no knowledge whatsoever as it regards the Cross concerning Sanctification. In other words, the part the Cross plays in our everyday living for God, which in fact is the single most important aspect of our daily living, is all but unknown in the modern Church. Consequently, most of the Church not having this knowledge, is ruled by the sin nature, which means that works of the flesh are predominant within their lives (Gal. 5:17, 19-21). As stated, they are *"practicing sin."*

Now this is not something that such a Believer desires to do. In fact, most fight against it with all of their strength, but find, that is if they are honest with themselves, that all of their struggle does not make the problem better, but rather worse. So what happens in such a situation?

The sad truth is, this which I have just described is not isolated cases, but rather the majority. And I base my statement on the following:

If the Believer doesn't understand the part the Cross plays in his everyday living for God, and almost none do, then it is impossible for that Believer to live a victorious, overcoming, Christian life. I'm not saying that person isn't saved. In fact they are saved, and because they are trusting Christ for Salvation; however, they don't know how to trust Christ for Sanctification, which simply means that the Believer understands that everything he receives comes to him through the Cross; consequently, he must at all times maintain his Faith in the Cross of Christ as it regards his daily living (Lk. 9:23; Rom. 6:3-14; I Cor. 1:17-18; 2:2). With Faith properly placed in the Cross of Christ, which we have stated over and over again in this Volume, the Holy Spirit will then work mightily within that Believer's heart and life, and victory will be assured, for the simple reason that the Holy Spirit can do anything. He is God! (Rom. 8:1-2, 11, 13). But not knowing this, the Believer struggles in his own strength.

In fact, the entirety of Romans, Chapters 6, 7, and 8, along with the entirety of the Epistle to the Galatians, deals with this very subject. To be sure, if it wasn't such a problem, the Holy Spirit wouldn't have devoted so much space to the subject.

WHAT HAPPENS TO SUCH A CHRISTIAN?

Once again let's keep it in mind that we are not dealing here with isolated cases, but with almost the entirety of the Church. In the last several decades there has been so little teaching on the Cross of Christ, which means there has been so little teaching on Sanctification, that for all practical purposes, the modern Church is Cross illiterate, which means that it is also lacking in knowledge regarding the Sanctification process. In fact, Sanctification is almost a foreign subject in most modern Churches. In other words, most Believers don't have the foggiest idea as to what it is. That's tragic, considering that there is nothing more important for the Child of God. Unfortunately, much of the modern Church has majored in super-faith, when in reality, they've had precious little faith at all, and at the present, they are majoring in money, with the results being tragic.

Sanctification simply means *"to be set apart exclusively to God."* The problem is, the modern Church has little idea as to how to be set apart. In fact, it goes from one silly fad to the other. At one period it's the *"laughing phenomenon,"* and at another period it's the *"family curse,"* and at another period it's other type of *"manifestations,"* etc. In years past it was *"confession,"* and then *"casting*

demons out of Christians," and as well *"humanistic psychology"* has been big.

So again what happens in all of this?

We have Christians, including Preachers, who are failing in every respect. To get around this, millions lie, or they try to hide the true picture, while all the time claiming grandiose things in the Lord. So we have a modern Church filled with hypocrisy.

In all of this, many draw up their own plans and criteria for Righteousness. In other words, Righteousness is according to the standard they have laid down, which conveniently overlooks their own problems. God calls it self-righteousness! However, this fake righteousness helps them to deceive themselves. And that's exactly what is happening, self-deception.

There is no Righteousness outside of Faith in Christ and what Christ did at the Cross. And if we add anything to what Jesus did at Calvary, we nullify the Righteousness which Christ Alone can give. So the Believer had better understand the following:

RIGHTEOUSNESS OR
SELF-RIGHTEOUSNESS?

As I've already said a number of times in this Volume, the Cross of Christ is the dividing line between the True Church and the Apostate Church. And to be sure, this line is going to be so divisive that if one accepts the Cross, they will bring upon themselves the ire of the Apostate Church. It cannot be any other way. Even as John will mention in the coming Verses, Cain was not satisfied to attempt to formulate his own righteousness, at the same time he felt he must kill his brother Abel, who had put his Faith in the Cross of Christ. That spirit has prevailed from then until now.

The reason that much of the Church world hates this Evangelist, and I speak of me personally, is because of the Cross. Do we accept totally what Christ has done on our behalf, or do we accept man's ways? To be sure, man's ways, and I speak of religious ways, denies the Cross, so if man's ways are accepted, it will mean the loss of Christ. One cannot have both! It's either the Cross or religion!

Back to our original subject, if the Believer doesn't understand the Cross as it relates to our ongoing Christian experience, such a Believer will find himself being ruled by the sin nature, and thereby, *"practicing sin."* There is only one answer to this dilemma, and that is, as we have stated, the Cross of Christ. Only by Faith in that Finished Work can the Believer no longer *"practice sin."*

HIS SEED

The phrase, *"For His seed remaineth in him,"* refers to the Word of God. The *"seed"* is the Word of God. This *"seed"* is referred to in several ways, i.e., *"the light"* (I Jn. 1:6-7), *"the truth"* (I Jn. 1:8; 2:4), *"the Commandment"* (I Jn. 2:7), etc. It makes no difference whether we say that the Word remains in us, or that we remain in the Word, the Truth, etc. *"Seed"* is figurative, but the figure extends only to the fact that a seed has life in it. The Word of God is a living power (I Pet. 1:23).

It is not necessary to extend this figure, to talk about vegetable seed and human seed, or life germ, and to seek for analogies in natural life, seed growth, etc. Jesus and the holy writers dominate their figures and are not dominated by them. Does this interpretation of the *"Seed"* as the Word lose the Holy Spirit? Indeed not! The great means by which the Spirit quickens, kindles life, keeps life alive, is the Word, in which He is, by which He works.

When the Believer has the Living Word in his reborn heart he is not able to go on sinning simply *"because he has been born from God."*

In October of 1991, I laid my Bible on the table in front of me and others in the room, stating, *"I don't know the answer, but I know the answer is in the Word of God. And by the Grace of God I'm going to find that answer."*

By the Grace of God I did find that answer. The Lord took me to Romans, Chapter 6 and thereby told me, *"That for which you seek is found in the Cross."* He opened up the Word to me, planting this *"Seed"* deep within my heart, as it regards victorious, Christian living, showing me as well how the Holy Spirit works upon the Word (Rom. 8:2). To say that it changed my life would be a gross understatement! And to be sure, what the Lord gave me is not something new, but rather that which He had given to Paul so

long, long ago. It has changed the lives of untold millions, and in fact, there is no other seed, but this *"Seed!"*

CANNOT PRACTICE SIN

The phrase, *"And he cannot sin, because he is born of God,"* refers to the repugnancy of sin in the heart of the true Christian.

"Cannot sin" in the Greek is *"dunamai,"* and means, *"I am not able."* In other words, as a Christian I am unable to practice sin. Again let us state, the Greek Text here holds no warrant for the erroneous teaching of sinless perfection; however, the Word of God definitely does teach us that sin will not have dominion over us (Rom. 6:14). This speaks of the *"sin nature,"* and refers to Faith in the Cross which alone overcomes the sin nature (Rom. 6:3-5).

(10) "IN THIS THE CHILDREN OF GOD ARE MANIFEST, AND THE CHILDREN OF THE DEVIL: WHOSOEVER DOETH NOT RIGHTEOUSNESS IS NOT OF GOD, NEITHER HE THAT LOVETH NOT HIS BROTHER."

The diagram is:

1. *"In this"* refers to Righteousness and Love which will be the hallmark of the true Child of God.

2. Likewise, the lack of these attributes proclaims the fact that such a one is a child of the Devil.

3. A Child of God will habitually do Righteousness and will habitually love his brother. Otherwise he's not a Child of God.

THE CHILDREN OF GOD

The phrase, *"In this the Children of God are manifest, and the children of the Devil,"* proclaims the fact that none are half and half; there is only an either/or. John has presented the manifest, plain, even visible difference. To say it even clearer, Verse 10 sums up the matter in a terse distinction: all mankind are either Children of God or children of the Devil. As stated, there is no half and half. In fact, God doesn't look at the world as we do. He doesn't see the five races, but rather two ranks: Believers or unbelievers.

In the time of the Romans, they actually labeled Christians as *"the third race."* They looked at themselves as one race, and all who were not Romans as the other race, and all who were Christians as *"the third race."* That's how distinct they were!

While today we look at the five races, brown, yellow, white, black, and red, perhaps we should think of a sixth race, those who are truly Christians; however, I wonder presently, if there is enough distinction to warrant such?

John tells us in this Verse that there will be a certain manifestation as it regards who is a Child of God and who is a child of the Devil. That manifestation for the Child of God is *"Righteousness and Love."* At the same time, such are absent in the child of the Devil.

RIGHTEOUSNESS

The phrase, *"Whosoever doeth not Righteousness is not of God,"* proclaims the fact that Righteousness will be the hallmark of the Child of God, and definitely will be absent in the child of the Devil. But let the Reader understand that it is Christ who defines and standardizes what is Righteousness.

In fact, this is the great dividing line between the True Church and the Apostate Church. It is God's definition of Righteousness or man's definition of Righteousness. That's actually what it's all about!

There are religious denominations with which I cannot associate, because I cannot agree to their definition of Righteousness. And we must remember, if we get this definition wrong we lose our souls. That's how critical all of this is.

WHAT IS GOD'S DEFINITION OF RIGHTEOUSNESS?

The Scripture says of Abraham: *"And he believed in the LORD; and He counted it to him for Righteousness"* (Gen. 15:6). Paul quoted this very Verse in Romans 4:3.

In fact, God gave to Abraham the meaning of Righteousness and how it was to be obtained. By stating it in this fashion, *"Abraham believed God,"* we are led to believe that Righteousness cannot be obtained by merit or works of any nature. In other words, Righteousness cannot be earned.

Paul said: *"Even as David also describeth the blessedness of the man, unto whom God imputeth Righteousness without works"* (Rom. 4:6).

NOTES

The word *"impute"* means to *"freely give."* What did Abraham and David believe?

When it speaks of believing God as it referred to Abraham or David, it is referring to believing in what God would do regarding the Redemption of the human race, which was in fact, the giving of His Only Son. In fact the whole of this matter, is summed up in the one Scripture: *"For God so loved the world, that He gave His only Begotten Son, that whosoever believeth in Him, should not perish but have everlasting life"* (Jn. 3:16).

So we learn that the way to receive Righteousness is to simply believe in Christ and what Christ did for us at the Cross. We must not try to earn it, or try to work for it in any manner, but just simply believe in Christ and the Cross (I Cor. 2:2).

Upon such Faith, a spotless, pure Righteousness is awarded to the Believer, which in effect, is the Righteousness of Christ (Rom. 1:16-17; 5:18; 9:30; 10:4; II Pet. 1:1).

THE RIGHTEOUSNESS OF GOD

God has always had a Perfect Righteousness. In fact, God is Righteousness (I Jn. 3:7). But the question was how could God award His Righteousness to sinful man? And when we speak of sinful men, we're speaking of *"children of the Devil."* That would be like granting a pardon to a confessed killer who is claiming that he will continue to kill and murder if released from prison. Any society that would do such a thing would soon find itself in anarchy. So God could not merely award Righteousness to confessed felons, which in fact, was and is the human race.

To answer this question, a laborious process would have to be enacted. At the very outset, God showed how it could be done, by His introduction of the sacrificial system. He in effect told Adam and Eve that He would send a Redeemer into the world Who would bring man out of his dilemma (Gen. 3:15; Gen., Chpt. 4). In the meanwhile, the human race had become so wicked that God would have to destroy the whole of humanity with the Flood, with the exception of Noah and his family (Gen. 6:11-16).

Some 400 years after Noah, and about 2,000 years after Adam, God revealed to Abraham how all of this would be done. He proclaimed to him, as stated, the way and manner that Righteousness would be obtained, and that it would be brought about through God giving His Only Son, of which He used Abraham to present this truth by a tremendous object lesson (Gen., Chpt. 22).

Some 400 years after Abraham, God gave to Moses *"the Law,"* which was His Standard of Righteousness. In other words, if man was to be accepted by God, he would have to live up to this Standard. It was summed up in the Ten Commandments (Ex., Chpt. 20). Due to the Fall, man was unable to do this which God commanded, which of course, God knew at the beginning. The Law was given in order to set a standard for Righteousness, to define sin, and to show man how incapable he actually was.

God gave man approximately 1,600 years and during that time, not one single individual totally kept the Law. At the end of that period, Christ came, Who had been promised all along, Who would keep the Law perfectly in every respect.

There was Righteousness in the Law, but for such Righteousness to be obtained, one had to keep it perfectly. Jesus kept it perfectly and thereby, gained its Righteousness, and did so as the *"Last Adam,"* or the *"Second Man"* (I Cor. 15:45-47).

Having gained this Perfect Righteousness, which He had to do as a Man, and which He did do, that is if fallen humanity was to be saved, He then went to the Cross to satisfy the curse of the broken Law. In other words, it was not enough for Christ to merely gain the Righteousness which He did, the matter of man's crime, man's terrible sin debt against God, had to be addressed as well. In other words, somebody had to pay the penalty, and that Somebody was Christ.

In order to pay this price, He would have to be *"made a curse for us"* (Gal. 3:13), which He was.

This means that He gave His Own Life as a Sacrifice *"that He might deliver us from this present evil world, according to the Will of God and our Father"* (Gal. 1:4).

Inasmuch as He did this, thereby satisfying the terrible sin debt owed by man to God, then the Promise made to Abraham by God could come into full bloom. All man has to

do is simply trust in Christ Who served as our Substitute, which means to trust in what He did at the Cross, and then a Perfect Righteousness will be awarded to such a believing sinner, even as it has been to untold millions.

This is the only Righteousness which God will honor, i.e., *"the Righteousness of Christ awarded to men who simply evidence Faith in Christ and what He did at the Cross"* (Eph. 2:8-9).

THE APOSTATE CHURCH

Perhaps the word *"Righteousness"* will define the True Church and the Apostate Church as no other word. As stated, the True Church looks to what Jesus did at the Cross whereby Righteousness is obtained strictly by Faith. The Apostate Church either ignores the Cross altogether, thereby formulating its own brand of Righteousness, or else it claims to believe in the Cross, but adds something to the Finished Work of Christ, which in effect, nullifies what Christ has done. To attempt to add to the Finished Work is just as bad in one sense as denying the Finished Work.

For instance, many, if not most, Churches are not content to trust completely in what Christ has done at the Cross as it regards the sin question, but rather feel that they have to add a regiment of punishment, etc.

We believe that the Bible teaches that there is only one Sacrifice for sin, and that is what Jesus did at the Cross (Heb. 10:12). And this means the only way that sin can be forgiven and washed clean, is for the Believer to trust completely in what Christ has done; however, at least as it regards Preachers, most Churches all but ignore what Christ has done at the Cross, rather instituting their own regiment of punishment which runs the gamut all the way from the Preacher not preaching for a period of time, to a number of other rules that must be kept, etc.

First of all, most Christians commit sin, and that goes for Preachers as well, simply because they do not properly understand the part the Cross plays in our everyday life and living; consequently, they try to live the life in all the wrong way, which guarantees failure.

The answer to this problem is for the Cross to be properly explained to such an individual, which is the proper method of restoration

(Gal. 6:1). It's surely not going to help the individual for them to perform some other type of silly things. In fact, such doings only make matters worse. And something else should be said as well:

It is not only very wrong Scripturally for Churches to impose such foolishness, but it's wrong for any Christian, Preachers included, to obey such demands. At whatever cost, at whatever price, the Word of God must be the criteria for all things.

The only way that Righteousness can be obtained is by simply trusting in what Christ has done at the Cross on our behalf. There is no other answer for sin and failure. It's bad enough for a Christian to fail the Lord in any capacity; however, to compound the problem, by attempting to add to the Finished Work of Christ only exacerbates the situation.

LOVE

The phrase, *"Neither he that loveth not his Brother,"* presents the second hallmark of the true Child of God, Righteousness being the other.

"Loveth" is *"agapao"* in the Greek, which refers to Divine love which is self-sacrificial in its essence, the love produced in the heart of the yielded Saint by the Holy Spirit, the love defined by Paul in I Corinthians, Chapter 13, the love shown by God at Calvary. In fact, Calvary was the greatest display of love that humanity has ever known and ever will know. Consequently, I would have to say that the Christian cannot really understand and know the true Love of God, unless he as well understands the Cross of Calvary. Calvary which at the same time says *"the Cross,"* was totally for others. Jesus did not die for Angels or even Himself, but only for others. And to be sure, these *"others"* were not those who loved Him, but rather hated Him. To die for those who love you is one thing, but to die for those who hate you is something else altogether. This Jesus did! So I think the reason there is so little love seen in the modern Church, is because there is so little understanding of the Cross.

The idea of all of this is our relation to God at once involves our relation to each other. By John saying that *"the one not loving his*

Brother" is not of God, the Apostle draws a decisive circle about *"the Children of God"* and presents us as being separated from *"the children of the Devil."* They are separated at the very source, their respective fathers; the One is the Heavenly Father, God, the other the Devil (Jn. 8:44). This origin and source is itself secret and invisible, but the tangible, visible evidence is plain: love and the absence of love.

The reason John says *"not loving his Brother"* instead of *"not loving God,"* he will tell us in I John 4:20; his pattern will be completed in due time. Love for the Brother is a part of *"doing the Righteousness."* It is, we might say, a good example. Hence true evidence that is fully understood by what it reveals is so important, and John points it out to his Readers. The evidence furnished by love is both clear and unmistakable. John is as much the Apostle of knowledge as of love; so is Paul who really wrote the grandest description of love (I Cor., Chpt. 13).

One might say that Righteousness and Love are inseparable; since they are inseparable in the Character of God and in His Revelation in Christ, so they must be inseparable in the lives of His people.

Righteousness involves the fulfillment of all law, of relation to God and to man, both personally and socially. The love of Christian for Christian, resting on the sense of a Divine fellowship carries forward to its loftiest embodiment the Righteousness which man can reach (Westcott).

John, then, is not stressing absolute moral conformity or *"sinless perfection"* but the one requirement by which all other requirements are measured — love for one's Brother. For this there is no substitute, its violation allows for no excuse, its application permits no compromise. Here there are no gray areas, no third possibilities. One either loves his Brother and proves he is God's child or does not love his Brother and proves he belongs to the Devil (Gaebelein).

(11) "FOR THIS IS THE MESSAGE THAT YOU HEARD FROM THE BEGINNING, THAT WE SHOULD LOVE ONE ANOTHER."

The composite is:

1. The first attribute made evident in the new Christian is love.

2. The Holy Spirit refers to *"love"* as a *"message."*

3. To understand the Cross is to understand love.

THE MESSAGE

The phrase, *"For this is the Message that you heard from the beginning,"* presents the greatest word known to man, that of love.

This is not the Mosaic Commandment of love to one's neighbor but what Jesus says in John 15:12, 17 to the effect that His Disciples love one another.

As Christians, we love all men as our fellow creatures, but as spiritual Brothers we can love only those who are such Brothers. Because of love we do all manner of good to all men as opportunity offers, but especially to our spiritual Brothers who are of the household (family) of Faith (Gal. 5:10). This is true with reference to God Himself. He is able to give gifts of love to His children which those who are not of His children will not receive.

The very first thing that the new convert notices, is the new found love that is now in his heart — in fact, a love that is so different that it amazes him. It is the God kind of love, actually love from another world. The new convert senses this immediately, and it is meant to grow from that moment, and definitely will, if the Holy Spirit has His way. With Christ as our ever present example, there is no limit to the degree of love which can accrue in one's heart.

LOVE ONE ANOTHER

The phrase, *"That we should love one another,"* proclaims the first Message of Christianity. Since the nature of God as light is the foundation of the Gospel that was received from the beginning, so the command to *"love one another"* has the same origin. Love is not merely the application of the *"Message"* but the goal established *"from the beginning."* The whole aim of the Gospel is the creation and strengthening of love. The words *"love one another"* do not simply give the content of the Message, but its aim, its purpose (Westcott).

(12) "NOT AS CAIN, WHO WAS OF THAT WICKED ONE, AND SLEW HIS BROTHER. AND WHEREFORE SLEW HE

HIM? BECAUSE HIS OWN WORKS WERE EVIL, AND HIS BROTHER'S RIGHTEOUS."

The composite is:

1. Cain was of the Devil.

2. The cause of his position was the rejection of the Cross.

3. Cain cut his Brother's throat.

4. All works are evil which do not have their foundation in the Cross.

5. All works are Righteous which have their foundation in the Cross.

CAIN

The phrase, *"Not as Cain, who was of that wicked one, and slew his brother,"* presents the prototype of evil.

In Cain, John carries forth the idea that whoever lives a life of habitual sinning is the moral child of the Evil One — though he may be a very religious man like Cain.

The mention of Cain points back to I John 3:8 and reminds us that hatred as love is also from the beginning. The choice between the Children of God and the children of the Devil, between *"hatred and love, life and death, murder and self-sacrifice"* stems from the earliest moment of man's existence. It also probably points to John 8:37-47, where some Jewish opponents of Jesus had exhibited the same kind of hatred toward Jesus that Cain expressed toward Abel. There Jesus says to them, despite their claim to be Abraham's children: *"As it is, you are determined to kill Me . . . if God were your Father you would love Me . . . you belong to your father, the Devil, and you want to carry out your father's desire. He was a murderer from the beginning, not holding the truth"* (Jn. 8:40, 42, 44). The overlap of language and ideas between the two Passages supports the contention that John, Chapter 8 was probably in the author's mind when he wrote this section.

MURDER

The question, *"And wherefore slew he him?"*, presents the idea that it was not by Cain murdering his Brother that made him a child of the Devil; but, being a child of the Devil, his actions were evil and culminated in the murder of his Brother. The main point is not the *"fact"* that Cain slew Abel but the *"reason"* that he did so.

WHY DID HE KILL HIS BROTHER?

To *"do Righteousness"* is to act as Abel did. He humbled himself and accepted God's way of Righteousness, which was the Cross. To *"commit sin"* is to act as Cain did. His religious works, which were a rejection of the Cross, were evil. He was a religious man but not a righteous man.

His worship would have secured the admiration of *"modern thought"* but the Holy Spirit says here it was evil. He rejected the Divine Way of Righteousness and thus showed that he was *"out of"* the Evil One.

Popular modern Preachers teach that both religions were equally good; but God did not think so, for He accepted the one and rejected the other.

THE TWO WAYS OF SALVATION BY SATAN

Satan has two ways of salvation: one by *"sacraments,"* and the other *"ethics."* Christ's Atonement — possessing infinite moral value — condemns and destroys both these false ways of seeking acceptance with God. Christ is the measure of the Believer's acceptance; and, therefore, that acceptance is perfect, full, and eternal. In that Righteousness no one can find a flaw; and it needs neither ecclesiastical ceremonies nor human merits to add to its perfection.

So the first murder was caused by Abel accepting the Cross, which was typified in the sacrifice of the innocent victim, a Lamb, which his Brother Cain rejected, in effect stating that he did not need a Redeemer.

The words *"wicked one"* are the translation of the Greek *"poneros,"* which means *"evil in active opposition to the good."* Such a person seeks to drag everyone else down with himself into the corruption and destruction that awaits him. That is Satan and, therefore, that was Cain.

The word *"slew"* in the Greek is *"sphazo,"* which means, *"to slay, slaughter, butcher, by cutting the throat."* It was used in classical Greek of slaughtering victims for sacrifice by cutting the throat, also of animals tearing by the throat, of any slaughter by knife or sword.

The usual word meaning *"to kill"* in the Greek is *"apothnesko."* The inspired writer goes out of his way to use a specialized word to describe the murder of Abel by Cain. The latter cut his Brother's throat.

God said to Cain, *"What have you done? The voice of your Brother's blood crieth unto Me from the ground"* (Gen. 4:10).

The method Cain used to kill his Brother was one in which much blood would be shed. The cutting of the jugular vein would fit that description. So what are we saying?

We are saying that Cain grew so incensed over God accepting the sacrifice of Abel, which sacrifice had been dispatched by the slitting of its throat, all which typified the death of Christ on the Cross, that he would slit his Brother's throat in the same fashion. It was a violent opposition to the Cross and, therefore, a violent opposition to the one who had accepted the means and ways of the Cross. That spirit has not died from then until now.

Those who follow Cain are not satisfied to merely reject the Cross, they feel they must reject the messenger as well, and do so in the most violent terms. There is no evil like religious evil. Let us say it again:

Cain was a very religious man. He offered up sacrifice the same as his Brother Abel. The difference was that Abel offered up that which God had demanded, which was a Lamb, which would serve as a symbol until Christ came. Cain offered up the labor of his own hands, which God could never accept. Cain's rejection of the blood sacrifice that typified Christ was symbolic of the untold millions who have followed in his train. It speaks volumes. Such a way denies the need for a Redeemer and, therefore, denies Christ. It all comes down to an acceptance or a rejection of the Cross of Christ.

EVIL WORKS AND RIGHTEOUS WORKS

The phrase, *"Because his own works were evil, and his Brother's righteous,"* points directly to the Cross.

The rejection of God's way, which is the Cross, is labeled by the Holy Spirit as *"evil."* The acceptance of that way is labeled by the Holy Spirit as *"righteous."*

I think one can say without fear of contradiction that all *"evil"* and all *"righteousness"* can be defined by the way and manner that one looks at the Cross.

(13) "MARVEL NOT, MY BRETHREN, IF THE WORLD HATE YOU."

The exegesis is:

1. Expect no better treatment from the world than Abel received from Cain.

2. This hatred is tendered because of one's Faith in the Cross of Christ.

3. If the world hated Him, and they definitely did, then the world will hate us.

MARVEL NOT

The short phrase, *"Marvel not,"* portrays the fact that the Christian should not be surprised concerning the animosity of the world tendered toward those who follow Christ. To be frank, even the world itself doesn't know the reason for this animosity. The true reason is guilt.

Man is guilty of sinning against God, and man does not want to admit that.

God says there is only one solution for man's dilemma, and that is the acceptance of the crucified Christ. Man does not want to accept that!

The Cross says that man is so wicked that it took the death of God's only Son to address the problem. Man does not want to admit that!

God says that if a person is to be saved, he must accept Jesus Christ and what Christ did at the Cross on his behalf. There is no other way of Salvation. Man doesn't like that at all!

HATRED

The phrase, *"My Brethren, if the world hate you,"* puts such hatred in the same class of Cain hating Abel, and hating him enough to kill him. However, the part of the world generally which hates the true Child of God, is the religious part. It must be remembered that it was the Pharisees, the most religious sect in Israel, who murdered Christ. The Sadducees, who were little religious, at least by comparison to the Pharisees, registered very little opposition to Christ, until they thought it in their interest to do so. They then joined with the Pharisees, whom they incidentally hated, in order to kill Christ. But it was the Pharisees who took the lead in the crime of the ages.

As well, it is the religious sector of the world that generates the greatest degree of

NOTES

hatred toward those who are truly of Christ. And once again, it stems from a rejection of the Cross.

The religious sector is not too very much opposed to *"Christ the Healer,"* or *"Christ the miracle worker,"* but it's rather *"Christ Crucified"* which they hate. They want to devise their own way, exactly as did Cain, which God could not accept then, and cannot accept now. So the hatred is really a religious hatred!

(14) "WE KNOW THAT WE HAVE PASSED FROM DEATH UNTO LIFE, BECAUSE WE LOVE THE BRETHREN. HE THAT LOVETH NOT HIS BROTHER ABIDETH IN DEATH."

The diagram is:

1. Life without God is reckoned as *"death."*

2. To be in the Lord is reckoned as *"life."*

3. Love for the Brethren is the first sign of this *"life."*

4. If love is not present for the Brethren, the individual isn't saved.

FROM DEATH UNTO LIFE

The phrase, *"We know that we have passed from death unto life, because we love the Brethren,"* presents the first principle or sign of Salvation. The test is not the hatred of the world but our love.

In the Greek Text it is *"the death"* and *"the life,"* specifying a particular death and a particular life. This portrays the two spheres in which men must be, *"death or life."*

The Holy Spirit likens the proposed life without God, as *"death."* When Adam and Eve failed God in the Garden of Eden, they died immediately, which speaks of *"spiritual death,"* which speaks of separation from God. Before the Fall, Adam and Eve were destined to bring sons and daughters of God into the world. Now, and we speak of after the Fall, they can only bring offspring into the world after the likeness of Adam, which refers to every baby being born in *"original sin"* (Gen. 5:3). This means that the *"sin nature"* now controls every human being, which is the cause of all of man's inhumanity to man.

This *"death"* could only be addressed by *"life,"* which alone could come from God, Who Alone has Spiritual Life. It can be gained only by the *"born again"* experience (Jn. 3:3, 16), which can only be gained by the acceptance of Christ and what Christ has done for lost humanity at the Cross. That's why Paul said, *"We preach Christ Crucified"* (I Cor. 1:23).

Having accepted Christ, being spiritually dead, we are then made spiritually alive.

There are many professors of Salvation, but John says the profession is hollow, if the one doing the professing is lacking in love for the Brethren.

At the moment of Salvation, the Divine nature comes into the Believer, which is a result of Regeneration, all carried out by the Holy Spirit, Who functions on the premise of the Sacrifice of Christ, which makes it all possible. In this Divine nature is the Love of God. In other words, it's impossible to have the Divine nature without having the Love of God. So if one is truly saved, one will truly love the Brethren.

Now *"born again,"* and a member of the Family of God, it is as natural for Believers to love one another, as do blood brothers and sisters, actually, even more so!

ABIDETH IN DEATH

The phrase, *"He that loveth not his Brother abideth in death,"* turns around and says the same thing again in another way, placing emphasis on the fact that love for the Brethren must characterize the Salvation profession. The one not-loving presents the plain evidence that Salvation has not come to the heart of such an individual. John once more writes the verb *"remains,"* or *"abideth,"* which appears through this Letter. The fact that love always shows itself, just as does the absence of love, John will add presently.

This is a characteristic instance of John's logic. From the terseness and pregnancy of his style, he does not give all the steps of an argument, but frequently turns it upside down, in order more speedily to bring out a forcible spiritual truth.

But for this he would have written, *"We love the Brethren, because we have passed from death unto life; but he that abideth in death loveth not."* But wishing to put the ideas in the form of a direct encouragement, in the face of a hating world, he puts the reason as the conclusion, and the conclusion as the

NOTES

reason. This unexpected turn rivets the attention far more than a rigid deduction.

The Holy Spirit through the Apostle doesn't mince words. He plainly says that if love is lacking, the person is not saved. Irrespective of his profession, he *"abides in death."*

Once we properly take this to heart, it is a chilling thought. Let me make the following statement which I think will put it even in a clearer spectrum:

When one is down and can do nothing to defend oneself, and anyone can do any negative thing to him they so desire and can do so without any fear of being reprimanded, but will rather be applauded, one finds out very quickly just how much love there is among professing Christians.

It's very easy to show love, or what passes for love, to those who are popular and favored, but such is never a test of true love. We must remember that Christ loved us while we were yet sinners, which tells us that irrespective of our profession of love, we haven't really loved until we love the one who is unlovable. That and that alone shows what true love really is.

Somebody made the statement once, *"Many times people are friends simply because of what you can do for them or to them,"* which means they aren't really friends at all.

We need to consider very carefully what the Holy Spirit through the Apostle is saying here. If love really is the criteria, and John plainly says here that it is, then we must come to the conclusion that the ranks are thinned considerably. Love is the evidence that we have been brought from death to life, and if love is lacking, that means that we *"abide in death"* still!

(15) "WHOSOEVER HATETH HIS BROTHER IS A MURDERER: AND YE KNOW THAT NO MURDERER HATH ETERNAL LIFE ABIDING IN HIM."

The composition is:

1. Where love is not, there is hatred.
2. Where hatred is, there is murder.
3. Where murder is, there can be no eternal life.

MURDERER

The phrase, *"Whosoever hateth his Brother is a murderer,"* goes back to Cain. So the world hates us and thereby attests its Cain-like nature. Whether blood is actually shed or not makes no difference. We are reminded of Matthew 5:21-22, where Jesus made the two equivalent. In the heart there is no difference; to hate is to despise, to cut off from relationship, and murder is simply the fulfillment of that attitude.

The private malice, the secret grudge, the envy which is cherished in the heart, is murderous in its tendency, and were it not for the outward restraints of human laws, and the dread of punishment, such attitudes would often lead to the act of murder.

The Apostle does not say that he who hates his Brother, though he does not in fact commit murder, is guilty to the same degree as if he had actually done it; but he evidently means to say that the spirit which would lead to murder is there, and that God will hold him responsible for it. Nothing is wanting but the removal of outward restraints to lead to the commission of the open deed, and God judges men as He sees them to be *"in their hearts."*

What a fearful declaration, then, is this! How many real murderers there are on the Earth besides those who are detected and punished, and besides those open violators of the laws of God and man who go at large!

And who is there that should not feel humbled and penitent in view of his own heart, and grateful for that sovereign mercy which has restrained him from open acts of guilt? — for who is there that has not at some period of his life, and perhaps often, indulged in feelings of hatred, envy, and malice toward others, which, if acted out, would have led to the commission of the awful crime of taking human life? Any man may well shudder at the remembrance of the secret sins of his own heart, and at the thought of what he would have been but for the restraining Grace of God. And how wonderful is that Grace which, in the case of the true Christian, not only restrains and checks, but which effectually subdues all these feelings, and implants in their place the principles of love (Barnes).

ETERNAL LIFE

The phrase, *"And you know that no murderer has eternal life abiding in him,"* comes back to the absence of love.

John speaks of the murderers who murder by hating, this is not a crime in the eyes of the world; it is in fact, what the world does the world over.

Is John saying here that if love is absent, hate there abides? Let's be clearer.

Is it possible to not have love and at the same time to not have hate? I think the implication is clear.

If love does not abide, then in some way, hate does, and hatred leads toward murder whether the act is ever carried out or not.

And let the Reader understand that the love of which John speaks here, is the love of God, which the world cannot have. To be sure, they do have a form of love; however, it's not the Love of God. In fact, the love which the world has, can be turned to hate in almost a moment's time, hence man's inhumanity to man.

We are given a very clear lesson here as it regards the origin of evil, which pertains to the wicked hearts of men, and the cause of evil, which is a lack of love. And let it be clearly understood, the type of love of which John speaks, comes about only with one's acceptance of Christ. It cannot be obtained in any other fashion.

(16) "HEREBY PERCEIVE WE THE LOVE OF GOD, BECAUSE HE LAID DOWN HIS LIFE FOR US: AND WE OUGHT TO LAY DOWN OUR LIVES FOR THE BRETHREN."

The structure is:

1. In Christ we are given an example of the Love of God.

2. He laid down His life for us.

3. As our example, true love within our hearts will cause us to lay down our lives for the Brethren as well.

THE LOVE OF GOD

The phrase, *"Hereby perceive we the Love of God,"* speaks of knowledge gained by experience.

This *"knowledge"* in essence tells us what the Love of God actually is. It pulls no punches and leaves absolutely no room for misunderstanding.

In this explanation that is given by the Holy Spirit through John, we see the real nature, the real power, the real sacrifice of love. We see it in its highest form, when the

Son of God gave Himself to die on a Cross. This is the example used by the Holy Spirit, and the reason that I say that one cannot truly know and understand the Love of God, unless one truly understands the Cross of Christ. And what do we mean by that?

Of course, a human being is limited in his understanding, but the point I wish to make, is the point of faith. In other words, our Faith is to be 100 percent in the Cross of Christ, understanding that it is through the Cross that we receive all blessings from God. Everything comes through the Cross, and without the Cross nothing can come to us.

So that means that if we evidence faith in things other than the Cross, we cut ourselves off from God. The Cross is the means by which everything is made possible. We should know that, understand that, have faith in that, which means to make the Cross, ever the Cross, the object of our Faith. Then and only then can we truly understand the Love of God, or anything else from the Lord for that matter.

THE CROSS

The phrase, *"Because He laid down His life for us,"* proclaims the fact, as previously stated, that the highest proof of love is the sacrifice of that which is most precious: nothing could be more precious than the life of the Word made flesh. The idea is Jesus died for sinners! No evidence of love can go beyond this.

In Romans 5:6-10 Paul states in so many words why this evidence of Christ's love is supreme. What person in all the world ever laid down his life for another except in the rare cases where the other was a good man? But Christ did this for *"ungodly ones,"* for actual enemies. Oh love Divine, all love excelling!

As well, Jesus went into this death voluntarily. And for Him, we know what this death meant. It was *"on our behalf," "for us," "for our benefit," "instead of."* It is substitution, and without it Christ's Death would be of no benefit to the ungodly. In I John 1:7 John says: *"The Blood of Jesus, His Son, cleanses us from all sin"*; in I John 2:2: *"He Himself is the expiation for our sins,"* etc. It is sacrificial, substitutionary blood that expiates. Such love *"that One"* put into action and evidence, and we have realized it, we have stepped over from the death into the life by

means of His substitutionary Death. Once again let us state the case:

Jesus died for the ungodly, for sinners, for enemies, which we were. There could be no greater love than that. *"He laid down His life for us."*

FOR THE BRETHREN

The phrase, *"And we ought to lay down our lives for the Brethren,"* proclaims Christ as our example, and what the meaning of true love actually is.

The love we have realized begets like love in us with a like visible evidence. Let us understand what the Holy Spirit here is actually saying:

It is not often that the Lord calls upon a Believer to actually lay down his life for a fellow Believer. To be sure, this definitely has happened, but not often. The general meaning has to do with putting others first, which means to deny self for another's gain. It is doing what Jesus Himself would do.

While the Lord doesn't often call upon us to actually lay down our lives for someone else, to be sure, He is constantly calling upon us to stretch forth our hand to that individual who is in need. This we face on a daily basis, even which John will address in the next Verse.

We may encourage ourselves with romantic ideas of giving up our lives for another, when the chances of such are remote. But to be sure, if we show little or no love at all in our everyday dealings, we are only fooling ourselves!

(17) "BUT WHOSO HATH THIS WORLD'S GOOD, AND SEETH HIS BROTHER HAVE NEED, AND SHUTTETH UP HIS BOWELS OF COMPASSION FROM HIM, HOW DWELLETH THE LOVE OF GOD IN HIM?"

The exegesis is:

1. The world's *"good"* or *"goods,"* speaks of food, clothing, shelter, the necessities of life.

2. The one who has need, truly has need.

3. Even though the Christian has the capacity to help in such a case, he refuses to do so. There is no love in such a one, John says!

THE NECESSITIES OF LIFE

The phrase, *"But whoso hath this world's good,"* refers to the necessities of life.

There are some Christians who have a greater business sense than others and are thereby able to accumulate money and property. John is not stating here that such is wrong, but that if such be the case, the one so blessed, should share with those who are not so blessed, but which there is a qualification, which we shall see.

First of all, any and all good things are blessings from the Lord. This means that we really do not deserve them, but God in His Grace has made such possible. As Believers, if we are so blessed, we must never forget this.

It's so easy to give the credit to ourselves, which refers to our own ability, etc. But as it regards a Child of God, it is the Lord Who has made all good things possible, irrespective of our so-called acumen, etc.

Possibly this is the reason that God cannot bless many people. They quickly take the credit themselves, while paying lip service to the Lord.

Every person who truly belongs to the Lord is now placed in a position totally unlike those in the world. Now that we belong to Christ, and have been paid for with such a price, every single thing that happens to us is either allowed or caused by the Lord. While of course, the Lord doesn't cause us to sin or to do wrong, that being our own foolishness, still, we are in His control. He will never violate our free moral agency, and if we go in wrong directions, we will definitely have to pay the price. But still He doesn't leave us, always working on our behalf, seeking to bring us to the right place. He wants to guide us and control us in all things, but this is always control that must be freely given to Him. He will never take it by force, inasmuch as the Holy Spirit is always a Perfect Gentleman.

Therefore, we are to ever understand that every blessing is always from Him, and even the chastisement will prove to be a blessing in the long run. So if we have been blessed with this world's goods, we must remember that such a blessing is also at the same time *"a test."* How will we use these goods? To whom will we give the praise and the glory?

NEED

The phrase, *"And seeth his Brother have need,"* needs qualification.

"Seeth" in the Greek is *"theoreo,"* and means, *"to look with interest and purpose."* It means to *"deliberately contemplate."* This is not a hasty glance. It is seeing a Christian in need of the necessities of life over a long period.

It doesn't speak of momentary need, and it certainly doesn't speak of laziness. Paul addressed laziness by saying: *"That if any would not work, neither should he eat"* (II Thess. 3:10).

Unfortunately, Christianity has its share of loafers. They make it their business to sponge off others. They always have something physically wrong with them that they can't work, mostly back trouble. To be sure, John is not speaking of this type of individuals.

He is speaking of individuals who have tried their best, and have run into a series of unfortunate events, which have put them in a negative position. This type of person, and actually, there aren't very many of them, should be helped by those who have the means to help.

BOWELS OF COMPASSION

The phrase, *"And shutteth up his bowels of compassion from him,"* presents the individual who has the means to truly help one who is truly in need, but refuses to do so.

The word *"bowels"* would probably have been better translated *"heart."* The idea in the word is that of *"tender affections."* In II Corinthians 7:15, the word is translated *"inward affection."*

In the Gospel statements concerning our Lord, such as *"He was moved with compassion,"* the Greek word is *"splagchnizomai,"* the same word translated *"bowels,"* but in the verb form. The word in its root, therefore, refers to a heart of compassion, kindness, pity, mercy, to the tenderer affections as produced in the heart of the yielded Believer by the Holy Spirit.

For someone, as stated, who is able to help, and who sees someone who is truly in need, and who will not help, the Holy Spirit through John plainly asks the question, *"How dwelleth the Love of God in him?"*

THE LOVE OF GOD

The question, *"How dwelleth the Love of God in him?"*, once again puts the situation as to where the rubber proverbially speaking, meets the road. John has a way of saying the same thing but in a different way. Consequently, the Truth which he is bringing out is further emphasized. Love and Righteousness are the criteria for Salvation. The expression of love as labeled here, translates into Righteousness. In other words, Love does Righteousness!

(18) "MY LITTLE CHILDREN, LET US NOT LOVE IN WORD, NEITHER IN TONGUE; BUT IN DEED AND IN TRUTH."

The diagram is:

1. To love in word only, is not truly love.

2. In these cases, action speaks louder than words.

3. For love to truly be love, it will be portrayed *"in deed and in truth."*

TRUE LOVE

The phrase, *"My little children, let us not love in word, neither in tongue,"* refers to sham, empty evidence. To use only *"word"* and *"the tongue"* are mere hypocritical pretense of loving.

John is not condemning kind words which are comforting and cheering, which every Christian should give constantly. But the Apostle is saying that our love should not be confined only to mere words. There should be action expressed as well, and if it's not, then it's really not love.

John hints that there is some danger of this conventionality among Christians, and earnestly exhorts to genuineness. He forbids all the traitorous babble of heartless insincerity, and urges that just, active, straightforward, all-embracing affection, which was complete in Christ alone (Rom. 12:9; Eph. 4:15; James 2:15-17; I Pet. 1:22; II Jn., vs. 1; III Jn., vs. 1).

DEED AND TRUTH

The phrase, *"But in deed and in truth,"* proclaims the fact that love demands simple acts, which anyone can see, which meets the needs of Brothers and Sisters in distress. Any expression of love that fails here is not only empty but also blasphemous. James said: *"Suppose a Brother or Sister is without clothes and daily food. If one of you says to him, 'Go, I wish you well; keep warm and well fed' but does nothing about his physical needs, what good is it?"* (James 2:15-16; I Cor. 13:1).

(19) "AND HEREBY WE KNOW THAT WE ARE OF THE TRUTH, AND SHALL ASSURE OUR HEARTS BEFORE HIM."

The structure is:

1. The evidence of love is the guarantee of truth.

2. Am I as loving as I ought?

3. Our hearts will tell us.

THE TRUTH

The phrase, *"And hereby we know that we are of the truth,"* refers to the fact that we are not deceived in what we profess to be; that is, we are true Christians. To be of the truth stands opposed to cherishing false and delusive hopes. All that was said about love for the Brother and the true evidence for such love is so vital because it reflects our relation to God. The question asked about our love for God in Verse 17 reverts to this. The Children of God cannot be such children if we do not also love each other and show the evidence of such love.

THE ASSURANCE OF OUR HEARTS

The phrase, *"And shall assure our hearts before Him,"* proclaims the fact that a true Christian does not attempt to conceal the fact that there is much for which his own heart and conscience might justly accuse him; but he finds, notwithstanding all this, evidence that he is a Child of God, and he is persuaded that all will be well.

"The truth" means all of the eternal nature, purpose, and Will of God which it concerns us to know — revealed in Christ, brought home by the Spirit, exemplified in Christian lives.

"The heart" means the affections, the seat of the moral feelings, as distinct from the intellect; the emotional side of the moral nature, of which the intellectual side was called by Paul *"the conscience"* (Acts 24:16; Rom. 2:15; 9:1; 13:5; I Cor. 8:7; II Cor. 5:11).

Concerning this Verse, Barker asks: *"How may we know that we belong to the truth and how do we deal with our own condemning hearts?"*

He then answers: *"If we know that we love truly, with actions and not mere words, that knowledge will not only assure us 'that we belong to the truth' but will also act to 'set our hearts at rest in His Presence whenever our hearts condemn us'."*

(20) "FOR IF OUR HEART CONDEMN US, GOD IS GREATER THAN OUR HEART, AND KNOWETH ALL THINGS."

The composite is:

1. Our failures in duty and service rise up before us, and our heart condemns us.

2. The worst that is in us is known to God, and still He cares for us and desires us. Our discovery has been an open secret to Him all along.

3. He *"reads everything"* so to speak, which means He sees the deepest things, and to be sure, the things of the heart are the real things. This is the true test of a man.

THE CONDEMNATION OF THE HEART

The phrase, *"For if our heart condemn us,"* does not really express *"why?"* Apparently it is not important.

John's readers, like all others, know how easily the conscience can render us ineffective. Doubt, guilt, and failure are never far from any of us. Sometimes our misgivings are the result of our own actions or inactions. Sometimes it is the *"accuser"* who seizes our weaknesses and shortcomings and so elevates them that we wonder whether we can really be in the truth. What can we then do?

We can remember that God understands everything. His Word and His Truth are greater than our feelings or our conscience. We may rest ourselves in His love for us and live in that love and by that love. We will not excuse ourselves of any sin, but neither will we needlessly accuse ourselves (I Cor. 4:3-5).

GOD IS GREATER

The phrase, *"God is greater than our heart, and knoweth all things,"* presents God alone knowing our hearts. This is the true test of a man.

Is the deepest that is in him the best? Is he better than he seems? His failures lie on the surface: is there a desire for goodness deep down in his soul? Is he glad to escape from superficial judgments and be judged by God Who *"reads everything"*? Who sees *"with larger eyes than ours,"* to make allowance

for us all? David was a man after God's Own heart because the general tenor of his life was habitually Godward. The Psalms give the real David, and not the account of his failures as given in some of the other Books of the Old Testament.

Regarding the statement, *"God is greater than our heart, and knoweth all things,"* Vincent asks this question and makes the following statement: *"Is this superior greatness to be regarded as related to God's 'judgment' or to His 'compassion?' If to His 'judgment,' the sense is: God Who is greater than our heart and knows all things, must not only 'endorse' but 'emphasize' our self-accusation. If our 'heart' condemn, how much more 'God,' Who is greater than our heart. If to His 'compassion,' the sense is: when our heart condemns us we shall quiet it with the assurance that we are in the hands of a God Who is greater than our heart — Who surpasses man in love and compassion no less than in knowledge."*

CONDEMNATION?

Think of what John has said in Verse 16 about the real evidence of love! Many an honest Christian heart will question whether it is able to go that far. Even regarding Verse 18 many a heart will question whether it has always lived up to that as it should. Note that *"we"* includes John himself as it did in I John 1:10. This is what John means with *"if in regard to anything the heart condemn us."*

A judge recognizes something as being valid against us, on which he must pronounce against us. The judge is in this instance our own heart which knows our inner motives (like conscience) and how often, at least inwardly, our love for a Brother falls short of what it ought to be.

John does not deny the finding and the verdict of our heart or imply that our falling short escapes God or amounts to nothing in His sight. That would be lying, to use John's own expression.

To be sure, the Lord knows all our failures in love, all that our own heart finds against us; but He knows vastly more, namely all about our real spiritual state, that the measure of love we do have shows that we have stepped over from the death into the life, that although we are yet imperfect in love, and our own hearts penitently acknowledge it, we have been born from Him and are His children (Lenski).

(21) "BELOVED, IF OUR HEART CONDEMN US NOT, THEN HAVE WE CONFIDENCE TOWARD GOD."

The exegesis is:

1. The words *"If our heart condemn us not,"* do not claim sinless perfection, but represent the heart attitude of a Saint that so far as he knows has no unconfessed sin in his life.

2. *"Confidence"* speaks of boldness and assurance.

3. *"Toward God"* speaks of Justification by Faith.

NO CONDEMNATION

The phrase, *"Beloved, if our heart condemn us not,"* does not claim sinless perfection, but rather represents the heart attitude of a Saint that so far as he knows has no unconfessed sin in his life, has nothing between himself and the Lord Jesus, a Saint who is yielded habitually to the Holy Spirit and living in close fellowship with his Lord (Wuest).

This is not the case of a heart that fails to accuse us when it ought to, but of one that does so and yet does not do so because of that stated in Verses 19 and 20.

The main point is the dealing of our heart with God, which refers to an appearance before God as the Judge. So now, when we are sure of God's verdict despite our faults, we have assurance, confidence, and joyful fearlessness.

There is only one way that our heart can be such before God, and I speak of an uncondemning heart. So please read very carefully what we have to say here.

If the Believer is looking exclusively to Christ as it regards his Salvation, his walk with God, his Righteousness before God, in other words, everything that he possesses from the Lord, which means to trust exclusively in what Christ has done at the Cross, which then gives the Holy Spirit latitude to work within our hearts and lives, such a Believer knows no condemnation. This is what Paul was speaking of when he said: *"There is therefore now no condemnation to them*

which are in Christ Jesus, who walk not after the flesh, but after the Spirit" (Rom. 8:1).

Everything that we receive from the Lord, everything we are in Christ, the entirety of the foundation of our Salvation and our victorious walk, all and without exception are found in the Sacrifice of Christ. Consequently, one's Faith must rest exclusively in that Sacrifice, and do so unfailingly and, therefore, constantly.

If in fact, our faith is elsewhere, and it really doesn't matter where else it might be, our heart is definitely going to condemn us. The reason is simple; whatever direction our faith may be other than the Cross, ultimately it concludes in self. In other words, it's either Faith in Christ or faith in self. Two things are wrong with the latter:

REBELLION AGAINST GOD

First of all, the very act of us not trusting in the Cross of Christ but rather self, is sin within itself. In fact, doing such a thing is the highest act of rebellion against God, and will always fall out to wreckage and ruin in one way or the other. Whether we realize it or not, it is the same identical thing as what Cain did, when he ignored the command of the Lord as it regarded the sacrifice of the innocent lamb and the pouring out of its blood, all which typified the coming Christ, rather replacing that with the labor of his own hands (Gen., Chpt. 4). However, there is a difference with most Christians:

First of all, most Christians do no really intend to rebel against the Lord as did Cain. They want to obey the Lord and thereby live a Godly life; however, most Christians simply do not know the way of the Cross as Paul taught, and because it's not taught behind their pulpits; therefore, they try to live this life the best way they can, but which always leads to failure. Let the Reader understand the following:

No Believer will ever accidentally stumble upon the Message of the Cross (I Cor. 1:18). In fact, it is impossible for such to happen. There are too many opposing forces against such a position. So what am I saying?

I'm saying if the Believer doesn't hear the Word of God taught in this manner, he will never know God's way, and will continue to stumble in failure and defeat, irrespective as to who he might be or how hard he may try otherwise. That's the reason these Commentaries are so very, very important. This is the reason I plead with Christians to get them, and for you the Reader to get a copy to give to a friend, and especially your Pastor. We are not speaking here of mundane matters, but rather the very issues of life and death; consequently, nothing could be more important!

DEPENDENCE ON SELF LEADS TO CONTROL BY THE SIN NATURE

Paul tells us how to live victoriously over the sin nature in Romans, Chpater 6. Some 17 times he mentions the word "sin" in that one Chapter. All but two times, if I remember correctly, in the original Greek, it has what is referred to as the definite article before the word "sin," actually making it read "the sin." Consequently, it's not speaking of particular acts of sin, but rather "the sin nature."

When the Believer has his faith in "self" instead of Christ, the ultimate results will always be and without exception, failure. The Believer then tries to overcome this "failure" by the efforts of "self." He doesn't realize he's doing this, simply because he covers it all up with religious phraseology, and in fact does spiritual things. But the truth is, he's simply not trusting in what Christ did at the Cross, but rather in his own religious efforts.

No matter how hard he may try in this capacity, he will not succeed, and the end result will be the "sin nature" not only being present within his life as it is all Believers, but rather "ruling and reigning."

So the upshot of all that I've said is, the great sin of rebelling against God's prescribed order of victory, always leads to acts of sin, which always leads to the "sin nature" ruling the Believer's life, exactly as it did before the Believer came to Christ (Rom. 6:12).

Is such a Believer still saved?

Of course they are! To be sure, their life will be far less than it ought to be and in this mode, they will never know the "more abundant life" which Jesus promised (Jn. 10:10), which regrettably, is the state of most modern Christians presently.

Even though we've already dealt with this in this Volume, simply because of its great

NOTES

significance, please allow me the latitude of briefly looking at the subject again.

WALKING AFTER THE SPIRIT

Even though John didn't go into any detail, as it regards condemnation, Paul definitely did.

If we are to live a life in which our heart does not condemn us, then we must "walk after the Spirit" (Rom. 8:1). However, the truth is, most Christians don't have the foggiest idea as to what "walking after the Spirit" actually is. If pressed for a definition, most would think that it refers to doing spiritual things such as reading the Bible more, praying more, being more faithful to Church, giving more money to the Work of the Lord, or witnessing to more souls about Christ, etc.

While these things mentioned are definitely spiritual and very good, and which all good Christians will definitely do, the truth is, these things have absolutely nothing to do with "walking after the Spirit."

We find the definition of walking after the Spirit in Romans 8:2. In other words, Paul's statement in Romans 8:1, answers itself in Romans 8:2. The Apostle said:

"For the Law (this is a Law made by the Godhead which the Spirit will not violate) of the Spirit (Holy Spirit) of life (the opposite of sin and death) in Christ Jesus (which refers to all that Christ did at the Cross) has made me free from the law of sin and death."

The key to this Verse is found in the phrase "in Christ Jesus," which Paul uses in one way or the other nearly 170 times in his 14 Epistles. In fact, these three words, or their derivates such as "in Him," etc., explain the Biblical way more so than any other statement.

Always and without exception, it refers to what Christ did for us in His great Sacrifice. So the idea is this:

"Walking after the Spirit" simply refers to placing one's faith exclusively in the great Sacrifice of Christ, realizing that all we receive from the Lord, and without exception, comes to us through the Cross (Rom. 6:3-5). It's not a matter of "doing," but rather a matter of "believing." But it's believing the right thing!

The Spirit of God and without fail, will always lead one's Faith to the Cross of Christ. Listen again to Paul:

"But now in Christ Jesus you who (Gentiles) *sometimes were far off are made nigh by the Blood of Christ . . . And that He* (Christ) *might reconcile both* (Jews and Gentiles) *unto God in one body* (the Church) *by the Cross* (this is the way it was done), *having slain the enmity thereby* (Jesus removed the enmity between God and man by what He did at the Cross) *. . . For through Him* (through Christ) *we both* (Jews and Gentiles) *have access* (access to the very Throne of God) *by one Spirit* (the Holy Spirit) *unto the Father"* (Eph. 2:13, 16, 18).

ACCESS

In fact, this Eighteenth Verse tells us that the Holy Spirit will not allow access to the Father, except we evidence Faith exclusively in the Finished Work of Christ. One might say that He guards the entrance to the Holy of Holies against all who would attempt to come other than by virtue of the slain lamb (Jn. 10:1, 8-9).

This means that God will accept no worship but that it be based on the premise of what Jesus did for us at the Cross. This means that God will accept no works except on the basis of Faith in the Finished Work of Christ. In other words, proper Faith will always produce proper works, but proper works will never produce proper Faith. We must never forget that!

The Believer must understand, and without fail, how critical all of this is. The truth is, the Believer cannot even receive forgiveness for sin, unless he seeks such from the Father on the basis of the shed Blood of the Lamb (Jn. 1:7, 9). The Message in totality is, *"Jesus Christ and Him Crucified"* (I Cor. 2:2).

THE EFFECT OF THE CROSS

This statement *"the effect of the Cross,"* is without a doubt one of the single most important statements that any human being could ever make. But the tragedy is, if our believing is wrong, which means that our understanding is wrong, then we will *"make the Cross of Christ of none effect."* Listen to what Paul said concerning this:

"For Christ sent me not to baptize, but to preach the Gospel: not with wisdom of words, lest the Cross of Christ should be made of none effect" (I Cor. 1:17).

NOTES

Let's first of all look at the effect of the Cross:

The *"effect of the Cross"* pertains to everything that we receive from God. In other words, no one is going to receive anything from the Lord, unless they evidence Faith in the Cross of Christ. It's just that simple!

The *"effect"* pertains to Salvation, which refers to Justification, Sanctification, Reconciliation, Grace, Peace, Hope, Love, Fruit of the Spirit, Gifts of the Spirit, in fact, the entirety of everything the Spirit does within our hearts and lives.

However, if the Church specializes in things other than the Cross, and irrespective as to how important these other things might be, even Water Baptism which Paul uses as an example, such emphasis, will and without fail, *"make the Cross of Christ of none effect."* If that is done, the Christian has just cut himself off from all victory, all power, all overcoming grace, in fact, he has just frustrated the Grace of God, which spells disaster (Gal. 2:20).

Once again, I come back to the tragedy of what is presently happening in the modern Church. Being all but Cross illiterate, the modern Church for all its blow and bluster, walks in defeat. We've had more teaching on faith in the last several decades, than all the balance of the history of the Church put together. But the truth is, there is less Faith presently in the modern Church than ever. And I think I exaggerate not!

The faith that's been taught these last few decades has not been faith in the Cross, but rather faith in self, whatever its claims might have been. In fact, it has almost destroyed the Church! Due to its great significance, please allow me to make this statement again:

If it's not Faith in the Cross of Christ, which refers to the Finished Work of Christ, then it's not faith that God will recognize. We can claim it to be faith in the Word, or whatever type of *"spin"* we would desire to use. But the truth is, if it's not faith exclusively in the Cross of Christ, which is truly faith in the Word, then it's bogus faith.

Going back to what Paul said, how many Churches do you know which emphasize the Cross of Christ, exclusive of all other things?

When we look at the modern Church, we see Preachers majoring in Water Baptism,

NOTES

the Lord's Supper, particular Church Denominations, speaking in tongues, faith in self, confession, humanistic psychology, etc.

In fact, some of these things mentioned are very good in their place; however, we must not forget, that even as Paul says here, we do terribly wrong when we emphasize these things. The emphasis and without fail must always be on the Cross of Christ, or else we will make the Cross of none effect. When we do that, we have just destroyed the potential for all victory within hearts and lives. What did Jesus say?

"And as Moses lifted up the serpent in the wilderness, even so must the Son of Man be lifted up . . . And I, if I be lifted up from the earth, will draw all men unto Me" (Jn. 3:14; 12:32).

He was speaking of being lifted up on the Cross. The idea is, all men can come to Him through the Cross, and in fact must come to Him through the Cross, or they will not be accepted.

CONFIDENCE

The phrase, *"Then have we confidence toward God,"* actually means that we are able to stand *"face to face"* with God, or *"facing God,"* which implies, *"no condemnation."*

Incidentally, the definite article appears here in the original text before *"God"* making it read *"the God,"* thereby referring to *"God the Father."*

This *"confidence"* comes about because one is exclusively trusting Christ, which refers to trusting in what Christ did at the Cross, all on our behalf, and not trusting in self. Because of its great significance, let us say it again, but in another way:

The confidence or boldness which we have towards our Maker is founded solely on the evidence that He will graciously accept us on the basis of what Christ did for us at the Cross, and our Faith in that Finished Work; not in the belief that we deserve His favor.

In Philippians 3:3-6, Paul makes it clear that we can have no confidence in mere human effort. He reviews his own experience and his faultless qualifications as far as legalistic righteousness is concerned. He concludes that his moral accomplishments are *"rubbish."* Only a Righteousness that comes from God through Faith in Christ will do.

Yet at other times, Paul speaks of his confidence in his fellow Believers — even as he did the Corinthians (II Cor. 2:3; 7:4, 16). Paul's expressions of confidence, however, are not based on qualities he observed in these members of the Corinthian Church. They are founded on the fact that *"if anyone is in Christ, he is a new creation; the old has gone, the new has come"* (II Cor. 5:17).

The argument of this Passage is that we should not evaluate our fellow Believers by what we presently see of their lives. What we see now is temporary (II Cor. 4:18) and will change. Paul looks instead at the heart. There he finds Christ and is convinced that Christ's love is a compelling, motivating force that will surely bring about moral transformation (II Cor. 5:12-15). It is because God was at work in the Corinthians that Paul could speak so confidently of their future.

Paul put it this way in Philippians 1:6: *"Being confident . . . that He Who began a good work in you will carry it on to completion until the day of Christ Jesus."*

PROGRESS

John in his First Epistle, the Epistle of our study, looks at the question of Christian confidence from another perspective. Paul wrote of the theological certainty that God, Who takes up residence in the Believer, will do a transforming work, that is if our Faith is properly placed. John explores the subjective basis for confidence that God is even now at work in us. John's stress is on following Jesus' Commandments, especially the Commandment that we love one another.

If we live obediently, so that *"our hearts do not condemn us,"* then we *"have confidence before God"* (I Jn. 3:21; 4:16-17).

We may at times feel discouraged because we cannot see much progress in our transformation. God's Message to us at such times is this: *"Do not throw away your confidence; it will be richly rewarded. You need to persevere so that when you have done the Will of God, you will receive what He has promised"* (Heb. 10:35-36).

ON THE BASIS OF THE SACRIFICE OF CHRIST

Paul in Hebrews 4:16 invites us to *"approach the Throne of Grace with confidence."*

NOTES

We've come boldly because we are assured of a welcome on the basis of the Sacrifice offered for us by our High Priest, Jesus Christ (Heb. 5:1-10).

Picking up the same theme, Hebrews 10:19 affirms, *"We have confidence to enter the Most Holy Place by the Blood of Jesus."* Only through Faith in Christ, and because of Him (what He did for us at the Cross), may people *"approach God with freedom and confidence"* (Eph. 3:12).

It is our relationship with Jesus, then, that brings us confidence. Because Jesus is resident within us, and we are depending on what He did for us at the Cross, we have confidence that we and our Brothers and Sisters will grow in Christlikeness. Because Jesus has died for us, we are sure that we are always welcome when we turn to God (Richards).

(22) "AND WHATSOEVER WE ASK, WE RECEIVE OF HIM, BECAUSE WE KEEP HIS COMMANDMENTS, AND DO THOSE THINGS THAT ARE PLEASING IN HIS SIGHT."

The exegesis is:

1. The word *"ask"* as given here, speaks of prayer, and that we must keep on asking for that which is desired. It speaks of repeated and continuous praying, day after day.

2. The prerequisites for answered prayer are an uncondemning heart, and . . .

3. The habitual keeping of God's Commandments, and . . .

4. The habitual doing of those things which please Him, with all of these things summed up as Faith in the Cross of Christ.

ASKING IN PRAYER

The phrase, *"And whatsoever we ask, we receive of Him,"* tells us several things:

First of all, the word *"ask"* in the Greek is *"aiteo,"* and means, *"to ask for,"* and in the Greek *"speaks of continuous action."* It speaks as stated, of repeated and continuous praying, day after day, until the answer comes.

Unfortunately, as it regards the modern erroneous teaching on faith, we are told that if we have to ask more than once, we are lacking in Faith. The Bible does not teach such a thing, as should be overly obvious. In fact, it teaches the very opposite.

As well, this erroneous teaching on faith totally ignores the Will of God, rather claiming that the will of the Christian is always the same as the Will of God. How foolish can we be!

All the Promises of God mean exactly what they say (Mat. 21:22; Mk. 11:24; Jn. 15:7); however, they are all predicated on the Will of God and never on the will of man. We go back to Faith in the Cross or faith in self.

The only way we can properly know and understand the Will of God is to have proper Faith in the Cross. Faith in self will always seek to pervert the Will of God. And that's where the modern faith message primarily is. It is in *"self"* and not in Christ or in the Word.

The Saint with his Faith properly placed in the Cross, will know the Will of God, and because *"the Holy Spirit makes intercession for the Saints according to the Will of God,"* and only according to the Will of God (Rom. 8:27).

The Will of God having been ascertained, which is not so difficult to come by once one properly places his Faith, the Believer is to then *"ask,"* and not stop asking until the answer comes. Jesus said, and concerning this very thing:

"I say unto you, though he will not rise and give him, because he is his friend, yet because of his importunity (persistence) *he will rise and give him as many as he needeth"* (Lk. 11:5-13).

COMMANDMENTS

The phrase, *"Because we keep His Commandments,"* refers to that which definitely will be done, and gladly so, providing our Faith is properly placed. Otherwise, it is impossible!

The *"keeping of His Commandments"* is a foregone conclusion, if the Believer is properly looking to Christ. Paul said:

"I am crucified with Christ (Rom. 6:3-5)*: nevertheless I live* (I was raised in newness of life — Rom. 6:4-5)*; yet not I* (I do not live this Christian life through my own machinations)*, but Christ lives in me* (through the Person and Work of the Holy Spirit)*: and the life which I now live in the flesh* (my everyday life and living) *I live by the faith of the Son of God, Who loved me, and gave Himself for me"* (Gal. 2:20). The phrase *"but

Christ liveth in me," actually refers to the fact that I am *"in Christ,"* which came about as a result of my Faith in Him and what He did at the Cross for me, when I was initially saved. My continued Faith in that Finished Work guarantees me all that Christ has done for me, which means that through Christ every Commandment is kept.

In keeping these Commandments, I do not look at all to myself, but always to Christ. If I get up each morning and think that I have got to keep these Commandments today, such thinking shows that I'm trusting in *"self,"* and not in Christ. The keeping of the Commandments should never cross one's mind, and because it all has been done in Christ, and it all is being done in Christ.

John mentions this as he does, simply because he was dealing with individuals who were teaching and believing false doctrine, which claimed that it really didn't matter what a person did, it was only their flesh which did it, and not their spirit. In other words, breaking the Commandments, even not loving one's Brother and Sister in the Lord, were not looked at as sin by these false teachers. That's the reason that John makes these statements as he does.

If one has proper Faith, one is going to *"keep His Commandments,"* but will do so exclusively through Christ, which refers to Faith in what He did at the Cross.

CHRIST LIVING IN ME

About all of my Christian life, I heard certain individuals speak of Christ living in us; however, I knew it was a correct statement, but I really didn't know what it meant, and looking back, most of those who made the statement little knew as well what it meant. In fact, most Christians will make the statement presently, *"Christ living in me,"* but regarding most of them, they really don't know what it means.

First of all, when Paul speaks of Christ living in us, he is actually speaking of us being *"in Christ,"* which refers to his first statement, *"I am crucified with Christ."* Jesus addressed this as well by saying:

"At that day (after I have gone to the Cross and the Holy Spirit has come) *you shall know that I am in My Father, and you*

in Me, and I in you" (Jn. 14:20). Let's look at this Passage:

1. *"I am in My Father"*: This refers to the Deity of Christ. Jesus Christ is God.

2. *"You in Me"*: This refers to Romans 6:3-5, where the Believer exhibits Faith in what Christ did at the Cross, and in the Mind of God, the believing sinner is literally placed *"in Christ."*

3. *"I in you"*: Due to the Believer now being *"in Christ,"* and by virtue of Faith in what Christ did at the Cross, Christ can now abide in the Believer, which He does, through the Person of the Holy Spirit. In fact, Christ is at this moment seated at the Right Hand of the Father (Heb. 1:3). So He is in the Believer one might say by proxy, i.e., *"through and by the Person of the Holy Spirit."*

Christ has already kept all Commandments, which He did in His spotless, pure, Perfect Life. My Faith in Him, and what He did at the Cross, now makes me a Law-keeper, instead of a Lawbreaker. Simple Faith and trust in the Cross, which means what He did there, guarantees the help of the Spirit within my life, which guarantees that the Commandments are automatically kept.

PLEASING IN HIS SIGHT

The phrase, *"And do those things that are pleasing in His sight,"* points to Faith. Paul said: *"Without faith it is impossible to please Him: for he who cometh to God must believe that He is* (God is faithful), *and that He* (God) *is a rewarder of them who diligently seek Him"* (Heb. 11:6).

Let's pinpoint what Paul is speaking about when he mentions Faith.

Without exception, he is speaking of Faith in what Jesus did at the Cross on our behalf, through which all things come. When we exhibit Faith in Christ, this pleases God. When Jesus was baptized in water, the Scripture says: *"And there came a voice from Heaven, saying, 'You are My beloved Son, in Whom I am well pleased'"* (Mk. 1:11).

God was well-pleased with Christ for many reasons as would be obvious; however, the great thing that pleased Him, was that Christ would offer Himself up in sacrifice, which would effect Redemption for mankind; hence, John the Baptist would say of Him:

"*Behold the Lamb of God, which taketh away the sin of the world*" (Jn. 1:29). Jesus took away the sin of the world, by being offered up on the Cross, hence being referred to by the Holy Spirit as "*the Lamb of God.*"

So the key to all things, at least as it regards the Lord, and we speak of that which pleases Him, is for the Believer to exhibit Faith in Christ at all times, and what He did for us at the Cross, realizing and understanding that all things that we receive from God are made possible exclusively by the Cross (Gal. 6:14; Col. 2:14-15).

(23) "AND THIS IS HIS COMMANDMENT, THAT WE SHOULD BELIEVE ON THE NAME OF HIS SON JESUS CHRIST, AND LOVE ONE ANOTHER, AS HE GAVE US COMMANDMENT."

The diagram is:

1. Christianity has actually one Commandment, and that is to believe on Christ, which will produce love in our hearts for others.

2. The whole tenor of a Saint's life should be Christward.

3. This belief is an intellectual assent to all that the Bible states is true of our Lord and a heart submission to Him Personally.

4. Love will always be the product of such a consecration.

HIS COMMANDMENT

The phrase, "*And this is His Commandment,*" is given to us in the singular.

In Verse 22, John uses the plural "*Commandments.*" Yet when we look at all of them, they coalesce into just one, the one that John names. These are not two Commandments: to believe and to love. These two are one. You cannot believe without loving nor love without believing.

If it is to be noticed, the word "*Commandment*" as given here by the Holy Spirit through John is totally different than the Commandments of the old Jewish Law. That involved "*doing,*" while this involves "*believing.*" As should be obvious, they are two different things.

There is absolutely nothing that one must "*do,*" as effecting Salvation. Jesus has already done it all. But there definitely is something that one must "*believe,*" without which one cannot be saved.

NOTES

In fact, what John here says, is exactly what Jesus had already said.

The Scripture says that a lawyer asked him a question, saying: "*Master, what is the great Commandment in the Law?*

"*Jesus said unto him, 'You shall love the Lord your God with all your heart, and with all your soul, and with all your mind.*

"'*This is the first and great Commandment.*

"'*And the second is like unto it, you shall love your neighbor as yourself.*

"'*On these two Commandments hang all the Law and the Prophets'*" (Mat. 22:35-40). In fact, everything that is taught in the Epistles had already been taught by Christ.

FAITH

The phrase, "*That we should believe on the Name of His Son Jesus Christ,*" stands for all that the Son of God is in His wonderful Person.

First of all, John emphasizes the Deity of Christ by saying, "*His Son Jesus Christ,*" referring to Christ as God's Son. In I John 1:7, John says: "*And the Blood of Jesus Christ His Son cleanseth us from all sin,*" which proclaims the purpose of Christ. This points to the Son incarnate in Jesus and includes His Blood by making it "*the Blood of His Son,*" which thereby proclaims the mission of "*His Son.*"

The entire Gospel reveals His Son Jesus Christ. And in effect, we might say that His Name alone is the Son brought to us. By His Name alone we apprehend Him in Faith.

The name "*Jesus*" in both the Greek and the Hebrew means "*Savior*" or "*Deliverer.*" And what does the Scripture say about that?

"*Who gave Himself for our sins, that He might deliver us from this present evil world, according to the Will of God and our Father*" (Gal. 1:4).

And exactly how did He bring this about?

"*And that He might reconcile both* (Jews and Gentiles) *unto God in one body* (the Church) *by the Cross, having slain the enmity thereby*" (Eph. 2:16).

And exactly what did He do at the Cross to effect this?

"*But now in Christ Jesus you who sometimes were far off are made nigh by the Blood of Christ*" (Eph. 2:13).

Christ atoned for our sins by the shedding of His Own Precious Blood, which refers to the pouring out of His Life, which He gave in order that man's terrible crime against God could be settled, which it was.

"*Christ*" means "*Messiah,*" or "*Anointed One.*" In other words, the name "*Christ*" refers to the fact that Jesus fulfilled all the promises as it regards His Person. In other words, He was the One to Whom all the Prophets pointed, Who was to come.

"*Believe*" or "*faith*" in all of this presents the key word. Do you believe that Jesus Christ is the Son of God? Do you believe that He gave Himself on the Cross, and died so for us, which made it possible for man to be redeemed? Do you believe that one must express Faith in Christ and what He did for us at the Cross in order to be saved? It is "*His Commandment*" that we believe these things stated, or else we cannot be saved (Acts 16:31).

LOVE

The phrase, "*And love one another, as He gave us Commandment,*" presents that which will definitely happen once one has definitely and truly believed on the Name of the Lord Jesus Christ. Once again the Apostle comes back to love. If the person has truly been Born-Again, has truly believed on the Name of the Lord Jesus Christ, there will definitely be an instant change in that person's life. The Divine nature now becomes a part of such a Believer as generated by the Holy Spirit, and love is the automatic response. As impossible as it is to have this love without Christ, as impossible it is to *not* have this love with Christ. So obedience and love demonstrate the presence of the new nature in the Believer and the Spirit makes the fact of this indwelling conscious to the Believer.

The mention of faith (believe) in Verse 23 suggests to John the necessity of a still further discussion of truth and error, lest it should be thought that all religious fervor is of the truth, which he will address in the next Chapter.

(24) "AND HE THAT KEEPETH HIS COMMANDMENTS DWELLETH IN HIM, AND HE IN HIM. AND HEREBY WE KNOW

THAT HE ABIDETH IN US, BY THE SPIRIT WHICH HE HATH GIVEN US."

The structure is:

1. Faith in Jesus Christ and what He has done for us at the Cross proclaims the fact that we are dwelling in Him, and He is dwelling in us.

2. The knowledge of the fact that God is abiding in the Saint comes from the Holy Spirit.

3. He bears witness in connection with our human spirit as energized by Him, that we are born-ones of God (Rom. 8:16).

DWELLING IN HIM AND HE IN US

The phrase, "*And he who keeps His Commandments dwells in Him, and He in him,*" can be said, "*He who dwells in Him and He (Jesus) in him (in the Believer), keeps His Commandments.*"

The idea is, as the Believer keeps on believing on the Name of Jesus Christ, which keeps on producing love in the heart of the Believer, Christ will keep on abiding in the Believer and the Believer in Christ.

We dwell in Christ by faith, i.e., "*by believing on His Name.*" However, it's Faith which has the Cross of Christ as its object.

Whenever you as a believing sinner evidenced Faith in Christ when you were initially saved, in the Mind of God, you were literally crucified with Christ, or rather "*baptized into His Death,*" buried with Him, and raised with Him in newness of life (Rom. 6:3-5). As we have previously stated, that is your "*in Christ,*" position. Consequently, you are to build everything from henceforth on that fact, and I continue to speak of you being "*crucified with Christ*" (Gal. 2:20).

We are "*in Him*" by Faith, and we must continue to exhibit Faith in Him as we go forward in Christ. As stated, this refers to the fact that the Cross of Christ must ever be the object of our Faith. We never outgrow that, and for the simple reason that the Atonement is inexhaustible. In fact, it is so inexhaustible that Paul refers to it as "*the Everlasting Covenant*" (Heb. 13:20).

As a result of Faith in Him, which refers to a continued Faith in the Cross, He also abides in us, and does so, through the Person of the Holy Spirit, even as John will say in the next phrase.

THE HOLY SPIRIT

The phrase, *"And hereby we know that He (Christ) abides in us, by the Spirit which He has given us,"* in effect refers to the Trinity.

John is actually referring to God dwelling in us, which He does by virtue of what Jesus did at the Cross on our behalf, and our Faith in that Finished Work, which the Holy Spirit reveals to us. The solid proof of the indwelling, and, therefore, the Sonship of the Believer, is the demonstrable Presence of the Spirit.

Hitherto the thoughts by John have been chiefly about the Father and the Son where any direct reference was made to Persons in the Trinity. Here the Divine Spirit comes into prominence; formerly He had only been alluded to in the anointing (I Jn. 2:20, 27). Paul in effect said the same thing: *"The Spirit itself* (Himself) *beareth witness with our spirit, that we are the Children of God"* (Rom. 8:16).

This *"witness"* by the Spirit, covers every aspect of the Believer's life. Please understand that the Spirit is never silent. While some Believers would definitely have a greater knowledge of these things than others, still, even the newest convert knows that the Holy Spirit is living within him. There is always constant conviction by the Holy Spirit, and constant leading. To be sure, He will readily inform the Believer, even the youngest convert, when he has done something wrong.

A fellow Preacher of my acquaintance, related this incident as it regarded his own experience.

The next morning after he was saved the night before, he went on the job where he was a driller on an oil rig.

There was one particular individual on this rig with whom he had constant problems. And this particular morning true to form, the man did something that could have caused serious injuries among the other workers. My friend approached him, and in the course of the conversation as to how the man had endangered others, the fellow smarted back at my friend.

Before he realized what he was doing, he knocked him down.

NOTES

Now he was this type of man before he got saved. In other words, he didn't brook any foolishness. But this time something happened that was different.

Instantly, after doing this thing, he was convicted by the Holy Spirit, and convicted sharply. Despite the fact that the man was wrong, he had to go to him and apologize for his actions.

Of course, the moment this was done, Satan immediately informed him that if he was truly saved he would not have done such a thing. But then the Spirit of God countered by informing him that before he was saved, he did this with impudence, and thought nothing of it. But now, that he is *"born again,"* and the Spirit of God abides within him, instantly, he was convicted of his wrongdoing, which is the clearest proof of Salvation.

If the professing Christian doesn't know what we are speaking about here, this is a sure sign that he really isn't saved. As stated, the Spirit within us is in constant movement, leading, guiding, and directing in all things. However, in all of this, He is always a Perfect Gentleman. In other words, while He definitely wants total control within our lives, He will never take that control. We must always freely give it to Him. And let us never forget the following:

He is limited to what He can do within our lives, according to our Faith in the Finished Work of Christ (Rom. 8:2). He doesn't require much of us, but He does require that. He functions strictly on the basis of what Jesus has done at the Cross. That excellent Finished Work of Christ is what has made it possible for the Holy Spirit to come into our lives, and to perform His work within us. So it requires that we evidence Faith constantly in the Sacrifice of Christ, which then gives the Holy Spirit the latitude to do what He has been sent to do (Rom. 8:27).

THE BAPTISM WITH THE HOLY SPIRIT

Incidentally, *"the Spirit"* as mentioned here by John, and His abiding in us, is different than the Baptism with the Holy Spirit, which can only come to a Saint after conversion, and which is always accompanied by the speaking with other tongues (Acts 2:4).

Every Believer at the moment of Salvation receives the Spirit, even as addressed here by John. But being *"born of the Spirit"* which is the case here, is totally different than being *"Baptized with the Spirit"* (Mat. 3:11). Being *"born of the Spirit"* regards Sonship, while being *"Baptized with the Spirit"* involves power (Acts 1:8). But yet, being *"Baptized with the Spirit"* is not optional as it regards the Christian. In fact, Jesus *"commanded them that they should . . . wait for the Promise of the Father"* (Acts 1:4-5).

They were then instructed to wait, simply because the Holy Spirit had not yet been given. After the Day of Pentecost, no more waiting was required. They were Baptized with the Spirit instantly, upon Faith (Acts 2:4; 8:17; 9:17; 10:45-46; 19:1-7). As stated, we believe that the Bible teaches that every single recipient of the Holy Spirit Baptism will, and without exception, speak with other tongues at the time of being filled (Acts 2:4; 10:45-46; 19:1-7).

"Tongues" are to then be a constant part of our praying and worship, even as Paul outlined in I Corinthians, Chapter 14.

Once again allow us to emphasize the fact that Jesus commanded this, which means that it's not a mere suggestion (Acts 1:4). That being the case, we greatly shortchange ourselves, if we in fact ignore this command. Unfortunately, about half of the Church world does ignore this which Jesus said, thereby consigning themselves to little more than spiritual oblivion.

And even with those who claim the Spirit Baptism, if He is not properly addressed within our lives, which refers to constant Faith in the Cross, He will be greatly hindered in that which He desires to do. To preach the Spirit without the Cross is to invite *"spirits"* to take control, which has regrettably happened in many cases regarding modern Pentecost.

The Spirit-filled life is the greatest life there is. This life alone makes Jesus real in one's heart and life; however, the true Spirit-filled life is always based strictly on the Cross of Christ, which demands constant Faith in the Finished Work of Christ. Without this proper foundation the Holy Spirit is greatly limited in what He can do in us and for us.

NOTES

"We have heard the joyful sound: Jesus saves! Jesus saves!
"Spread the tidings all around: Jesus saves! Jesus saves!
"Bear the news to every land, climb the steeps and cross the waves;
"Onward! 'Tis our Lord's command; Jesus saves! Jesus saves!"

"Waft it on the rolling tide: Jesus saves! Jesus saves!
"Tell to sinners far and wide: Jesus saves! Jesus saves!
"Sing ye islands of the Sea; echo back, ye ocean caves;
"Earth shall keep her jubilee: Jesus saves! Jesus saves!"

"Sing above the battle strife: Jesus saves! Jesus saves!
"By His death and endless life, Jesus saves! Jesus saves!
"Sing it softly through the gloom, when the heart for mercy craves;
"Sing in triumph o'er the tomb, Jesus saves! Jesus saves!"

"Give the winds a mighty voice! Jesus saves! Jesus saves!
"Let the nations now rejoice, Jesus saves! Jesus saves!
"Shout salvation full and free; highest hills and deepest caves;
"This our song of victory: Jesus saves! Jesus saves!"

CHAPTER 4

(1) "BELOVED, BELIEVE NOT EVERY SPIRIT, BUT TRY THE SPIRITS WHETHER THEY ARE OF GOD: BECAUSE MANY FALSE PROPHETS ARE GONE OUT INTO THE WORLD."

The composite is:

1. Behind every doctrine there is a *"spirit,"* the Holy Spirit if it's true Doctrine, evil spirits if it's false doctrine.

2. We are not to believe everything we hear, but rather to *"try"* or *"prove"* the spirits whether they are of God.

3. *"False prophets"* are generic, meaning that it can stand for false teachers, false

pastors, in other words, anyone who claims to be preaching and teaching the Word of God.

4. The Holy Spirit says there are *"many"* of these people.

EVERY SPIRIT

The phrase, *"Beloved, believe not every spirit,"* presents the Apostle dealing with false prophets, i.e., *"false teachers."*

The mention of the Holy Spirit and those whom He inspires gives occasion for this parenthesis which instructs with respect to evil spirits and those whom these spirits inspire.

The Apostle provides two tests which decide whether a teacher in the Church spoke by Divine or by Satanic influence. The two tests are: A. The confession of Jesus the Messiah having come in the flesh (vs. 2); and, B. Subjection to Apostolic doctrine (vs. 6).

Christ come in the flesh, i.e., in actual physical and perfect humanity involves Atonement and Resurrection; for in order to die as the Sin-Offering He must become man, for God could not die; and that His Atoning Death should have a demonstration of Divine acceptance He must be raised from the dead, otherwise His oblation failed in its purpose and did not satisfy the claims of Righteousness.

The false teachers of that day, like some presently, taught that the Messiah was an Illusion, a Power that influenced Jesus of Nazareth. The Messiah, therefore, at least as they taught this error, had no proper actual humanity.

What the Apostles taught was by the Holy Spirit committed to writing, and all teachers of truth teach what they taught (vs. 6).

These two tests, i.e., presenting Christ as a personal Saviour, and subjection to the Holy Scriptures as the Divine fount of doctrine, reveal the true Minister of the Gospel.

To confess Jesus Christ having *"come in the flesh"* is more than the intellectual acceptance of the doctrine of Incarnation. It is a confession to Him and of Him Personally that involves conversion and the New Birth; and, a presentation of Him to give to men as the only Savior of man (Williams).

By John using the word *"spirit"* in the way that he does here, tells us two things:

1. He is speaking of human beings, and in this case, Teachers and Preachers of the Gospel.

NOTES

2. But more particularly, he is speaking of the *"spirit"* which is promoting them, whether the Holy Spirit, or evil spirits.

BELIEVE?

As Christians we are not to believe everything we hear. The truth is, every single Preacher and Teacher claims to be of God. They claim that what they are teaching and preaching is truth. But the facts are, some are of God and some aren't.

In this Chapter, the Holy Spirit through John will proclaim to us in no uncertain terms, how we can tell which ones are of God, and which ones aren't. Consequently, this is one of the most important Chapters in the entirety of the Bible.

TRY THE SPIRITS

The phrase, *"But try the spirits whether they are of God,"* refers to the fact that everything we hear is to be put to the test.

And what test do we use? Well of course the correct answer is that we test everything to the Word of God; however, that is sometimes complicated. Peter said:

"Which they that are unlearned and unstable wrest, as they do also the other Scriptures, unto their own destruction" (II Pet. 3:16). In other words, Preachers and Teachers can put an erroneous interpretation on the Scripture, making it mean something which was not originally intended. In fact, this is done constantly. Verse 2 will help us to understand more so the test we are to use as it regards *"trying the spirits."*

FALSE PROPHETS

The phrase, *"Because many false prophets are gone out into the world,"* refers to Satan attempting to sow tares among the wheat.

Every person reveals what kind of a personality or spirit he is by his word and his action although he may try to hide what he really is. Proper testing will penetrate the deception, will show whether what is in his spirit or heart is *"out of,"* i.e., *"derived from, God"* or from some ungodly, unscriptural source. John wants all his Readers to apply this testing to all who come to them as Prophets in order to teach them.

It is vital to find out whether *"the spirits"* of these Prophets, their inner spiritual character, and what is in their hearts, *"are really from God."* If the source, the spring, is Divine and pure, one may drink; if the source is otherwise, it is poison.

Note well that all Christians are told to do this testing. It is not taken out of their hands and reserved for the clergy of the Church. Unfortunately, some Pastors or Denominational heads, attempt to do the testing themselves, and then force all who are in their respective Churches to accept their findings. The implication here is that every single Christian should conduct the test himself, and not take someone else's word.

Christians will, of course, help each other in making the proper tests; some are more capable than others, have more experience than others; to be frank, Pastors should be especially trained for this work. We accept all such aid; in fact, John is offering it here to his Readers. Yet in the last analysis every Christian is personally responsible. Whom he believes or does not believe affects himself primarily. In essence, John wants himself to be tested by his Readers. Every true Preacher will definitely fall into this category. As stated, the Second Verse will bring out more clearly what that test ought to be.

(2) "HEREBY KNOW YE THE SPIRIT OF GOD: EVERY SPIRIT THAT CONFESSETH THAT JESUS CHRIST IS COME IN THE FLESH IS OF GOD:"

The composite is:

1. As Believers, we are to know what the Spirit of God sanctions.

2. The Incarnation of Christ speaks of the Cross of Christ.

3. The Spirit of God will place His sanction on the Cross and the Cross alone. Anything else is not of God.

THE SPIRIT OF GOD

The phrase, *"Hereby know ye the Spirit of God,"* refers to the fact, that we as Believers are to know what the Holy Spirit sanctions. We are to be acquainted with Him enough that we will know His leading, etc.

The idea is, we as Believers are to be so familiar with the Holy Spirit, which pertains to His leading and guidance, which means that we know the Word very, very well, that we will recognize instantly what is of Him

NOTES

and what is not of Him. The Holy Spirit is actually the giver of the Word, and as such, it is impossible to be properly acquainted with Him, unless we know the Word. And to turn it around, it's impossible to properly know the Word, unless one is properly acquainted with the Holy Spirit.

And now we will see what all of this actually means:

THE CROSS OF CHRIST

The phrase, *"Every spirit that confesseth that Jesus Christ is come in the flesh is of God,"* proclaims the test which we are to use.

Now, what is involved in the statement, *"Jesus Christ is come in the flesh"?*

The name *"Jesus"* is the English form of the Greek *"Iesous,"* and this is the Greek form of the Hebrew name *"Jehoshua"* which means *"Jehovah saves."*

"Christ" is from *"Christos," "the Anointed One."*

The words *"is come"* speak of the God of the Old Testament Who in the Person of His Son became Incarnate in human flesh without its sin, died on the Cross to satisfy the just demands of His Law which man broke, and was raised from the dead in the body in which He died, to become the living Saviour of the sinner who places his faith in Him in view of what He did for him on Calvary's Cross. The person who teaches that, John says, is actuated by the Holy Spirit. Otherwise, such a teacher who does not agree with that Doctrine is not of God. He is actuated by the spirit of Antichrist who denies and is against all that the Bible teaches regarding the Person and Work of the Lord Jesus.

So there will be absolutely no misunderstanding as to what is being said here, please note the following:

The Bible teaches us, even as we've already related in this Volume, that *"Jesus Christ is the Living Word"* (Jn. 1:1).

The Scripture then says: *"And the Word was made flesh, and dwelt among us"* (Jn. 1:14).

John the Baptist then said concerning Jesus: *"Behold the Lamb of God, which taketh away the sin of the world"* (Jn. 1:29).

The idea is the Living Word became flesh in order to die on a Cross, which in fact, was planned from before the foundation of the world (I Pet. 1:18-20).

Therefore, any Preacher who denies the Cross in any manner is labeled by the Holy Spirit as a *"false prophet."*

WHAT DOES IT MEAN TO PREACH THE CROSS?

The meaning of the New Covenant was revealed to Paul by Christ, which in effect, was and is the meaning of the Cross (Gal. 1:11-12).

Now this means that the entirety of the New Covenant, which refers to all that the Holy Spirit does, is wrapped around what Jesus did at Calvary. In other words, the Cross of Christ is not merely a doctrine, but rather the foundation of all Doctrine. Paul in effect, was the great Preacher of the Cross, which is the foundation of the Church. He said, and as it regards the Cross:

"For Christ sent me not to baptize, but to preach the Gospel: not with wisdom of words, lest the Cross of Christ should be made of none effect.

"For the preaching of the Cross is to them that perish foolishness; but unto us which are saved it is the power of God" (I Cor. 1:17-18).

"But we preach Christ crucified, unto the Jews a stumbling block, and unto the Greeks foolishness" (I Cor. 1:23).

"For I determined not to know anything among you, save Jesus Christ and Him Crucified" (I Cor. 2:2).

In Romans, Chapter 6, Paul gave us what some refer to as *"the mechanics of the Spirit."* In other words, in that Chapter he brought to us in detail the manner and way in which victory is won and maintained by the Saint, which tells us how the Holy Spirit works as it regards the Cross.

In Romans, Chapter 8, which some refer to as the *"dynamics of the Holy Spirit,"* the Apostle in that Chapter tells us what the Holy Spirit does, as a result of the Believer properly placing his Faith in the Cross of Christ, which is outlined in Romans, Chapter 6.

The preaching of the Cross is actually embodied in one principle, which means that everything comes to us through the Cross; however, to make it easier for the Believer to understand, I will break it down into two parts:

NOTES

1. The Preacher is to preach the Cross, which refers to what Jesus did there, as the only means of Salvation. This means that no one can be saved, unless they accept Christ as their own personal Saviour, which means to believe in Him and what He did at the Cross on our behalf (Jn. 3:16). To be sure, the believing sinner has almost no knowledge whatsoever of Christ and the Cross, but to be sure, when the Holy Spirit initially convicts the sinner, He does so on the premise of the fact that Christ is the only Saviour, and that He saves through what He did at the Cross (Jn. 16:7-11).

If the Preacher doesn't hold up the Cross as the only answer for sin and sinners, he is not preaching the Gospel, and will not see anyone saved.

2. Along with preaching the Cross as it regards the initial Salvation experience, the Preacher must as well preach the Cross as it regards the Christian having victory over the world, the flesh, and the Devil. This is where many Preachers let down.

Many Preachers preach the Cross as it regards the initial Salvation experience, but not at all as it regards the everyday life and living of the Child of God. For those who sit under such teaching and preaching, they are consigned to spiritual weakness and defeat. The Cross of Christ has just as much to do with our ongoing Christian experience, as it did with our initial Salvation experience. To be frank, it has even more, and for all the obvious reasons. As stated, this is what Romans, Chapters 6 and 8 are all about.

MODERN FALSE TEACHING

As I hope we have adequately brought out, this which John addresses as it regards the Incarnation, centers up on the reason for the Incarnation, which was the Cross of Christ. In other words, the Cross was the very purpose and reason for God becoming man (I Pet. 1:18-20). Consequently, there is nothing more important!

It's not pleasant to address false doctrine, and worse still, it is even more unpleasant to address those who are preaching false doctrine. Nevertheless, if we are to properly obey the Word, we must point out the error as well as portray the Truth (Ezek., Chpt. 3).

It is my personal feeling that the Church as a whole is no longer preaching the Cross as it should. Of course, there are definitely exceptions to what I have said, but I think as a general rule my statement is correct.

For instance, most every religious Denomination, and I especially speak of the major Denominations, whether Pentecostal or otherwise, have opted wholly for humanistic psychology. We believe the Bible teaches that the Cross is the only answer for the sins, perversions, and aberrations of the human race. This means that the situation was and is so bad that it is only the Cross which could address this terrible problem.

By contrast, humanistic psychology claims that man holds the answer to this dilemma. We cannot have it two ways, and neither can we join the Bible with psychology. The two will not at all mix. One must be believed and the other rejected.

If one teaches and preaches that the Cross is the answer, then at the same time, one is teaching and preaching that humanistic psychology isn't the answer. And conversely, if one teaches that humanistic psychology is the answer, they are at the same time teaching that the Cross holds no answer. As stated, one cannot have it both ways. It is either one or the other! So if the modern Church has opted for psychology, I have to believe at the same time, it has rejected the Cross. And as stated, every major Denomination of which I am aware, at least in the United States and Canada, has opted wholly for the psychological way.

The Word of Faith people fall into the category of rejecting the Cross as well. They do so by openly repudiating the Cross, claiming that it was the greatest defeat in human history. One of their bright lights refers to it as *"past miseries."* Many of their teachers openly claim that the Blood does not atone; consequently, they will sing no songs about the Blood or the Cross in their services, I am told!

They teach that the Cross was incidental, claiming that Salvation was brought about by Jesus dying as a sinner on the Cross, actually taking upon Himself the Satanic nature, and going to Hell where He remained for some three days and nights. Suffering agony those particular three days and nights, they claim, God then said, *"It is enough,"* and at that time, Jesus was Born-Again, actually being the firstborn of many Brethren, they continue to claim. He was then raised from the dead.

They claim that Salvation comes by having faith in the sufferings of Jesus in the burning side of Hell and in His Resurrection.

Now there are many problems with all of this, but the main problem is, it is all pure fiction from beginning to end. Not a shred of that which we have stated is found in the Bible. It is made up out of whole cloth!

Jesus did not die as a sinner on the Cross. Actually, He was a Sin-Offering on the Cross, which means that He poured out His Life's Blood, which atoned for all sin. While He did go down into the part of Hell called *"Paradise,"* and as well also preached to the fallen Angels who were imprisoned, there is nothing in the Bible that states that Jesus went to the burning side of Hell and there suffered as a sinner (Ps. 16:10; Acts 2:31; Eph. 4:9; I Pet. 3:19).

There are thousands of Word of Faith Churches across the nation and around the world. I've never heard of anyone being saved in these Churches; however, I'm not saying that such is the case altogether. But I am saying, regarding those who have been saved, it was not by heeding the Message these people preach as it regards the Cross. It's impossible for one to be saved believing such error. And let the Reader understand, misunderstanding anything in the Bible is serious; however, misunderstanding the Atonement, or misinterpreting the Atonement, is as serious as it can get. That's why Satan fights the Cross so hard.

(3) "AND EVERY SPIRIT THAT CONFESSETH NOT THAT JESUS CHRIST IS COME IN THE FLESH IS NOT OF GOD: AND THIS IS THAT SPIRIT OF ANTICHRIST, WHEREOF YOU HAVE HEARD THAT IT SHOULD COME; AND EVEN NOW ALREADY IS IT IN THE WORLD."

The composite is:

1. Every person who denigrates or even minimizes the Cross in any way is not of God.

2. The spirit that denies the Cross is the spirit of the Antichrist.

3. The denial of the Cross was prevalent in John's day, and is even more prevalent now.

A WRONG CONFESSION

The phrase, *"And every spirit that confesseth not that Jesus Christ is come in the flesh is not of God,"* presents one of the boldest statements in the entirety of the Bible as it concerns the Atonement.

The Doctrine of the Cross is essential to the Christian system; and he who does not hold it cannot be regarded either as a Christian, or recognized as a Christian Teacher.

The test that we are to apply is to examine the person's confession. The Scriptures nowhere ask us to look into a man's heart. God Alone sees the heart; no man can see into another's heart. And yet, it is precarious to assert: *"The man's heart is alright!"* when the man's confession is wrong. The Lord has given us the one safe test, the confession. Beyond this our responsibility ceases. *"What is the man's real confession?"* is for us the only question. Since one confesses not only with his lips but also with his practice and his acts, we are to examine both.

If the Preacher denigrates the Cross, he is false through and through. This means he is not of God, which means he is a false prophet, which means he is not saved. It doesn't really matter what else he might say, how smooth he may seem to be concerning other Biblical matters, if he denigrates the Cross, he is false.

There are two groups of people in the modern Church who fall into this category, at least of whom I am aware:

The first is the Modernists. These people do not believe that Jesus Christ is the Son of God, or that His Death on the Cross with the shedding of His Life's Blood availed anything. Unfortunately, there are many of these in the old-line Churches.

The other group, which we have just addressed, goes under the heading of *"Word of Faith,"* or some such name. They aren't in the same category as the Modernists, which means they do not exactly deny the Cross, but rather pervert its meaning. In other words, they make the Cross of Christ of none effect (I Cor. 1:17). I've already addressed their particular beliefs several times in this Volume, so I will not go into detail here;

NOTES

however, to refer to the Cross as the *"greatest defeat in human history,"* shows a complete misunderstanding of the Atonement; consequently, those who follow this teaching, will bring upon themselves serious spiritual harm, and could even lose their souls.

And now we come to the apostasy of most major religious Denominations, including the Pentecostals. Almost all, at least as it regards the leadership of these Denominations, have opted for humanistic psychology, which is a direct affront to the Cross of Christ. As we've already said several times, one cannot have both — and I speak of the ways of the world and the ways of God. Humanistic psychology is man-devised while the Bible Way is of course, God-devised and instituted. One is all of man and the other is all of God. As stated you cannot join the two.

PROPER PERSPECTIVE

Let the Reader understand the following:

We are speaking of the end result. We are maintaining that whatever God gives to humanity comes exclusively through the Cross of Christ. All other proposed ways and means projects the idea that these things come from God by other means. That's really what it boils down to.

Using Cain and Abel as an example, both men offered up sacrifices. Cain offered up one that God wouldn't accept, which was the labor of his own hands, while Abel offered up an innocent victim, a Lamb, which God would accept, and because it was a type of the coming Christ.

So when we talk about *"trying the spirits"* or *"false prophets,"* or error of any nature, we are basically speaking of the end result, and how that end result is attained. We believe the Bible teaches that everything that God gives to humanity comes exclusively through the Cross of Christ. We believe that the Bible also teaches that any proposed way other than the Cross, is error, and those who teach such error are false prophets, etc.

THE SPIRIT OF ANTICHRIST

The phrase, *"And this is that spirit of antichrist,"* in effect says, that if any other way than the Cross is proposed as the answer to hurting humanity, that such way is *"antichrist."*

The story of the Bible is the story of the fall and Redemption of humanity, and the story of that Redemption is *"Jesus Christ and Him Crucified"* (I Cor. 2:2). So this means that the Cross of Christ, i.e., *"the Finished Work of Christ,"* is not merely a doctrine, but actually the foundation on which all Doctrine is built. It is the *"house built upon the rock"* (Mat. 7:24). Everything else is *"the house built upon the sand"* (Mat. 7:26).

The word *"antichrist"* used here actually means *"pseudochristos."* In other words, these false teachers pretend to be of Christ, but they actually aren't. These would be those of whom Paul spoke of as *"preaching another Jesus"* (II Cor. 11:4).

ANOTHER JESUS?

Paul spoke of *"preaching another Jesus,"* which is done by *"another spirit,"* which presents *"another gospel"* (II Cor. 11:4).

This falls under the heading of *"antichrist,"* or *"pseudochristos."* Once again to make it crystal clear, it refers to the following:

Basically the sum total of Christianity can be characterized by the means which God uses to reach fallen humanity. As stated, we teach and preach what the Bible teaches, that He does so exclusively through the Cross of Christ. If any other way is taught, it is false.

THE FALSE WAY

The phrase, *"Whereof you have heard that it should come; and even now already is in the world,"* speaks of Satan immediately trying to counter the great message of Redemption.

Of all the ways which Satan attacks, I think he reserves his greatest energy for attacks against the Cross. He seldom proposes that God has no answers, but rather proposes a false way of receiving from the Lord. Most of the ways which he suggests are good within themselves, and this deceives us. Listen to what Paul said:

"Was then that which is good made death unto me? God forbid. But sin, that it might appear sin, working death in me by that which is good; that sin by the Commandment might become exceeding sinful" (Rom. 7:13).

Most Christians do not really understand what Paul is saying here.

NOTES

First of all, the Apostle is talking about how that the Law is *"holy, just, and good"* (Rom. 7:12).

The problem was, he was trying to keep the Law in his own ability and strength, which fell out to failure, as it always will. So he is saying that the Law is good, which it is, and that his efforts as well were good; however, his trying to live for God in the wrong way, caused sin to appear within his life, which worked death in him *"by that which is good."*

Now all of this happened to Paul before the Lord revealed to him the Message of the Cross, which then brought victory. But the sadness is, most modern Christians fall into the same category presently as Paul did so long, long ago.

Not understanding the Cross, most Christians attempt to live for God by doing *"good things."* But the doing of these good things, whatever they might be, and as well intentioned as the individual might be, does not fall out to victory, but the very opposite. And that leaves Christians in a state of confusion. Instead of victory the failure becomes worse and worse.

What is wrong?

The good things they are doing aren't wrong. And the desire to do right certainly isn't wrong. The wrong comes in with our misplaced faith. In other words, trying to live for God in this way, in effect says that what Christ did at the Cross was not enough and needs some other things added. Because these *"other things"* are *"good things,"* it deceives us (Rom. 7:11). The problem is we are trying to achieve results in the wrong way.

The only way that we can successfully live for the Lord is to understand that Jesus did everything for us at the Cross. We are to place our Faith exclusively in that great Sacrifice, which will then guarantee the help of the Holy Spirit. Victory will be the result. Any other way, and no matter how good it may seem on the surface, is in effect *"the spirit of the antichrist."*

(4) "YE ARE OF GOD, LITTLE CHILDREN, AND HAVE OVERCOME THEM: BECAUSE GREATER IS HE THAT IS IN YOU, THAN HE THAT IS IN THE WORLD."

The structure is:

1. The indication is that some of these Christians had been tempted to believe this false doctrine, but had overcome that temptation.

2. The reason for their victory, is that the Holy Spirit Who resides in Believers, was and is greater than Satan.

3. These Saints understood the manner and way in which the Holy Spirit works.

OVERCOMING POWER

The phrase, *"You are of God, little children, and have overcome them,"* refers to several things.

First of all, there is indication here that Satan had initially come on forcefully. His presentation by these false teachers had at first seemed plausible; but these Saints, knowing the Word of God, and being helped by the Holy Spirit, had prevailed. They had refused to believe these lies!

It is not promised the Child of God that Satan will not be allowed to attack; however, the Lord has made a way that we can overcome every single effort made by the Evil One, but we must do it God's way. In His seven Messages to the seven Churches of Asia, Jesus admonished Believers seven times, that we must be an overcomer (Rev., Chpts. 2-3). The question is, how?

The answer is found in the might and power of the Holy Spirit Who resides within us. But the great problem is, most Christians simply do not know how He works, simply thinking that His mere Presence guarantees the victory. It doesn't!

THE HOLY SPIRIT

The phrase, *"Because greater is He Who is in you, than he who is in the world,"* refers to the Holy Spirit being greater than Satan. The Holy Spirit is God!

First of all, every single thing that is done on this Earth as it regards the Godhead, is done by, through, and of the Holy Spirit. This begins with Genesis 1:2 with Moses writing, *"And the Spirit of God moved upon the face of the waters."* The Canon of Scripture closes out with John writing, *"And the Spirit and the Bride say, Come. And let him that heareth say, Come. And let him that is athirst come. And whosoever will, let him take the water of life freely"* (Rev. 22:17). And everything

NOTES

done between Genesis and Revelation, with the exception of Jesus Christ coming to this world and redeeming man by dying on the Cross, was all done by the Holy Spirit. And He was involved in every single thing done by Christ, from His conception, throughout His Ministry, even unto the Cross, where Jesus died, and did so only when the Holy Spirit said it was time (Heb. 9:14). As well, it was the Spirit of God Who *"raised up Jesus from the dead"* (Rom. 8:11).

Concerning how the Spirit works, the Cross changed everything. As we've already related in this Volume, before the Cross the Holy Spirit was very limited as to what He could do as it regards the Saints. It was because the sin debt had not yet been paid, due to the fact that the Blood of bulls and goats could not take away sin (Heb. 10:4). But when Jesus paid the price on Calvary's Cross, which means He atoned for all sin, this made it possible for the Holy Spirit to now abide in the heart and life of the Believer on a permanent basis (Jn. 14:16-17).

On the Day of Pentecost the Holy Spirit came to this world in a brand-new dimension. The Cross having addressed many questions, the Holy Spirit now has latitude to work to a far greater degree than previously. We see this in the Book of Acts. In fact, the Book of Acts is an account of the acts of the Holy Spirit in the Early Church. So this means, if the modern Church is to be what it ought to be, it must have the earmarks of the Book of Acts, or else it's not really Church as it ought to be Church.

TWO OUTPOURINGS

The Word of God mentions two great outpourings of the Holy Spirit after the Cross. The Prophet Joel in referring to the Holy Spirit mentioned *"the former rain"* and *"the latter rain"* (Joel 2:23-29). The former rain refers to the Early Church, with the latter rain referring to the outpouring of the Holy Spirit which took place at approximately the turn of the Twentieth Century, and continues unto this hour. During the last 100 or so years, it is estimated that over one hundred million people have been baptized with the Holy Spirit, with the evidence of speaking with other tongues (Acts 2:4).

Unfortunately, a great part of the modern Church, especially the old-line Denominations rejected this outpouring. For all practical purposes, there is no moving or operation of the Holy Spirit within these Churches, which means they are man-instituted and man-directed, which means there is very little, if anything, actually done for the Lord.

Unfortunately, even in the ranks of those who refer to themselves as *"Pentecostal,"* which means they believe in the Baptism with the Holy Spirit with the evidence of speaking with other tongues, most even in these ranks little know and understand the Holy Spirit. He is somewhat taken for granted, which means that it is believed if one is baptized with the Holy Spirit, all problems are then solved; however, it is very obvious that this isn't the case at all.

While the Baptism with the Holy Spirit is definitely the necessary first step, His work thereafter in our hearts and lives is not automatic. It requires cooperation on our part. The Holy Spirit is always a Perfect Gentleman. He wants control in our lives, but He will never take control unless it is freely given to Him.

HOW THE SPIRIT WORKS

The problem with most Pentecostals is that they little know and understand how the Spirit of God works within their hearts and lives. As stated, they take Him for granted thinking that His work is automatic. As a result, we have Christians, even though Spirit-filled, who are at the same time, failing. Let the Reader peruse the following very carefully:

First of all, the Holy Spirit works exclusively by and through what Jesus did at the Cross. In other words, the Cross is what gives latitude to the Holy Spirit regarding all that He does for us.

Paul plainly says: *"For the Law of the Spirit of Life in Christ Jesus has made me free from the law of sin and death"* (Rom. 8:2).

This one particular Scripture tells us plainly how the Holy Spirit works. And the way He works is actually referred to as a *"Law,"* which means that this is a law devised by the Godhead, and from which the Holy Spirit will not deviate.

However, this *"Law"* by which the Spirit works, is *"in Christ Jesus."* What does that mean?

It refers to the Cross. Any time Paul uses the phrase *"in Christ Jesus,"* or one of its derivatives, without exception he is speaking of what Jesus did at the Cross, by and through which the Spirit works. So what does this mean?

It means simply that we as Believers must understand as well that everything we have from God comes exclusively through the Cross of Christ, which Paul aptly outlined in Romans 6:3-5. Consequently, we are to express Faith in the Cross constantly, ever making that the object of our faith (I Cor. 1:17-18, 23; 2:2; Gal. 6:14; Col. 2:14-15).

Placing our faith exclusively in the Cross of Christ, understanding that this is the means by which all things come to us from God, gives the Holy Spirit the latitude within which to work within our lives. The major reason that Spirit-filled Christians do not experience the power and victory which the Spirit Alone can give is because their faith is in something else other than the Cross. That being the case, the Holy Spirit simply will not function. If He did, He would be breaking the *"Law,"* and we refer to the *"Law of the Spirit of Life in Christ Jesus,"* and that He will not do.

The Child of God can overcome only by the means which I have stated. If we try to do so any other way, failure will always and without exception be the result.

To be sure, the Holy Spirit being God is definitely greater than Satan and all of his minions of darkness. And to be sure, He strongly desires to exert His almighty power on our behalf. But He will not do so outside of the parameters of the Cross. Our Faith must ever be in that Finished Work. That being the case, He will develop the Fruit of the Spirit within our lives, give us Gifts of the Spirit, make us Christlike in every respect, developing Holiness and Righteousness. In fact, He Alone can develop these things within our lives. There is no way that we can do such within our own strength and ability. He only asks that we express Faith in the Finished Work of Christ on a continuous basis. This being done, He will work mightily for us and within us. Only in this manner can we be *"overcomers."*

(5) "THEY ARE OF THE WORLD: THEREFORE SPEAK THEY OF THE WORLD, AND THE WORLD HEARETH THEM."

The exegesis is:

1. These false teachers have their source in the world system of evil, this present pernicious age.

2. The demons of Satan are part of this world system, and the source of all heresy.

3. Those who are of the world accept their teaching, for it recognizes its own language.

OF THE WORLD

The phrase, *"They are of the world,"* refers to the false teachers of Verse 3. These false teachers are successful *"in the world"* because their thinking, their theology, is accommodated to the world's beliefs. So their teaching is philosophically congenial to the prevailing currents of the day. Naturally the world hears such teachers gladly.

The term *"world"* is probably to be understood in two ways: as a system of thought antithetical to the Christian belief and as a description of those members of the Church who are led astray by false teachers.

THEREFORE THEY SPEAK

The phrase, *"Therefore speak they of the world,"* refers to the fact that the source of their false doctrines is the world. As stated, the demons of Satan are part of this world system, and the source of all heresy. Paul said:

"Now the Spirit speaketh expressly, that in the latter times (the times in which we now live) *some shall depart from the faith, giving heed to seducing spirits, and doctrines of Devils"* (I Tim. 4:1).

For all their utterance they have no higher source, draw from no Divine fountain, and no stream rises above its source. What they have may be religious, and may even be papered with Scriptures; however, it is not from God, simply because it is not the True Gospel, i.e., *"Jesus Christ and Him Crucified."*

THE WORLD HEARS THEM

The phrase, *"And the world heareth them,"* answers a lot of questions.

There have always been two Churches, the True Church and the Apostate Church. The

Apostate Church will always hear the false prophets. The message will appeal to them simply because both are from the same source, the world. They do not have the Spirit of God; therefore, they do not follow the Spirit of God. Actually, they are greatly opposed to the Spirit of God, and will do everything within their power to stop its flow.

The modern *"money gospel"* is an excellent case in point. It professes to be the Gospel; however, its source is the world; therefore, it attracts the Apostate Church. They have a kindred spirit.

As another example, Christian Contemporary music comes from the same source — the world. Therefore, it attracts those who think like the world, who have not the Spirit, and once again which constitutes the Apostate Church.

There is no way the two can mix. Each is distinct within itself. The ways of the True Church are the ways of the Spirit and the Bible. The ways of the Apostate Church are the ways of the world. As stated, the two are antagonistic to each other. They always have been, and they always will be. In fact, one of the very reasons for the Rapture of the Church is to separate these two. The Lord will take His unto Himself, while the other will be left in this world. It is of the world, so it should be in the world. The True Church is of Heaven, so it should be in Heaven.

(6) "WE ARE OF GOD: HE THAT KNOWETH GOD HEARETH US; HE THAT IS NOT OF GOD HEARETH NOT US. HEREBY KNOW WE THE SPIRIT OF TRUTH, AND THE SPIRIT OF ERROR."

The diagram is:

1. In contradistinction to the false teachers, we are of God.

2. Men's attitude to the Message of the Incarnate Saviour ranks them on this side or on that — on God's side or the world's.

3. *"The Spirit of Truth"* is the Holy Spirit Who teaches the truth, and *"the spirit of error"* is the spirit which comes from the Devil, teaching lies and seducing men into error.

OF GOD

The phrase, *"We are of God,"* refers to John himself and to those who believed his Gospel. The line is drawn.

John feels a grave duty, in condemnation of Cerinthus and others of like ilk, to assert the genuine Truth and Divine authority of the Apostolic Gospel. There could be no spiritual pride in this; it was a conscientious obligation. God spoke in them, and their loyalty forbade both disclaimer and accommodation (Jn. 18:37).

Paul, also, not infrequently refers to the same thing respecting himself; to the fact — a fact which no one would presume to call in question, and which might be regarded as the basis of an argument — that he and his fellow-Apostles were what they claimed to be (I Cor. 15:14-15; I Thess. 2:1-11).

By John making the bold statement, *"We are of God,"* he is at the same time saying that those who repudiated Christ in the sense of His atoning work, pure and simple *"are not of God."* The Preachers of a false unity dare not read these statements as given by the Apostle. He minces no words, pulls no punches, in effect, says it just like it is.

Any Preacher who is not as sure of his Gospel as John was of his, should not preach. We are handling Words of Life. We are dealing with the issues of life and death. As a result, we must be sure of the Gospel we preach. We must be certain that it is unequivocally the Word of God. One day every single Preacher will answer to the Lord for his Ministry and his Message; consequently, we must be as dogmatically certain even as was the beloved Apostle John.

At the same time, the true Preacher must understand that the Apostate Church is going to oppose him and will do so severely. If it doesn't oppose him, it's because he's not adequately preaching the Word. Let the Preacher remember the following:

The True Gospel will make many glad and many mad, but to be sure, it will not be ignored.

The condition of the Church is always a product of the Gospel. It cannot be any other way. What we preach is what we get! And one might at the same time say, what we get is what we preach!

WHAT DO YOU HEAR?

The phrase, *"He that knoweth God heareth us,"* presents a bold, bold statement, which in effect, draws the line in the sand.

If one Preacher is preaching the Truth, and another is preaching error, then it is obvious that the former is being led by the Holy Spirit while the latter is being led by spirits. Consequently, one is of God while the other isn't. It's just that simple!

As John has made a bold statement, let me by the guidance of the Holy Spirit make the same statement.

I am preaching the same Gospel which Paul and John preached; consequently, all who are of God will hear me and all who aren't won't. We are preaching the Cross exactly as Paul preached the Cross, or rather we're doing our very best to preach the Cross exactly as he did. So why wouldn't a true Christian desire to hear this message?

Some may counter by pointing to the fact that I am not of their particular Denomination. If that is the case, then they are serving their Denomination and not Christ. Others may counter by saying that Preachers whom they respect have told them not to listen to us. If that is the case, then they are being led by Preachers instead of the Holy Spirit.

If I am preaching the truth, and that goes for any other Preacher as well, then those who are of God will hear me. In fact, it cannot be any other way.

NOT OF GOD

The phrase, *"He that is not of God heareth not us,"* once again, draws the proverbial line in the sand.

From this, we know that there were some professing Christians in John's day who would not hear him. That seems inconceivable, considering who he was; nevertheless, it is obvious that this was the case. Some professing Christians would rather follow false teachers than to follow the Apostle John, who was one of the chosen Disciples of Christ, and whom the Lord used to write five Books in the Bible. Such portrays the evil of the human heart.

The argument as given here by John parallels that of Jesus in John 8:47: *"He who belongs to God hears what God says. The reason you do not hear is that you do not belong to God"* (Jn. 10:4-5; 18:37).

The implication of all of this is that when John spoke, as would be the case with all

God-called Preachers, he drew from a correspondingly high Source, from God. He had the Light, the Truth, the Word, and the Commandment. And the clincher is this:

The Gospel as preached by John changed people's lives. In other words, it brought forth good fruit. This is the acid test as given by Christ (Mat. 7:15-20).

Regarding all of this, Smith comments: *"Men's attitude to the message of the Incarnate Savior ranks them on this side or on that — on God's side or the world's."*

Two situations are brought into play here:

1. If the Believer is prejudiced toward the Preacher, and for whatever reason, no matter how much truth the Preacher delivers, it will not be heard by that particular Saint. This can be tragic, because that particular Preacher, whomever he might be, may be the only one whom God will use to deliver His particular Word to that particular Saint. So what am I saying?

I'm saying that every Saint must search his heart very closely. He must not allow thoughts of bias or prejudice to get into his heart, which means he must not be swayed by the opinions of others, etc. He must judge every man and woman according to the Word of God. If not, he may miss the very Word which he so desperately needs.

2. Exactly as Smith said, the Cross of Christ is the dividing line one might say, for everything. Men's attitude to this Message ranks them on God's side or the world's. The Cross of Christ stands as the center point of all things. Martin Luther said, *"As one viewed the Cross, so they viewed the Reformation."*

One might paraphrase the Reformer's statement by saying, *"As one views the Cross, one views Christ."*

THE CHANGED CENTER
THROUGH THE CROSS

As we've already stated, Paul portrayed the great Truth of the Cross as no other Apostle. While all other Apostles complemented what Paul gave us, it was to Paul that the Holy Spirit gave the meaning of the New Covenant, which in fact, was and is the meaning of the Cross.

As we read II Corinthians 5:13-18, we cannot fail to see how deeply, in this Passage, the Cross is the very center of the life of the

Apostle, and must be the center of our lives as well. This is what the Holy Spirit through the Apostle said:

"For whether we be beside ourselves, it is to God: or whether we be sober, it is for your cause.

"For the love of Christ constraineth us; because we thus judge, that if one died for all, then were all dead:

"And that He died for all, that they which live should not henceforth live unto themselves, but unto Him which died for them, and rose again.

"Wherefore henceforth know we no man after the flesh: yea, though we have known Christ after the flesh, yet now henceforth know we Him no more.

"Therefore if any man be in Christ, he is a new creature: old things are passed away; behold, all things are become new.

"And all things are of God, Who hath reconciled us to Himself by Jesus Christ, and hath given to us the ministry of reconciliation."

Let me draw your attention to Verses 14 and 15, which read, *"For the love of Christ constrains me, because I thus have judged, that if one died for all, then all died* (in Him), *and that He died for all, that the living might live no longer to themselves but to Him. . . ."* These words taken alone unmistakably teach the identification of the Believer with Christ in His Death, and his emergence into a life where he lives wholly and entirely unto Christ, and not self. But if the words are read in connection with the context, preceding and succeeding Verse 14, the veil is lifted in a remarkable way, showing that Verse 14 is the very center of a striking Passage, revealing the circumstances and conditions which brought forth from Paul his reference to the Cross.

THE CROSS

Let me try to picture the situation behind the words of the Apostle. His critics at Corinth were charging him with exalting himself, and being *"beside himself"* with vanity, but he replies, *"If I exalt myself it is for God's cause: if I humble myself, it is for your sakes."*

"For the love of Christ constrains me," and then he points to the Cross as the reason why he should say this about himself. He knew that it was not *"self exaltation"* or vanity

manifested in his zeal and intense abandonment to God, because of his identity with Christ in death. *"Self"* was no longer the dominant center of his being, *"self"* was no longer the focal base from which he acted, either in *"exaltation"* or *"humility."*

How expressive, in the light of this, are the words of the Apostle in Verse 16. *"We therefore"* — here the pronoun, is emphatic. *"We therefore view no man carnally,"* i.e., as you have viewed me. You call me vain and mad in my zeal, but that is a carnal view — the view of the flesh. I know that I have died with Christ, and that I am no longer living unto myself. It is the love of Christ dwelling in me which constrains me — *"Whosoever then, is 'in Christ,' is a new creation; his old being has passed away . . . all comes out of God. . . ."*

"You are calling me crazy, in saying this, that and the other about me, but I know it is not 'I' which is dominating me, for I have seen the 'I' on the Cross. I have judged the true meaning of Christ's death. I see that if 'One' died for all, then 'all died,' so that those who are thus 'in Christ' become 'new creations." Their center is changed. They have a new center — Christ — all is new and all comes out of God, as the central spring of their lives.

"It is thus that the 'love of Christ' is constraining me, bursting out of me like a torrent from the central spring of His life, and not the mere zeal and enthusiasm which you carnally judge to be the power at work in me. . . ."

THE MEANING OF THE CROSS

How in line this is with God's way of revealing the meaning of the Cross to His children. The inner knowledge of the Cross can never be grasped merely by the intellect. The death of Christ at Calvary was something so awesome and terribly real that only they who enter experimentally into that death can get even a glimpse into it. The Message of the Cross (I Cor. 1:18) can never be merely a *"doctrine,"* for it was something more than a *"doctrine"* to Christ, and, as we see in the life of the Apostle of the Cross, to Paul. God's way of revealing truth is to work it into a man's experience — wrought out in the life, before it can penetrate the intellect. We shall only

NOTES

get Paul's knowledge of the Cross as we get Paul's experience, i.e., we must be brought to the same experimental point from which he spoke, if we are to understand his message.

THE CHANGE OF THE CENTER

Now it is the change of the center, so to speak, which Paul describes in this Passage in Corinthians, which I want to dwell upon for awhile. We have spoken of the Cross and death to sin, as shown in Romans, Chapter 6, the Cross and death to the world as in Galatians, Chapter 6; and sometimes of the *"grain of wheat"* death-life depicted in John 12:24, but we may get light about all these aspects of the Cross, and experience a measure of deliverance through the truth, and yet not know deep, deep down in our innermost being, this change of the *"I"* center which the Apostle speaks about in II Corinthians 5:14. To put in other words, there is something needing dealing with deeper than *"sin"* or the *"world."* It is the selfhood — the *"ego"* — the *"I."* Has the Cross penetrated there?

"I," said Paul, *"henceforth view no man carnally."* When the *"I"* center is dealt with, the outlook is entirely changed.

We learn from this that even the *"view"* of *"Christ"* can be *"carnal"* — that is, from the viewpoint of the self-center instead of the *"new creation"* viewpoint which comes *"out of God."* It is this bedrock basis of the inner life which we must get down to and examine in the light of the Cross. No other way can the Lord set free in us His rivers of living water, nor can we be brought into the place of authority over the powers of darkness, for the selfhood is poisoned at its source by the fallen nature of the first Adam.

THE SPIRIT OF CHRIST

Before passing on to further elucidate this from the Scriptures, let me quote you a passage from the Appendix to *"The Spirit of Christ,"* by Dr. Andrew Murray, in which he gives an extract from the writings of Dr. Dorner. He says:

"The character of Christ's substitution is not repressive of personality, but productive . . . He is not content with the existence in Himself of the fullness of the spiritual life,

into which His people are absorbed by faith . . . Christ's redeeming purpose is directed to the creation, by the Holy Spirit Whom He sends, of 'new personalities' in whom Christ gains a settled, established being . . . As a new Divine principle, the Holy Spirit creates, though not substantially, new faculties, a new volition, knowledge, feeling, a new self-consciousness. In brief, He creates a 'new person,' dissolving the old union-point of the faculties, and creating a pure union of the same. The new personality is formed in inner resemblance to the Last Adam, on the same family type, so to speak . . . Through the Holy Spirit the Believer has the consciousness of himself as a new man, and the power and living impulse of a new, holy life . . . mere passivity and receptiveness are transformed into spontaneity, and productiveness. . . ."

THE LIFE PRINCIPLE

Dr. Andrew Murray comments on this:

This thought that the Spirit of God, as the Spirit of the Divine Personality, becomes the life principle of our personality, is one of extreme solemnity, and of infinite fruitfulness. The Spirit not only dwells in me as a *"locality,"* or within me, alongside and around that inmost Ego in which I am conscious of myself, but, within that *"I"* becomes the new and Divine life principle of the new personality. The same Spirit that was and is in Christ, His inmost Self, becomes my inmost Self.

What new meaning it gives to the word *"He that is joined to the Lord is one spirit"* with Him! And what force to the question, *"Know ye not that the Spirit of God dwelleth in you?"* The Holy Spirit is within me as a Personal power, with a will and a purpose of His Own. As I yield up my personality to His I shall not lose it, but find it renewed and strengthened to its highest capacity.

Here we have clearly set forth the change of *"center"* which Paul so acutely realized through the light he had on the Cross.

A NEW PERSONALITY

Three times the Apostle affirms this basic *"new creation"* as his experience.

"I live; yet not I . . ." (Gal. 2:20).

"I command; yet not I, but the Lord . . ." (I Cor. 7:10).

"I laboured . . .! yet not I . . ." (I Cor. 15:10).

In the Church at Corinth, in Paul's words in I Corinthians 1:12, we have a glimpse of a contrast to this. *"Every one of you saith 'I' . . . 'I' of Paul, 'I' of Apollos. . . ."* But Paul did not say *"I"* in the sense of *"I"* being the originating and moving spring of his words and actions. *"I"* — yes, it is *"I"* still, but a new *"I"* — a new personality. A new *"ego"* as Dr. Dorner says — not *"Christ and I,"* with *"I"* at the center, but Christ, so to speak, by His Spirit alongside the *"I."* But a *"creation"* by the Holy Spirit of a new *"I,"* because of the old *"I"* nailed to the Cross with Christ (Gal. 2:20).

NEW CREATION WORK

This is something wholly beyond our power to grasp mentally. The *"new creation"* work must be done by the *"Creator"* as much as in the first creation in Eden. Let us not be self-deceived, and imagine that *"not I but Christ"* is but a motto, a choice, a purpose. It is that, but far, far more. The Holy Spirit will do His part if we see our need and set ourselves for His deepest work of Grace in us.

Here we need to go back to the most vital Passage on the meaning of the Cross which is to be found in the New Testament. It is part of the great doctrinal Epistle to the Romans, wherein the Apostle lays down the foundational truths for the Christian Church, upon which the whole superstructure of the Christian life alone can be built.

Passing over the first necessary unfolding of the death of the Christ as *"Propitiation for sin,"* Godward (Rom. 3:25), and then as *"Substitutionary for the sinner"* (Rom. 5:6-10), we come to the very bedrock focal point of the sinner's death in the death of his Substitute, in Romans, Chapter 6. It is the spiritual fact which lay at the base of Paul's words in Galatians 2:20. *"I have been crucified with Christ, yet I live, no longer I but Christ lives in me. . . ."*

Familiar as we are with the words, and to some extent with the truths of Romans, Chapter 6, let us take one word only in the Chapter, strip it of the context, and through this word see how deep and real the basic central fact of *"I"* crucified is meant to be.

It is the word *"dead"* in Romans 6:2. It is also rendered in one version as *"died,"* so as to bring out the tense of the Greek term which is so strongly embodied in it.

DEAD

The Greek word for *"dead"* is *"apothnesko."* The Greek Lexicon says of this word that it has a prefix *"rendering the verb more vivid and intense, and representing the action of the simple verb as consummated and finished."* It also gives as the meaning of the word, *"to die out, to expire, to become quite dead."*

The same word is used again in Romans 6:7. *"He that is 'dead'* (apothnesko) *is freed from sin,"* and Romans 6:8, *"If we be 'dead' with Christ."* Now it is obvious that if Paul used such language of the Believer's identification with Christ in His death, he meant something more than a *"likeness"* or a figure.

Let us for a moment picture the Apostle dictating these words to the Romans. We know from other parts of His Epistles, how magnificently he would break out with bursts of truth flooding his spirit and mind, as with the very light of Heaven. And it was always *"truth"* revealed by the Spirit in response to need.

Here we have Paul dictating his letter. Dealing with the question of *"grace"* overflowing beyond the deepest depth of the outbreak of sin in the human race, an objection made by Judaising disputants against his doctrine, occurs to him, with the result that there bursts out of his spirit the most wonderful unveiling of the Cross. These Jews *"argued that if the sin of man called forth so glorious an exhibition of the Grace of God,"* then the *"more men sinned, the more God was glorified."* But, says, the Apostle, *"the Cross deals not only with the sin,"* but with the *"sinner."* Then he bursts out, in vivid and intense language:

HOW SHALL WE WHO ARE DEAD TO SIN LIVE ANY LONGER THEREIN?

That is, in Christ's death we have *"died to sin,"* as an act consummated and finished, and he that is thus *"dead"* is freed from (slavery to) sin (Rom. 6:7).

Again let us note that this same word, (apothnesko), *"dead,"* is used in II Corinthians 5:14, Galatians 2:19 and 21, Colossians 2:20, as well as in Colossians 3:3, *"For you are dead . . ."* but let us be careful here.

It does not speak at all in these Passages of the experimental outworking of the Cross, but of a *"position"* — a central basic position of identification with the death of Christ — which has to be recognized and *"reckoned"* upon by the Believer before the Holy Spirit can do His part of the work.

The point I want to press is that all Paul's Epistles, with their marvelous unfolding of the Life of Christ for the Church, had at their base Paul's own personal experience of the *"I"* — the *"self"* — crucified, and that we must get to the same basic position as the Apostle himself, *"I have been crucified with Christ." "I live, yet not I . . ."* if we also are to enter into all that the *"heavenly life"* means experimentally.

THE EXPERIMENTAL OUTWORKING

Now having laid the foundation of the need of a new center, of a new creation, a new *"ego,"* so to speak, let us look at a few other Passages showing that on the basis of having *"died out"* to sin, as shown in Romans 6:2, the Apostle uses other words to describe the experimental outworking of the Cross.

In Romans 8:13, he writes, *"If you through the Spirit do mortify the deeds of the body . . .",* the margin of one translation says, *"make to die the doings of the body."* The Greek word used is *"thanatoo."*

The Greek Lexicon says of this, *"to take away the vital principle, the aspect being the lifelessness of that from which the life has been taken away."*

Here is the work of the Holy Spirit with which the Believer has to cooperate. On the faith basis of *"dead"* (Rom. 6:2), the Believer must now *"make to die"* the *"deeds"* of the body, i.e., yield to the Cross all the activity of the fallen nature, and as he does so, *"that activity will cease,"* for the *"Cross"* deals with the fallen life which energizes the *"deeds"* incited by it.

There is yet another word used by Paul in the same connection. This is *"nekroo,"* in Colossians 3:5, in reference to the members of the body. One translation says, *"mortify."* Another translation says, *"make dead."* The

Lexicon note is *"to make a dead body or a corpse,"* the aspect being toward the corpse and the deed by which it becomes such, i.e., the *"members"* of the *"body"* must be brought in all their actions into harmony with the central fact of *"death with Christ."*

The *"members"* are to be made *"dead,"* in that they are no longer to be energized by the fallen life of Adam, but brought under the power of the Cross. They are thereby made *"dead to sin"* and alive unto God for His service (Rom. 6:13).

THE PERPETUAL DEATH-LIFE

And yet there is more. These words *"apothnesko* (to die out of sin),*" "thanatoo* (to bring the deeds of the body under the power of that death),*" "nekroo* (to deprive the members of the body of the activity of the old life),*"* do not cover the whole ground. II Corinthians 4:10-11 gives another word, showing that there will be no point in our life on Earth where the need of the application of the Cross will cease.

II Corinthians 4:10 reads in one translation, *"Always bearing out in the body the dying of the Lord Jesus."* The word dying is *"nekrosis"* — a *"putting to death."*

The Lexicon says it is *"expressive of the action being incomplete and in progress."* In II Corinthians 4:11, the word *"death"* is *"thanatos."* The deep work of God at the center is but the beginning of all that has to be wrought out in us by the Holy Spirit. How clearly the Greek words used bring out the *"position"* basis of having *"died out"* in Christ's death, and the progressive *"putting to death"* perpetually which must of necessity be done day-by-day. *"In my body I bear about continually the dying of Jesus,"* writes the Apostle, but again the verbal exactitude of the Greek as shown in the use of the word *"thanatos* (death)*"* in Verse 11.

The Lexicon says that this describes the cessation of life of any kind, i.e., the *"putting to death"* of Verse 10 to which the Believer is always handed over by the Holy Spirit, is for the purpose of bringing about the cessation of the activity of the old life of nature — and this is *"not once for all, but continuously."* In other words, this is what Jesus meant when He said: *"If any man will*

come after Me, let him deny himself, and take up his cross daily, and follow Me"* (Lk. 9:23).

So it means that from center to circumference, the identification of the Believer with Christ in His death, is a necessity for the growth of the new life as it comes out from the center of our being, changed by the power of God, into full maturity.

(The above material on *"the changed center through the Cross"* is derived from the work of Jessie Penn-Lewis.)

THE SPIRIT OF TRUTH AND THE SPIRIT OF ERROR

The phrase, *"Hereby know we the spirit of Truth, and the spirit of error,"* presents the power of recognition. This power of recognition belongs to all Believers.

"The spirit of Truth" is the Holy Spirit Who teaches the truth, and *"the spirit of error"* is the spirit who comes from the Devil, teaching lies and seducing men into error. The spirit that comes from the Devil teaching heresy, Paul declares to be a demon (I Tim. 4:1) (Westcott).

So if the power of recognition is available to all Believers, why is it that some Believers forsake the *"truth,"* and embrace *"error"*?

Although many things could be said in answer to this question, with most having some validity; still, if the bottom line is to be reached, the reason that some Christians accept *"error,"* is because they have an improper view of the Cross (I Cor. 1:17-18; 2:2, 5).

The Holy Spirit through Paul said: *"For it is written, I will destroy the wisdom of the wise, and will bring to nothing the understanding of the prudent"* (I Cor. 1:19).

However, this is done only for those who have placed their Faith in the Finished Work of Christ (I Cor. 1:18).

"The wisdom of the wise" as Paul uses the phrase here, regards those who are outside of Christ. Or else they claim to be in Christ, and in fact do have wisdom, but it's not the wisdom of God, but rather of the carnal mind. Therefore, if the faith of the Believer is not properly placed in the Cross, this particular *"worldly wisdom"* will sound very attractive to the carnal ear. Hence they are enticed and drawn away. The *"spirit of error"* is anything that's outside of the Finished Work of Christ,

which refers to anything that's outside of the Word of God.

(7) "BELOVED, LET US LOVE ONE AN-OTHER: FOR LOVE IS OF GOD; AND EV-ERYONE THAT LOVETH IS BORN OF GOD, AND KNOWETH GOD."

The composite is:

1. *"Beloved"* refers to *"Divinely-loved ones,"* that is, *"beloved ones, loved by God."*

2. If we are loved by God, and we definitely are, we should as well *"love one another."*

3. The kind of love of which John speaks here, comes only from God. In other words, it is the God kind of love.

4. If one is truly Born-Again, one truly loves. Otherwise, one is not Born-Again.

LOVE ONE ANOTHER

The phrase, *"Beloved, let us love one an-other,"* presents the Apostle coming back to his theme.

Fellowship with God and His Son involves fellowship with one another; this correlative fact is noted already in I John 1:7. It com-bines us in God, in the light, the truth, the confession, etc.; it joins us to each other in love; it separates us from the world and from all heretics who talk of fellowship with God and yet are not in the truth but in the darkness, who deny Christ's Deity and His Blood, etc.

All this is now carried still farther; it is centered on love but is enriched by the weav-ing in anew of other pertinent facts that also have been treated. More glorious light is shed on the whole and on every detail. The whole pattern, woven as a unit, nears completion, grows richer and more beautiful as so much of it is unrolled.

LOVE IS OF GOD

The phrase, *"For love is of God,"* speaks of agape love, of which the world knows noth-ing and in fact, cannot have to any degree.

Actually, the phrase *"love is of God,"* should be translated *"this love is from God."* Strictly speaking, this means that love in general is from God as its one Fountain and Source.

But is the love of the world for its own from God (Jn. 15:19); or the love of publican for publican (Mat. 5:46)? Are we not told not to love the world (I Jn. 2:15)?

Only *"the love,"* the one that John urges, the one of one Christian toward another, is from God. It is the love of our fellowship with one another (I Jn. 1:7) which results from our fellowship with God and with His Son Jesus Christ.

There is no need to worry about our lov-ing also our neighbor who is not a Christian. God loves all men and yet loves His children in a special way by bestowing all manner of loving gifts on us. He loves us in a way in which He cannot love the wicked. This is also true with regard to us. John speaks of this narrow range of love because this love exhibits so clearly our fellowship with God, our origin from Him.

BORN OF GOD

The phrase, *"And everyone that loveth is born of God, and knoweth God,"* evidences our origin from God, our birth into God's family as His children (I Jn. 3:1), and proves that we are no longer *"the children of the Devil"* (I Jn. 3:10).

Our proper love for non-Christians is not considered, for our love for our fellow Christians exhibits our Spiritual Birth from God in the way that nothing else can; it does this so clearly because the world does not love us.

(8) "HE THAT LOVETH NOT KNOWETH NOT GOD; FOR GOD IS LOVE."

The exegesis is:

1. The one who is not habitually loving *"knoweth not God."*

2. God as to His nature is love.

3. The Cross of Christ is the greatest ex-hibition of that love that the world has ever known or seen.

DOESN'T KNOW GOD

The phrase, *"He that loveth not knoweth not God,"* presents itself as blunt and to the point.

"Knoweth not" actually says in the Greek *"never knew."* True knowledge of God will always be accompanied by a true love on the part of the proposed Believer. Without such an effect it is not knowledge, but a mere mental deception. Inasmuch as God is love, a man who does not love does not know God and in fact, never knew Him. Love is the

nature of God; and by virtue of the New Birth the Believer becomes a partaker of that nature, and his actions exhibit the affections of that nature. Thus, he knows God and begins to know what love is in its fullness.

By fixing his attention on the perfection of God's love as exhibited at Calvary, the Believer is saved on the one hand from mysticism and on the other hand from doubt.

But it is a knowledge of the perfection of God's love as exhibited in the Gift of Christ and in His atoning sacrifice for sins, and it is occupation with that love, which perfects love in the heart of the Believer (Williams).

GOD IS LOVE

The phrase, *"For God is love,"* should read, as stated, *"God as to His nature is love."*

In the early part of the Epistle John had defined God as Light, and the thoughts had been grouped round and in relation to that central idea. It would of course be impossible to ever exhaust all the definitions of God; but just as our nature may be roughly classified as intellectual and moral, mind and heart, thought and emotion, so, when we have thought of God as Light (embracing all such attributes as truth, knowledge, purity, health, power, and justice), we shall not have traversed and outlined all that we can know of His nature, or all that concerns us to know, until we have also thought of Him as Love, the Author and Source of all true affection, kindness, pity, friendliness, rejoicing in the creation of infinite life for the sake of its infinite happiness, and offering eternal bliss to all His human family, that He may be forever surrounded by inexhaustible illustrations of the joy and glory of perfection (Ellicott).

GOD

In the darkness of this world of sin — and all the sorrows that come now upon the race, and that will come upon the wicked hereafter — we have the assurance that a God of infinite benevolence rules over all; and though we may not be able to reconcile all that occurs with this declaration, or see how the things which He has permitted to take place are consistent with it, yet in the exercise of faith on His Own declarations we may

NOTES

find consolation in believing that it is so, and may look forward to a period when all His universe shall see it to be so.

In the midst of all that occurs on the Earth of sadness, sin, and sorrow, there are abundant evidences that God is love.

Even in this world of confusion, disorder, and darkness, we have evidence sufficient to prove that He is benevolent, but the full glory and meaning of that truth will be seen only in Heaven. Meantime let us hold onto the truth that He is love. Let us believe that He sincerely desires our good, and that what seems dark to us may be designed for our welfare; and amidst all the sorrows and disappointments of the present life, let us feel that our interests and our destiny are in the hands of the God of love.

(9) "IN THIS WAS MANIFESTED THE LOVE OF GOD TOWARD US, BECAUSE THAT GOD SENT HIS ONLY BEGOTTEN SON INTO THE WORLD, THAT WE MIGHT LIVE THROUGH HIM."

The diagram is:

1. The Love of God was manifested to the human race.

2. *"Only begotten"* in the Greek is *"monogenes,"* and means, *"single of its kind, only."*

3. Our Lord is the uniquely begotten Son of God in the sense that He proceeds by eternal generation from God the Father, possessing coeternally with God the Father and God the Spirit, the essence of Deity.

4. It is only through Christ and what He did at the Cross, that we can find life, and as well, live through Him.

THE MANIFESTED LOVE OF GOD

The phrase, *"In this was manifested the Love of God toward us,"* presents the fact that love, infinite love, as one of God's attributes, staggers us most of all. No mind and no heart can fully fathom John 3:16 or what John reveals about God's love. God's love reveals itself in wondrous acts and reaches out to its object.

It is unwarranted to state that when we speak of God's love as an energetic attribute that we reduce the force of what John says, into a mere manifestation of love. Every attribute of God, is nothing but His indivisible essence, His entire being revealed and perceived in one respect. The revelation of the supreme manifestation of God's love is for us the revelation that God is love. Without this manifestation no sinner could know God, could know that God is love.

Consequently, it is impossible for one to be truly born of God and at the same time be *"not loving,"* for the simple fact that *"God is love."* If one doesn't love, one is far from the loving God.

A PROPER DEFINITION?

That we may somewhat understand His love, we might say that God is all that He is, not for Himself, but for us. Love as well as life reveals its presence by its acts. In I John 3:1 it is the Father's gift that makes us His children. So, the Holy Spirit doesn't stop with merely stating the fact that God is love, but rather that this love was manifested toward us, and as we shall see in the next phrase, the greatest manifestation of all was God giving *"His only begotten Son,"* and in fact, giving Him up to the Cross, in order that man might be saved.

In all of our definitions of love, in all of our explanations of attempting to explain it, in our trying to define the Greek language in which these words were originally written, irrespective of all efforts, we fall woefully short of a proper summation. Again we come back to the Cross.

The greatest example of love that man has ever known, and ever will know, is what God did in order to redeem fallen, Hell-bound, lost humanity. Calvary stands as the greatest beacon, the greatest object lesson of love that man will ever know.

It is impossible to define the Love of God beyond the Cross, simply because the Cross cannot be exhausted. The Atonement covers the length, the breadth, the height, the width of all that we can know and think, and in fact, there is no end to these dimensions.

It is the Cross that melts the hard, cold, human heart. It is the Cross that portrays the fact of Who God is more so than anything else. It is the Cross that links the great divide, making it possible for a thrice-Holy God to reach sinful, wicked man, and for sinful, wicked man, to reach God. The Cross

stands at the intersection of humanity, and is not only the hope of humanity, but in fact, the only hope.

HIS ONLY BEGOTTEN SON

The phrase, *"Because that God sent His only Begotten Son into the world,"* portrays, as stated, the most graphic manifestation of all as it regards the Love of God.

In the Greek Text, the object *"His Son"* is placed emphatically forward; the verb and the subject are reversed, and thus the subject is emphasized: His Son He has sent, God has sent. In the Greek Text *"Only Begotten"* contains the definite article, in which it actually reads *"the Only Begotten."*

On *"His Son,"* John alone calls Him *"The Only-Begotten."* Both *"His Son"* and *"The Only-Begotten"* avow the Deity of the Saviour. He was *"The Logos," "The Son," "The Only-Begotten"* in eternity before His Incarnation, and is that still in His Incarnation.

The idea of all of this is actually beyond our comprehension. God's love required Him to send His Son. And as an addendum, God's love in us requires deeds by which we show our love for one another.

SENT

"Sent" in the Greek is *"apostello,"* and means *"to send on a commission as an envoy, with credentials* (the miracles), *to perform certain duties."* Here it refers to dying for sinners, providing a Salvation to be offered on the basis of justice satisfied to the one who places his Faith in Him as Saviour.

The place that God's Son was sent is *"the world,"* which speaks of that which is the opposite of Heaven. Satan is the god of this present world, the prince of the powers of the air. While the Earth per se belongs to the Lord, its system belongs to Satan. In fact, almost the entirety of mankind follows their god, Satan. Consequently, they are in a cauldron of stealing, killing, and destroying (Jn. 10:10).

But into this cesspool, for that's what it is, God sent His Only Begotten Son. He didn't send an Angel, but His Son.

As well, He was sent for a purpose, and that purpose was to *"destroy the works of the Devil,"* which He did at the Cross, which if believed by fallen man, will set the captive free.

TO LIVE THROUGH HIM

The phrase, *"That we might live through Him,"* refers not only to God's initial plan of the believing sinner coming to Christ and being saved, but as well, our daily, ongoing life and living, as long as we are in this world. One might even say that the purpose of this sending and commission is *"that we may live through Him."* This indicates mediation. He is the Personal Mediator, and the execution of His commission makes Him the channel for bestowing spiritual, eternal life upon us. He is the fount of life for us.

The mission of the Son, the Only-Begotten, includes His entire office, the part which He executed while He was here on Earth plus the part that He is still executing as our Advocate (I Jn. 2:1), our eternal High Priest, and our King.

To send the Son, the Only-Begotten on this mission and for this purpose is, indeed, the supreme manifestation of God's love (Lenski).

What did John mean by the phrase, *"Live through Him"*?

The Sixth Chapter of Romans gives us this information. Whenever the believing sinner is initially saved, Salvation comes by believing in Jesus and what He did at the Cross. But in the Mind of God, something else happens which is much more detailed.

In the Mind of God, the believing sinner is literally baptized into the death of Christ. He is buried with Christ and raised with Him in newness of life (Rom. 6:3-5).

Jesus did all of this as our Substitute, and our Faith in Him, gives us all the benefits for which He died.

The truth is, we had to die in Him, for the simple reason that what we were before Salvation was totally depraved and could not be salvaged. So in the Mind of God the *"old man"* died with and in Christ, and was raised a *"new man."* What we once were we no longer are. We are now a new creation in Christ Jesus, with old things having passed away, and all things having become new (II Cor. 5:17).

As a Believer ever after, we are to understand that all that we are in Christ, is because of what happened to us when we were

NOTES

initially saved, *"baptized into His death."* And please understand that the word *"baptize"* as Paul uses it here in Romans 6:3, has nothing to do with Water Baptism, but rather speaks of the death of Christ on the Cross.

Understanding what happened to us at our initial Salvation experience, we are from henceforth to *"reckon ourselves to be dead indeed unto sin, but alive unto God through Jesus Christ our Lord"* (Rom. 6:11).

This means that we are to place our Faith exclusively in the Cross, understanding that what Jesus did there affords us all things, whether Salvation or victorious, Christian living. Continuing to express Faith in the Cross, which is to never end, actually constitutes *"walking after the Spirit"* (Rom. 8:1). Continued Faith in the Cross guarantees the continued help of the Holy Spirit, and in that case, *"sin shall not have dominion over you"* (Rom. 6:14).

This is how we *"live through Him,"* and the only way we can *"live through Him."* That's why Paul said:

"I am crucified with Christ: nevertheless I live; yet not I, but Christ liveth in me: and the life which I now live in the flesh I live by the faith of the Son of God, Who loved me, and gave Himself for me" (Gal. 2:20).

If we try to live for God any other way than by the way of the Cross, we will be *"walking after the flesh,"* and *"they that are in the flesh cannot please God"* (Rom. 8:1, 8).

THE PATHWAY OF THE CROSS

Inasmuch as this is so very, very important, and I continue to speak of *"living through Him,"* which in effect, refers to living through what He did for us at the Cross, let us examine this even further.

Let's look at the outworking of the Cross subjectively as a law of life which comes out of His death, and in a sense, out of our death as well, as it regards fruit-bearing. We must be brought into a real fellowship with Christ, which we are as we were *"baptized into His death."*

There is an experimental knowledge of the Cross. The Spirit of God applies the death of Christ to us, and then the life-power of the Resurrection follows (Rom. 6:5). But we must ever remember that we cannot have *"the likeness of His Resurrection,"* and we speak of resurrection life, unless we first understand that *"we have been planted together in the likeness of His death."*

The Holy Spirit begins at the center of our being, and works out to the circumference so to speak. In the pathway of fellowship with His death we learn first, the liberation of the spirit (and I speak of our human spirit), and then find out how it works out to the realm of the soul, and then to the body.

But we must point out that although this may be the sequence of God's working, He does not always work in this order. The Lord working in us is limited to that which we understand, which sometimes is very little. Sometimes Believers begin at one of the later stages, and then have to be taken back to learn the first elements of truth. Much depends upon their environment, and the knowledge of those on whom they depend at the beginning of their Christian life. Moreover, with some the Lord cannot work very quickly. He fits His dealings to the limitation of the soul, and has all kinds of methods, and ways of working (I Cor. 12:6).

THE CORN OF WHEAT

Now turn to John 12:24, where we read: *"Except a corn of wheat fall into the ground and die, it abideth alone: but if it die, it bringeth forth much fruit."* Then the Lord applied the meaning of this saying of His to the individual Disciple, and set forth at the same time, a law in the spiritual realm analogous to the law of nature.

He said, *"He that loveth his life shall lose it: and he that hateth his life in this world shall keep it unto life eternal. If any man serve Me, let him follow Me"* (Jn. 12:25-26).

This is clearly *not* the same aspect of the Cross as *"death to sin."* This is a gradual experience, and there is no gradual deliverance from sin, no gradual process of death to sin or deliverance from the world, or the flesh. The Spirit of God regarding sin does not say *"a little bit today,"* and *"a little bit tomorrow,"* but to all sin and all workings of the flesh, as soon as you become aware of either, it is to be put away from us!

Romans, Chapter 6, therefore, bids you *"reckon"* yourself *"dead"* to sin, but John

12:24 speaks of a gradual and progressive law of death in respect to fruitfulness. It speaks, not of parting with that which is wrong, but that which is lawful — that which we have by nature — life. It is this *"life"* which the Lord calls those who follow Him to lay down for His sake, and in fulfillment of the law of death for fruitfulness, i.e., the *"life"* we have by nature has to go into *"death,"* to enable the *"life"* of God in us to bring forth fruit.

LIFE

In Verse 25 this is clearly seen in the Greek original, for the two words rendered into English, *"life,"* are not the same in the Greek. One Greek word means the lower form of life, the life of nature — that which we share in common with the animals. The other is the eternal life — the life we have from God in the new birth wherein we are made partakers of the Divine nature. The Passage could be read thusly:

"He who loves his (natural) *life shall lose it* (the fruit of it in eternity), *and he who hates his* (natural) *life in the world shall keep it* (save it from eternal loss) *unto life* (eternal life)."

The Lord's children are, to a great extent, mostly concerned with the question of victory over sin, and it is necessary that we should be, but when we know the way of victory over sin, we forget that there is another and deeper phase of the Cross beyond that period. It is then a question — not of sin, but of the *"life"* by which we live and act. As someone has said, the life of nature has no *"carrying"* power in the spiritual sphere. It has no power of fruitfulness in the spiritual realm. That is why some Believers toil so much, and get so little fruit. They know victory over sin, but the life of nature is their animating power and service, and in the ordinary use of their faculties, the intellect is animated by this particular type of life, as well as the affections and the emotions! It need not be anything sinful in the use of the intellect, or affections, but the very virtues of these things, are from the life of nature, and not from the life of God within them.

The life of nature as the animating power in the Believer, instead of the life of God, means powerlessness in the spiritual conflict, for a spiritual foe cannot be fought by the *"natural man,"* with natural weapons. Therefore, insofar as we walk in the life of nature, in other words do so naturally, to that extent we are powerless in the warfare with the powers of darkness. They are supernatural, and can only be met by spiritual power, i.e., *"the Holy Spirit."*

THE OLD LIFE AND RESURRECTION LIFE

The old life of the Believer and dependence on that life, which refers to *"self,"* must be completely eradicated in the Believer. That way is dependence on self, which Paul likened to *"walking after the flesh"* (Rom. 8:1). That's what Jesus was talking about as well, when He said: *"Except a corn of wheat fall into the ground and die, it abideth alone: but if it die, it bringeth forth much fruit."* The old self, the old way of doing things, the dependence on self, all of that must die before we can bring forth fruit.

Resurrection life, that which we derive solely from Christ, which is another kind of life altogether, can come about only through the Cross. In fact, this is the idea of the Cross. As we've already stated, in the Mind of God, when the believing sinner trusts Christ, which means to be *"baptized into His death,"* the old life is laid aside, and the new life is gained. The new life comes exclusively from Christ, but more particularly, by and through what Christ did at the Cross. That and that alone is *"resurrection life,"* but we must never forget that it comes about through the Cross. Let us say again what Paul said:

"For if we have been planted together in the likeness of His death, we shall be also in the likeness of His resurrection" (Rom. 6:5).

Every Christian wants *"resurrection life,"* and rightly so! However, this *"resurrection life"* depends solely on our understanding that we have been *"planted together in the likeness of His death."* In other words, the death of the Cross produces this life.

Our understanding of that, our Faith in that, and our faith on a continuing basis, is what Paul was referring to when he spoke of *"walking after the Spirit."* The Holy Spirit will always lead one to dependence on the new life that is in Christ, and not at all in the old life that came from our old way before Christ. But let the Believer understand that

it's not possible to function in this new life, without understanding the Cross, and that this new life comes by the means of the Cross. In that way alone we can *"live through Him."*

(10) "HEREIN IS LOVE, NOT THAT WE LOVED GOD, BUT THAT HE LOVED US, AND SENT HIS SON TO BE THE PROPITIATION FOR OUR SINS."

The structure is:

1. *"Herein is love"* actually says in the Greek *"herein is the love."* It is the particular love that inheres in God's nature, Divine love.

2. The unconverted human race does not love God; nevertheless, He loved the human race.

3. The English word *"propitiate"* means *"to appease and render favorable."*

LOVE

The phrase, *"Herein is love,"* pertains to the true love that alone deserves the name *"love."* This love has its origin wholly in God Who, in fact, is love itself, which is not in any way in us who had nothing but our sins, the opposite of love for God.

The difference in understanding between John and the false teachers is never greater than in their understanding of love. The false teachers claim to love God but understood love not in Christian terms but in those of Greek philosophy.

Love in the Hellenistic world became a cosmic principle, and the mystical craving for union with the Eternal is given a metaphysical basis (metaphysics referring to a system of principles underlying a particular study or subject). In religious terms, love from that source is perceived as *"essentially the love of man for God — that is to say, the insatiable craving of limited, conditional, and temporal beings for the Infinite, the Absolute, the Eternal."* Two things derive from this understanding of love.

First, love for God as it was expressed by the false teachers becomes primarily an exercise in self-gratification. As such, it expresses the vanity of those teachers.

Second, one can never attribute love to God and say, for example, that God loves us. God as the Absolute is always passionless and unmoved. In other words, God doesn't love us more at certain times than others.

HE LOVED US

The phrase, *"Not that we loved God, but that He loved us,"* refers to the fact that the human race has not loved God with the present result that it does not possess any love for Him.

What love is this, that, distasteful, uncongenial, unloving, unlovely as we must have been in His sight, He did this great thing for us!

PROPITIATION

The phrase, *"And sent His Son to be the propitiation for our sins,"* comes out to a new meaning as John uses the word, than it did in paganistic thinking.

The pagan worshipper brought gifts to his god to appease the god's wrath and make him favorable in his attitude towards him. But the God of Christianity needs no gifts to appease His wrath and make Him favorable towards the human race.

Divine love springs spontaneously from His heart. His wrath against sin cannot be placated by good works. Only the infliction of the penalty of sin, which is death, will satisfy the just demands of His Holy Law which the human race violated, maintain its government, and provide the proper basis for His bestowal of mercy, namely, Divine justice satisfied.

This is the propitiation, that sacrifice which fully satisfies the demands of the broken Law. It was our Lord's death on Calvary's Cross. Thus does this pagan word accrue to itself a new meaning as it enters the doctrinal atmosphere of the New Testament (Wuest).

(11) "BELOVED, IF GOD SO LOVED US, WE OUGHT ALSO TO LOVE ONE AN-OTHER."

The composition is:

1. *"If God so loved us,"* harks back to God giving His Son.

2. If God did this great thing for us, surely we can *"love one another."*

3. The love of God is portrayed more so in the Cross than anything else, and for us to understand His love, we have to first understand the Cross.

GOD SO LOVED US

The phrase, *"Beloved, if God so loved us,"* places the emphasis on the sending of His Son, the Only-Begotten, that we may live through Him. His Son and our Saviour shed His Blood

in expiation (to pay the price) for our sin so that, cleansed from them, we live indeed.

This statement as given by John is aimed at Cerinthus, at his following, and at all who are of a similar mind. To them Jesus was the son of Joseph; the Spirit, Who was bestowed on Jesus at His Baptism, they say, left Him before His passion and His death. The Deity of Jesus, the expiating efficacy of His Blood were thereby denied.

We see why John emphasizes in this way: *"In 'this' was manifested the love of God — in 'this' is the love, etc. — if 'thus' God did love,"* etc. Everything centers up on what Jesus did for us at the Cross. If this be in any way denied, the efficacy (effectiveness) of His Blood is thereby denied.

It doesn't really matter to Satan in what manner the Blood is denied, or what type of spin is put upon the erroneous proposal. If in any way, the effectiveness of the Cross is denied, which in effect portrays the pouring out of the Life Blood of the Saviour, Salvation is forfeited. The only way that one can be saved, is by trusting in what Christ did at the Cross (Jn. 3:16; Eph. 2:13-18).

Regrettably, the *"Word of Faith"* doctrine falls into this category. It denies the Blood Atonement of Christ, rather substituting, as we have previously stated, a fictitious concoction of Jesus purchasing man's redemption in Hell of all places.

Unfortunately, most of the followers of this doctrine are little interested in the Sacrifice of Christ, but rather in money, etc. So it seems they pay little attention to the erroneous, blasphemous statements made about the Cross, rather focusing their attention on the means by which they hope to get rich.

I realize what I'm saying is blunt, but I do not know of any other way to couch my terminology. Understanding the seriousness of all of this, one can at the same time understand the reason that Paul said:

"But though we, or an Angel from Heaven, preach any other gospel unto you than that which we have preached unto you, let him be accursed" (Gal. 1:8).

LOVE ONE ANOTHER

The phrase, *"We ought also to love one another,"* speaks of a moral obligation.

John claims our love to God through the evidence of this love, and this evidence is the fact that we who are in the family of God as *"the Children of God"* (I Jn. 3:1) love one another. John leads us step by step, from fact to fact, until he brings us to the top. Many leap over these intervening steps and shout, *"We love God!"* They need to understand where alone this love is born, not what alone is the evidence of this love, namely that we who have Spiritual Life through the Son's expiation love one another, love those born from God to this life, His children indeed. It is thus that John begins with the admonition which he has voiced already in Verse 7: *"We, too, ought to be loving one another."*

As God has bestowed His affection so gratuitously on us, and we benefit by it in such an inconceivable degree, and in essence can bestow upon Him no return, we can only address the debt, even though it could never be paid, by bestowing our poor equivalent on our fellow men. Although our happiness depends strictly on God, still He has allowed us to be stewards for Him in some small degree for the happiness of those about us (Ellicott).

(12) "NO MAN HAS SEEN GOD AT ANY TIME. IF WE LOVE ONE ANOTHER, GOD DWELLETH IN US, AND HIS LOVE IS PERFECTED IN US."

The exegesis is:

1. The idea is, Deity in all its essence, no one has ever yet seen.

2. Consequently, no one has the capacity of totally beholding Him.

3. If Saints have this agape love habitually for one another, that shows that this love which God is in His nature, has accomplished its purpose in our lives.

4. The words *"His love"* do not refer to our love for Him, or to His love for us, but to the love which is peculiarly His Own, which answers to His nature.

5. His love being perfected in us makes us loving and self-sacrificial in our characters (Wuest).

HAS SEEN GOD?

The phrase, *"No man has seen God at any time,"* refers to all of His character, all of His essence, and all of His nature. One might say, *"Deity in all of its essence no one has*

ever yet seen." Wuest says that the expanded translation reads, *"Deity in its essence no one has ever yet beheld, with the present result that no one has the capacity of beholding Him."*

As far as actually seeing God, many men have seen Him with the eyes (Gen. 18:2, 33; 32:24-30; Ex. 24:10; 33:11; Josh. 5:13; Isa., Chpt. 6; Ezek. 1:26-28; Dan. 7:9-14; 10:5-6; Acts 7:56-59; Rev. 4:2-5; 5:1-7).

One might say that John is saying, *"The Only Begotten Son Alone has fully comprehended and experienced God in all His fullness. No man ever has or ever will."*

LOVE AND THE PRESENCE OF GOD

The phrase, *"If we love one another, God dwelleth in us,"* presents the Apostle going back to the greatest attribute of God that a Believer can have, which is Love.

After saying that no man has seen God at any time, instead of then saying, *"God the only Son, Who is at the Father's side, has made Him known"* (Jn. 1:18), he turns rather to love: *"If we love each other,"* we know that God is present with us. As God was and is present in His Son, so now He is present in Believers. Stott warns against weakening this assertion: *"We must not,"* he says, *"stagger at the majesty of this conclusion. God's love which originates in Himself and was manifested in His Son is perfected in His people."* Westcott says, *"It is through man that the 'love of God' finds its fulfillment on earth."*

Though we cannot see Him, yet there is a way by which we may be assured that He is near us, and that He even dwells in us. That way is by the exercise of love.

John mentions all of this as an admission of the limits of human nature and the condition of faith, but only in order to state the richness of the substitute, which is the Presence of God within the soul, verified and substantiated by the historical Person of Christ.

PERFECTED IN US

The phrase, *"And His love is perfected in us,"* doesn't mean that the love of God needs perfecting. God's love is ever Perfect, which means that it is never subject to perfecting.

The idea is His love aims at reaching a certain goal in us, which means that we are to keep loving one another. Our loving one another is the evidence that God's goal has been attained in us. This is evidence that we can see; the stronger our love, the clearer and the stronger is the evidence.

(13) "HEREBY KNOW WE THAT WE DWELL IN HIM, AND HE IN US, BECAUSE HE HAS GIVEN US OF HIS SPIRIT."

The diagram is:

1. God dwells in us and we dwell in Him.

2. *"Dwells"* speaks of fellowship between two or more individuals. In this case, God and ourselves.

3. The Spirit has been caused to take up His permanent resident in us.

THE DIVINE ENTRANCE

The phrase, *"Hereby know we that we dwell in Him, and He in us,"* presents reciprocal abiding, which is the final expression of fellowship with God.

Our love for one another is evidence that God is remaining in us, that His love for us has not been in vain but has been brought to this goal, namely God's union with us. Valuable as this evidence is, it must be taken together with what underlies it, namely God's gift of the Holy Spirit to us. It is the Spirit Who produces the love of one to another in our hearts. All holy impulses and actions are His work, and so also is brotherly love with all its deeds of love.

Were it not for the Holy Spirit, we could never realize that we remain in God and He in us, for who would dare say that his love for God has been perfected? Even if a hybrid degree of love gives one this knowledge, are we ready to claim such a degree of love? No we aren't.

If this is the basis for our really knowing that we are united with God, we should have a slender basis, indeed, and should wrestle with constant doubt. That's why God's gift of His Spirit to us is here introduced.

THE HOLY SPIRIT

The phrase, *"Because He has given us of His Spirit,"* refers to the greatest gift of all to the Saint.

"Love" is an attribute of God; however, the Holy Spirit is God, and is the One Who perfects God's love within us.

As well, the statement as given here in Verse 13, doesn't mean that God has given the Saint only part of the Holy Spirit, for such isn't possible. The Holy Spirit is a Person, and a Person cannot be divided and parceled out in parts. Each Saint receives the Holy Spirit Himself in His entirety.

Now even though every Saint has the Holy Spirit in His entirety, this doesn't mean that the Spirit will function in such a life according to all His graces. It takes cooperation from the Saint for that to happen.

Even though John here doesn't go into any detail, concerning the Holy Spirit there are two things which must be said:

THE BAPTISM WITH THE HOLY SPIRIT

Even though all of the Holy Spirit comes into the heart and life of the believing sinner at conversion, which is true of all who are Born-Again, it remains then for the Believer to be baptized with the Spirit, which is always accompanied by the speaking with other tongues as the Spirit of God gives the utterance (Acts 2:4). In fact, it's not possible for the Believer to be *"baptized with the Spirit,"* until first the Believer has been *"born of the Spirit."* The work of Regeneration must take place first, which refers to the Saint being washed, sanctified, and justified (I Cor. 6:11), which to be sure is also a work of the Spirit, before the Saint can then be Baptized with the Spirit. Jesus said: *"Even the Spirit of truth; Whom the world cannot receive"* (Jn. 14:17).

The Baptism with the Spirit opens up the Saint to the *"power of God,"* in a way heretofore unknown (Acts 1:8). To be sure, this Spirit Baptism, which Jesus commanded all Saints to receive (Acts 1:4), affects the Child of God in every other way as well.

Many claim that the Believer receives everything at conversion. In other words, they claim there is no separate experience of the Baptism with the Holy Spirit; however, the Bible doesn't teach that. It teaches the Baptism with the Holy Spirit as a separate work, apart from Salvation, which in fact, follows Salvation. As stated, Jesus commanded all Believers to receive this experience.

In Acts, Chapter 8 we are told of the great Revival preached by Philip in Samaria. Many came to Christ, but none were Baptized with the Holy Spirit. The Scripture says concerning this:

"Now when the Apostles which were at Jerusalem heard that Samaria had received the Word of God, they sent unto them Peter and John:

"Who, when they were come down, prayed for them, that they might receive the Holy Spirit:

"For as yet He was fallen upon none of them: only they were baptized in the Name of the Lord Jesus."

The Scripture then says: *"Then laid their hands on them, and they received the Holy Spirit"* (Acts 8:14-17).

Now if all Believers receive everything at conversion, why did Peter and John go to Samaria and pray for these individuals to be baptized with the Holy Spirit?

As well, Acts, Chapter 9 gives us the account of the great conversion of Paul on the road to Damascus; however, some three days later, at the command of the Lord, a Believer by the name of Ananias went to where Paul was staying in Damascus, and said to him: *"Brother Saul, the Lord, even Jesus, Who appeared unto you in the way as ye came, has sent me, that you might receive your sight, and be filled with the Holy Spirit"* (Acts 9:17).

If we get it all at conversion, in other words, if there is no second experience of the Baptism with the Spirit, what was Ananias doing praying for Paul to be filled with the Spirit some three days after his conversion?

In Acts, Chapter 19, we are given the experience of the Ephesian Believers.

The Scripture says: *"Paul having passed through the upper coasts came to Ephesus: and finding certain disciples,*

"He said unto them, have you received the Holy Spirit since you believed?"

First of all, to try to explain this away as individuals who had never been saved is wrong. Every time the word *"Disciples"* is used in the Book of Acts, it always and without exception, speaks of those who were followers of Christ.

The truth is, these men had accepted Christ as their Saviour, but they *"had not so much as heard whether there be any Holy Spirit."*

The Scripture says, *"When Paul had laid his hands upon them, the Holy Spirit came on them; and they spoke with tongues and prophesied"* (Acts 19:1-7).

So I think these examples prove beyond the shadow of a doubt, that the Baptism with the Spirit is not received at conversion. It is a second experience, a Work of Grace, that is received after Salvation.

Actually, when John spoke of God the Father giving us of His Spirit, he wasn't speaking of the Baptism with the Spirit, but rather the entrance of the Spirit at Regeneration. But we should ever understand, that the entrance of the Spirit now makes it possible for the Baptism with the Spirit. In fact, it is an insult to Christ for the Believer not to ask for and receive the Holy Spirit Baptism. John the Baptist said of Jesus: *"He shall baptize you with the Holy Spirit, and with fire"* (Mat. 3:11). The Baptist was speaking that day of the Holy Spirit Baptism, the Second Work of Grace.

As well, we teach that every recipient of the Spirit Baptism will speak with other tongues at the time of reception, which in fact, is the initial physical evidence that one has been filled (Acts 2:4; 10:45-46; 19:1-7). In fact, speaking with other tongues after one has been baptized with the Spirit will become a part of one's worship and prayer.

Gifts of the Spirit are then made available to Spirit baptized Believers (I Cor. 12:1, 8-10). Without the Spirit Baptism, I do not personally think the Gifts of the Spirit are possible. In fact, I have never heard of anyone having these Gifts who wasn't baptized with the Holy Spirit.

(For a complete description of the Gifts, please see our Commentary on I Corinthians.)

THE SANCTIFYING POWER OF THE SPIRIT

As we've said elsewhere in this Volume, someone has well said that Romans, Chapter 6 presents the *"mechanics of the Spirit,"* which in effect, tells us *"how"* the Spirit works within our lives. They have also said that Romans, Chapter 8, gives us the *"dynamics of the Spirit,"* which tells us *"what"* the Spirit does, after we learn from Romans, Chapter 6 *"how"* He does it.

We learn from Romans, Chapter 6 that the Cross of Christ is the foundation of our Faith. In other words, everything that we receive from the Lord comes to us exclusively by and through what Jesus did at the Cross.

In fact, the Believer is so closely connected to the Crucifixion of Christ that the Spirit through Paul says that when we were initially saved, we were actually *"baptized into His death,"* speaking of the death of Christ. Of course we were not literally there when all of this happened; however, in the Mind of God, when we evidenced Faith in Christ at our initial Salvation experience, this is what happened. Jesus was our Substitute, and Faith in Him, grants us all that He did. In fact, He did it all for us, and not at all for Himself (Rom. 6:3-5).

Understanding the initial process, which is given to us in Romans 6:3-5, we are to then understand that our Faith must ever remain in the Cross of Christ, which is the means by which God gives us all things. Everything is tied to the Sacrifice of Christ.

Understanding this, we now go to Romans, Chapter 8, where Paul speaks of *"walking after the Spirit."* In fact, *"walking after the Spirit"* is not actually doing spiritual things as most believe, but rather evidencing constant Faith in the Cross of Christ. We learn this from Romans 8:2.

Paul said, *"For the Law of the Spirit of Life in Christ Jesus has made me free from the law of sin and death."*

Without a doubt, this is one of the single most important Scriptures in the entirety of the Bible. We are told here how the Spirit works, and what He does.

The *"Law"* by which He works within our lives, pertains strictly to Christ and what He did at the Cross, summed up in the phrase *"in Christ Jesus."* Every time Paul uses this phrase, which he does often, without exception, he's always speaking of what Christ did at the Cross on our behalf.

Samuel Brengle, a gifted leader in the Salvation Army, wrote in 1918 of spiritual authority. He said:

"It is not won by promotion, but by many prayers and tears. It is attained by confession of sin, and much heart searching and humbling before God; by self-surrender, a

courageous sacrifice of every idol, a bold, uncomplaining 'embrace of the Cross,' and by an 'eternal, unfaltering looking unto Jesus crucified.' It is not gained by seeking great things for ourselves, but like Paul, by counting those things that are gain to us as loss for Christ. This is a great price, but it must be paid by the leader who would not be merely a nominal but a real spiritual leader of men, a leader whose power is recognized and felt in Heaven, on Earth, and in Hell."

When the Believer places his Faith in the Cross of Christ exclusively, he can then expect the help of the Spirit, Who will do great and mighty things in one's heart and life. It is all through and by what Jesus did at the Cross, hence Paul saying, *"But God forbid that I should glory* (boast), *save in the Cross of our Lord Jesus Christ, by Whom the world is crucified unto me, and I unto the world"* (Gal. 6:14).

(14) "AND WE HAVE SEEN AND DO TESTIFY THAT THE FATHER SENT THE SON TO BE THE SAVIOUR OF THE WORLD."

The composite is:

1. John was an eyewitness of Jesus Christ, both as to Who He was, and as well, as to What He was.

2. He can testify as an eyewitness to the fact of the purpose of the Son of God.

3. His mission was to redeem lost humanity, which He did at the Cross.

WE HAVE SEEN

The phrase, *"And we have seen,"* considering John's advanced age when he wrote this Epistle, probably tells us that he was the only one left alive in the world who had actually seen Christ, had touched Him, and had been with Him for a protracted period of time. In fact, tradition says that in the last months of John's life he said repeatedly, *"When I'm gone, there will be no one left who saw Him, who touched Him, and who actually heard Him."*

As John pens these words in his First Epistle, his hair is now gray, his skin is wrinkled from age, but his mind is sharp, as he remembers those glorious days. He with a few other men had been privileged to walk by His side for nearly three and one half years. During this time there is no record that they ever doubted

Who He was. That He was the Son of God, the Messiah of Israel, of that there was no doubt; however, at the beginning they did not fully understand the purpose of His mission. It was hard for them to understand that He was both the suffering Servant and the exalted King. As all of Israel, they wanted a conquering David. To be sure, this is what they would get, but not in the way they had thought.

They wanted Jesus to conquer Rome and make Israel once again the leading nation in the world. But Jesus came to conquer sin, which was the greatest enemy of all. John now knows that beyond the shadow of a doubt.

There seems to be many in John's day who came up with fanciful notions about Christ. But only John could say, *"I have seen!"*

And yet, as the Holy Spirit had the Apostle to use the pronoun *"we,"* it certainly referred to the Apostles, all who were now dead with the exception of John, but it ought not to be limited merely to them.

Every individual who is truly saved has the Spirit of God working in them Who permits us to *"see"* in the historic event of Jesus' death God's act for our Salvation. And even though we have never personally seen God or seen Christ, we do *"see"* by faith that the Cross lifted up in Israel was for our sins and for our Salvation. We do *"see"* in Jesus our own Saviour and Lord. We do *"see"* in the fellowship of faith the presence of His love. And because His Spirit in us gives us this *"seeing"* experience, we are commissioned to bear witness to the event.

WE DO TESTIFY

The phrase, *"And do testify,"* proclaims the fact that we must tell what we have seen. Jesus said:

"When the Counselor comes, Whom I will send to you from the Father, the Spirit of Truth Who goes out from the Father, He will testify about Me; but you also must testify, for you have been with Me from the beginning" (Jn. 15:26-27).

Therefore, since there is such a close connection between *"seeing"* and *"testifying"* and the Gift of the Holy Spirit, it is likely that John meant his words to include his Readers and as well, to be applied to all Christians now as well as in the past.

NOTES

To what are we to testify?

In fact, we are as Believers, as those who have been changed by the miracle working power of God, to testify to the entirety of the Person and Ministry of Christ; however, the emphasis must ever be on His Sacrificial, Atoning Death. If we are to truly live and preach the Gospel, we must live and preach the Cross (I Cor. 1:17-18, 21, 23). If the Cross ever ceases to be the emphasis of our life and Message, we have then stopped living and preaching the Gospel, and have in essence, *"made the Cross of Christ of none effect"* (I Cor. 1:17). And that is the sin of the modern Church.

The emphasis is not on the Cross but rather on other things. And to be sure, Satan little cares what those other things are, just as long as it's not the Cross.

Satan was not defeated in the healings and miracles of Christ, as wonderful and glorious as they were. He wasn't defeated by the greatest Message the world has ever known which fell from the lips of the Master, as great as that was. As necessary as was the Virgin Birth, that did not defeat the Evil One. Neither did His Perfect, spotless Life, even though all of these things certainly played an extremely important part. Satan wasn't even defeated by the Resurrection of Christ, even though that put the icing on the cake so to speak.

To the contrary, Satan was totally and completely defeated by what Jesus did on the Cross in the giving of Himself in the pouring out of His Life's Blood, which satisfied the justice of a thrice-Holy God, and thereby, atoned for all sin (Eph. 2:11-18).

We must ever understand that the death of Christ on the Cross did not merely represent a doctrine. In fact, it is and must be, the foundation of all Doctrine. And any doctrine which doesn't have the Cross as its foundation is not Biblical.

THE SAVIOUR OF THE WORLD

The phrase, *"That the Father sent the Son to be the Saviour of the world,"* presents an outsized statement. The Holy Spirit through John over and over again, links the great Sacrifice of Christ to the entirety of the world, which includes all time as well. It was John the Beloved who wrote, *"For God so loved the world, that He gave His only Begotten Son . . ."* (Jn. 3:16).

And then he said: *"And He is the propitiation* (the One Who satisfied) *for our sins: and not for ours only, but also for the sins of the whole world"* (I Jn. 2:2).

In all of this, John puts the entirety of the world on notice, that in the eyes of God there are only two types of people in this world, *"the saved and the unsaved,"* i.e., *"those who have accepted Christ and those who have rejected Christ."* This lays waste every religion in the world, every philosophy, etc. All is Christ, and more particularly, *"Christ and Him Crucified."* There is only One *"Saviour of the world,"* and that is the Lord Jesus Christ.

The expression, *"the Saviour of the world"* has a reference to the fact that the Roman Emperor was also called *"the Saviour of the world."*

No doubt, the Samaritan men also had the above in mind when they said to the woman, *"We have heard Him ourselves, and know that this is the Christ, the Saviour of the world"* (Jn. 4:42).

Emperor worship was the state religion of the Roman Empire, and the binding factor that united its far-flung, subject-peoples together in a union stronger than that of any military force. Consequently, to recognize our Lord as the Saviour of the world instead of the Emperor was a capital offense, for such recognition was a blow to the very vitals of the Empire. In fact, that was the quarrel which Rome had against Christianity, and that was the reason for the bloody persecutions (Wuest).

(15) "WHOSOEVER SHALL CONFESS THAT JESUS IS THE SON OF GOD, GOD DWELLETH IN HIM, AND HE IN GOD."

The composite is:

1. The confession of which John speaks here, is a lifetime confession, and represents the sustained attitude of the heart.

2. The confession is that Jesus is the Saviour of the world, is my own personal Saviour, and is the Son of God, thus, God the Son, thus very God of very God.

3. This confession proclaims the union of Christ and the Believer already accomplished.

CONFESSION

The phrase, *"Whosoever shall confess that Jesus is the Son of God,"* proclaims the fact that such is open evidence for the invisible inward union with God. Its substance is *"Jesus Christ having come in the flesh"* (I Jn. 4:2), and this is proof that one is *"from God," "born from Him"* (I Jn. 2:29), or in other words, *"that Jesus is the Son of God."* It is not only an admission as to Who He is, but as well that He is that to my personal heart and life.

In this confession of faith, for that's what it is, we have not only the fact of Who Christ is, but in the Name Jesus, what He did, which refers to the Cross. Jesus is the Son of God, and this Son of God is the Saviour of the world.

During the time of the Early Church, there were many false teachers who denied the reality of the Incarnation. As a result, great stress was laid upon this great Truth, and understandably so.

In those days, if one accepted the Incarnation, in other words, God becoming Man, and the physical death of Christ to atone for sins, plus His bodily Resurrection, more than likely that person would accept the Lord as his Saviour. In modern times, that is not necessarily true. Millions presently confess that Jesus is the Son of God, but that doesn't mean that they are saved, even though many of them may think they are. They have given a mental assertion of this fact, but they have never really accepted Christ in their hearts.

When one truly accepts the Lord, there will be a change in that person that will be evident to all. In other words, it will be obvious that that person has been born again. This means that merely confessing that Jesus is the Son of God, even though that is necessary, is not enough to be saved. One must surrender one's life completely to Christ, understanding that He Alone is the Saviour. In such a surrender, one is Born-Again, and alone with such a surrender (Rom. 10:9-10; 12:1-2; II Cor. 7:10; I Jn. 1:7-9).

UNION WITH GOD

The phrase, *"God dwelleth in him, and he in God,"* proclaims the union of Divine fellowship in which the Father is in Believers and Believers are in the Father.

Initially John connected the fellowship

NOTES

with obedience to the command to love one another (I Jn. 3:24). Then he showed its dependence on the gift of the Holy Spirit, which definitely comes to all Believers at conversion (I Jn. 4:13). Here he shows that the fellowship is built on Jesus, Who must be acknowledged as being One with the Father (I Jn. 2:23), as the One Who came in the flesh (I Jn. 4:2), and as the Son of God Who was sent to be the Saviour of the world (I Jn. 4:14-15), which He accomplished by going to the Cross.

John speaks of God dwelling in the Believer, while Paul speaks of Christ dwelling in the Believer (Gal. 2:20).

However, the actual representation of the Godhead in the Believer is in the Person of the Holy Spirit (Jn. 14:16-17). As it regards the Trinity, to have One is to have All. But at the same time, one cannot have God at all, unless one accepts the Lord Jesus Christ, exactly as John proclaims here, which means to accept what Christ did for us at the Cross.

(16) "AND WE HAVE KNOWN AND BELIEVED THE LOVE THAT GOD HAS TO US. GOD IS LOVE; AND HE WHO DWELLS IN LOVE DWELLS IN GOD, AND GOD IN HIM."

The structure is:

1. The love that God has shown to us is manifested in Him giving His Son to die on the Cross. We know that and believe that.

2. *"God is love,"* which is proved by His act of the giving of His only Son.

3. If one truly knows the Lord, one will truly dwell in love, which shows that God is dwelling in him.

THE LOVE OF GOD

The phrase, *"And we have known and believed the love that God has to us,"* in effect says, *"We have known and still know, and have believed and still believe."* This, John implies, is back of our confession. To know as John speaks of knowing is to believe, and vice versa. No inner realization can be without a corresponding confidence, no true confidence without such a realization.

As John uses the words *"God has to us,"* it does not mean *"to us"* as it seems to mean, or *"in us,"* or *"in our case,"* but rather *"in connection with us."* God's love has succeeded in connecting itself with us.

The sequence of thought is this: First, we must know and rely on the fact that God loves us. Second, we come to realize through relying on His love (or having faith in His Son — the meaning is the same) that in His very nature God is love. Third, we discover that to live in God means to live in love. The fellowship we have with the Father and with the Son (I Jn. 1:3), the fellowship in which He lives in us and we live in Him, is perceived as nothing other than a fellowship of love (Barker).

GOD IS LOVE

The short phrase, *"God is love,"* finds John repeating from Verse 8. His wording is always most exact.

As stated, the idea of all of this is that God's love has succeeded in connecting itself with us through what Jesus did at the Cross, i.e., *"the expiation of our sins."*

All of this is connected to the Cross. The Holy Spirit through John is saying here that the way and means by which we know and understand the Love of God, in fact, understanding that He in fact *"is Love,"* is by and through what He did in the sending of His only Son to this world, and Christ giving up Himself on the Cross in order that we might be redeemed. Philosophically or intellectually, it's not really possible for one to understand the Love of God. It must be seen by and through the Cross, and if seen in that connection, will become obviously clear.

As amply proved here, everything comes to the Believer through the Cross. The Cross stands at the intersection of all humanity. By and through the Cross, which of course proclaims what Christ did there, man can know God and a thrice-Holy God, can reach out to sinful man — but only through the Cross!

After seeking the Lord day and night for some five years, and doing so with tears, as to the way of Sanctification, when He began to answer me, He took me first of all to Romans, Chapter 6. He then related to me in prayer, *"The answer for which you seek is found in the Cross and the Cross alone!"*

I will never forget that day or that moment. I knew instantly that it was right, and because it was Biblical. From that moment He has continued to add to this Revelation, which in fact, opens up the Word, which has wondrously and gloriously revolutionized my life.

I believe I can now say and without fear of contradiction, that I know more about the Love of God than I have ever previously known. Once the Cross becomes the center of one's thinking, then self ceases to be that center, which is the purpose all along. But only the Cross can accomplish this fact. Any other direction leads only to more self, while the Cross leads to more Christ.

This Scripture tells us that God dwells in a light that cannot be approached by any man; as well, no human being has seen God in all of His Glory, nor can one see such (I Tim. 6:16). When one says that *"God is Love,"* it must be understood that this does not constitute the entirety of the *"Being"* of God. God is *"Love,"* even as He is *"Light,"* but these things in no way totally describe Who or What God actually is.

God is all of these things, plus so much more, but yet none of these things do away with His personality. In other words, God is a Person, which means that He has a personality.

DWELLING IN LOVE

The phrase, *"And he who dwells in love dwells in God, and God in him,"* refers to this great union being made possible by the Love of God, which is made possible by Christ, which is made possible by what He did at the Cross.

To help us properly understand this statement, it could probably be better translated, *"And he who remains in love remains in God, and God in him."* This means that all that John has said about the manifestation of God's love and about the goal that it has attained in us, must at the same time, be retained. Without the Son's expiation, without Jesus dying for the world, without our confession of the Son, which means that we know and believe this love of God, this double remaining so to speak, is impossible. The *"double remaining"* referring to us dwelling in God, and God dwelling in us.

The heretics of John's time may talk as they please about God's love while they deny the Deity and the expiation by means of the Blood of Jesus. In doing so, they do *not* remain in God, and God does not remain in them. This is still true with regard to all who are like them today.

True fellowship with God is His remaining in us and our remaining in Him and not a mere claim of fellowship. Because of its great importance let's be clearer:

For God to dwell in us, and for us to dwell in Him, our Faith must be in the Cross of Christ, and our Faith must remain in the Cross of Christ. We can say without fear of contradiction, that all of this hinges completely on what Jesus did for us at the Cross, and our constant Faith in that Finished Work.

The heretics of John's day denied forgiveness and cleansing from all sin by means of the Blood of Jesus, and regrettably, their modern counterparts do the same thing presently. The modernists claim that the Blood of Jesus atones for nothing, while the so-called Word of Faith people say the same thing. As the belief system of the heretics in John's day was blasphemy, the belief system of their modern counterparts is blasphemy as well!

(17) "HEREIN IS OUR LOVE MADE PERFECT, THAT WE MAY HAVE BOLDNESS IN THE DAY OF JUDGMENT: BECAUSE AS HE IS, SO ARE WE IN THIS WORLD."

The exegesis is:

1. Our love is brought to fruition, i.e., *"made complete,"* by a continued confession of Jesus Christ as the Son of God, and what He did for us on the Cross.

2. The judgment addressed here, is the coming *"Judgment Seat of Christ."*

3. We will then be able to stand before Christ with *"boldness,"* and because our Faith was not at all in ourselves, but altogether in Him and what He did for us at the Cross.

4. Christ is totally victorious, and through Him we can be totally victorious in this world as well.

LOVE MADE PERFECT

The phrase, *"Herein is our love made perfect,"* refers to confidence. This confidence relates at least in part to the coming time of judgment (the Judgment Seat of Christ), though John as well taught that *"confidence"* is the mark of a Believer in every relationship to God (I Jn. 3:21; 5:14).

He may have introduced the judgment theme in the context of the Commandment to love because Jesus Himself made this command so specific and established love as the basis for judgment. Not to love, therefore, is to disobey Christ and to spurn the Father's Own love in sending Jesus. To live in love, however, is to live in God; and this results in complete confidence for prayer and judgment (Barker).

HOW THIS LOVE IS OBTAINED

For the Believer to attempt to perfect this love himself, which means by his own machinations, efforts, and ability, presents itself as a fruitless exercise. In other words, it simply cannot be done.

In the first place, this love of which John speaks, is the *"God kind of love,"* which means that the world doesn't have this love, and as well, means that it's not possible for it to originate in man. It only originates in God.

At the moment of conversion, the Love of God comes into the believing sinner. This is all done at the moment of Regeneration, worked out by the Holy Spirit. In fact, it is impossible for the Divine nature to come into the person without at the same time the Love of God being a part of that Divine nature. They are one and the same!

So the Believer starts off with the Love of God, automatically given to him at conversion. But now the Holy Spirit sets about, to *"perfect"* this love. And please understand, this is strictly and purely a work of the Spirit, which means that man cannot accomplish this task, even the Born-Again Christian. In fact, *"love"* heads up the Fruit of the Spirit (Gal. 5:22-23).

So if one automatically has the Love of God at conversion, what is it that the Spirit is doing as it regards His Fruit?

One might say that the seed of the Love of God is planted in the heart and life of the new Believer at conversion. The Holy Spirit is then to develop that seed, and have it grow into a proper *"Fruit."* This is a process which takes time, and cooperation on the part of the Believer. But the great question is how does the Spirit do this?

HOW THE SPIRIT DEVELOPS HIS FRUIT

As we've already stated, it is only the Spirit of God Who can do these things within our hearts and lives. It is impossible for the

Christian to bring about any type of Christlikeness through his own efforts, personal strength, ability, or machinations. But yet this is the great problem for the Child of God. Most do not know how the Spirit works, and thereby try to see these things done in all the wrong ways.

The only requirement of the Believer is that we understand, as previously stated, that all things come to us from God through the Cross, i.e., *"the Atoning Work of Christ."* Consequently, we are to anchor our Faith in that which Jesus has done on our behalf in the giving of Himself in Sacrifice, and in fact, not allow our Faith to be moved from that Finished Work. Ever making the Cross of Christ the object of our Faith (Rom. 6:3-14), the Holy Spirit will then work mightily within us, doing what He Alone can do (Rom. 8:1-2, 11, 13). *"Herein"* and *"herein alone,"* is our love made perfect.

The following is a Message by Miles J. Stanford, which I think, adds beautifully to the statements I have just made. We are indebted to him for the following:

THE CROSS

Studying these truths is hard work, is it not?! Although spiritual hunger and need are prime requisites for light and understanding, the Holy Spirit does not release the treasures of the Word quickly or easily. *"Deep calleth unto deep."* We have to be prepared, and even then there is much time, digging, praying, meditation, yearning, and experiencing involved. True spiritual reality comes in no other way, but, praise the Lord, it does come in this way!

Understanding and appropriating the facts of the Cross proves to be one of the most difficult and trying of all phases for the growing Believer. Our Lord holds His most vital and best things in store for those who mean business, for those who hunger and thirst for His very best as it is in our Lord Jesus Christ. The Believer's understanding of the two aspects of Calvary gives the key to both Spiritual Growth, and life-giving service.

Calvary is the secret of it all. It is what He did there that counts, and what He did becomes a force in the life of a Christian when it is appropriated by Faith (Rom., Chpt. 6). This is the starting point from which all Godly living must take its rise. We shall never know the experience of Christ's victory in our lives until we are prepared to count (reckon) upon His victory at the Cross as the secret of our personal victory today (Rom. 6:11). There is no victory for us that was not first His. What we are to experience He purchased, and what He purchased for us we ought to experience.

The beginning of the life of Holiness is a Faith in the Crucified Saviour which sees more than His substitutionary work. It is a Faith which sees myself identified with Christ in His Death and Resurrection.

DEATH TO SIN

Actually, our Father has trained every one of us for clear-cut, explicit Faith in this second aspect of Calvary, and I speak of our individual identification with the Lord Jesus in His death to sin and rising to resurrection ground.

The first aspect of Calvary concerns believing and appropriating the finished work of His dying for our sins of which is Justification. Now we are asked just as definitely to believe and appropriate the further aspect: *"Knowing this, that our old man is crucified with Him"* (Rom. 6:6): *"Likewise reckon ye also yourselves to be dead indeed unto sin, but alive unto God"* (Rom. 6:11).

Our intelligent Faith standing on the facts of Calvary gives the Holy Spirit freedom to bring that finished work into our daily lives. We stood on the fact of His dying for our sins, and this act of Faith allowed the Holy Spirit to give us freedom from the penalty of sin — Justification. Now, once we come to see this further fact, we are urged in the Word to stand on the liberating truth of our dying with Christ in His death to sin, which allows the Holy Spirit to bring into our lives freedom from the power, the enslavement, of sin — progressive Sanctification. And of course when we stand with Him in Glory, we will be forever free from the presence of sin — entirely sanctified and glorified.

OUR SUBSTITUTE AND OUR REPRESENTATIVE MAN

As our Substitute He went to the Cross alone, without us. To pay the penalty of our

sin; as our Representative, He took us with Him to the Cross. And there, in the sight of God, we all died together with Christ. We may be forgiven because He died in our stead: we may be delivered because we died with Him (as our Substitute He died *"for"* us; as our Representative Man He died *"as"* us).

God's way of deliverance for us, a race of hopeless incurables, is to put us away in the Cross of His Son, and then to make a new beginning by re-creating us in union with Him, the Risen, Living One (II Cor. 5:17). It is the Holy Spirit Who will make these great facts real and true in our experience as we cooperate with Him; and so the plague of our hearts will be stayed, and we shall be transformed into the likeness of Christ.

Through the crucifixion of the old man with Christ, the Believer has been made dead unto sin, he has been completely freed from sin's power. He has been taken beyond sin's grip, the claim of sin upon him has been nullified. This is the flawless provision of God's Grace, but this accomplished fact can only become an actual reality in the Believer's experience as faith lays hold upon it and enables him moment by moment, day-by-day though temptation assail him, to reckon it to be true. As he reckons, the Holy Spirit makes real; as he continues to reckon, the Holy Spirit continues to make real. Sin need have no more power over the Believer than he grant it through unbelief. *"If he is alive unto sin it will be due largely to the fact that he has failed to reckon himself dead unto sin."*

SPIRITUAL GROWTH

The Reformation brought into focus once again the emphasis on Spiritual Birth, without which there can be no beginning. What is lacking among Believers to this day is the proper emphasis on *"growth"* — not just to be saved, and Heaven by and by. What sort of Salvation would we have if our Father simply saved us from the penalty of sins, and then left us on our own to deal with the power of sin in our Christian life and walk? But most Believers feel this is about as far as He went, and are struggling to get on the best they can, with His help.

And this is the Galatian error, so prominent even now throughout Born-Again circles. We must be brought back to the basics: freed from the *"penalty"* of sin by His finished work; freed from the *"power"* of sin by His finished work; *"justified by faith"* (Gal. 3:24); *"we walk by faith . . ."* (II Cor. 5:7); *"As you have therefore received Christ Jesus the Lord, so walk ye in Him"* (Col. 2:6).

We are not left to deal with the old life ourselves; it has been dealt with by Christ on the Cross. This is the fact which must be known, and upon that fact is built the New Testament principle and Doctrine of holiness. In other words, Calvary is as much the foundation of Sanctification as of Justification. Both gifts spring from the same work and are two aspects of the same Salvation.

Now, as long as the Believer does not know this dual aspect of his Salvation, the best he can do is seek to handle his sins by confession (I Jn. 1:9) — that is, after the damage has been done! This takes care of the penalty of the product, but not the source.

Is it not time we allowed the Holy Spirit to get at the source, and cut off this stream of sins before they are committed? Is this not infinitely better than the wreckage caused by sin, even though confessed?

When Believers get sick and tired of spinning year after year in a spiritual squirrel cage — sinning, confessing, but then sinning again — they will be ready for God's answer to the power of sin, which is death to self, brought forth from the completed work of the Cross.

THE SIN NATURE

When God's light first shines into our heart our one cry is for forgiveness, for we realize that we have committed sins before Him: but once we have known forgiveness of sin, we make a new discovery — the discovery of sins, and then we realize that we still have the nature of a sinner. In other words, there is an inward inclination to sin. There is a power within that draws us to sin, and when that power breaks out we commit sins.

We may seek and receive forgiveness, but then we sin again: and life goes on in a vicious circle — sinning and being forgiven, but then sinning again. We appreciate God's forgiveness, but we want something more than that, we want deliverance. We need

forgiveness for what we have done, but we need deliverance from what we are, or we might say, we need to more properly understand the deliverance that's already been wrought for us by Christ. That's why Jesus said, *"You will know the truth, and the truth will make you free"* (Jn. 8:32).

SELF

Our reckoning on the finished work of our death to sin, in Christ at Calvary, is God's one way of deliverance — there is no other way because that is the way He did it. We learn not to add to the finished work in the matter of Justification, and now we must learn not to add to the finished work of emancipation. We will be freed when we enter His prepared freedom — there is no other. The Believer can never overcome the old man even by the power of the new apart from the death of Christ and, therefore, the death of Christ unto sin is indispensable, and unless the Cross is made the basis upon which we overcome the old man, we only drop into another form of morality; in other words, we are seeking by self-effort to overcome self, and the struggle is hopeless (C. Usher).

I must recognize that the enemy within the camp — the flesh, the old nature, self, I, the old Adam — is a usurper. By faith I must reckon him to be in the place that God put him — crucified with Christ. I must realize that now my life is hid with Christ in God; that He is my life.

THE CROSS, OUR FAITH,
AND THE HOLY SPIRIT

The Message I've just given you from Miles J. Stanford says it and says it well; however, I'm afraid as it regards the Christian who is unacquainted with the Cross as it pertains to our Sanctification experience, that some of the statements as given by our Brother need qualification.

For instance, he said that we learned when we got saved, not to add to the finished work of Christ in the matter of Justification. In other words, we were saved simply by trusting in Christ and what He did at the Cross, and we must not try to add works or merit to our faith. The entire scenario of Salvation pertains to faith, but more particularly, Faith exclusively in what Christ did at the Cross on our behalf.

Most Christians understand that, but as it regards the Cross, that's about as far as they go in their thinking, and simply because they have been taught next to nothing concerning the Sanctification process as it regards the Cross.

The Believer must know and understand that every single thing we receive from the Lord, which includes our Salvation, and then our victorious walk on a daily basis, comes exclusively through what Jesus did at the Cross. Consequently, our Faith must be placed in the Cross, must remain in the Cross, and must not be moved away from the Cross.

With this done, the Holy Spirit will then help us mightily and greatly, simply because all that He does, is done exclusively within the parameters of the Finished Work of Christ. So if we want the help of the Spirit, which we definitely must have if we are to be what we ought to be in the Lord, then our Faith must be exclusively in the Finished Work of Christ (Rom. 8:1-2, 11, 13).

THE FINISHED WORK OF CHRIST

First of all, what do we mean by the statement *"the Finished Work of Christ"*?

Paul said, *"When He* (Jesus) *had by Himself purged our sins* (which He did at the Cross) *sat down on the Right Hand of the Majesty on high"* (Heb. 1:3).

The Apostle then said: *"But this man* (Christ), *after He had offered one sacrifice for sins forever* (which He did at the Cross), *sat down on the Right Hand of God"* (Heb. 10:12).

By the Holy Spirit emphasizing the fact that Jesus has *"sat down on the Right Hand of God,"* tells us that His work was total and thereby completed. In other words, there is nothing else that needs to be done as it regards our Salvation, and in fact, all that we receive from the Lord.

These type of statements have to do with the old Levitical Priesthood. As it regards all of the sacred utensils of the Tabernacle and Temple, there was not a single chair among these vessels, and for the reason that the work of the Priests was never finished. In other words, they had to continue to offer up more and more sacrifices because *"the*

blood of bulls and goats could not take away sin"; therefore, it was necessary that more sacrifices continued to be offered (Heb. 10:4). So the work of the Priests in that Old Testament system was never finished.

But when Jesus came, to Whom the sacrifices pointed, and gave Himself on the Cross, what He did was so total, so complete, that it will never have to be repeated in all of eternity. In fact, Paul referred to His Sacrifice of Himself as *"the Blood of the Everlasting Covenant"* (Heb. 13:20).

Now if what Jesus did is 100 percent sufficient, this then means that we now have a perfect Salvation, a perfect victory, which means that we cannot add anything to what He has already done, and in fact, we must not add anything to what He has already done. We must get this in our minds, understanding that His work is a *"Finished Work."* So why am I stressing this?

WORKS

Paul said, *"And if by grace, then it is no more of works"* (Rom. 11:6).

The Apostle also said: *"Even as David also describeth the blessedness of the man, unto whom God imputeth righteousness without works"* (Rom. 4:6).

He then said: *"Knowing that a man is not justified by the works of the law, but by the faith of Jesus Christ . . . for by the works of the law shall no flesh be justified"* (Gal. 2:16).

When most Christians read these words, they think of Salvation. And of course, they do refer to Salvation, but they also refer to our everyday living before God. And what do we mean by that?

The modern Church is very bad about preaching faith for Salvation, and then preaching *"works"* for Sanctification. They do it in two ways, both of them grossly wrong:

1. The Church for all practical purposes teaches that one can be Sanctified by works. In other words, most Christians think that we draw closer to God, or become Christlike, by doing certain good things. And Believers believe this and try to do this, because this is what they are taught.

However, we do not become Christlike by doing good things, as good as those things may be in their own right. We become

Christlike, which means to get closer and closer to the Lord, which means to walk victorious over the world, the flesh, and the Devil, strictly by evidencing Faith in what Christ did at the Cross on our behalf. When we do this, even as we've already stated, the Holy Spirit who works completely within the parameters of the Finished Work of Christ, then develops His Fruit within our hearts and lives.

This is the only way that one can become Christlike, get closer to God, walk in victory, etc.

2. When it comes to sin, most in the modern Church believe that in some way a Christian ought to be punished for failure, and especially Preachers. Whether they realize it or not, they are in essence saying that one has to earn one's forgiveness, which is totally contrary to the Word of God.

In the first place, such an attitude loudly states that Jesus Who in fact was punished on our behalf, was in fact, not punished quite enough, and we need to add to what He has already suffered. I would certainly trust that upon proper contemplation of such thinking, we would see how sinful and wicked that it really is.

Considering what Jesus suffered, and then for us to think that He didn't suffer enough is an insult to Him of the highest magnitude.

There is only one sacrifice for sin, whether it's a Preacher or the laity, and that is the Sacrifice of Christ. And to be sure, what He did at the Cross is enough to satisfy every single sin debt (Jn. 2:1-2).

So the idea of punishment is to say the least, an insult to Christ.

In both of these points, the Church is engaging in *"works,"* which God can never accept. This shows that they do not really understand the work of Christ as a *"Finished Work."* If they did, they would dispense with the *"works,"* and rely strictly on Faith in what He has done on our behalf.

FAITH

Most Christians will readily state that they are *"trusting Christ,"* which means that they have Faith in Christ. However, the truth is, most Christians really don't understand totally what faith actually is.

Before we comment on the subject, let me first of all say that when the Bible speaks of *"believing"* or *"Faith,"* without exception, it is always speaking of Faith in Christ, and more particularly, what Christ did for us at the Cross. Irrespective as to what the statement may be, whether it's in the Old or New Testaments, if we trace it back to its roots, always and without exception, it centers up on Christ, and more particularly, the Sacrifice of Christ. In fact, that is the story of the entirety of the Bible.

So as it regards Faith, the Believer must always understand that the object of faith, and that's what is so very, very important, must always be in *"Christ and Him Crucified"* (I Cor. 2:2, 5). As I've said repeatedly in this Volume, we must not separate Christ from the Cross, or the Cross from Christ. To do so, is to conclude by preaching and believing *"another Jesus"* (II Cor. 11:4).

Millions of Christians, who mostly have been taught wrong incidentally, keep trying to increase their faith. In reality, the increase of faith is not actually the idea. The idea is, the correct object of faith. The correct object must always be Jesus Christ and Him Crucified.

To make Christ the object of our faith without including the Cross, denies the very purpose for His coming to this world, and the very cause of our Redemption. The truth is, the Cross of Christ was a settled fact before the world was ever created (I Pet. 1:18-20).

Jesus mentioned to His Disciples how that He must go to Jerusalem, *"and suffer many things of the Elders and Chief Priests and Scribes, and be killed, and be raised again the third day."*

When He said these things, the Scripture says that *"Peter took Him, and began to rebuke Him, saying, 'be it far from Thee, Lord: this shall not be unto Thee'."*

Jesus was very upset over the statement as given by the big fisherman, and, thereby, turned, and said unto Peter: *"Get thee behind Me, Satan: you are an offense unto Me: for you savor not the things that be of God, but those that be of men"* (Mat. 16:21-23).

We learn here that any idea which turned Christ away from the Cross, which was the very reason He came to this world, is an idea fostered by Satan. So, we learn from this that any denigration of the Cross, any put down of the Cross, any misinterpretation of the Cross, is in fact, a misinterpretation of the entirety of the Plan of God. In fact, all such thinking is of Satan. It cannot be stated in any other way.

FALSE DIRECTIONS

Several times in this Volume I have mentioned the *"Word of Faith"* doctrine. It goes under several names, but this is I think, the most common designation.

I have mentioned it numerous times, simply because this teaching has had a powerful impact on the modern Church. Because of its view of the Cross, I maintain that this doctrine is not of God, but is in fact of the Evil One. In truth, it has caused more damage to the modern Church, than possibly any other error of the last half of the 20th Century.

For the most part, this particular gospel which in reality is *"another gospel"* (II Cor. 11:4), has degenerated into what I refer to as the *"money gospel,"* or *"greed gospel."* It comes back to the statement as given by Paul that *"a little leaven leaveneth the whole lump"* (Gal. 5:9).

Any doctrine that's wrong, if not corrected, will only get more and more wrong. And the fundamental wrongness of this doctrine is its viewpoint of the Cross. In other words, it's not Faith in the Cross, but rather faith in self. It may claim to be faith in the Word, but it is a perverted Word, i.e., *"the Word taken out of context."*

E. W. Kenyon wrote: *"We have sung 'near the Cross' and we have prayed that we might be 'near the Cross' but the Cross has no salvation in it. It is a place of failure and defeat"* (Advanced Bible Course, p. 279). It is from Kenyon that Kenneth Hagin and Kenneth Copeland get their unfundamental ideas. No Salvation in the Cross? Paul says in I Corinthians, Chapter 1 that there is no Salvation apart from the Cross.

Copeland says in his Reference Edition of the Bible, p. 129: *"Satan conquered Jesus on the Cross and took His Spirit to the dark regions of Hell."* To put such a statement in the Commentary notes in a Bible shows one's contempt for the truth.

NOTES

What did Jesus say on the Cross? Did He say, *"It is unfinished"*? Or did He say, *"It is finished"*? Of course we know that He said, *"It is finished"* (Jn. 19:30). The term *"it is finished"* means *"paid in full."* This doesn't sound like Satan conquering Jesus to me, and I don't think it does to you as well.

Kenneth Copeland also said: *"Jesus' death on the Cross was not enough to save us."* This is from his Message *"What Happened From the Cross to the Throne,"* (Tape 000303).

Fred Price, another devotee to the *"Word of Faith"* doctrine, said: *"After He died spiritually He* (meaning Jesus) *is not made alive* (Born-Again) *until He suffers for our sin in Hell."* He then went on to say, *"Do you think that the punishment for our sin was to die on the Cross? If that were the case, the two thieves could of paid your price. No, the punishment was to go into Hell itself and to serve time in Hell separated from God . . . Satan and all the demons of Hell thought they had Him bound and they threw a net over Jesus and dragged Him down to the very pit of Hell itself to serve our sentence"* (Ever Increasing Faith Messenger, June 1980).

There are many things wrong with this statement, but the main thing is that it is pure fiction. The Bible has nothing to say about these things, simply because they didn't happen.

The evidence of Scripture is overwhelming in its testimony to the fact that Christ's death on the Cross was a physical death only. There was no suffering in Hell (Jn. 2:19-21; Eph. 2:15; Col. 1:22; Heb. 10:10; I Pet. 2:24; 3:18; 4:1).

In fact, I Peter 3:18 plainly says: *"For Christ also has once suffered for sins, the just for the unjust, that He might bring us to God, being put to death in the flesh, but quickened by the Spirit."* *"Put to death in the flesh,"* plainly tells us that He only died physically and not spiritually.

This doctrine claims that Jesus Christ became a sinner on the Cross, actually taking upon Himself the nature of Satan, died and went to Hell, and when we say *"Hell,"* we are speaking of the burning side of the pit, where He suffered there for three days and nights, they claim. At the end of that three days and nights during which Satan and his cohorts laughed in hellish glee, because in their minds Jesus was defeated, God then said, *"It is enough."* At that time, Jesus was *"born again,"* becoming the firstborn of many Brethren, which means that He had to be Born-Again as any sinner is Born-Again, that is if they are to be saved. He was then resurrected from the dead.

That's the reason that this teaching claims that the Cross was the greatest defeat in human history; consequently, they will not sing songs about the Cross or the Blood in their Churches, etc.

There are many things wrong with these statements, but the main problem is, and as we have said some paragraphs back, it is pure fiction from beginning to end. In other words, you will not find it in the Bible.

As far as I know, this doctrine is believed by all the adherents of the *"Word of Faith"* message. This includes Kenneth Hagin, Kenneth Copeland, Fred Price, Benny Hinn, Joyce Meyer, etc.

Every cult and pseudo-Christian sect disparages the Cross and/or the Person of Christ. An enemy of the Cross is one who even suggests that the Sacrifice of Christ on the Cross was insufficient for Salvation. Anyone who disparages the Cross is teaching another gospel. And the destiny of such teachers is destruction (Phil. 3:19). Therefore, we must come to the conclusion that no enemy of the Cross can be a Brother in Christ.

THE DAY OF JUDGMENT

The phrase, *"That we may have boldness in the day of judgment,"* refers to the coming *"Judgment Seat of Christ"* (I Cor. 3:11-15).

There will be no unredeemed at the Judgment Seat of Christ, their judgment taking place at the Great White Throne over a thousand years later (Rev. 20:11-15).

At the Judgment Seat of Christ, motives and works will be judged. If it's works tendered by the effort of trying to produce faith, that will be judged very negatively. If it's works as a result of Faith, which is the right way, then motives will be judged.

If our Faith is properly placed in the Cross of Christ, and not at all in ourselves, we have boldness now, even as we will have boldness then. The way it's translated in the King James

makes it seem as if it is boldness we will come by on that coming day; however, the Greek Text puts it in the present. *"We have boldness in connection with the day of judgment."* We are looking forward to that day and to the fact that on that day we shall stand with God.

Incidentally, the Judgment Seat of Christ will have nothing to do with the penalty of sin, for the simple reason that this was taken care of at the Cross. And yet wrongs toward fellow Brothers and Sisters in the Lord, which have never been settled, will have to be settled at the Judgment Seat of Christ.

If our Faith is totally in the Cross of Christ, and that refers to our basing our life totally and completely on what Jesus did there for us, and not at all on ourselves, then we have boldness now, even as we will have boldness then. In other words, even as John will say in the next Verse, *"There will be no fear."* But let the Reader understand that this *"boldness"* of which John speaks, is predicated totally and completely on the Finished Work of Christ, and our Faith in that great Sacrifice.

AS HE IS, SO ARE WE

The phrase, *"Because as He is, so are we in this world,"* refers to the Christlike life. This makes the Saint as he dwells in the midst of a world of sinful people, like Christ. And the Lord Jesus will not at the Judgment Seat of Christ condemn those who while they lived on Earth, were like Him.

Christ as He stands before the Throne of God in the glory represents the Believer while yet in the world. All that He is in the sinless perfection of His nature is the property of the Believer, who can, therefore, say: *"Thus I stand before God!"*

(18) "THERE IS NO FEAR IN LOVE; BUT PERFECT LOVE CASTETH OUT FEAR: BECAUSE FEAR HATH TORMENT. HE THAT FEARETH IS NOT MADE PERFECT IN LOVE."

The diagram is:

1. The type of *"fear"* spoken of here is not a Godly fear or filial reverence, but rather a slavish fear of a slave for a master, or of a criminal before a judge.

2. It is guilt that makes men fear what is to come; that he whose sins are pardoned, and whose heart is filled with the Love of God,

has nothing to dread in this world or the world to come. This type of love casts out fear.

3. The Love of God and such fear are totally incompatible.

4. If we as Christians fear the coming Judgment Seat of Christ, or anything for that matter, then this shows that our love for Christ has not been fully developed.

NO FEAR IN LOVE

The phrase, *"There is no fear in love,"* speaks, as stated, not of a Godly fear, but rather a slavish fear.

The idea is, if we love God as we ought to, in other words, our love is not diluted, there will be no fear. Proper love at the same time demands proper Faith. In other words, it's impossible for a Believer to properly love the Lord, if that Believer does not properly exhibit Faith in the Lord as well. And when we speak of Faith, we are speaking of the Cross.

This means, if our faith is not properly placed in the Cross, but rather other things, our faith is improper, and will translate into improper love, which will translate into fear.

The love of which John speaks here, is not known by the poor results of its action in man but rather by its perfect action in God; and that perfection manifested itself at Calvary. This perfect love is a fact, and it manifested itself outside of man in order to the Salvation of man.

The Believer knows it by the Gift of God's Son, and he enjoys it by the Gift of God's Spirit. It is at Calvary that we learn what love is; and that when we had no love for God, God loved us perfectly though we were far from Him and dead in sins.

Man has no love for God, and I speak of unredeemed man; his pretension to possess it is self-deception. He cannot find it by searching within himself, but he can know it as manifested in the atoning Sacrifice of Christ. He gave the Life which loves and made propitiation for sins.

Those who really possess this Divine nature love because they are loved. It is especially a fraternal love; it loves fellow-Believers more intimately than the nearest relatives who are unconverted. It binds the heart with a stronger bond to persons never seen than to the dearest companions of childhood:

NOTES

it is a new nature, a realm outside of natural human affection — a realm of Divine love — of fellowship with God and with all who know Him. There is in truth no love outside that realm (Williams).

PERFECT LOVE

The phrase, *"But perfect love casteth out fear,"* presents the fact that love and fear are incompatible. They cannot coexist. For the Christian love is first an experience of the Father's love for us. This *"love"* is so powerful and life changing that when we know it we are forever removed from *"fear."*

As we have stated, the fear spoken of here is not to be confused with reverence for God. Reverence will only deepen through the experience of God's love. The experience of the Holiness of God's love makes us desire to be even more obedient to His commands. But it also removes us from the power of fear.

Whatever may take place in this world cannot nullify the power of His love nor separate us from it. Similarly, if we experience fear in any portion of our life, to that extent we deny God's love and fail to trust Him.

Going back to the previous Verse, *"fear"* is the opposite of *"boldness"*; where the one is, the other is not. The love of God, which translates into the Sacrifice of Christ, has removed all our sins (I Jn. 1:9; 2:1-2; 4:10); what is there left to make us afraid?

TORMENT

The phrase, *"Because fear hath torment,"* actually should have been translated *"punishment."* John states this in order to show why, in being brought to its goal, God's love necessarily throws out all such fear. This love would not reach its proper goal without that.

Punishment from God should have no place in the thinking of the Christian, Christ having suffered in our stead. If the Believer fears punishment from God, this means the Believer does not fully understand the Cross and what Jesus did there.

Now of course, this doesn't mean that we can trifle with the Word of God. Anyone who takes lightly the Word of God will suffer its consequences.

But if sin has been committed, it must be confessed before the Lord and forsaken. That being the case, there is no fear of punishment, for Jesus took all of that at the Cross. While there definitely may be chastisement from the Lord, and in fact always is, that is if we are truly a Child of God, this is not to be looked at as punishment. It is rather to be looked at as correction, which is altogether different from punishment. Punishment is for the mere purpose of inflicting pain, while chastisement is correction in the sense of bringing us to the right way.

WHAT IS PERFECT LOVE?

The phrase, *"He that feareth is not made perfect in love,"* presents such a statement as always and without exception, translating back to the Cross.

Perfect love always centers up on the Cross. This was the perfect demonstration of God's love for man, and demonstrated itself accordingly. In the first place, this type of love must originate with God, and is, therefore, perfect, and because God doesn't have anything less than perfect.

As we have stated, this perfect love is not demonstrated by the poor results of its action in man but by its perfect action in God. We continue to speak of the Cross.

Consequently, the only way the Believer can evidence this perfect love, is by loving the One Who is Perfect, namely the Lord, and understanding what He has done for us in the realm of Calvary. As it centers up in the Cross, at the same time of course, it centers up in Jesus.

If we do not properly understand the Cross, then we are not made perfect in love. If we properly understand the Cross, thereby placing our Faith and trust in that Finished Work, of necessity the Love of God will then be generated in our hearts, and of necessity, that love is perfect, i.e., *"made perfect."*

To be *"made perfect,"* involves a process, which again refers to our Faith in the Sacrifice of Christ.

When we talk about loving God, we must understand that we can only do such through a proper understanding of His Son the Lord Jesus Christ, and what He did for us in the Sacrifice of Himself. Placing our Faith totally and completely in that Finished Work, at the same time makes perfect the Love

NOTES

of God within our hearts, which drives out all fear.

(19) "WE LOVE HIM, BECAUSE HE FIRST LOVED US."

The structure is:

1. Unredeemed man has no love for God.

2. He cannot find love by searching within himself, but he can know it as manifested in the atoning Sacrifice of Christ.

3. The first initiation of Love, as was necessary, was on the part of God, and not us.

LOVE

The phrase, *"We love Him,"* proclaims that which comes only after He has first loved us.

Love must never be conceived as a *"natural"* experience of the natural man. There is such a *"natural love,"* but it must not be confused with the Divine love (agape). The love John speaks of originates with the Father. It became manifest in and through the Son and now characterizes the life of the children of God. Therefore, he begins this summary by saying, *"We love."*

Although the Greek verb form expresses either exhortation or description, here it is better to understand it descriptively: as the Father loves, and as the Son loves, so also will we love.

The love with which we love is not our own. We do not create it, nor do we even have the power to express it. It is always God's love or Jesus' love in us. But because we abide in the Father and in the Son, the love becomes also our own love. It is not that God reveals His love apart from us, or in spite of us, but that He invites us to love even as He loves. So we return to Him His Own love and love Him with the gift of His love (Barker).

HE FIRST LOVED US

The phrase, *"Because He first loved us,"* proclaims Him as the originator of all good things.

God loving us made it possible for us to love Him: otherwise we should not have known Him, or had the faculty of loving Him even had we known Him. And yet, to suppose that John is merely putting a case of gratitude before us is to rob him of the dignity and depth of his meaning.

John's statement corresponds with Paul's, *"But God commendeth His love toward us, in that, while we were yet sinners, Christ died for us"* (Rom. 5:8). This means that He loved us when we were unlovable. This is the God kind of love.

All of this places us and our loving beside God and His act of love, and states that God's love is the cause of ours.

(20) "IF A MAN SAY, I LOVE GOD, AND HATES HIS BROTHER, HE IS A LIAR: FOR HE WHO LOVES NOT HIS BROTHER WHOM HE HAS SEEN, HOW CAN HE LOVE GOD WHOM HE HAS NOT SEEN?"

The composite is:

1. We cannot hate our Brother, and at the same time love God.

2. Anyone who claims to love God, and hates his Brother, the Holy Spirit calls *"a liar."*

3. If a professed Christian, therefore, does not love one who bears the Divine image, whom he sees and knows, how can he love God Whose image he bears, Whom he has not seen?

LIAR

The phrase, *"If a man say, I love God, and hates his Brother, he is a liar,"* presents the sense, that no man, whatever may be his professions and pretensions, can have any true love for God, unless he also loves his Brethren.

The essential thing in our loving is that we love God. This truth no one contradicts or questions so that John simply proceeds by taking this for granted. But this is true only in the Christian sense. Because God loved us *"God"* is the supreme object of our love.

And now John gives a simple test by which we may verify both regarding ourselves and regarding others whether the claim: *"I love God,"* is true or not. He who makes this claim *"and hates his Brother is a liar."* This also means that he who makes this claim and loves his Brother speaks the truth.

It is impossible for anyone to love God, Whom he has not seen, when he does not love his Brother, whom he has seen. To claim that this is possible, to say, *"I am doing it,"* is to lie. Such supposed love for God is not love, it is a fiction. The God Whom this person claims to love is also a figment of his mind, namely a self-made god who lets him hate his Brother, which our God, Who is love itself, cannot do.

LOVING GOD

The question, *"For he who loves not his Brother whom he has seen, how can he love God Whom he has not seen?"*, presents the objects of love, and even juxtaposes them in order to give a greater effect. John states only a part of the thought when he declares that it is impossible to love the latter while not loving the former; he states the rest in Verse 21 and in I John 5:1-3, especially in I John 5:1-2, for there we learn why this is impossible.

The explanation that loving the Brother is loving God Who is in the Brother so that not loving the Brother makes it impossible to love God, the Brother being visible, God invisible, is on the right track but does not go far enough. As we will see, John goes much farther (Lenski).

God's love for us and in us sets us free to love our Brother even as God loves him. To fail this test of love proves that one's claim to love God is a lie — just as the previous claims to have fellowship with God while walking in darkness (I Jn. 1:6), to know Him while disobeying His commands (I Jn. 2:4), or to possess the Father while denying His Son were lies — and establishes the one making this claim as a liar.

Bultmann shows that *"liar"* has a double sense: the liar does not speak the truth in that what he claims is false; and, second, his action shows that he has divorced himself from the reality of God. The liar's life is a lie because it betrays the Being and Essence of God (Barker).

(21) "AND THIS COMMANDMENT HAVE WE FROM HIM, THAT HE WHO LOVETH GOD LOVE HIS BROTHER ALSO."

The exegesis is:

1. The Holy Spirit through John proclaims all of this as a *"Commandment."*

2. How can love be commanded, when its very nature demands free will?

3. The command is explicit; he who claims to love God must at the same time love his Brother.

COMMANDMENT

The phrase, *"And this Commandment have we from Him,"* presents that as given by the Holy Spirit, as should be obvious.

John is taking the word *"Commandment"* from the teaching of the Master Himself. The quotation *"Whoever loves God must also love his Brother,"* presents an unmistakable echo of Jesus' words in Mark 12:28-31, in answer to the question, *"Which is the most important Commandment?"* Jesus answered, *"The most important one is this: 'Hear, O Israel, the Lord our God, the Lord is One. Love the Lord your God with all your heart, and with all your soul, and with all your mind, and with all your strength.' The second is this: 'Love your neighbor as yourself"* (Jn. 13:34).

John makes it clear that obedience expresses itself in a single command. Love for God and love of neighbor are inseparable. The one is not possible apart from the other. If one loves God, he cannot refuse love to the image of God that meets him in his Brother. Dodd puts it thus: *"Being the object of God's love, we are to love our neighbor in Him and Him in our neighbor; and that is what it is to remain in His love"* (Barker).

The idea here is not that God is commanding that we love someone, for love cannot be commanded. It must be of one's free will or else it's not love.

The command is in the entirety of the subject matter. If we claim to love God, we must at the same time love our neighbor, or else our claim is false. The command has nothing to do with the *"act"* of love, but rather the *"fact"* of love!

LOVING GOD

The phrase, *"That he who loves God love his Brother also,"* proclaims the command. The Scripture is clear, even as the Holy Spirit through John has said, if one claims to love God and doesn't love his Brother, or even hates his Brother, pure and simple, he is lying.

"And can it be that I should gain an interest in the Savior's Blood?
"Died He for me, who caused His pain, for me Who Him to death pursued?
"Amazing love! How can it be that Thou, my God, should die for me?"

"'Tis mystery all! The immortal dies! Who can explore His grand design?
"In vain the firstborn seraph tries to sound the depth of love Divine!
"'Tis mercy all! Let Earth adore; let Angel minds inquire no more."

"He left His Father's throne above, so free, so infinite His grace;
"Emptied Himself of all but love, and bled for Adam's helpless race.
"'Tis mercy all, immense and free! For, O my God, it found out me."

"Long my imprisoned spirit lay fast bound in sin and nature's night;
"Thine eye diffused a quickening ray. I woke, the dungeon flamed with light;
"My chains fell off, my heart was free; I rose, went forth, and followed Thee."

"No condemnation now I dread; Jesus, and all in Him, is mine!
"Alive in Him, my living Head, and clothed in Righteousness Divine,
"Bold I approach the eternal throne, and claim the Crown through Christ, my own."

CHAPTER 5

(1) "WHOSOEVER BELIEVETH THAT JESUS IS THE CHRIST IS BORN OF GOD: AND EVERYONE WHO LOVES HIM WHO BEGAT LOVES HIM ALSO WHO IS BEGOTTEN OF HIM."

The diagram is:

1. The Cerinthian Gnostics denied the identity of Jesus and the Christ. In other words, they denied that Jesus was also the Christ. The word *"believeth"* is not a mere intellectual assent to the fact of the Incarnation, but a heart acceptance of all that is implied in its purpose, the substitutionary death of the Incarnate One for sinners.

2. Such a person who believes accordingly has been born of God and as a result is a Child of God.

3. *"Him that begat"* is God. *"Him that is begotten of Him"* is the Child of God.

4. The person who loves God as his Father

also loves God's children because of the fact of the family relationship, that of having a common Father.

BELIEVING THAT JESUS IS THE CHRIST

The phrase, *"Whosoever believeth that Jesus is the Christ is born of God,"* refers to several things:

1. In previous Passages, John strikes out at the heresies of Cerinthus and of his following. In fact, John does this from the very beginning of this Epistle, even as we have noted at times. John, the Beloved as he is often called, is not a sentimental pacifist, but rather the very opposite. The word *"liar"* (I Jn. 1:6, 10; 2:22; 4:20) is hurled like a bolt from his pen.

2. Since John used the unmodified name *"Jesus,"* we know that he had in mind the man Jesus, Who walked here on Earth as a man. The heretics said, *"That is all that He was and that He is."* In other words, the Cerinthian Gnostics denied that Jesus was also the Christ. John confronts this head on!

3. To believe that the man Jesus is *"the Christ,"* is to believe in the Deity of Jesus, the expiation (to pay the price for) of His Blood, the remission and the cleansing which this Blood effects, in fact, the whole love of God that is expressed in the whole Saviorhood of Jesus, the whole Gospel. John is not presenting the minimum content of Faith but its full, normal, true content.

4. One who believes this which we have just said with all of his heart *"is born of God."* It's impossible to believe this without being born of God, and impossible to be born of God without believing this.

Above all, this doesn't refer to a mere intellectual acknowledgment of the proposition that Jesus is the Messiah, etc.

If, in the proper sense of the phrase, a man does believe that Jesus is the Christ, receiving Him as He is revealed as the Anointed of God, and the Saviour, it is undoubtedly true that this constitutes him a Christian, for that is what is required of a man in order that he may be saved (Jn. 3:16; Rom. 10:9-10, 13). As we've already said, there must be a heart acceptance of all that is implied in the purpose of Christ, His substitutionary death for sinners, thus making a way of Salvation in which God could bestow mercy on the basis of justice satisfied.

NOTES

Only what Christ did at the Cross could satisfy the demanded justice of God. God's very nature demanded that justice be satisfied, or else justice becomes a mockery. Only Christ could do this thing, and He could only do this by giving of Himself in Sacrifice on the Cross. That and that alone, would satisfy the justice of God, making it possible, for God, as stated, to bestow mercy, on the basis of a satisfied justice.

The Church is fond of saying that if one sins, one must take responsibility. That is right, but only if the definition is correct. If they are meaning that one must pay for their sin, then that is Scripturally off base, and in fact, off base badly!

There is no way that one can pay for one's sin. Such is impossible, and to think such, shows a terrible ignorance of the Word of God.

In the first place, it's impossible for man to do such, whatever it is he might try to do to atone for his wrongdoing; second, Jesus Christ has already taken responsibility for sin, and did so in the most graphic way possible. He atoned for all sin, past, present, and future, by the giving of Himself on the Cross. And for the Church to claim that more is owed insults Christ in no uncertain terms. In other words, such an assumption is gross sin, even blasphemy!

BEGOTTEN OF HIM

The phrase, *"And everyone who loves Him who begat loves him also who is begotten of Him,"* simply states that those who love God as their Father also love God's children. This is because of the fact of family relationship, that of having a common Father and that of sustaining the relationship with other Believers, that of children in the same family (Wuest).

As we've already stated, *"Him who begat"* is God. *"Him who is begotten of Him"* is the Child of God.

The general idea is that as all Christians are the children of the same Father; as we constitute one family; as we all bear the same image; as we share His favor alike; as we are under the same obligation of gratitude to Him, and are bound to promote the same common cause, and are to dwell together in the same home forever, we should, therefore, love one another. As all the children in a family love their common father, so it should be in the great family of which God is the Head (Barnes).

A SURE LOVE

John does not say, *"He ought to love."* The truth that the Child of God loves the Father Who begot him as His child and thus loves also his Brother whom the Father has likewise begotten, is a simple fact. To imagine the opposite, namely that one who is so begotten should not love him, who has likewise been begotten, is to imagine the impossible.

John always goes to the root of it all. In other words, he heads straight for the jugular. He weaves into one fabric all the threads of his Epistle, all that he says about the Father, about Jesus, His Son, the Christ, and this Son's Blood and mission, about our connection with the Father and the Son, about life (I Jn. 1:1-2; 4:9), about passing from the death into the life, and about remaining in the death (I Jn. 3:14).

In fact, a full exegesis of this Verse would include the exegesis of all that precedes. This is John's wonderful way of writing: each brief, crystal-clear statement involves all that precedes (Lenski).

(2) "BY THIS WE KNOW THAT WE LOVE THE CHILDREN OF GOD, WHEN WE LOVE GOD, AND KEEP HIS COMMANDMENTS."

The structure is:

1. Our perception of the existence of love to our Brethren is developed on every occasion when we exercise love and obedience toward God.

2. Love on the part of a Saint for his Brother in Christ is shown when that Saint observes the Commandments of God, for obedience to the Commandments puts that Saint in right relationship to his brother Christian, which relationship results in his acting in a loving manner toward that Christian.

3. The converse also is true, namely, when a Saint is acting in an unloving way toward his fellow-Saint, he is disobeying God's Commandment.

HOW DO WE KNOW?

The phrase, *"By this we know that we love the Children of God,"* presents the presentation of the same truth in another form.

As it is universally true that if we love Him Who has begotten us we shall also love His children, or our Christian Brethren, so it is true also that if we love His children it will follow that we love Him. In another place, the Apostle says that we may know that we love God if we love those who bear His image (I Jn. 3:14).

Even though this Scripture is said in the way that John intended for it to be said, to properly understand it, it would have to be reversed.

"When we love God, and keep His Commandments, by this we know that we love the Children of God."

In effect, this says there are three boxes. The outer one is doing what God wants. Open that, and in it is loving God, the Father of all His children. Open that, and in it is loving His children. Now we know. If all the boxes aren't complete, then we are not obeying the Scriptures.

Findley says: *"If love to men proves the worth of our love to God, love to God proves the worth of our love to men."*

COMMANDMENTS

The phrase, *"When we love God, and keep His Commandments,"* in effect says, that if this is truly done, we will also at the same time *"love the Children of God."* It is as simple as that.

Here are God's Commandments. Review all that John says about *"Commandments,"* notably in I John 2:3-8, also in I John 3:22-24, and finally in I John 4:21. By doing these Commandments, Gospel Commandments which ask for both faith and love (I Jn. 3:23), you are loving God; and by loving God you are loving the Children of God. Just look at what you are doing with the Commandments of God, Who is love, then you cannot help knowing, i.e., *"realizing."* The negative is, of course, equally true.

Not to be doing God's Commandments (I Jn. 3:23) leaves you with nothing but the lying claim that you are loving God (I Jn. 4:20) and having fellowship with Him (I Jn. 1:6); and then any proposed love for God's children, in fact, any claim that you are a Child of God and are born from God becomes mere fiction.

NOTES

Simply put, love and obedience to God will assure us of the truth of our love to others. In I John 2:3 and I John 4:20-21, obedience to God and love to our fellows were the signs of knowledge of God and love to Him. The two are really inseparable. If love of God is absent, then our love of our fellows is not genuine — it is earthly, it is a mockery. All friendship must be tested by loyalty to God; all love to Him must be tested by charity.

(3) "FOR THIS IS THE LOVE OF GOD, THAT WE KEEP HIS COMMANDMENTS: AND HIS COMMANDMENTS ARE NOT GRIEVOUS."

The composite is:

1. In effect, John is saying *"the love for God."*

2. We show our love for God by keeping His Commandments.

3. His Commandments not being grievous, love for Him makes the keeping of such a delight rather than a burden.

LOVE FOR GOD

The phrase, *"For this is the Love of God,"* in effect, says, as stated, *"love for God."*

The connection between love for God and obedience is meant as a protection against thinking of love for God as mere *"emotional feelings"* about God. True love (agape) requires action. In respect to humankind, it means willingness to lay down one's life. In respect to God, it means a life of willing obedience, a relation of sonship with God, and service on behalf of God. It requires laying down one's life as being one's own possession and taking up a new life in response to our Lord and Master (Barton).

KEEP HIS COMMANDMENTS

The phrase, *"That we keep His Commandments,"* are actually summed up in the following:

"And you shall love the Lord your God with all your heart, and with all your soul, and with all your mind, and with all your strength: this is the first Commandment.

"And the second is like, namely this, you shall love your neighbor as thyself. There is none other Commandment greater than these" (Mk. 12:30-31).

HIS COMMANDMENTS ARE NOT BURDENSOME

The phrase, *"And His Commandments are not grievous,"* speaks of that which is burdensome, severe, stern, violent, cruel, unsparing. Love for God makes the keeping of His Commandments a delight rather than a burden (Wuest).

The meaning is the Laws of God are not unreasonable; the duties which He requires are not beyond our ability; His government is not oppressive. It is easy to obey God when the heart is right; and those who endeavor in sincerity to keep His Commandments do not complain that they are hard. All complaints of this kind come from those who are not disposed to keep His Commandments.

They, indeed, object that His Laws are unreasonable; that they impose improper restraints; that they are not easily complied with; and that the Divine government is one of severity and injustice. But no such complaints come from true Christians.

In fact, we find His Service easier than the service of sin, and the Laws of God more mild and easy to be complied with than those which are fashioned of men. The service of God is freedom; the service of the world is bondage.

No man ever yet heard a true Christian say that the Laws of God, requiring him to lead a holy life, are stern and *"grievous."* But who has not felt this in regard to the inexorable laws of sin?

Is it a burden to believe in the Son of God Who died in expiation of our sins (I Jn. 2:2; 3:23; 4:10)? There is no greater joy than this confidence and trust.

Is it a burden to be called one of God's children (I Jn. 3:1), children of Him Who is love (I Jn. 4:8, 16), and for the love of Him Who first loved us (I Jn. 4:10) to love Him and thus also His children even as He loves us, and as they love us?

Can there be any greater joy than to stand in this circle of love, to have this love poured out upon us, to be warmed into answering love by this love? No, His Commandments are not burdensome! (Barton)

In fact, every single thing that God has commanded is for our highest profit and happiness. Were we perfect, we should not find them commands at all, for they would be our natural impulses. The more sincerely we serve God, consequently, the more enjoyment we shall derive from them. Only to those whose inclinations are distorted, perverted, and corrupted by sin can God's Laws seem irksome.

To the natural man the Will of God is strange; the requirement for Righteousness, foreign and hard. Even the law of love to such a person is a burden. But when God has entered into us and when we trust God's Son, then *"His yoke is easy and His burden is light"* (Mat. 11:30).

We who have been born of God have within us a desire and a yearning for the Father. Seeking and hungering after Righteousness becomes our joy. Living the life of love becomes our delight. The Commands of God bring us the freedom and the liberty we so ardently long for (Barton).

(4) "FOR WHOSOEVER IS BORN OF GOD OVERCOMETH THE WORLD: AND THIS IS THE VICTORY THAT OVERCOMETH THE WORLD, EVEN OUR FAITH."

The composite is:

1. If we follow God's prescribed order, we will overcome the world.

2. It is our Faith that overcomes the world.

3. Overcoming the world is *"victory,"* which means deliverance from the world.

4. The *"world"* speaks of the *"world system"* governed by Satan, which is evil.

OVERCOMING THE WORLD

The phrase, *"For whatsoever is born of God overcometh the world,"* proclaims beyond the shadow of a doubt, that towards which the Holy Spirit ever drives.

In John 16:33, the Saviour says: *"Be of good cheer; I have overcome the world."* He obtained a complete triumph over him *"who rules the darkness of the world,"* and laid the foundation for a victory by His people over all vice, error, and sin.

The way that John phrases this statement, presents the idea that every single Believer, with no exceptions, is meant to overcome the world, and in fact, provision has been made that every single Believer would overcome the world. That provision is Christ and the

NOTES

Cross, which is all done by Faith, even as John says in the last phrase of this Verse.

FAITH

The phrase, *"And this is the victory that overcometh the world, even our faith,"* in a very abbreviated way, gives us the key to living an overcoming life.

First of all, we are plainly told here, and rightly so, that we overcome by *"faith."* Even though in the next few Verses, John briefly alludes to the way in which Faith operates, still, it remains for Paul to tell us exactly how this is done. In fact, the entirety of his fourteen Epistles addresses this very thing, but more specifically, Romans, Chapters 6 and 8, along with the entirety of the Epistle to the Galatians.

As we've said previously in this Volume, there are two aspects to the great work that Jesus carried out at Calvary. The first is Justification where the penalty of sin was dealt with. This most Christians understand, and they understand it, because it doesn't require much comprehension to obtain the results.

In other words, all the believing sinner has to do to be saved is to simply call on the Name of the Lord (Rom. 10:13). Upon doing that, the Justification process is immediately enacted (I Cor. 6:11). But regrettably, most Christians are taught almost nothing about the second aspect of the Cross, which is Sanctification. Unlike the first aspect, the second aspect requires knowledge on the part of the Believer. Unfortunately, even most Preachers know almost nothing about this second aspect. As a result, most Christians stumble from one fad to the other, trying to find *"the victory that overcomes the world."*

I remember some years ago speaking with two of the biggest *"names"* in Christendom regarding this very thing. Both of these men, who are literally household names, had no knowledge at all as it regards the Sanctification process. Their solution for Christians with problems was to lay hands on these individuals, and rebuke the demon spirits causing them problems.

To be sure, demon spirits always get involved in any type of sin or failure; however, even though demon spirits definitely are real, and even though they definitely oppress

Christians at times, that is not the answer. There is nothing in the Word of God to substantiate such thinking. Jesus plainly said, *"You shall know the truth and the truth shall make you free"* (Jn. 8:32). And as one of my associates said some time back, *"Believers need the truth a whole lot more than they need a touch."*

While the touch may be real, and very helpful as it regards the short term, if the truth is not known, the individual before very long, will be right back to the place he was before the touch.

I remember back in the late 1980's, one Preacher, who incidentally pastored a very large Church, told me that the answer to this problem was a Christian finding someone in whom he could confide, and the two putting their strength together, would give power to overcome. In the 1970's, the great way and manner of victory over the world, was *"confession,"* which to a certain extent, continues unto this hour. In the early 1990's it was the *"laughing phenomenon."* It was taught that if one had this experience, one had *"overcome the world."* In the late 1990's, the *"family curse"* thing was big. Christians with problems were taught that such were caused by a *"family curse."*

While all of these things, plus some we haven't named, may have some validity, there is no victory that overcometh the world in these particular practices. The Holy Spirit through John plainly tells us here that it is *"even our faith,"* which is the answer. Now what exactly did he mean by that?

GOD'S PRESCRIBED ORDER OF VICTORY

Unfortunately, most Christians really do not understand faith as they should. When they think of *"faith,"* they think of believing in the Lord, or His Word, or in the Name of Jesus, all which are very valid. However, that's about as far as their faith goes, simply because they have not been taught anything else.

When John mentions Faith here, or in reality, when *"believing"* or *"faith"* are mentioned anywhere in the Word of God, and especially in Paul's writings, without fail, it is speaking of Faith in Christ and what Christ did at the Cross. The two *"Christ and the Cross"* must never be separated. It is the Cross which has made everything possible, and so it is the Cross that must ever be the object of our Faith.

We are to understand that Jesus addressed every single problem that faces humanity at the Cross. He completely and totally satisfied the demands of the broken Law, and did so all on our behalf. As well, in the doing of this, He also atoned for all sin, past, present, and future, at least for all who will believe (Jn. 3:16).

And in the atoning of sin, which took away the sin penalty which incidentally was death, He also broke the power of sin, which addresses the Sanctification process. And in removing all sin, in effect *"taking it away,"* which means to take away its penalty, He also took away Satan's legal right to hold man in captivity. As a consequence, He *"spoiled principalities and powers, making a show of them openly, triumphing over them in it"* (Col. 2:14-15).

So there is no problem that you as a Christian might have that Jesus didn't address at the Cross. Therefore, for you as a Christian to walk in victory, and I speak of overcoming the world in every capacity, you must understand that your answer is found only in the Cross of Christ. Consequently, you must make the Cross the object of your Faith, and not allow it to be moved to something else.

When this is done, the Holy Spirit, Who works solely within the parameters of the Finished Work of Christ, will grandly and gloriously help you, Who Alone has the power to do anything, for the simple reason that He is God. So there you have God's prescribed order of victory: A. The Cross; B. Your Faith in the Cross; and, C. The help of the Holy Spirit (Rom. 8:1-2, 11, 13).

THE OLD MAN IS DEAD

The following are the things you must learn and understand as a Christian, which deals with the second aspect of Calvary. Now let's say that again:

There are two aspects to what Jesus did at the Cross: A. He took away the *"penalty"* of sin, which has to do with one's Justification; and, B. He broke the *"power"* of sin, which has to do with your Sanctification. Now let's see what this means:

Paul said: *"Knowing this, that our old man is crucified with Him, that the body of sin might be destroyed, that henceforth we should not serve sin"* (Rom. 6:6).

Paul is speaking here to Believers. And when he uses the term *"knowing this,"* he is referring to the information he has just given in Romans 6:3-5, which speaks of the Crucifixion of Christ, and our part in that Crucifixion. In other words, when Jesus died on the Cross, and when we evidenced Faith in Him, when we were originally saved, in the Mind of God, we were literally *"baptized into His death"* (Rom. 6:3). That's how closely that God identifies us with what Christ did at the Cross, and what makes the Cross so very, very important. Jesus died there as our Substitute. Actually, as our Substitute He died *"for"* us, and as our Representative Man, He died *"as"* us (I Cor. 15:45-47).

While Romans 6:3-5 has to do exclusively with our initial Salvation, the Holy Spirit through Paul is letting us know that everything that we have thereafter is based upon what Jesus did at the Cross. At Salvation we were literally placed *"in Christ,"* which was all done by our having Faith in Christ and what He did for us. In other words, we were crucified with Him, buried with Him, and raised with Him in newness of life, all which are found in Romans 6:3-5.

Now the Apostle says, *"knowing this,"* we are to understand that what we once were, which speaks of what we were before Salvation, was *"crucified with Him."* And when that was done *"the body of sin was destroyed,"* which means that the power of sin was broken, which has to do with the second aspect of the Cross. Consequently, we do not any more have to serve sin. And incidentally:

Whenever the word *"sin"* is used in this Sixth Chapter of Romans, with the exception of a couple of times, it always carries in front of the word that which is known in the Greek Text as the definite article. In other words, it reads *"the sin,"* which actually refers to the *"sin nature."*

Before we were saved, we were ruled by the sin nature. Paul says here that due to the Cross, and our Faith in that Finished Work, we no longer have to serve *"the sin."* So what comes next?

NOTES

OUR FAITH

Paul now says: *"Likewise reckon ye also yourselves to be dead indeed unto sin, but alive unto God through Jesus Christ our Lord"* (Rom. 6:11).

This is where our faith comes in. We are to believe that Jesus addressed every single need we might have at the Cross; consequently, our Faith must be anchored in all that Christ there did. Total trust and confidence in what Christ did at the Cross, is to be exercised in that great Sacrifice. The Cross is the means of our victory, the means of the Grace of God, the means by which the Holy Spirit works within our lives. If it's failure here, it is a failure of faith. This we must understand. It means our faith is not properly in the Cross but rather in something else, etc.

SIN NATURE DOMINION BROKEN

With Faith properly placed, the sin nature will no longer have dominion over us. And if that's not the case, once again we need to look at our faith. Is it in the proper object? And of course that proper object is the Cross.

This is the Faith of which John spoke, and the Faith that overcomes the world.

Most Christians understand very little about the sin nature, having had almost no teaching on the subject. The truth is if one doesn't understand the sin nature, it is almost certain that the sin nature is going to dominate the Believer.

Many Preachers erroneously teach that once the person comes to Christ, there is no more sin nature.

In Romans, Chapter 6, Paul mentions sin about 17 times. Fourteen of those times, if I remember correctly, in the original Greek Text, even as we've previously stated, he placed the definite article before the word *"sin,"* making it read *"the sin."* This means that he is not talking about acts of sin, but rather the sin nature. And what is the sin nature?

When Adam and Eve fell in the Garden of Eden, they lost the Divine nature which they had, which was a total God consciousness, and it was replaced by the sin nature, which means that they now had a propensity or nature toward sin and in every capacity.

When the believing sinner comes to Christ, the sin nature loses its power. Paul plainly says this in Romans 6:6. Ideally it shouldn't cause the Christian any problem. In fact, it is dormant one might say, with the Divine nature now ruling the Child of God.

However, most Christians not knowing or understanding the Cross, try to live this Christian life outside of faith in the Cross, which always results in failure. When this happens, the sin nature springs to life. Still not understanding the Cross, the Believer tries to function by and through the flesh, even though he thinks it's the Spirit of God. Failure continues to be the result, and in a very short period of time the sin nature is once again ruling the Christian. In other words, it is ruling exactly as it did before the person was saved. That's why Paul said:

"Let not sin (the sin) *therefore reign in your mortal body, that you should obey it in the lusts thereof"* (Rom. 6:12).

For those who claim that the Christian has no sin nature, why would the Apostle say such a thing? If no sin nature exists, it's pointless to even address the problem. No! He addressed it because the Christian does have a sin nature. However, even though it does abide, it is not to rule, i.e., *"reign."* But until the Christian understands the Cross, thereby placing his Faith in that Finished Work, it is certain that the sin nature will rule in that Christian's life.

Even though I've already given the following in this Volume, because of its great importance, please allow me to give it again. I'm speaking of the formula for victory:

1. Focus: The Cross of Christ must ever be the focus of the Child of God (Rom. 6:3-5).

2. The Object of our Faith: This must always be the Finished Work of Christ, understanding that everything we receive from the Lord comes exclusively through the Cross (Gal. 6:14).

3. Power Source: Once our Faith is properly placed in the Cross, the Holy Spirit will grandly help us to live the life we ought to live (Rom. 8:1-2, 11).

4. Result: Victory! As John said, *"This is the victory that overcometh the world, even our Faith."*

(5) "WHO IS HE THAT OVERCOMETH THE WORLD, BUT HE THAT BELIEVETH THAT JESUS IS THE SON OF GOD?"

The diagram is:

NOTES

1. The Holy Spirit through John holds up by example the one who overcomes the world.

2. It is not he that *"does,"* but he that *"believeth."*

3. Believe what? That *"Jesus is the Son of God,"* which refers to all that He did at the Cross, even as the next Verse proclaims.

WHO IS THE ONE WHO OVERCOMES?

The beginning of the question, *"Who is He that overcometh the world . . .?"*, in effect proclaims the fact that there is only one way the world can be overcome. This should give us pause for thought!

Where is there one who can pretend to have obtained a victory over the world, except he who believes in the Saviour? All else are worldly, and are governed by worldly aims and principles.

It is true that a man may gain a victory over one worldly passion; he may defeat some one evil propensity; he may abandon one unprofitable direction, may even break a particular habit of profanity; but still, unless he has Faith in the Son of God, which refers to believing in Christ and what Christ did at the Cross, the spirit of the world will reign supreme in his soul in some form. In other words, the sin nature will rule within his life. And please understand, we are speaking here of Believers.

HE THAT BELIEVETH

The phrase, *"But he that believeth that Jesus is the Son of God,"* proclaims to us two great things:

1. First of all, we learn from the Word of God that it's not so much what we do, but rather what we *"believe."* Unfortunately, most of the modern Church has it backwards. To be sure, what we believe will definitely affect what we do, and as well, what we do will affect what we believe. However, the emphasis must always be on *"believing."*

But the question must be asked, believing what?

That brings us to the second part of this statement:

2. To give the answer immediately, and then we will comment, one must believe in Jesus Christ and what He did for us at the Cross. In this statement as given by John, we find the entirety of the answer.

First of all, Jesus Christ is God. He is God manifest in the flesh, which we refer to as the Incarnation.

Second, the very Name *"Jesus,"* means *"Saviour."* The manner in which this was and is done is by and through what Jesus did at the Cross. So any time you speak the Name *"Jesus,"* you are in effect speaking of Christ as Saviour, and as well, of the way, means, and manner in which He has saved humanity, which is by the Cross.

The sinner is saved not by doing certain things, but by simply believing in Christ and what Christ did at the Cross on his behalf (Jn. 3:16; Rom. 10:9-10, 13; Rev. 22:17).

Likewise, the Christian is able to walk in victory, and do so on a perpetual, daily basis, and we mean victory over all things as it refers to the world, the flesh, and the Devil, by continuing to believe in what Jesus did in His great Sacrifice. The problem is, after we are saved, we then try to perfect Righteousness and Holiness within our hearts and lives, by the things we *"do."* Such an effort is impossible. While of course, what we do is definitely important; still, if our faith is in what we do, it will only tend to breed self-righteousness, and definitely will not breed the Righteousness which God can accept, i.e., *"Christlikeness."*

Despite the fact of being a Christian, which refers to being a new creation, all in Christ Jesus, the Believer cannot perfect any of the attributes of Righteousness within his life by his own efforts and abilities. It is simply impossible. All of these things are a work of the Holy Spirit, which comes under the heading of the *"Fruit of the Spirit"* (Gal. 5:22-23). As we've said over and over in this Volume, the Holy Spirit only requires one thing of us as it regards Him carrying out this work within our lives, and that is that we evidence Faith totally and completely in Christ and what He did at the Cross (Rom. 8:1-2, 11).

When the Believer anchors his Faith in the Cross of Christ (Gal. 6:14), he is making a statement. He is saying that he knows he cannot do this thing himself, which is certainly correct, and as well, that Christ has done everything that is needed for us at the Cross. The unfortunate thing is, we attempt to do that which we cannot do, and in fact,

NOTES

which Christ has already done.

The very reason that Christ came to this world is because we could not do these things which are required. So He came and did them all for us. He was our Substitute in all things, doing for us, what we could not do for ourselves.

However, once we become a Christian, we tend to forget that these things are beyond our grasp. We have a tendency to stop trusting Christ, and start trusting in our own efforts, while all the time, claiming that we're trusting Christ.

TRUSTING CHRIST

Let the Reader understand the following:

No matter what the Christian might say, no matter how much the Christian may claim to be trusting Christ, and no matter how loudly he may claim it, if he's not trusting in what Christ did at the Cross, then he's really not trusting Christ, irrespective of his claims.

In fact, almost every Christian claims to be trusting Christ. But the truth is, only those who are truly denying themselves and taking up the Cross daily are actually following Christ as they should (Lk. 9:23).

When Jesus spoke of *"denying oneself,"* He wasn't speaking of asceticism, which is the denial of all things which are comfortable or pleasurable, He was rather speaking of denying our own strength, efforts, and ability to live this Christian life, and rather depending totally and completely upon Him (Christ).

When He spoke of taking up the Cross daily, He wasn't speaking of suffering, which most Christian believe, but rather trusting in the benefits which come from the Cross.

As well, He told us to do this even on a *"daily"* basis, which is in effect, a renewal of faith on a daily basis. By that we speak of a renewal of Faith in the Cross on a daily basis, believing that what Jesus did there has continued results, and in fact results that will never be discontinued, and results that can meet my every need. It is somewhat like the Manna which came on a daily basis in Old Testament times.

THE MESSAGE OF THE CROSS

The Message of the Cross is not a mere doctrine, but rather the foundation on which all Doctrine is built. Let's explain it in another way:

What Jesus did on the Cross is not a mere doctrine. In fact, what He did there is the entirety of the New Covenant. So when we teach the Cross, we are in effect teaching the entirety of the New Covenant, typified in that which we refer to as *"the Lord's Supper."* As what He would do (future tense) was typified in the Old Testament Sacrifices, what He has done (past tense) is typified in the Lord's Supper.

So this means the story of the Bible is the story of the Cross. And if we don't understand the Bible in that fashion, then we really don't understand the Bible. The *"Cross"* stands at the center of all that God has done and is doing for humanity. So every single Doctrine must be built upon the foundation of the Cross, or else in some way, it is unscriptural.

Therefore, understanding the Cross in that fashion, we begin to come to the conclusion as to how important all of this is. In fact, the Message of the Cross, as would be obvious, is the single most important aspect of the Plan of God. In fact, it is the Plan of God.

When we understand this, and then at the same time realize that the modern Church knows next to nothing about the Cross, we then begin to understand the precarious position in which the modern Church now finds itself. Being for all practical purposes Cross illiterate, it has little knowledge as to where it has been, where it is, or where it's going. Not understanding the Cross, the far greater majority of Christians now live in the Seventh Chapter of Romans. That is tragic but true! Of course there is an exception here and there, and thank God for that, but the truth is, those exceptions are few and far between.

This can only be remedied by the Message of the Cross (I Cor. 1:18), being taught to the Church. The Scripture still says, *"So then Faith cometh by hearing and hearing by the Word of God"* (Rom. 10:17).

When one begins to understand the Message of the Cross, such understanding will affect the entirety of one's belief system. In other words, one will find their understanding of every subject in the Bible changing somewhat. By that I refer to everything being brought into line with the Cross of Christ. One will

NOTES

read the Bible differently than before. One will see and understand oneself differently than previous. And above all, one will understand the Lord in a different fashion than ever before. The Cross puts its own interpretation on every single thing in the Bible.

And when one begins to understand the Cross, one will then begin to enjoy the *"more abundant life,"* promised by Christ (Jn. 10:10). It's a shame, every single true Christian in the world has more abundant life, but only those who properly understand the Cross are enjoying that more abundant life. Once the Cross begins to be understood, this Christian experience takes on a brand-new complexion. It becomes a joy unparalleled in living for Christ. All fear is gone, replaced by love and Faith.

No, this doesn't mean that such a Christian will never have any more problems. But it does mean that every Christian who properly understands the Cross, will know where the solution to that problem can be found. As well, a proper understanding of the Cross doesn't mean that such a Christian has total victory. It means that Christian knows where the victory is found, and is definitely going that way.

All of this is a growing process; however, while the growing process is sometimes painful, that is still a million times better than no growth at all. And without an understanding of the Cross, there can be no proper growth. In fact, Jesus plainly said, *"For without Me you can do nothing"* (Jn. 15:5). In fact, the entirety of the Fifteenth Chapter of St. John bears this out. It is all in Christ, and more particularly, what Christ did at the Cross.

(6) "THIS IS HE THAT CAME BY WATER AND BLOOD, EVEN JESUS CHRIST; NOT BY WATER ONLY, BUT BY WATER AND BLOOD. AND IT IS THE SPIRIT THAT BEARETH WITNESS, BECAUSE THE SPIRIT IS TRUTH."

The composite is:

1. *"This is He that came,"* refers to the first Advent of the Son of God, when He embraced human nature without its sin through the Virgin Birth.

2. His coming to make an atonement for sin was accompanied by and made effective through water and blood. The water witnessed

to His full and proper humanity, while the blood witnessed to the nature of His atoning death.

3. *"Not by water only,"* refers to the fact that Jesus Christ being born into this world, and in effect being the *"Godman,"* very God and very man, within itself couldn't save anyone. This Living Word Who became flesh, had to shed His Blood at Calvary's Cross in order for men to be saved.

4. The Holy Spirit bears witness to the humanity and Deity of Christ, as well as His Atonement. He bears witness by making it effective in the hearts and lives of Believers in the *"born again"* experience.

5. The Holy Spirit is truth, which guarantees the effectiveness of Christ's atoning work.

WATER AND BLOOD

The phrase, *"This is He that came by water and blood, even Jesus Christ,"* refers to the Living Word becoming flesh (Jn. 1:1, 14), which is symbolized by *"water,"* and then at the same time being the Lamb of God Who took away the sin of the world, which was effected by the shedding of His Blood on the Cross of Calvary.

Concerning the Born-Again experience, which Jesus made possible by His becoming flesh and dying on the Cross, He said: *"Except a man be born of water and of the Spirit, he cannot enter into the kingdom of God."*

And then to tell us what He meant by that, He said: *"That which is born of the flesh is flesh* (which speaks of the baby being born into this world)*; and that which is born of the Spirit is spirit* (which speaks of the Born-Again experience)*"* (Jn. 3:5-6).

Some have tried to make the water as mentioned here by Christ refer to Water Baptism, exactly as some have tried to do as it regards John's statement, claiming that it refers to the Baptism of Christ. However, if this is done, it reduces the Salvation experience to a mere ceremony, which cannot be upheld Scripturally.

No, the *"water"* refers to humanity, in the case of our study, God becoming man, while the *"blood"* refers to the Atonement.

NOT BY WATER ONLY

The phrase, *"Not by water only, but by*

water and blood," testifies to the absolute necessity of the Atonement. In other words, God becoming Man, The Man Christ Jesus, being born of the Virgin Mary, and living a Perfect Life as a man, all represented by the *"water,"* as important as all of this was, and even as necessary, still, this within itself could not redeem anyone. It took both, His coming into this world as a human being, and dying on a Cross, which latter is represented by the *"Blood."*

Some time back I made the statement to a group of people that our Salvation didn't come to us merely because Jesus is God. The truth is, He has always been God. But that fact never saved anyone. God had to become flesh, which He did; nevertheless, if it had stopped there, as wonderful as that was, and as necessary as it was, still, that fact wouldn't have saved anyone. The truth is, the Living Word (Jn. 1:1), became flesh (Jn. 1:14), for the specific purpose of dying on the Cross, which had to be, in order to redeem humanity (Jn. 1:29).

"Blood" refers to the special work of Christ Himself — the work of reconciliation and atonement by His death and passion, the realization of all that the sacrifices and types of the former state of Judaism had meant. That He was the True Sacrifice was proved by the perfection of his life, by the signs and wonders with which He had attracted and convinced His followers, by the fulfillment of prophecy, by the marvels of His teaching, by the amazing events which had happened at the different crises of His life; however, had it stopped there, there would have been no atonement. He had to go to the Cross, which He did, which necessitated the shedding of His Life's Blood, which atoned for all sin. It was for this reason that the Word was made flesh and dwelt among us.

John constantly upholds the humanity of Christ, represented here by the water, as well as His Deity, and does so throughout this Epistle.

The Cerinthian Gnostic heresy claimed that the Divine element came upon Jesus at His Baptism and left Him before His death on the Cross. Consequently, during this time they denied His humanity, and before this time, they denied His Deity. So by John making these statements as he does, he proclaims Christ as Very Man and Very God, and all at the same time.

There are two things that must not be confused. The first is the *"Person"* of Christ, as it regards His humanity and Deity, and the second is the Atonement as carried out by Christ, which concerns His work on the Cross. And to be frank, one might say that all false doctrine in some way begins here.

THE HOLY SPIRIT

The phrase, *"And it is the Spirit Who bears witness,"* proclaims the fact that the Holy Spirit, using the Person and Work of Christ, will bring about a satisfactory work in the hearts and lives of all who believe. This means that His witness is more than an affirmation of truth. It is that, but as well, it is the bringing about of that for which Jesus came and died.

TRUTH

The phrase, *"Because the Spirit is truth,"* refers to the fact that the Spirit, Who is ultimate Truth, is the only one capable of so bearing witness (I Jn. 3:24; 4:13). Man cannot receive the witness by himself. There are no human categories available to him through which he can understand it. God's redemptive act in Christ is not a bit of data humankind can deduce for itself by analogical reasoning. Like the Resurrection, it can only be announced. And this time it is not made known by Angels as the Resurrection (Lk. 24:6) but by the Spirit of God.

This statement as given by John concerning the Holy Spirit, does not take away from the conception of the Holy Spirit as one of the Persons of the Trinity, for the Lord Jesus also referred to Himself as the Truth (Jn. 15:26). The idea is that it is the Holy Spirit Whose characteristic is Truth, to Whom John refers.

This tells us that John no longer stresses the fact that he himself and the Apostles are the ones testifying as he did in I John 1:2 and I John 4:14, but he does not do this because their Apostolic testifying is not sufficient for faith, i.e., *"the doctrine of the Apostles."* John advances from the intermediate bearers of testimony to the ultimate

One Who testifies. As the Epistle progresses it advances as it goes along.

THE ULTIMATE ONE

The ultimate One bearing testimony, from Whom all the Apostles also derive their testimony, on Whom their own faith also rests, is the Holy Spirit, none less. This refers to the Third Person of the Godhead.

The Spirit is above all the ones giving testimony, and is thus the ultimate Testifier, *"because the Spirit is the truth,"* the truth itself. Jesus calls Him *"the Spirit of the Truth"* (Jn. 15:26; 16:13). Jesus adds:

"He shall testify concerning Me." To the Apostles Jesus says: *"And you, too, testify, because from the beginning you are with Me"* (Jn. 15:27). All of this agrees with what John says in I John 1:2 and in I John 4:14 about the Apostles' testifying and now about the Spirit as the One testifying. The relation of the Apostles to the Spirit is plain: Jesus gave them the Spirit. In fact, they speak as being borne along by the Holy Spirit (II Pet. 1:21), the Spirit being the ultimate Testifier.

As well, the One testifying, is in the present tense, because the Spirit has never ceased testifying, and does so unto this hour (Lenski).

(7) "FOR THERE ARE THREE THAT BEAR RECORD IN HEAVEN, THE FATHER, THE WORD, AND THE HOLY SPIRIT: AND THESE THREE ARE ONE."

The structure is:

1. The Law has ever required and requires to this day that two or three testify (Deut. 17:6; 19:15; Mat. 18:16; II Cor. 13:1); God Himself adheres to this principle (Heb. 10:28-29); so does Jesus (Jn. 5:31-37; Heb. 6:18).

2. *"The Father, the Word, and the Holy Spirit,"* refer to the Trinity. Jesus Christ is the Word (Jn. 1:1).

3. It is impossible that *"three"* can be *"one"* except in unity. This is clear from John 17:11, 21-23. Three can easily be one in unity, but three cannot be one in number.

THREE

The phrase, *"For there are three that bear record in Heaven, the Father, the Word, and the Holy Spirit,"* specifically proclaim the Trinity.

Most Scholars claim that Verse 7 is not in the original Greek Text, and is, therefore, not a part of the Scripture. Whether that is true or not, I cannot tell; however, what is said in this Verse is correct, so we'll leave it at that.

UNITY

The phrase, *"And these three are one,"* as previously stated, proclaims unity.

I suppose there has been more discussion regarding the Trinity than any other subject found in the Bible. The phrase, *"these three are one,"* in effect says that there is one God, Who is manifest in Three Persons, *"God the Father, God the Son, and God the Holy Spirit."*

TRINITY

The Christian doctrine of God is distinguished by its emphasis on Divine Three-in-Oneness, that is, the eternal coexistence of God the Father, God the Son, and God the Holy Spirit, all in the inner personal life of the Godhead. Evangelical theology affirms that the living, speaking, and acting God is a Personal Divine Trinity of Father, Son, and Holy Spirit in the eternal unity of God Himself, and then His Work. The one God, the subject of all Divine Revelation is self-disclosed — as the Bible authoritatively teaches:

1. As the invisible Father: From Whom all Revelation proceeds.

2. The Son: Who mediates and objectively incarnates that Revelation in an historical manifestation.

3. The Holy Spirit: Who is Divinely outpoured and subjectively applies that Revelation to men.

A BIBLICAL TERM?

The term *"Trinity"* is not necessarily a Biblical term, although I personally believe that it definitely is Biblical. The Scripture gives the doctrine of the Trinity, not in formulated definition, but in fragmentary units, similar to many other elements of the Christian system of Truth.

B. B. Warfield remarked that the entire New Testament *"is Trinitarian to the core; all its teaching is built on the assumption of the Trinity; and its allusions to the Trinity are frequent, cursory, easy, and confident."*

There is in the New Testament, as in the

Old Testament, only One True and Living God; and in its view, Jesus Christ and the Holy Spirit are each God in the fullest sense; and Father, Son, and Spirit stand related to each other as *"I," "Thou,"* and *"He."*

Many Passages in the Gospels teach Jesus' Divinity and the Son's unity with the Father. In the context of such Passages, it is emphasized that the same essential interrelationship extends to the Holy Spirit (Jn. 14:16-26; 15:26; 16:5).

The importance of the Baptismal formula (Mat. 28:19) lies in the fact that it most nearly approaches the Doctrine in the words enunciated by the Lord Himself, preserved, moreover, by one of the synoptic writers. This formula impressively asserts the unity of Father, Son, and Holy Spirit by embracing them as a single name, yet emphasizes the distinctiveness of each Person by repeating the article: *"In the Name of the Father and of the Son and of the Holy Spirit."*

The Pauline letters, for instance, likewise, not only repeatedly refer to God the Father and to Jesus Christ in juxtaposition, as joint objects of adoration, but the Holy Spirit appears with Them as a Personal Source of all Divine Blessing. In the early as well as the later writings of Paul, all three Persons are mentioned together as Co-Sources of the Blessings of Salvation (I Thess. 1:2-5; II Thess. 2:13; I Cor. 12:4; II Cor. 13:14; Eph. 2:18; 3:2; 4:4; 5:18; Titus 3:4; II Tim. 1:3, 13). In fact, the other New Testament writings repeat the same pattern (Heb. 2:3; 6:4; 10:29; I Pet. 1:2; 2:3; 4:1; I Jn. 5:4; Jude Vs. 20; Rev. 1:4).

ST. JOHN, CHAPTER 17

As stated, the evidence of the Trinity is obvious throughout the entirety of the Bible, and especially throughout the New Testament; however, possibly the greatest concentration of Divine Personalities evidenced is found in the Seventeenth Chapter of the Gospel according to John.

In this Chapter, the *"Son"* prays to the *"Father,"* and is anointed by the *"Holy Spirit"* to do so, inasmuch as the entirety of the Bible is inspired by the Holy Spirit. In this Chapter, five times our Lord prays for *"oneness,"* as it regards the Body of Christ, as well as the Trinity.

He said:

"That they may be one, as We are" (Jn. 17:11).

And then:

"That they all may be one; as You, Father, are in Me, and I in You."

He then said:

"That they also may be one in Us" (please note the plurality of the pronoun *"Us"* [Jn. 17:21]).

He then said clearly and plainly:

"That they may be one, even as We are One" (Jn. 17:22).

And finally:

"I in them, and You in Me, that they may be made perfect in one" (Jn. 17:23).

Most clearly, this defines the Trinity. It does not mean one in number, but it most definitely means *"one in unity."* Moreover, regarding the Trinity, it definitely means one in Essence, and regarding the Body of Christ, it means the same in principle.

As stated, there is one God, manifested in three Persons, *"God the Father, God the Son, and God the Holy Spirit."*

(8) "AND THERE ARE THREE THAT BEAR WITNESS IN EARTH, THE SPIRIT, AND THE WATER, AND THE BLOOD: AND THESE THREE AGREE IN ONE."

The exegesis is:

1. Once again the three witnesses come into view. As in Heaven so on Earth.

2. *"The Spirit, and the water, and the blood,"* speak of the Holy Spirit, the humanity of Christ, while never ceasing to be Deity, and the Atonement, i.e., *"the Cross."*

3. These three agree that Christ is Very Man while at the same time being Very God, Who died on the Cross to redeem fallen humanity.

THE THREE ON EARTH

The phrase, *"And there are three that bear witness in earth,"* once again stands by the three witnesses, holding to Scripture.

These three witnesses have borne record on Earth from the very moment that Jesus died on the Cross, with His Righteousness being accepted in Heaven. As a result, the Holy Spirit was sent to this Earth in a dimension in which He had not heretofore known. As stated, all of this was made possible by the Cross. From that moment He has been bearing witness

in this Earth of what Calvary produced.

I think I can say without fear of exaggeration that hundreds of millions of lives during this span of time (the age of the Church) have been gloriously and wondrously changed by the Power of God. The witness of these miraculous conversions is clear and plain for all to see.

THE SPIRIT, THE WATER, AND THE BLOOD

The phrase, *"The Spirit, and the water, and the Blood,"* has to do with the Holy Spirit and with Christ, and especially what He did at the Cross on behalf of dying humanity. These are the three witnesses on Earth.

As we've said repeatedly, the Holy Spirit works exclusively within the parameters of the Finished Work of Christ. This is what Paul was talking about in Romans 8:2. In fact, the Holy Spirit works so closely with Christ, and especially as it refers to His Sacrifice, that in the vision that John had of the Throne in Heaven, we find the following:

"And I beheld, and, lo, in the midst of the Throne and of the four beasts, and in the midst of the Elders, stood a Lamb as it had been slain, having seven horns and seven eyes, which are the seven Spirits of God sent forth into all the earth" (Rev. 5:6). Several things are here said:

1. This which John saw is at the Throne of God in Heaven, signifying the highest place and position.

2. The fact that this which John saw is in the *"midst of the Throne and of the four beasts,"* proclaims such as most holy. The very function of these *"Beasts"* or *"Cherubim"* is to say, *"Holy, holy, holy, LORD God Almighty, which was, and is, and is to come"* (Rev. 4:8). This tells us that there is nothing more holy than what Jesus did at the Cross on behalf of lost humanity.

3. This vision is as well *"in the midst of the Elders,"* refers to the fact that this great Sacrifice was made on behalf of humanity.

4. Jesus is referred to here as *"a Lamb as it had been slain,"* signifying the Cross. In other words, this is the manner and way in which Christ appears before God at the Throne. As such He is our Great High Priest and Intercessor.

5. The Holy Spirit is so closely intertwined

with Christ that They are looked at as one and the same. One could say, *"these two are one."*

6. The Holy Spirit is shown as *"having seven horns and seven eyes, which are the seven Spirits of God sent forth into all the earth."*

All of this of course, is symbolic, with the number *"seven"* referring to totality, perfection, and completion; *"horns"* referring to perfect dominion; with *"eyes"* referring to perfect illumination.

Everything the Holy Spirit does within our hearts and lives as Believers, He does strictly on the basis of justice satisfied by and through the Finished Work of Christ. The *"water"* signifies the humanity of our Lord, while the *"blood"* signifies what He did in His humanity — die on the Cross, which necessitated the shedding of His Life's Blood.

AGREEMENT

The phrase, *"And these three agree in one,"* refers to the one purpose of all of this, the redemption of mankind, which Christ effected by what He did at the Cross.

We had best understand that this *"agreement"* centers up in what Christ did at the Cross. The purpose of the Spirit is to witness to this great act. The purpose of the *"water"* is to guarantee the Incarnation of Christ, God becoming man. The purpose of course, of *"the blood"* is to signify the price paid, and the Holy Spirit guarantees that it will never have to be paid again, inasmuch as that which Christ did was and is totally sufficient. *"These three agree in this one Atonement."*

(9) "IF WE RECEIVE THE WITNESS OF MEN, THE WITNESS OF GOD IS GREATER: FOR THIS IS THE WITNESS OF GOD WHICH HE HATH TESTIFIED OF HIS SON."

The diagram is:

1. Why can't we receive the witness of God, if we, in fact, receive the witness of sinful men? The latter practices deception, while the former cannot possibly deceive.

2. The Son is the Witness of God, and is far greater than the witness of men.

3. This witness centers up on the Cross.

THE WITNESS OF GOD

The phrase, *"If we receive the witness of men, the witness of God is greater,"* in effect

NOTES

says, *"Since we are in the habit of receiving the testimony of men, we should understand that the testimony of God is infinitely greater, and therefore should be received."*

What the Spirit, the water, and the blood say is God's Own testimony; these three testifiers are furnished by Him, by Him because this testimony of His deals with His Own Son. This constitutes its greatness. Once given, it stands now and ever — the perfect testimony.

When the Father sends us three Testifiers and through them in the most legal way testifies about His Own Son, can we who daily receive the testimony of men refuse to accept this great testimony, which is great because it is given by God and is given about His Son? I think the answer to that is obvious!

This Divine witness proclaims the Trinity. We have the witness of the Spirit and we have the witness of Christ, and now we have the witness of the Father. It was His voice that confirmed that Jesus' *"passion"* was an act in which God would glorify Himself (Jn. 12:28-30). So also it is God's Own Voice that is being heard again in the threefold witness.

THE CROSS

The phrase, *"For this is the witness of God which He has testified of His Son,"* centers up on the Cross. In fact, it can be no other way.

God the Father testifies as to Who the Son is, i.e., *"His Son"* (Mat. 3:17), and as well testifies to the veracity of what His Son did in the giving of Himself on the Cross. He testified to the veracity of the Cross in two ways:

1. The moment Jesus died, God rent the Veil in the Temple, which hung between the Holy of Holies and the Holy Place, signifying that the way to the very Throne of God was now opened, and made possible by what Jesus did at the Cross (Mat. 27:51).

2. He raised Christ from the dead, which testified to the fact that Jesus had atoned for all sin by His death on the Cross, and thereby, death could not hold Him (Mat. 28:2-6).

In fact, the very reference as given here by the Holy Spirit through John, referring to Christ as *"God's Son,"* testifies as to Who He is, and What He has done. All of this was that He might go to the Cross offering up Himself in Sacrifice, which would make it possible for man to be redeemed on the basis of justice satisfied. The very appellative *"Son"* and more particularly *"His Son,"* proclaims this great Truth.

(10) "HE THAT BELIEVETH ON THE SON OF GOD HAS THE WITNESS IN HIMSELF: HE THAT BELIEVETH NOT GOD HAS MADE HIM A LIAR; BECAUSE HE BELIEVETH NOT THE RECORD THAT GOD GAVE OF HIS SON."

The diagram is:

1. The key is in *"believing,"* and not so much doing; however, when one properly *"believes,"* one will properly *"do."*

2. Our *"believing"* must be in Christ and what Christ has done for us at the Cross.

3. When this happens, there is a definite witness in the heart of the Believer that he has been Born-Again.

4. The person who does not believe in the Son of God with a heartfelt faith is in effect calling God a liar.

5. There is no excuse for unbelief as it regards the Lord Jesus Christ, considering the witnesses to this great truth which God has given the world.

FAITH

The phrase, *"He that believeth on the Son of God has the witness in himself,"* refers to a know so Salvation. As we've already stated, it refers to *"believing"* or *"faith"* rather than *"doing."* And what do we mean by that?

The greater problem with faith is not so much having faith, but is rather the proper object of Faith.

First of all, the Holy Spirit through John is telling us that our Faith must be centered up in Christ. And more specifically, it must be centered up in what Jesus did at the Cross on our behalf. There are several problems one might say regarding Faith, and some of them are as follows:

1. There are untold millions of people in the world who claim to have some type of overall faith in God, but in this type of faith, the Lord Jesus Christ is just sort of a part of the mix. In other words, faith is not really centered up in Him. This type of faith will not be honored by God.

2. There are millions who have faith in Christ, but it is really *"another Jesus"* in which they are having faith (II Cor. 11:4).

NOTES

What do we mean by that?

If our thinking regarding Christ is not exclusively in Him and what He did to redeem us, which He did by going to the Cross, then it is *"another Jesus"* in whom we are evidencing faith. God will not honor such faith.

3. Now we speak of the proper Faith. *"Jesus Christ and Him Crucified"* must ever be the object of our Faith (I Cor. 2:2, 5). In other words when we think of Jesus, we are to automatically think of the Cross. To be sure, every attribute of Christ, every work of Christ, every action of Christ, all and without exception, are of extreme significance; however, every single thing He did, was leading up to the central purpose of His Coming, which was to die on the Cross. It was the Cross and the Cross alone that made our Salvation possible and as well, our victorious, overcoming life and living. That is why Paul said:

"For Christ sent me not to baptize, but to preach the Gospel: not with wisdom of words, lest the Cross of Christ should be made of none effect" (I Cor. 1:17).

In other words, Water Baptism, and all the other ordinances of the Church for that matter, are greatly important; however, the emphasis must never be placed on those things, but always on Jesus Christ and Him Crucified. The Cross must ever be held up as the central theme within our hearts and lives.

Once this is done, and I speak of Faith in Christ and His Finished Work, there will definitely be a *"witness"* in the heart and life of the Believer that he is saved, that his name is written down in the Lamb's Book of Life, that he is a Child of God, etc.

The love of Jesus satisfies the deepest need of our nature. When He is welcomed, the soul rises up and greets Him as *"all its Salvation and all its desire"* and the testimony is no longer external in history but an inward experience and, therefore, indubitable. Thus, the one who believes on the Son of God and what He has done for us at the Cross has the testimony in him to the effect that he thus believes. Paul in Romans 8:16 tells us that the Holy Spirit bears testimony in connection with our human spirits as energized by the Holy Spirit that we are Children of God. That is, our human spirit, energized by the Holy Spirit, gives us the consciousness that we as Believers are Children of God. The Holy Spirit testifies to us that the same thing is true (Wuest).

All of this means that to the real Believer the threefold Testimony of God no longer remains merely an outward object of thought to be contemplated and grasped: it has become part of our own nature.

UNBELIEF

The phrase, *"He that believeth not God hath made Him a liar,"* presents the problem of unbelief as the basic difficulty in the human race. This tells us that unbelief is not merely a difference of opinion, but in actuality a deep and abiding affront toward God. It is in effect, and as stated, calling God a *"liar."*

If we are to notice about John, he doesn't mince words. He cuts straight through to the bottom line.

So the unbeliever may try to claim that they aren't calling God a liar, but the Holy Spirit here through John, says that's exactly what is happening. Let's be more specific:

How is it that such a position is in effect calling God a liar?

In effect, God is saying, that the sinner cannot be saved, and neither can the Believer walk in victory, unless they place their Faith in Christ, and more particularly, *"Jesus Christ and Him Crucified"* (I Cor. 1:23). If the sinner thinks he can be saved some other way, he is calling God a liar, because God says he can't. If the Christian thinks he can walk in victory by placing his faith and trust in things other than the Cross, whether he realizes it or not, he is calling God a liar, because God said in His Word that the victorious life cannot be maintained without proper faith in the Cross (Rom. 6:3-5, 11, 14).

In other words, man cannot receive anything from God unless he goes through the Cross. This is the Word of the Lord (I Cor. 1:17). If he thinks he can, he's calling God a liar.

To be a little more blunt, this means that the part of the Church which advocates humanistic psychology, is in effect calling God a liar. It means that the part of the Church which denigrates the Cross, referring to it as *"past miseries,"* and *"the greatest defeat in human history,"* is calling God a liar. This

means that any Christian who tries to live for God by means other than explicit Faith in the Cross of Christ, is calling God a liar.

As should be obvious, these are very serious charges. I think no sane Christian would want to be caught in such a position. To make God out a liar is blasphemy!

THE RECORD

The phrase, *"Because he believeth not the record that God gave of His Son,"* proclaims the fact that the proof is undeniable.

It is making God a liar when one refuses to believe God's Testimony regarding anything; however, it is making God a liar in the worst possible way when one refuses to believe God's Testimony about His Own Son.

One must note that believing is not a matter of the head and the intellect alone but that it ever appeals to the heart. Faith is the confidence of the heart, in the Believer, the objective testimony of God and thus all that God's testimony contains as John now makes plain.

When we claim fellowship with God outside of the Cross, we are in effect making Him a liar, because He tells us there is no fellowship outside of the Cross, and on top of that, we are claiming that He fellowships liars! (Eph. 2:13-18).

The *"record"* that God gave of His Son, is found in His Word, and as well in the hearts and lives of untold millions who have given themselves to Christ.

(11) "AND THIS IS THE RECORD, THAT GOD HAS GIVEN TO US ETERNAL LIFE, AND THIS LIFE IS IN HIS SON."

The diagram is:

1. The *"record"* is the Word of God, which is the story of the Cross.

2. God has given to fallen man, who was dead in trespasses and sins, the gift of Eternal Life, at least to those who will believe.

3. This life is contained in Jesus Christ, and more particularly, what He did at the Cross on behalf of lost mankind.

THE CREED

The phrase, *"And this is the record,"* in effect tells us that the story of the Bible, is the story of Jesus Christ Who gave Himself for sinners, and did so on the Cross.

The Christian creed is reduced here to a

very small compass: the gift of Eternal Life and the dependence of receiving that life upon His Son. Eternal life does not mean here the mere continuance of life after death, whether for good or evil; it is the expression used throughout John's writings for that life in God, thought of without reference to time, which can have no end, which implies Heaven and every possible variety of blessedness, and which consists in believing in God the Father and His Son.

Its opposite is not annihilation, but the second death! Existence but excluded from God.

ETERNAL LIFE

The phrase, *"God has given to us Eternal Life,"* presents, one might say, the greatest words that were ever given to the human race.

"Eternal Life" as stated, is not mere existence, but rather the Life of God flowing into and literally becoming a part of the individual.

In the coming First Resurrection of Life, this Eternal Life will translate into a future without physical death. This will be brought about by the glorified body, which will be like that of the physical body of Christ (I Jn. 3:2).

On the part of God, this Eternal Life that is given to every Believer, came at great price. Even though we know and understand that the price was the giving of His only Son, at the same time, our comprehension of this, the most unselfish act in history, can only go so far. In other words, the price paid is beyond our magnitude of comprehension.

LIFE IN THE SON

The phrase, *"And this life is in His Son,"* refers to what Christ did at the Cross. This means that Eternal Life is only in Jesus. All who are in Him have this Eternal Life and all out of Him do not have it.

Most certain in Romans 6:3-5, Paul explains how this Life which is in the Son, can come to the Believer.

In these three Verses, we are given a brief description of the Crucifixion of Christ, but more particularly our part in that death. Christ was our Substitute, which was the very reason that He became a man.

Whenever we as a believing sinner evidenced Faith in Him, and I speak of the time that we were initially saved, in the Mind of God, we

NOTES

were literally baptized into His death. We were also buried with Him, and raised with Him in newness of life. In other words, in the Mind of God we literally died. It was a death of the *"old man"* (Rom. 6:6-7).

As a result of His Death and Resurrection, and our Faith in that Finished Work, we were literally placed *"in Christ."* Actually, that was the idea! It all came by faith on our part, but was just as real in the Mind of God, if we had been the one who had died there; however, it really would have done us no good to have gotten on a Cross inasmuch as we were an unfit sacrifice. Only Christ could fit this bill. In our place He was born Perfect. In our place He lived a Perfect Life without sinning even one time. In other words, He kept the Law of God in every respect. In our place He went to the Cross, in order that the terrible sin debt could be addressed. The penalty must be paid, and only a Perfect Sacrifice would be sufficient. Christ Alone, as stated, fit that bill. So to be *"in Him,"* which refers to all *"life,"* our Faith must be in Him exclusively, and more particularly, what He did at the Cross.

It is not enough to merely believe in Christ, we must believe in what Christ has done for us, and that refers to the Cross. If Christ is separated from the Cross, and done so in any manner, and at any time, He then becomes *"another Jesus"* (II Cor. 11:4), which faith God can never accept. That's the reason that Paul hammered this subject constantly, that it must be *"Jesus Christ and Him Crucified"* (I Cor. 1:17-18, 21, 23; 2:2, 5).

When the Holy Spirit through John said, *"This Life is in His Son,"* He is referring to what Christ did at the Cross. One might say that this Life was in Christ always and be Scripturally correct; however, the Cross became the means by which this Life was transferred from Christ to the believing sinner. In fact, this is what John 3:16 actually says.

(12) "HE THAT HATH THE SON HATH LIFE; AND HE THAT HATH NOT THE SON OF GOD HATH NOT LIFE."

The structure is:

1. The only way to have Eternal Life is for one to accept Christ as their Saviour and Lord, which refers to accepting what He did at the Cross.

2. It doesn't matter how religious a person

may be, if that person has not made the Lord Jesus Christ their Saviour, they do not have Eternal Life. This completely voids all the religions of the world.

3. Once again we emphasize, all of this which Christ has done for us, was made possible by the Cross.

LIFE

The phrase, *"He that hath the Son hath life,"* refers to accepting the price that Christ paid, which was paid at the Cross, which made it possible for this Eternal Life to be given to sinners. This is why Jesus said:

"I am the Door: by Me if any man enter in, he shall be saved, and shall go in and out, and find pasture" (Jn. 10:9).

John binds everything together. God's testimony brings us His Son; Eternal Life is in His Son, is in Him for us; it is given us in and by this testimony; to believe it is to have the Son, and to have Him is to have this Life; not to believe it is not to have the Son and this Life. It is all as simple and as lucid as these brief statements make it.

John can say for himself and for his readers: *"God gave to us Life Eternal,"* gave it to us when we believed His testimony and thereby received the Son into our possession with all that He is for us. Regarding the heretics he can now let the general statement suffice: *"The one not having the Son does not have this Life."*

WITHOUT THE SON THERE IS NO LIFE

The phrase, *"And he that hath not the Son of God hath not life,"* presents no room for argument.

It is not an idea, a system of belief, or even a fact that is the ultimate object of faith; it is a Person. That Person is Jesus Christ. He is to live in us (I Jn. 3:24). His love is to abide and be made complete in us (I Jn. 4:12). We are to live in Him (I Jn. 4:13). And this is life eternal.

Every religion in the world projects an idea. Christianity, which incidentally is not a religion, but rather a relationship, projects a Person. That Person is Christ, and one's relationship with Him, which is carried out by Faith in Him and His Finished Work on the Cross, gives us Eternal Life.

NOTES

By John using the phrase *"Son of God,"* he is telling us two things:

1. He is telling us that Jesus Christ is God.

2. He is also telling us that He gave of Himself on the Cross, which was necessary if we were to be redeemed.

(13) "THESE THINGS HAVE I WRITTEN UNTO YOU THAT BELIEVE ON THE NAME OF THE SON OF GOD; THAT YOU MAY KNOW THAT YOU HAVE ETERNAL LIFE, AND THAT YOU MAY BELIEVE ON THE NAME OF THE SON OF GOD."

The composite is:

1. The purpose of this Epistle is not merely that we may have Eternal Life by believing, but that we may know that we have it.

2. The Gospel exhibits the Son of God, the Epistle commends Him. It is a supplement to the Gospel of John, a personal application and appeal.

3. To *"believe,"* is to make Christ not only the Saviour of the soul, but the Lord of one's life as well.

FAITH

The phrase, *"These things have I written unto you that believe on the Name of the Son of God,"* carries within the structure of the sentence, not only Who Christ was, but as well, What He did to redeem humanity, which was to go to the Cross. The whole of what John writes, is to bring to the mind of his readers the fact that they have life eternal, and because they believe on the Name (Revelation) of the Son of God.

What does it mean to truly believe?

"Believe" in the Greek is *"pisteuo,"* and means *"persuasion, conviction of the truthfulness of God, constancy in such profession, assurance."* It is believing something with all of one's heart, in effect, giving oneself totally to that which is believed, and in this case, to the One in Whom one has believed, namely Christ. It is belief, faith, and confidence, without reservation. In the case of Christianity, it is far more a Person than it is an ideal. With all the religions in the world it is the opposite, but with Christianity, the central focus is always Christ.

As well, to believe in Christ, is to give oneself wholly to Him, in effect, as Paul used the term, becoming His bond slave. As should be obvious, this is far more than merely giving mental assent to something. Millions believe to that extent as it regards Christ, but they aren't saved. This is far more than a mere acknowledgment as to Who He is or what He has done; but rather, the giving of oneself to Him, which refers to what one has been, what one is, and what one shall be. It refers to ambition, place, position, love, wants, desires, etc., everything centers up in Christ.

And as everything centers up in Christ, the thrust of our faith goes to not only as to Who He is, but as well, to what He has done, and we refer to the Cross.

If one is to notice, in every way the Holy Spirit presents Christ, He does so in the capacity of what Christ has done to redeem fallen humanity. For instance, when He mentions the *"Name of the Son of God,"* He is not only referring to Deity, but as well, for the very reason that He became the Son, which was to go to the Cross. Had He said *"Jesus Christ,"* He would have been saying the same thing. The very Name *"Jesus,"* means *"Saviour,"* even as *"Christ"* means *"Messiah,"* or *"The Anointed."* So the Anointed One came to this world in order to save lost humanity, which He did by going to the Cross.

A KNOW SO SALVATION

The phrase, *"That you may know that you have Eternal Life,"* actually proclaims the central purpose of this Epistle which is not merely that we may have Eternal Life by believing, but that we may *"know that we have it."*

"Know" in the Greek is *"oida,"* and means not a mere experimental knowledge, but of absolute, beyond the shadow of a doubt knowledge, a positive knowledge.

I suppose that one of the most oft asked questions is, *"How can one know positively that one has Eternal Life?"*

This is where both subjective and objective truth are brought to bear.

Subjective truth is not very reliable, and because it is subject to circumstances, situations, feelings, etc. To the contrary, objective truth has as its objects the Lord Jesus Christ, which includes God's Word and the Holy Spirit (Jn. 14:6; 17:17; I Jn. 5:6). Such Truth is not subject to variances or feelings, so it cannot change. But yet, when it comes

NOTES

to the Salvation process, both subjective truth and objective truth are brought to bear, but subjective truth here is subject to the Word of God and, therefore, in this case, is correct. Let me give a personal illustration:

MY PERSONAL SALVATION

I was saved at a most unusual time and in a most unusual place. The year was 1943. It was a Saturday afternoon at approximately 2 p.m., that is if I remember the time correctly. It was either late spring or early summer. I was eight years old.

That early Saturday afternoon, I got into the line with other kids, waiting for the ticket window to open, in order to go see the Saturday afternoon movie. Our little town of Ferriday, Louisiana, only had one movie theatre. And every Saturday afternoon they showed one of the *"shoot 'em ups."* As an 8 year-old boy, that particular type of thing was somewhat attractive to me.

As we stood there in line waiting for the window to open, without any previous warning, the Spirit of God came upon me, with the Lord speaking to my heart, saying, *"Do not go into this place. Give me your heart. I want to use you in My service."* Beyond the shadow of a doubt I knew it was the Lord.

SALVATION CAME TO OUR HOUSE

My Mother and Dad had given their hearts to Christ about two years earlier. After coming to Christ, they never missed Service; consequently, I also went to Church every time the doors were opened. Hearing the preaching of the Word during these couple of years, laid the groundwork for what was to happen that Saturday afternoon.

Some may ask as to how as an 8 year-old child, I could know that this was the voice of the Lord?

First of all, it was not an audible voice, but rather a voice in my spirit. But yet, it was so forceful, so powerful, so unmistakable, that I had absolutely no doubt that it was the Lord. No, I had never experienced anything like this before, and in fact, had never heard of anything of this nature. But still, I knew it was God.

One can either believe that God is able to do all things, or else, one does not believe. If

God is in fact, Almighty, even as the Scripture says He is, then He would have no difficulty whatsoever in speaking to an 8 year-old child, or anyone else for that matter.

When the Lord spoke to me that afternoon, I did not respond immediately. I knew it was God, but in my spirit I said nothing, and in my actions I did nothing.

About that time, the ticket window opened and the kids began to purchase their tickets with the line moving forward.

I guess I must have been two or three kids away from the window, when the Lord spoke to my heart again. The words were identical, and if possible, even more forcible.

"Do not go into this place. Give Me your heart. I want to use you in My service."

By this time I was at the window. I remember laying my quarter down on the table-like projection in order to purchase the ticket. In my spirit I was in a great quandary.

About that time, the spool of tickets jammed, and the lady selling the tickets diverted her attention to freeing the spool.

I'll always believe that the Lord jammed that spool of tickets in order to give me a few more moments. At about the same time she freed the spool, in my heart I said *"Yes"* to the Lord. I grabbed my quarter, and bolted from the line.

I remember walking past the Piggly Wiggly supermarket, Doris' Dress Shop, and Ellis' Five and Dime. I walked into Vogt's Drug Store on the corner, and I'll never forget it, Vogt, Jr. was behind the counter. I took my quarter that I was supposed to use to go to the movies, and bought a triple-decker ice cream cone, vanilla, strawberry, and chocolate. Those were the only flavors we had in our little town in those days.

I took my dime change and walked outside.

I stopped on the corner facing the street with the ice cream cone in my hand. All of a sudden I felt something like I've never felt in my life. It was like 500 pounds were lifted from my shoulders.

I've often thought about that! I was only a child, only 8 years old. But if I felt that wonderful, that good, when I came to Christ, considering that I knew next to nothing about sin, how must someone feel who

NOTES

has been delivered from the worst type of sinful bondages?

But yet, every child is born in original sin, and when Salvation does come, whether early or late, a miraculous transformation takes place, and does so to such an extent, that it is obvious.

SUBJECTIVE TRUTH

Of course, I'm certain that each person is different. Their feelings are different, their reactions are different. Some are more emotional than others, but in some way, I believe that every person who comes to Christ, senses something within his heart and life that's different than he has ever sensed before. This is subjective truth, but it is truth based on the Word of God; therefore, it is not erroneous by any means.

I don't want to leave the idea that *"feelings"* are a part of Salvation. Actually they aren't, and that's the reason I refer to this particular type of truth as *"subjective."* But still, as human beings, we have emotions and feelings. And Salvation affects such a powerful change within our hearts and lives that I think I can say, without any fear of exaggeration, Salvation in some way can be felt by every single human being, irrespective as to the type of personality they might be. It is impossible, I think, for such a miraculous change to take place in one's heart, which refers to the entrance of the Holy Spirit, with thereby the Divine Nature becoming a part of the individual, without that person feeling something. It may not come at the exact moment of Salvation, but at some point, come it will.

OBJECTIVE TRUTH

However, the bedrock of our Salvation, that by which we know beyond the shadow of a doubt, that we now have Eternal Life, is because the Word of God says that if certain things are done, Eternal Life will accrue to the Believer. It says it and we believe it. Irrespective as to what I feel, or don't feel, my faith is to believe, and when I believe, I am guaranteed that which the Word promises.

The Scripture plainly says: *"That if you shall confess with your mouth the Lord Jesus, and shall believe in your heart that God has*

raised Him from the dead, you shall be saved
. . . For whosoever shall call upon the Name
of the Lord shall be saved" (Rom. 10:9, 13).

If we do what the Word says to do, and
thereby believe it with all of our heart, we have
the guarantee of the Word that we are saved,
i.e., "have Eternal Life." As stated, whatever
we feel, or don't feel, God's Word cannot lie.
We are saved! That is objective truth.

MY REACTION

That memorable day in 1943 when I gave
my heart to the Lord, I knew beyond the
shadow of a doubt that I was saved. There
was no doubt in my heart.

Not having gone to the movies, I got home
early. My Mother was surprised to see me
home at that time, and immediately asked
as to what had happened. I said to her, "I
didn't go to the movies!"

"Why didn't you go?" she immediately
asked.

Somewhat matter-of-fact I answered her,
"I got saved!"

"You what?" she exclaimed.

I then told her what had happened, and
then I'll never forget her reaction. She put
her arms around me, and began to cry.

A few months later I was baptized with
the Holy Spirit with the evidence of speaking with other tongues. And then began my
love for the Word of God which continues
unto this hour. But going back to the original subject, make no mistake about it, this is
a "know so Salvation."

WHAT IS THE NAME OF
THE SON OF GOD?

The phrase, "And that you may believe
on the Name of the Son of God," actually says
in the original text, "That you may know that
you have eternal life, unto you that believe
on the Name of the Son of God."

The Name of the Son of God is "The Lord
Jesus Christ"; however, John uses the
appellative "the Son of God" because of the
denial of the heretics who claimed that Jesus
was not really the Son of God. The Readers
must know this with a clear mental perception in order to meet and to refute these
Gnostic heretics when they come with the
claim that they are the ones who know.

NOTES

This is the purpose of John's instructive,
clear, simple presentation. John has already
said that he is writing nothing new and
strange (I Jn. 2:7), also that his Readers have
for a long time realized and believed (I Jn.
2:13; 4:16); John writes in order to fortify
his Readers just as we must also constantly
be informed and fortified anew. Therefore,
John's first Epistle is addressed to those who
have accepted Christ but still need assurance
that through this Name they have indeed
received Eternal Life. So the Apostle refers
16 times to what we Believers know:

1. We do know that we know Him (I Jn.
2:3).

2. Hereby know we that we are in Him (I
Jn. 2:5).

3. Because you know . . . the truth (I Jn.
2:21).

4. We know that we have passed from
death unto life (I Jn. 3:14).

5. And hereby we know that we are of the
truth (I Jn. 3:19).

6. And we know that He abideth in us (I
Jn. 3:24).

7. Hereby know ye the Spirit of God (I
Jn. 4:2).

8. Hereby know we the Spirit of Truth (I
Jn. 4:6).

9. Hereby know we that we dwell in Him
(I Jn. 4:13).

10. By this we know that we love the Children of God (I Jn. 5:2).

11. That you may know that you have Eternal Life (I Jn. 5:13).

12. Whatsoever we ask, we know that we
have the petitions that we desired of Him (I
Jn. 5:15).

13. We know that whosoever is born of
God sinneth not (I Jn. 5:18).

14. And we know that we are of God (I Jn.
5:19).

15. And we know that the Son of God is
come (I Jn. 5:20).

16. That we may know Him that is true (I
Jn. 5:20).

The false teachers present a different
"knowledge" as well as a different lifestyle.
John counters with a series of tests by which
the Believers can evaluate the false teachers' claims and practices. Walking in the
light, obeying His commands, loving one's

brother, being steadfast in the community of faith, doing what is right — these serve as tests of whether the life that is from God has been received.

When it has been received, it is only because God's witness to His Own Son as the Source of that Life has been accepted and believed. On this basis, we can expect God to hear us in prayer, free us from the presence and power of sin, and forgive our transgressions. Those who know these things know that they have received Eternal Life (Barker).

(14) "AND THIS IS THE CONFIDENCE THAT WE HAVE IN HIM, THAT, IF WE ASK ANY THING ACCORDING TO HIS WILL, HE HEARETH US:"

The exegesis is:

1. Proper believing gives us proper confidence, which is proper assurance.

2. *"According to His will"* does not mean that we should first ascertain His Will and then pray, but that we should pray with the provision, expressed or implicit, *"if it be Thy will."*

3. The promise is not that He grants it, but that He hearkens to us. He answers in His Own way.

CONFIDENCE

The phrase, *"And this is the confidence that we have in Him,"* refers here to that which relates to the answer to prayer. The Apostle does not say that this is the only thing in respect to which there is to be confidence in Him, but that it is one which is worthy of special consideration.

The confidence we have in our life with Christ belongs not only in the future time of His Coming (I Jn. 2:28) and of Judgment (I Jn. 4:17) but also in the present and especially in the fellowship of prayer. We know that we have access to Him (I Jn. 3:21) and that *"He hears us."*

In John *"hearing"* does not mean simply to be listened to but to be heard favorably (Jn. 11:41-42). The expectation is, of course, linked to the qualifying phrase *"if we ask according to His will."*

This seems to reflect a natural dependence on Jesus' Own teaching — *"Thy will be done"* (Mat. 6:10) — and His example in

NOTES

Gethsemane — *"Not what I will, but what You will"* (Mk. 14:36).

THE WILL OF GOD

The phrase, *"That, if we ask anything according to His Will, He heareth us,"* presents the proper and necessary limitation to all prayer.

God has not promised to grant anything that shall be contrary to His Will, and it could not be right that He should do it. We ought not to wish to receive anything that should be contrary to what He judges to be best. It is one of the most desirable of all arrangements that the promise of any blessing to be obtained by prayer should be limited and bounded by the Will of God.

The limitation here, *"According to His Will,"* probably implies the following things:

1. In accordance with what He has declared that He is willing to grant. Here the range is large, for there are many things which we know to be in accordance with His Will, if they are sought in the proper manner and way — as the forgiveness of sins, the Sanctification of the soul (I Thess. 4:3), comfort in trial, the needful supply of our wants, grace that we may do our duty, wisdom to direct and guide us (James 1:5), deliverance from the evils which beset us, the influences of His Spirit to promote the cause of Christ in the world, and our final Salvation. Here is a range of subjects of petition that may gratify the largest wishes of prayer.

2. The expression, *"according to His will,"* must limit the answer to prayer to what He sees to be best for us. Of that we are not always good judges. We never perceive it as clearly as our Maker does, and in many things we might be wholly mistaken.

Certainly we ought not to desire to be permitted to ask anything which God would judge not to be for our good.

3. The expression must limit the petition to what it will be consistent for God to bestow upon us. We cannot expect that He will work a miracle in answer to our prayers, which will at the same time harm someone else. We cannot ask Him to bestow blessings in violation of any of the laws which He has ordained, or in any other way than that which He has appointed. It is better that the

particular blessing should be withheld from us, than that the laws which He has appointed should be disregarded.

It is better that an idle man should not have a harvest, though he should pray for it, than that God should violate the laws by which He has determined to bestow such favors as a reward of industry, and work a special miracle in answer to a lazy man's prayers.

4. The expression, *"according to His will,"* must limit the promise to what will be for the good of the whole. God presides over the universe; and though in Him there is an infinite fullness, and He regards the wants of every individual throughout His immense creation, yet the interests of the whole, as well as of the individual, are to be consulted and regarded.

In a family, it is conceivable that a child might ask for some favor which bestowment would interfere materially with the rights of others, or be inconsistent with the good of the whole, and in such a case a just father would of course withhold it. With these necessary limitations the range of the promise in prayer is ample; and, with these limitations, it is true beyond a question that He does hear and answer prayer (Barnes).

MODERN ERROR

The modern *"Word of Faith"* teaching has greatly hindered the Church as it regards prayer and receiving from the Lord:

1. This group little believes in prayer, but rather in *"confession."* They claim that prayer is an admission that something is wrong, and in their teaching, nothing can ever be wrong with a *"new creation man."*

2. They teach that Jesus was literally born again as a sinner, which He experienced of all places in Hell, and that when we are born again we are then placed in the *"God class."* As a result, they claim we can create things by what we say, and in a sense, have the same creative power as Christ. He is a *"born again man,"* they say, and us being born again, puts us in His class.

As such, the Will of God about any matter is little, if ever, consulted, because we are now in the *"God class"* and, therefore, automatically know the Will of God in all things.

In this capacity, they teach that it's never proper for us to ask the Lord for something,

and say, *"if it be Thy will,"* but rather to merely *"confess it into existence."* Anything we say or do, they say, is the Will of God.

As a result of this teaching which has made great inroads in the modern Church, and especially among the Pentecostals and Charismatics, prayer has almost become a thing of the past. We have Christians running around all over confessing all sorts of things.

I would hope the Reader can see that all of this caters to pride, and not at all to Christ. In fact, it is the very opposite of Christ; as well, this teaching is basely unscriptural and, therefore, Satanic. It is fostered by seducing spirits, and is in fact, *"doctrines of Devils"* (I Tim. 4:1).

As we've said elsewhere in this Volume, this particular doctrine makes too little of Christ and too much of man. It humanizes Christ to a fatal degree, and deifies man to a fatal degree.

(15) "AND IF WE KNOW THAT HE HEAR US, WHATSOEVER WE ASK, WE KNOW THAT WE HAVE THE PETITIONS THAT WE DESIRED OF HIM."

The diagram is:

1. God answers our prayers in His Own way.

2. *"We have our request"* not always as we pray but as we would pray were we wiser.

3. God gives us not necessarily what we ask but what we really need.

WE KNOW THAT HE HEARS US

The phrase, *"And if we know that He hear us, whatsoever we ask,"* presents the fact that we are assured of this, even though we may not see immediately that the prayer is answered. Still, we have the utmost confidence that it is not disregarded, and that it will be answered in the way best adapted to promote our good, if we ask in His Will.

The argument here is derived from the faithfulness of God; from the assurance which we feel that when He has promised to hear us, there will be, sooner or later, an answer to prayer.

THE CROSS

As we've been saying throughout this Volume, everything comes to the Child of God from God by the means of the Cross. In other words, it is the Cross that makes it possible for God to deal with mankind, whether the sinner to be saved, or whether blessing the Christian. No one ever outgrows the Cross! No one ever dispenses with the Cross! No one goes beyond the Cross! To go beyond the Cross is to lose one's way, for the simple reason there is nothing beyond the Cross.

In truth, it's impossible for one to go beyond the Cross, simply because it's impossible for one to exhaust the benefits of what Jesus did in the giving of Himself. In understanding this, no Christian can have a proper prayer life, unless that Christian properly understands the Cross. Listen to what Paul said:

"But we preach Christ crucified . . . unto them which are called, both Jews and Greeks, Christ the Power of God, and the Wisdom of God" (I Cor. 1:23-24).

In the Message of the Cross, we find both the *"Power of God"* and the *"Wisdom of God."* Both come through the Holy Spirit. In effect, that's what John was speaking about when he gave us the account of his Vision of the Throne of God. He said:

"And I beheld, and, lo, in the midst of the Throne and of the four beasts, and in the midst of the Elders, stood a Lamb as it had been slain, having seven horns and seven eyes, which are the seven Spirits of God sent forth into all the earth" (Rev. 5:6).

The *"horns"* stand for dominion and power, while the *"eyes"* stand for wisdom. The number *"seven,"* as we've already stated several times in this Volume, stands for totality, perfection, and completion. It is God's number. In other words, the *"power"* of God is *"all-power,"* and His wisdom is *"all-wisdom."* This is all in the Holy Spirit, but as we can see from this Sixth Verse, the Holy Spirit is so intertwined with the *"slain Lamb,"* that they are for all practical purposes, one and the same. The idea is this:

THE HOLY SPIRIT

The Holy Spirit works within our lives strictly on the basis of the Sacrifice of Christ. This great Finished Work is what gives Him the legal right to do all that He does. And here is what the Reader must understand:

The Spirit will not work in our lives regarding His *"power"* and *"wisdom,"* unless our faith is properly placed in the Cross. Listen again to what Paul said:

"For the preaching (Word) *of the Cross is to them that perish foolishness; but unto us which are saved it is the Power of God"* (I Cor. 1:18).

To be sure, the Cross itself has no power, and in actuality, the death of Christ on that Cross contains no power. The power without exception is in the Holy Spirit (Lk. 4:18). But the Holy Spirit works 100 percent within the parameters of the Finished Work of Christ. He demands that we have Faith in what Christ has done for us, and that our Faith be there exclusively. Paul again said:

"For the Law of the Spirit of Life (the Holy Spirit works through a law) *in Christ Jesus* (this law is in what Christ did at the Cross) *has made me free from the law of sin and death"* (Rom. 8:2).

Some Pentecostals and Charismatics think that because they speak in tongues once in awhile, this means the Holy Spirit is working mightily within their lives. As Paul said, I speak in tongues almost every day of my life, and to be sure, every Christian would benefit greatly from this given to us by the Spirit of God; however, the *"Power of God"* and the *"Wisdom of God"* don't work on that basis. And how do I know that?

I know it because there are millions of Spirit-filled Christians who are praying and worshiping in tongues quite often, which they should do, but are at the same time failing the Lord on a constant basis. In other words, the *"sin nature"* is ruling these Christians despite the fact they are Baptized with the Holy Spirit, etc. Now that comes as a shock to most Christians; however, it shouldn't, and for the simple reason, that the problem which I now address, is literally pandemic among Spirit-filled Christians. In fact, there are millions of Spirit-filled Christians who are greatly confused and perplexed, because they don't understand what is happening to them. How can they be Spirit-filled, and at the same time failing, and despite the fact that they are doing everything within their power not to fail? (Rom. 7:15).

SPIRIT-FILLED BUT FAILING JUST THE SAME

Most Pentecostals and Charismatics refuse to address this subject, simply because they don't understand what is happening and they don't know the answer. So most try to cover up their failure in various different ways. And let me say it again:

We are not speaking here of an isolated few, but in reality virtually all Spirit-filled Christians. Why?

Most modern Christians, including the Spirit-filled variety, have little or no knowledge of the Cross. There has been so little teaching on this subject in the last several decades, that for all practical purposes, the modern Church is Cross illiterate. That means it doesn't know where its foundation is? Where its victory is? Where its power is? In other words, the modern Church doesn't know how to live for God.

I realize these are strong statements, but they just happen to be true!

To prove my point Scripturally, let's go to Romans, Chapter 7. This is the account of the experience of the Apostle Paul immediately after he was saved. Now let's understand it correctly:

This man was saved on the road to Damascus (Acts, Chpt. 9). In fact, his Salvation was probably one of the most dramatic in the history of mankind. Three days later he was baptized with the Holy Spirit, as Ananias prayed for him (Acts 9:17). As well, he was called from that moment to be an Apostle (Acts 9:15).

So we now have a man who is redeemed, Spirit baptized, called to be an Apostle, with the Spirit of God working in him. And yet, according to the Seventh Chapter of Romans, despite these things we've just said, Paul found that he couldn't live a victorious life, and no matter how hard he tried. Listen to what he said:

"For that which I do I allow (understand) *not: for what I would* (to live right) *that do I not; but what I hate* (fail the Lord regarding sin), *that do I"* (Rom. 7:15).

In fact, this Fifteenth Verse is the exact place where most modern Christians are as well. In fact, if the Christian doesn't understand the Sixth Chapter of Romans, then he is doomed to relive the Seventh Chapter of Romans.

Now if we know anything at all about Paul, we know that he was a man of strong courage

NOTES

and fortitude. And yet even Paul couldn't live for God, at least in victory, without knowing and understanding the Cross. And if he couldn't do this thing, how do you think you can do it?

Now many Preachers try to place Romans, Chapter 7 Paul's experience before he was saved; however, even an elementary perusal of this Chapter will prove the fallacy of that thinking. No! The Seventh Chapter of Romans deals with a saved, Spirit-filled man, who was trying to live for God outside of the means and ways of the Cross. That's why Paul said:

"Oh wretched man that I am! Who shall deliver me from the body of this death?" (Rom. 7:24).

To Paul's credit, there was no one else in the world of his day who knew the victory of the Cross, that truth having not yet been given. But out of the desperation of Romans, Chapter 7, the Lord gave to Paul God's prescribed order of victory.

GOD'S PRESCRIBED ORDER OF VICTORY

The Lord has only one way of victory, and that is what He gave Paul which is outlined in Romans, Chapter 6. He gave to the Apostle the meaning of the Cross, which in effect, is the meaning of the New Covenant. In other words, in that particular Chapter we are told how to live a victorious life, and to do so on a perpetual basis.

Even though this can be outlined in several different ways, perhaps the following will help. The Sixth Chapter of Romans teaches us the following:

1. The Cross: In Romans 6:3-5, we learn how through the Cross that we are placed *"in Christ."* We are crucified with Him (baptized into His death), buried with Him, and raised with Him in newness of life. We must learn that everything in our Christian living must always come through the foundation of this experience. We never outgrow this, simply because it's not possible to outgrow this. In fact, it's not even possible to exhaust the potential of the Cross.

2. Death: Paul then said, *"Knowing this, that our old man is crucified with Him, that the body of sin might be destroyed,*

that henceforth we should not serve sin" (Rom. 6:6). Before the *"new man"* could be, the *"old man"* had to die, which it did at the Cross. That's why the Cross is so very, very important. There the *"old man"* died, and the *"new man"* was raised in resurrection life.

3. Faith: Understanding this, we are to *"reckon ourselves to be dead indeed unto sin, but alive unto God through Jesus Christ our Lord"* (Rom. 6:11). Pure and simple, this means that our Faith is to be totally and completely in what Christ did for us at the Cross. Now this is so very, very important!

If we have a problem, this is the place where the problem will surface. And if there is a problem in us living victorious, it is a problem with our *"faith."* Our Faith must ever be anchored in the Finished Work of Christ, for there and there alone, was all victory purchased.

4. Victory: Paul then said, *"For sin shall not have dominion over you: for you are not under the Law, but under grace"* (Rom. 6:14). If our Faith is properly placed in the Cross, and our Faith properly remains in the Cross, then the *"sin nature"* will no longer have dominion over us. Now let's go back to what we originally said:

Concerning most of the modern Church, the sin nature does have dominion over them. This means, and despite the fact that many are Spirit-filled, that sin in some way is dominating that particular individual. And it is dominating them because they don't understand the things that we've said in the last few paragraphs. In other words, they do not understand Romans, Chapter 6. Please read the following very carefully:

LAW AND GRACE

Most Christians erroneously think that because this is the day of Grace, or rather the Dispensation of Grace, that this means that we're automatically under Grace.

In fact, this *is* the Dispensation of Grace, and has been ever since the Cross; however, believe it or not, despite that fact, most Christians are living as though this was still the Dispensation of Law. To be sure, there is a little Grace mixed in their thinking, which without they couldn't be saved; however, for

NOTES

the most part, most are living under Law. Let me say it this way:

If the Believer doesn't understand the things I've said here concerning the Cross, whether the Believer knows it or not, that Believer is living under Law in some way. Why do you think Paul said this in this fashion?

When Paul was living his experience of Romans, Chapter 7, he was living under Law. He didn't know what else to do! Now what does it mean to live under Law?

It means that we're trying to live this Christian life by means other than Faith in the Finished Work of Christ. We're trying to live for God by the means of rules and regulations made up by our Church, or made up by ourselves, or someone else. For instance:

Most Christians think that being consecrated means that they are faithful to Church, faithful with their tithe, and that they read their Bible a little each day, and pray a little each day, or a regimen to that effect.

To be sure, every good Christian will definitely do these things, but not for the purpose and the reason we have just mentioned. The problem is this:

Such Christians are putting their Faith in the *"doing"* of these things, which is what makes it wrong. Now don't misunderstand and think that I am saying that being faithful to Church is wrong, etc. I'm not saying any such thing. In fact, I'm saying the very opposite. Again let me emphasize, every good Christian will definitely be faithful to Church, will definitely be faithful with his tithes, will definitely be faithful in his Bible study, etc. But to be sure, we aren't good Christians because we do these things. In fact, we do these things because we already are a good Christian. But the tragedy is, most are doing these things in order to try to be a good Christian, which means, that they've placed their faith in the doing of these things and not in the Cross.

And if a Christian does this, and the far greater majority do, then whether the Christian realizes it or not, he is living under *"law."* To be sure, it's not the Law of Moses, but rather a law that he's made up himself, or that someone has made up, but still it is law. And when we do this, what happens in the spirit world?

THE FRUSTRATION OF GRACE

If we are living our Christian lives in this fashion, and I mean by putting our trust in these *"good things"* which we do, then we are frustrating the Grace of God. Listen again to Paul:

"I am crucified with Christ (again we come back to the Cross)*: nevertheless I live* (raised with Christ in newness of life)*; yet not I, but Christ liveth in me: and the life which I now live in the flesh I live by the Faith of the Son of God, Who loved me, and gave Himself for me* (gave Himself on the Cross).*"*

The Apostle then said: *"I do not frustrate the Grace of God: for if Righteousness come by the law, then Christ is dead in vain"* (Gal. 2:20-21).

The Apostle plainly says here that if we can become righteous by doing certain things, then Jesus didn't need to come down here and die on a Cross. In effect he is saying, that all the great Plan of God as it regards the Cross was a wasted effort, if we can live this life by doing good things.

No, we live this life by Faith. And that means that we place our Faith totally and completely in Christ, which means to believe in what He did for us at the Cross. When we do this, the Holy Spirit can then work mightily on our behalf, which is outlined in Romans, Chapter 8.

WHY DO CHRISTIANS WANT TO HOLD ON TO LAW?

Law which refers to our own efforts, our own doings, is the product of our own ingenuity, ability, and strength. And it goes against the grain for somebody to tell us that all of these laborious things we are doing to try to make ourselves holy, are in fact, not succeeding at all. And again, there is something in all of us that likes to think that we are contributing something toward our Holiness and Righteousness.

I think all would agree that no one could have a better teacher than the Apostle Paul. And yet, after he had labored in bringing in the Churches in Galatia, which goes without saying that he had brought them in right; still, after Paul had gone on to other fields of labor, teachers of the law came in to these Churches, telling the people that the Cross

wasn't enough, and that they needed to have law added to their Christian experience; consequently, the Apostle wrote the entirety of the Epistle to the Galatians to correct this terrible error. And to be sure, he was not too very nice in this Epistle. In fact, I think one could state and without fear of contradiction, that the man was downright angry.

He knew if these Galatians abandoned the Cross, accepting law instead, that it would destroy them. So we would ask the following question:

How could these people who had been grounded correctly, throw over the Cross in favor of the law which was going to wreck their Christian experience?

As stated, there is something in all of us that loves *"law."* We love rules and regulations! As someone has well said, the doing of religion is the most powerful narcotic there is. Let's go to the Old Testament for a perfect example.

ABRAHAM AND ISHMAEL

The effect of the birth of Isaac was to make manifest the character of Ishmael. Ishmael hated him, and so did his mother. Prompted by her he sought to murder Isaac (Gal. 4:29), and with his mother was justly expelled. Both merited the severer sentence of death. Thus, the birth of Isaac which filled Sarah's heart with mirth, filled Hagar's with murder.

Isaac and Ishmael symbolize the *new* and the *old* nature in the Believer. Sarah and Hagar typified the two covenants of works and grace, of bondage and liberty (Gal., Chpt. 4). The birth of the new nature demands the expulsion of the old. In fact, it is impossible to improve the old nature.

The Holy Spirit says in Romans, Chapter 8 that *"it is enmity against God, that it is not subject to the Law of God, neither indeed can be."* Therefore, if it cannot be subject to the Law of God, how can it be improved?

Therefore, how foolish the doctrine of moral evolution appears! The Divine way of holiness is to *"put off the old man"* just as Abraham *"put off"* Ishmael. Man's way of holiness is to improve the *"old man,"* that is, to improve Ishmael. The effort is both foolish and hopeless. Now we come to the real problem:

The casting out of Ishmael was *"very grievous in Abraham's sight,"* because it always costs a struggle to cast out this element of bondage, that is, salvation by works. For legalism is dear to the heart. Ishmael was the fruit, and to Abraham the fair fruit of his own energy and planning. But the Epistle to the Galatians states that Hagar, the bondwoman, represents the covenant of the Law, and that her son represents all who are of *"works of law,"* that is, of all who seek Righteousness on the principle of works of Righteousness. But the bondwoman cannot bring forth a free man! The Son Alone makes free, and He makes free indeed (Jn. 8:32). Sarah, the freewoman, symbolizes the covenant of Grace and Liberty. *"So then, we are not children of the bondwoman but of the free."*

Going back to what we previously said about Abraham, he didn't give up Ishmael easily, and neither do we give up our *"works of religion"* easily.

THE STRUGGLE

As there was a struggle in the heart of Abraham to give up Ishmael, who was a type of the flesh, and because Ishmael was the product of Abraham's planning and scheming, it is likewise very hard for the Christian to give up all these things in which he has placed his faith, in favor of the Cross, and the Cross exclusively. But the Reader must understand if we are to walk in perpetual victory, we can only do so through and by Faith exclusively in Christ, and exclusively in what Christ did for us at the Cross. There is no other way!

The way of the *"law,"* will lead to more and more failure. It cannot be otherwise. The Holy Spirit will never help us in such an effort, and without the help of the Spirit, we are doomed to failure. And failure puts the *"sin nature"* in charge, which means that the same nature that ruled you before you were saved, can very well rule you after you are saved, and in fact, will definitely rule you, unless your Faith is anchored squarely in the Finished Work of Christ.

You, who are reading these words, now know. So you will from henceforth have no more excuse. In other words, the Lord through this Commentary has brought the truth to you. If you ignore it, and insist upon

NOTES

retaining the efforts of holiness by law, the spiritual deterioration will accelerate, and do so at a frightful pace. If the light is given, we must walk in that light.

So you have before you, the way of Grace and the way of Law. Which will you choose?

WHAT IS GRACE?

The Grace of God is simply the Goodness of God extended to undeserving Believers.

The idea is, all that we need from the Lord, we cannot at all provide for ourselves. In other words, we are helpless to bring about Righteousness, Holiness, Purity, Grace, Love, etc. Despite the fact that we are Believers, even as Romans, Chapter 7 exemplifies, within ourselves there is nothing we can do. In fact, every single thing done in our lives, that is the things which are from God, must be brought about by the Holy Spirit.

So all of these things we have mentioned, must be granted to us by the Lord. We cannot earn them, we cannot merit them, and we certainly aren't worthy of them. But the Goodness of God, which is Grace, extends all of these things to us, but does it only on one merit.

That merit is *"Jesus Christ and Him Crucified"* (I Cor. 2:2). In other words it is the Cross that makes it possible for the Goodness of God to be extended to us. And when we try to obtain this Goodness or Grace by other methods, for instance by our good works, etc., we only seek in frustrating the Grace of God. In other words, we stop its flow to our lives, which spells catastrophe (Gal. 2:21).

What needs to be done, we cannot do, but Jesus has done it for us at the Cross. If we do not understand that, and attempt to do ourselves what we in fact cannot do, we only seek to displease God. Paul plainly said: *"So then they that are in the flesh cannot please God"* (Rom. 8:8).

In fact, in Romans 8:7, the preceding Verse, Paul said: *"Because the carnal mind is enmity against God: for it is not subject to the Law of God, neither indeed can be."* In other words, no Believer can properly keep the Law of God, as was proven by Paul's experience in Romans, Chapter 7.

Now most Believers would counter by saying, *"but I'm not trying to keep the Law. All of that was done away with by Christ."*

Regarding the latter part, they are absolutely correct. It was done away with by Christ; however, if we are trying to live this life in any way other than by Faith in the Cross, then whether we realize it or not, we are trying to keep the Law all over again, which is impossible for us to do. Only Christ kept the Law, and He did it on our behalf, and because we couldn't do it for ourselves. So for us to try to live for God outside of the Cross, in effect states that God doesn't know what He's talking about, and that we in fact, can keep the Law, which means that all that Jesus did was a wasted effort.

I realize that these thoughts aren't in our minds; however, by our actions, that's the way it translates in the Mind of God.

Paul mentioned *"the carnal mind,"* and he mentioned *"the spiritual mind."* What was he talking about? (Rom. 8:6-7).

Most Christians think that being *"carnally minded,"* is watching too much television, etc. At the same time, they think that being *"spiritually minded"* is reading the Bible, etc. Such thinking is basely incorrect.

Being *"carnally minded"* refers to trying to live for God by means other than Faith in the Cross. Being *"spiritually minded"* is living for God by the means of Faith in the Cross. It is just that simple!

In fact, being *"carnally minded"* and being *"in the flesh,"* both mean the same thing — trying to live for God by means other than Faith in the Cross.

The Christian is *"under Grace"* (Rom. 6:14), if the Christian places his faith exclusively in the Finished Work of Christ, and not at all in himself. Any faith in anything other than the Cross of Christ automatically places such a Christian *"under the law."* He may not understand it, but that's exactly what is happening. And to be sure, if he is functioning *"under law,"* he is going to stop the Grace of God, which means that he is now doomed to failure, which means that he will now be ruled by the sin nature.

The Christian can be ruled by the sin nature or by the Spirit of God. He cannot be ruled by both. Listen again to what Paul said:

"For if you live after the flesh (by your own efforts and strength outside of the Cross), *you shall die: but if you through the*

Spirit do mortify the deeds of the body (which means to have Faith in the Cross of Christ), *you shall live* (be victorious)*"* (Rom. 8:13).

THROUGH THE SPIRIT

The Passage we've just quoted, tells us clearly and plainly that the only way we can walk in victory, i.e., *"mortify the deeds of the body,"* is *"through the Spirit."* If we try to do this thing *"after the flesh,"* which refers to our own efforts outside of the Cross, and thereby, outside of the Spirit, the Scripture plainly says, *"you shall die."* This means that you will fail; you will sin; the sin nature will rule you, which will lead to worse and worse action.

When Paul uses the term *"the flesh,"* almost all the time, he's speaking of our own strength and ability outside of the Holy Spirit. And as we found in Romans, Chapter 7, even the great Paul couldn't live this life by his own strength, ability, and means. It couldn't be done then, and it cannot be done now.

But most Christians would counter by saying, *"I am trusting Christ, but I'm still failing!"*

The trouble is, most Christians think they're trusting Christ, when they really aren't. The truth is, they are trusting Christ as it regards their Salvation, i.e., *"being saved."* But when it comes to living on a day-to-day basis, they in fact, aren't trusting Christ. And how do I know that?

I know that because most Christians don't know anything about the Cross, as it regards their day-to-day living. About all they know is *"Jesus died for me."* While that is certainly correct, they do not translate that into their daily living, but only as it regards their initial Salvation experience. Consequently, they are attempting to live for the Lord by the means of their own efforts, and because they don't know any better. In such a case, which includes almost the entirety of the modern Church, Paul said: *"Christ is become of no effect unto you, whosoever of you are justified by the Law* (seek to be justified by works, etc.)*; you are fallen from Grace"* (Gal. 5:4). Now let's look at it in another way:

Paul also said: *"For Christ sent me not to baptize, but to preach the Gospel: not with wisdom of words, lest the Cross of Christ should be made of none effect"* (I Cor. 1:17).

If we make the Cross of Christ of none effect, then *"Christ is become of no effect."* That being the case, I think we should understand that we are in trouble.

Now look carefully at what I've just said: If we make the Cross of Christ of none effect, we thereby make Christ of none effect.

HOW CAN A CHRISTIAN MAKE THE CROSS OF CHRIST OF NONE EFFECT?

If we read carefully I Corinthians 1:17, which I have just quoted, we can see how this can easily be done. It is placing the emphasis on things other than the Cross. Paul mentioned Water Baptism; however, it could be anything, and in fact, very good things; but, Satan doesn't care how good the other things are. He knows if emphasis is placed on anything other than the Cross of Christ that the Cross is then made of none effect, which leaves the Believer without the help of the Holy Spirit, and guarantees a failing life.

The reason I say the things I do about the modern Church is because of this very problem. How many Preachers presently behind pulpits are emphasizing the Cross? There are a few, but precious few to say the least! The truth is, the modern Church is emphasizing everything but the Cross. It is emphasizing Water Baptism, manifestations, humanistic psychology, healings and miracles, which most turn out to be illegitimate, and about everything else that one could think. But the facts are, most are not emphasizing the Cross whatsoever, and this means that most, irrespective of the erroneous claims, aren't living victorious lives.

While most of these things we have named are helpful and significant in their own right, they are not to be emphasized above the Cross, hence Paul making his strong statement.

The Lord has only one prescribed order of Salvation and victory, and that is the Cross of Christ. If we emphasize other things, we consign those who look to us for instruction, to spiritual failure. And to be sure, we aren't meaning merely that the growth of such a Believer will be stunted, but rather that Satan, the enemy of their souls, will take full advantage of their wrong direction, and wreak spiritual havoc on them. We are speaking here of the issues of life and death, which

NOTES

means we are speaking of the most important thing there is.

INDEPENDENT OF THE CROSS

Most of the modern teaching regarding the Bible centers up on *"self,"* instead of Christ. To be sure, Christ is used, but only used. And I say that because of the following:

If we do not link Christ with the Cross, and do so every time we think of Christ, then we aren't properly preaching Christ, but rather *"another Christ"* (II Cor. 11:4). To make a Christian independent of the Cross is to guarantee spiritual failure on the part of that Christian. Such teaching consigns that individual to spiritual oblivion. Let's say it another way:

Any teaching that pulls a Christian away from the Cross, irrespective of what it may seem like on the surface, is in fact a promotion of *"self."* There is simply no other way to go. We're either depending on the Spirit or the flesh (Gal. 5:16). If we preach the Cross, we are *"walking in the Spirit."* If we preach anything else other than the Cross, we are *"walking in the flesh,"* which always caters to *"self."* In that case, *"works of the flesh"* are going to manifest themselves in some way.

WORKS OF THE FLESH

Paul said: *"Now the works of the flesh are manifest, which are these; adultery, fornication, uncleanness, lasciviousness, idolatry, witchcraft, hatred, variance, emulations, wrath, strife, seditions, heresies, envyings, murders, drunkenness, revellings, and such like"* (Gal. 5:19-21).

When most Christians think of works of the flesh, they only think of the first four, *"adultery, fornication, uncleanness, lasciviousness."*

Most dismiss idolatry as not applying to this age, when in reality, many Christians are neck deep in idolatry. Let me give you an example:

Millions have made and do make idols out of their Churches, Denominations, or even Preachers.

"Witchcraft" is likewise relegated to another age; however, witchcraft is just as prominent as idolatry in the modern Church. The

truth is, if we try to deal with people in any manner other than the Spirit of the Cross, in one way or the other, we are engaging in witchcraft. In other words, we are dealing in the spirit world by ways and means other than the Cross, which will lead to spiritual disaster.

For instance, *"heresies"* are as well, works of the flesh. This refers to any doctrine that is taught, which has as its foundation something other than the Cross. Most Christians wouldn't think of such as a work of the flesh, but that's exactly what Paul says it is. This means that whatever particular, erroneous doctrine is being taught, it was not birthed by the Holy Spirit, but rather by the flesh, aided and abetted by demon spirits (I Tim. 4:1).

The only way that works of the flesh can be avoided, and in fact must be avoided, is by the Believer placing his Faith and trust totally and completely in Christ and what Christ did at the Cross on our behalf, which guarantees the help of the Holy Spirit (Rom. 8:1-2, 11, 13). Any other way is the way of defeat and disaster. Of these erroneous ways, there are many, whereas the Message of the Cross is one. It is *"Jesus Christ and Him Crucified"* (I Cor. 2:2, 5).

PETITIONS

The phrase, *"We know that we have the petitions that we desired of Him,"* proclaims the conclusion regarding the means and ways of the Holy Spirit respecting prayer. These ways are as follows:

1. Our Faith must rest solely within and upon *"the Son of God,"* which in its very nature speaks of the Cross.

2. Proper Faith breeds proper confidence.

3. We must pray within His Will, and definitely will do so if our Faith is properly in Christ and the Cross.

4. Our Faith properly placed, and praying according to His Will, guarantees that He *"hears us."*

5. Having Faith in the Christ of the Cross, which gives us confidence, and praying according to His Will, which guarantees that He hears us, guarantees as well that whatever we ask will be granted.

All too often, we forget the qualifications to answered prayer. After studying John we have no more excuse.

(16) "IF ANY MAN SEE HIS BROTHER SIN A SIN WHICH IS NOT UNTO DEATH, HE SHALL ASK, AND HE SHALL GIVE HIM LIFE FOR THEM THAT SIN NOT UNTO DEATH. THERE IS A SIN UNTO DEATH: I DO NOT SAY THAT HE SHALL PRAY FOR IT."

The composite is:

1. By the use of the word *"Brother,"* we know that John is speaking here of Believers.

2. The *"sin not unto death,"* while wrong, and because it's going in the wrong direction; still, there is hope that the person can be turned to the right way.

3. The sin not unto death refers to direction other than the Cross, and done in ignorance.

4. The Believer who understands God's prescribed order of victory which is the Cross, should pray for those who are ignorantly going in a direction opposite of the Cross.

5. The *"sin unto death,"* speaks of unbelief. This group is not opposing the Cross because of ignorance, but rather because they simply do not believe in the atoning work of Calvary.

6. While it is pointless to pray that God would forgive such a person, it is proper to pray that the blindness of their unbelief will be removed.

A SIN WHICH IS NOT UNTO DEATH

The phrase, *"If any man see his Brother sin a sin which is not unto death,"* as is obvious speaks of professing Christians, and in actuality, true Christians. Such a person has been genuinely saved, and is saved; however, they are rebelling against Christ and His Finished Work, through ignorance.

The idea is, such a Brother not knowing the way of the Cross, is living a life of spiritual failure, but yet he is saved. While what is being done will not cause the loss of the soul, it will cause the loss of all victory, in effect, making life miserable.

The author of the Fourth Gospel learned a whole mystic language from the Life and Ministry of Jesus. Death, in the great Master's vocabulary, was more than a single action. It was again wholly different from bodily death.

There are two realms for man's soul coextensive with the universe and with itself. One which leads towards God is called Life; one which leads from Him is called Death. There is the case by which the soul is translated from the death which is death indeed, to the life which is life indeed. There is another case by which we can pass from life to death, which John is addressing in this Verse.

As stated, the sin not unto death, refers to the Christian who is truly saved, which means that he's passed from death to life, but yet is trying to live this life outside of total dependence on the Cross. To be sure, his wrong direction, which constitutes rebellion against God, is definitely sin, but it's not a sin unto death, meaning that even though such a life is miserable, the soul will not be lost. In fact, any and every Christian who doesn't understand the Cross falls into this category, which regrettably, includes almost all of the modern Church.

Their trust is in Christ as it regards their initial Salvation, but it is in self as it regards their Sanctification, which is sin, but is done mostly in ignorance. In other words, they do not know the way of the Cross as it regards their daily living, i.e., *"Sanctification,"* and because this great foundational truth hasn't been taught them behind the pulpit. *"Faith comes by hearing and hearing by the Word of God"* (Rom. 10:17), and if one cannot hear the True Gospel in this respect, then one cannot exercise proper faith. As stated, this particular position characterizes almost all of the modern Church.

LIFE

The phrase, *"He shall ask, and he shall give him life for them that sin not unto death,"* refers to praying for such individuals. However, the Believer who understands the Cross should understand that such prayer, within itself, will not open the eyes of the individual or individuals in question, but is meant to be engaged in the sense that the true Message will be given to these particular people. That's what Paul was talking about when he said: *"Finally, Brethren, pray for us, that the Word of the Lord may have free course, and be glorified, even as it is with you"* (II Thess. 3:1).

The word *"life"* as we've already stated, refers to what the Believer is in Christ, and what the Spirit does within our hearts and

lives, that is when we properly understand the Cross. Listen to what Paul said:

"Even so we also should walk in newness of life" (Rom. 6:4). He is speaking here of resurrection life, which every Believer in effect has. However, we can only be in the *"likeness of His Resurrection,"* if we know and understand that *"we have been planted together in the likeness of His death"* (Rom. 6:5).

As well, the Holy Spirit is referred to as *"the Spirit of Life"* (Rom. 8:2).

When it comes to *"life,"* Christ has always had life, and in fact, is the very epitome of life, i.e., *"the Source of Life."* However, the life which He has always had, and in fact always is, could not be given to Believers, at least in the manner in which we now have such, until the Cross. In other words, the Cross made everything possible.

The moment any person comes to Christ, at that moment they have *"Eternal Life."* But that's not actually the *"life"* which John is addressing here. He is speaking here of the Life of Christ flowing in and through us, and doing so on a constant basis, simply because we are trusting solely in Christ and what Christ has done for us at the Cross. This is what Paul was speaking of when he said:

"I am crucified with Christ: nevertheless I live; yet not I, but Christ lives in me: and the life which I now live in the flesh, I live by the faith of the Son of God, Who loved me, and gave Himself for me" (Gal. 2:20).

THE SIN UNTO DEATH

The phrase, *"There is a sin unto death,"* continues to speak of Believers.

This *"sin unto death"* constitutes Believers who are in effect ceasing to believe. In fact, the entirety of the Epistle to the Hebrews, was written in respect to this very thing. Many Jews who had accepted Christ, were now turning their backs on Christ, actually denying Him, which means if they remained in that state, they would lose their souls. This is the sin of unbelief, and we must quickly ask, *"What type of unbelief?"*

As it regards the Cross, the Church is divided into three camps. They are:

1. The few who have placed their Faith totally and completely in Christ and what He has done for them at the Cross.

2. The group who is saved, but is trying to sanctify themselves by their own efforts and ability. They are doing so through ignorance, which means they do not know the way of the Cross, simply because it has not been taught to them.

3. The last group, which is large indeed, has abandoned the Cross and gone to other things, simply because they no longer believe that the Cross avails as it regards the perversions, aberrations, and sins of humanity. It is not a case of ignorance with these people, but rather rank unbelief. If they continue on that path, they will ultimately lose their souls, because to deny the Cross is to deny Christ. Most of these Preachers and laity alike, recommend humanistic psychology as the solution for man's problems. Many in such a state, have long since lost their way, which means they are no longer trusting Christ, even though they may continue to be very religious. Others are on the very brink!

PRAYER

The phrase, *"I do not say that he shall pray for it,"* refers to the fact that it is useless to pray that the Life of Christ could be imparted to these people, simply because they do not believe in such. However, it is proper to pray for them that their spiritual eyes of unbelief shall be opened, and they will truly see God's way. As stated, their problem is not ignorance but rather unbelief.

(17) "ALL UNRIGHTEOUSNESS IS SIN: AND THERE IS A SIN NOT UNTO DEATH."

The structure is:

1. *"Unrighteousness"* refers to any deviation from the Word, which the Holy Spirit here constitutes as sin.

2. All sin and all wrong are dangerous to our Spiritual Life.

3. All sins and all sinning, while greatly debilitating to the Believer, are not unto death. By confessing and fleeing to the intercession of our Advocate we may have our sins remitted and cleansed (I Jn. 1:8-2:2).

UNRIGHTEOUSNESS

The phrase, *"All unrighteousness is sin,"* refers to such as defined by God. Man's definition of unrighteousness is one thing, while God's definition is something else. We might

say that this refers to any deviation from the Word of God, which would be absolutely correct; however, the *"letter of the Law"* is one thing, while the *"spirit of the Law,"* is something else.

For instance, concerning the *"spirit of the Law,"* which refers to the Word of God, if we in any way take lightly the Sacrifice of Christ, we have embarked upon an unrighteous path. Such a direction constitutes rebellion against God's Way, which is the way of the Cross. And yet, most people would not think of such as sin, but God calls it sin. Listen to what Paul said:

"And he that doubteth is damned if he eat, because he eateth not of faith: for whatsoever is not of faith is sin" (Rom. 14:23).

The *"faith"* of which Paul here speaks, is Faith in Christ and what Christ did at the Cross, all on our behalf. Our Faith is to ever be anchored in that Finished Work. If it's not that kind of Faith, it's not only faith that God will not honor, but in fact, is *"sin."* And this wrong direction, which is away from the Cross, constitutes, I think, the origination of all sin, for it is rebellion against God and His way.

Righteousness which is the opposite of unrighteousness, as well can only be properly defined by understanding Christ. Man has a form of righteousness which God refers to as self-righteousness, which He will never honor.

"Righteousness" refers to that which is *"right,"* and is what God refers to as *"right."* Within himself, man has no righteousness, but in fact, has much unrighteousness.

The only Righteousness which God will honor, is the spotless, pure, Perfect Righteousness, which comes from His Son and our Saviour, the Lord Jesus Christ, and is made possible to us through the Cross, and our Faith in that Finished Work. Faith in what Christ did there, is the only way that this spotless, pure Righteousness of Christ, can be freely imputed to the Believer. And when this Righteousness comes in, which it does upon Faith in Christ, all unrighteousness departs (I Cor. 6:11). However, we must never forget, even as all righteousness comes to us solely by Faith in Christ and what He has done for us at the Cross, likewise, all unrighteousness departs the same way. As it's impossible for man to generate righteousness within himself, it is also impossible for man to rid himself of unrighteousness by his own means. All, the righteousness comes and the unrighteousness goes, due to what Christ did at the Cross (Rom. 4:25; 5:1-2, 16-19, 21; 8:2, 11, 13; I Cor. 1:17-18, 21, 23; 2:2, 5).

SIN

The phrase, *"And there is a sin not unto death,"* goes back to the previous Verse. It speaks of the individual who has trusted Christ for Salvation, which refers to trusting in what Christ did on the Cross, but not trusting Him as it refers to our daily living. The lack of trust in the latter instance is due to ignorance and not unbelief; therefore, such a sin, even though bringing upon the individual great disturbance, will not cause one to lose their soul.

This type of person lives a life of *"sinning and repenting, sinning and repenting."* That is a very debilitating way to live, but in fact, most Christians live this way, simply because they do not know God's prescribed order of victory. And because it's so serious, let us state the following again:

The *"sin unto death,"* constitutes the Believer who, as stated, is ceasing to believe. Such a person, places no stock in the Cross of Christ, but rather trusts in other things.

It's not always easy to properly define these people, simply because much of the time, their terminology is the same as the ardent Believer; however, even though the terminology may be very similar, the meaning held by unbelievers is totally different than that which is held by the Believer. When I use the term *"unbelievers,"* I'm not speaking of the unsaved who profess no faith in Christ, but rather to those who claim to be Christians, but in actuality, do not believe in the Cross. The problem is, many of these people will claim to believe in the Cross, while all the time advocating other things as it regards solutions to the ills of man.

As we have stated in previous commentary, if the emphasis is placed on things other than the Cross, such emphasis will find a place of lodgment in the hearts of those who listen to such Preachers. Consequently, due

NOTES

to their emphasis being wrong, many of these people will little understand the error when they are actually hearing it. Their emphasis being elsewhere, their minds are not on that of which we speak, so they do not really catch what is actually being said.

WRONG HEARING

If it is to be noticed, in the four Gospels, Jesus constantly said: *"He who has ears to hear, let him hear"* (Mat. 11:15; 13:9, 43; Mk. 4:9, 23; 7:16; 8:18).

If one is to preach and teach the Truth, one at the same time has to point out erroneous direction constituted by wrong doctrine. We do this at times over our Radio programs as well as the Telecast.

If the situation is serious enough, in other words if the erroneous doctrine is impugning the Cross, we will at times call the Preacher's name and quote verbatim what they have said.

Regarding this, a particular Brother wrote us a letter, which was most interesting. He had been listening to our daily Radio program, *"A Study in the Word"*, where we are teaching on the Cross, and at times pointing out wrong directions. He had heard this, and related as to how upon hearing our statements, he simply didn't believe what he was hearing. In other words, he didn't believe these Preachers were saying the things we had said, in effect, ridiculing the Cross. In this case, we were speaking of the Word of Faith doctrine.

After hearing our program that particular morning, and as stated registering unbelief regarding what we were saying, the very next morning he turned on one of these Preachers. To his amazement, he went on to say, this particular Preacher was saying the very things that we had claimed they were saying.

He went on to state how he couldn't understand how that he had not caught this before! Actually, the reason is simple.

Most of the people who heed the Word of Faith doctrine, do so because they think this will show them how to get rich. In other words, the doctrine caters to greed! As a result, they are little interested in whatever else is said, their emphasis being on *"money."*

Most of the time, people don't hear what they don't want to hear. They've made up their minds, and they don't want anyone disturbing them with the truth.

But let the Reader understand, while all things that relates to the Word is of utmost significance, still, when we deal with the Atonement we are dealing with that which is the most important of all. A person can be saved while at the same time believing many wrong things; however, if he believes wrong as it regards the Atonement, he cannot be saved. So this means that of all things in the Bible, the Atonement stands at the very heart of the Gospel. In fact, the Atonement is the Gospel.

(18) "WE KNOW THAT WHOSOEVER IS BORN OF GOD SINNETH NOT; BUT HE THAT IS BEGOTTEN OF GOD KEEPETH HIMSELF, AND THAT WICKED ONE TOUCHETH HIM NOT."

The exegesis is:

1. *"Is born"* speaks of a past complete act of Regeneration with the present result that such a person is a born-one of God.

2. The one born of God does not keep on habitually sinning.

3. The *"begotten of God"* is Christ.

4. The *"wicked one"* refers to Satan.

5. *"Toucheth him not"* refers to the fact that Satan cannot grasp, or lay hold of.

6. Our security is not in our grip on Christ but His grip on us (Wuest).

BORN OF GOD

The phrase, *"We know that whosoever is born of God sinneth not,"* refers to the fact that such a one does not practice sin, does not habitually sin. It doesn't mean that a Christian cannot sin, or if a Christian sins, they aren't truly saved. That's not what the Apostle is saying. He has already said, *"If we say that we have no sin* (sin nature), *we deceive ourselves, and the truth is not in us"* (I Jn. 1:8). He is saying here that the Christian does not habitually sin.

However noble the sentiments expressed by the false teachers, the test of the truth of God is conduct. A sinful life is totally incompatible with the life received from God. John is not unaware of the difficulties involved in living the new life or of the quality

of the opposition from the Evil One. The Apostle knows the wiles of the Devil and expects them. Nonetheless, he is adamant in his confidence that the Evil One need not prevail. It is not the quality of strength in the life of the Believer that gives him hope of prevailing but the presence of the Power of God.

John is showing here that he who lives in Christ will not habitually sin. No one born of God possessing the Divine Life of God will fall victim to the life of sin. Now that's quite a statement!

If the Believer doesn't understand the Cross, inevitably the sin nature will rule within his life. In such a case, he is habitually sinning; however, if such a person is truly serious with the Lord, somehow and someway, the Holy Spirit will lead that person to the truth, and I speak of the truth of the Cross, where perpetual victory can be found. The facts are, there are millions who claim Christ, but who aren't really saved. In fact they've never been saved, only religious! The sadness is, most of those people, although religious, will never come to Christ. Some few will, but only a few!

If in some way the Cross of Christ isn't preached, people cannot be saved. Due to the fact that the Cross is preached not at all in untold thousands of Churches, this means, that not a single person in these respective Churches is actually saved. But there are millions who are truly saved, who know next to nothing about the Cross, as it refers to the Sanctification process. Until these people learn the Cross, they are bound to live the Seventh Chapter of Romans all over again. It is impossible for it to be otherwise. Romans, Chapter 7 cannot be placed in the past tense, until Romans, Chapter 6 is properly understood and in fact lived. Then and only then can the *"sin nature"* be completely throttled (Rom. 6:14).

BEGOTTEN OF GOD

The phrase, *"But He that is Begotten of God keepeth himself,"* should have been translated, *"But He* (Christ) *that is Begotten of God keepeth him."* *"Himself"* in the Greek is *"autos,"* and should have been translated *"him."* Smith says: *"There is no comfort in the thought that we are in our own keeping; our security is not in our grip on Christ but His grip on us."*

"Is begotten" speaks of the Son of God, Who is by eternal generation from God the Father in a birth that never took place because it always was (Wuest). Pure and simple, the idea is, *"Christ keeps us."*

HOW DOES CHRIST KEEP US?

He keeps us through the power of the Holy Spirit Who is constantly working within us; however, the Holy Spirit works solely within the parameters of the Finished Work of Christ. Consequently, even as the Sixth Chapter of Romans demands, we are to express unending Faith in the Cross of Christ, understanding that everything we receive from the Lord is made possible by what Jesus did at the Cross. In that manner and that manner alone, Christ keeps us.

If we do not express Faith in the Cross, and I speak of Faith in the Cross for victory over the world, the flesh, and the Devil, we have clipped the wings of the Holy Spirit so to speak. In such a case, we are left on our own, which means that the Holy Spirit will not help us, at least in this respect, which as should be understood, translates into abject failure.

Jesus paid a terrible price for us at the Cross. If we forget that price, or try to circumvent that price, or else we do not properly understand the price that He actually paid, which is the case regrettably with most Christians, very negative results will be the conclusion.

Everything the Lord has told us that He will do, will definitely be done; however, it must all be done His way, which is always, and without exception, the way of the Cross. And that's where the problem begins.

Many in the modern Church do not believe that which I've just stated. And even many who claim to believe the statement, in fact, do not! They pay lip service to the Cross, if any service at all. Man loves to design and develop his own way, and concludes it to be very spiritual, because he does it in a very spiritual way. In other words, he uses good things; however, let the Reader understand, religious flesh is flesh still and, consequently, that which God can never accept.

NOTES

The Begotten of God will keep us, providing we do things His way. This is an absolute, an imperative!

THE WICKED ONE

The phrase, *"And that wicked one toucheth him not,"* means that Satan will not be able to grasp or lay hold of such a Believer.

I can remember the day that I would read these Passages and literally weep. I knew what the Scripture said, and I knew that it was true; however, I didn't know how it was true. The *"wicked one"* was touching me, even though I was struggling with all of my strength that he not do so.

In those days, I did not know or understand the Message of the Cross. To be sure, I understood it as it regards the initial Salvation process, and preached it strongly. In fact, in that capacity I preached the Cross so strongly that many in Leadership became upset with me. But God rewarded my Message with hundreds of thousands of people being brought to a saving knowledge of Jesus Christ. But when it came to understanding the Cross as it regards our Sanctification, I had no understanding in that capacity, and the lack of such understanding, caused me untold grief and trouble.

In those days, not knowing the right way, I thought I could pray my way to victory. To be sure, the Lord greatly blessed me in my seeking His Face, but victory over the world, the flesh, and the Devil could not be found in that capacity. That may come as a shock to many Christians, but it happens to be true (Jn. 8:32).

There is nothing I think, more sacred than prayer. In fact, I do not see how that any Christian can have any type of proper relationship with Christ, unless they have a proper prayer life.

As I dictate these notes (April 2, 2001), I have just returned from prayer meeting. As I sought the face of the Lord, He moved mightily within my heart concerning certain particulars that I was bringing before Him. So do not think I am knocking prayer. But the problem was this:

My faith for victory was in my prayer life, and not the Cross of Christ. As holy and sacred as a proper prayer life may be, if our faith for victory is placed in such, it then becomes an improper object of faith, which God cannot bless. Let the Reader understand the following:

There is only one Sacrifice for sin, which includes all victory and in every capacity, and that is the *"One Sacrifice"* of Christ (Heb. 10:12).

When the Lord began to reveal to me the capacity of this *"One Sacrifice,"* and that it included my victory over the world, the flesh, and the Devil, at that moment I began to know the Christian experience as I had not previously known. And that experience has enlarged itself even on a daily basis from that very moment. In other words, it keeps getting greater and greater, even as my understanding of the Cross becomes more and more enlarged.

Now I have an assurance that surpasses all understanding, an assurance that only the Cross can provide. Even as John said *"that wicked one toucheth him not."*

(19) "AND WE KNOW THAT WE ARE OF GOD, AND THE WHOLE WORLD LIETH IN WICKEDNESS."

The diagram is:

1. God looks at the entirety of the world as having only two kinds of people, the Redeemed and the unredeemed.

2. Because of trusting in Christ and what He has done for us at the Cross, *"we know that we are of God."*

3. The *"whole world"* being in wickedness, refers to the world system.

WE KNOW

The phrase, *"And we know that we are of God,"* goes back to I John 4:4 and restates what is said objectively in Verse 18: *"Everyone who has been born from God,"* for that's what the Greek actually says. In *"from God"* there lies the fact that all our Spiritual Life has its origin in God. How this origin shows itself John has just stated in Verse 18, which sums up all that the Apostle has said to the same effect throughout the Epistle.

This *"know so Salvation"* is not based on boastful claims, like those made by the false teachers, but on the basis of the *"test of eternal life"* which are substantiated by life and action. As Bruce says: *"To claim to belong to the Family of God is one thing; to exhibit*

the marks of His family, in the light of the criteria of obedience, love, and perseverance, is another thing. In the case of John and his 'little children,' these criteria have been met."

THE WHOLE WORLD AND WICKEDNESS

The phrase, *"And the whole world lieth in wickedness,"* means to lie prostrate in his power domain. *"Wicked one"* is an excellent translation (vs. 18), simply because Satan is actively, viciously wicked. In this lies the idea of passivity which does not even struggle against the Devil, because it already belongs to him. He does not need to fasten himself on the world; he already has the whole of it completely in his power. This in no way contradicts I John 2:2, for John has also written I John 3:8.

As we see here with John, clearly there is no middle ground. To be born of God is to be safe from the power of the wicked one. Not to be born of God is to be wholly under the power of the wicked one.

(20) "AND WE KNOW THAT THE SON OF GOD IS COME, AND HATH GIVEN US AN UNDERSTANDING, THAT WE MAY KNOW HIM THAT IS TRUE, AND WE ARE IN HIM THAT IS TRUE, EVEN IN HIS SON JESUS CHRIST. THIS IS THE TRUE GOD, AND ETERNAL LIFE."

The structure is:

1. The words *"we know"* proclaim the assurance and guarantee of it all — the Incarnation, the Cross, an overwhelming demonstration of God's interest in us and His concern for our highest good.

2. He has come, and has given us an understanding of Himself, *"that we may know Him that is true."*

3. We are in Jesus Christ by virtue of being *"baptized into His death"* (Rom. 6:3-5).

4. Jesus Christ is truly God, and Faith in Him guarantees *"Eternal Life."*

JESUS HAS COME

The phrase, *"And we know that the Son of God is come,"* presents that which is not simply a historic fact, but rather an abiding operation.

Regarding the words *"is come,"* John does not use a verb here which speaks only of the act of coming, but rather that which includes in the idea of His coming, the fact of arrival and Personal Presence. It is, *"the Son of God has come"* (Incarnation), has arrived, and is here. While He departed in His glorified body to Heaven, yet He is here in His Presence in the Church, i.e., *"His Body, which constitutes all Believers."* His coming was not like that of a meteor, flashing across the sky and then gone. He remains in His followers on Earth.

Consequently, the third and final affirmation of John is in fact the summary of the Epistle. It affirms the point of dispute with the false teachers. Christian Faith has to do with Jesus Christ. He is the *"Word of Life"* (I Jn. 1:1), *"the Eternal Life"* (I Jn. 1:2) Who was with the Father and through the Incarnation came into human history.

By His coming, humankind is enabled to know the True God and to have fellowship with Him. But the false teachers said that this relationship was apart from the Son. Fellowship with God as they taught it came through Divine knowledge of the subject. It was received through a process of speculative inquiry.

From the beginning John denied this teaching. The reality of God can be known only through apprehending the reality that is in the Son. This comes through Revelation, but it is a Revelation grounded in the facts of history. It requires that one know Jesus Christ as God's Son and that one live his life entirely in Him. One knows by this experiential life in the Son that He is also in the Father and that the Son is none other than the True God, the Author of Eternal Life.

UNDERSTANDING

The phrase, *"And has given us an understanding, that we may know Him that is true,"* refers to spiritual sense and ability to understand. We know the real One, namely God. This is *"the real One"* as opposed to spurious gods.

At the end of this Epistle, which has dealt with the antichrists who deny both the Son and the Father and has not dealt with pagans and with their idols or Divinities, John writes *"the real One"* as opposed to the fictional god of the heretics, the god that they made for themselves in their unregenerate, lying claims as men still do today. No one knows Who

God really is save the Son and He to whom the Son reveals Him (Mat. 11:27; Jn. 1:18).

IN HIM

The phrase, *"And we are in Him that is true, even in His Son Jesus Christ,"* concerns the fact that the Son of God has placed us in connection with the real God by giving us Salvation and thus making us know God. There is nothing fictional about either the God with Whom we are connected or about our being in Him, about our fellowship and connection with Him. It is the Son of God Himself Who made this real God known to us and joined us to Him. The heretics have no Son of God, have not the Father (I Jn. 2:22-23), have only an illusion which they call *"god,"* so that their claim of having fellowship with God is a lie (I Jn. 1:6). They do not have fellowship with what they call *"god"* because their *"god"* does not exist.

Concerning being in God, we are in the real One (God) in His Son Jesus Christ. Only in this way are we in God. Apart from the Son no one is in God (Jn. 14:6). He who denies the Son has not the Father (I Jn. 2:23). This in fact, is the burden of the entire Epistle. This meaning cannot be eliminated at the climax. We are in the real One in Christ; no man is in God without Christ.

But this Christ is not a mere man. The early Gnostics conceived Him to be such, to them He was nothing more than the physical son of Joseph. That is why at the end of this Epistle, in the summary, *"the Son of God"* is once more strongly emphasized: *"The Son of God has come,"* etc. He made the real God known to us. We are in the real God only in and not apart from this real God's Son Jesus Christ; John now adds His Name *"Jesus Christ."*

The Gnostics dreamed of an *"eon Christ,"* which *"eon"* joined Jesus at His Baptism but left Him before His passion so that only a poor, helpless man died on the Cross, or so they say! But we must ever understand, that the Blood of Jesus is *"the Blood of His* (God's) *Son"* (I Jn. 1:7), the expiation for the world's sin (I Jn. 2:2; 4:10).

ETERNAL LIFE

The phrase, *"This is the true God, and Eternal Life,"* puts us in the clear for the clinching statement. *"This One is the real God and Life Eternal."*

Everything depends on His Deity, and His Deity means no less than this, that as the Father Who is made known to us by Him is the only real God (I Thess. 1:9), so also His Son Jesus Christ *"is the real God"* and Eternal Life.

If the Son is less, if He is not real God even as the Father is the real God, then this entire Epistle and all that it declares about His Blood, expiation, our fellowship with God, etc., are futile. That, too, is the reason the predicate that refers to Jesus Christ is doubled: *"This One* (His Son Jesus Christ) *is the real God, and Life Eternal."*

"His Son Jesus Christ" takes us back to I John 1:3; this Son is now defined as no less than what He is: *"the real God,"* God's *"Son"* in no inferior sense.

"And Life Eternal" takes us back to I John 1:2 and to the double designation: *"the Life was made manifest"* — *"the Life, the Eternal One, Who was with the Father."* In effect, John ends as he began (Lenski).

The idea of all of this is for John to ascribe full Deity to Jesus. After all, this is the crux of his argument and the basis for his statement that he who is in Jesus is in the Father as well.

(21) "LITTLE CHILDREN, KEEP YOURSELVES FROM IDOLS. AMEN."

The composite is:

1. *"Little children"* actually says *"little born-ones."*

2. *"Keep"* means *"to guard, to watch, to keep watch."* It is used of the garrison of a city guarding it against attack from without. The heart is a citadel, and it must be guarded against insidious assailants from without.

3. *"Idols"* here are not referring to the heathen worship of Ephesus, Artemis and her Temple, but of the heretical substitutes for the Christian conception of God. In effect, it also means to guard against everything which occupies the place of God.

LITTLE CHILDREN

The phrase, *"Little children,"* was probably used by John alone. He was now probably near 90 years of age, or at least past 80. Being the only original Disciple of Christ left, he could easily use the term *"little children"*

when referring to the Saints. No one could deny him this place of maturity, even in a sense, a father of the Church, if not at this time *"the father."* Such an affectionate note serves to remind his readers of his genuine commitment to them. Whereas the false teachers had other things in mind, John truly and sincerely loved those who were followers of Christ. He wanted to teach them in order that they may grow in Grace and the knowledge of the Lord. His business was to develop them, as the business of the false teachers was to exploit them.

Exploitation is a dreadful thing, a gross sin against God, and is altogether too prevalent in the modern Church.

Just the other night I watched a Preacher over Television for a few minutes, as he importuned people to send money. If they would pick up the phone and make a sizeable pledge, he would pray for all of their needs, guaranteeing those needs to be met. He concluded his statement by claiming that *"the anointing was even then all over him."*

Pure and simple, that type of thing is no more than a *"scam."* I suppose the implication was, that if they did not pledge money, he wouldn't pray for them. But the absolute guarantee that if they gave money, he was going to pray for them, and all of their needs were then going to be met, presents the absolute chicanery of the whole business.

First of all, everything that God has is a *"gift."* When we put a price tag on it, we have negated the gift, which is to make a mockery of the Cross. And then to claim the anointing of the Holy Spirit on such shenanigans, is blasphemy. This is exploitation at its highest. Jesus referred to such as *"false prophets in sheep's clothing"* (Mat. 7:15).

Paul referred to them as *"Satan's ministers"* (II Cor. 11:13-15).

It's not wrong for a Preacher to ask for money regarding the need to pay expenses, but it's terribly wrong to place it on that level.

That network was T.B.N., and the Evangelist was Benny Hinn.

IDOLS

The phrase, *"Keep yourselves from idols,"* probably represents a final characterization of the *"heresy"* represented by the false teachers. False teaching is ultimately *"apostasy from the true faith."* To follow after it is to become nothing better than an idol worshipper, especially if it is a matter of the truth of one's conception of God. John is blunt. The false teachers propose not the worship of the True God, made known in His Son Jesus, but a false god — an idol they have invented.

Presently, we are not in danger, indeed, of bowing down to idols, or of engaging in the grosser forms of idol-worship. But we may be in no less danger than they to whom John wrote were, of substituting other things in our affections in the place of the True God, and of devoting to them the time and the affection that are due to Him.

Our children it is possible to love with such an attachment as shall effectually exclude the True God from the heart. The world — its wealth, and pleasures, and honors — we may love with a degree of attachment such as even an idolater would hardly show to his idol-gods; and all the time which he would take in performing his devotions in an idol-temple, we may devote with equal fervor to the service of the world.

There is practical idolatry all over the world; in nominally Christian lands as well as among the heathen; in families that acknowledge no God but wealth and fashion; in the hearts of multitudes of individuals who would scorn the thought of worshipping at a pagan altar; and it is even to be found in the heart of many a one who professes to be acquainted with the True God, and to be an heir of Heaven. God must have the supreme place in our affections. The love of everything else should be held in strict subordination to the love of Him. He must reign in our hearts; be acknowledged in our homes, our families, and in the place of public worship; be submitted to at all times as having a right to command and control us; be obeyed in all the expressions of His Will, by His Word, by His providence, and by His Spirit; be so loved that we shall be willing to part without a murmur with the dearest object of affection when He takes it from us; and so that, with joy and triumph, we shall welcome His messenger, when He shall come to summon us into His presence.

NOTES

In truth, anything that comes between us and God is an *"idol."* In fact, religion is the biggest idol of all! This means that to some Christians, their Church or Denomination is their idol. Preachers can be idols, or whatever! As we've already stated, false doctrine, which is the product of an Angel of light, is always an idol.

In fact, the only way that this admonition *"to keep ourselves from idols,"* can be properly upheld, is for the Believer to properly understand the Cross. That and that alone will keep a fence around the Child of God.

Amen!

"Take up thy Cross and follow Me,
"I heard my Master say;
"I gave My life to ransom thee,
"Surrender your all today."

"He drew me closer to His side,
"I sought His Will to know,
"And in that will I now abide,
"Wherever He leads I'll go."

"It may be through the shadows dim,
"Or o'er the stormy sea,
"I take my Cross and follow Him,
"Wherever He leadeth me."

"My heart, my life, my all I bring,
"To Christ Who loves me so;
"He is my Master, Lord, and King,
"Wherever He leads I'll go."

INTRODUCTION TO THE
II AND III EPISTLES OF JOHN

It is believed that the Apostle John in all probability wrote these two short Letters in Ephesus, and wrote them on the same day, and they were to be sent to the same place. This place and the date of composition are unknown. Regarding the date we venture to say merely that the interval between the writing of these two Letters and the composition of John's First Epistle cannot have been long.

The fact that the name of the writer is not affixed to the Epistles is much in the manner of John. Paul, in every case except in the Epistle to the Hebrews, affixed his name to his Epistles; Peter, James, and Jude did the same thing. John, however, has never done it in any of his writings, except in the Book of Revelation. He seems to have supposed that there was something about his style and manner which would commend his writings as genuine; or that in some other way they would be so well understood to be his, that it was not necessary to specify it.

THE HARSHNESS OF THE BELOVED

The apparently severe and harsh remarks made in the Epistle in regard to heretics, may be adverted to as evidence that these Epistles are the genuine writings of John the Apostle. Thus, in the Second Epistle, Verse 10, he says, *"If there come any unto you, and bring not this doctrine, receive him not into your house, neither bid him God speed."* So in the Third Epistle, Verse 10: *"If I come, I will remember his deeds which he doeth, prating against us with malicious words,"* etc.

It has been made an objection as to the genuineness of these Epistles, that this is not

in the spirit of the mild and amiable *"Disciple whom Jesus loved"*; that it breaths a temper of uncharitableness and severity which could not have existed in him at any time, and especially when, as an old man, he is said to have preached nothing but *"love one another."*

But these two circumstances will show that this, so far from being an objection, is rather a proof of their genuineness. One is, that in fact these expressions accord with what we *"know"* to have been the character of John.

The truth is, there was a remarkable mixture of gentleness and severity in the character of John; and though the former was the most prominent, and may be supposed to have increased as he grew old, yet the other also often manifested itself.

We are not to think that one cannot be mild and gentle, and at the same time, be somewhat harsh and severe, especially when it comes to false doctrine. We must never forget that we aren't dealing here with mundane matters, but rather with the very issues of life and death. In other words, if people miss it here, they miss it altogether.

So one should thank God for one such as John, who not only loudly and brilliantly proclaimed the Love the God, but also warned against false doctrine, which would bring upon one the Judgment of God.

LETTERS

Letters of this nature must have been put into the hands of many Missionaries in apostolic times. We are unable to say how these particular two came to be preserved, except by the watchfulness of the Holy Spirit.

NOTES

The first short Letter, John wrote to one he referred to as *"the elect lady."* She likely had a Church in her home. She was a married woman, for her children are also greeted. No husband is mentioned so perhaps she was a widow who entertained many ministers and traveling Evangelists in her home. Beyond that we know little.

Regarding the Third Epistle, it is addressed to one by the name of *"Gaius."* It seems that John is sending some Preachers to this particular city where Gaius is located, and he asks this man to provide lodging for these men and to help them on their way. Gaius has been aiding the Gospel in this manner, and John strongly commends him for this.

Gaius already knows the reason for sending these men. Diotrephes, the domineering spirit in this particular, local congregation, is hostile to John and refuses to lodge and to help Preachers who come from John and also forbids the other members to do so under threat of expulsion from the congregation. So John asks Gaius to provide for these men whom he is sending.

In this Letter, what John tells the members of the congregation is plain enough: admonition to hold to what they had from the beginning; warning against the many deceivers who have gone out into the world. Some of these false apostles will come also to them. John forbids them to receive such men; they are not even to greet them.

More than likely, these deceivers are the same as those referred to in the First Epistle of John: Gnostics, followers of Cerinthus who denied the Deity of Jesus. One may well conclude that Diotrephes was favorable to these Gnostics and wanted their Preachers lodged and helped and not those who came from John. To what extent Diotrephes had already imbibed the Gnostic heresies is not indicated. John will bring matters to an issue when he presently arrives in person.

As stated, it is believed that both of these Letters were written within the same time frame, possibly even on the same day. It is also believed they were written from Ephesus, although that is not certain. Both Letters were addressed to an individual and not to a particular Church, although what was said definitely involved the Church.

In these two short notes were are given an idea as to the manner of writing for those days, and as well, some of the problems that persisted in the Early Church. To be sure, there are lessons to be learned, for which reason the Holy Spirit has preserved these Texts, and included them in the Canon of Scripture.

"Like the woman at the well I was seeking
"For things that could not satisfy;
"And then I heard my Savior speaking:
"Draw from My well that never shall run dry."

"There are millions in this world who are craving
"The pleasure earthly things afford;
"But none can match the wondrous treasure
"That I find in Jesus Christ my Lord."

"So, my brother, if things this world gave you
"Leave hungers that won't pass away,
"My blessed Lord will come and save you
"If you kneel to Him and humbly pray."

THE
BOOK OF II JOHN

—■—

(1) "THE ELDER UNTO THE ELECT LADY AND HER CHILDREN, WHOM I LOVE IN THE TRUTH; AND NOT I ONLY, BUT ALSO ALL THEY THAT HAVE KNOWN THE TRUTH;"

The composite is:

1. John refers to himself as *"the Elder."*

2. He writes unto a particular woman in a particular place, whom he refers to as *"the elect lady."*

3. The bond that has pulled this aged Apostle to this dear lady, and her to him, is *"truth."*

ELDER

John refers to himself as *"the Elder."* If it is to be noticed, it is *"the Elder"* and not *"an Elder,"* which we will address momentarily.

"Elder" in the Greek is *"Prespyteros,"* which can mean, *"Pastor,"* or simply a *"Preacher of the Gospel."* In fact, the titles *"Elder, Pastor, Bishop, Presbyter, Shepherd, Overseer,"* all referred to the Pastor of a local Church, or a Preacher in general. In fact, these particular titles are used interchangeably by Paul, etc. It was only when men began to usurp authority over the Holy Spirit that more was made of some of these titles than intended.

For instance, the title *"Bishop"* is the same as Pastor, i.e., *"Pastor of a local Church"*; however, in the Second Century and especially into the Third, the title of Bishop began to refer to something different than it was originally intended by the Holy Spirit, and made so by men. Today the title *"Bishop"* infers that one who holds such a title is in charge of a particular locality containing a number of Churches. This is a designation that did not exist in the Early Church, which in essence, means that it's not Scriptural.

John uses the title *"the Elder"* to designate himself in a sense that is still more distinct. He does not mean: one of the Apostles who may be called an *"Elder"* when, like Peter, he addresses Elders of a Church (Pastors); John is not addressing such Elders. He is *"the Elder"* in the sense that this title belongs only to him.

John is *"the Elder"* because the Churches it seems, gave him this title in an eminent sense as we speak of *"the President,"* *"the Governor,"* etc.

When they titled John in this manner, the Churches intended to honor the aged Apostle who alone had survived the other Apostles. This honor was combined with the recognition of John's apostolic calling as being that of the one Apostle who still remained to guide, teach, and direct the Churches. Of course, we are speaking of the original Twelve. Because he understood it in this sense John accepted the title.

When one said *"the Elder,"* all the members of the Churches, and wherever those Churches may have been, knew who it meant; when here and in III John the Apostle himself writes *"the Elder,"* the Readers knew who this was. The addition *"John"* is not only unnecessary but would also be misleading, for it would convey the thought that there were others like him, when in reality, there were no more like John. There was only this one *"the Elder,"* and there were no others who were to be ranked with him.

We are not to infer from this that the Holy Spirit is placing His sanction on higher ecclesiastical offices than *"Apostle, Prophet, Evangelist, Pastor, and Teacher"* (Eph. 4:11). John referring to himself as *"the Elder,"* or *"the*

Presbyter," for that's actually what it meant, was strictly something that was honorary. It had to do with his advanced age, and more than all, with him being a selected Disciple of our Lord, and more particularly, the last one of that original Twelve remaining alive.

While it is obvious that John's word carried authority in the Churches of that day, and rightly so, this again was not intended by the Holy Spirit as a recognition of ecclesiastical authority. Paul carried that same authority and because he was the master builder of the Church. John carries this authority because of who he is, as should be obvious. Even then some in the Church did not heed him, even as these two Letters bear out.

More than anything else, these two short Letters, proclaim the leadership of the Apostle, which all along has been intended by the Holy Spirit. Whereas *"Prophets"* spearheaded the move of God under the old economy, namely Israel, it is Apostles who fill this role in the Church. In other words, it is God-called Apostles who serve in the capacity of leadership in the Church, as it regards doctrine and direction. A grand mistake is made, when Religious Denominations attempt to usurp this God-ordained authority.

Even then the authority recognized, is always done in a limited way. True Apostles never exercise a dictatorial authority, but always in the spirit of *"I beseech you."*

ELECT LADY

The phrase, *"Unto the elect lady and her children,"* probably means exactly what it says, a Christian woman of some prominence in the Church.

The Apostle addresses his Letter to her and her children, and mentions the fact that in his travels he met her other children, and reports that they were ordering their behavior in the sphere of the Truth. He also sends greetings from the children of this elect lady's sister.

The word *"lady"* in the Greek is *"kuria."* It is the feminine form of *"kurios,"* which means *"lord, master."* It was a common name in those days. It is the Greek form of the name *"Martha"* which means *"mistress."*

It is believed that she was a devout Christian who lived near Ephesus. It also seems that her home was the meeting-place of the local assembly, there being no Church buildings in those days (Wuest).

The word *"elect"* from the Greek is *"eklektos,"* and means *"one picked out, chosen."* The reference is to the fact that this lady was one of the elect of God, one of the chosen-out ones of God, chosen-out from among mankind by the sovereign Grace of God for Salvation.

However, the word *"elect"* is not meant to refer to some special designation regarding this woman, but as well, was honorary, even as *"the Elder"* was honorary, other than John's original calling.

Some have claimed that John was actually addressing a Church, thereby referring to it as *"elect lady and her children,"* but the general consensus of the entirety of the Text as it regards the Letter, militates toward the fact that this individual was actually a prominent woman. She was a married woman, for her children are also mentioned. No husband is mentioned so possibly her husband was dead. Quite possibly the Church was actually in her house, which was the custom in those days, there being no Church buildings.

The word here rendered *"children"* would include in itself both sons and daughters, but as the Apostle immediately uses a masculine pronoun, it would seem more probable that this woman's children were sons only. In other words, she had no daughters. At all events, the use of such a pronoun proves that some at least of her children were sons. Of their number and character we have no information, except that a part of them, or possibly all of them, were Christians.

WOMEN IN THE CHURCH

I think it should be obvious from the account given in the New Testament that the Holy Spirit makes no distinction between men and women in the Work of God, other than what Paul said:

"Wives, submit yourselves unto your own husbands, as unto the Lord.

"For the husband is the head of the wife, even as Christ is the head of the Church: and He is the Savior of the body.

"Therefore as the Church is subject unto Christ, so let the wives be to their own husbands in every thing" (Eph. 5:22-24).

Even then there are qualifications in all of this. The wife is to submit herself to her husband who loves her even as Christ loves the Church (Eph. 5:25). As should be obvious, it wouldn't be difficult to submit to someone of this nature.

Concerning the great Plan of God for the human race, the Holy Spirit through Paul said: *"There is neither Jew nor Greek, there is neither bond nor free, there is neither male nor female: for ye are all one in Christ Jesus"* (Gal. 3:28).

Some claim that it's not proper for a woman to preach; however, the Bible does not bear out such a thing. Peter quoting the Prophet Joel said: *"And it shall come to pass in the last days, saith God, I will pour out of My Spirit upon all flesh: and your sons and your daughters shall prophesy"* (Acts 2:17).

He also said: *"But every woman that prayeth or prophesieth . . ."* (I Cor. 11:5).

The word *"prophesieth"* in the Greek is *"propheteia,"* and means *"to predict or fore-tell or to serve as an inspired speaker."* This tells us that women can also preach. Inasmuch as women are baptized with the Holy Spirit the same as men, this tells us that they can do anything that a man can do.

WHAT DID PAUL MEAN BY THE STATEMENT, *"LET YOUR WOMEN KEEP SILENCE IN THE CHURCHES"*?

In giving instruction to the Church at Corinth as it regards the operation of the Gifts of the Spirit, the Apostle made the statement, *"Let your women keep silence in the Churches: for it is not permitted unto them to speak"* (I Cor. 14:34).

What did Paul mean by this statement?

In those days, wherever it was that the people assembled to worship, the women sat on one side of the room and the men on the other. Many things were taking place then such as Gifts in operation, with many of the women not really understanding what was actually happening; consequently, they were calling out across the Church, asking their husbands as to the meaning of certain things.

Concerning that, Paul said, *"If they will learn any thing let them ask their husbands at home"* (I Cor. 14:35).

Paul wasn't talking about preaching or anything of that nature, but rather this of which we have addressed. So for Preachers to use this Passage as a claim that women cannot preach, proverbially speaking, holds no water.

To my knowledge, the Baptists are the only Religious Denomination that bans women Preachers. And yet even they claim that it's satisfactory for a woman to teach children, or to serve as a Missionary overseas. In other words, she can preach to adults overseas but not in the United States. Such thinking, if in fact that is correct, is silly! If it's wrong for a woman to preach, it's wrong for her to preach anywhere.

The truth is, and as stated, whatever men can do as it regards work for the Lord, women can do as well. There is no discrimination in the Gospel.

TRUTH

The phrase, *"Whom I love in the truth,"* refers to this particular lady, and refers to the Love of God.

The particular word he chooses is *"agapao,"* not *"phileo."* Had he used the latter word, he would have been expressing a human fondness for her, which would have been a grave mistake in a man of John's position in the Church. He says that he loves her and her children with a Christian love, a love produced in his heart by the Holy Spirit, a pure, self-sacrificial, Heavenly, nonhuman love devoid of any sexual connotations. It is as if he said, *"I love you in the Lord."*

But he is not satisfied with thus carefully delineating his love for her by the use of the Greek word *"agapao,"* which means the God kind of love. He adds the qualifying phrase, *"in the Truth."*

That is, the love with which he loved this well-known woman of position in the Church was circumscribed by the Truth as it is in Christ Jesus. It was in connection with the Word of God that he loved her. His love for her had to do with Christian relationships in the Church life and work (Wuest).

KNOW THE TRUTH

The phrase, *"And not I only, but also all they that have known the truth,"* refers to the fact, that all in that local Church who truly knew the Truth, loved her as well.

The linking of *"truth"* and *"love"* is of great importance. Because John's readers are in the Truth — i.e., they know Jesus as the Christ, the Father's Son — they are also the recipients of God's love as it is known and manifested in the community of faith. And the love received by the Church comes from all who know the Truth. The community of love is as encompassing as the truth that is believed and lived.

John is speaking in clear contrast to the heretics. They do not have the truth nor do they know what it means to be in the community of love (Barker).

By now the Reader should well understand that John will not tolerate the slightest false doctrine. *"Truth"* is his foundation, and truth must not be compromised or diluted. With his many years of experience, he now sees the efforts of Satan to dilute the truth with that which is false. The Apostle recognizes it instantly.

There seems to be a fear in his heart that the Gospel will be more hindered in this way than in any other manner, and rightly so! So he determines to stand boldly for truth. And that statement is not meant to infer that this was a struggle within his heart. Quite the contrary. If there was a struggle, it pertained to the degree of forcefulness and nothing else.

As should be obvious, John is addressing Truth in the sense of Christ. Christ is Truth, even as the Word is Truth, even as the Spirit is Truth (Jn. 14:6; 17:17; I Jn. 5:6). The central theme of *"Truth"* is *"Christ and Him Crucified"* (I Cor. 2:2).

This means if the central core of Truth, which is the Cross, is compromised in any way, the entirety of one's understanding of the Word will be compromised as well. The story of the Bible, i.e., *"the Truth,"* is the story of the Cross. Therefore, to know Truth and then to understand Truth, one must without fail, understand the Cross of Christ. In fact, the explanation of the New Covenant is the understanding of the Cross (I Cor. 1:17-18, 21, 23).

(2) "FOR THE TRUTH'S SAKE, WHICH DWELLETH IN US, AND SHALL BE WITH US FOREVER."

The exegesis is:

1. *"For the Truth's sake,"* could just as easily be translated *"For Christ's sake."*

2. As Christ dwells in us, Truth dwells in us. And only as Christ dwells in us, does Truth dwell in us.

3. This is *"forever,"* with the principle of truth bringing growth.

THE TRUTH'S SAKE

The phrase, *"For the Truth's sake,"* proclaims the fact that love is a product of Truth. God's Word is Truth; consequently, if we veer from the Truth in any manner, as it regards the understanding of the Word, we suffer negative consequences to the degree in which we embrace error. It cannot be any other way.

John also wrote concerning the Holy Spirit, Who as well is Truth, as it regards the Saints, *"He will guide you into all Truth."* In this process, *"He shall glorify Christ: for He shall receive of Mine* (of that which belongs to Christ), *and shall show it unto you"* (Jn. 16:13-14).

When it speaks of glorifying Christ, and taking the things of Christ and showing them to Believers, Christ is speaking of what He did at the Cross, and the great benefits thereof.

For years I lived for God, even accomplishing great things for Him, which of course we were able to do only by His help and grace, but yet I didn't know during that time, the tremendous part the Cross plays in our Sanctification. Not understanding this part of the Truth, I suffered drastic consequences, which will be the case in one way or the other, with all who do not understand the Finished Work of Christ in this capacity. Some Believers erroneously think that because they are saved God overlooks their wrong thinking, or else doesn't hold them responsible for their lack of understanding. Nothing could be farther from the truth. To the degree that we do not understand the Word, to that degree we will suffer loss.

In Romans 6:3, Paul says, *"Know ye not,"* implying that the Saints should know the great truth on which he is about to expound, which is the Truth of the Cross.

"No" in the Greek is *"agnoeo,"* and means *"lack of information or by implication to ignore through disinclination."* In other words,

some Believers do not *"know"* simply because they've never heard the Truth of the Cross preached. But others do not know, simply because they have little or no interest. Either way will cause great problems, but the latter will always and without exception bring about disastrous results. In other words, for a Believer to show no interest in the Cross, such an attitude could lead to the loss of the soul.

The Holy Spirit gave us the truth for a specific reason. We are to know and understand that truth, and the cop-out that we don't read the Bible simply because we can't understand it, proverbially speaking, will not hold water.

Every Believer has the Holy Spirit Who in effect is the Author of the Word of God, and Who as well, is Truth. His very purpose, as stated, is to *"guide into all Truth."* If the Believer is sincere before the Lord, and irrespective of his lack of formal education, if he will ask the Lord to help him understand the Word, to be sure, such knowledge will be forthcoming. The problem with most Christians is they do not cooperate in the slightest with the Holy Spirit, and to be sure, He will not force the issue on anyone.

COMMENTARIES

In 1992 the Lord began to deal with my heart about writing these Commentaries. I sought the Lord earnestly for an extended period of time before undertaking this project. In the first place, I felt woefully inadequate, and to be sure, I definitely was woefully inadequate. Consequently, I knew that if I was to do this thing that I would have to have the help of the Lord in every capacity.

When I set out to obey the Lord in this respect, I had the idea that I would write one Volume. But as I began to get into the effort, I soon realized that would be impossible, so in my mind, I lengthened it to three Volumes. I soon realized that wouldn't work either, soon coming to the place that it would require 30 or more Volumes to properly accomplish this task.

The Lord instructed me to write these in a certain way, actually to slant them toward the Laity. This we have tried to do.

In 1996 the Lord in answer to prayer, actually some five years of seeking His face,

NOTES

began to open up to me the Message of the Cross. It was the most revolutionary thing that I had ever encountered as a Christian. It completely changed my life and Ministry. At this particular time I was writing the Commentary on Romans; consequently, from that Volume forward, information on the Cross took on a far greater intensity. In effect, as I complete each Volume, the information continues to expand, as the Revelation becomes all encompassing. To be sure, that which the Lord has given me is not something new. It is actually that which the Apostle Paul was given by the Lord, and which he gave to us in his Epistles.

IS THERE SUCH A THING AS NEW TRUTH?

In a word, no! Anything that the Lord gives to anyone, it is already in the Word. It might be a truth long overlooked, and so long overlooked that it seems new, however, if what is given is truly from the Lord, to be sure it is already in the Word. When people come up with things that they claim is from the Lord, and there is no Biblical foundation for what they are saying, pure and simple what they are claiming is not from the Lord but out of their own minds, or else being given to them by an Angel of light (II Cor. 11:13-15). The Word of God is always the final criteria for all things. Jesus said:

"Man shall not live by bread alone, but by every word that proceedeth out of the Mouth of God" (Mat. 4:4).

The *"Word"* which has proceeded out of God's Mouth is that which we know as *"the Bible."* And while Words to be sure, continue to come out of God's Mouth, it will always be something that He has already said, and is found somewhere in His Word.

That which the Lord has given me on the Cross is definitely not a new truth. It is as old as the Cross itself, and in fact, as old as the Promises of God through the Prophets, as it regards what the Lord would do concerning the Redemption of humanity.

DWELLS IN US

The phrase, *"Which dwelleth in us,"* refers to the fact that it is not merely apprehended by the intellect but welcomed by the heart.

NOTES

"Dwelleth" in the Greek is "meno," which refers to "one living as a guest in the home of another." Thus, the Truth is a welcomed guest in the heart of the Christian.

This implies that it hasn't always been there, but in fact came in when we were "born again."

Even though it came into our hearts at conversion, proper understanding of the truth, and its enlargement, are a process. In fact, this continues all the days of our lives. Even the great Paul said: "Not as though I had already attained, either were already perfect: but I follow after, if that I may apprehend that for which also I am apprehended of Christ Jesus.

"Brethren, I count not myself to have apprehended: but this one thing I do, forgetting those things which are behind, and reaching forth unto those things which are before,

"I press toward the mark for the prize of the high calling of God in Christ Jesus" (Phil. 3:12-14).

FOREVER

The phrase, "And shall be with us forever," proclaims the fact that Truth cannot change. Our understanding of truth may change, or be enlarged; however, it's the person who has changed and not Truth.

(3) "GRACE BE WITH YOU, MERCY, AND PEACE, FROM GOD THE FATHER, AND FROM THE LORD JESUS CHRIST, THE SON OF THE FATHER, IN TRUTH AND LOVE."

The diagram is:

1. Grace, Mercy, and Peace all stem from Truth.

2. The Truth is, God the Father and the Lord Jesus Christ.

3. This salutation does not differ from those commonly employed by the sacred writers, except in the emphasis that is placed on the fact that the Lord Jesus Christ is "the Son of the Father."

GRACE, MERCY, AND PEACE

The phrase, "Grace be with you, Mercy, and Peace," all speak of the realm of Sanctification and not Justification. While all of these attributes definitely came to the Believer as a result of the Justification process, the Apostle is primarily speaking here of these attributes manifesting themselves to Believers and within Believers, on a daily basis. What does John mean by these statements?

Grace is God's undeserved favor toward Believers; Mercy is his pity for those who are in trouble and distress; Peace is the well-being that results when Grace and Mercy are ours.

As far as the attributes of God are concerned, all and without exception, come to each Believer at the moment of conversion. However, these attributes have to be cultivated. This is done by the Holy Spirit, but the problem is most Christians don't know how the Holy Spirit works. As a result, most Believers think that these attributes just automatically begin to work in one's life, or else they try to cultivate them by their own efforts. Both ways are wrong.

The Holy Spirit works on the premise of the Finished Work of Christ, which of course, is the Cross. He will not work outside of these boundaries.

This means that the Believer is to specialize in the Cross. That means that he is to understand that all of his Blessings come to him exclusively through what Jesus did in the great Sacrifice of Himself. Even though I've already given the following in this Volume, due to its great significance, and knowing that we have to have repetition in order to properly remember and understand something, please allow me to give it again:

GOD'S PRESCRIBED ORDER OF VICTORY

1. Focus: The Cross of Christ must ever be the focus of the Saint, understanding as stated, that everything comes to us from God through the Cross. Knowing that, this is where our focus must be (I Cor. 1:17-18, 21, 23; 2:2, 5).

2. The Object of our Faith: This must always be the Finished Work of Christ, realizing that Jesus addressed at the Cross every single problem that we might have, irrespective as to what it might be (Rom. 6:3-14).

3. Power Source: With our Faith focused completely on the Cross, the Holy Spirit will then help us, actually becoming our power source (Rom. 8:1-2, 11).

4. Results: Victory. John said it well, *"This is the victory that overcometh the world, even our faith"* (I Jn. 5:4).

Now let me give the opposite of this, which regrettably, is where most modern Christians are:

1. Focus: The Law. To cut straight through to the reason, if the Christian doesn't have his focus on the Cross, whether he realizes it or not, it's going to be on law, and because there is no other place for him to be. He may not understand that, and may think that he is doing something very spiritual, but if it's not the Cross it's always law. And when we say law, we are not actually speaking of the Law of Moses, but rather law that we've made up ourselves, or that someone else has made up.

2. The Object of our Faith: Instead of it being the Finished Work of Christ, if our focus in on law, or anything other than the Cross, then the object of our faith becomes *"works."*

3. Power Source: With our focus on law, which constitutes rules and regulations that we've made up or someone else has made up, and with the object of faith being *"works,"* our power source becomes *"self."*

4. Results: Failure.

The Reader needs to study these two outlines very closely, simply because he is one or the other. If we're in the first one, the Holy Spirit will definitely develop these great attributes of Grace, Mercy, and Peace, plus all the other Blessings from the Lord. Faith in the Cross of Christ guarantees this, while faith in other than the Cross cancels out these great things.

GOD THE FATHER AND THE LORD JESUS CHRIST

The phrase, *"From God the Father, and from the Lord Jesus Christ,"* presents the two Givers. In fact, these two are equal (I Jn. 5:20). The perfect independence, parallel equality, and mutual connection of the two Persons of the Trinity given here are noticeable. In fact, it cannot be otherwise. In having John state the case in this manner, the Holy Spirit is proclaiming the Deity of Christ, and in effect, making Him coequal with the Father. This as well combats the heresy concerning the Person of Christ held by some that He was a mere man and not God.

All of these attributes are *"from God the Father,"* and *"from the Lord Jesus Christ,"* due to what He did for us at the Cross. In fact, God has always had these qualities. But it took the Cross to open up the way for these gifts to be given unto men. This is what Paul was speaking of when he said: *"Wherefore He saith, when He ascended up on high, He led captivity captive, and gave gifts unto men"* (Eph. 4:8). The Cross made it possible for the great Gifts of God to be given unto the human race. However, all of this is given strictly on the basis of what Jesus did at the Cross, and our Faith in that Finished Work. As repeatedly stated, this is the manner in which the Holy Spirit works, and the only manner in which He works. Once we begin to understand this, we then are beginning to understand the Plan of God for the human race.

THE SON OF THE FATHER

The phrase, *"The Son of the Father,"* presents the only time this expression is used in this way. It emphasizes that Jesus is not the Father, but the Son of the Father (Jn. 1:14, 18; 3:16), but yet that He is Deity, equal with the Father.

This particular statement as given by John serves to bring out distinctly the twofold personal relation of man to the Father and the Son. Brooke comments: *"The Fatherhood of God, as revealed by One Who being His Son can reveal the Father, and Who as man (Jesus) can make Him known to men."* The Son has interpreted the Father to man, *"not merely in truth,"* enlightening the intellect, but *"in love,"* engaging the heart.

Whenever the term or name *"Son"* is used, it always streams back to Calvary. Maybe one can say that it is defined more so in Grace, Mercy, and Peace, than in anything else.

To show you how all of this springs from the Cross, the word *"Grace"* or *"Charis"* as it's given in the Greek, referred to a favor conferred freely with no expectation of return, and finding its only motive in the bounty and free-heartedness of the giver. Of course, this favor was always done for a friend, never for an enemy.

When *"Charis"* is taken into the New Testament, it leaps an infinite distance forward, for the *"favor"* God did at Calvary in paying the penalty for sin in the place of man, all was done for a race that bitterly hated Him, a race, unlovely, and humanly speaking, unlovable. Mercy is God's *"kindness and good will toward the miserable and afflicted, joined with a desire to relieve them."* Grace meets man's need in respect to his guilt and lost condition; mercy, with reference to his suffering as a result of that sin.

Trench says: *"In the Divine mind, and in the order of our Salvation as conceived therein, the 'mercy' precedes the 'grace,' God so loved the world with a pitying love* (therein was the mercy), *that He gave His only-begotten Son* (herein the grace), *that the world through Him might be saved. But in the order of the manifestation of God's purpose of Salvation, the grace must go before the mercy and make way for it. It is true that the same persons are the subjects of both, being at once the guilty and the miserable; yet the Righteousness of God, which it is quite as necessary should be maintained as His love, demands that the guilt should be done away before the misery can be assuaged; only the forgiven may be blessed. He must pardon before He can heal . . . from this it follows that in each of the apostolic salutations where these words occur, grace precedes mercy."*

Concerning *"Peace,"* our Lord made it possible through the Blood of His Cross when He made it possible for a Holy God in perfect justice and holiness to bind together a believing sinner and Himself in an indissoluble, living union (Wuest).

TRUTH AND LOVE

The phrase, *"In truth and love,"* is not to be connected with the expression *"the Son of the Father,"* as if it meant that He was His Son *"in truth and love."* It is rather to be connected with the *"Grace, Mercy, and Peace"* referred to, as a prayer that they might be manifested to this family. Truth was to absorb and regulate all their intellectual faculties; love, all their emotional.

True Christian love is based upon truth and is exercised in the interests of truth, and it is only in the realm of truth and love that grace, mercy, and peace can be enjoyed. Those

who love in the truth also love because of the truth (Williams).

In fact, the words *"truth and love"* provide the transition to what follows, where they become the chief topic.

Actually, John is not praying that God would grant these attributes, but that they will definitely be ours if we truly remain in His Truth and love.

(4) "I REJOICED GREATLY THAT I FOUND OF THY CHILDREN WALKING IN TRUTH, AS WE HAVE RECEIVED A COMMANDMENT FROM THE FATHER."

The diagram is:

1. Evidently the children of this lady to whom John writes, lived elsewhere, possibly having families of their own. John, evidently having been with them for some time, now commends their consecration to the Lord.

2. They were *"walking in truth."*

3. It was truth having as its foundation the Word of God, which all truth must have, or else it's not Truth.

WALKING IN TRUTH

The phrase, *"I rejoiced greatly that I found of thy children walking in truth,"* refers to the fact that the Apostle had some connection with these individuals.

"Walking" in the Greek is *"peripateo,"* and means *"to order one's behavior, to conduct one's self."* Her children were conducting themselves in the sphere of the Truth as it is in Christ Jesus, and doing so on a daily basis. Their actions and words were circumscribed by the Word of God. Their conduct was governed by the Word of God. All of this speaks of one's Sanctification. One is able to *"walk in truth"* only as one understands his *"in Christ"* position. As stated, this pertains to our daily living, and is the acid test of Christianity.

I believe I can say without fear of contradiction, that if one is to *"walk in the Truth,"* one must walk according to the Message of the Cross (I Cor. 1:18). Otherwise it is impossible.

COMMANDMENT

The phrase, *"As we have received a Commandment from the Father,"* relates the fact that the truth by which they were walking, was not their own concoction, but rather was according to the Word of God.

The word *"Commandment"* is a covering term for the Gospel as delivered by the Lord Jesus from the Father to the Apostles. In fact, Paul specifically stated as it regards the Gospel, that He *"neither received it of man, neither was taught it, but by the Revelation of Jesus Christ"* (Gal. 1:11-12).

The *"Father,"* in the Scripture, is everywhere represented as the Source of law, i.e., *"Commandment."* In fact, everything that God does is based on laws that He Himself has formulated and instituted. For instance, we have *"the law of faith"* (Rom. 3:27); *"the Law of God"* (Rom. 7:22); *"the law of the mind"* (Rom. 7:23); *"the law of sin"* (Rom. 7:23); *"the law of the Spirit of Life in Christ Jesus"* (Rom. 8:2). In fact, I think that one can say without fear of exaggeration or contradiction that God governs the entirety of His creation by and through the laws that He Himself has made. And to be sure, God is the author of all laws, even *"the law of sin and death"* (Rom. 8:2).

This is somewhat confusing to some, considering that the Holy Spirit through Paul tells us that we must be *"dead to the law"* (Rom. 7:4). Paul is meaning this:

First of all, the Law which Paul is speaking of in Romans 7:4, is the ancient *"Law of Moses."* More particularly, he is speaking of the part of that Law referred to as *"the Ten Commandments,"* which is God's Standard of Righteousness.

Naturally, the Law of Moses demanded obedience, even as it must. But yet man in his fallen condition, even with the best of intentions, simply couldn't keep the Law. But Jesus totally and completely kept it for us, and when we came to Christ, we were literally crucified with Him, and thereby died to all that we were before coming to Christ, which means that we died to the Law as well! Christ kept and obeyed the Law in every respect, all in our place, actually as our Substitute. He then died for us, and we in effect, died with Him. This means that the Law of Moses has no claim on me whatsoever, and because of my Faith in Christ. This means that I'm to live this life, not by trying to keep the Law of Moses, but by Faith and

trust in Christ and what He has done for us at the Cross.

As I continue to exhibit Faith in Christ and His Cross, the Holy Spirit will work mightily in me, and the Law will be kept in every respect. But it is done not through my efforts to try to obey it, but rather through my trust in Christ.

(5) "AND NOW I BESEECH THEE, LADY, NOT AS THOUGH I WROTE A NEW COMMANDMENT UNTO THEE, BUT THAT WHICH WE HAD FROM THE BEGINNING, THAT WE LOVE ONE ANOTHER."

The structure is:

1. The great Apostle does not command, but rather beseeches (begs).

2. The Commandment of which he speaks is not new, but rather that which the Church had from the beginning.

3. It is the Commandment that we love one another.

I BESEECH YOU

The phrase, *"And now I beseech thee, lady,"* proclaims the heart of the great Apostle.

John was not only an Apostle, he had as well been selected personally by Christ for this high and holy office. He had walked with Christ for some three and a half years, and now was the last of the original Twelve left alive. As should be obvious, he is also a very old man. All of this speaks of seniority, place, and position. Think of the following:

I have no doubt that scores of people constantly plied John with questions about the Person of Christ, and about the great miracles He performed. John was there. He saw these miracles, and not just one or two, but literally hundreds, if not thousands. He saw blinded eyes instantly opened, lepers instantly cleansed, the dead raised, etc.

How he must have related these incidents over and over, with a far away look in his eyes, as he recalled those glorious times. I can well imagine that time after time, his voice would choke, and he would be unable to proceed. At other times, and perhaps very often, the Spirit of God would come upon him greatly as he would relate the Life and Ministry of the Master. As stated, it is said that he repeated over and over in his closing days, *"When I'm gone, there will be no one else who saw Him, who heard Him, and who touched Him."*

But still, when it comes to dealing with fellow Believers, the great Apostle, the one whom Jesus loved, John the Beloved, he never threatened or commanded, only *"beseeched."*

What an example of true humility! What an example of the love of God! What an example of Christlikeness!

NO NEW COMMANDMENT

The phrase, *"Not as though I wrote a new Commandment unto you,"* proclaims the fact that the command to love one another was understood as far as the Gospel was known; and he might well presume it, for true Christianity never prevails anywhere without prompting to the observance of this law.

It is clear that for John the Commandment of Love has precedence here as it does in I John 4:21: *"And He has given us this Command: Whoever loves God must also love his Brother."* It is not that love precedes truth or belief but that love offers the clearest test of the truthfulness of the confession and the sincerity of the obedience given to God's Commands.

Belief may be feigned and confession only of the lips, but love cannot be counterfeited.

LOVE ONE ANOTHER

The phrase, *"But that which we had from the beginning, that we love one another,"* presents love as the Christian's moral disposition of mind, which embraces all other virtues and graces. It implies Faith, because it is founded on Christian principle, and can only be tested by a right belief.

It implies purity, because it is modeled on the Love of God, and has replaced the *"old man"* (Rom. 6:6).

It implies unselfishness, because it desires the good of the other for his own sake and God's.

It implies humility, because it distrusts self, relies on God, and thinks more of others than of self (Jn. 13:14; 15:12; I Cor., Chpt. 13; Eph. 5:2; I Pet. 4:8; I Jn. 3:11, 23; 4:7, 21).

John is not requiring something new but that which has been the supreme and final word *"from the beginning."* What the Father required (I Jn. 4:7), the Son manifested (I Jn.

3:16), and the Spirit makes available to Believers through Life in Him (I Jn. 4:13-15).

The command *"that we love one another"* was that on which, in the Apostle's old age, he loved to dwell; and he had little more to say than this, to exhort all Believers to obey this injunction of the Saviour.

Of course we know that the Holy Spirit was promoting this through the Apostle. If one truly loves God, one will truly love one's Brother and Sister in the Lord, and love them with a Godly love. If that is obvious, one might say it is guaranteed that *"Grace, Mercy, and Peace,"* will be present as well. If it is to be noticed, *"Love"* is the first Fruit of the Spirit (Gal. 5:22-23).

This Commandment of love was given to us by the Father through His Son Jesus Christ, which God Himself made basic for all who know the truth. Consequently, this is not a Commandment that has been newly invented by John.

As well, it pertains to all of us, to John, to the lady to whom he was writing, to the congregation of the Church to which she belonged, and to all Christians everywhere.

DEFINITION

This love with which Saints are to love one another needs to be defined. The English word *"Love"* may mean any one of a dozen kinds of love. There are as many meanings to it as there are persons in a Preacher's audience, for a speaker is understood in the definition his audience puts upon a word, unless he defines it himself. Wise is the Preacher who defines it for his people.

This love with which a Saint should love another Saint is produced by the Holy Spirit in the heart of the Saint, and its amount and intensity are determined by the degree of yielding to the Spirit on the part of that Saint. It is self-sacrificial in its essence (Jn. 3:16).

It is longsuffering in its character, kind, self-abasing, humble, well-behaved, altruistic, is not provoked, thinks no evil, does not rejoice in iniquity, rejoices in the truth, bears all things, believes all things, hopes all things, endures all things, never fails (I Cor. 13:4-8).

The words *"one another"* are a reciprocal pronoun in the Greek text. That is, there must be reciprocity among the Saints as to this love. A Saint must reciprocate the love shown him by a fellow-Saint (Wuest).

(6) "AND THIS IS LOVE, THAT WE WALK AFTER HIS COMMANDMENTS. THIS IS THE COMMANDMENT, THAT, AS YOU HAVE HEARD FROM THE BEGINNING, YOU SHOULD WALK IN IT."

The composite is:

1. The text actually says, *"And this is the love."*

2. As given here, *"walking after His Commandments,"* is *"loving one another."*

3. We are to order our behavior, conduct ourselves, dominated by the Commandments of God. They are to be the dominating factor in our behavior.

4. We should conduct ourselves in the sphere of love.

5. Divine love, produced in the heart by the Holy Spirit, is the motivating factor that impels Saints to observe the Commandments of God (Wuest).

THIS IS LOVE

The phrase, *"And this is love, that we walk after His Commandments,"* presents the proper expression or evidence of love to God.

Four times in Verses 4 through 6 John uses the noun *"command."* This is his way of making clear that what he is saying is a direct expression of God's will.

And how does one know that he fulfills the Will of God? The test of love is obedience to God's Commands, and the test of obedience is whether one *"walks in love."*

The argument is intentionally circular. Love of God that does not result in obedience to the Word of God cannot be the love that is God's Gift in Jesus Christ. Jesus' Own love was manifested by His obedience even to death. Love of God can finally be expressed only in action and truth (I Jn. 3:18). Do we love our Brother? Are we prepared to die for him? Obedience that does not lead to the life of love in which we love one another even to death, if such would be necessary, is not obedience offered to God. Not to love means to remain in darkness (I Jn. 2:11) and in death (I Jn. 3:14). Hatred of one's Brother can never be defended as obedience to God. It is rather obedience and gratification of one's own sin — one's own evil nature (I Jn. 3:12) (Barker).

THE COMMANDMENT

The phrase, *"This is the Commandment, that, as you have heard from the beginning, you should walk in it,"* presents the Commandment by which the followers of the Lord are to be peculiarly characterized, and by which we are to be distinguished in the world.

Loving one another is not one doing of one Commandment among many others; it is doing all God's Commandments. However, when John speaks of *"Commandments,"* he is not really speaking of the Mosaic Law, but rather of the Gospel and of what it asks of us. We are walking in the whole Gospel when we love one another as Brethren in Jesus Christ, God's Son. Love itself is hidden in the heart, and thus John writes, *"that we walk,"* meaning that this love displays itself in our walk, in word, and in deed.

THE FIRST EPISTLE

Supremely, and above all else, the First Epistle of John contained three warnings, very necessary for those times, and as well for us:

1. There was a danger of losing the True Christ, the Word made Flesh, Who for the forgiveness of our sins did shed His Own precious Life's Blood, in order that we might be saved. A shadowy Christ was being proposed by some false teachers, whom Paul referred to as *"another Jesus"* (II Cor. 11:4).

2. There was a danger of losing true love, therefore, Spiritual Life, with truth.

3. With the True Christ and true love there was a danger of losing the True Commandment — love of God and of the Brethren.

THE SECOND EPISTLE

Now in the Second Epistle these very three warnings were written on a leaflet in a form more calculated for circulation and for remembrance:

1. Once again we address the peril of faith, of losing the True Christ. John said, *"Many deceivers are gone out into the world — they who confess not Jesus Christ coming in the flesh. This is a deceiver and an antichrist."*

With the True Christ, the True Doctrine of Christ would also vanish, and with it all living hold upon God. While progress was the watchword, in reality, if the false teaching of these false teachers was heeded, it was in reality regress. *"Everyone who abideth not in the doctrine of Christ has not God."*

2. Against the peril of losing love. *"I beseech thee, lady . . . that we love one another."*

3. Against the peril of losing the True Commandment (the great spiritual principle of charity), or the true Commandments (that principle in the details of life). *"And this is love, that you walk after His Commandments. This is the Commandment, that even as you heard from the beginning you should walk in it"* (Alexander).

(7) "FOR MANY DECEIVERS ARE ENTERED INTO THE WORLD, WHO CONFESS NOT THAT JESUS CHRIST IS COME IN THE FLESH. THIS IS A DECEIVER AND AN ANTICHRIST."

The exegesis is:

1. A *"deceiver"* is a false teacher who leads others into heresies.

2. *"Entering in the world,"* means that these deceivers were trying to set up another way, in effect, another Church.

3. *"Jesus Christ come in the flesh,"* does not refer to the totally-depraved nature, but to the physical body and human life with its human limitations of our Lord. The denial here is that of the Incarnation.

4. Such a false teacher is a *"deceiver,"* and irrespective as to how much he might proclaim Christ, in fact, is anti-Christ.

DECEIVERS

The phrase, *"For many deceivers are entered into the world,"* refers to those who function with the help of *"seducing spirits"* (I Tim. 4:1). Paul referred to what they taught as *"doctrines of Devils."*

Not content to be deceived themselves, these individuals cannot rest until they have deceived others, as many as possible. They do not bother pagans, and for the simple reason that their gospel will not draw anybody to Christ. They must prey on true Christians.

While Satan opposes the True Church from both without and within, he has his far greater success in opposing from within. He comes as *"an angel of light"* (II Cor. 11:13-15).

"Are entered into the world" could be translated, *"Have gone out into the world."*

This speaks of a particular crisis in the First Century Church when these false teachers suddenly broke with the Saints in matters of doctrine, and went forth teaching heresy, in effect, attempting to start another Church, one might say. They didn't do this by attempting to win souls to Christ, for their false message would not win anyone to the Lord; consequently, they had to try to turn the Saints who were true followers of Christ, into following this false doctrine. How could they do this?

Going back to I Timothy 4:1, their message was empowered by *"seducing spirits."*

Even though there are many such like doctrines in the world presently, the *"Word of Faith"* doctrine is probably one of the most visible, and one of the most successful. Let the Reader understand, all false doctrine begins with a false impression of the Person of Christ or His Mission, and by His Mission, we primarily speak of the Cross. If there is error, that's where it usually begins.

This is not new, having begun with Cain and Abel. Man ever since has been attempting to change God's order as it regards Redemption and Victory. Paul said:

"And I, Brethren, if I yet preach circumcision, why do I yet suffer persecution? Then is the offense of the Cross ceased" (Gal. 5:11).

As Cain was offended by the Cross, many in the modern Church are as well.

WHY IS THE CROSS AN OFFENSE?

In the first place, the very fact of the Cross says that man's problem is so bad, in fact, so terminal that he cannot address it himself, thereby, God would have to take steps to address the problem from the position of the Godhead. The Cross was the answer (I Pet. 1:18-20). Man keeps thinking he can solve his own problem; unfortunately, many in the Church think the same thing. So the Cross is an offense to them.

The truth is, man, not even redeemed man, can alleviate his situation. In other words, Believers cannot live for God, and by that I speak of having victory over the world, the flesh, and the Devil, by their own strength. It is literally impossible (Rom. 8:1,

8). In fact if he tries to live for God by his own machinations and ability, the Holy Spirit simply will not help, and without the help of the Spirit, man is doomed to failure, irrespective that he is redeemed, etc. (Rom. 8:1-2, 11, 13).

As the sinner is saved by trusting in Christ and what Christ did at the Cross, which is the only way he can be saved; likewise, the Christian can walk in victory and on a perpetual basis, only as his Faith is 100 percent in the Finished Work of Christ, which then gives the Holy Spirit the latitude to provide His help, which is always more than enough. That's the reason that Paul said:

"But unto them which are called, both Jews and Greeks (Jews and Gentiles), *Christ the Power of God, and the Wisdom of God"* (I Cor. 1:24).

What did Paul mean by the statement that Christ is the Power of God, and the Wisdom of God?

Regarding the *"Power of God"* it simply means, that what Jesus did at the Cross, which was to atone for all sin, made it possible for the Holy Spirit to come in and abide within the heart and life of the Believer, and to do so on a perpetual basis. The power is in the Holy Spirit, but the Holy Spirit is able to do the things He does simply because of what Christ did at the Cross.

The *"Wisdom of God"* concerns itself with the actual fact of Calvary and what happened there.

As stated, Jesus atoned for all sin at the Cross, and did so by the giving of Himself in the pouring out of His Own Life's Blood, which served as a Sacrifice that God would and did accept. In the doing of this, Christ atoned for all sin, past, present, and future, at least for all who will believe (Jn. 3:16). When Christ did this, He *"destroyed the works of Satan,"* by making it impossible for Satan to any more hold man in captivity, at least for those who will believe. Sin gave Satan the legal right to exert captivity over mankind. With all sin removed, which it was at the Cross (Jn. 1:29), Satan lost his legal right to hold man in bondage. This is the *"Wisdom of God,"* i.e., *"the Cross."* So this means that the Cross is both the Power of God and the Wisdom of God, irrespective

NOTES

as to what the world or even the Church might think.

THE INCARNATION

The phrase, *"Who confess not that Jesus Christ is come in the flesh,"* pertains to the Incarnation.

John is not using the word *"flesh"* here as Paul normally uses it, which speaks of human ability, etc. He is rather speaking of the physical body and human life of Christ with its human limitations, which characterize the Incarnation, God becoming man. The Apostle is coming here against the false teachers. A man by the name of Cerinthus was probably the most noted of the false teachers at that particular time. He did not deny that Jesus was a man; he regarded Jesus as the physical son of Joseph and of Mary. What he denied was the Incarnation, the fact that in Jesus Christ we have the Eternal Son of God, born of the Virgin, Whose shed Blood (I Jn. 1:7) is the expiation for the sins of the world (I Jn. 2:2; 4:9-10), and that *"this One is the real God and life eternal"* (I Jn. 5:20).

That which John says here proves the timeless character of the event. It is seen not simply as an event in history but as an *"abiding truth"* defining the union between humanity and Deity that is present in Jesus' Person. This union is not limited to Jesus' historical manifestation but remains true of Him as the One at the right hand of the Father. This means that the Incarnation was more than a mere incident, and more than a temporary and partial connection between the Logos and human nature. It was the permanent guarantee of the possibility of fellowship by redeemed humans with God, and the chief means by which it is brought about.

THE MANNER OF THE INCARNATION

The Incarnate Son is the supreme Word or Revelation of God to men. This is the force of John 1:1-3, 14, 18. He is the *"Image"* of God (II Cor. 4:4; Col. 1:15). By Him, as in no other way, God has spoken (Heb. 1:1-3). He who has seen Jesus has seen the Father (Jn. 14:9). God, as it were, placed Himself in the immediate presence of men, accessible even to observation by the common senses (I Jn. 1:1-3), not to be comprehended, however, except through the illumination of the Spirit (I Cor. 2:7-16).

It was through the realization of Who Christ was and of the nature of His relationship with the Father that gave men a new understanding of God and led them to see His triune nature.

THE IMAGE OF GOD

In a double sense Jesus Christ was the Image of God. As Son in an immediate and unique sense revealing the Divine nature, Jesus was the Image of God. As man He also was the perfect example of what was in the Mind of God when He said, *"Let us make man in Our Image"* (Gen. 1:26). In Him is revealed ideal man, man in true and perfect fellowship with God, man as the reflection of the grace and goodness of God, showing the inner graces of love, joy, goodness, and such like.

By this, Christ becomes a revelation of what sinful man is; by contrast with Christ man is so obviously short of the Glory of God (Jn. 1:14; Rom. 3:23). At the same time He reveals God's purpose for all who commit themselves to His saving purpose, for into this Image God transforms men (Rom. 8:29; II Cor. 3:18; 5:17; Col. 3:10).

There is nevertheless a certain hiddenness in the very form of the self-revelation of God in the Incarnation. God was, as it were, veiled in Christ so that men might look upon Him. Certainly, in human flesh the Son of God was not easily recognized (I Cor. 2:8; I Jn. 3:1). For the unrepentant sinner, the full vision of God will occasion unspeakable terror (Rev. 6:15-17); for the Believer, the final transformation (II Cor. 3:18; I Jn. 3:2).

THE NECESSITY OF THE INCARNATION

The Incarnation was essential in the Plan of God to deliver men from sin and all its dire consequences.

Through Christ becoming man, sinful men were able in an immediate and direct fashion to receive and acknowledge Him as Lord, or repudiate and reject Him. For the most part men rejected Him; in their laying hands upon the Incarnate Lord they were giving the fullest possible expression to sin, and in the act of crucifixion is exhibited as

in no other way the real nature of sin: man's willful refusal to accept the sovereign right and rule of his Creator Lord. Allowing men so to act He was still Lord, for it was ordained that in and through His death on the Cross He should bear the sins of men (Jn. 1:29, 36; Acts 2:23; 4:26-28; I Pet. 2:24; Rev. 5:6; 13:8). In Him God was reconciling men to Himself (II Cor. 5:19). This was the basic purpose in the Incarnation (Heb. 10:5, 10).

Furthermore, by virtue of His Incarnation, Death, and Resurrection, He became the new Adam and Head of the new race of redeemed men (Rom. 5:12; Col. 1:18).

These two purposes, Revelational and Redemptive, are inseparably related. God's revealing activity in all its forms, and supremely in Christ, is redemptive in purpose. This is His answer to man's ignorance through sin.

Christ is the light of the world (Jn. 8:12), the One through Whom God has shone into our hearts (II Cor. 4:6). The Son came that men might see their sin, learn of God's Grace, and so turn to God in true penitence and faith. God's revelatory activity always involves a certain giving of Himself to men, and especially was this so in the Incarnation. Then in self-giving, God is taking the initial act in restoring men to fellowship with Himself.

This restoration could not take place, however, without that to which the self-giving of the Incarnation led, namely the Cross.

The Cross, in turn, is a Revelation: in it is revealed as in no other way the inestimable love of the Father and of the Son (Rom. 5:8; I Jn. 4:9-10).

THE DOCTRINE OF THE INCARNATION

It has been suggested that the Incarnation was in the mind of God independently of His redemptive purpose for fallen man; that even had men not sinned, the Son would still have become Incarnate. Indeed, when Adam was created in the Image of God, the pattern was that Incarnate form which God purposed in due time for His Son. Of this idea, however, Scripture seems to give no clear direction.

Even within the Apostolic period the reality of the Incarnation was challenged. An early and persistent error, strongly denounced in I and II John, which we are now studying (known as Docetism, from the Greek *"to seem"*), was that Christ only appeared to be human, that His inner spirit was Divine, not human, or even that His body was not a truly human body.

Despite the emphatic Scriptural condemnation of this error, many attempts to define the Incarnation have tended to be in this vein. Any view which sees in Jesus less than a full humanity and a full experience of the limitations that essentially belong to human existence (not the additional limitations inherent in sinful humanity) is Docetic. Jesus Christ was *"made like His Brethren in every respect"* (Heb. 2:17).

With the early rise of conflicting views and a natural continued interest in the nature of Jesus of Nazareth, the Church had to give increasing and urgent attention to the doctrine of the Incarnation. There were two main issues around which there was great controversy in the early centuries after the Apostolic period:

1. The actual nature of Jesus Christ — to which the Church gave answer: He was both human and Divine.

2. This being so, how were these two natures united in one Person? In answer to the second, the tendency was, and in modern theology still is, to commence from and emphasize either the Deity or the humanity, to some diminution of the other.

AN UNDERSTANDING OF
THE INCARNATION

First of all, perhaps it is impossible to fully understand the Incarnation. Maybe our explanations raise as many questions as they provide answers. For instance, when we say that Jesus Christ was and is *"Very Man and Very God,"* we are meaning that at the same time he was fully man and yet fully God. Perhaps we could say it stronger by using the phraseology, *"Very Man of very man and Very God of very God."*

As one scholar has said, *"In the Incarnation God laid aside the expression of His Deity, while never losing possession of His Deity."* As stated, the problem with the Church is to emphasize either the Deity or the humanity, to some diminution of the other. This must not be done.

But to whatever excesses the Church has gone, one of the greatest problems facing the Church presently is, *"Christ has been too humanized and man has been too deified."*

ANTICHRIST

The phrase, *"This is a deceiver and an antichrist,"* says in the original, *"This is the deceiver and the antichrist."* The idea is, the teacher who denies the fact of an Incarnation is a deceiver and an antichrist, and as Alford says, *"A representative and precursor of antichrist himself."*

As we've already stated, all false doctrine begins with a misconception or misinterpretation of the *"Person"* of Christ and the *"Purpose"* of Christ. In other words, it's Who He was, and What He did!

The idea is, whenever false doctrine is presented, those who teach such are flirting with the great foe of Christ as he roams about the world, and we speak of Satan.

Some may take issue with us regarding the pointing out of false doctrine; however, I would remind the Reader that much of what John is saying here, even as it was with Paul, is the pointing out of false doctrine along with proclaiming that which is true. One of the great purposes of the Gospel is to warn of the false while at the same time pointing out the Truth.

If we are enjoying true fellowship with God, that fact will be manifested in certain ways. The first manifestation will be the absence of any hypocrisy. John prefaced this aspect of his message about genuine fellowship by announcing, *"that God is light and in Him there is no darkness."* This *"Message"* is not mere hearsay; it has always been the claim of God (Jn. 8:12). He cannot possibly possess duplicity, or He would not be God.

THE GNOSTICS

By way of contrast, the heretical Gnostics were shrouded with dissimulation. They made contradictory claims that the Apostle exposed as spurious. In fact, when he wrote *"if we say"* he may have been alluding to actual slogans propagated by these false teachers.

The Apostle was blunt when he said, *"If we contend that we have an unbreakable 'fellowship' with the Lord, yet walk in darkness, we lie."* He uses a present active verb that denotes a habitual lifestyle. It is not possible for us to be constantly walking in the light unless we are partaking of God's Divine nature.

An authentic relationship with God cannot be reduced to a mere adoption of a creed. If we assert that we are walking with God but are instead walking in darkness, the doctrine has not been translated into action. Assertion and action are not the same thing. In fact, John said, *"We are not practicing the truth."* People who are consistently practicing the truth of God's Word have no fear of the Light because they are walking transparently before the Lord (Jn. 3:21).

THE INVENTION OF A JUSTIFICATION FOR SIN

It is possible to rationalize and misinterpret the Scriptures until we invent Justification for sin. The Gnostics did it by claiming that all matter, including human flesh, is inherently evil. Hence, according to them the human body serves as a mere container in which the human spirit resides. This would mean, therefore, that what the material part of a human does has no bearing whatever on the immaterial portion (soul and spirit) of his being. In other words, how one lives does not matter; a certain type of knowledge is all that really counts, they say!

This unbiblical approach made it possible to justify a blatant lawlessness in which individuals could practice gross immorality and attest to a personal and abiding relationship with God at the same time. This is the worst kind of darkness because it involves knowing but not doing.

I John 1:7 contains the antidote to this hypocritical approach. The answer is not covering up sin. It is, rather, the direct opposite. The Biblical approach is to keep on walking totally exposed to *"the Light,"* or to the Truth of God expressed in Scripture, in other words, with Faith and trust expressly in the Sacrifice of Christ. The Divine order is *"union,"* then *"communion."* If we are truly united with God through Christ, that crucial condition will be revealed in two wonderful ways.

UNION AND COMMUNION

First, we will constantly have *"fellowship"* with *"one another,"* or with fellow Christians. Other bona fide Believers will acknowledge our living relationship with Jesus Christ, and they will want to participate with us in worshiping and serving Him. Now notice I said *"bona fide Believers,"* and not merely those who claim Christ but really do not possess Christ.

The second result is continuous cleansing *"from all sin,"* which gives us communion with God. *"Cleanses"* in the Greek constitutes another present active indicative verb which speaks of an ongoing process of purification. Notice that it happens through *"the Blood of Jesus His Son."*

The Gnostic leader Cerinthus taught that Jesus was a mere human when He was crucified, but John designated Him as the Eternal Son of God Who assumed a tangible body of flesh, bones, blood, etc. Because He is the Son of Man, His Blood was genuine human blood made available as the sacrifice for sin, and because He is the Son of God, His Blood is efficacious (effective) to cleanse humans from sin.

NO IMPENITENCE

In I John 1:8 we see the second claim of imposters who say they enjoy a relationship with the Lord. *"If we say that we have no sin"* is a blatant denial of the possession of a sinful nature. These are individuals who claim to be absolutely sinless, an assertion that even the Apostle Paul would not make for the conclusion of his earthly life (Phil. 3:12-14). Again, this claim reflects the Gnostic subtlety which relegated sin merely to the physical body, alleging that it had no influence on the human spirit.

John affirmed that such an approach signifies two things:

1. *"We deceive ourselves,"* or we keep on leading ourselves astray. We do not fool people and we certainly do not delude God.

This kind of approach was not peculiar just to Gnostics. Some Jews argued with Jesus that they were not subject to slavery to sin because they were Abraham's progeny (Jn. 8:31-41). The Lord quickly informed them that they were really children of the Devil (Jn. 8:42-47).

2. Denial of the principle of sin merely signifies that *the truth is not in us.* Why? Because God says all humans sin (Rom. 3:23; 5:12; etc.).

The Lord does not say that because He desires for us to practice sin. Of course not (Rom. 6:1-2)! He tells us this so we will turn to Him for the antidote. The solution to the problem is not to ignorantly deny the situation, but to follow God's instructions which are given to us in Romans, Chapter 6, so we can be victorious over the sinful nature.

NO SELF SUFFICIENCY

The third unscriptural claim as mentioned by John is, *"If we say that we have no sin* (no sin nature), *we deceive ourselves, and the truth is not in us"* (I Jn. 1:8).

John was blunt enough to say that people who claim personal, absolute, sinless perfection are really making God *"a liar."* This is far worse than lying (I Jn. 1:6) or deceiving oneself (I Jn. 1:8). Of course, God is not the One Who is the liar. Allegedly, D. L. Moody was approached one time by a man who claimed to be absolutely sinless in himself. Moody supposedly retorted, *"I would like to ask your wife if that is true."*

The Apostle John aggressively asserted that if we make such claims *"His Word is not in us."* God's written Word (the Bible) and His Living Word (Christ) do not condone such egotism. The Lord Jesus is the only One Who lived totally free from sin. How can we dare claim to place ourselves on the same level with Him? His sinless sacrifice is our only hope of forgiveness and deliverance from our sinful plight.

While the Bible does not teach sinless perfection, it does teach, however, that *"sin will not have dominion over us"* (Rom. 6:14). But of course, as is obvious, that is a far cry from sinless perfection.

The way that such a place of victory is assured is the Faith and confidence we express in Christ and what He did at the Cross on our behalf. If the Believer does not have his Faith anchored squarely in the Cross, understanding that it is from this Sacrifice that all blessings come, then he will have his faith

in *"self,"* which is what we mean by *"self-sufficiency."* Now let the Reader read these words carefully:

If the Believer is not trusting in the *"Cross,"* without fail, he is trusting in *"self."* The irony is, he will do so while loudly proclaiming that he is trusting Christ. But it is impossible to properly trust Christ, unless one properly understands the Cross.

SELF THE GREATEST HINDERER

When a person comes to Christ he doesn't cease to be a *"self."* In fact that's what we are. So the harm is not in self per se, but rather in our dependence on self.

Due to the Fall, dependence on self is the greatest problem of the human race. We think we can solve all of our problems, that we can pull ourselves by our own machinations, out of our dilemma. In other words, we think we can save ourselves, or if we are a Christian, then we can bring ourselves to victory through the machinations of self.

We must learn that self is woefully inadequate, even redeemed self. Coming to Christ in no way means that we are now done with the Cross, even as many Christians seem to think. In fact, the Christian will never be done with the Cross. The truth is, even Christian self is woefully inadequate, and if we attempt to live this life by the rudiments of self, we will find out this truth very quickly. That's why Jesus said that we must deny ourselves and take up our Cross daily and follow Him (Lk. 9:23).

When the Believer places his Faith solely in the Finished Work of Christ, this makes a statement. It says that he knows he cannot do it himself, and that in fact, Christ has already done it for us. Actually, the very reason He came to this world was to serve as our Substitute, in other words, to do for us what we couldn't do for ourselves.

The Christian is very quick to claim that the person who doesn't know Christ cannot save himself by his good works, etc., but he then turns around and tries to sanctify himself by his own efforts, in fact, doing what he claims the unsaved man cannot do. Let me say it again:

Coming to Christ in no way sets aside dependence on Christ. In fact, the very act of coming to Christ and belonging to Him proclaims our dependence on Him, and in fact, our dependence solely on Him. That is shown by our trust in the Cross of Christ, and in that Finished Work alone!

That is the only way that *"self"* can be overcome, or rather be placed in its rightful position, which is hidden *"in Christ."* That's why Paul said:

"For you are dead (when we accepted Christ, we were baptized into His death — Rom. 6:3), *and your life is hid with Christ in God"* (Col. 3:3).

As someone has well said, *"Jesus died on the Cross to save us not only from sin but as well from self."*

(8) "LOOK TO YOURSELVES, THAT WE LOSE NOT THOSE THINGS WHICH WE HAVE WROUGHT, BUT THAT WE RECEIVE A FULL REWARD."

The diagram is:

1. *"Look to yourselves,"* is the same as Paul's *"examine yourselves!"*

2. It is possible for us to lose what we have, even to the loss of our souls.

3. When we stand at the Judgment Seat of Christ, we will either receive a *"full reward,"* or less. It will be because of our motivation and consecration to the truth.

EXAMINE YOURSELVES

The phrase, *"Look to yourselves,"* is basically the same as Paul's, *"Examine yourselves, whether ye be in the faith; prove your own selves. Know ye not your own selves, how that Jesus Christ is in you, except you be reprobates?"* (II Cor. 13:5).

The only safeguard against false doctrine is that we are properly *"in the faith."* What does that mean?

When Paul speaks of *"Faith,"* and especially *"the Faith,"* without exception, he is always speaking of Christ, and what Christ has done to redeem us, which was to offer Himself in Sacrifice on the Cross of Calvary, thereby pouring out His Own Life's Blood, which atoned for all sin. Our Faith and confidence must be exclusively in that.

When error abounds in the world, our first duty is not to attack it and make war upon it; it is to look to the citadel of our own souls, and see that all is well-guarded there.

Continuing to use this as a metaphor, when an enemy invades a land, the first thing will not be to go out against him, regardless of our own strength, or of the security of our own fortresses, but it will be to see that our forts are manned as well as we think they are, and that we are thereby, secure from the assaults of the enemy. If that is so, we may then go forth with confidence to meet him on the open field.

This goes along also with Paul's admonition to Timothy: *"Fight the good fight of faith, lay hold on eternal life"* (I Tim. 6:12). In the Greek it actually says: *"Fight the good fight of the faith."* This is the only fight we are called upon to engage. And it pertains to *"the faith."*

Satan will attack us here, as he does no place else. While this is a fight, it is a *"good fight,"* and because of the payoff which is *"Eternal Life."*

WHAT DOES IT MEAN TO FIGHT THE GOOD FIGHT OF THE FAITH?

The idea can probably be summed up in *"the object of our Faith."* The object must ever be the Finished Work of Christ, and what does that mean?

It means that we are to understand that the answer to every question is found in the Cross; the solution to every problem is found in the Cross; the key to all victory is found in the Cross. Understanding that, we place our Faith in that great Sacrifice, and refuse to allow it to be moved.

After living for the Lord these many years, I am persuaded that almost all of Satan's attacks are for the purpose of moving our faith to something else. He knows if he can do this, he has won the battle. So the struggle poses itself in us not allowing our Faith to be moved to other things, despite the pressure of the attack. The key to living for God is faith; however, more particularly, the key is our Faith in the proper object, which always must be the Cross of Christ.

At this particular time, Satan is mounting an all-out attack on the Cross. It's mostly coming from two directions:

1. It's coming from the area of humanistic psychology. This doesn't affect the laity directly, but it definitely affects them

indirectly. Whenever the leadership of a Denomination abandons the Cross of Christ, which one has to do, when one accepts humanistic psychology, after awhile that particular position affects the entirety of the Denomination. And regrettably, the major Pentecostal Denominations in the United States and Canada have taken that route. Most of that particular leadership would vehemently deny that they have abandoned the Cross; however, these two particular directions are opposites. In other words, it's impossible to hold to both. If we're trusting what man produces, we're not trusting the Lord, etc.

2. The other major opponent of the Cross is the Word of Faith people. They are openly antagonistic to the Cross, referring to it as *"the greatest defeat in human history."* They openly state that the Blood of Jesus Christ does not avail for anything. Without a doubt, their attack which is frontal, is the most vicious at the present time.

I have every confidence, if that particular belief system had been in force during the time of John, that he would have made the same identical statements which he made concerning Gnosticism. In fact, some of the Gnostic system has been adopted by the modern Word of Faith teaching. Their modern counterparts teach that the spirit of man is perfect after Redemption, and whatever sin is committed is retained in the physical body, which is of little or no consequence.

From my study of the Word of God, I believe that we are presently living in the last of the last days. As such, these false doctrines are going to become worse and worse. But at the same time, the Lord is raising up a standard against these false teachings. That Standard is the Cross! Consequently, the Cross of Christ is the dividing line, I believe, between the True Church and the Apostate Church. In truth, it has always been that way, but I think it is going to be more pronounced now than ever.

LOSS

The phrase, *"That we lose not those things which we have wrought,"* proclaims the fact, coupled with the next Verse, that not only can reward be lost, but as well, the soul can be lost, all through accepting false doctrine.

NOTES

Let the Reader understand that any acceptance of false doctrine always and without exception, falls out to spiritual loss. In fact, it cannot be otherwise!

There is nothing more important than one's relationship with Christ. It has to do with eternal consequences, and eternity is a long, long time. Unfortunately, we seem to trade so very much which is eternal for that which is temporal, which cannot help but be a very bad trade.

Many Christians do not seem to realize that what we do here will decide what we will be there. In fact, everything is decided here! What kind of motives do we have? What is our purpose as it regards this Christian life? How much do we seek the Will of God in all things?

And then, many Christians take the position that if they barely make Heaven they'll be satisfied. That's a terrible attitude to have regarding something which is so important.

One should want to be the best that one can be. And how can one be that?

Everything is in Christ, but more particularly, what He did for us at the Cross. If we understand the Cross then we understand Christ. If we don't understand the Cross, our understanding of Him will then be very limited. Our Faith properly placed in Him and what He has done for us, is the key to all things.

REWARD

The phrase, *"But that we receive a full reward,"* refers to the coming Judgment Seat of Christ, where and when every true Christian will give account of our life lived on Earth for the Lord. Christ Himself will be the Judge, and of course, His Judgment will be perfect. Knowing the hearts of all, for the first time in human history, true judgment will be accorded.

As well, we are plainly told here that some part or even all of one's reward can be lost. If there is loss, it will be eternal, which means that the loss will be severe indeed!

What exactly the reward will be, we aren't told, but whatever it is, considering the character of our Lord and Saviour, it will be great.

For instance, at the very beginning of His Ministry, Jesus borrowed Peter's boat for about an hour, using it as a platform to preach to the people on the shore.

When He had finished, knowing that Peter and the other ship with him, had caught nothing, even though they'd fished all night long, He said to Simon, *"Launch out into the deep, and let down your nets for a draught."*

Peter answered by saying unto Him, *"Master, we have toiled all the night, and have taken nothing: nevertheless at Thy Word I will let down the net."*

The Scripture tells us that when this was done, they caught so many fish in that one haul, that the net began to break. In fact, they filled both ships so full of fish that the ships were in danger of sinking (Lk. 5:1-7).

If the Lord would tender such a reward in this case, one can well imagine what the reward might be for those who have been faithful, when they stand at the Judgment Seat of Christ.

(9) "WHOSOEVER TRANSGRESSETH, AND ABIDES NOT IN THE DOCTRINE OF CHRIST, HAS NOT GOD. HE WHO ABIDES IN THE DOCTRINE OF CHRIST, HE HAS BOTH THE FATHER AND THE SON."

The composite is:

1. This Scripture tells us that it's possible for a Believer to quit believing, and to thereby, lose their soul.

2. To *"abide in the Doctrine of Christ,"* one has to first accept Christ. So we're speaking here not merely of one who professes, but of one who has actually possessed Christ.

3. One must come to the Lord, which means to come by accepting Christ and what He has done at the Cross, and then to continue to abide therein, that is if one is to be saved.

4. The word *"both"* vividly proclaims the fact that there are at least two Persons in the Trinity. Considering that it is the Holy Spirit Who inspired these words, we now have the complete Trinity.

ABIDING IN THE DOCTRINE OF CHRIST

The phrase, *"Whosoever transgresseth, and abides not in the Doctrine of Christ, has not God,"* refers to someone who has truly accepted Christ and is, therefore, saved; however, they did not continue to abide in the True Doctrine of Christ, but rather began to believe error. Blunt and to the point, John says if such occurs, and regrettably it does quite often, that particular person *"has not God."* The idea is this:

The individual in question does not cease to believe, but rather shifts their faith from Christ and what He did at the Cross, to something else. As it is, such a person is no longer believing in that which is the True Gospel of Jesus Christ, but rather something else.

This Passage, plus scores of others similar, clearly proclaims the fact that a Believer can cease to believe, or else begin to believe in something that's wrong concerning Salvation, and thereby lose their soul. Consequently, such Passages completely refute the unscriptural doctrine of unconditional eternal security.

We must remember that John is addressing himself here to false teachers and false doctrine. He then warns those who believe these doctrines, plainly telling them that to believe such could cause the loss of their souls.

WHAT IS THE DOCTRINE OF CHRIST?

It is: *"For God so loved the world, that He gave His only Begotten Son, that whosoever believeth in Him should not perish, but have everlasting life"* (Jn. 3:16). The Doctrine of Christ pertains to *"Who"* Christ is, and *"What"* Christ has done.

First of all, as to Who He is, Jesus Christ is God. But more particularly, He is God manifest in the flesh, which means that He is *"Very Man and Very God."* He is the One of Whom the Prophet Isaiah predicted: *"Therefore the Lord Himself shall give you a sign; behold, a virgin shall conceive, and bear a son, and shall call His name Immanuel"* (Isa. 7:14).

John the Beloved also said of Him: *"In the beginning was the Word, and the Word was with God, and the Word was God"* (Jn. 1:1).

He then said: *"And the Word was made flesh, and dwelt among us, (and we beheld His glory, the glory as of the only Begotten of the Father,) full of Grace and Truth"* (Jn. 1:14).

Concerning the Living Word Who was made flesh, John the Baptist said of Him: *"Behold the Lamb of God, which taketh away the sin of the world"* (Jn. 1:29).

NOTES

Consequently, we are told here in the very First Chapter of the Gospel according to John, as to Who Jesus is, and What He came to do.

The very reason that God became man was in order to die on a Cross, which alone could redeem fallen humanity. In fact, this was decided long before the world was created (I Pet. 1:18-20).

God cannot die, so He would have to become man in order to pay the terrible price that His nature and justice demanded.

So the Doctrine of Christ is actually Who He was and is, namely God manifest in the flesh, and What He did, which was to die on a Cross. Men must believe in Him and as well believe in what He did in order to be saved. If we confuse the issue as to Who He is, and What He has done, we cannot be saved, and if we have already been saved by properly believing in Him to begin with, due to the fact that we no longer interpret His Person correctly, or what He did, which means that we no longer abide in the correct doctrine, we can lose our souls.

THE FATHER AND THE SON

The phrase, *"He that abideth in the Doctrine of Christ, he has both the Father and the Son,"* refers to the fact that the way to the Father is through the Son, and by using the title *"Son,"* the Holy Spirit is referring to both Deity and the Cross, as it refers to Christ.

There is such an intimate union between the Father and the Son that he who has just views of the One has also of the Other (Jn. 14:7, 9-11; I Jn. 2:23).

Much is being said presently about *"doctrine."* People say they do not want doctrine, and Preachers try to accommodate them. Do we not want the truth, the great facts and realities about God, about Christ, and about ourselves, to be put into the proper words so that we may hear, realize, and believe them? If we want that, and surely we do, then we want doctrine.

Or rather do we want sophisticated myths or fables? (II Pet. 1:16).

No matter in what direction one goes and does not remain in the Doctrine of Christ, clear and plain, *"he has not God"* although he may shout ever so loudly, *"I know Him!"* (I Jn. 2:4). This is the great delusion (I Jn.

2:23). God, the real God (I Jn. 5:20), is found only in Christ, and what Christ has done for us at the Cross (Jn. 10:30; 14:9, 11), hence only in the Doctrine of Christ (Jn. 1:18).

John does not need to add *"and has not Christ"* because he who forsakes Christ's Doctrine certainly also forsakes Christ.

The one remaining in the Doctrine, this one, this one alone, *"has Both the Father and the Son."* By having the One he has the Other; a separation of the two is impossible. To have them is to have Salvation.

Not for naught does John say *"has not God"* and now *"has Both the Father and the Son."* These Gnostics imagined that they had *"God,"* but in their estimation He was not *"the Father"* of *"the Son"*; to true Believers in Christ and in His Doctrine God is *"the Father"* of *"His Son Jesus Christ"* (I Jn. 1:3).

Paul Crouch of T.B.N. said: *"The heresy hunters that want to find a little mote of illegal doctrine in some Christian's eye and pluck that little mote out of their eye when they've got the whole forest in their own lives and in their own eyes. 'I say to Hell with you,' Oh, Hallelujah! Get out of God's way, quit blocking God's bridges, or God's gonna shoot you if I don't."*

In effect, this man is saying that doctrine doesn't matter!

The sadness is, the modern Church is so Scripturally illiterate and so lacking in discernment that it hardly knows what is of the Lord and what isn't any more. In fact, Satan has presently become so bold that for all practical purposes he has shed his *"sheep's clothing"* (Mat. 7:15), and is rather appearing boldly as a *"seducing spirit"* (I Tim. 4:1).

It's bad enough to refuse to support the Work of God, but to support that which is in actuality the *"work of the Devil,"* is the worst thing, I think, that a Christian can do. And that's pretty much what the modern Church is presently doing. It little knows what is of God and what isn't any more. It worships *"devils"* thinking it's worshiping the Lord. It chases *"spirits"* thinking it's following the Holy Spirit!

THE ONLY CURE FOR DECEPTION

The only cure is the Word of God preached in all of its purity, power, and done so without fear, favor, or compromise; however, when that's done, it's going to arouse anger as never before. But whatever the abuse, a stand must be taken, and simply because souls are at stake.

This conflict didn't begin yesterday. In fact, it began with Cain and Abel, as recorded in Genesis, Chapter 4. And if you remember correctly, Cain killed Abel, because Abel trusted in the Cross. That was the reason for the conflict then, and it is the reason for the conflict now — the Cross. For those who reject it, they will also try their best to stop the voice of those who accept it. Nevertheless, the Word must go forth in all of its purity and power.

(10) "IF THERE COME ANY UNTO YOU, AND BRING NOT THIS DOCTRINE, RECEIVE HIM NOT INTO YOUR HOUSE, NEITHER BID HIM GOD SPEED:"

The structure is:

1. John says in order to be saved, we must believe in the *"Doctrine of Christ."*

2. For those who claim Salvation, but yet do not believe in the *"Doctrine of Christ,"* with them we can have no fellowship.

3. We are not to receive false teachers into our Churches, nor pray God's blessings upon them. We can pray for their souls, as we certainly ought to do, and we can pray that they might see the light; however, we cannot bless their false doctrine.

FALSE TEACHERS

The phrase, *"If there come any unto you, and bring not this Doctrine,"* refers as stated, to the *"Doctrine of Christ."*

John is not speaking of those who have never heard or been instructed in the Doctrine of Christ; he means those who deliberately altered the Apostolic teaching.

The word *"transgresseth"* as given in Verse 9, means, *"to go beyond,"* and in this case, to go beyond the teaching respecting Christ. As today, so at that time, doctrines other than the *"Doctrine of Christ"* have many followers.

However, all who reject a Divine and atoning Saviour reject God. Only they who accept the teaching of the Holy Spirit respecting the Person and Work of the Lord Jesus Christ know God and possess Him. All who

reject His Godhead and Atonement have a god of their own imagination; and that god is an idol. Such cannot be accepted! Only the *"Doctrine of Christ"* can be accepted. Nothing must be taken from that Doctrine, or added to that Doctrine.

NO BLESSING

The phrase, *"Receive him not into your house, neither bid him God speed,"* presents the fact that false teachers must not be shown hospitality, as if they were Brothers in the Faith. Because they are deceivers, it would be a mockery of the Father and a sin against Christ to give those who deny the Son and in effect, are trying to destroy the Brethren, a place of respect within the community of faith. To do so would be to become a partaker in their unbelief and hatred of the truth.

This statement is all the more remarkable since it comes from the *"Apostle of love."* Moreover, the command to extend hospitality is at the same time deeply rooted in the tradition of Christianity (Rom. 12:13; I Tim. 3:2; 5:3-10; Titus 1:8; Heb. 13:2; I Pet. 4:8-10). In fact, it was an absolute demand that Brothers in Christ, and we speak of Preachers, be supported, fed, and housed by the local congregations they visited. Nevertheless, John invokes a higher principle here.

False prophets, antichrists, and deceivers are not to share in the provision of hospitality. Even the Christian greetings that might be given ever so casually are forbidden in the case of false teachers. One cannot serve God and mammon simultaneously (Mat. 6:24). One cannot be a partner of God and a partner of the Devil (I Cor. 10:20).

But let us say that John is not saying here that no acts of kindness, in any circumstances, were to be shown to such persons; but that there was to be nothing done which could be fairly construed as encouraging or countenancing them as true teachers and Preachers of the Gospel. The true rule would seem to be, in regard to such persons, that, so far as we have intercourse with them as neighbors, or strangers, we are to be honest, true, kind, and just, but we are to do nothing that will countenance them as Preachers and Teachers of the Word. We are not to attend on their instruction (Prov. 19:27); we are not to receive them into our houses, or to entertain them as true Teachers of the Word. We are not to commend them to others, or to give them any reason to use our names or influence in propagating their error.

A Christian who is truly consistent is never suspected of countenancing error, even when he is distinguished for liberality, and is ready, like the good Samaritan, to pour in oil and wine in the wounds of any waylaid traveler.

In no way is this admonition of John meant to imply that we as Believers should forego the Christian attributes of love, kindness, humility, and simply doing good to people. It simply means that we are not to do anything that might countenance the false doctrine of those who propagate such.

THE HOLY SPIRIT

John is speaking primarily to leaders in the Church, but of course, it also applies to every Believer.

If the Pastor countenances that which is wrong, more than likely, most of his people will follow suit. Wrong or right, most Christian follow those whom they consider to be their spiritual leaders. Unfortunately, many times they do so to their detriment. The truth is, the Word of God alone must be the criteria for what and who we accept. While Preachers should be loved and respected, their voice must not be the final decision. The final authority on all things must be the Word of God. Regrettably, far too many Christians little know the Word as it should be known, so they take the word of someone else as to what ought to be done about any and all matters.

"If there come" presents a Greek verb that is in the indicative mood intimating that such do actually come and are sure to come. True love shuts the door against such religious teachers, as teachers. Love should minister to them if in affliction or sickness, but it is not to help them in their propaganda of error.

As we have just mentioned, it is John the Beloved, at times called the *"Apostle of Love,"* who is saying these things. Many Christians not understanding love would think that the Apostle is being somewhat harsh; however, true love not only points out the good but as

well, points out the error. And in fact, if error is not pointed out, the one who refuses to do such doesn't have the Love of God, despite his or her claims.

It takes real love to say things which, even though the truth, you know are going to offend some people. It is much easier to say nothing, but to do so is a betrayal of all trust.

(11) "FOR HE THAT BIDDETH HIM GOD SPEED IS PARTAKER OF HIS EVIL DEEDS."

The diagram is:

1. No Believer is to become a sharer or partner in that which is false.

2. To do so, is to become a partaker of that which is extremely detrimental, and which the Holy Spirit refers to as *"evil."*

3. If the Believer is properly anchored in the Cross, he will not fall for false doctrine.

GOD SPEED

The phrase, *"For he who bids him God speed,"* presents a prohibition.

The issue here involves more than disagreements in interpretation or personal misunderstandings among members of the Body of Christ. It presents a radical and clearly defined unbelief, and it involves active and aggressive promotion of perversions of truth, which if believed, will strike at the very heart of true Christianity.

But ought not persons who have gone so far astray be dealt with all the more in love? Do they not require even more by way of Grace, Mercy, and Forgiveness of Christ?

At the personal level, Christians should always be prepared to turn the other cheek and seek tirelessly to be reconciled with others. But only those whose own faith is secure and whose understanding is beyond corruption can do this.

Unfortunately, the Church of which the elect lady was a part was not yet in this position. It was not mature enough to deal with such deadly deviations; in fact, it was more likely that it might be destroyed by them.

The responsibility of parents may furnish an analogy. Parents must discriminate as to whom even among their relatives they entertain in their home. Some relatives might be of such questionable character as to menace the moral, spiritual, and physical welfare of the children. If that is the case, such relatives must be excluded.

Parents must balance their concern for their relatives with their responsibility for their children.

Notice that John does not suggest that the elect lady and her children deal with the false teachers in hatred or retaliate against them. Instead, he counsels that the false teachers be kept at a distance lest their heresy seriously hinder or even possibly destroy the young Church.

We today can be grateful that men like John in the Early Church took heresy seriously regarding the Person of Christ. Christianity stands or falls with its Christology. From the human point of view, if John and other Apostolic leaders had tolerated the *"antichrists"* who denied the basic truth of the Incarnation, the Church would not have survived. We today are the beneficiaries of the spiritual discernment and moral courage of John and others like him. We should be thankful!

EVIL DEEDS

The phrase, *"Is partaker of his evil deeds,"* refers to the fact that we support what we are. That is so important that it must be said again:

Christians support what they are, whether right or wrong. That's the reason that the Word of Faith doctrine of money, which I refer to as the *"money gospel,"* is so palatable to many Christians. Covetousness responds to covetousness, or to be more blunt, greed responds to greed.

False doctrine cannot take hold in the heart and life of a Believer, unless there are base motives on which the false doctrine can be secured. In other words, it was impossible for false doctrine to find a safe haven in the heart and life of the Master. I think the same could be said for Paul, and no doubt many others. Their hearts are pure before God, and so there is no soil that welcomes that which is false or wrong.

Let the Reader understand, to support that which is evil, makes one a partaker of the evil. Let me be a little more blunt:

THE GOOD MIXED WITH THE BAD

Most false doctrine has in fact, some good doctrine within its confines. If there was no

NOTES

good doctrine, there would be no bait. However, good doctrine which speaks of truth, which is used to foster a lie, then becomes a lie itself. But unfortunately, it's the truth that is a part of a lie which serves well as bait.

A PROPHECY

The following is an excerpt from a Prophecy given at the Elim Bible Institute Summer Campmeeting in 1965 by the late Stanley Frodsham. I never had the privilege of meeting Brother Frodsham, but I did read several of his books, and held him in esteem as a man of God.

His life and ministry spanned the Pentecostal Revival. He also authored the well-known book, *"Smith Wigglesworth: Apostle of Faith."*

I think the Reader should study this Prophecy very carefully. I realize that there are many things presently which go under the heading of *"Prophecy,"* but which in reality, don't fit the Scriptural criteria. This of which we will print, does fit that criteria, and should be heeded by every Saint of God. I will place headings at various intervals to make it easier to read and hopefully to understand.

THE DARKNESS AHEAD

"When I visit My people in mighty revival power, it is to prepare them for the darkness ahead. With the glory shall come great darkness, for the glory is to prepare My people for the darkness. I will enable My people to go through because of the visitation of My Spirit.

"Take heed to yourselves lest you be puffed up and think that you have arrived. Many shall be puffed up as in the olden days, for many then received My Message but they continued not in it.

"Did I not anoint Jehu? Yet the things I desired were not accomplished in his life. Listen to the Messengers, but do not hold men's persons in admiration. For many whom I shall anoint mightily, with signs and miracles, shall be lifted up and shall fall away by the wayside. I do not do this willingly, I have made provision that they might stand. I call many into this Ministry and equip them; but remember that many shall fall.

"Keep your eyes upon the Lord.

"They shall be bright lights and people shall delight in them. But they shall be taken over by deceiving spirits and shall lead many of My people astray. Hearken diligently concerning these things, for in the last days will come seducing spirits that shall turn many of My anointed ones away.

"Many shall fall through various lusts because of sin abounding. But if you will seek Me diligently, I will put My Spirit within you. When one shall turn to the right hand or to the left you shall not turn with them, but keep your eyes wholly on the Lord."

THE COMING DAYS

"The coming days are most dangerous, difficult, and dark, but there shall be a mighty outpouring of My Spirit upon many cities. My people must be diligently warned concerning the days that are ahead. Many shall turn after seducing spirits; many are already seducing My people. It is those who do Righteousness that are Righteous.

"Many cover their sins by theological words. But I warn you of seducing spirits who instruct My people in an evil way. Many shall come with seducing spirits and hold out lustful enticements. You will find that after I have visited My people again, the way shall become more and more narrow, and fewer shall walk therein."

DECEPTION

"But be not deceived, the ways of Righteousness are My ways. For though Satan comes as an angel of light, hearken not to him; for those who perform miracles and speak not Righteousness are not of Me. I warn you with great intensity that I am going to judge my house and have a Church without spot or wrinkle when I come.

"I desire to open your eyes and give you spiritual understanding, that you may not be deceived but may walk in uprightness of heart before Me, loving Righteousness and hating every evil way."

EYES OF THE SPIRIT

"Look unto Me, and I will make you to perceive with eyes of the Spirit the things that lurk in darkness that are not visible to the human eye. Let me lead you in this way

NOTES

that you may perceive the powers of darkness and battle against them. It is not a battle against flesh and blood; for if you battle in that way, you accomplish nothing. But if you let Me take over and battle against the powers of darkness, then they are defeated, and then liberation is brought to My people.

"I warn you to search the Scriptures diligently concerning these last days. For the things that are written shall indeed be made manifest. There shall come deceivers among My people in increasing numbers who shall speak for the Truth and shall gain the favor of the people. For the people shall examine the Scriptures and say, what these man say is true. Then when they have gained the hearts of the people, then and only then shall Satan enter into My people."

SEDUCERS

"Watch for seducers. Do you think a seducer will brandish a new heresy and flaunt it before the people? He will speak the words of Righteousness and Truth, and will appear as a Minister of Light declaring the Word. The people's hearts shall be won. Then, when the hearts are won, they will bring out their doctrines, and the people shall be deceived.

"The people shall say, did he not speak thus and thus? And did we not examine it from the Word? Therefore, he is a minister of Righteousness.

"This that he has spoken we do not see in the Word, but it must be right, for the other things he spoke were true. Be not deceived. For the deceiver will first work to gain the hearts of many, and then shall bring forth his insidious doctrines. You cannot discern those who are of Me and those who are not of Me when they start to preach. But seek Me constantly, and then when these doctrines are brought out you shall have a witness in your heart that these are not of Me."

THE MIXTURE

"Fear not, for I have warned you. Many will be deceived. But if you walk in holiness and uprightness before the Lord, your eyes shall be opened and the Lord will protect you. If you will constantly look unto the Lord, you will know when the doctrine changes

and will not be brought into it. If your heart is right I will keep you; and you will constantly look to Me, I will uphold you.

"The Minister of Righteousness shall be on this wise: his life shall agree with the Word and his lips shall give forth that which is wholly true, and it will be no mixture. When the mixture appears, then you will know he is not a Minister of Righteousness. The deceivers speak first the Truth then error, to cover their own sins which they love.

"Therefore, I exhort and command you to study the Scriptures relative to seducing spirits, for this is one of the great dangers of these last days."

MY WORD

"I desire you to firmly be established in My Word and not in the personalities of men that you will not be moved as so many shall be moved. Take heed to yourselves and follow not the seducing spirits that are already manifesting themselves. Diligently inquire of Me when you hear something that you have not seen in My Word, and do not hold people's persons in admiration — for it is by this very method Satan will destroy many of My people."

(12) "HAVING MANY THINGS TO WRITE UNTO YOU, I WOULD NOT WRITE WITH PAPER AND INK: BUT I TRUST TO COME UNTO YOU, AND SPEAK FACE TO FACE, THAT OUR JOY MAY BE FULL."

The structure is:

1. All has not been said, but all has been said that the Holy Spirit wanted him to say here.

2. The Apostle was hoping to visit this Church shortly.

3. He desired not only to impart information, but as well to receive information, but above all to be able to personally greet this fellow laborer in the Lord.

MANY THINGS TO WRITE

The phrase, *"Having many things to write unto you, I would not write with paper and ink,"* presents a tremendous understatement.

John was used by the Lord to write one Gospel, three Epistles, and the great Book of Revelation. Only Paul and Luke penned more of the New Testament. After writing these

Second and Third Epistles which bear his name, which some Scholars believe that he wrote on the same day, about five or six years later he wrote the great Book of Revelation. It is believed he was in Ephesus when he wrote these Epistles, although that is not for certain. He was on the Isle of Patmos when he wrote Revelation, actually incarcerated there as a prisoner of the Roman Empire. The evidence is, I think, that he was released from Patmos and went back to Ephesus, where he died soon thereafter.

In his Gospel he wrote what the Holy Spirit wanted him to write about Christ. But it is certain that he could have written much more. In the closing years of his life, I suspect that his thoughts were upon those days spent with Christ and on those days exclusively. They were all gone now, the remainder of the Twelve. The great Paul had also long since gone. There was no one left but John. But yet millions would follow in this train, making Christ their eternal Saviour. And as the new Millennium of 2000 rolled around, there are more people on the face of the Earth who claim Christ, than any religion.

The things that John has said in this short Epistle concerning false doctrine have been said in general terms; however, when it came to personal cases, it seems that he desired more information, which could only be obtained by being there in person, which he hoped to do shortly.

The Apostle had received reports concerning false apostles and their false doctrine. Of that he warns, but feels it is unwise to go further regarding personalities, until he has more first-hand information.

PAPER

Paper, as that term is now understood, was not invented until long after this period. The material designated by the word used by John was the Egyptian papyrus, and the particular thing denoted was a leaf made out of that plant.

The sheets were made from membranes of the plant closely pressed together. This plant was found also in Syria and Babylon, but it was produced in greater abundance in Egypt, and that was the plant which was commonly used.

It was so comparatively cheap that it, in a great measure, superseded the earlier materials for writings — plates of lead, stone, or the skins of animals. It is probable that the Books of the New Testament were written on this species of paper.

The ink, which was commonly employed in writing in those days was made of soot and water, with a mixture of some species of gum to give it consistency and durability.

JOY

The phrase, *"But I trust to come unto you, and speak face to face, that our joy may be full,"* concerns information that the Apostle wished to receive about several things. His statement concerning *"joy"* is more so a benediction than anything else.

But yet, it seems that the conduct of some in the Church brought about by false teaching, had lessened the joy that normally was present in the Christian experience.

Living for Christ is the greatest life there is. There is absolutely nothing that can remotely compare with that which Christ Jesus does for the individual. *"Joy"* is an apt description of this great Salvation brought about by what Christ did at the Cross, and our Faith in that Finished Work. In fact, Jesus said concerning this great Salvation, *"I am come that they might have life, and that they might have it more abundantly"* (Jn. 10:10).

Every single true Believer in the world has *"more abundant life."* But the sad fact is, due to not understanding the Sanctification process, most Christians although having this life, are in fact, not enjoying it.

On a personal basis, I know what it is to not enjoy this Christian experience as one should, and to be sure, that's an understatement. But praise God, due to the Grace of God, I also know what it is to have *and* enjoy this *"more abundant life"* to the full. It has come through the knowledge of the Cross, what Jesus there did for me, and all who will accept His great Sacrifice.

The Evil One seeks to come in and push the Christian away from the Message of the Cross. In fact, and as we've already stated in this Volume, his greatest efforts are in this capacity.

FAITH

Many years ago, I heard the great Pentecostal Preacher A. N. Trotter make the following statement:

He said, *"Every attack by Satan, and irrespective as to whether the attack is in the realm of the spiritual, domestical, physical, or financial, is for but one purpose, and that is to destroy, or else to seriously weaken our Faith."*

When he said that, I immediately knew that it was right, even as the Holy Spirit did bear witness in my heart; however, not until I began to understand the Cross, did I really understand his statement.

The faith of which he spoke, concerns our Faith in the Cross of Christ. If Satan can weaken our faith there, he has succeeded in his task. And when we speak of him attacking our faith, for the most part he doesn't try to cause us to lose faith completely, but rather to shift our faith from the Cross to other things. He is most successful with new converts regarding this, simply because there is so little teaching and preaching presently as it regards the Cross.

The moment the believing sinner comes to Christ, they should then be taught extensively Romans, Chapter 6 and Romans, Chapter 8. Only in this manner can they understand the Sanctification process, or to say it in more simple terms, how they should live for the Lord. Getting saved is one thing, but knowing how to simply live for the Lord is something else altogether. It's a shame, but most modern Christians, not understanding the Cross, simply don't know how to live for Him. Most attempt to accomplish this task by their own means and machinations, which always fall out to hurt. It's very confusing, simply because most of the things that Christians do to bring about this end result, and I'm speaking of a victorious life, are good things. When the failure ensues, as it always will, Christians simply increase the good things they are doing because that's all they know to do, but this only tends to make a bad matter worse.

DOING AND BELIEVING

Everything we as Believers have in Christ is brought about and maintained through *"believing."* In other words, we are to believe something, and that something is Christ and what He did at the Cross on our behalf. Our *"believing"* which in effect, is the action part of our faith, must always be centered in Christ and His great Sacrifice. This shows that we understand that He has done for us what we cannot do for ourselves. When this is done and continues to be done, the Holy Spirit, Who works exclusively within the parameters of the Finished Work of Christ, will work mightily on our behalf, developing His Fruit within our hearts and lives.

And as a Christian, we must understand that it is literally impossible for us to properly believe, unless we understand the Sixth Chapter of Romans. It is absolutely essential that the Believer understand what Paul is saying there, even as Christ through the Holy Spirit gave to him. If not, we will remain in the Seventh Chapter of Romans, which was Paul's experience after he was saved and baptized with the Holy Spirit, but before he understood the Message of the Cross. To be sure, that's a place and position that no Christian wants to be, but yet regrettably, where most Christians presently are, simply because they do not understand God's prescribed order of victory.

When most Christians think of *"believing,"* they automatically think of believing in Christ, which is certainly correct. But the problem is, most don't really understand what believing in Christ actually is. Their faith in this respect, is a somewhat nebulous faith, simply because it does not have an end result.

The Believer must understand that believing in Christ, actually means to believe in Him regarding what He did at the Cross on our behalf. We must never separate Christ from the Cross, or the Cross from Christ. That's the reason that Paul said, *"I determined not to know anything among you, save Jesus Christ and Him Crucified"* (I Cor. 2:2). That's the reason he also said, *"For Christ sent me not to baptize, but to preach the Gospel: not with wisdom of words, lest the Cross of Christ should be made of none effect"* (I Cor. 1:17).

The Sacrifice of Christ is the apex of Christianity. Take that away, and you have nothing left but an ethic.

Every religion in the world is based upon the ideas of its founder. Christianity is based exclusively upon the Sacrifice of Christ. And if we pull Christ away from His Sacrifice, we have compromised the Gospel, in fact we have so diluted the Gospel, until it has lost all of its power (I Cor. 1:18). Paul also said:

"For the preaching of the Cross is to them that perish foolishness; but unto us which are saved it is the Power of God" (I Cor. 1:18).

When it comes to the Cross, most Christians understand this great Sacrifice as it regards their initial Salvation experience; however, that's about as far as most go. Most don't have the slightest clue as to what part the Cross plays in their Sanctification experience, or I can say, their everyday living for God. Most don't realize that without a proper understanding of the Cross in this respect, that they simply cannot live a victorious life. They can be saved, but they cannot be victorious!

In truth, they might be victorious over some things, but they will not be over all things. And as well, they may be victorious part of the time, but they will not be victorious all of the time. Again Paul said:

THE LAW OF THE SPIRIT OF LIFE IN CHRIST JESUS

"For the Law of the Spirit of Life in Christ Jesus has made me free from the law of sin and death" (Rom. 8:2).

We are plainly told here that there is only one way for the Believer to have victory over *"the law of sin and death,"* and that is by and through *"the Law of the Spirit of the Life in Christ Jesus."* In other words, the *"Law of the Spirit"* alone is greater than the *"law of sin and death."* However, we must understand how this *"Law of the Spirit"* actually works.

If the Reader is to notice, this *"Law of the Spirit of Life"* is *"in Christ Jesus."* What did Paul mean by that?

Every time Paul uses the term *"in Christ Jesus,"* or *"in Christ,"* or *"in Him,"* or one of its derivatives, which he does nearly 170 times in his 14 Epistles, always and without exception, he is speaking of what Christ did at the Cross. Let the Reader understand that carefully. *"In Christ Jesus"* doesn't merely speak of Christ as the Messiah, or even God manifest in the flesh. While Christ is definitely all of these things, and much more, and while all of these things are very, very important; still, without exception, the Holy Spirit through the Apostle is speaking of the great Sacrifice of Christ, in other words, what Jesus did for us at the Cross.

The Holy Spirit works exclusively within the parameters of this great, Finished Work. That's why the Bible says that this *"Law"* by which the Spirit works is *"in Christ Jesus."* It means that the Holy Spirit, due to the Cross, has the legal right to come into the heart and life of the Believer and to abide there forever, and to guarantee all victory to that Believer, providing their Faith is properly placed.

To have these great things which the Holy Spirit Alone can do, simply requires *"believing"* on our part, and I speak of believing in what Christ did at the Cross on our behalf.

Most Christians not understanding this, set about to live for God, not by *"believing,"* but rather by *"doing."*

WORKS

Every single Christian in the world, is either functioning in grace or law. If they are functioning by the Spirit, they are functioning in grace. If they are functioning by the flesh, they are functioning in law, which is proven by their trust in works. It is ironic, most Christians would look at you strange if you suggested that they were living under *"law,"* and I speak of laws they've made up themselves, or that someone else has made up, but in fact, that's actually what most are doing. The truth is, if the Believer doesn't understand the Cross, as I have attempted to explain it in this Volume, and I have attempted to explain it exactly as Paul explained it, then without fail that Christian is functioning in law. Why do you think the Apostle said the following:

"For sin shall not have dominion over you: for you are not under the law, but under grace" (Rom. 6:14)?

If it wasn't possible for the Christian to function in law, then the Apostle would not have mentioned it here. The truth is, as stated, regrettably, this is where most Christians presently are — under law.

NOTES

Any time we are trying to live this life by *"doing,"* that means we're functioning in law. *"Flesh,"* which speaks of one's own efforts, which constitutes *"works,"* and which translates into *"law,"* presents itself, as the greatest problem facing the Christian. In fact, the entirety of the Epistle to the Galatians was written to counteract this problem. What exactly do we mean by law?

LAW

First of all, we are not speaking of the Law of Moses, although in a roundabout way, we actually are. However, to make it easier to understand, we will approach it in a little different way.

Law is anything we try to *"do"* in order to live for the Lord. As I've already stated in this Volume, most Christians think that being a good Christian, translates into being faithful to Church, paying one's tithes, reading the Bible daily, having some sort of prayer life, and witnessing to souls about Christ. Now please don't misunderstand, every good Christian will definitely and without fail, do these things. But what the Christian must realize is, we aren't good Christians because we do these things.

Now that comes as a shock to most Believers, and most will find that hard to accept. And the reason we find it hard to accept is because there is something in all of us that wants to think that we have merited something from the Lord by our diligence, etc.

Now let me say it again so there will be no misunderstanding: to be sure, all of these things I've mentioned are very, very important, and to be sure, every good Christian will definitely do these things. So if you think that we are speaking disparagingly of being faithful to Church, etc., then you're misunderstanding what we're saying. What we are saying is this:

It is not really the doing of these things that is wrong. It's our having faith in our doing these things instead of Faith in the Cross of Christ which is wrong. Now think about what I've just said:

Are we saying that paying tithes is wrong? Definitely not! But we are saying that the placing of our faith in the doing of that, thinking it earns us something with the Lord, or will bring about some spiritual work within our lives, is definitely wrong. And if we do not understand the Cross, that's exactly what we're going to do. Our faith will be placed in the doing of these things, which in effect is *"law."* In other words, we have made these things a law, which in effect are not actually a law within themselves. And then we judge our spiritual temperature as to how well we do all of these things that we have mentioned, etc. We Christians shout *"faith"* a lot, but practice law. And that's the tragedy!

ROMANS, CHAPTER 7

What did Paul mean by the statement: *"For I was alive without the law once: but when the Commandment came, sin revived, and I died"* (Rom. 7:9)?

When he spoke of being *"alive without the law once,"* he was speaking of the time when he was initially saved. This is recorded in Acts, Chapter 9. The *"Life"* which he found in Christ had nothing to do with the Law, and in his case, he was speaking of the Law of Moses. He was not saved because he believed the Law, or was trying to keep the Law, with in fact, the Law having absolutely nothing to do with his conversion, as it's had nothing to do with anyone's conversion.

Then he said, *"But when the Commandment came, sin revived, and I died."* What did he mean by that?

After he had come to Christ, and as well had been Baptized with the Holy Spirit, he of course, set out to live for God, just as any Believer will do. At that time, not knowing or understanding the Message of the Cross, he set about to keep the Ten Commandments. He found he was unable to do so, thereby failing, which is what he means by the statement *"sin revived."* Actually, in the Greek it actually says *"the sin revived,"* meaning that the sin nature which had become dormant in his life as a result of him having come to Christ, now springs to life, and actually begins to rule in his life. Let's explain that.

Every unsaved person is ruled by the *"sin nature."* When a person comes to Christ, while the sin nature definitely remains, it now has no more effect in the life of the Christian, that is, if the Christian has his faith properly placed in the Cross. If he tries to

live for the Lord as Paul did here, he will find the sin nature reviving, and actually controlling him even as it did before conversion.

If the Christian attempts to live for the Lord by his own strength, which means he's not doing so by faith and trust in the Cross of Christ, irrespective as to how hard that Christian tries, he is going to fail. When he fails, as most certainly he will, sin, which is the fuel of the sin nature, causes that nature to spring to life once again.

The Christian then repents of the wrongdoing, which he most certainly should do (I Jn. 1:9), and then sets about to try to stop this failure from ever taking place again. Not knowing or understanding the Cross, he resolves in his mind to take every precaution. He must not fail, because he is now a Christian. But then he finds that he does fail again, and again, and again, which means, even as Paul said, that the *"sin nature"* is now ruling and reigning in the Believer's life. And it doesn't seem that he is able to stop it.

By now he is very confused; however, he will not say anything to anyone about the problem, resolving to *"try harder."* In fact, if he does say something to someone about the problem, that's probably what he will be told: *"You must try harder!"*

The sadness is, the very one giving him such advice, is being controlled by the *"sin nature"* just as much as he is. If that were not the case, they would not be giving him such instructions. They would be telling him about the Cross.

When it comes to Paul, many Christians find it very difficult to understand or even believe, that the great Apostle lived a life of spiritual failure, at least up unto the time that the Lord gave him the Message of the Cross, which showed him how to live victoriously. In fact, the Holy Spirit allowed the great Apostle to include the Seventh Chapter of Romans in this Epistle, which is his own experience, that we might learn from him. The idea is, if you don't learn what the Apostle said in Chapter 6, you're going to repeat Chapter 7 all over again.

When the Apostle said in that Ninth Verse of Romans, Chapter 7, *"And I died,"* he wasn't meaning that he physically died, but rather that he failed the Lord. If you will notice he uses such terminology throughout the

Chapter as it regards sin and failure. He says in Romans 7:10, *"I found to be unto death,"* and then in Verse 11, *"And by it slew me,"* etc.

When the Apostle said, *"But when the Commandment came,"* he was speaking of trying to live right, in effect, trying to keep the Ten Commandments. Most Christians would ask the question concerning this, *"But isn't this what we're supposed to do?"*

Most definitely we are! However, we cannot do it by *"doing it,"* but we rather have to do it by *"believing it."* What do I mean by that?

The Lord Jesus Christ has already kept every rudiment of the Law. In other words, he kept the Ten Commandments perfectly, never failing even one time, plus every other rudiment of the Law. He did this simply because we couldn't do it for ourselves. And let the Christian understand that even though you are now a Christian, you still cannot keep the Ten Commandments by your own ability and strength.

The truth is, the Ten Commandments have already been kept in Christ. He did so as our Substitute and Representative Man, i.e., *"The Second Man"* (I Cor. 15:45-50).

As Believers, we are to simply place our Faith and trust exclusively in Christ and what He did for us at the Cross, which will then give the Holy Spirit the latitude to help us, and we will find ourselves automatically keeping the Law, and doing so without even thinking about it. Godliness, Righteousness, Holiness, and Christlikeness will simply become a part of our lives when our Faith is properly in Christ (Rom. 6:3-5, 11, 14).

But if we set about to live for the Lord in any other way than by the Cross, we will find ourselves failing, with the sin nature then reviving, which makes for a miserable Christian. Such a Christian will find himself exactly as Paul had been before his understanding of the Cross: *"For that which I do I understand not: for what I would, that do I not; but what I hate, that do I"* (Rom. 7:15).

That always translates into: *"O wretched man that I am! Who shall deliver me from the body of this death?"* (Rom. 7:24).

THE HOLY SPIRIT

When the Believer properly understands the Cross as is taught in Romans, Chapter 6,

NOTES

and properly places his Faith therein, and does so on a continuing basis, the Holy Spirit will then do great and mighty things in that Believer's life. Paul said:

"But if the Spirit (Holy Spirit) *of Him* (God the Father) *that raised up Jesus from the dead dwell in you, He Who raised up Christ from the dead shall also quicken your mortal bodies by His Spirit Who dwells in you"* (Rom. 8:11).

He is telling us here that the same Holy Spirit Who raised Jesus from the dead, also lives in us, and will give us His help, exactly as Jesus said He would (Jn. 14:16-18). The Holy Spirit is God, which means there is nothing He cannot do.

In fact, every single thing done in our lives as it regards the Lord, is always done and without exception, by and through the Person, Office, Work, and Ministry of the Holy Spirit.

The way He works is by and through what Jesus did at the Cross, even as Romans 8:2 tells us. Consequently, our Faith is to ever be registered in that Finished Work as Paul also told us in Romans 6:3-5.

Things that are impossible for human beings, present no problem for the Holy Spirit at all. But let the Reader understand that even though the Holy Spirit has taken up abode in the heart and life of every true Believer, His work is definitely not automatic within our lives. He demands cooperation from us, and that cooperation centers up in faith, and more particularly, Faith in the Finished Work of Christ.

Living for the Lord is very, very simple. If it wasn't, most of us wouldn't make it. It is simply trusting in Christ and what He did for us at the Cross. But sadly and regrettably, we tend to make it so difficult and so complicated. We complicate it by functioning in *"works"* and *"law,"* when all the time, it is actually so very easy and simple.

Jesus clearly and plainly said: *"Come unto Me, all you who labor and are heavy laden, and I will give you rest.*

"Take My yoke upon you, and learn of Me; for I am meek and lowly in heart: and you shall find rest unto your souls.

"For My yoke is easy, and My burden is light" (Mat. 11:28-30).

John the Beloved said: *"For this is the Love of God, that we keep His Commandments: and His Commandments are not grievous"* (I Jn. 5:3).

Concerning the Scribes and Pharisees who functioned by *"Law,"* Jesus said of them: *"For they bind heavy burdens and grievous to be borne, and lay them on men's shoulders"* (Mat. 23:4). He was speaking as stated, of the Law. Unfortunately, many Churches follow suit. To be sure, the more law we have, the more grievous it will be. The more Grace we have, the more wonderful it will be!

(13) "THE CHILDREN OF THY ELECT SISTER GREET THEE. AMEN."

The diagram is:

1. John was speaking of the flesh and blood sister of the *"elect lady"* to whom he was writing.

2. She was a Believer, hence John using the word *"elect."*

3. He evidently knew the children of *"the elect lady's"* sister.

John closes this rather informal yet Divinely-inspired Letter by relaying greetings from the children of the sister of this Elect Lady. He may have been staying at this second matron's house; at any rate, the family knew he was writing.

The simplicity of the great Apostle, the personal friend of the Risen Lord, the last of the great pillars of the Church — in transmitting this familiar message, makes a most instructive finish to what is throughout a beautiful picture (Ellicott).

It would seem probable, from the fact that she is not mentioned as sending her salutations, that she was either dead, or that she was absent. John mentions her, however, as a Christian — as one of the elect or chosen of God.

"Oh God, our help in ages past,
"Our hope for years to come,
"Our shelter from the stormy blast,
"And our eternal home!"

"Under the shadow of Thy Throne,
"Still may we dwell secure;
"Sufficient is Thine arm alone,
"And our defense is sure."

"Before the hills in order stood,
"Or Earth received her frame,

"From everlasting Thou art God,
"To endless years the same."

"A thousand ages, in Thy sight,
"Are like an evening gone;
"Short as the watch that ends the night,
"Before the rising sun."

"Oh God, our help in ages past,
"Our hope for years to come;
"Be Thou our God while life shall last,
"And our eternal home!"

THE
BOOK OF III JOHN

—■—

(1) "THE ELDER UNTO THE WELL-BE-LOVED GAIUS, WHOM I LOVE IN THE TRUTH."

The exegesis is:

1. John in this Third Epistle as well, refers to himself as *"The Elder."*

2. Four times in this very short Epistle, the Apostle refers to Gaius as *"beloved"* (vss. 1, 2, 5, and 11).

3. It is the Gospel of Jesus Christ which has generated this love, and because it is *"the Truth."*

GAIUS

The phrase, *"The Elder unto the well-beloved Gaius,"* could well be the same one mentioned in Acts 19:29; 20:4; Romans 16:23; and, I Corinthians 1:14.

As the previous Letter was written to a wealthy woman telling her to shut her door against Preachers of a false gospel, so this letter was written to a wealthy man telling him to open his door to Preachers of the True Gospel.

Three men are named in this Epistle: Gaius, Diotrephes, and Demetrius. Gaius was evidently a man of substance and one of a small circle of friends who were true to the Scriptures, faithful to the Apostle John, and it seems, not looked at too kindly by the local Church. Diotrephes was the ruler of that Church, probably by self-appointment or popular election. It seems that he had bought into the false doctrine of Gnosticism. He and some, if not many, in that particular Church, had rejected the authority of John (vs. 9), were refusing to receive Preachers whom John recommended; and excommunicated those who did receive them (vs. 19).

Demetrius was an Evangelist, commended by the Apostle and many others, and accredited as a Preacher of the truth by the spiritual results of his ministry.

This short Letter shows to what degree that false doctrine and evil conduct had come at that early age; as well, it is a vivid picture of the present condition of the modern Church. Corruption in doctrine, rejection of Apostolic teaching, ecclesiastical assumption on one side, and a little group of those faithful to the Word of God on the other. This latter group is unrecognized by the Church, and actively opposed by its leaders.

BELOVED

The word *"beloved"* in the Greek is *"agapetos,"* and means *"Divine Love, or the Love which comes from God Alone."* Of this type of love, the world has no knowledge, cannot know what it means, and cannot possess it in any fashion. One has to be Born-Again before one can have this God kind of love, which in fact, automatically comes into the heart and life of every Believer at conversion. It is a part of the Divine nature. But yet it has to be cultivated as a *"Fruit of the Spirit,"* and in fact, is the very first *"Fruit"* listed in the order of that cluster (Gal. 5:22-23).

The Holy Spirit is the only One Who can cultivate love in our hearts and lives, and He does it on one premise and one premise alone. In fact, every single thing we receive from God, and irrespective as to what it is, comes by and through the Person and Office of the Holy Spirit.

From the emphasis that the Holy Spirit through John places on love in these three

231

Epistles, we learn that *"Love"* is the bedrock of the Faith, so to speak.

Paul said: *"And now abideth Faith, Hope, Charity* (Love), *these three; but the greatest of these is love"* (I Cor. 13:13). The idea is this:

While *"Faith"* is the premier ingredient through which the Holy Spirit works as should be obvious, the idea is, irrespective of the claims, if we truly have Faith as we ought to, it will be evidenced by *"love."* If not, our boasts are valueless.

As we will see in the last phrase of this First Verse, the true Love of God will be faithful to the truth, and will be faithful to express the truth, even as John does here, even though at times it has to be stated in a strong and possibly even harsh manner. All of Christendom talks about love, but it is only the one, as John, who will truly relate the truth, who truly has love.

THE CROSS

I think I can say without any fear of Scriptural contradiction, that it is impossible for the Believer to properly have any of these attributes of God, and we continue to speak of love as well as all things that come from the Lord, unless the Believer properly understands the Message of the Cross. Everything that we receive from the Lord comes exclusively through the means of the Cross. Everything that we think of as it pertains to God, He has always possessed. He didn't suddenly come into possession of these things on the Day of Pentecost, etc. God doesn't change, but what has changed is the following:

The Old Testament proclaims the fact that God was very limited in what He could do with or for His people, as a result of the blood of bulls and goats not being able to take away sin (Heb. 9:12; 10:4). Until Christ, the sin barrier remained between man and God. That was the reason for the Veil that hung between the Holy Place and the Holy of Holies. That Veil had Cherubim embroidered on it, which in essence said to unholy man, *"holy, holy, holy,"* which in effect said *"keep out, lest you die!"*

But when Jesus died on the Cross, and at the moment He died, the Scripture plainly tells us: *"The Veil of the Temple was rent in twain from the top to the bottom"* (Mat. 27:51).

In effect, this was saying to the whole of mankind that the price had now been paid, all sin had now been atoned for, past, present, and future, and the way to God was now clearly and plainly open; consequently: *"The Spirit and the Bride say, Come. And let him that heareth say, Come. And let him that is athirst Come. And whosoever will, let him take the water of life freely"* (Rev. 22:17).

Oh dear Reader, can you not sense the Presence of God even as you read these words. Can you not understand the price that was paid, that makes it possible for us to come into the very Presence of God. No wonder the songwriter said:

"I will praise Him, I will praise Him,
"Praise the Lamb for sinners slain.
"Give Him glory all ye people,
"For His Blood has washed away each
    stain."

As a result, every Believer must anchor his Faith 100 percent in the Cross of Christ. In other words, the Cross must ever be the object of our Faith, and not something else. That's why Paul said:

"For I determined not to know anything among you, save Jesus Christ, and Him Crucified" (I Cor. 2:2).

When Paul went to Corinth to plant the Church in that great city, he was faced with a double problem. The people of this city considered themselves to be intellectuals, having produced some of the greatest philosophers of that time. As well, Corinth was probably the most jaded city of the Roman Empire regarding vice. So we have here a double-barreled problem. How in the world could these people be reached?

The Holy Spirit told the Apostle, to *"preach the Cross,"* which the Apostle did in no uncertain terms. He did it even though to the Jews the Cross was *"a stumblingblock and unto the Greeks foolishness"* (I Cor. 1:23). In other words, he was preaching what the Holy Spirit told him to preach, irrespective as to the thinking of the inhabitants of that city, a rare trait in today's climate I might quickly add.

NOTES

Despite the Cross being the foundation of the Message preached by the Apostle Paul, which means that the understanding of the Cross is in effect, the understanding of the New Covenant, most modern Christians have little understanding of the Cross or what it means. Unfortunately, most every Christian automatically thinks that he or she does know and understand what the Cross means. But the truth is, about all the modern Church understands as it regards the Cross, is *"Jesus died for me."* While in fact that is the greatest statement ever uttered by man, still, it is only the surface of that taught by Paul.

To properly understand the Cross, one has to understand the Sixth Chapter of Romans. And the truth is, most Christians don't have the foggiest idea as to what that Chapter actually means. Not understanding that Chapter, they are bound to repeat Romans, Chapter 7, where in fact, most of the modern Church actually resides. It is sad but true!

That's at least one of the reasons, I think, that the Holy Spirit has instructed me to write these Commentaries. It is the Message of the Cross! It must be preached and it must be taught. Even though I am repetitive, and at times even overly repetitive, it is all for a purpose and reason. How many times have I had someone to say to me, *"Now I see it!"*, which means that despite the fact of reading and hearing this particular Message over and over, and with some a period of several years, that they had not in all of this time seen this Truth.

Going a step farther, I think I can also say that every single Christian has to hear this Message over and over, before it becomes open and clear to them. Our thinking has been so warped and twisted by false doctrine and false directions that it takes a complete *"renewing of the mind"* before one can properly understand what the Spirit is saying here (Rom. 12:1-2). Listen to what Jesus said to Peter:

"Simon, Simon, behold, Satan has desired to have you, that he may sift you as wheat:

"But I have prayed for you, that your faith fail not: and when you are converted, strengthen the Brethren" (Lk. 22:31-32).

"Converted" in the Greek is *"epistrepho,"* and means *"to revert, turn about, to reverse self."* As used here, it has nothing to do with

being initially saved. In fact, Peter was already saved. It meant that he must get his thinking and, therefore, his faith straightened out. And what does that mean?

Peter was trusting in *"self,"* and when his faith was straightened out as it should be, he would then trust in the Cross. That's why the big fisherman said:

"Forasmuch as you know that you were not redeemed with corruptible things, as silver and gold, from your vain manner of life received by tradition from your father;

"But with the Precious Blood of Christ, as of a lamb without blemish and without spot" (I Pet. 1:18-19).

If the Reader thinks that I dedicate too much of this Volume to instruction on the Cross, then the Reader still doesn't properly understand the Cross. If one properly understands the Finished Work of Christ, it will never grow weary of the telling.

THE TRUTH

The phrase, *"Whom I love in the truth,"* refers to the Word of God, and a proper interpretation of that Word. As stated, truth properly understood, will properly generate love in the heart and life of the Believer.

Jesus said: *"Everyone who is of the Truth hears My voice.*

"Pilate said unto Him, what is Truth?" (Jn. 18:37-38).

The Roman Governor literally dripped with sarcasm and cynicism as he asked the question, *"What is truth?"*

As we've said elsewhere in this Volume, *"Jesus Christ is Truth, the Holy Spirit is Truth, and the Word of God is Truth"* (Jn. 14:6; 17:17; I Jn. 5:6). This means that Truth is actually not a philosophy and because philosophy is actually a search for truth. It is a Person, and that Person is the Lord Jesus Christ. To know Christ is to know reality. So, to help us understand it a little better, one could say that *"truth is reality, but is reality as God has revealed it."* The truth is reality as Believers are able to experience it by making choices guided by God's reliable Word. Paul wrote the truth (II Cor. 12:6) and so described reality, but, beyond that, it is vital that his Readers respond to and obey the Truth (Gal. 5:7).

Over half of the Greek words pertaining to *"truth,"* appear in John's writings. At times the uses are commonplace, as in contrasting truths and falsehoods (Jn. 4:18). But while different shades of emphasis can be distinguished, it is helpful when reading of truth to keep in mind that concept's relationship to reality. What is said in God's Word is reliable, for God's Word is Truth, ever in harmony with reality (Jn. 17:17).

But even more than that, we can be sanctified by the Word; for it strips away our illusions, then takes us by the hand to guide our steps. Jesus is *"the Truth"* (Jn. 14:6), for all of reality finds its focus in Him. He, Who created and sustains the universe, is also man's Redeemer and the goal toward which all history strains (Col. 1:15-23).

We can *"know the Truth"* and thus be set free only by keeping Jesus' words (Jn. 8:31-32). Only by accepting what He has done for us at the Cross, and then following His teachings, which unveil reality, can we experience reality and so find the freedom in Christ to be who God knows us to be.

This view of *"truth"* is important in grasping the teaching of I John, Chapter 1 on fellowship with God. We have fellowship when we *"live by the truth"* (I Jn. 1:6). This is clearly not sinless perfection, for the context immediately speaks of Christ's Blood purifying us *"from all sin"* (I Jn. 1:7). The focus on the Passage, then, is squarely on reality, and Verse 8 deals with the claim of some *"to be without sin."* Such a claim is self-deceit, and if we hold such a view, *"the truth is not in us."* The reality is that even though we are redeemed beings, sin at times does find expression in our lives.

In fact, within ourselves, we are unable to deal with sin, but God is able through His Son the Lord Jesus Christ, and what He did for us at the Cross, to forgive us and cleanse us from all unrighteousness (I Jn. 1:9).

Once again we go to the Cross. The Word of God is Truth, and the story of the Word is the story of the Cross, i.e., *"God's redemption of mankind by the giving of His Son, and by Christ giving Himself on the Cross."* Proper Faith in the Cross brings the Truth of God's Word into proper focus, and helps us to understand the Bible correctly (I Cor. 1:17-31; 2:2, 5).

(2) "BELOVED, I WISH ABOVE ALL THINGS THAT THOU MAYEST PROSPER AND BE IN HEALTH, EVEN AS THY SOUL PROSPERETH."

The structure is:

1. God's Will for all Saints is that they may prosper financially, be in health, and above all, prosper spiritually.

2. Jesus paid for all of this at the Cross.

3. The one requirement is Faith on the part of the Believer, and more particularly, Faith in the Cross.

MATERIAL PROSPERITY

The phrase, *"Beloved, I wish above all things that thou mayest prosper,"* refers here to financial prosperity.

It is said that such a salutation during the time of John was common among all people, even unbelievers; however, while that no doubt was the case, it is only that which is said in the Name of the Lord, which can in fact, come to pass.

It is unfortunate that at the present time, undue emphasis has been placed on material gain as it regards Faith in the Lord. While such definitely was included regarding the Atonement, as should be obvious, it should never be the emphasis, that being our spiritual enrichment. In fact, Jesus plainly said: *"But seek ye first the Kingdom of God and His Righteousness; and all these things shall be added unto you"* (Mat. 6:33).

I think it is obvious throughout God's Word that the Lord is One Who blesses, and we speak of material gain; however, whenever the Church, or any part of the Church, makes this primary, even as many in the Word of Faith doctrine are presently doing, this particular wrong emphasis plays out to the very opposite. In other words, it shuts down everything, material prosperity and spiritual prosperity also!

If we deviate from God's Word in any capacity, the Holy Spirit simply will not honor our faith. The Church somehow has a problem in understanding and grasping that, but it happens to be true. The Lord cannot bless error, cannot reward such faith, and must of necessity penalize such efforts. And to be sure, the modern *"money gospel,"* which is based entirely upon greed, is definitely not Scriptural. Let me emphasize again:

The Lord definitely does bless His people. He blesses materially and financially and does so abundantly; however, when we place the emphasis on those particular things, we have become unscriptural and when we become unscriptural, the Holy Spirit shuts the door, so to speak. We must do our very best to follow the Word to the *"T."*

The modern money gospel is very much akin to gambling casinos. The gambler at the casino keeps thinking that he's going to win. Of course he never does, but the lure of greed keeps pulling him back. It is the same with the money gospel. The only one who gets rich is the Preacher. But the people keep going back, and because they are told repeatedly that riches are theirs, if in fact they are just a few steps beyond reach. It is in this particular *"gospel"* which in reality is *"another gospel"* (II Cor. 11:4), that I personally heard Fred Price say that the Blessing of Abraham had absolutely nothing to do with spiritual things, but altogether pertained to money.

It's the only time in my life, I ever found myself standing before a television set screaming at it, and because such error is so blatant and I might quickly add, so destructive!

The *"Blessing of Abraham"* is *"Justification by faith"* (Gal. 3:6-8, 14-18).

Once again let us state, that the Lord definitely blesses His people financially and materially. But those things are to never be the emphasis, but rather the Cross of Christ (I Cor. 1:17).

PHYSICAL HEALTH

The phrase, *"And be in health,"* speaks of physical prosperity, even as the first phrase spoke of financial prosperity. Jesus Christ is the Healer (Ex. 15:26; Ps. 91; 103:3; Isa. 53:4-5; 58:8; Mat. 8:17; Mk. 11:24; Jn. 15:7; James 5:14; I Pet. 2:24; etc.).

Many have argued as to whether Divine Healing is in the Atonement. To be sure, Divine Healing is in the Atonement, and in fact, every single thing that Adam and Eve lost in the Fall, was addressed in the Atonement. While we presently only have the *"Firstfruits,"* of all that Jesus did there, to be sure, we will have it all at the Resurrection of Life.

Some argue that if healing is in the Atonement, then every Christian ought to

automatically be healed of every particular affliction, etc.

That is not correct thinking as it regards the Atonement. Every Preacher who believes the Bible will surely agree that cleansing from all sin is in the Atonement. But yet, even though that is certainly correct, it doesn't mean that no Christian will sin again. Such thinking is foolish. To be sure, there will come a day when all sin will end, and I speak of the coming Resurrection, and to be sure at that time, all sickness will end as well for all Saints. But until then, we still live in a physical body of clay, which is not only subject to sickness but as well to sin.

A Christian getting sick after being saved, no more proves that healing is not in the Atonement, than the same Christian committing a sin after being saved, proves that cleansing from all sin is not in the Atonement. As stated, there is not a single thing that Adam and Eve lost in the Fall that Jesus didn't address in the Atonement. He covered all bases, leaving nothing unaddressed (Col. 2:14-15).

As well, we should understand that even though healing is in the Atonement, that doesn't mean these physical bodies will not grow old and wear out. Paul spoke of this *"earthly house,"* as he put it, *"dissolving"* (II Cor. 5:1). And that's exactly what it does. But thank God, the Apostle also said, *"We have a building of God, an house not made with hands, eternal in the heavens,"* which speaks of the coming glorified body, which we will have at the Resurrection of Life. The Atonement makes this possible as well; however, we will not have this until the Trump sounds (I Cor. 15:51-54).

IS IT ALWAYS GOD'S WILL TO HEAL THE SICK?

From the Life and Ministry of Christ, I must conclude that it definitely is always God's Will to heal the sick.

We never find one single time that Jesus ever turned anyone away who came for healing, not one single time! And I'm certain, if it had been God's Will to heal some and not heal others, considering the thousands healed by Christ, at least a few would have fallen into the category of it not being the

Will of God, had that actually been the case. But considering that Jesus not one single time ever said to one single person, *"I'm sorry, I cannot heal you, because it's not the Will of God!"* No sir! Not one single time did that ever happen, so that tells me that it's always God's Will to heal the sick.

That being the case, why then aren't all Christians immediately healed, when prayer is offered on their behalf?

To be blunt, I simply don't know! But this I do know, whatever the problem might be, it's not God's fault that we got sick in the first place, or that we aren't healed immediately, etc. Man is so prone to lay the blame on God, but let all understand, the fault is never with God. The Scripture plainly says: *"Let God be true, but every man a liar"* (Rom. 3:4).

If the person isn't healed, it's so easy for the Preacher to say, *"You don't have enough Faith!"* Or the person might say of the Preacher, *"I would have been healed, if you had enough faith on my behalf!"*

While one or the other may be right, it is not necessarily so. The Church has been taught in the last several decades that if we have enough faith, we can do anything, etc. The wrongness of that thinking should be obvious on the surface. Were that so, then man would be bigger than God.

While faith is certainly a factor, the Wisdom of God is also a factor. In other words, it may be God's Will to do many things, but due to circumstances, it may not be His wisdom at the time. His Will and His Wisdom are two different things. While certain things may always be the Will of God that doesn't necessarily mean that it's His Wisdom. Let me give you an example:

If a father has a son who is acting badly, it is certainly that Father's will to do good things for the boy, but due to the son's actions, the wisdom of the Father may dictate otherwise. It's the same with Believers. While it's always God's Will, I believe, for every one of His children to prosper financially, at times it may not be His Wisdom. In that case, the fault is definitely not His but rather ours.

A PERSONAL EXPERIENCE

Getting back to our original subject of Divine healing, even though I have related the following in other Volumes, due to the manner in which Commentaries are normally studied, I think it would be profitable for me to repeat the following episode:

The Lord wondrously and gloriously healed me when I was about 10 years old.

My Mother and Dad took me to every doctor in our area trying to find the cause of the problem, but to no avail. Whatever the problem was, I stayed nauseous constantly, and would simply go unconscious at times. In fact, this happened several times while I was at school, with the Principal at one point telling my Dad that if something wasn't done, they were going to have to remove me from school. His exact words were, *"We don't want him dying on our hands."* That's how bad the situation was.

As stated, the doctors treated me for malaria, and other things as well, but couldn't seem to find the cause of the problem.

During this particular time, I was prayed for several times by the Pastor and others in our local Church. And please allow me to make this statement at this juncture:

I'm so glad that I attended a Church that believed that Jesus saves, Jesus heals, Jesus baptizes with the Holy Spirit, and Jesus is coming again. It was a very small Church, and not looked at favorably by the world at all. But had I been associated with many, if not most, Churches of that particular time, I do not believe I would be alive today.

I will never forget the day of my healing. It was a Sunday. My parents had just left the Church and actually the Pastor and his wife were with us, all going out to lunch after the Sunday morning service.

But before going to lunch, they were to go by the home of a particular parishioner who was ill in order to pray for this Brother. I remember the occasion vividly.

We had gone into the bedroom of the little simple home and had prayed for the man in question. We had walked out to the front room and were about to leave. In my mind's eye, I can still see all of us standing there, with my parents and others making conversation. Our Pastor was standing there as well, with a bottle of oil in his hands that he had just used to pray for the Brother who was ill. My Dad spoke up and said:

"Brother Culbreth, would you anoint Jimmy with oil and pray for him? If the Lord doesn't heal him, we're going to have to take him out of school."

Those words are freeze-frozen in my mind. I was standing next to the door, and I remember the Pastor smiling, taking the top off of the little bottle of oil, turning it upside down so that his finger may be moistened with its contents, and then walking toward me.

Now this same Pastor had prayed for me many times in the last year or so, but seemingly to no avail. That being the case, why would it do any good for him to pray for me now?

I cannot answer that question, and I don't think anyone else can either. But this I do know, I thank God that my Mother and Dad didn't quit believing. It would have been very easy for them to have said in their hearts that it was useless to continue praying. But they didn't do that! They kept believing, and thank God they did.

I don't know why the Lord didn't heal me previously. I don't know why He waited until I was in this particular house on that particular Sunday afternoon. I just know that we kept believing, and I am absolutely positive that had a lot to do with it.

The Pastor touched my head anointing me with oil, and began to pray. I don't recall what he said, and actually I don't think that matters a lot. But this I do know:

All of a sudden, the Power of God came into that room. It was unmistakable!

Starting at the top of my head I felt something like a ball of fire slowly go down through my body, all the way to my feet. And at that moment I knew that I was healed. I didn't have any doubt about it! It was gloriously done.

And true enough, from that day until this, I have never been bothered with that particular problem again. It left instantly, and has never returned, and I know it will never return.

Does that happen to everyone who is healed, and I speak of the ball of fire going down through their physical bodies?

No it doesn't! So why did it do that with me? That as well I cannot answer. I do know what John the Baptist said of Christ:

"I indeed baptize you with water unto repentance: but He Who cometh after me is mightier than I, Whose shoes I am not worthy to bear: He shall baptize you with the Holy Spirit, and with fire" (Mat. 3:11).

I know what happened to me that early Sunday afternoon, was the *"fire of the Holy Spirit."* Of that I have no doubt. But let me be quick to say the following:

The Lord is not limited to that manner of healing. His ways are past finding out. He can heal with manifestations or without manifestations. He is able to do all things. The songwriter said:

"There's a river of life flowing out from me,
"Makes the lame to walk and the blind to see,
"Opens prison doors and sets the captive free,
"There's a river of life flowing out from me."

Even as I relate this experience that took place so long, long ago, I greatly sense the Presence of God. And I believe if you the Reader need healing for your physical body, or a loved one needs healing, if you'll believe Him at this very moment, Jesus Christ is the same today as He was when He healed me, and when He healed untold millions of others down through the many centuries. He hasn't changed from the time He walked this Earth unto this moment, and in fact, He will never change. As the Word graphically states: *"Jesus Christ the same yesterday, and today, and forever"* (Heb. 13:8). So believe Him now for your healing!

THE PROSPERITY OF THE SOUL

The phrase, *"Even as thy soul prospereth,"* speaks of spiritual prosperity, which is the greatest prosperity of all. In this and this alone the Church must major. While we as Preachers must preach financial prosperity in Christ, and while we must preach Divine healing in Christ, the emphasis must always rather be, however, on spiritual prosperity.

Unfortunately, great segments of the Church have violated this principle in the last few decades. For instance, many in the

NOTES

Word of Faith camp are emphasizing financial prosperity to the exclusion of spiritual prosperity.

I don't enjoy being so blunt; however, spiritual deception is a powerful thing, actually being nurtured and fostered by seducing spirits; consequently, the Preacher, that is if he is to preach the Truth, must at times, even as John did in his Epistles, be very clear in the statements made, even specifically pointing out the wrong.

The Christian can be close to the Lord and make Heaven his eternal home, and still not be financially prosperous. Likewise, they can do the same and not be physically prosperous; however, they cannot be close to the Lord without being spiritually prosperous. Let's say it another way:

You can go to Heaven even though financially poor or physically sick, but you can't go to Heaven without being spiritually prosperous; consequently, it should be obvious as to the emphasis.

THE CROSS OF CHRIST

If the Believer properly has the Cross as the foundation of his Faith, which is in effect, having the Word as the foundation of his Faith, he will not have to worry about proper emphasis. The Cross always places the emphasis where it belongs. It is to be on Christ and what He did for us at the Cross. And of all the great things He did there, the price He paid centers up on the problem of sin, more so than anything else. To be frank, Jesus could have readily addressed the problem of financial difficulties without going to the Cross. He could have done the same as it regards physical problems, or many other things we could name. But He couldn't address the sin problem without going to the Cross; consequently, we should understand this, and I speak of sin, as the greatest problem with humanity, and by far! And to be sure, it continues to be a problem with Believers, hence the necessary faith to be continued in the Cross after Salvation. There is only one answer for sin, and that is the Cross of Christ (Heb. 9:14; 10:12). All the other things, while definitely important, are but side issues. So, whatever we do, let us make certain that whatever else happens, *"the soul prospers."* Nothing is more important!

NOTES

(3) "FOR I REJOICED GREATLY, WHEN THE BRETHREN CAME AND TESTIFIED OF THE TRUTH THAT IS IN THEE, EVEN AS THOU WALKEST IN THE TRUTH."

The structure is:

1. John now discloses the source of his information regarding the prosperous condition of the inner heart-life of Gaius.

2. Christian workers were always going out from Ephesus on preaching and teaching missions, and bringing back to John, reports from the various Churches.

3. The report was very favorable concerning Gaius, and the doctrine which he now held, and that it furnished a holy walk.

THE TRUTH

The phrase, *"For I rejoiced greatly, when the Brethren came and testified of the Truth that is in thee,"* pertains to more than meets the eye.

Whatever Church it was with which Gaius was associated, as this third Epistle implies, there had been problems. It seems that some were pulling away after false doctrine, which possibly was the teaching of Cerinthus. At any rate, it seems the Church was split, with some going with the false teaching and others with the teaching of John the Beloved.

Whoever it was who was reporting to John, testified that Gaius had not wavered in his allegiance to the Truth as taught by the Apostle, but had held, and was holding firm.

The short phrase *"I rejoiced greatly,"* tells us that this was great news to John, and for several reasons. The idea seems to have been, if Gaius had wavered, it could have meant the loss of the entirety of the Church. But with him holding firm, John has every hope that the Church will be saved.

How could any Christian at that particular time, repudiate John in favor of some false prophet? The life of the Apostle was impeccable. The Power of God with him, and was a constant testimony to what he was in Christ. In line with all of that, this man was the only one left alive at this time, who had actually been with Christ. In fact, he had been one of the chosen three, *"Peter, James, and John."* He had personally witnessed Jesus performing miracle after miracle, to such an extent that it defied all description. He had been there when the Master had been raised from the dead. He had personally witnessed His resurrected body, and was there when Jesus ascended back to Heaven. He was there on the Day of Pentecost when the Holy Spirit fell in a brand-new dimension. He had been an eyewitness of the Power of God as possibly no one else. And yet, some of these Believers would turn against John. Again I ask the question, how could that be?

As we have repeatedly stated, false doctrine presented by false teachers presents a powerful influence. The reason is *"seducing spirits"* (I Tim. 4:1). In other words, there is a power behind false doctrine that is nurtured and fostered by demon spirits, and in this case, *"seducing spirits."* The word *"seduction"* or *"seducing,"* means that however the approach is made, it is done so very subtly, which makes it seem so right. Unfortunately, many, if not most, Christians are not very versed in the Word; consequently, they are an easy prey for the wrong direction.

To be sure, as that problem existed in John's day, as is quickly obvious, it continues to exist unto this hour, and I think one could say, even in a greater measure now than ever before. In fact, the Bible teaches us the following concerning false doctrine in the last days:

"Now the Spirit (Holy Spirit) *speaks expressly* (speaks distinctly), *that in the latter times* (the times in which we now live) *some shall depart from the faith* (depart from the Cross), *giving heed to seducing spirits, and doctrines of Devils"* (I Tim. 4:1).

This problem of which the Holy Spirit spoke through Paul so long, long ago, is now upon us. And please remember, that which is false, will in fact have some truth in it, which will make it even more seductive. In fact, even as we've already addressed in this Volume, the small amount of truth serves as the *"bait."* But even that which is false, will sound like God, look like God, and act like God! Those who are not anchored solidly in the faith will be pulled aside. What is the faith?

THE FAITH

Paul said that *"some shall depart from the Faith."*

"The faith" goes much farther than simply *"believing God,"* or *"believing His Word."*

It rather refers to the entire system or body of belief as it regards Christianity. Paul also referred to it as *"the Faith of the Son of God"* (Gal. 2:20).

By that statement, he wasn't meaning that Jesus had faith, which of course He did, but that is not Paul's emphasis here.

He is referring to what Christ did in order to redeem fallen and lost humanity. In other words, he is speaking of the Cross. It is the work of Atonement that Christ carried out on the Cross, by the shedding of His Life's Blood, which atoned for all sin, and thereby made Redemption possible. In fact, to properly explain this, Paul often used the word *"Cross"* as a synonym, which means that this one word embodies all that Christ did in the Atonement. So when the Apostle said that *"some would depart from the Faith,"* he was in essence saying that *"some would depart from the Cross."*

In effect, that's what they were doing in John's day, which has always been the direction of all false doctrine. It always involves in some way, a false interpretation of the Person of Christ and of the Mission of Christ.

For the last several decades, the Church as a whole has had precious little teaching and preaching on the Cross of Christ. Consequently, at the present time, the Church is all but Cross illiterate. As a result, it doesn't understand its place and position in Christ, thereby becoming a target for all types of false doctrines. It is exactly what Jesus said would happen in the last days.

His words were: *"The Kingdom of Heaven is like unto leaven* (false doctrine), *which a woman took, and hid in three measures of meal* (the Word of God), *till the whole was leavened* (ruined)"* (Mat. 13:33).

Jesus is speaking here of the end of the Church age (Mat. 13:49).

"Leaven" in Biblical terms, always refers to that which is evil. As well, whenever *"a woman"* is used in symbolism in this fashion, she speaks of evil.

The *"meal"* speaks of the Word of God, in which the *"leaven"* is placed. As leaven does, it enlarges itself, until the *"whole is leavened,"* or corrupted.

In this very short Parable, Christ portrays to us what the condition of the Church will be in the last days.

In fact, in the preceding Parable (Mat. 13:31-32), Jesus speaks of the Church becoming large, which it did, but with the *"birds of the air coming and lodging in the branches thereof."* This means that the Church will become a refuge, a home, and a sphere of operation for demon powers. In fact, that's exactly what has happened. Presently, for every good Church, there are scores of Churches that are cesspools of false doctrine. Regrettably, the situation will not grow better but worse.

But at the same time, there is a group of Godly people in the Church who love God supremely, and who are growing stronger in Christ. By comparison to the whole, this number is small; however, it is in fact, *"a glorious Church."* It is the part of the Church that looks to *"Jesus Christ and Him Crucified"* (I Cor. 2:2). This is the True Church, the part in fact, which will go in the Rapture (I Thess. 4:13-18).

WALKING IN TRUTH

The phrase, *"Even as you walk in the Truth,"* refers by the word *"walk,"* the manner of one's behavior. What you believe will ultimately fall out to how you live.

John is saying here that the Truth believed by Gaius, translated into a Godly and holy walk before the Lord, which the truth will always do. Error cannot produce Godly living. It is impossible!

"Thou" is emphatic in the Greek, showing that there were others, of whom this could not be said. In other words, they had succumbed to false doctrine, and it translated into an ungodly walk, i.e., *"lifestyle."*

Even though John only casually mentions the *"walk"* of the Believer, as should be obvious, this is the single most important aspect of our Christian experience, other than our initial Salvation. Being saved is one thing, while living for the Lord is something else altogether. The latter translates into our Sanctification, which sadly and regrettably, is almost an unknown word in modern Christian circles. In other words, Sanctification, which means *"to be set apart exclusively for the Lord and from the world,"* is so little taught and preached in our modern Churches that modern Christianity

hardly knows the meaning of this most important Doctrine.

Immediately at conversion, the Holy Spirit comes into our hearts and lives to abide, but with the purpose of making us Christlike, which means to set us apart exclusively for God. In other words, it is the business of the Spirit to bring our *"condition"* of Righteousness and Holiness up to our *"position"* of the same thing, which we hold in Christ. Again, this refers to our *"walk."*

This is a work that the Believer cannot bring about of his own strength and ability. That's why Paul said: *"For I know that in me (that is in my flesh,) dwelleth no good thing: for to will is present with me; but how to perform that which is good I find not"* (Rom. 7:18).

The Apostle is simply saying here that by our own strength, ability, and machinations, we cannot be what we ought to be in the Lord. It just simply cannot be done that way; consequently, it must be done by the Holy Spirit, Who Alone can *"perform that which is good."* And how does He do this?

THE HOLY SPIRIT

As we've already explained any number of times in this Volume, the Holy Spirit is God; however, He works strictly within the guidelines of the Godhead, and what are those guidelines?

It is the Cross that has made it possible for the Spirit to abide permanently within our hearts and lives (Jn. 14:17). In fact and as we've already explained, He works exclusively within a particular *"Law,"* which has been devised by the Godhead. It's called *"The Law of the Spirit of Life in Christ Jesus"* (Rom. 8:2). He will not deviate from this *"Law,"* so if we want His help as it regards living a holy life, we as well, have to function within this *"Law."*

What is this Law?

In effect, it is what Jesus did at the Cross on our behalf; hence, it is referred to as being *"in Christ Jesus."* The Work of Christ on the Cross was a legal work, which incidentally satisfied the demands of a thrice-Holy God. In other words, the Cross wasn't carried out to appease the Devil, but rather to appease God. The crime had been committed against God, and it was to God that man owed this monstrous debt – a debt incidentally, which he could not within himself even remotely hope to pay. But Jesus paid it all at the Cross, by the giving of Himself, in the pouring out of His Life's Blood, which atoned for all sin.

Consequently, when the Believer expresses Faith in Christ, which actually means that we have Faith in what He did at the Cross, we are functioning within this *"Law,"* which guarantees the help of the Holy Spirit, which guarantees victory on our part. In this capacity and in this capacity alone, can we *"walk"* victoriously. And the reason we can is because we are *"walking in truth."* To attempt this walk in any other manner, translates into spiritual failure.

(4) "I HAVE NO GREATER JOY THAN TO HEAR THAT MY CHILDREN WALK IN TRUTH."

The structure is:

1. The importance for the Church of Gaius' stand for the truth is seen in John's response.

2. There is no more important news than for Christians to live in fidelity (to the Truth).

3. By the phrase *"my children,"* John may have been inferring that Gaius was his convert.

NO GREATER JOY

The phrase, *"I have no greater joy,"* presents the fact of the emphasis in John's life and Ministry. To hear that Gaius and others were walking in truth, which means they had not fallen for the false doctrine, is an occasion of great joy to the Apostle, and should be to us in similar circumstances as well.

In 1996, the Lord began to give to me the Revelation of the Cross. To be sure, it was not something new, actually being what Paul had already taught in his Epistles. I use the word *"began,"* simply because that Revelation has continued unto this hour, which I trust will ever continue, and because it is literally impossible to exhaust the potential of the Atonement.

As I preach and teach this subject, and watch Believers begin to hear this Truth, almost all of them for the first time, and then watching it take effect within their lives, provides the occasion of tremendous joy. So in a small measure, I know what the Apostle was saying.

When I speak of the Message of the Cross, I am referring to the part the Cross plays in our everyday living. Unfortunately, about all that most modern Christians know about the Cross, is the part it plays in their initial Salvation experience. Beyond that, most have no teaching. But let the Reader understand, that as critical as the Cross is in our initial Salvation experience, as critical it is in our ongoing walk before the Lord. Paul explains all of this in Romans, Chapter 6.

MY CHILDREN

The phrase, *"Than to hear that my children walk in truth,"* refers to the fact, as stated, that quite possibly Gaius was a convert of John.

But in a greater sense, I think John the Beloved at this stage, felt a tremendous responsibility for the entirety of the Church of that day, which included every single Christian, of course with him not knowing many of them. Nevertheless, due to his age, and especially as to who he was, I think to a great extent, that the Church in those days, may very well have been divided between those who followed the teaching of *"the Elder,"* or the teaching of others who did not subscribe to what John taught. In effect, John taught the same thing which Paul taught, although he would not have gone into the detail as did Paul, and especially as it refers to the Cross. But basically, there would have been no difference in their doctrine. So, when he says *"my children,"* I think his statement covered the entirety of the True Church.

The joy of this aged Disciple was rooted completely in the truth. Many do not have their joy thus rooted.

John knew that to *"walk in truth,"* presented itself as the highest form of Christianity. In other words, this is that for which Christ died. He knew of course that if one did not abide in the truth, one simply could not walk in the truth. In other words, the *"works of the flesh"* would some how and some way manifest themselves in such lives and living. And please understand, it has not changed from then until now.

Paul tells us, in no uncertain terms, that it's impossible for the Believer to walk victorious before the Lord, unless he does so

NOTES

through Faith in the Cross of Christ, which guarantees the help of the Holy Spirit. But if one doesn't understand the Cross as it refers to one's Sanctification, then it's virtually impossible for such a Believer to walk in victory, irrespective as to how consecrated and dedicated to the Lord he might be.

A HYPOTHETICAL CASE

Please read the following very carefully, which I would hope would properly explain what we are attempting to say.

Hypothetically let's select a dear Brother who loves the Lord supremely, and who is accordingly, very consecrated and dedicated. Let's say that in his dedication, he will devote at least an hour a day without fail, to seeking the Face of the Lord in prayer. Let's say that he will as well devote at least a half an hour each day to studying the Word.

Considering that praying Christians are about as scarce as the proverbial hen's teeth, I think almost all Christians would agree that such a man would be concluded to be a very strong Christian, someone who is totally devoted to the Lord. And they would be right!

However, at the same time, continuing to use this case in a hypothetical way, lets say that this dear Brother doesn't know anything about the Cross of Christ as it relates to his living for the Lord. He perfectly understands the Cross as it regarded his initial Salvation experience, but regarding Sanctification he has no knowledge. In other words, the Preachers under whom he has sat, simply didn't preach anything about the Cross, and for the most part, simply because they knew little about the Cross themselves. At any rate, our dear Brother in question simply does not understand God's prescribed order of victory.

SHOCKING STATEMENTS

Now I'm going to make some statements that most modern Christians would question. But that's quite alright!

If our Brother, whom we are using as an example, doesn't understand the Cross, despite his zeal, despite his consecration and dedication, despite his love for God, in some way he will walk in failure. In other words, the works of the flesh will manifest themselves in his life to some degree. Now don't misunderstand what I'm saying:

We aren't saying that our Brother's prayer life or Bible study are wrong, or all the other things he might be doing in this capacity. In fact, they are very right, and in many ways God will bless him abundantly so; however, when it comes to victory over sin, these things he's doing, and these things in which he is placing his faith, simply will not suffice.

No, we're not telling our Brother to quit praying or studying his Bible. God forbid! Let me emphasize again, it's not his prayer life or Bible study time which are wrong. As stated, these things are very right. Where the wrong comes in is according to the following:

Not understanding the Cross, our dear Brother is placing his faith in the doing of these things instead of the Cross, and that's where the wrong comes in. In other words, the object of his faith is wrong.

We aren't telling him, to stop praying. Again I will use Paul's favorite term, *"God forbid!"* What we're telling him is this:

Instead of having faith in these things that he is doing, he must place his faith instead in what Christ has already done at the Cross. When the object of his faith is correct, then to be sure, his prayer life and Bible study time will be even more productive, in fact, much more productive. And as well, he will begin to have victory over the world, the flesh, and the Devil.

BELIEVING OR DOING?

The very ingredient of Christianity as the Bible proclaims this relationship with Christ, is *"believing"*; however, most of the Church is rather occupied with *"doing."* And yet, most all of these Christians will think their major thrust is in believing. But actually it isn't! In fact, unless the Christian understands the Cross, his major thrust cannot be *"believing,"* but will rather be *"doing."* It just simply cannot be otherwise.

Now please understand, we are not criticizing the *"doing."* More than likely, the things that most Christians are doing for the Lord are within their own right, good things. It's not really the *"doing"* that's wrong, but rather the placing of our faith in the doing, which makes it wrong. And whether they will admit it or not, that's where the faith of most Christians actually is.

Regarding their way with the Lord, if they don't understand the Cross, they are going to immediately think, *"I'm right with God, or close to the Lord,"* or whatever terminology, *"because I do these things."*

What we have done, is to turn these things, whatever they might be, into *"works,"* which God can never sanction. In other words, our faith is in the doing of these things, instead of in Christ and what Christ has done for us at the Cross. That and that alone constitutes the wrong.

The Reader must understand that everything we are in Christ, our closeness to Him, our walk with Him, all and without exception, are due to what we *"believe,"* and not what we *"do."* To be sure, correct believing will turn into correct doing; however, incorrect doing will never turn into correct believing. Listen to what Paul said:

"And if by Grace, then is it no more of works: otherwise Grace is no more Grace. But if it be of works, then is it no more Grace: otherwise work is no more work" (Rom. 11:6).

The Apostle is saying here that it cannot be both *"Grace"* and *"works"* at the same time. If we're trusting totally and completely in the Grace of God, then we're not trusting in works. If we're trusting in works, then we are not trusting in Grace. It's just that simple!

And to be sure, the Lord will not accept works, but only Faith that is founded on the Word of God, all made possible by the Grace of God. Paul said:

"For by grace are you saved through Faith; and that not of yourselves: it is the Gift of God:

"Not of works, lest any man should boast" (Eph. 2:8-9).

MUCH OF THE MODERN CHURCH IS STILL MIRED IN WORKS

And how do I know that?

I know it by the way they approach sin. It is approached in two ways:

1. They try to hide sin. They do this in a variety of ways.

One way is by false doctrine, which claims that once a person comes to Christ, they have no problem with sin anymore. They claim if

sin is never mentioned, then it will present no problem. The mentioning of sin, they say, creates a sin consciousness, which in turn, leads one to sin, etc.

Others do not take that tact, but rather deny the problem they have, whatever the problem might be.

A great part of the Church, actually almost all of the modern Church, has pretty well limited sin to what I refer to as the big five: *"alcohol, immorality, drugs, gambling, and nicotine."* If an individual is not bothered with one of those problems, everything else is pretty well overlooked. This means that the *"works of the flesh"* listed by Paul in Galatians 5:19-21, have been greatly diluted. In their eyes, it's only a certain few things that constitute sin.

In this scenario, Christians are running all over the world trying to find a Preacher whom they think God is using, who will lay hands on them and solve all their problems. As well, every type of ridiculous method is being promoted in order to overcome sin. However, the word *"sin"* is never used openly in this fashion, at least most of the time. Irrespective, and whatever label may be applied, however, it's really *"sin"* that's the problem.

2. I know that the modern Church is trusting mostly in works because of the way that it addresses sin, when it does have to admit that something untoward has happened. Not understanding the Cross and thereby functioning in works, most modern spiritual leaders subscribe to the idea that if someone sins, it is simply because they wanted to do whatever it is that was done. For the most part in the thinking of these people, this means that the victim is judged very harshly. And if he committed some sin because he wanted to do such, meaning that he could have simply said *"No,"* then he must be punished.

They take great delight in punishment, simply because in their minds, if they take a very hard line against the one who has failed, then it makes it seem like they are very hard on sin. The ironic thing is, most of the time, the ones doing the punishing, are in worse spiritual condition than the one they are punishing. They conveniently overlook their own wrongdoing, whatever it might be, while loudly proclaiming the faults of the one who has failed. Somehow they seem to think that the harder they are on this particular individual that such action and attitude atones for their own wrongdoing.

I suspect the Reader has started to catch the drift of what I'm saying. We're dealing here with hypocrisy! Pure and simple, it can be defined as nothing else than hypocrisy! And regrettably, the Church is rife with such doings.

HOW SHOULD THE CHURCH FUNCTION IN GRACE?

First of all, precious few true Christians, if any, actually want to sin. I realize that the Church is fond of saying that *"sin is a choice."* In one sense of the word that is correct, but not as they are saying it. The truth is, if the Believer doesn't understand the Cross, Satan can actually force the Believer's will (Rom. 7:18). I realize a lot of Christians don't want to believe that, but to deny it, is to deny the Word of God. Let me say it in another way:

If the Believer is attempting to ward off temptation by any means other than Faith in the Cross, such as with his willpower, that Christian will find that he is unable to carry the task to a successful conclusion. In other words, Satan will ultimately override his will, and the Christian will be forced to do something that he doesn't want to do.

Yes, despite that fact, he definitely is responsible for his actions, and here's how:

While the *"will"* of the Christian is definitely very important, it is important really in one particular way.

The Christian has the power of choice as it regards depending on Christ or depending on himself or other things. That's where the power of choice actually is. If he decides for Christ, which refers to placing his Faith in what Christ has done at the Cross, he will then get the help of the Holy Spirit, which will guarantee victory. If he makes the decision to trust in other things, then he's left with nothing but his own willpower, meaning that the Holy Spirit will not help in such circumstances, which means he is then doomed to failure.

However, most Christians do not really have the opportunity of making that choice, because most don't know anything about the

Cross. The Bible plainly states that *"faith cometh by hearing, and hearing by the Word of God"* (Rom. 10:17). But if the Believer doesn't hear the Word as it regards the Cross, then he is left with but one choice, and that is to try to make it by his own ways and means, and that Believer, as stated, is doomed to failure.

In such a case, which is mostly the case with most failures, with so-called spiritual leaders coming in and punishing such a person, they are only adding insult to injury. And please allow me to state the case again: such individuals are not qualified to punish anyone. And if they are dead set on doing such things, let them begin with themselves.

In the case of failure, the Believer who is spiritual (Gal. 6:1), which means he understands the victory of the Cross, should explain to the one who has failed, why he has failed, and then explain to him as to how he can have victory in the Cross of Christ. That is true restoration. That's Grace! Anything else is *"law"* and *"works,"* which God can never accept.

But unfortunately, most of the modern Church has adopted the ways of the world instead of the Biblical way. And of course, when they adopt the ways of the world, the world applauds such action, as understandably it will. But to be sure, God doesn't applaud such wrong direction.

I'm assuming the Reader wants to be Biblical. If instead, we want other directions, then that's something else altogether. But if we want to be Biblical, we will have to follow the way of the Cross, which is the way of Grace. And it's the most beautiful way in the world. As John said, that is *"walking in truth."* Anything else, also as John said, *"is a lie."*

(5) "BELOVED, THOU DOEST FAITHFULLY WHATSOEVER THOU DOEST TO THE BRETHREN, AND TO STRANGERS;"

The exegesis is:

1. Gaius and those with him had been faithful in their duties.

2. What Gaius did was not merely a kind and generous act, but he considered it a spiritual service to the Lord.

3. Little did this man know that what he was doing, would be heralded in the Word of

God, and would be known all over the world, and for all time.

FAITHFUL

The phrase, *"Beloved, thou doest faithfully,"* presents the greatest compliment that could ever be given to a Child of God. As someone has well said, the Lord has not called us to be successful, but He has called us to be faithful. Jesus said:

"Well done, thou good and faithful servant: thou hast been faithful over a few things, I will make thee ruler over many things: enter thou into the joy of thy Lord" (Mat. 25:21).

Unfortunately, in the modern Church, *"faithfulness"* doesn't carry much weight, the key word now being *"success"* or *"successful."* However, God's definition of success is far different than that of man.

The Church defines success by the amount of money taken in and the size of the crowds. God defines success as *"faithfulness."*

WHATEVER YOU DO

The phrase, *"Whatsoever thou doest to the Brethren, and to strangers,"* presents John asking Gaius to take care of these Preachers without really asking him. No greater compliment could be paid to this man than that John should take for granted that Gaius will do what is not even asked but is only implied. In fact, John does better than to ask, he commends what Gaius will do for these Preachers as though Gaius had already started upon the doing. The Apostle certainly knew how to call out and how to acknowledge the best that is in a man. This enhances all that Gaius will do for them, and John does not fail to note it and to credit Gaius in advance (Lenski).

(6) "WHICH HAVE BORNE WITNESS OF YOUR CHARITY BEFORE THE CHURCH: WHOM IF YOU BRING FORWARD ON THEIR JOURNEY AFTER A GODLY SORT, YOU SHALL DO WELL:"

The diagram is:

1. The word *"charity"* here should have been translated *"love."*

2. To *"bring forward"* as used here, refers to standing good for the maintenance and expenses of visiting Preachers.

3. *"After a Godly sort"* refers to that which is *"worthily of God,"* which means, *"to treat them as God would have treated them."*

LOVE

The phrase, *"Which have borne witness of thy charity before the Church,"* presents *"charity"* as an unfortunate translation. The Greek word is *"agape,"* the particular word for the Divine love which is produced in the heart of the yielded Saint by the Holy Spirit, a love which is self-sacrificial in its essence, always giving of itself for the benefit of others (Wuest).

"Church" in the Greek is *"Eklesia,"* and means *"a called-out body of people,"* and as one might say, called out from among the world and called unto God. Before what Church they had borne this testimony is unknown.

ON THEIR JOURNEY

The phrase, *"Whom if you bring forward on their journey after a Godly sort, you shall do well,"* refers to the fact that the entirety of the Church should have shared in this responsibility; however, due to a man in that particular Body by the name of Diotrephes, a man incidentally who had embraced false doctrine and had as well, influenced the majority of the Church, the responsibility was left totally in the hands of Gaius, and we continue to speak of these visiting Preachers.

Gaius will lodge these Preachers, but this is the least that he will do; he will also send them forward on their journey, which does not mean with only a friendly goodbye but rather with adequate supplies.

Since they traveled on foot and often covered considerable distances until some other congregation or some friend like Gaius gave them new supplies, this sending forward required money. Consequently, the love of Gaius would not be miserly.

John knows that Gaius will send these Brethren forward *"in a manner worthy of God,"* of Him in Whose cause they are assuming no little hardship, even when they receive such help.

As John mentions the *"journey"* of these Preachers, Preachers incidentally who breathed, practiced, and preached the Truth, conversely, he tells Believers not to bid the proclaimer of false doctrine Godspeed on his journey (II Jn. 10-11). The former is to be helped, the latter not at all!

(7) "BECAUSE THAT FOR HIS NAME'S SAKE THEY WENT FORTH, TAKING NOTHING OF THE GENTILES."

The structure is:

1. It was for the sake of the Name of Jesus that these Preachers went forth.

2. *"The Name"* is an Old Testament expression speaking of all that God is in His glorious attributes. It refers here and in Philippians to all that the Lord Jesus is in His glorious attributes.

3. These Preachers would accept no support from the pagans to whom they went, and rightly so, lest they be accused of commercializing their Ministry, with Paul having first set this example.

HIS NAME'S SAKE

The phrase, *"Because that for His Name's sake they went forth,"* proclaims *"Christ,"* but always with the full Revelation of Christ (I Jn. 3:23).

These Preachers whomever they may have been, were first of all called of God. As well, they had sought the Lord earnestly as it regards the place or places to where they should go, and felt they had the mind of the Lord in this respect. As a result, they had the privilege of using His Name, the Name of Jesus, in whatever capacity it would be needed, which would be honored in the spirit world, but as well, felt they had direction given by the Lord. In other words, they knew where they were going, what they were going to do, the message they were going to preach, and the people to whom it would be preached. From the next phrase, the evidence is that they were going into new territory in order to plant Churches.

THE GENTILES

The phrase, *"Taking nothing of the Gentiles,"* refers to virgin territory as it regards the Gospel, different places where they would plant Churches.

Most of the people who would be won to the Lord would be Gentiles. But yet they would take no money from these individuals, at least at the outset, and of course, the question is, why?

As stated, Paul had set the example regarding this practice. Almost all the Gentiles who came to Christ in those days had been associated before conversion with some of the heathen temples. Not to mention other things, the *"priests"* of these heathen temples, used every strategy possible to wheedle money out of the devotees to these particular temples, which in effect, were devotees to particular gods. As stated, Paul set the example. When he went into a certain city and the Lord would give him favor by Gentiles being saved, at the outset he would not seek any support from them in a financial sense. He wanted them to know and understand that Christianity had no kindred spirit whatsoever with the practice of these heathen temples. Money was the name of their game, and he didn't want such a spirit to characterize Christianity. So he asked for no help whatsoever from the newly converted Gentiles. It seems that John and others continued to follow this example, and rightly so.

After these Gentiles had become seasoned in the Lord, then it is evident that offerings were received. In fact, part of the Letter to the Philippians is devoted to thanking the Gentiles in that particular Church for the offering they had sent the Apostle while he was in prison in Rome (Phil. 1:5). As well, the Philippians had supported him in other places also (Phil. 4:15-18). Also, the Apostle gives the greatest dissertation concerning giving, found in the entirety of the Bible in his Second Epistle to the Corinthians, who incidentally were mostly Gentiles (II Cor., Chpts. 8-9).

So the refusal to accept monetary help from the Gentiles, who had just come to Christ, was done for good reason. No doubt the Holy Spirit led Paul in this practice, with the other Apostles being very wise to follow suit.

(8) "WE THEREFORE OUGHT TO RECEIVE SUCH, THAT WE MIGHT BE FELLOWHELPERS TO THE TRUTH."

The composite is:

1. Those who are truly called of God must be received by the Church.

2. All Believers are to be fellowhelpers in the Work of God.

3. However, we must be very careful that we in fact are *"fellowhelpers to the truth,"* and not rather helping to spread error.

TO RECEIVE SUCH

The phrase, *"We therefore ought to receive such,"* refers here to Preachers of the Gospel who are truly called of God. In other words, if God has called them, and anointed them, and it is obvious that this is so, the Church is under obligation to receive such. If the Church refuses to do so, they aren't so much saying *"No"* to the individual or individuals, as they are to God Himself; consequently, as I would pray is obvious, this becomes quite a serious matter. In fact, there is very little that is more ungodly than refusing to accept that which God has accepted. Why am I making an issue of this?

I'm making an issue of it simply because I believe the Holy Spirit is making an issue of it. So the question must arise as to why certain segments of the Church wouldn't accept these God-called men?

If it weren't true that some in the Church at that particular time were refusing to accept God-called Preachers, then the Holy Spirit wouldn't have mentioned the situation.

The reason this was done then, and the reason it is done now, is because the Church begins to adhere in some way to false doctrine. That was the case then, and it is the case now.

AN EXAMPLE

A very close friend of mine, who pastors a large Church in a major city, and who is associated with a large Pentecostal Denomination, ran into this problem.

A certain position was being taken by this Denomination, which my friend felt to be unscriptural. He wrote the General Superintendent about the matter. If I remember correctly, he wrote twice, but received no answer.

Several months after his initial inquiry, he either called the man on the phone about the matter, or the man called him. I don't remember which; at any rate, the discussion over the phone centered up on the question at hand.

The General Superintendent insisted that what was being done was Scriptural, but could provide no Scriptural foundation for his claims, despite being pressed about the issue.

The truth is, what this particular Denomination was and is doing as it regards the question at hand, is basely unscriptural.

The Laity may read these words, and automatically conclude that this concerns Preachers only; however, please understand that every single Believer, even as John is addressing here, has to make the decision as to what Preachers they are going to receive. Unfortunately, most so-called Christians receive only those whom their Denomination recommends, or their local Pastor.

Totally and completely, this is the wrong position for any Layman to take, even as it is the wrong position for any Preacher to take. We must judge every Preacher of the Gospel according to the Word of God, and not according to what other people may say about them. Is the man Scriptural? And is the Spirit of God prevalent within his life and Ministry? For a good Christian, that's not difficult to ascertain.

To flippantly accept someone simply because Denominational heads say so, or even the local Pastor, or to reject someone on the same basis, will ultimately lead to terrible, spiritual declension. In the first place, if the Believer has no more knowledge of the Word of God than that, whether he realizes it or not, he has just stopped all Spiritual Growth. The results will be at least a *"leanness of the soul,"* and possibly even the loss of the soul.

THE EARLY CHURCH

The problem of which we speak was already beginning in John's day. In fact, a few years after John's death, little by little, unspiritual men began to gain ascendancy in the Church, until finally, all who were Godly were on the outside.

Correct Doctrine was the first thing to go, even as we are studying here, with correct government being the next thing to fall by the wayside. Government as laid down by the Holy Spirit in the Book of Acts began to be pushed aside, with men making up the rules that had no Scriptural bearing, or else the Scriptures were perverted, until in the early part of the Seventh Century, the Bishop of Rome began to be called *"Pope."* Thus began the Catholic Church, which had actually begun, regarding the seedbed of corruption, some 300 years earlier. Organized religion is very seldom Godly. In fact, its very nature leads toward ungodliness. It becomes political and almost without exception. And becoming political, it ceases to be spiritual. The tragedy is, millions of Christians link their Salvation with these particular Denominations, which means, whether they realize it or not, they are rejecting Christ. In fact, Satan destroys more people through religion than any other way. As well, religion probably causes more people to be eternally lost, than all the vices put together.

SPIRITUAL ADULTERY?

In the first few Verses of Romans, Chapter 7, the Holy Spirit through Paul uses an analogy that is quite apt.

He illustrates a woman who is married to one man, with the implication being that she divorces this man without any Scriptural reason and marries another. The Scripture says: *"So then if, while her husband lives, she be married to another man, she shall be called an adulteress"* (Rom. 7:3).

Paul then said: *"Wherefore, my Brethren, you also are become dead to the law by the Body of Christ* (the Crucifixion of Christ)*; that you should be married to another* (married to Christ)*, even to Him Who is raised from the dead, that we should bring forth fruit unto God"* (Rom. 7:4).

The idea is, we as Christians cannot be married to Christ and to the law at the same time. If in fact that is the case, we are looked at by God as committing *"spiritual adultery."*

Now most Christians would read these Verses and automatically think, *"that doesn't include me, because the Law has nothing to do with me."* The truth is, sadly and regrettably, these Passages given here by Paul in fact include most modern Christians. And how does it do that?

Most Christians don't understand anything about the Cross, at least as it regards their Sanctification; consequently, they are attempting to sanctify themselves, which means they are engaging in law whether they realize it or not, which makes them a *"spiritual adulterer."* In other words, they are married to Christ, but at the same time are serving the law. Admittedly, it's not the Law of Moses, but it definitely is a law made up by themselves or their Church or Denomination.

I want to make a statement now that is very shocking, but at the same time is regrettably true:

The very fact of joining and belonging to some Churches, or Denominations, automatically makes one a *"spiritual adulterer."* As stated, that's a shocking statement, but it happens to be the truth.

How is it the truth?

Most Churches and Denominations subscribe to a system of *"law."* In other words, they claim that if one is loyal to their particular Church or Denomination, and I speak of keeping all its rules and regulations, etc., that this means that the person is a good Christian, etc. In other words, they are advocating something other than the Cross of Christ. They are trying to be holy and righteous, by means other than simple Faith in Christ and what Christ did for us at the Cross.

Actually, in today's modern religious climate, *"Righteousness"* and *"Holiness"* are seldom even mentioned any more. It's just loyalty to the Church, etc. Let me say it again:

If one associates oneself with the Church, where the emphasis is not on the Cross but rather something else, this means that particular individual is married to Christ and at the same time married to the law. This makes that person a *"spiritual adulterer."* And please understand, even though the person may not comprehend the fact that they are engaging in *"law,"* the truth is, if they are not trusting what Christ did at the Cross, and doing so 100 percent, whether they realize it or not, they are engaging in law, which makes them a *"spiritual adulterer."*

While the act of joining such a Church doesn't make one a spiritual adulterer, at least within itself, adhering to what it teaches, definitely does!

WHAT DOES IT MEAN TO BE A SPIRITUAL ADULTERER?

As we've already stated, a spiritual adulterer is one who is married to Christ, but at the same time is married to the law. That's hard for modern Christians to understand, because when *"law"* is mentioned, they automatically think of the Law of the Moses, and automatically assume that it doesn't apply to them. But what the Reader must understand is, anything that we do to try to live a holy life, or to just simply try to live for God, whatever that might mean, other than simple Faith in Christ and what Christ did for us at the Cross, is defined by God as *"law."* In other words, we are trying to live according to rules and regulations of some sort made up by ourselves or our Church, etc. We don't think of it as *"law,"* because most of these things are very spiritual; however, if it's not the Cross, which translates into Grace, then it's *"law."* Listen to what Paul said:

"For I am jealous over you with Godly jealousy: for I have espoused you to one husband, that I may present you as a chaste virgin to Christ."

He then said, *"But I fear, lest by any means, as the serpent beguiled Eve through his subtilty, so your minds should be corrupted from the simplicity that is in Christ"* (II Cor. 11:2-3).

In essence, Paul is saying the same thing here that he said in the first four Verses of Romans, Chapter 7. He mentioned *"one husband,"* and that is *"Christ."* The problem is, many, if not most, Christians, and we're speaking in the spiritual sense, have *"two husbands,"* Christ and the law.

To answer the question of our heading, as to what such means, it falls out to a total lack of victory on the part of the Believer. In other words, trying to live for God in this manner frustrates the Grace of God. While we're trusting in *"Law,"* we automatically stop the flow of *"Grace."*

What makes all of this so destructive is, while most Christians understand the Cross as it refers to their initial Salvation experience, they don't have the foggiest idea as to the part the Cross plays in their ongoing Christian experience. And to be sure, 95 percent of the instruction given by Paul as it regards the Cross, had to do with our Sanctification rather than our initial Salvation. But regrettably, most Christians don't know that. *"Faith comes by hearing, and hearing by the Word of God"* (Rom. 10:17). This means that if the Believer doesn't *"hear"* the Word of God taught and preached in this manner, and I speak of the Cross, there is no way they can have Faith in the Finished Work of Christ. And regrettably, most pulpits are

silent on this, the single most important subject of all! So, most Christians succumb to spiritual adultery by default. In other words, they simply don't know any better; nevertheless, that in no way lessens the wreckage.

HOW CAN SPIRITUAL ADULTERY BE CORRECTED?

First of all, the Christian needs to repent, not only of the sinful failures, but also of trusting in things other than the Cross. The idea is, if we trust in anything other than what Christ did at the Cross, we are sinning. That's why Paul said: *"Whatsoever is not of faith is sin"* (Rom. 14:23).

When Paul speaks of *"Faith,"* always and without exception, he is speaking of Faith in Christ and what Christ did at the Cross on our behalf. He never separates the two. It is always *"Jesus Christ and Him Crucified"* (I Cor. 1:23; 2:2).

Once the Believer places his Faith exclusively in Christ and what Christ did at the Cross, which means that he makes Christ and what Christ did the total object of his Faith, which also means, that he doesn't have faith in other things, at that moment, he ceases to be a spiritual adulterer. It is all a matter of *"faith,"* and more particularly, the correct object of our faith. That correct object must always be the Cross of Christ.

So when we speak of Repentance on the part of the Christian, it should be Repentance not only for the bad things that are done, but also we should repent of our trust in the good things we are doing. In fact, the latter is no doubt the greatest problem in Christendom. Trusting in the good things we do, means that we are not properly trusting Christ. We must repent of that, which means to cease doing what we're doing, and begin to do the right thing.

RIGHTEOUS ACTS AND RIGHTEOUSNESS

Many, if not most, Christians confuse *"righteous acts"* with *"Righteousness."* In other words, they think that because one does righteous acts, which to be certain every Christian ought to do, that this then means the person performing such acts is righteous. It doesn't!

In fact, in a strict sense of the word, *"righteous acts"* don't really have anything to do with *"Righteousness."*

"Righteous acts" is what we do, while *"Righteousness"* is what Jesus has done, or rather what Jesus actually is. Righteous acts cannot translate into Righteousness, simply because all Righteousness must come exclusively from Christ, and more particularly, what Christ did at the Cross. The Cross made it possible for Christ to give us of His spotless, pure, Righteousness, which we can receive by Faith only. And that's the key, *"faith"* and not *"works."*

Righteous acts, as good as they may be, and as much as every Christian ought to do these things, pure and simple are works. But not knowing and understanding the Cross, and I speak of the Cross as it concerns our Sanctification experience, almost all Christians revert to works. In fact, there is no other place to go. As we've already stated, it's either the Cross as it refers to Grace, or it is law as it refers to works. Those two positions are the only positions in which a Christian can place himself. And if one doesn't understand the Cross, one will automatically revert to law, i.e., *"works."*

One has to make a conscious decision to go to the Cross and to trust in what Jesus did there, but when it comes to law, that automatically happens without any decision on our part at all. The reason is this:

The Cross requires Faith on our part, while the law requires no faith at all.

FELLOWHELPERS

The phrase, *"That we might be fellowhelpers,"* proclaims the fact that God calls men and women for particular tasks regarding Ministry, but at the same time, He calls every Believer to help in this task, hence the Holy Spirit using the word *"fellowhelpers."*

As the one called is held responsible by God regarding the particular task in question, likewise, all Believers, in one way or the other, are held responsible regarding their help. This thing is so designed by the Lord that one cannot do without the other. The one *"sent"* by its very nature, must have *"senders."* As the one *"sent"* has no choice but to obey, at least if he wants to do the

NOTES

Will of God, likewise, the *"senders"* have no choice but to be a *"fellowhelper."* We are joint workers with those sent when we help support them.

A PERSONAL EXAMPLE

For instance, the Lord has told me to minister over Television and over Radio. In fact, He has given us a very unique Radio ministry, in that the Ministry owns the Radio Stations, which means that we broadcast 24 hours a day, 7 days a week. These Stations are scattered all over the United States, with more being installed almost on a weekly basis.

And yet, I cannot do these things, unless I have the support of the Body of Christ. Consequently, the *"fellowhelpers"* become very, very important!

Now as should be obvious, Satan will fight such an effort with all of his strength. He does it in a variety of ways. Many Believers function according to Denominations. In other words, if the Preacher in question is not a member of their particular Denomination, then they will not support him. This means that the Believers who subscribe to such direction, are not really following the Lord, but are rather being led by their Denominational leaders. Others refuse their support simply because of prejudice or bias, both based on rumor or gossip. As we've previously stated, the Word of God and nothing else, must ever be the criteria for all things.

Is the man preaching the Word? And is he doing so under the anointing of the Holy Spirit? That alone is the criteria. If that is the case, and we're certain that it is the case, then such a Preacher deserves our support.

THE TRUTH

The phrase, *"To the truth,"* means that no one should help support something that is not *"the Truth."* This cements exactly what I've been saying.

The facts are, only a few Preachers are actually preaching the truth. Such a ministry will see people saved, Believers baptized with the Holy Spirit, the sick truly healed, and lives gloriously changed by the Power of God.

Now almost every Preacher claims all of these things, but much of the time it's claims only. In other words, the *"fruit"* of what they claim cannot actually be found. The truth is, and I say this regrettably, most Christians are supporting Preachers who are not preaching the truth, which in essence means that the people are supporting nothing, which translates into nothing being done, or they are actually supporting that which is of the Devil. Listen to what Paul said:

"For such are false apostles, deceitful workers, transforming themselves into the Apostles of Christ.

"And no marvel; for Satan himself is transformed into an angel of light.

"Therefore it is no great thing if his ministers also be transformed as the ministers of righteousness; whose end shall be according to their works" (II Cor. 11:13-15).

"His ministers" can be translated "Satan's ministers." And yet these individuals, according to Paul, were claiming to be "apostles of Christ." In fact, they look like the Lord, sounded like the Lord, and of course claimed to be of the Lord. In effect, they were "angels of light," which actually means they were pretending to be something they were not.

Some of the Believers in the Church at Corinth were supporting these Preachers with their money and by other ways as well. Now let me ask the Reader this question:

Were these people actually supporting the Work of God? Well of course not! They were in effect, supporting the work of Satan. But they were deceived into believing otherwise.

And so are millions of modern Christians. They are supporting those who claim to be of God, but are in effect, "Satan's ministers." So this means that the support of such Christians going to these individuals is actually going to support the work of the Evil One. And let me say again, that's where many, if not most, Christians presently are. They think they're supporting the Work of God, when in reality, they are supporting the very opposite. If it's not the Truth, then it's not of God.

(9) "I WROTE UNTO THE CHURCH: BUT DIOTREPHES, WHO LOVETH TO HAVE THE PREEMINENCE AMONG THEM, RECEIVETH US NOT."

The structure is:

1. The reference is to a Letter that John had written to the local Church of which Gaius was a member. The verbiage suggests that the Apostle did not regard the communication as especially important.

2. "Diotrephes" is a Greek name that means "Zeus-nursed." Zeus was the chief of the gods of the Greek pantheon. The custom in the Early Church was for a Christian Greek to discard his pagan name and take a Christian name, which Diotrephes did not seem to do.

3. He was an ambitious leader and sympathizer with the Gnostics. He opposed John, with John warning Gaius against him.

THE CHURCH

The phrase, "I wrote unto the Church," speaks of a local Church, but of its location we aren't told. As we have stated, the Letter that John wrote, was not in the class of an Epistle, and probably had something to do with Preachers John was recommending.

Some claim that the Apostle is speaking of II John; however, even though that is possible, it is speculation at best.

There were problems in this local Church, and as always, they were caused by someone stepping outside of the Word of God, in this case, Diotrephes.

As always, Satan's greatest hindrance comes from within the Church.

The idea seems to be that the Letter, which John mentions, was sent to Diotrephes. That Letter is lost, perhaps destroyed by Diotrephes himself. Its contents are not, however, difficult to imagine. On the basis of what the Elder wrote Gaius, we can surmise that he had written the Church asking them to extend hospitality to certain traveling Preachers he had sent out. It may also have included a request for support that would speed them on their way. Diotrephes chose to thwart John's intention either by suppressing the Letter or publicly opposing the request before the congregation. It seems he also had threatened the expulsion of any in the Church who were considering offering hospitality to those who had been recommended by John. In fact, some may already have been forced out of the Church.

DIOTREPHES

The short phrase, "But Diotrephes," tells us something about this person even as it regards his name.

As stated, his name means, *"Zeus-nursed."* Considering that it was the custom for Christian Greeks to discard their pagan name and to take a Christian name, and considering that Diotrephes didn't do this, tells us something about this man's person. In other words, it speaks of rebellion in his spirit.

Some claim that his problem was not false doctrine, but rather a desire for preeminence as John will say; however, I think that is incorrect.

The Apostle stressed heavily the *"truth"* which was in Gaius, which means that Diotrephes was not abiding by the truth, which means that he was following false doctrine. It seems to have been the Gnostic problem.

During Paul's time, the great problem had been Judaism. As someone had well said, Christianity has its roots in Judaism, but Judaism almost became its grave as well! This consisted of Teachers from Jerusalem coming into the Churches which had been planted by Paul, and trying to mix Law with Grace, which occasioned much of Paul's teaching, as it regarded coming against this error.

Jerusalem was totally destroyed in A.D. 70 by the Romans, which meant that the Church was there destroyed as well. So, the Law/Grace issue was not nearly as volatile now as it had been in Paul's day. It had been cured by drastic circumstances. The problem now, and I speak of that which occasioned the Letters of John the Beloved, was the beginning stages of Gnosticism. It also was the beginning stages of man-directed Church Government, which ultimately evolved into the Catholic Church. In other words, the type of Government laid down in the Book of Acts and the Epistles by the Holy Spirit was little by little abandoned in favor of that instituted by man. It proved to be the ruin of the Church.

PREEMINENCE

The phrase, *"Who loveth to have the preeminence among them,"* concerns itself with a place and position in the Church which was not designed by the Holy Spirit. In other words, whatever position Diotrephes occupied in that particular Church was a position instituted of himself, and not the Lord. In other words, he gained this position by political means.

NOTES

"Preeminence" is made up of two Greek words, *"phileo,"* and *"protos."* They mean in succession, *"to be fond of,"* and *"to be fond of being first."* Smith says that the Church was disturbed by two problems, *"intellectual arrogance and personal aggrandizement."* To be sure, those two problems persist unto this hour.

"Intellectual arrogance" falls into the position of the *"wisdom of man,"* which means that the Wisdom of God has been rejected. As the First Chapter of I Corinthians describes this, it is *"the Cross of Christ being made of none effect."* Paul said:

"For Christ sent me not to baptize, but to preach the Gospel: not with wisdom of words, lest the Cross of Christ should be made of none effect" (I Cor. 1:17).

If men do not rely on the Cross, and rely on the Cross exclusively, they will every time resort to their own wisdom, which the Holy Spirit cannot abide.

The Holy Spirit through Paul plainly says: *"For after that in the Wisdom of God the world by wisdom* (human wisdom) *knew not God, it pleased God by the foolishness of preaching* (the Cross) *to save them who believe"* (I Cor. 1:21).

The foray of the modern Church into humanistic psychology is a prime example of *"intellectual arrogance."* In fact, one particular writer, who calls himself *"Pentecostal,"* who is as well a Psychologist, said in one of his books, that modern man was facing problems that are not dealt with in the Bible; consequently, he had to turn to psychology for help. This is a prime example of intellectual arrogance. What does the Bible say about this man's statement?

"According as His Divine Power hath given unto us all things that pertain unto life and Godliness, through the knowledge of Him that has called us to glory and virtue:

"Whereby are given unto us exceeding great and precious promises: that by these you might be partakers of the Divine nature, having escaped the corruption that is in the world through lust" (II Pet. 1:3-4).

Now either the Holy Spirit gave us *"all things that pertain unto life and Godliness,"* or else He didn't, which means that He lied. And if He lied, then we must turn to the likes of Freud, etc.

What does the Bible say about that question?

"Let God be true, but every man a liar" (Rom. 3:4).

Paul also said: *"Professing themselves to be wise, they became fools"* (Rom. 1:22).

Those who would say such things about the Bible, the Holy Spirit calls *"fools!"*

TO BE RECEIVED

The phrase, *"Receiveth us not,"* presents that which is always the case when false doctrine overtakes the Church. John of course, was of God, so there was no way that false doctrine was going to receive him.

During Paul's day, there is no record that anyone gained preeminence in the Church, at least in the Churches planted by Paul, who was in error, although they tried! But now, some 20 odd years later, we find that greater inroads have been made.

As we have previously stated, it is inconceivable that some in the Church at that time, wouldn't receive John. Here is the man who had walked and talked with Jesus, the man who had witnessed all, or at least most, of His miracles and healings, who at this time knew more about the Spirit of God than any human being alive, and yet some in the Church wouldn't receive him! Unthinkable! Unbelievable! But let us remember the following:

For those who would not receive John, at the same time, they wouldn't receive the Holy Spirit. It is no different presently. If the man or woman who is definitely of God is rejected, at the same time, God is also rejected. You cannot reject the Messenger of the Lord, without at the same time, rejecting the Lord.

(10) "WHEREFORE, IF I COME, I WILL REMEMBER HIS DEEDS WHICH HE DOES, PRATING AGAINST US WITH MALICIOUS WORDS: AND NOT CONTENT THEREWITH, NEITHER DOES HE HIMSELF RECEIVE THE BRETHREN, AND FORBIDS THEM WHO WOULD, AND CASTS THEM OUT OF THE CHURCH."

The composite is:

1. The words, *"If I come,"* presents the fact that the aged Apostle with his failing strength can only hope to undertake the journey.

2. If the Apostle is able to come to this particular Church, he will recite, he says, to the people, the things that Diotrephes has done against him.

3. Not content with undercutting John with pernicious words, Diotrephes refuses to accept the Preachers whom John has commended to the Church.

4. Concerning those who desired to welcome these Preachers sent by John, Diotrephes excommunicated them from the Church, thereby strengthening his hold.

IF I COME

The phrase, *"Wherefore, if I come,"* proclaims to us several things:

First of all, the Apostle by now was very aged. Considering that travel in those days was very difficult to say the least, it seems that he was not at all certain, due to his advanced age, if he could make the trip.

As well, the statement shows that he evidently, at this particular time in his ministry, traveled to many Churches as much as possible. To be sure, they needed his strong hand, and simply because Satan was ever trying to insert leaven into the purity of the Word of God.

How are we to explain the sharp words and drastic response on the part of the Apostle of love? Do they not represent a contradiction to his teaching? More probably they represent the response of one who sensed that the very nature of the Gospel was being threatened by such hypocritical conduct on the part of one of its Ministers. Diotrephes' actions against John were reprehensible by any standard; but they were even more so on the part of one who probably had once been the friend of John and had then walked true. But now his head had been swayed by false direction. For such a leader of the Church to give way to a false direction, added to by personal pique and selfish ambition was unthinkable.

EVIL DEEDS

The phrase, *"I will remember his deeds which he does, prating against us with malicious words,"* presents John writing this, we must remember, by the inspiration of the Holy Spirit. In other words, the Spirit of God not only allowed him to say these things, but also strongly impressed upon him to say these things.

"I will remember," could be translated *"I will remind."* It means that John, that is if he is able to come, will appear in the public assembly of the congregation and will there in public remind all the members what this man's works are. The members know John needs only to remind them.

What Diotrephes has been doing with his vicious tongue, John puts into bold relief: *"with wicked words prating against us,"* which means, *"to babble without sense, to spout or prate."* Nothing is too wickedly vicious for Diotrephes to hurl at us.

There is no evidence whatever that this is said in a vindictive or revengeful spirit, or that John spoke of it merely as a personal matter. If it had been a private and personal affair only, the matter might have been dropped, and never referred to again. But what had been done was public. Consequently, it pertained to the authority of the Apostle, and the duty of the Church, and the character of the Brethren who had been commended to them.

If the Letter was written, as is supposed by the aged John, and his authority had been utterly rejected by the influence of this one man, then it was proper that the authority should be asserted. If it was the duty of the Church to have received these men, who had been thus recommended to them, and it had been prevented from doing what it would otherwise have done, by the influence of one man, then it was proper that the influence of that man should be restrained, and that the Church should see that he was not to control it (Barnes).

OPPOSITION TO THE WORK OF GOD

The phrase, *"And not content therewith, neither does he himself receive the Brethren, and forbids them who would, and casts them out of the Church,"* proclaims this man doing four things:

1. He is running down John the Beloved.

2. He will not receive the Brethren whom John has sent to minister in the Church, and as well to be helped by the Church to go to other places in order to take the Gospel.

3. Not only will he not receive the Brethren, but he forbids anyone else in the Church to do so as well.

NOTES

4. Those who would side with John, he casts them out of the Church, or else seeks to do so.

Had Diotrephes thrown Gaius out of the Church? These present tenses say what Diotrephes is engaged in doing, they do not say that he accomplished his will in every case. Very likely, however, in most cases he succeeded in enforcing his demand that the rest also do so. In fact, he attained so much authority that John could send no Preachers to the congregation as such to be lodged with various members. We see this from the fact that John sends his Preachers directly to Gaius. It seems that Diotrephes had created so much trouble in the congregation that taking care of the Preachers on the part of the congregation was practically at an end.

As to the actual throwing out, this, I think, was probably no more than a vicious attempt. From the way in which II John reads, it is doubtful that Diotrephes had achieved the actual expulsions that he demanded. But his raging against the members who did not obey him, may well have caused them to stay away from the Church for the time being, totally interrupting the Work of God, which is what Satan intended.

Such contradiction to the Gospel by word and deed as done by Diotrephes could not be condoned, and indeed it was not. It was no longer Diotrephes who was on trial for his action but rather John and all those who believed like him. Silence on their part in the face of such total rejection of the Truth and the life of the Gospel would have been as hypocritical as Diotrephes' earlier action.

(11) "BELOVED, FOLLOW NOT THAT WHICH IS EVIL, BUT THAT WHICH IS GOOD. HE WHO DOES GOOD IS OF GOD: BUT HE WHO DOES EVIL HAS NOT SEEN GOD."

The exegesis is:

1. In effect, John is referring to Diotrephes as *"evil."*

2. At the same time, John is boldly stating that what he preaches is *"good,"* and, therefore, *"of God."*

3. Despite the claims of Diotrephes and those like him, he who opposes the True Gospel, is in effect *"doing evil,"* which means, despite their claims, they don't know God.

EVIL

The phrase, *"Beloved, follow not that which is evil,"* in effect says to Gaius, that he must not follow Diotrephes, because the man *"is evil."*

The intimation is that Diotrephes and his supporters had exerted intense pressure on Gaius to give up his support for John and the Gospel that John preached. In that event, Gaius would have no option but to take his stand on principle. To give in to pressure against one's convictions is to submit to evil. Whatever its source or whoever its advocates, evil can never be reconciled to God. Even to contemplate giving in to evil means that loyalty to God's revealed Will is jeopardized.

John has appealed to Gaius and others, not to *"imitate what is evil but what is good."* He does this, because it is the nature of God's Revelation that truth (vss. 1, 3), love (vs. 6), and Righteousness (vs. 11) have been modeled first in Jesus Christ and then by those who are faithful to His Commandments.

Humankind does not have in its nature a dependable standard by which to judge itself. It must always measure its understandings and actions by God Himself, for Whom love, truth, and Righteousness are absolute attributes. In Christ these same attributes have become available to all who love God and desire to obey His commands. To show them forth in our lives proves that we are *"from God."* All goodness proceeds from Him; our perseverance in goodness demonstrates that in Jesus Christ we have seen God (Barker).

GOOD

The phrase, *"But that which is good,"* presents the terms *"evil"* and *"good"* in a different light.

While the Apostle is definitely speaking of sin and sinful impulses, the greater thrust of *"evil"* and *"good"* as it is used here, has to do more so with *"truth"* than anything else. If it's not *"truth"* or *"the truth,"* which is the Gospel of Jesus Christ, which pertains to the price that He paid at the Cross, then whatever it is that's being presented, even as here with Diotrephes, is *"evil."* That which is the True Gospel, which in effect, is the Message of the Cross, is that which is *"good."* Satan would

get our eyes off the things that are the most important, and have us major in minors.

For instance, the Church will wink at false direction, which means opposition to the Cross, which is the worst sin that can be committed, and at the same time take a great stand against abortion. Don't misunderstand! The Church must take a strong stand against abortion, and such like sins, but its greater emphasis always must be that it proclaim the right Message. The reason for that should be obvious:

If we are not preaching the Truth, after awhile we're not going to be living the Truth. And if we preach the Truth, such preaching will help us to live the Truth.

THE CROSS

So that the Reader will have absolutely no problem understanding what I'm saying, I will say it in this manner:

If the Preacher is not preaching the Cross, and the Christian is not living the Cross, then whatever direction they are taking can be concluded as none other than *"evil."* Listen to what Paul said:

"For when we were in the flesh (trying to live for God by our own strength and ability), *the motions of sins, which were by the law* (the Law defined sin), *did work in our members to bring forth fruit unto death"* (Rom. 7:5).

The whole idea of this Passage is Paul trying to live for God without dependence on Christ and what Christ did at the Cross, but rather by his own strength. In other words, he was trying to keep the Law by his own strength, which was impossible. This is *"evil,"* but we little recognize it as such, and because our efforts are so religious. This took place immediately after he was saved, and before he was given the Revelation of the Cross.

That which is *"good,"* pertains to trusting solely in what Christ has done for us at the Cross (Lk. 9:23-24). Therefore, we can reduce *"good"* and *"evil"* to living by the *"Cross of our Lord Jesus Christ,"* or *"not living by the Cross of our Lord Jesus Christ."* We must *"follow"* that *"which is good."*

DOING GOOD

The phrase, *"He who does good is of God,"* proclaims the characteristic of God that the

Saint definitely will have, that is if he is truly a Saint. However, in the final analysis, we greatly shortchange the statement, if we limit this to good deeds only, etc.

The idea to its fullest extent as it regards the statement, pertains to our trust and faith in what Christ did at the Cross on our behalf, which God looks at as *"good."* If we limit this only to good deeds, far too often, *"self"* is lifted up, which the Lord can never abide. Only by one placing one's Faith exclusively in the Cross of Christ, can self be properly addressed, and Christ be properly glorified.

If the Believer properly understands the Cross, and thereby looks to the Cross, understanding that through this means God reveals Himself to us, that being done, and done on a perpetual basis, will always be followed by good deeds. But when the good deeds are carried out as a means of Righteousness or Holiness, which regrettably most of the Church presently does, the end result is the opposite of these things mentioned, in fact, self-righteousness.

THE DOING OF EVIL

The phrase, *"But he who does evil has not seen God,"* once again in the final analysis, refers to one trying to make one's way, by means other than the Cross. God looks at all such ways as *"evil,"* and even the *"doing of evil."* God can never be reached except by and through Jesus Christ, and what Jesus did at the Cross on our behalf. That's why Paul said, *"We preach Christ crucified"* (I Cor. 1:23). The *"doing of evil"* falls out into two directions:

1. In trying to gain victory, if the object of our faith is in anything other than the Cross, even *"good things,"* God looks at all such efforts as *"evil."* This means that one can turn prayer into that which is *"evil,"* or the giving of money, or many other goods things of this nature. In fact, such things certainly aren't within themselves evil. It is only placing our faith and trust in such which God constitutes as evil. That's why He said, *"Whatsoever is not of faith is sin"* (Rom. 14:23).

Concerning this, Paul also said: *"Was then that which is good made death unto me? God forbid. But sin, that it might appear sin, working death in me by that which is good . . ."* (Rom. 7:13).

2. If the Believer doesn't understand the Cross, and attempts to live this Christian life by means other than faith in the Finished Work of Christ, ultimately, wicked deeds will most definitely follow. It cannot be otherwise. And these things will happen, irrespective of the efforts of the Believer to do otherwise. Listen again to Paul:

"For that which I do I allow (understand) *not: for what I would* (I want to live righteously), *that do I not; but what I hate* (to fail the Lord), *that do I"* (Rom. 7:15).

THE PRINCIPLE OF GOOD AND EVIL

God does not work from the principle of good and evil, as we think of such, if He did, He wouldn't do anything at all. He works rather from the principle of Faith in His Son, and more particularly, what Jesus did at the Cross on our behalf.

But yet, most of the Church definitely does work on the principle of *"good and evil."* Does the Reader understand what I'm saying?

Most Christians judge their Christian experience by the *"good things"* they do, and the *"bad things"* they don't do. Now of course, those things are definitely important; however, that system is self-righteousness, which God can never honor.

As we've just stated, God functions entirely on the principle of Faith in Jesus Christ and Him Crucified (I Cor. 1:17-18; 2:2, 5). But it's very hard for most Christians to make the transition from the *"performance"* mode, to the *"Faith"* mode. And yet, most all Christians while functioning in the *"performance"* mode claim to be functioning in the *"Faith"* mode.

Most modern Christians do not at all understand the Old Testament Saints. They do not at all understand how Samson could be listed in the great Eleventh Chapter of Hebrews, in fact, listed with such great men as Abraham, Moses, and others. They don't understand how God could continue to use Moses, even after he killed a man, or David, after he committed the terrible sins of adultery and murder. In the thinking of most, how in the world could God use the sons of Jacob, who seemed to be anything but righteous, thereby naming the tribes of Israel after them, and far above that, inscribing their names on the twelve gates of the New Jerusalem? (Rev. 21:12).

The answer to all of this is simple, but yet which most Christians don't understand.

The Lord didn't judge these people by their performance, but rather by their faith. That doesn't mean that He overlooked their sins. Far from it! They suffered terribly for their wrongdoing, whatever it may have been; however, despite the failures, they didn't give up, they kept believing God. And it's Faith that God honors. As stated, He doesn't function from the principle of good and evil, but rather from the principle of faith.

It hasn't changed presently. God still functions from the same principle now as He did in Old Testament times. That's why Paul said: *"But without faith it is impossible to please Him: for He who comes to God must believe that He is, and that He is a rewarder of them who diligently seek Him"* (Heb. 11:6).

And as well, I must quickly add, the type of *"faith"* which the Old Testament worthies evidenced, was the same as our Faith now. Their Faith and trust was in Christ and Him crucified. Of course, they only saw that then in shadow. Their understanding was not near what ours is presently; nevertheless, Jesus Christ and Him crucified, was always the object of their Faith, as it must be the object of our Faith presently.

The object of one's faith actually began in the Garden of Eden, with God telling Satan through the serpent, that the seed of the woman would bruise his head (Satan's head). And then He said, *"You shall bruise His heel"* (Gen. 3:15). This last statement referred to the Cross. In outlined description, it was taken up in Genesis, Chapter 4 with the sacrificial system, with such system continuing until Christ came, Who was then offered up (Gal. 1:4).

(12) "DEMETRIUS HAS GOOD REPORT OF ALL MEN, AND OF THE TRUTH ITSELF: YES, AND WE ALSO BEAR RECORD; AND YOU KNOW THAT OUR RECORD IS TRUE."

The diagram is:

1. Demetrius was probably the bearer of this Letter to Gaius. He was a stranger to the members of the local Church of which Gaius was a member, and needed a word of commendation from the Apostle (Wuest).

2. John uses the perfect tense in his statement, which means that the testimony to the Christian character of Demetrius that was given in the past, stood at the same level at the time of the writing and sending of this Letter as it did when it was first spoken.

3. John says that this testimony comes from three sources, the community as a whole, the truth itself, and from John himself and his colleagues (Wuest).

DEMETRIUS

The phrase, *"Demetrius has good report of all men,"* gives us here all that we know of this man.

It would seem that Demetrius was the leader as it regards the Preachers who were sent by John, whom Gaius was to lodge and to send forward. The entire weighty endorsement of this man, the leader of the delegation that John is sending, is a part of the recommendation and the certification that John is sending along with and for those Preachers whom he sends, and thus goes with Verse 7.

Endorsing the leader in a special way in addition to endorsing the delegation as such (vs. 7) is entirely in place because so much depends on the leader. Paul does the same in II Corinthians 8:16-29 where he sends a delegation of two men, Titus being the leader, the other not being named. Paul recommends the latter but makes Titus chief and tells especially that Titus consented to come.

As a result, we have three men mentioned in this Third Epistle as written by John. They are *"Gaius," "Diotrephes,"* and *"Demetrius."* Two of these followed John, with one following false doctrine. How wonderful it was, to be placed in the column of *"truth,"* even as was Gaius and Demetrius. And how awful to be placed in the column of error, as was Diotrephes. Consequently, let us look at this short Epistle very carefully, because in the Books of Heaven, such is being written of us constantly, whether of the truth or whether of error.

TRUTH

The phrase, *"And of the truth itself,"* presents that which is extremely noteworthy.

Insistence on the Truth as the test for the last days in receiving, or not receiving

Preachers, is very remarkable. The question of authority to preach is not even hinted at. What was preached was the fundamental matter and question.

Further, it is instructed to observe that Gaius persevered in his independent action despite the condemnation of the Church and its erroneous government. The authority of the Preacher lay altogether in his fidelity to truth. This must never be forgotten! The Apostle pointed to no authority that sanctioned his mission, the absence of which would prove it to be false or unauthorized.

The Apostle himself had no other way to judge of the authority of these Preachers. There was, therefore, no other than the truth itself, for had there been any other authority it would have been vested in the Apostle. So he did not instruct Gaius or Demetrius to examine their papers but to test their doctrines. If they brought the truth they were to be received, if they did not bring the truth, the doors were to be closed against them (Williams).

Today, for all practical purposes, truth has fallen to the ground. It carries little or no weight in modern Church circles. Where the authority of the Preacher in John's day, lay altogether in his fidelity to truth, presently, such authority is in Denominational association, irrespective of what he preaches. This is the ruin of the Church!

THE PREACHER AND TRUTH

There is really only one thing that matters with the Preacher, and that is that he preach *"the Truth."* And what is the Truth?

As we've said repeatedly in this Volume, the Truth is that we preach *"Jesus Christ and Him Crucified"* (I Cor. 1:23). If that is not the undergirding foundation of all that we preach, then we're not preaching the truth. We may be preaching some of the truth, or part of the truth, but until we preach the Cross, we aren't preaching all the Truth.

Considering how little is presently known about the Cross, we must at the same time consider how little truth is actually being preached at present.

The modern Church world can pretty well be divided into three parts:

1. The old-line Denominations, for the most part, have totally and completely rejected the Holy Spirit, which means they are presently preaching much of nothing. There is an exception here and there, but not many.

2. The Pentecostal world for the most part, has abandoned the Cross in favor of humanistic psychology, which the old-line Denominations have done as well.

3. Many in the Charismatic world, openly repudiate the Cross, claiming that the Blood of Jesus availed for nothing, which can be construed as none other than rank blasphemy.

As stated, in all of this there definitely are exceptions. But for the most part what I've just stated holds true. So, if the Preacher preaches the Cross as he should, he will pretty well be blacklisted by these groups we have just mentioned, which refers to the greater majority of the modern Church world. Unfortunately, most Preachers aren't willing to pay such a price. But it is only the Preachers who truly preach the Cross, who will truly see something done for God, which translates into changed lives (I Cor. 1:17-18, 21, 23; 2:2, 5).

BELIEVERS AND THE TRUTH

It is my belief that the Holy Spirit is fastly making the Cross of Christ the dividing line between the True Church and the apostate church. In fact, the Cross has always been the dividing line, but the Holy Spirit, I believe, is going to make this line so obvious that every Believer is going to have to make a decision whether to make the Cross the object of their faith, or something else.

So the Believer is left with a choice. He can look for Preachers who preach the Cross, which means they are preaching the truth, which are the true credentials, or he can look for the Preacher who is sanctioned by the modern Church world. And to be sure, if the Preacher is sanctioned by institutionalized religion, there is a good chance he's not preaching the Cross.

THE RECORD

The phrase, *"Yes, and we also bear record; and you know that our record is true,"* refers to the recommendation of John and his colleagues, as it regarded Demetrius.

We may ask why John felt that he must endorse the leader of his delegation in so strong a manner?

When a delegation arrives from afar in a place where there is serious trouble as there is here, when the leader of this delegation also bears a special letter to the congregation, which he will either read to the congregation or will place into the hands of one who certainly will read it, everything depends on this leader. John would make Gaius feel easy on this score. Gaius may trust Demetrius completely, he need not worry in the least, need not himself take any steps about the Letter to the congregation. John has sent the right man (Lenski).

(13) "I HAD MANY THINGS TO WRITE, BUT I WILL NOT WITH INK AND PEN WRITE UNTO YOU:"

The structure is:

1. John ends this letter in much the same way he ended his Second Epistle.

2. As would be obvious, the Apostle has much information to give to Gaius, but would not try to say these things in the form of a letter, but would hope to shortly say them to Gaius in person.

3. We must conclude that whatever these things were, the Holy Spirit did not want them to be now said.

MANY THINGS TO WRITE

The phrase, *"I had many things to write,"* probably tells us that John had seriously considered writing much more, but felt led of the Lord not to do so. Of course, in reading this, we wish that he had continued. But yet, the Holy Spirit knows best.

We must understand that every single Book or Epistle in the Bible is inspired by the Holy Spirit. This means they are error free, and it means that every word is of the Lord, meaning that it was given by the Lord.

The inspiration of the Word of God simply means that the Holy Spirit literally searched through the vocabularies of the writers in question, and thereby selected each word regarding that which He wanted said. To be sure, He used the personalities and educational backgrounds of each individual; however, it was He, the Holy Spirit, Who directed all things that were written. That's why Peter said:

"For the prophecy came not in old time by the will of man: but holy men of God spoke as they were moved by the Holy Spirit" (II Pet. 1:21).

INK AND PEN

The phrase, *"But I will not with ink and pen write unto you,"* refers to the *"many things"* of the opening phrase. Evidently, the Apostle felt that it would take too long to put all of his thoughts on paper concerning whatever situations were in mind, so he decides to say no more. As stated, evidently this is all the Holy Spirit wanted him to write, at least at this time. It is believed that about five or six years later, he wrote the Book of Revelation while on the Island of Patmos.

(14) "BUT I TRUST I SHALL SHORTLY SEE YOU, AND WE SHALL SPEAK FACE TO FACE. PEACE BE TO YOU. OUR FRIENDS SALUTE YOU. GREET THE FRIENDS BY NAME."

The exegesis is:

1. John planned to visit this particular Church shortly.

2. He would then deal with Gaius as it regarded particular problems in the Church.

3. John, like a true shepherd of God's flock, it seems, knew them all by name. So this means that the Church evidently was small.

A PERSONAL VISIT

The phrase, *"But I trust I shall shortly see you, and we shall speak face to face,"* presents a possible visit, of which we have no record. In other words, we do not know if John was able to visit this Church or not. Without a doubt, the aged Apostle was trying his best to visit as many Churches during that particular time as possible. And to be sure, his visit to any Church proved to be a spiritual boon to that Church, as should be obvious.

From the things he wrote, it seems beyond doubt that his chief concern was that *"the Truth"* be preached, proclaimed, and upheld. As possibly no other man, at least at that particular time, he saw the danger of false doctrine, and how that Satan was doing his best to compromise the Message. As usual, he was attempting to do so from inside the Church.

PEACE

The phrase, *"Peace be to you,"* is as is obvious, a benediction; however, in the full scope of what the Apostle is saying, he is speaking of *"sanctifying Peace."*

Such Peace can only come as one places one's faith totally and completely in the Finished Work of Christ, understanding that it was all done at the Cross. It is Faith, but it's Faith in the correct thing, that being the Sacrifice of Christ.

Such provides a Peace that passes all understanding. This Peace is the greatest antidote for stress, worry, anxiety, fear, etc.

FRIENDS

The phrase, *"Our friends salute you. Greet the friends by name,"* presents those, both with John and those with Gaius, who were loyal to the Truth. Otherwise, and as should be obvious, they wouldn't be a friend.

"I'm pressing on the upward way,
"New heights I'm gaining every day;
"Still praying as onward bound,
"'Lord, plant my feet on higher
    ground'."

"I want to live above the world,
"Though Satan's darts at me are
    hurled;
"For faith has caught the joyful sound,
"The song of Saints on higher ground."

"I want to scale the utmost height,
"And catch a gleam of glory bright;
"But still I'll pray 'til Heaven I've
    found,
"'Lord, lead me on to higher ground'."

NOTES

THE
BOOK OF JUDE

―■―

THE GENERAL EPISTLE OF JUDE

Jude along with James, the Senior Pastor of the Church in Jerusalem, was a brother of our Lord and Saviour, Jesus Christ. Actually, the record tells us that Jesus had four brothers, *"James, Joseph, Simon, and Jude."* He also had several sisters, exactly how many we aren't told (Mat. 13:55-56). In essence, these would be called half-brothers and half-sisters of our Lord. Christ's Brethren did not believe on Him until after the Resurrection (Jn. 7:5). This must have hurt our Lord deeply!

"Jude" is an English form of *"Judas,"* the Greek form of *"Judah,"* the name of Jacob's fourth son, founder of the Tribe of Judah. Due to the perfidiousness of Judas Iscariot practically all major English versions use the form *"Jude"* rather than *"Judas."*

The First Verse identifies the author of this Letter as *"Jude, a servant of Jesus Christ and a brother of James."* The only James who is well enough known to the Early Church that the unspecified use of his name would be generally recognizable was James of Jerusalem. Paul called him *"James, the Lord's Brother"* (Gal. 1:19). Later, according to Hegesippus, he became known as *"James the Just."*

All of this means that Jude was the brother of the Senior Pastor of the Jerusalem Church (Acts 12:17; 15:13; 21:18; I Cor. 15:7; Gal. 1:19; 2:9, 12) and the half-brother of Jesus of Nazareth (Mat. 13:55; Mk. 6:3). As we have stated, Jude did not believe in the Messiahship of Jesus until after the Resurrection. This probably explains the humility with which Jude introduces himself as a servant (slave) of the Brother (now recognized as the Messiah) he had denied.

THE HUMILITY OF JUDE

In a story that comes from Hegesippus and is related by Eusevius, this trait of humility was as well, shown by the grandsons of Jude, *"said to have been the Lord's Brother according to the flesh."*

The story tells how the grandsons were brought before Domitian, the Roman Emperor (A.D. 81-96), and accused of belonging to the royal house of David. The Emperor questioned them about the Christ and His Kingdom, and they explained that it was a Heavenly Kingdom that would come at the end of the age. So the Emperor dismissed them as simple peasants with no royal pretensions.

Irrespective of their appearance before Caesar, this tells us, that the grandsons of Jude were continuing to bear the Name of Jesus with pride, which means that they were grandly serving Him.

THE PURPOSE OF THIS EPISTLE

The Book of Jude has been called *"the most neglected Book in the New Testament."* There may be various reasons for its neglect, yet Christians and the Church today need to listen to Jude's contribution to Biblical Revelation. The emphasis on a *"fixed"* core of truth known as *"the Faith"* needs to be pondered. Jesus is God's Word to man (Rom. 6:17; Heb. 1:1-4). *"God is light; in Him there is no darkness"* (I Jn. 1:5) presents John's summary of the Revelation of God in Jesus. Consequently, we learn from these witnesses that God is Righteous and True and that He hates sin and error, which should be obvious!

Jude warns us of the dangers in the mixture of error with Truth. We had best soberly heed his warning.

While it may be granted that some Christians have been and are still intolerantly dogmatic about relatively minor theological issues, there is also the great danger of accepting uncritically all teaching or positions as being valid and thus compromising God's once-and-for-all self-disclosure in Jesus. In other words, *"Jesus Christ and Him Crucified"* must ever be the Message, and its purity must not be diluted.

JUDE AND THE SECOND
CHAPTER OF II PETER

One of the most remarkable things respecting this Epistle, is its resemblance to the Second Chapter of the Second Epistle of Peter — a similarity so striking as to make it quite certain that one of these writers had seen the Epistle of the other, and copied from it, or else the Holy Spirit inspired both of them to say the same thing.

It is most probable that Jude wrote his Epistle after Peter wrote his Second Epistle, and there is no doubt that Jude, if in fact that was the case, read that written by Peter. I cannot imagine otherwise; however, this in no way means that the Holy Spirit didn't inspire what Jude said. Whenever the Spirit says something once, it is of course, of extreme significance; however, when He says it twice, which He is prone to do at times, then it is significant to a greater degree than ever.

Both the Second Chapter of II Peter and the one Chapter of Jude, deal with false prophets and false doctrine, no doubt the most serious problem which plagues the Church. Considering that, it should not be uncommon at all for the Holy Spirit to repeat these warnings. The question should not be as to why He did such, that in fact, should be obvious. The question should be as to how we can more perfectly heed what is being said.

In reading other Commentary writers' introductions to Jude, paragraph after paragraph is spent on the *"why"* of the similarity between these two Chapters; consequently, the real purpose of the writing of Jude is then lost.

THE LAST DAYS

The apostasy of the last days prior to the Coming of the Lord will be, as predicted in the New Testament, both doctrinal and moral. This Epistle develops the history of that apostasy, and reveals its root — both doctrinal and moral — in the self-will of Cain. His followers, like himself, doctrinally went out from the presence of Jehovah (Gen. 4:16; I Jn. 2:19), and then crept back into the visible Church, like Lamech (Gen. 4:19-24), returned to corrupt it morally.

The Epistle foretells that there will be no arrest to these double apostasies, and it predicts their continuance up to the appearing in judgment of the Lord Jesus with the Angels of His might (II Thess., Chpt. 1). This prophecy in fact, conflicts with the belief that Christendom will be recovered from its present corruption; that the Gospel will conquer and purify the nations; that God's moral government will be established thereby in the Earth; that is what is meant by the Coming of the Lord; and that His Personal visible return is not a doctrine of the Scriptures.

II Peter and this Epistle envisage the same period of time — the former views its sin; the latter, its apostasy. Both Epistles trace these doctrinal and moral rebellions to their root in the self-will of man.

"I've tried in vain a thousand ways,
"My fears to quell, my hopes to raise;
"But what I need, the Bible says,
"Is ever, only Jesus."

"My soul is night, my heart is steel — I
*   cannot see,*
"I cannot feel; for light, for life I must
*   appeal*
"To simple Faith in Jesus."

"He died, He lives, He reigns, He pleads;
"There's love in all His words and
*   deeds;*
"There's all a guilty sinner needs
"Forever more in Jesus."

"Tho' some should sneer, and some
*   should blame,*
"I'll go with all my guilt and shame;
"I'll go to Him because His Name,
"Above all names, is Jesus."

(1) "JUDE, THE SERVANT OF JESUS CHRIST, AND BROTHER OF JAMES, TO THEM THAT ARE SANCTIFIED BY GOD THE FATHER, AND PRESERVED IN JESUS CHRIST, AND CALLED:"

JUDE

It is certain that Jude was the half-brother of the Lord Jesus Christ. But yet we know so little about him. He is mentioned in Matthew 13:55, Mark 6:3, and of course at the beginning of the short Epistle which bears his name. And yet from the silence we learn some things.

John 7:5 emphatically states: *"For neither did His Brethren believe in Him."* This includes Jude, and speaks volumes.

What is it that they didn't believe?

Despite living with Christ on a one-to-one basis, they didn't believe at this particular time, that He was the Messiah of Israel, the Son of God, the fulfillment of the prophecies, God manifest in the flesh. But I guess the question must be asked as to *why* the Brothers of Christ didn't believe in Him?

WHY?

Through the entirety of His childhood, into His teenage, formative years, in fact all of His life, Christ was totally and completely sinless. This means He was sinless in word, thought, and deed. Such to us is absolutely incomprehensible.

It is impossible for the balance of humanity to even remotely comprehend perfection. There being no such spirit of sinless attitude among humanity, we have nothing relative by which to form an opinion, or come to a conclusion. In other words, we do not even remotely know what perfection actually is. Such has only been registered one time in history, at least as far as man is concerned, and that, as stated, was in Christ. But there is one thing we do know:

Man has a sin nature, which Christ didn't have. This sin nature has a constant bent toward iniquity, and in every shape and form. As well, it has an animosity toward anything that is righteous. This is the detriment of the sin nature, and is incumbent in every human being who doesn't know the Lord.

Understanding this, I suppose we have answered our own question. The unrighteousness that incorporated itself in the hearts and lives of the Brethren of Christ, opposed the Perfect Righteousness that was in Christ, and in fact, which was Christ.

That explains it, but at the same time, doesn't explain it! Others accepted Christ, even though they were plagued with the same problem of the *"sin nature."*

Quite possibly, the flesh and blood brothers of Christ (one might say) had grandiose ideas as to Who and What the Messiah would be. Despite His perfection, Jesus was a peasant. As such, there was absolutely nothing there which spoke of royalty.

But yet, they knew full well and understood that had the Davidic dynasty continued, that their father Joseph would now be king of Israel. They knew that Joseph went all the way back to David through Solomon, and that their mother Mary went back to David through another son of David, Nathan. Consequently, the genealogy was perfect. As well, all of this could be easily checked in the Temple, where genealogies of every family in Israel were kept.

I have no doubt also that Mary related to her family, no doubt time and time again, the visit of the great Angel Gabriel to her, in order to announce the conception of Christ. She knew the prophecies by heart, *"Thou shall call His Name JESUS: for He shall save His people from their sins"* (Mat. 1:21).

But until He was 30 years of age, the Son of God worked as a carpenter, i.e., *"the carpenter's son."* Tradition says that he made plow yokes; consequently, He could be seen at any time plying His trade, although honest, but yet menial. So in Christ, despite His perfection in personality, nature, demeanor, attitude, and spirit, He was still a peasant. The perspiration streamed from His face, as He swung the ax to the tree; therefore, they couldn't see His Deity for the humanity.

THE BEGINNING OF HIS MINISTRY

Quite possibly what we have just attempted to explain could be in some measure understandable; however, when He began His Ministry at 30 years of age, which incidentally was the age that a Levite could begin his

Priesthood under the Mosaic Law, from then on there was no excuse, if in fact, there had ever been one. (While Jesus was not of the Tribe of Levi, but rather of the Tribe of Judah, He was not in the strict sense of the word, a Priest. But yet, He in fact, would be after the Cross, our Great High Priest. In fact, Christ filled all roles of Prophet, Priest, and King.)

After the Spirit came upon Him regarding the beginning of His Ministry, He began to perform miracles of such astounding proportions as to defy all description. In fact, there has never been anything even remotely like Christ in the annals of human history. Quite possibly, He performed thousands of miracles, all the way from the opening of blinded eyes, to the raising of the dead. But yet, it was during this particular time that the Scripture plainly says that His Brethren didn't believe in Him (Jn. 7:5).

WHEN DID JUDE ACCEPT CHRIST?

We aren't told! Quite possibly it was at the time when Christ after His Resurrection appeared to James, the oldest after Christ (I Cor. 15:7). Whatever happened at that appearance we aren't told, but James became an ardent follower of Christ immediately thereafter. Quite possibly, Jude did as well! Beyond that, we have no knowledge, except that he definitely accepted Christ at some point in time, which was almost certain after the Resurrection.

THE SLAVE

The phrase, *"The servant of Jesus Christ,"* could have been translated, *"the slave of Jesus Christ,"* because *"servant"* in the Greek is *"doulos,"* and means *"a bond slave."* Vincent says: *"He does not call himself an Apostle, as Paul and Peter in their introductions, and seems to distinguish himself from the Apostles in Verses 17 and 18."*

It is my personal belief that Jude was an Apostle. I think he would have to be to have his short Epistle included by the Holy Spirit in the Canon of Scripture. The fact that he didn't designate himself as such, in effect means nothing. It's what the Holy Spirit intended that counts.

It is my personal opinion that Jude along with James, didn't refer to themselves as

Apostles, simply because they didn't feel worthy to do such. As we have stated, they had not believed in Christ during His earthly Ministry, and no doubt, this was ever a source of grief for them. Irrespective, Paul referred to *"James the Lord's Brother,"* as an Apostle (Gal. 1:19). Jude, I think, would have to be included as well!

It is, I think, easy to understand the feelings of Jude, in that he was much more comfortable in addressing himself as *"the slave of Jesus Christ."*

JAMES

The phrase, *"And Brother of James,"* is said in this manner I think, because James was the better known of the two. Being the Senior Pastor of the great Church in Jerusalem, most everyone in Christendom at that time, knew who James actually was.

While Jude identified himself as the brother of James, and we speak of the physical sense, he does not identify himself as the brother of Christ, even as James didn't as well, and we think for the reasons we have given. He rather refers to himself as the slave of Jesus Christ, even as did both Paul and Peter. This means *"one whose will is wholly that of his Divine Lord."* As such a slave, Jude addresses his readers who will be glad to hear what such a man has to say, especially considering that he was the actual half-brother of the Lord, which most all Believers then knew.

It is sometimes said that Jude does not intend to identify himself by this reference to his brother. But he does certainly thereby identify himself; if it were not for this apposition, we could not know just which *"Jude"* is writing, considering that this name was quite common at that particular time.

The real question is: Did *"brother,"* on the other hand, of *"James"* intend to convey more?

The opinion that this type of statement is a roundabout way of calling himself *"a brother of the Lord"* since James was known as such a brother (Gal. 1:19), does not commend itself in view of Acts 1:14 and I Corinthians 9:5 where the plural is used.

And yet, quite possibly, when Jude wrote this short note, his brother James had just been executed. (It is believed that James was killed in Jerusalem at Passover in 66.) If that in fact was the case, Jude it is believed, is stepping in where his brother James might otherwise have done so.

Does this make the readers Jewish Christians?

While of course, Jewish Christians would definitely read this Epistle, due to the prophetic nature of Jude, it does not stand to reason whatsoever that the Brother of our Lord was writing mainly to Jews. He was writing in fact, to the entirety of the Church, which of course, included both Jews and Gentiles.

Going back to the person of Jude, and the incident of his two grandsons appearing before the Roman Caesar and enlarging upon that illustration already given, we note the following:

THE FAMILY OF JUDE

We know that he was married, not merely from the general statement made by Paul respecting the Brethren of the Lord (I Cor. 9:5), but from the interesting story told by Hegesippus, and preserved by Eusevius, that two grandsons of Jude were taken before Domitian as being of the royal family of David and, therefore, it was thought, dangerous to his rule. *"For,"* says Hegesippus, *"he was afraid of the appearance of the Christ, as Herod was."*

In answer to his questions, they stated that they were indeed of the family of David, but they were poor and humble persons, who supported themselves by their own labor; in proof of which they showed their calloused hands.

When further questioned respecting the Christ and His Kingdom, they said that it was not earthly, but Heavenly, and would arise at the end of the age, when He came to judge the living and the dead. Whereupon Domitian contemptuously dismissed them as too simple to be dangerous, and ordered that the persecution of the descendants of David should cease.

These two men were afterwards honored in the Churches, both as strong confessors of Christ and as being near of kin to the Lord. It is also said that their names were Zocer and James.

LOVE

The phrase, *"To them that are sanctified by God the Father,"* should have been translated, *"To them who are loved by God the Father."* The major Texts have *"agapao,"* which means, *"to love,"* instead of *"hagiazo,"* which means, *"to sanctify."* The Greek terminology speaks of a past complete act having present results.

The distinctive word for *"love"* here is the word for God's Self-sacrificial love that was shown at Calvary. This love here is the outgoing of God's love for the Saints in which He gives of Himself for our good. He will do anything within His good will for the Saints.

He went all the way to Calvary for us when we were unlovely and naturally unlovable. He will do as much and more for His Saints who in Christ are looked upon by God the Father with all the love with which He loves His Son. The original Greek Text speaks here of the fact that the Saints are the permanent objects of God's love.

Jude is, therefore, writing to those who have been loved by God the Father with the present result that we are in a state of being the objects of His permanent love, and that love extends not merely through the brief span of this life, but throughout eternity (Wuest).

PRESERVED

The phrase, *"And preserved in Jesus Christ,"* in effect says, *"God the Father is keeping the Saints guarded for Jesus Christ."* Our Lord prayed (Jn. 17:11), *"Holy Father, keep (preserve) through Your Own Name those whom You have given Me, that they may be one as We are."* Our Lord committed the Saints into the watchful care of God the Father, and the Father is keeping us for Jesus Christ, not in the sense that the Father is keeping the Saints in lieu of His Son keeping us, but in the sense that the Father is keeping us so that we might continue to be forever the possession of the Lord Jesus (Wuest).

The idea is, the Grace of God keeps us, and were it not for the Grace of God, we simply could not be kept, i.e., *"preserved."*

HOW ARE WE KEPT?

Knowing that this is done is one thing, but knowing how it is done is something else altogether.

Unfortunately, most Christians upon reading this, would simply think that what is being said here, is simply an automatic situation, which takes place simply because the person is a Christian. That isn't correct!

The shores of Christianity are littered with the wrecks of those who once knew Christ, but now no longer even make any attempt to live for Him. In other words, even as Paul said, they have *"made shipwreck of their faith"* (I Tim. 1:19).

Other millions of Christians, while continuing to attempt to live for God, find themselves in the position which Paul mentioned, *"for that which I do I allow not* (understand not)*: for what I would, that do I not; but what I hate, that do I"* (Rom. 7:15). In fact, most of Christendom is actually living in a state of *"spiritual adultery"* (Rom. 7:3-4).

Are all of these people being kept? And if they aren't being kept, why not?

First of all let us establish the fact that the *"keeping"* is not automatic. Romans, Chapter 7 graphically bears that out, plus the entirety of the Epistle to the Galatians. Paul said there: *"Christ is become of no effect unto you, whosoever of you are justified by the Law* (try to be justified by the Law)*; you are fallen from Grace"* (Gal. 5:4).

God has one prescribed order of victory, which guarantees the keeping of the Saints. If the Believer subscribes to that order, most definitely the Believer will be kept (Gal. 2:20). If the Believer doesn't subscribe to that prescribed order, he will find himself *"frustrating the Grace of God,"* which will wreak havoc in his life (Gal. 2:21).

GOD'S PRESCRIBED ORDER OF VICTORY

For God to preserve the Saint, in other words, to keep His Grace flowing to the Saint, which we all must have, that is if we are to live a victorious, overcoming life, the Believer must understand and subscribe to the following:

THE CROSS

Everything comes from God to the Believer through the Cross: in other words, the Cross is the means by which all the great things of God are given to the Believer. The Cross makes everything possible.

NOTES

The actual meaning of the Cross is *"A Sacrifice which happened in the distant past, and was so effective it will never have to be repeated, and has continuing results, which continue up unto this very hour, and in fact, will never be discontinued."* It is the results of the Cross, or all the things that the Cross made possible, which gives us what we need. As a result, the emphasis must be always on the Cross. Paul said:

"For Christ sent me not to baptize, but to preach the Gospel: not with wisdom of words, lest the Cross of Christ should be made of none effect" (I Cor. 1:17).

He also told us exactly how the great change was brought about in our lives as a result of the Cross. He said:

"Know ye not, that so many of us as were baptized into Jesus Christ (the Crucifixion of Christ, not Water Baptism) *were baptized into His death?*

"Therefore we are buried with Him by Baptism into death: that like as Christ was raised up from the dead by the Glory of the Father, even so we also should walk in newness of life.

"For if we have been planted together in the likeness of His death, we shall be also in the likeness of His Resurrection" (Rom. 6:3-5).

This Passage tells us that when we accepted Christ, whenever that was, and I speak of our initially being *"born again,"* that as far as God was concerned, we actually died with Christ, were buried with Him, which means all of our old, past life was buried with Him, and then raised with Him in newness of life, which refers to His Resurrection.

The problem of sin was so awful, so bad, so horrible, that in effect, the Lord has to start over with each and every individual. In other words, in a spiritual sense, that person has to die, which is what the Cross of Christ was all about. Of course, we were not there when Jesus died, and it would not have done us any good had we been there. That's not the idea.

The idea is, Jesus died as our Substitute and our identification with Him grants us all that He did. He actually died as our Representative Man. Simple faith in Him and what He did for us at the Cross, grants us all of this in the Mind of God. Upon Faith in His death, burial, and resurrection, we become *"new creations in Christ Jesus, with old things passing away, and all things becoming new"* (II Cor. 5:17).

The Cross and the Cross alone, is what removed the barrier of sin, thereby making it possible for sinners to be cleansed, and actually to come into the very Presence of God (Heb. 9:12).

THE OBJECT OF OUR FAITH

Understanding that everything comes to us through the Cross, the object of our faith must always be the Cross of Christ. This is very, very important! In fact, this is where most of the Church goes wrong.

Most Christians understand the Cross at least somewhat, as it refers to their initial Salvation experience. But beyond that, they don't have the faintest clue as to the part the Cross plays in our ongoing Christian experience. On that, they draw a blank!

As a result, they place their faith in something else. And it really doesn't matter what else it might be, or how good it might be in its own right, faith placed in anything other than the Cross of Christ, will not bring the desired results as it regards a victorious, overcoming, Christian life. Now let the Reader understand:

We're speaking here of living victorious over the world, the flesh, and the Devil. We're speaking here of the Fruit of the Spirit being developed within our hearts and lives, in other words, us becoming more and more Christlike. We're speaking here of Righteousness and Holiness. All of these things pertain to victory over sin. And let the Reader also understand there is only one Sacrifice for sin, and that is the Cross of Christ (Heb. 10:12).

If we put our faith in our Church, a particular Preacher, or a Denomination, while those things may or may not be good in their own right, that's not what died on the Cross for you. So, such faith can only be construed as misplaced faith. In other words, faith placed in those things means that it's not in the correct object. Let's look at faith a little closer:

Christians have been taught in the last several decades that if they can just increase their faith level they can do anything, etc. In other

words, the key to receiving from the Lord, they have been taught, is to increase the Faith level. Consequently, in order to try to do this, they are taught to select particular Scriptures which they think pertain to their situation, whatever their situation might be, memorize those Scriptures, and then quote them over and over again, which is supposed to somehow bring God into action. This error is not much different than witchcraft.

While it's always good to memorize the Scriptures, and it's always good to quote them, doing it in this fashion, however, which means our Faith is placed in ourselves, will never bring the desired results. In fact, I think I can say without any fear of Scriptural contradiction, that such efforts done in that particular way, greatly displeases the Lord. And the reason it does, is because it's not really faith that's being practiced, but rather *"the flesh"* (Rom. 8:8).

Satan doesn't really care too very much where you place your faith, just as long as it's not in the Cross of Christ. In fact, he fights the Cross as he fights nothing else. That within itself should give us a clue as to where the real victory is. What did Paul say?

"But God forbid that I should glory (boast), *save in the Cross of our Lord Jesus Christ, by Whom the word is crucified unto me, and I unto the world"* (Gal. 6:14).

It's not enough to just have faith. In fact, every single person in the world has faith. Even those who claim they don't, actually have faith in the very fact that they don't have faith. But all of this faith of which we speak, God will not honor. Even the faith of Christians placed in something other than the Cross, God will not honor.

So the problem of the Christian is not really in having faith, for all Christians have faith (Rom. 12:3). The idea is that you have the correct object of faith, which is the Sacrifice of Christ (Rom. 6:3-14; I Cor. 1:17-18, 21, 23).

THE HOLY SPIRIT

Everything the Saint needs from God is done exclusively by the Holy Spirit. As well, He works exclusively according to what Christ did at the Cross; consequently, He demands that we have Faith in the Finished Work of Christ, which in effect, gives Him the

NOTES

legal right to do all the things for us that we need (Rom. 8:2). Listen to what the Lord said about this:

"Not by might (human might), *nor by power* (human power), *but by My Spirit, saith the LORD of Hosts"* (Zech. 4:6).

We are here plainly told that what needs to be done in our lives, we cannot do. Only the Holy Spirit can do it, and He works exclusively within the parameters of the Sacrifice of Christ. The idea is this:

If you want the Holy Spirit to work on your behalf as it regards victory over sin, and all the powers of darkness, then your faith must be in the Sacrifice of Christ, exclusively through which the Spirit works. It is just that simple!

We have Christians doing all types of things trying to bring about victory, and I speak of things outside of faith in the Cross of Christ, and they wonder why the Holy Spirit isn't helping them. Let me venture this scenario:

At this very moment as you read these words, there are millions of Christians who are being overcome by the powers of darkness, despite all of their efforts not to be, and they are wondering why the Holy Spirit doesn't help them?

To be sure, He wants to help. That's the very reason He is in our hearts and lives. Jesus referred to Him as *"the Comforter,"* which means *"helper"* (Jn. 14:16). But He will give us this help only on the premise of what Christ did at the Cross, and our Faith in that Finished Work (Rom. 8:1-2, 11, 13).

TRUST IN CHRIST

Almost every Christian I suppose, claims to trust Christ. If you question them for just a few moments, they will quickly reiterate that their trust is in Christ, etc.

My statements here are not meant to impugn such Christians, for without a doubt, they are sincere; however, most only think they are trusting Christ, when in reality they aren't.

If you were to ask them what they mean by the statement *"trust in Christ,"* most would just look at you somewhat blank. They would say something like, *"I believe His Word,"* or something to that effect.

While that is not an incorrect answer, at the same time it's not correct.

For one to correctly trust Christ, one must trust exclusively in what He did for us at the Cross. That trust must pertain to our initial Salvation experience, as well as our ongoing, Christian experience. Concerning the latter, of that, most Christians don't have the slightest knowledge. Consequently, they aren't trusting Christ in that respect, and in fact, they cannot trust in something of which they have no knowledge. And when it comes to understanding the Cross as it pertains to our everyday living, most Christians have little or no knowledge of that part of the Finished Work of Christ; consequently, when they claim to be trusting Christ, most really don't know what they're talking about. As a result, despite loving the Lord, they live lives of spiritual failure. In other words, in some way the works of the flesh manifest themselves within such lives (Gal. 5:19-21).

ANOTHER JESUS

In II Corinthians Paul spoke of *"another Jesus,"* *"another spirit,"* and *"another gospel."* What did he mean by that?

In simple terms, if it's not *"Jesus Christ and Him Crucified,"* pure and simple, what is being preached, and who is being preached, is *"another Jesus."* This will always cause people to *"receive another spirit,"* which is not the Holy Spirit, but rather spirits of darkness. All of this falls out to *"another gospel,"* which means that it's not the Gospel of Jesus Christ, although it proposes to be that particular Gospel.

In fact, and I think I can say without fear of exaggeration, most Preachers are in reality preaching *"another Jesus."* This means they aren't preaching the Cross, which means their emphasis is on Jesus in some other capacity. The Holy Spirit will never honor such preaching, and will never be a part of such proclamation. The Message without exception must be, *"Jesus Christ and Him Crucified"* (I Cor. 1:23; 2:2).

Let's be plain, even blunt, so that no one will have any problem understanding what we're saying:

If the Preacher is not preaching the Cross (I Cor. 1:21), then pure and simple, he is proclaiming *"another Jesus."*

As a result, people will not be saved under such a ministry, will not be baptized with the Holy Spirit, will not be truly healed, will not be delivered, in fact, no lives will be changed.

That's the reason that the far greater majority of the message preached in the *"Word of Faith"* camp, specializes in *"money."* That particular message will not get anyone saved, will not see anyone baptized with the Holy Spirit, and will not see lives changed. It is pure and simple, *"another Jesus"* which is being preached in that particular doctrine. It cannot be thought of in any other manner, at least if we hope to be Scriptural.

The same can be said for humanistic psychology. The Church Denominations and Preachers which espouse this secular philosophy, and at the same time claim to be preaching Jesus, in truth they are proclaiming *"another Jesus."* It is impossible for any Preacher to Scripturally preach both humanistic psychology and the Cross of Christ. One cancels out the other. In other words, if one is going to believe one of these, the other will have to be laid aside.

THE PENALTY OF SIN AND THE POWER OF SIN

Romans, Chapters 4 and 5, proclaim to us the manner and means of Justification by Faith. It tells us how that Jesus addressed the *"penalty of sin,"* which He did by going to the Cross. That penalty was death, and with Him dying in our stead, thereby offering Himself up as a Sacrifice, and with God accepting this Sacrifice, which He definitely did, our Faith in that Finished Work, grants us Salvation on the basis of Justice satisfied. My Faith in Christ means that the penalty of sin was handled on my behalf, and done so at the Cross. This is what John the Baptist was speaking of when he said of Christ:

"Behold the Lamb of God, which taketh away the sin of the world" (Jn. 1:29).

If it is to be noticed, he didn't say *"sins"* but rather *"sin."* If it had said *"sins,"* that might have meant that some sins were not atoned for. But inasmuch as the singular *"sin"* is used, this means that all sin was atoned for, past, present, and future. In other words, the total and complete penalty of sin was absolutely handled. The debt is paid.

With the debt being completely paid, there is no more place for a penalty. It was paid by the Shed Blood of Jesus Christ.

The *"power of sin"* being broken, pertains to the sin nature being defanged so to speak, and is addressed in Romans, Chapter 6.

Even though the penalty of sin has been addressed, it is still possible for Christians to commit *"acts of sin."* And that's what Paul addresses in the Sixth Chapter of Romans.

He tells us that everything we need is found in the Cross (Rom. 6:3-5).

He then tells us that our Faith must be exclusively in the Cross, in other words, that the Cross must ever be the object of our Faith. Pertaining to this he said:

"Likewise reckon you also yourselves to be dead indeed unto sin, but alive unto God through Jesus Christ our Lord" (Rom. 6:11).

In fact, he actually said *"dead indeed unto the sin,"* which speaks of the sin nature, and which means that in the original Greek, the word *"sin"* is preceded by what is referred to as the definite article, making it read *"the sin."*

How can we reckon ourselves to be dead indeed unto the sin nature?

We do so on the basis of what happened to us when we accepted Christ, which means that we died to all sin, and all that sin means. That's what the crucifixion was all about (Rom. 6:3-5).

With our faith properly placed, the power of sin is then broken. We then have the assurance that *"sin shall not have dominion over us"* (Rom. 6:14).

However, this is not a once-for-all thing. This is something that must be carried on even on a daily basis, and I speak of our continued Faith in the Cross. Listen to what Jesus said:

TAKE UP YOUR CROSS DAILY

"If any man will come after Me, let him deny himself, and take up his cross daily, and follow Me.

"For whosoever will save his life shall lose it: but whosoever will lose his life for My sake, the same shall save it" (Lk. 9:23-24).

Knowing that Jesus Personally said these things, all Christians know them to be true and of course, very important; however, not properly understanding what they actually mean, most steer clear of what the Master is saying here.

The error that is believed concerning these Passages is about as bad as it gets as it regards a false interpretation of the Word of God.

For instance, most Christians think that the two words *"deny himself,"* refer to asceticism, which is the denial of all things that are comfortable or pleasurable. In other words, most think that Christ is saying, that if anyone wants to be a good Christian, they can never enjoy anything anymore.

As well, most think that taking up the Cross refers to *"suffering."* Consequently, if some person has to go through something that's very negative, most Christians will say, *"I pray the Lord never makes me do that,"* or words to that effect.

And when it comes to saving our life or losing it, most don't have a clue as to what that means. In other words, they don't even try to interpret it.

The truth is, these two Scriptures are some of the most wonderful in the entirety of the Word of God. In fact, they mean the exact opposite of what most Christians think.

For instance, *"denying oneself,"* has nothing to do with asceticism, as Jesus uses the term here. It rather speaks of the Believer not trying to live this Christian life by his own strength and ability.

As well, *"taking up the Cross daily,"* has nothing to do with suffering, but rather availing ourselves of the many benefits of the Cross, in other words, having Faith in what Christ did there. Trusting totally and completely in what Christ did at the Cross is in effect, *"denying oneself."*

Also, considering this is a daily struggle, we are to somewhat renew our Faith in the Finished Work of Christ each and every day, for that's what Jesus has said here.

As it regards the *"saving of our lives,"* the idea is, if we take our life in our own hands we will lose it. But if we will lose our life in Christ, rather living in Him, for Him, and through Him, in the losing of our life in this fashion, we will *"save it."* In effect, Paul said this very same thing:

"I am crucified with Christ (I have placed my life completely in Christ)*: nevertheless I live* (in the losing of my life, I will find it)*; yet*

NOTES

not I, but Christ lives in me (which is what makes life grand and glorious)*: and the life which I now live in the flesh* (my everyday living) *I live by the faith of the Son of God* (what Christ did for me at the Cross)*, Who loved me, and gave Himself for me"* (Gal. 2:20).

CALLED

The short phrase, *"And called,"* is placed at the end of the sentence for emphasis. It is an adjective used to describe those who were called in the sense of being invited, for instance, to a banquet.

The word here speaks of that effectual call of God whereby the sinner called to Salvation is constituted willing to receive that which he by nature rejects, namely, Salvation, this being the pre-Salvation work of the Holy Spirit in which He brings the sinner to the place of repentance and the act of faith in the Lord Jesus as Savior (Wuest).

The idea as presented here by the Holy Spirit through Jude, is that God does not want to lose the people whom He has called to be His Own through false doctrine. They are those *"who have been loved in God* (the) *Father and have been kept for Jesus Christ."* All this must now not be ruined by the false men who have stolen in among the Believers.

Once again, we come face-to-face with the knowledge as to how dangerous false doctrine actually is.

A PERSONAL EXAMPLE

For the last few months (this is dictated on April 18, 2001), we at the Ministry have felt led of the Lord to address ourselves to some of the false doctrine that has penetrated the Church in the last few decades. My son Donnie has especially felt led of the Lord in this direction, and as well, my associate Loren Larson. And please understand this was not at all of my prompting, but strictly between these Brethren and the Lord.

In fact, the first Message that Donnie preached on this subject was in the Thursday night Service of the 2000 Thanksgiving Campmeeting, conducted here at Family Worship Center, in Baton Rouge, Louisiana. I had no idea what he was going to preach that night, as I've never had any idea as to what he is going to preach.

A little ways into his Message, he made the statement that he was going to address some false doctrine, and was going to give the exact quotes of the Preachers, and call their names. He went on to state that he would do so as diplomatically as possible, but due to the seriousness of the matter, considering that we are dealing with the issues of life and death, he wanted the people to know what was being said and who was saying it.

The Lord anointed him greatly that night to minister, and after the Service, I felt in my heart that God was using him as a prophetic voice.

Over our Radio Program, *"A Study In The Word,"* aired daily, seven days a week, we have addressed these subjects as well. I speak primarily of the *"greed gospel,"* which is very popular at present, and as well the *"Jesus died spiritually doctrine."* In fact, my associate Loren Larson dealt with this latter doctrine in our Easter Campmeeting, in the 8 a.m. Services, Thursday through Saturday.

To which we have already briefly addressed in this Volume, the Jesus died spiritually doctrine, teaches that the Cross was of no consequence as it regards our Salvation experience. It also claims that the Blood of Jesus didn't avail or atone for anything.

This erroneous doctrine teaches that Jesus died on the Cross as a sinner, actually taking upon Himself the Satanic nature, and then dying and going to the burning side of Hell, even as all sinners do. For three days and nights, they teach, He suffered the agonies of the damned, with Satan and his cohorts thinking that Christ was now defeated.

But at the end of the three days and nights, God suddenly said, according to their teaching, *"It is enough,"* with Jesus then being born again in Hell, actually becoming the *"firstborn among many Brethren."* He was then raised from the dead.

Faith in His agony in Hell, and in His Resurrection, these teachers claim, is what saves the soul of those who believe.

They then teach that everyone who is *"born again,"* graduates instantly into the *"God class,"* the same as Christ, and if the necessity arose, could redeem men themselves by doing exactly what Jesus did. Coming into

the class of a *"little god,"* all Believers can now do great and mighty things through the power of confession, etc.

All of this is pure fiction. It cannot be found in the Word of God, because it's not in the Word of God.

It is most serious, because it is a serious attack upon the Atonement. As a result, these Churches who believe this lie, and a lie it is, will not sing any songs about the Cross, or the Blood, claiming that such is *"defeatist,"* actually claiming that the Cross was the greatest defeat in human history.

These particular Preachers (Teachers), and they number into the thousands, very seldom make any attempt to get anyone saved. The major reason is, despite whatever other excuse they might give, people cannot be saved by believing such foolishness. As well, there is no victory in such lives, despite the great boasts of such. Without Faith being placed in the Cross, there can be no Salvation, and there can be no victory. Considering that these people do not believe in the Cross, this means there is no Salvation and there is no victory.

FIRSTBORN

Incidentally, the word *"firstborn"* as used in the New Testament, at least in this fashion, doesn't mean what they think it means. Paul said:

"For whom He did foreknow, He also did predestinate to be conformed to the Image of His Son, that He might be the firstborn among many Brethren" (Rom. 8:29).

The word *"firstborn"* here doesn't mean that Jesus was Born-Again, as sinners are Born-Again. In fact, concerning the Greek word that is used, there is no English equivalent thereof. The word *"firstborn"* is the closest that the translators could come.

Its actual meaning is that Christ is the Father so to speak, of the Redemption process, which makes it possible for sinners to be Born-Again.

Again, Paul said: *"Who (meaning Christ) is the Image of the invisible God, the firstborn of every creature"* (Col. 1:15).

By the use of the word *"firstborn"* in this fashion, it makes it seem as though Christ is a created being. That's not true at all!

Again, the word *"firstborn"* is the nearest English equivalent, but does not really state the case properly.

The actual meaning is, Christ is the Creator of all things.

Paul again uses this word when he said: *"And He* (Christ) *is the Head of the Body, the Church: Who is the beginning, the firstborn from the dead"* (Col. 1:18).

The actual meaning is far greater than Christ being the first One to be resurrected. It actually means that what He did at the Cross, made the Resurrection possible for all who believe.

THE RESPONSE

Almost all the people who have taken exception to our pointing out this false doctrine, have not taken exception at all to the Doctrine we are proclaiming as it regards the Cross, but rather that we're calling the names of these Preachers who are preaching this false doctrine. In other words it seems as if they didn't really care what these men preach, how erroneous it is, even as it concerns the Atonement. They seem to have no concern about doctrine. There could be nothing more dangerous.

It's certainly nothing wrong with loving Preachers; however, we aren't these men's enemies because we tell them the truth. In fact, we are their friends. Actually, it takes a real friend to take the abuse we are taking, and continue to tell the truth.

We are not dealing here with mundane matters, but rather the issues of life and death. In other words, there is nothing more important. In fact, as one looks at the Atonement, it is so important that every step must be taken in order that the True Gospel be given to the people. And to be certain, if what we preach cannot be backed up by the Word of God, then it's wrong. And again to be sure, the *"greed gospel"* and the *"Jesus died spiritually doctrine"* cannot be backed up at all by the Word. So that means these doctrines are wrong, and if people heed them, it can only fall out to their detriment.

Why do you think that Paul, Peter, John, Jude and even others, said so much about false doctrine, and warned us so much about this which is so dangerous? They did it because

it must be done. As well, if we are to be the Preachers we should be, and in fact, must be, we also, must stand as proper *"watchmen"* (Ezek., Chpt. 3).

The Holy Spirit is emphatic about what will happen if we don't:

"When I say unto the wicked, you shall surely die; and you give him not warning, nor speak to warn the wicked from his wicked way, to save his life; the same wicked man shall die in his iniquity; but his blood will I require at your hand" (Ezek. 3:18).

(2) "MERCY UNTO YOU, AND PEACE, AND LOVE, BE MULTIPLIED."

The diagram is:

1. Mercy is a product of Grace.
2. The *"Peace"* of which Jude mentions here, is *"Sanctifying Peace."*
3. The Saints are the permanent objects of God's love.
4. Mercy, Peace, and Love, will continue to expand in the heart and life of the Believer who has placed his trust and faith in Christ and what Christ has done for him at the Cross.

MERCY

The phrase, *"Mercy unto you,"* presents itself as the product of the Grace of God.

"Mercy" in the Greek is *"Eleos,"* and means *"the pity of God on undeserving humans."*

Some time in the distant past, God chose *"Grace"* as the means by which He would deal with men. No doubt, this was done before man was ever created (I Pet. 1:18-20). And incidentally, Grace has to be a choice, or else it isn't Grace.

But once Grace was chosen, God literally had no choice but to grant Mercy, in that Mercy is a product of Grace. In other words, in the choosing of Grace, Mercy would naturally follow.

But yet in the Divine Mind, and in the order of our Salvation as conceived therein, Mercy precedes Grace. God so loved the world with a pitying love, which speaks of Mercy, that He gave His only Begotten Son, which speaks of Grace. So the Mercy preceded the Grace.

But in the order of the manifestation of Salvation, the Grace must go before the Mercy. It is true that the same persons are the subjects of both, being at once the guilty and the miserable, yet the Righteousness of God demands that the guilt should be done away with before the misery can be assuaged. Only the forgiven can be blessed. So it's the Grace of God that is extended first, and done in the Salvation process, with Mercy following, which brings about the joy of sins forgiven.

With God the legal work is accomplished first, which is a work of the Grace of God. The joy follows, which is Mercy, which is the guilt assuaged.

PEACE

"Peace" in the Greek is "Eirene," and means, "to join." Therefore, to make peace is to join together that which has been separated. Our Lord through the Blood of His Cross has made Peace between a thrice-Holy God and sinful man in the sense that He has joined together those who were by sin separated, who are God and the believing sinner. This is justifying Peace (Eph., Chpt. 2).

However, Jude, in writings to the Saints, is not speaking here of Justifying Peace, but rather of "Sanctifying Peace," which is that state of tranquility that is the result of the Mercy of God assuaging the evil results of sin.

Every Saint in the world has "Justifying Peace," which was received at the moment of Salvation, and cannot change. However, even though every Saint can have "Sanctifying Peace," the truth is, only a few do.

HOW IS SANCTIFYING PEACE OBTAINED?

First of all, Sanctifying Peace is perhaps the greatest attribute provided by the Holy Spirit for the Child of God. To attempt to explain is well nigh impossible. But I will try.

This particular "Peace" does not reflect an absence of problems, but it does reflect peace despite the problems. It is a sense of well-being, of security, that is impossible to obtain any other way.

Countless times, I have gone to the Lord in prayer, and have been greatly troubled about situations or problems in the Ministry. But then the Presence of God would come, with the Lord giving me Peace about the situation, whatever the situation may have been. That has happened, and continues to happen countless times.

NOTES

However, that which we have just stated is more than anything else, the icing on the cake. Real Sanctifying Peace, and I speak of a perpetual Peace, comes about only as one properly understands the Cross of Christ as it refers to the Sanctification process. Actually, that's the reason we refer to this as "Sanctifying Peace."

When one understands the Cross, which means that one understands that every single thing the Believer needs was provided by Christ at the Cross, and we obtain all of these things by simply having Faith in what Jesus did there. It is not a matter of "doing," but rather a matter of "believing," and when we speak of "believing," we are speaking of Faith placed exclusively in the Cross of Christ.

When one completely trusts in the Cross, this means that one is not trusting in one's self. And this is the key.

When we trust in ourselves, this means we aren't trusting in the Cross, which means the Holy Spirit is not helping us, which translates into "fear." But when one trusts solely in the Cross, one then has the help of the Holy Spirit, Who along with His help provides the Peace of which we are addressing here. This is "Sanctifying Peace," and as stated, is the greatest assurance and serenity on the face of the Earth (Rom. 8:1-2, 11, 13).

This is what Jesus was speaking about when He said: "But the Comforter, which is the Holy Spirit, Whom the Father will send in My Name, He shall teach you all things, and bring all things to your remembrance, whatsoever I have said unto you.

"Peace I leave with you, My peace I give unto you: not as the world giveth, give I unto you. Let not your heart be troubled, neither let it be afraid" (Jn. 14:26-27).

The "Peace" of which Jesus here spoke, is "Sanctifying Peace."

Justifying Peace is that which is given to sinners upon coming to Christ. Sanctifying Peace is that which is given to Saints. Both, Justifying Peace and Sanctifying Peace, were made possible solely by the Cross.

LOVE

The short phrase, "And love," is the God kind of love. It is that which is shed abroad in the heart of the yielded Saint. Mayor says:

"The Divine love is infused in us, so that it is our own, and becomes in us the source of a Divine life" (Rom. 13:10). *In virtue of this gift we are inspired with a love which is like the Love of God, and by this we truly claim the title of Children of God as partakers of His nature"* (I Jn. 4:7, 10).

Paul declared love to be the greatest of the Christian graces (I Cor. 13:13). John stated that God Himself is love, and that love emanates from God (I Jn. 4:7). Jesus showed that love was the identifying badge of Divine Sonship (Mat. 5:44).

ATTRIBUTES

Though love itself is an attribute of God, it in turn consists of attributes. It is through these attributes, functional characteristics, and fruits that love is portrayed in the Bible rather than through definitive terms. From the earliest Patriarchal records (Gen. 24:12), the durability and permanence of love is portrayed in the continual recurrence of the phrase *"steadfast love."* The phrase in one form or the other occurs in nearly every Book in the Old Testament, totaling at least 171 times. It is particularly frequent in the Psalms. Actually, it appears 26 times in Psalm 136. Even though it is translated, *"For His Mercy endureth forever,"* the actual Hebrew rendition is, *"For His steadfast love endures forever."* So an attribute of love is that it is *"steadfast."*

Another attribute of love is power. The young lady said that *"love is strong as death"* (Song of Sol. 8:6); and then with fire as a metaphor says, *"Many waters cannot quench love, neither can floods drown it"* (Song of Sol. 8:7). In fact, the power of love holds the family together, binds Church members together, and tethers man to God.

Charity is another attribute of love. Certainly, giving is Godlike. *"For God so loved the world that He gave . . ."* His dearest and best to save man (Jn. 3:16). Likewise, Jesus so loved people that He willingly died for them (Eph. 5:2). The Christian philosopher Thomas Aquinas said that creation itself sprang from God's love of giving. Love separates the givers from the getters. Consequently, 11 Disciples left all that they had to give themselves to Jesus and His work,

whereas Judas grabbed thirty pieces of silver. The reward of the former was membership in the infinite kingdom of love; the reward of the latter an untimely and ignominious death.

Other attributes of love are compassion, tenderness, and sympathy. In fact, it is probably impossible to exhaust all the attributes of love. There is no downside to love, only an upside.

THE LOVE OF GOD

To experience the love of God is to experience God; to know the love of God is to know God. God is inseparable from His nature. It is significant that Paul wrote both of *"the God of Love"* and *"the Love of God"* (II Cor. 13:11, 14). The former signifies the nature of God, and the latter, the expression of that nature. Both claim and reward man's noblest self.

Love as a part of the nature of God, has its ultimate origin in God. Every expression of the God kind of love, therefore, whether of God or man, emanates from God. *"God is love"* (I Jn. 4:8), and consequently all love has its roots in the Godhead. To love is to be like God. The essence of God's nature is portrayed by John as *"life"* (Jn. 1:4), *"spirit"* (Jn. 4:24), *"light"* (I Jn. 1:5), *"truth"* (Jn. 14:6), and *"love"* (I Jn. 4:8).

Although love is an eternal attribute of God, which always benefits man, it was through the long process of Revelation that man became more aware of this significant fact. It was not until the decline of the northern Kingdom of Israel that the Love of God, in Hosea's prophecy, was presented as a dominant theme (Hos. 11:1).

Later, at the fall of the southern Kingdom of Judah, Jeremiah portrayed the Lord as a God of love, compassion, and tenderness, not only to the Jews but also to all mankind (Jer. 31:3). In the dark days of Judah, Isaiah sang, *"I will recount the steadfast love of the LORD . . . His mercy, according to the abundance of His steadfast love"* (Isa. 63:7).

THE EXPRESSION OF GOD'S NATURE

The love of God may be seen in all His created works. At times and places law and power are more in evidence in nature, but

God's love is undergirding all (Rom. 1:20). Love is manifested in duty and orderliness, and in the balance and sustenance of natural life. Nature in turn becomes an instrument of God's love for man in providing food and plants (Gen. 1:29) and in fish, birds, and animals (Gen. 9:2). God's promise to Noah after the Flood summarizes His loving care for man through natural laws: *"While the earth remains, seedtime and harvest, cold and heat, summer and winter, day and night shall not cease"* (Gen. 8:22). God's love also transcends the area of ecology.

Enoch and Noah experienced the personal love of God. Abraham achieved Divine favor and was chosen as the fountainhead of God's immeasurable redeeming love (Gen. 12:2; 22:15). Subsequently, God progressively revealed His love to man until it reached its fullest measure in the Gift of Jesus Christ.

Early in His Ministry, Jesus revealed to Nicodemus, a ruler and teacher of Israel, that *"God so loved the world that He gave His only Son, that whoever believes in Him should not perish but have eternal life"* (Jn. 3:16).

Luther called this Verse *"the Gospel in miniature."* It reveals both the extent and power of God's love. It reveals the Fatherhood of God and His compassionate care for His children on Earth. Jesus' entire Ministry expressed God's love.

LOVE AS THE EXTENSION OF GOD'S NATURE

Christ is the foremost object of God's love (Jn. 17:24), yet long before Christ made His appearance in history God was manifesting His love to man. When Moses returned from Mount Sinai with the two new tables of stone, God disclosed Himself as *"abounding in steadfast love and faithfulness, keeping steadfast love for thousands, forgiving iniquity, transgression, and sin . . ."* (Ex. 34:6-7). Subsequently, it became increasingly evident that Israel was the object of God's love.

Even in Israel's apostasy, God revealed to the Prophet Hosea His undying love for His chosen people. Divine compassion that would not let Israel go was realistically portrayed through Hosea in the domestic drama of a faithful husband's love to an unfaithful wife (Hos. 1:2; 3:1-5). Hosea related God's

consoling promise, *"I will heal their faithlessness; I will love them freely, for My anger has turned from them, I will be as the dew to Israel; he shall blossom as the lily . . ."* (Hos. 14:4-5).

When there was valid reason to reject Israel, God revealed Himself as a husband whose persistent love ultimately reclaims His wayward wife. This advance in revelation portrays more of the love of God, and more of its availability to man. It becomes more intimate, more personal, and consequently more vital in human affairs.

THE JEWS

In Judah's darkest hour — her beloved city ravaged, her sacred Temple destroyed, her nobility deported to Babylon, and her land desolate and wasted — God supported His people with His hand of love. Just before this dark hour, Jeremiah declared God as One *"Who showest steadfast love to thousands"* (Jer. 32:18).

He delivered God's Promise that restoration would occur and that His people would again sing their former song of praise, *"Give thanks to the Lord of hosts, for the Lord is good, for His steadfast love endures forever!"* (Ps. 136:1). *"For I will restore the fortunes of the land as at first, says the Lord"* (Jer. 33:11).

God's love was never confined to the Jews, but was from their progenitor mediated through them (Gen. 12:3). In due time Jesus could declare that *"Salvation is from the Jews"* (Jn. 4:22).

He also said that *"God so loved the world,"* not just Israel; that He provided eternal life for all who would believe (Jn. 3:16). As God was fully revealed in Jesus Christ, His Nature of extending and comprehending love became manifest. Henceforth it would be known that God loved Gentiles and Jews, sinners and righteous, aliens and neighbors, rich and poor, black and white — all men everywhere (Mat. 28:19; Acts 1:8), not just the favored ethnic or religious groups.

In three parables — the lost sheep, the lost coin, and the lost son (Lk. 15:3-32) — Jesus illustrated God's love for an individual, its searching mission accomplished, and the consequent joy in Heaven. This lends credence to Paul's assertion, *"Love never ends"* (I Cor. 13:8).

THE LOVE OF CHRIST

The love of Christ is unique in that Jesus is both the Personification and Mediator of God's love. From this approach may be seen the donation, degrees, and demands of love.

Christ is the Gift of God's love to man, and sufficient for all his needs: life, liberty, healing, happiness, fellowship with man and with God. Paul admonished the Roman Christians to *"Owe no one anything, except to love one another"* (Rom. 13:8). Therefore, love is a personal product of supreme value, and a debt that every Christian owes his brother; but love is a free gift from God, unmerited by man.

God does not owe it, but man does, because he is placed under obligation by the free gift from God to share it with others. When Jesus sent the Twelve on their initial tour of home missions, He said to them, *"You received without pay, give without pay"* (Mat. 10:8).

Jesus specifically declared to His Disciples His mediation of God's Gift of love: *"As the Father has loved Me, so have I loved you; abide in My love. If you keep My Commandments, you will abide in My love, just as I have kept My Father's Commandments and abide in His love"* (Jn. 15:9-10). Jesus' fourfold ministry of preaching, teaching, healing, and redeeming was God's love in action, as well as an expression of Jesus' Own love (Mat. 4:23; 20:28).

THE DEGREES OF LOVE

There are degrees of love as there are varieties of love. *"For God so loved"* implies degree, in this case the fullest degree.

Sinners who only *"love those who love them"* (Mat. 5:43-48) limit their love to small degrees. Jesus admonished His Disciples to do better than that. An example of degrees of love was pointed out by Jesus as He sat at the table in the house of Simon the Pharisee.

During the meal, a sinful woman poured ointment on Jesus, at the same time weeping and wiping His feet. The Pharisee inaudibly scorned the act because Jesus allowed a sinful woman to touch Him.

In response Jesus told Simon a parable of two debtors, with unequal debts, whose creditor forgave both, and asked Simon which one

NOTES

would love most. Then Jesus contrasted Simon's limited love with that of the woman, declaring that, *"Her sins, which are many, are forgiven, for she loved much; but he who is forgiven little, loves little"* (Lk. 7:47).

The postresurrection scene at the seaside provides another example of the degrees of love. Here Jesus asks Peter, *"Do you love Me more than these?"* (Jn. 21:15). The question recalled Peter's former boast when he implied that he loved Jesus more than the other Disciples did (Mk. 14:29).

The Gospels record that Jesus stated the measure of love. Man was to love God with *"all his faculties and being; and he was to love his neighbor as himself"* (Mat. 22:37, 39). The law then was summarized in the expression of love as stated in these two Commandments (Deut. 6:5; Lev. 19:18).

To these Jesus added a new Commandment of love by which His Disciples were to be bound in spiritual brotherhood: *"This is My Commandment, that you love one another as I have loved you. Greater love has no man than this, that a man lay down his life for his friends"* (Jn. 15:12-13). That was the supreme measure of love, the highest degree possible to man. Soon afterward Jesus laid down His life for His friends, and challenged them to comparable devotion.

THE DEMANDS OF LOVE

Paul wrote to the Corinthians, *"The love of Christ controls us"* (II Cor. 5:14). Christians are controlled, constrained, and motivated by the love of Christ.

As Jesus faced the Cross, He said, *"He who loves his life loses it"* (Jn. 12:25). Jesus was ready to lose His life to save it and others. Thus, He also said, *"And I, when I am lifted up from the earth, will draw all men to Myself"* (Jn. 12:32).

Paul felt the pull of that love on the Cross, and he saw its effects in Christian converts. Love like that could not end at the Cross; it would find response in the hearts of people and make demands upon their lives.

THE LOVE OF CHRIST IN
THE LIFE OF PAUL

The love of Christ placed Paul *"under obligation both to Greeks and to Barbarians, both to the wise and to the foolish"* (Rom. 1:14). Throughout this masterful treatise, Paul made it clear that his impelling drive to share his Spiritual Blessings came out of his experience in Christ. His rejoicing, endurance, and hope, even in suffering, were *"because God's love has been poured into our hearts through the Holy Spirit which has been given to us"* (Rom. 5:5). This love he traced through Christ from God, climaxed in the Crucifixion. *"But God shows His love for us in that while we were yet sinners Christ died for us"* (Rom. 5:8).

All the commands of the Ten Commandments could not be as effective as this one act of supreme love. Paul was willing to live for it and to die for it. It was his drive and demand, in work and in death. *"We know that in everything God works for good with those who love Him"* (Rom. 8:28). Triumphantly he asks, *"Who shall separate us from the love of Christ?"* and answered that no power or person *"will be able to separate us from the Love of God in Christ Jesus our Lord"* (Rom. 8:35-39).

However, it must be quickly added here that this is so only if we understand Romans, Chapter 6 which presents *"how the Holy Spirit works within our hearts and lives,"* and Romans, Chapter 8, which tells us *"what"* the Holy Spirit does in us, by us, and through us, providing we understand Romans, Chapter 6. Understanding this, and putting it to practice within our lives, only then can the Believer say, *"Who shall separate us from the love of Christ?"*

THREE AREAS OF CONTROL

For clarity it may be seen that *"the love of Christ controls"* in three areas of the Believer's life:

A. His faith; B. His manner of life; and, C. His ministry.

All are evident in New Testament Christians, particularly in the boldness and persistence of the Apostles in their preaching. Paul said, *"Woe to me if I do not preach the Gospel!"* (I Cor. 9:16).

Peter and the other Apostles deliberately disobeyed the Jewish council's order not to preach, and then boldly defied the council and court, declaring, *"We must obey God rather than men"* (Acts 5:29).

Stephen, a deacon, not an Apostle — was so impelled by Christ's love that he gave his life after preaching one Message to the Sanhedrin (Acts 7:2-60). Thousands of men and women since have followed the examples of these early Christians for the love of Christ.

SPURIOUS LOVE

Love that is limited to selfish interests of a worldly and temporal nature is spurious. It expresses itself in a number of ways. One is extramarital sex indulgence, the prostitution of honorable members of the body by spurious love (I Cor. 12:23). Two of the Ten Commandments, the Seventh and the Tenth, forbid adultery and sexual lust respectively (Ex. 20:14, 17). Jesus speaks strongly against illicit sexual desires (Mat. 5:28). In the Wisdom literature (Prov., Chpt. 7), men are warned against the enticing flattery and seduction of a harlot or adulteress who says, *"Come, let us take our fill of love until morning; let us delight ourselves with love. For my husband is not at home"* (Prov. 7:18).

Admittedly, this is speaking more of spiritual adultery, i.e., *"forsaking the Ways of God and replacing them with the ways of the world,"* than it is physical adultery, but it definitely includes the latter.

In the unfaithfulness of Hosea's wife, the heartbreaking effects of Israel's apostasy is illustrated (Hos. 3:1). With vivid metaphor, Ezekiel drew a sordid picture of Judah's apostasy: *"The Babylonians came to her into the bed of love, and they defiled her with their lust"* (Ezek. 23:17).

GREED

Spurious love, which in reality is lust, also takes the form of greed for material things — houses, lands, money, all kinds of worldly possessions. Jesus called these things mammon, and uttered strong warnings against their influence. He said, *"No one can serve two masters; for either he will hate the one and love the other, or he will be devoted to one and despise the other. You cannot serve God and mammon"* (Mat. 6:24).

He often warned against riches and, in two parables — the rich farmer (Lk. 12:16-21), and the rich man and Lazarus (Lk. 16:19-31) — against the fatal consequences of being a slave to riches. Summarily, Paul said, *"The love of money is the root of all evil"* (I Tim. 6:10). Later he wrote to Timothy, *"Demas, in love with this present world, has deserted me"* (II Tim. 4:10).

SELFISHNESS

Jesus pointed out that even love for one's family could be selfish. *"He who loves father or mother more than Me is not worthy of Me; and he who loves son or daughter more than Me is not worthy of Me"* (Mat. 10:37).

Moreover, He said, *"He who loves his life loses it"* (Jn. 12:25; Rev. 12:11).

VAINGLORY

A fourth type of spurious love is *"vainglory."* It is most prevalent and most tempting, making its appeal to the ego. It can destroy the effectiveness of faith by replacing God with self, as did the Jewish leaders in Jesus' day.

Jesus called them hypocrites who *"love to stand and pray in the Synagogues and at the street corners, that they may be seen by men"* (Mat. 6:5). His renunciation was strong: *"Woe to you Pharisees! For you love the best seat in the Synagogues and salutations in the marketplaces"* (Lk. 11:43). He warned against the Scribes for the same conduct plus their love for *"the places of honor at feasts"* (Lk. 20:46).

To these may be added the love of pleasure and the love of wine (Prov. 21:17; Isa. 47:8), and anything else that may come under the heading of *"the world or the things in the world. If anyone loves the world, love for the Father is not in him"* (I Jn. 2:15).

SPIRITUAL LOVE

The highest form of man's love is spiritual. It is the God kind of love, or rather, the love that proceeds only from God, which the world doesn't have, and in fact cannot have. It is only those who are *"born again,"* thereby having the Divine nature, who can have the Love of God. In fact, in the Godly man it is both spontaneous and commanded. Jesus defined the bond of Believes in a love sequence. *"As the Father has loved Me, so have I loved you; abide in My love. If you keep My Commandments, you will abide in My love,*

NOTES

just as I have kept my Father's Commandments and abide in His love" (Jn. 15:9-10).

Hence, the spiritual family is man in love, and love in man, and both in God. With God and His Kingdom as the focal attraction of man's love, all other objects of man's love may properly and acceptably fall into subordinate categories. The Kingdom of God and His Righteousness, however, are to be sought first for man to keep his love in proper perspective (Mat. 6:33).

Love on a lower plain is based on emotion and, therefore, prompted by feeling, whereas spiritual love (agape) can be commanded. Consequently, in New Testament Righteousness, Jesus could and did make a threefold command to love. Man must love God completely, his neighbor as himself, and his Christian Brother as Christ loves him (Lk. 10:27; Jn. 15:12).

PAUL

As Paul discussed various activities of the Christian life, he concluded by pointing out *"a still more excellent way"* (I Cor. 12:31) with his immortal classic on love (I Cor., Chpt. 13).

In it he virtually personified love, and this portrayal may very well be a picture of Jesus Christ. It is at once the greatest of the spiritual gifts, the attributes of Christ, and the example of perfection for Christians. It lacks jealousy, boastfulness, arrogance, rudeness, selfishness, and irritability; it rejoices in the right, bearing all things, believing, hoping, enduring; and never fails in any endeavor, nor ends in time or circumstance. This is spiritual love — excellent and eternal — and attainable by man through the Love of Christ.

JOHN

On the same high plain, John emphasized brotherly love of Believers. He is persuasive in his logical presentation: God's love is seen in sending His Son for the expiation of our sins; to love one another is the primary authentication that we know God, Whom no man has ever seen; the testimony of the Holy Spirit and man's confession that Jesus is God's Son insures man's dwelling in God and God in him; and this perfected love allays any fear of judgment in us; and finally that love originates with God, and that love for a Brother is essential to love for God (I Jn. 4:7-21).

According to the enlightened quality of love, John wrote, *"He who loves his brother abides in the light, and in it there is no cause for stumbling"* (I Jn. 2:10). Thus, Jesus, Paul, and John, show the necessity, nature, and rewards of man's spiritual love, i.e., *"the love of God."*

A PERSON — THE SON OF GOD

Jesus Christ is God's preeminent Gift to man, since through Him all other gifts were and are administered. He is love in Person, offering to man the rich legacies of love. He makes available to man not only eternal life, but abundant life with joy, gladness, peace, assurance of God's daily care, and hope (Mat. 5:12; 6:25-33; Jn. 10:10; 14:27).

The Person, works, and teachings of Jesus constitute the world's richest legacy. He set the perfect example of ethical love. In His brief and busy Ministry, He supplied man's need in tenderness and love; *"He went about doing good and healing all that were oppressed of the Devil"* (Acts 10:38).

Finally He mediated God's love in its deepest expression by His voluntary death on the Cross (Mat. 20:28; Jn. 10:17). He helped men to live, and He gave life beyond death. Beyond the grave He gave us hope: *"Because I live, you will live also"* (Jn. 14:19).

He showed the world the immortality of love. Paul, like other Believers, got the Message and boldly asked, *"Who shall separate us from the love of Christ?"* (Rom. 8:35).

Triumphantly, he answered his own question with the assurance that neither invisible powers *"nor anything else in all creation, will be able to separate us from the love of God in Christ Jesus our Lord"* (Rom. 8:39). The crowning Gift of God's love is His Son.

A POWER — THE SPIRIT OF GOD

Someone has said that in the Old Testament, God was for man; in Jesus Christ, God was with man; and, in the Holy Spirit, God is in man (Jn. 14:17). God not only sent Jesus, He sent His Holy Spirit to dwell in those who love Jesus and keep His Commandments (Jn. 14:15). *"He who has My Commandments and keeps them, he it is who loves Me; and*

he who loves Me will be loved by My Father, and I will love him and manifest Myself to him" (Jn. 14:21).

Subsequently, Paul could rejoice in suffering, *"because God's love has been poured into our hearts through the Holy Spirit which has been given to us"* (Rom. 5:5). In turn, Paul says, *"The Fruit of the Spirit is love . . ."* (Gal. 5:22; Col. 1:8).

Jesus identified the Holy Spirit as God's legacy to Believers who love Christ and keep His Commandments; a legacy given in response to Jesus' prayer. *"I will pray the Father, and He will give you another Counselor, to be with you forever, even the Spirit of truth, Whom the world cannot receive"* (Jn. 14:16-17). This is a unique legacy for Believers only, imparting to them Christ's life, uniting them to God, and giving peace of heart and guidance of mind (Jn. 14:18-31). In Christ's service, the Holy Spirit is the Source of power for the Believer in sustaining us, in our preaching the Gospel, and in our warfare against Satan (Acts 1:8; Rom. 15:13; I Cor. 2:4).

HOW IS THE HOLY SPIRIT THIS POWER?

Every Christian knows that the Holy Spirit is God. Consequently, considering that He is God, He has all power. This means that He is Almighty, which means that He can do anything.

However, one of the first things the Christian learns after coming to Christ, is that the evidence of this power is not automatic within our lives. Even those who are Spirit-filled, soon find that out.

Most, if not all, Christians know that the Holy Spirit is in our hearts and lives to help us, but they have little understanding as to how this help comes about. Most are led to believe that this is automatic; however, as stated, they soon find out that such is not the case.

The Believer must understand that the Holy Spirit does many things. His *"help"* includes every type of help of which one could think. He is not limited to merely one avenue of endeavor. In fact, He wants to take complete control of our lives; however, it's control that we must freely give Him, because He will never take it by force. Unfortunately,

He doesn't have much cooperation from many Christians.

We must understand that the Holy Spirit abides within us, strictly on the premise of what Jesus did at the Cross. Before the Cross, while the Holy Spirit could definitely come into the hearts and lives of certain ones to help them carry out a particular task, the evidence is, when that task was completed, He left. In other words, He could not at that time abide in their hearts and lives permanently. The reason was simple:

The terrible sin debt which man owed to God could not be assuaged by the blood of bulls and goats. In fact, the Scripture bluntly says: *"For it is not possible that the blood of bulls and goats should take away sins"* (Heb. 10:4).

While those animal sacrifices did provide a stopgap measure so to speak, that was in essence all they could do. Therefore, due to the sin debt remaining, the Holy Spirit was limited in what He could do. In fact, of this very thing Jesus said:

"Even the Spirit of truth (Holy Spirit)*; Whom the world cannot receive, because it sees Him not, neither knows Him: but you know Him; for He dwells with you, and shall be in you"* (Jn. 14:17).

Jesus was addressing His Disciples and followers here before the Cross. He was telling them that the Holy Spirit, due to their being saved, definitely did dwell with them; however, He would not be able to permanently be in them, until the Cross was a fact. Then, *"He may abide with you forever"* (Jn. 14:16).

THE LAW OF THE SPIRIT OF LIFE IN CHRIST JESUS

As stated, while the Holy Spirit works within our lives in every capacity, the greatest thing He does for us, and by far, is to give us victory over *"the law of sin and death"* (Rom. 8:2).

Despite being saved, and even baptized with the Holy Spirit, which means that one is a new creation in Christ Jesus, the greatest problem for the Believer is *"sin."* Now some may argue that this isn't the case; however, if it's not the case, why did Paul take up so much space in explaining this situation? The entire Sixth Chapter of Romans is given over to the mechanics of the Holy Spirit as it regards victory over the sin nature. The Eighth Chapter of

Romans tells us what the Holy Spirit can do within our hearts and lives, once we understand the Sixth Chapter of Romans, thereby placing our Faith exclusively in the Cross of Christ. As well, the entirety of the Epistle to the Galatians is given over to this problem of victory over sin, as well as much of the material in all of the Epistles written by the Apostle. Yes, the greatest problem for the Child of God is victory over sin in all of its forms.

Romans, Chapters 4 and 5 tell us how Justification by Faith is brought about, which refers to the penalty of sin being addressed, which it was by Christ at the Cross. This explains the principle of sin and how it was defeated, hence John the Baptist saying when introducing Christ: *"Behold the Lamb of God, which taketh away the sin of the world"* (Jn. 1:29).

If it is to be noticed, John used the singular *"sin,"* because he was speaking of the principle of sin being addressed by Christ at the Cross, and that it would be answered in its entirety.

While Romans, Chapters 4 and 5, deal with the penalty of sin, and how it was addressed, Romans, Chapter 6, deals with the power of sin being broken, which refers to acts of sin being stopped in the hearts and lives of Believers, who place their Faith entirely in Christ and what He did at the Cross on our behalf (Rom. 6:14).

Many Christians are confused because they sense the Holy Spirit helping them grandly in many ways, but seemingly not helping them when it comes to the sin problem. In other words, there are millions of Christians who are being dominated by the sin nature in some way, and they don't understand why this is so, simply because they don't want it this way, and in fact, they are trying very, very hard to overcome, but not succeeding. In fact, I greatly suspect that many of you holding this book in your hands have asked yourself the question many times, *"Why won't the Holy Spirit help me?"* And speaking of a particular problem in your life. I'm going to tell you now how that help can be brought about.

THE CROSS

Understanding that the Cross alone is what made it possible for the Holy Spirit to come in and abide within our hearts and lives on a permanent basis, in other words, giving the Holy Spirit the legal right to do all that He does, this means that our Faith as a Christian must be anchored permanently in the great Sacrifice of Christ. In other words, the Cross of Christ, even as we have repeatedly stated, must ever be the object of our Faith. The Holy Spirit demands that (Rom. 6:3-6, 11, 14). Read carefully what Paul said:

"For the Law (a Law made by the Godhead within which the Spirit always works) *of the Spirit* (Holy Spirit) *of Life* (victory over the world, the flesh, and the Devil) *in Christ Jesus* (this Law is centered up in what Christ did at the Cross) *has made me free from the law of sin and death"* (Rom. 8:2).

Please notice that this *"Law"* in which the Holy Spirit always works is *"in Christ Jesus."* That means it's predicated on what Christ did at the Cross and that alone!

Now if the Christian abides by this particular *"Law,"* which gives the Holy Spirit latitude within his life, the Spirit to be sure, will *"make you free from the law of sin and death."* This is the only manner in which sin can be defeated in one's life. It cannot be defeated by willpower, by personal strength, by personal ability, etc., only by the *"Law of the Spirit of Life in Christ Jesus."*

That *"Law"* is simple! It refers exclusively to what Christ did on our behalf at the Cross. In other words, it pertains totally and completely to the great Sacrifice of Christ, or in other words, *"The Finished Work of Christ."*

At the Cross, Jesus addressed the demands of the broken Law, and the Law of which we now speak, the Law of Moses, which in effect, was God's Standard of Righteousness that was demanded of man. Man being unable to keep this Standard, God became man, and kept this Standard perfectly for us, thereby gaining its Righteousness, and then as well, addressed its penalty. Regarding the Law of Moses, two things had to be done:

1. The Law had to be kept perfectly, and in every respect. This was done totally and completely by Jesus Christ in that He never failed at all. As our Substitute He did for us what we could not do for ourselves, and as our Representative Man He literally functioned as us (I Cor. 15:45-50). We obtain

NOTES

all that He did for us, by identifying with Him. It's *"The Law of Substitution and Identification."*

2. The second thing that Christ had to do as it regards the Law of Moses was to address its penalty. The Scripture bluntly tells us *"the wages of sin is death"* (Rom. 6:23). So, to satisfy the demands of the broken Law, in order to satisfy the Nature and Righteousness of God, Jesus had to die on the Cross. That was the penalty, and He had to suffer that penalty in its totality. Therefore:

"For He (God) *has made Him* (Christ) *to be sin* (a Sin-Offering) *for us, Who knew no sin; that we might be made the Righteousness of God in Him"* (II Cor. 5:21).

Now what does that mean?

Paul explains it in Colossians, Chapter 2:

"Blotting out the handwritings of ordinances that was against us (the Law of Moses), *which was contrary to us, and took it out of the way, nailing it to His Cross* (meaning that He settled all the demands of the Law against humanity, by paying its debt, which He did by dying on the Cross);

"And having spoiled principalities and powers, He made a show of them openly, triumphing over them in it" (Col. 2:14-15).

When Jesus died on the Cross, He did so as a Sin-Offering, which had been perfectly typified by the untold millions of lambs which had been offered up in the Old Testament economy. The lamb that was offered up was an innocent victim, which had done nothing wrong, but would die in place of the sinner who definitely had done something wrong. This typified Christ Who was perfectly sinless, and thereby had to be, in order to be a perfect Sacrifice that God would accept. It was all done at the Cross!

When He died, at that moment the price was paid. Some think the price being completely paid awaited His Resurrection. Not so! Due to the fact that Jesus had atoned for all sin, the Resurrection was never in question. While it is true that if one single sin had been left unatoned, and due to the fact that the wages of sin is death, then Jesus could not have been raised from the dead, but due to the fact that all sin was atoned for, past, present, and future, at least for those who will believe, the Resurrection was never in question. The great work of Redemption was finished the moment that Jesus died, and I'll prove it from the Word of God.

In the first place, Jesus Himself plainly said at the moment of His death: *"It is finished,"* with the Scripture then saying: *"And He bowed His head, and gave up the ghost"* (Jn. 19:30).

In fact, the chronology of those last moments and what He said were most likely: *"It is finished: Father, into Thy hands I commend My spirit"* (Jn. 19:30; Lk. 23:46).

Immediately before that, the Scripture implies that He said, *"'Eli, Eli, lama sabachthani?' That is to say, 'My God, My God, why have You forsaken Me?'"* (Mat. 27:46).

God in fact, did forsake Him at the moment of His death, but then returned to Him immediately after dying, proven by the fact that Jesus said, as just quoted, *"Father, into Thy Hands I commend My spirit."* If God forsook Him completely at death, and for the entirety of the three days and nights He was dead, as some teach, then He couldn't have commended His spirit to the Father, which He definitely did!

No! God forsook Christ only at the moment of death, and for the simple reason that death is the wages of sin, of which God can Personally have no part. Therefore, at the moment that Jesus breathed out His breath and purposely died, God at that moment, turned His back on Him, so to speak. In fact at that time, there was an eclipse of the sun, which darkened that part of the world, and did so for three hours (Mk. 15:33).

Jesus was placed on the Cross at 9 o'clock in the morning, the time of the morning Sacrifice. At noon, the Earth turned black, and stayed that way until the ninth hour, which was 3 o'clock in the afternoon, the time of the evening Sacrifice, the time that Jesus died. During those three hours, the evidence is, Christ was bearing the penalty of the sin of the world, and during that three hour span, God was separated from Him, which lasted until the time of His death. The moment He died, the darkness lifted, and because the price had been paid, with God now embracing His Son once again. It definitely was *"finished!"*

NOTES

The second reason I know that it was all finished at the Cross is because the Scripture plainly tells us that when Jesus died, at that moment: *"The Veil of the Temple was rent in twain from the top to the bottom"* (Mat. 27:51).

This says that the Way to the Holy of Holies, the very Presence of God, was now open. Now please notice, the renting of this Veil did not await the Resurrection as some teach, but took place immediately upon the death of Christ. Everything was paid at the Cross! There was nothing left owing. In effect, this is the *"Law of the Spirit of Life in Christ Jesus."* And to be sure, if this *"Law"* is followed, it will *"make us free from the law of sin and death."*

When the Believer places his faith exclusively in this great Sacrifice of Christ, the Holy Spirit will then work mightily on behalf of that Believer, giving him victory totally and completely over all of the law of sin and death. In fact, that is God's prescribed order of victory. Our faith must ever be in the Finished Work of Christ, which Work was completely totally and absolutely at the Cross.

In the entirety of the Book of Hebrews, Paul deals with the Cross in every way that one could begin to think. He only mentioned the Resurrection one time (Heb. 13:20). Now of course, the Resurrection is very, very important; however, as important as it is, it had nothing to do with our Redemption, that being effected totally and completely by what Jesus did at the Cross. Any attack against the Cross of Christ is an attack against the Atonement. In fact, one cannot be saved unless they place their faith and trust in Christ and what Christ did at the Cross. Any other type of faith, in other words, faith placed in other things, is a spurious faith, which God will never recognize. Over and over again, in one way or the other, the Scripture constantly says:

"For God so loved the world, that He gave His only Begotten Son, that whosoever believeth in Him, should not perish but have everlasting life" (Jn. 3:16).

A PROVINCE — THE KINGDOM OF GOD

The initial note in the preaching of John the Baptist and of Jesus was: *"The Kingdom of Heaven is at hand"* (Mat. 3:2; 4:17). In His teaching, Jesus sought, primarily through parables, to portray the image of the Kingdom. It is in essence a spiritual Kingdom (Lk. 1:33; 13:29; 17:21; Jn. 18:36) whose citizens are bound together by bonds of God's love.

In His Sermon on the Mount, sometimes called the Magna Carta of the Kingdom of God, Jesus enumerated both the blessings to be received (Mat. 5:3-11) and the blessings to be given. Disciples were not only to receive the legacy of love, but they were also to convey it. It is not enough to *"love those who love you,"* but you are to *"love your enemies . . . so that you may be sons of your Father"* (Mat. 5:44-46).

Jesus commanded the strongest kind of love for binding together members of the Kingdom (Jn. 15:12). Paul was pleased that the Laodiceans were *"knit together in love"* (Col. 2:2); and his prayer for the Philippians was *"that your love may abound more and more"* (Phil. 1:9). Similarly, Peter commanded Believers to *"Love the brotherhood"* (I Pet. 2:17), and to have *"love of the Brethren"* (I Pet. 3:8; II Pet. 1:7).

A PORTRAIT — THE NATURE OF GOD

In all the various aspects of God's self-disclosure, the most far-reaching and fruitful knowledge that ever came to man was the revelation that *"God is love,"* demonstrated fully and magnificently in Jesus Christ.

The portrait of God as a loving Father was revealed by Christ (Jn. 17:20-26). John was deeply impressed with this revelation of God. He exclaimed, *"See what love the Father has given us, that we should be called Children of God; and so we are"* (I Jn. 3:1; Jn. 1:12; Rom. 8:15). In fact, John portrays God so dominantly as love that other attributes are hardly seen. Thus, Christ and the early Christians bequeathed to the Church a glowing portrait of the God of love.

A PERMANENCE — THE CITY OF GOD

The final legacy of love is an eternal dwelling place with God. From that night in old Jerusalem when Jesus told Nicodemus that God's love purchased eternal life for man (Jn. 3:16), to the closing scenes envisioning the New Jerusalem (Rev. 21:10-22:5), the New

Testament shows that man's eternal home is a Gift of God's love. Jesus told His Disciples that He was going to prepare a place for them, and return to take them home with Him (Jn. 14:2). Paul said, *"For we know that if the earthly tent we live in is destroyed, we have a building from God, a house not made with hands, eternal in the heavens"* (II Cor. 5:1).

Final transaction, however, is made in possession secured when man reciprocates with love. So, *"it is written, 'no eye has seen, nor ear heard, nor the heart of man conceived, what God has prepared for those who love Him'"* (I Cor. 2:9; Isa. 64:4).

James gave the same conditional promise: *"Blessed is the man who endures trial, for when he has stood the test he will receive the crown of life which God has promised to those who love Him"* (James 1:12). Again, *"Has not God chosen those who are poor in the world to be rich in faith and heirs of the Kingdom which He has promised to those who love Him?"* (James 2:5).

Furthermore, man's assurance of his eternal heritage lies in his love on Earth, *"We know that we have passed out of death into life, because we love the Brethren"* (I Jn. 3:14).

Paul gave the assurance that *"He destined us in love to be His sons through Jesus Christ"* (Eph. 1:5). The ultimate destiny of the Disciples' journey in His *"Father's house"* (Jn. 14:2), and the way is paved with love.

HARMONY

The final word on love cannot be said, but a treatise may well be concluded with some Scriptural highlights on the subject. Paul admonished Believers to *"Make love your aim"* (I Cor. 14:1). There are three obvious reasons for doing so:

First, love is the essence of harmony. Without love there would be universal chaos. By it all other attributes of God are harmonized; by it all Heavenly Beings are in harmony; and wherever it prevails on Earth there is harmony.

"Above all hold unfailing your love for one another, since love covers a multitude of sins" (I Pet. 4:8).

Love is spiritual healing of frictions and fractures in interpersonal relations. It makes possible the boundless reach of God's Kingdom on Earth. Love holds together and harmonizes various human elements. It binds the brotherhood. *"In the love of God"* (Jude, vs. 21) is peace and harmony. Without love, man is beastly, greedy, suspicious, selfish, murderous, and always at enmity with others. With love man builds homes, Churches, and communities, and lives in harmony with God and his fellow man.

LIFE

Second, love is the essence of life. *"He who does not love remains in death"* (I Jn. 3:14). To love is to give and to give is to live. Whoever loses himself in the love of God finds his life in the greatness of God (Mk. 8:35).

Without love one does not risk the outward reach, but is driven by fear into the suffocating bonds of self until he dies. However, *"There is no fear in love, but perfect love casts out fear"* (I Jn. 4:18). It alleviates all fear of punishment here and hereafter. It releases the life-giving forces in man, and enables him to grow toward Christian maturity. Love is an essential ingredient for man's sustenance, and all people all the time need it.

SERVICE

Finally, love is the essence of occupational service. All occupations grow out of supply and demand in such areas as food, clothing, shelter, health, education, and spiritual welfare. The supply of God's love is abundant, and the demand is great. Agents are needed to deliver the goods.

This constitutes an occupation in which there is no threat of unemployment. Every Christian is employed in the business of sharing love. Jesus closed His earthly Ministry with this emphasis. Someone must take His love to the unlovely and the unloved, and keep his own supplied.

At His postresurrection appearance by Galilee, after breakfast Jesus gave Peter a second test on love. Peter had failed the first in thinking that the sword was more powerful than love. Things were different now. Love had broken the bonds of death, to which he was witness. In reminiscence of his former boast of love (Mk. 14:29), and subsequent denial (Jn. 18:17, 25-27), Jesus asked him, *"Simon, son of Jonas, do you love Me more than these?"* (Jn. 21:15).

NOTES

The question was repeated three times, providing the opportunity for three affirmative answers, to revoke the three denials. Peter answered with the Greek word *"philo"* in all three instances, which means *"Lord I am fond of you."* Jesus used the Greek word *"agapas"* in the first two, which refers to the God kind of love. Peter passed the test, and how did he pass that test?

In the first place, Peter did not now boldly exclaim his love as he once had done. In other words, he was saying in essence, *"Lord, I think I love you with all of my heart, but I cannot really know until I'm put to the test."* In effect, that's what Jesus wanted him to say. It's easy to boast, but not so easy to carry out the boast.

Jesus then gave Peter a special threefold assignment to express his love: *"Feed My lambs . . . Tend My sheep . . . Feed My sheep"* (Jn. 21:15-17).

And this is the assignment of love for all Christians until the Lord of love comes again!

(Bibliography: J. H. Thayer, Greek-English Lexicon of the New Testament. F. W. Robertson, Robertson's Sermons. A. T. Robertson, Greek Grammar of the New Testament. G. W. Truett, A Quest for Souls. D. M. Baillie, God Was in Christ.)

MULTIPLIED

The phrase, *"Be multiplied,"* proclaims the fact that these attributes can grow and expand. In fact, if our faith is properly placed, which always refers to Christ and what He did at the Cross, these attributes definitely will advance in our hearts and lives.

Unfortunately, much of the modern Church is busily engaged in attempting to multiply money, while the Holy Spirit proclaims the fact here that *"Mercy, Peace, and Love,"* are to be multiplied. What a contrast!

(3) "BELOVED, WHEN I GAVE ALL DILIGENCE TO WRITE UNTO YOU OF THE COMMON SALVATION, IT WAS NEEDFUL FOR ME TO WRITE UNTO YOU, AND EXHORT YOU THAT YOU SHOULD EARNESTLY CONTEND FOR THE FAITH WHICH WAS ONCE DELIVERED UNTO THE SAINTS."

The diagram is:

1. The word *"diligence"* proclaims a compulsion generated by the Holy Spirit.

2. He had at first thought to write of the *"common Salvation,"* which means that his Epistle would have been similar to Romans. But the Holy Spirit, although the Author of the compulsion, did not lead in this direction.

3. The Holy Spirit intended for him to exhort the Saints to contend for the Faith.

4. The faith mentioned here is not faith exercised by the individual, but Christianity itself in its historic doctrines and life-giving Salvation.

5. *"Earnestly contend"* refers to the fact that with intense effort, the Saints must defend the Doctrines of Christianity.

6. *"Once delivered unto the Saints,"* refers to the fact that no other faith will be given. The idea is that God gave the Christian Doctrines to the Saints as a deposit of truth to be guarded.

THE COMMON SALVATION

The phrase, *"Beloved, when I gave all diligence to write unto you of the common salvation,"* proclaims the fact that Jude was thinking of writing an Epistle explanatory of the way of Salvation, such probably as the Epistle to the Romans. The word *"diligence"* implies that he was being compelled to write, and that the compulsion was generated by the Holy Spirit. We derive this from the subject matter. The Holy Spirit was definitely the One Who was urging him to write, but not on the subject which he first had in mind. This should be a great lesson for us:

We must first of all be led by the Spirit. And then led by the Spirit, we must be given direction by the Spirit. So we have both *"leading"* and *"direction."* *"Leading"* is that something is to be done, and *"direction"* is that which is to be done. We see in this the guidance of the Spirit in all things as it regards the Child of God. Jesus plainly said of Him, *"He* (the Holy Spirit) *will guide you into all truth* (not just some truth, but all truth)*: for He shall not speak of Himself; but whatsoever He shall hear, that shall He speak* (shall speak of that which was carried out by Christ at the Cross)*: and He will show you things to come"* (Jn. 16:13). Three things are said here by Christ concerning the Holy Spirit:

1. Guidance into all truth: at this particular time, it had come to the attention of

NOTES

Jude that some were *"turning the Grace of God into lasciviousness, and denying the only Lord God, and our Lord Jesus Christ."* Consequently, he must contend for truth, which he does in no uncertain terms.

2. Whatsoever He shall hear that shall He speak: the idea as presented here is the Glorification of Christ (Jn. 16:14). Jesus said: *"For He* (the Spirit) *shall receive of Mine, and shall show it unto you."* This refers to what Jesus did at the Cross, which was done on behalf of sinners, but which also made possible the victorious living of the Saint. In other words, the Holy Spirit is to make real to the Saint all the benefits of the Cross, which He will do, as the Saint evidences Faith in the great Sacrifice of Christ (Rom. 6:3-5, 11, 14; 8:1-2, 11).

3. He will show you things to come: the Holy Spirit showed to Jude what would happen in the Church, if the false direction continued. However, the broader sweep of this statement refers to all the great benefits that the Cross will bring about, that is if the Believer continues to evidence Faith in the Finished Work. In other words, the Holy Spirit will show us things to come in our lives, all made possible by the Cross, that is if we continue to believe.

On a personal basis, I believe the Lord has given me assurance, in other words, has shown me things to come, as it pertains to my own life and Ministry. I hold to these Promises, definitely believing that each Promise shall come to pass. To be sure, He will do for any and every Saint the same thing, if they will only believe the Lord, ever drawing closer to Him, and ever keeping their Faith in the great Sacrifice of Christ. He is no respecter of persons.

A PERSONAL EXPERIENCE

In the Saturday morning Service of our Easter Campmeeting, which date was April 14, 2001, the Lord gave me a Word, which was an encouragement to say the least, and that which was meant not only for me, but for you the Reader as well, and in fact, any Christian who will dare to believe God.

At the particular time when the Lord spoke to my heart, the Service had progressed to the point where the people were worshipping and doing so grandly. In other words, there was a great spirit of worship that had swept over the entirety of the congregation, as God began to move.

A dear Brother had been singing, and the Spirit of God had begun moving.

Between the verses of his song, while the people were praising and worshipping, he made a statement that was intended for me. I'm not sure if even he realized what he had said. But the moment it was said, the Spirit of God quickened it mightily to my heart, and which it continues to thrive unto this very hour. The statement was:

"If you can believe it, I can do it!"

It was a Word from the Lord, and is in essence saying that the emphasis is not on whether the Lord can carry out the necessary things which need to be done, because that is a given, in that He is able. The emphasis must be upon whether we can believe it or not? *"If you can believe it, I can do it!"*

That Word burned into my heart. *"If you can believe, I can do it!"* Why would the Lord give me that type of Word?

Of course, no human being can ascertain as to why the Lord does all things; however, as it regards my own personal experience, many of the things which I believe the Lord has told me to do, and which I believe He has said that He will also do within my heart, life, and Ministry, are totally and completely impossible, at least as the natural is concerned. That being the case, one easily gets one's eyes off of the Lord onto the difficulties and problems. So the Lord was telling me, not to look at circumstances, but to look to Him and keep believing.

Now what I've just given you is a very simple *"Word"*; however, just about everything the Lord does falls into that category. In other words, He makes it very easy for us to understand, so we will have no excuse.

As well, the manner in which the Lord gave this *"Word"* to me, I firmly believe was not given for me alone. I believe it was intended for *you* as well.

I do not know the needs or the crying of your soul. I do not know that for which you have cried unto the Lord. But of course the Lord knows, and this Word, *"If you can believe it, I can do it,"* I think is definitely meant

for you, just as much as it was meant for me. In fact, the Lord spoke to my heart about two years ago that whatever He gave to me is also meant for all those who love and support this Ministry. Therefore, this Promise is meant for you just as much as it was meant for me. *"If you can believe it, I can do it!"*

COMPULSION

The phrase, *"It was needful for me to write unto you,"* is far stronger in the original text. The word implies that whatever was to be written, had to be written at once and could not be prepared for at leisure, like the one he had previously contemplated. It was no welcomed task: *"Necessity was laid upon him."* What was this necessity?

It had to do with false doctrine that had come into the Church. In some way, whether revealed to him by others or revealed to him by the Holy Spirit, Jude had seen the danger that had come into the Church from false teachers. He was determined to call attention to this problem.

Unfortunately, many in the modern Church, and perhaps this has always been the case, do not desire that error be pointed out. But I have found out, through many years of preaching this Gospel of Jesus Christ, that if we aren't too very much opposed to error, we will not too very much be in defense of Truth.

Some contend that we are only to preach Truth and never mention the error. They say that this is the right way for error to be addressed.

While Truth most definitely, and as should be obvious, should certainly be preached, at the same time, error has to be graphically pointed out, or most Christians will never see what needs to be seen.

Error has a seductive spirit to its very nature and character. Paul said so:

"Now the Spirit (Holy Spirit) *speaketh expressly* (speaks pointedly), *that in the latter times* (the times in which we now live) *some shall depart from the faith* (Jesus Christ and Him Crucified), *giving heed to seducing spirits, and doctrines of Devils"* (I Tim. 4:1).

This plainly tells us that the *"spirits"* promoting these *"doctrines of Devils,"* are *"seducing spirits."* This means that the error that is presented is done in such a way that many

Christians do not see the error, but rather something else. Let me give you an example:

In our Easter Campmeeting of 2001, which I have just mentioned, on Thursday night, Donnie preached a Message that addressed itself not only to truth, but also to error. In the body of the Message, he gave quotes from certain Preachers, actually quoting them verbatim, and then told the names of the Preachers who were preaching false doctrine.

In the Sunday night Service, a man related to Donnie as to how he had heard Donnie's Message, and had grown somewhat angry, because in effect, he really didn't believe that these men were saying these things.

Strangely enough, he happened to catch one of them on Television that Sunday morning. The man was preaching exactly what Donnie had said that he was preaching, in other words, that which was false.

The man went on to relate to Donnie, as to how he didn't understand as to why he had not seen this previously? Had Donnie not preached this Message, more than likely he would have never seen this error, and that goes for most Christians like him.

Why is it that he had not seen it previously until Donnie expressly pointed it out?

As stated, all false doctrine is generated by seducing spirits, which means that it is so presented that many Christians will hear what is being said, but yet not hear what is being said! That's why Jesus over and over again said: *"He who has ears to hear, let him hear"* (Mat. 11:15; 13:9, 43; Mk. 4:9, 23; 7:16, etc.).

The doctrine of which I'm speaking of here, and which Donnie addressed, is the *"Word of Faith"* doctrine. The Preacher in question was Kenneth Copeland. Let me say it here kindly but bluntly:

This particular doctrine is not of the Lord. While it has many things in it that are right, just as most false doctrine does, its general thrust is totally wrong. And why do I say that?

The entirety of the *"Word of Faith"* doctrine stems from its interpretation of the Atonement, which is completely unbiblical. As we've already said in this Volume, it teaches that Jesus took upon Himself the Satanic nature while on the Cross. In other words, He literally, they claim, became a sinner on the Cross, and then died and went to

NOTES

Hell, and we speak of the burning side of Hell, where all sinners go. Copeland bluntly and plainly states that *"the Blood of Christ did not atone for anything."* Pure and simple that is blasphemy!

They then teach that Jesus atoned for the sins of man by suffering three days and nights in Hell, tormented in the flames, etc. At the end of the three days and nights, according to their version, God then said, *"It is enough,"* which at the time, Jesus was then *"born again,"* becoming the *"firstborn of many Brethren."* He was then raised from the dead.

I've already explained the *"firstborn"* synopsis, so we'll not go into that again, but several things must be said here:

1. The brief synopsis I've just given of their doctrine concerning the Atonement is not found at all in the Bible. In other words, their account is pure fiction. It does not Scripturally exist! In fact, one of their chief devotees, Joyce Meyer said concerning this false doctrine, *"You won't find this in the Bible, but you'll feel it in your spirit,"* or words to that effect! She's right about one thing, you won't find it in the Bible, because it's not Biblical.

2. The faith they teach that one must have in Christ is not what Christ did for us at the Cross, but rather His suffering in Hell for three days and nights. Consequently, a person cannot be saved believing this particular doctrine.

Paul said: *"For Christ sent me not to baptize, but to preach the Gospel: not with wisdom of words, lest the Cross of Christ should be made of none effect"* (I Cor. 1:17).

In the worst sort of way, these people have made the Cross of Christ of none effect. They have shifted people's faith from the Cross to Hell itself.

The Apostle then said: *"For the preaching of the Cross is to them that perish foolishness; but unto us which are saved it is the Power of God"* (I Cor. 1:18).

Paul spoke here of *"preaching the Cross!"* He didn't say anything about preaching the suffering of Christ in Hell, which would effect Salvation.

He also said: *"But we preach Christ crucified"* (I Cor. 1:23). Again, he didn't say anything about *"preaching Christ burning in Hell."*

And finally: *"For I determined not to know anything among you, save Jesus Christ, and Him crucified"* (I Cor. 2:2). Evidently, Paul didn't know anything about this *"Jesus died spiritually"* doctrine. And then I must add the following:

The Apostle also said: *"That your faith should not stand in the wisdom of men, but in the Power of God"* (I Cor. 2:5).

The *"Power of God"* is found in *"the preaching of the Cross"* (I Cor. 1:18). It is not found in the *"wisdom of men,"* and it's certainly not found in the *"doctrines of Devils."*

WHAT DOES IT MATTER?

Let the Reader understand that when we speak of the Atonement, we are speaking of the single most important thing in the history of man. According to what you believe about the Atonement, will determine whether you will be eternally saved or eternally lost. In other words, there is absolutely nothing more important than this.

As we've previously stated in this Volume, all false doctrine begins with a false interpretation of the Person of Christ or a false interpretation of the Mission of Christ, or both. In the case of the so-called *"Word of Faith"* doctrine it is a misinterpretation of both. They far too much, humanize Christ and deify man.

This is at least one of the reasons that the Holy Spirit had Jude to write this short Epistle. Attention must be called to false doctrine, and the Truth must be presented. We are not speaking here of mundane matters, but of the very issues of life and death.

Let me give you another example as to why most in the modern Church world don't like Jimmy Swaggart. While they may use other things as an excuse, the real reason is our insistence upon Faith in the Cross, and Faith in the Cross alone!

HUMANISTIC PSYCHOLOGY

I've already dealt with this subject several times in this Volume. But due to the fact that what we are addressing here is of such significance, I feel in my heart that I must make doubly certain that the Reader understands exactly what is being said.

A little over a hundred years ago (as I dictate these notes in 2001), Sigmund Freud

NOTES

presented to the world the beginning of the psychological way. It was an effort to attempt to understand man outside of the Word of God. In fact, at the time of Freud, Theology, which is the study of God and His Word, was the queen of the sciences in the universities of the land. I speak of the United States and Canada. Now, psychology is the queen of the sciences, with Theology given no place at all. In fact, the differences between the Bible and humanistic psychology cannot be bridged at all. Please note the following:

• The Bible is the Word of God (Jn. 1:1). The *"bible"* for psychology is man's opinion, which changes almost on a daily basis.

• The Bible holds all answers relative to human behavior (II Pet. 1:3). Psychology claims to hold all answers relative to human behavior, and those answers are not at all the same as are in the Bible.

• The Bible says man is an eternal soul (Jn. 3:16). Psychology has its roots in evolution.

• The Bible says man is a sinner (Rom. 3:23). Psychology says man is a victim.

• The Bible says the problem is man's evil heart (Jer. 17:9). Psychology says man's problem is his environment.

• The Bible says man is inherently evil (Jer. 17:9). Psychology says man is inherently good.

• The Bible treats the core of man's problem, which is an evil heart (Jer. 17:14). Psychology treats man's symptoms only.

• The Bible says that Jesus Christ is the answer (Mat. 11:28-30). Psychology says psychotherapy is the answer.

• The Bible says that we should deny self (Mat. 16:24). Psychology says we should love self.

• The Bible directs us to the Spirit of God (Zech. 4:6). Psychology directs us to the flesh.

• The Bible directs us to faith in God (Mk. 11:22). Psychology directs us to self-effort.

• The Bible directs us to Repentance (Acts 26:20). Psychology directs us to remorse.

• The Bible directs us to the Cross as the answer to man's dilemma (I Cor. 1:18). Psychology directs us to psychologists.

• The Bible directs us to Truth (Jn. 17:17). Psychology directs us to man's opinions.

- The Bible directs us to a relationship with Christ (Jn. 3:16). Psychology directs us to idolatry.
- The Bible directs us to personal responsibility (Rev. 22:17). Psychology directs us to irresponsibility.
- The Bible directs us to free will (Rev. 22:17). Psychology directs us to determinism (causes other than one's self).
- The Bible deals with a *"cure of souls"* (Mat. 11:28-30). Psychology deals with a *"cure of minds."*
- The Bible says God's Truth is unchangeable (Ps. 119:89). Psychology says truth is determined by majority and culture.
- The Bible says it is sufficient (II Pet. 1:3). Psychology says the Bible is insufficient.
- The Bible leads to love for God and man (Mat. 22:37-39). Psychology leads to love for self.

Psychology is actually the religion of humanism. Humanism puts man in the center of all things. Hence, psychology puts man in the center of all things.

Conversely, the Bible puts Christ in the center as the only answer for man, and more particularly, *"Christ and Him Crucified."* Psychology (psychotherapy) and the Bible, therefore, are total opposites and cannot be reconciled.

CHRISTIAN PSYCHOLOGISTS

The term *"Christian Psychologists"* is a misleading term causing unsuspecting seekers of help to think that such individuals have a body of learning that is not available to, or is different than that of secular Psychologists — or to Preachers of the Gospel for that matter.

However, let the Reader understand that there is no such thing as *"Christian Psychology."* It simply does not exist. There are some Psychologists who claim to be Christians, but no such thing as *"Christian Psychology"* or *"Christian Psychologists."*

This means there is no training or education that *"Christian Psychologists"* receive that is any different from secular Psychologists. The education in that realm that is given to a Christian who aspires to be a Psychologist is the same education that is given to the individual who has no regard for Christianity whatsoever.

NOTES

However, the term *"Christian Psychologist"* subtly leads the seeker of help to believe that the practitioner has a body of knowledge that is not given in the Word of God. In other words, there is an implication that the Word of God does not hold the answer to the problems that beset modern man.

One so-called Christian Psychologist said: *"It is not a question of whether therapists rely upon the Holy Spirit or upon their counseling skills."*

In other words, he was saying that it really doesn't matter where the help originates, whether it is from the Holy Spirit or from Psychology. They then claim that we *"must equip ourselves with the best tools available,"* insinuating, as stated, that the Bible is woefully lacking in this category. In fact, the same man who claimed that it didn't really matter where the help came from, also stated that modern man is facing problems that the Bible does not address. In other words, he was saying that the Bible is simply insufficient.

PSYCHOLOGY, A TOOL?

Is Psychology a tool?

When it was suggested that modern-day Psychology is not found in the Bible, one Preacher stated that neither is the automobile, the airplane, or the computer. We do not, he reasoned, resist utilization of these tools in our lives, so why should we resist the tool of Psychology (or any other self-help method or technique we might develop)?

My answer is, admittedly, the Bible has nothing to say about the automobile, computer, or a host of other crafts developed since it was written. In fact, the Bible does not claim to be a handbook on engineering, science, etc. (although, whatever it does say on these subjects is 100 percent accurate).

The Bible doesn't mention these things, because these are not man's problems. A man can be an expert scientist, a qualified engineer, or a host of other things — and still be a moral and spiritual wreck. However, the Bible *"does"* claim to be a handbook on the *"human condition,"* and it *"does"* claim to hold all the answers in this particular human area:

"According as His Divine power has given unto us all things that pertain unto life and

Godliness, through the knowledge of Him Who has called us to glory and virtue:

"Whereby are given unto us exceeding great and precious Promises: that by these we might be partakers of the Divine nature, having escaped the corruption that is in the world through lust" (II Pet. 1:3-4).

Now either the Bible did give us all things that pertain unto life or it didn't. If it didn't, it is a lie and we then need to turn to other sources.

Regarding Psychology, Christian educators have taken an ungodly, atheistic, anti-Christian, unbiblical, worldly system and attempted to integrate it into Biblical counseling. And the Church, regrettably, has bought it hook, line, and sinker.

There is no help, and I mean no help whatsoever in humanistic psychology. It in fact does not hold any answers. It is a zero. Actually, it not only has no positive answers for man, it actually causes harm.

There is only one answer for the sins, perversions, aberrations, and foibles of man, and that is *"Jesus Christ and Him Crucified."* In other words, what Jesus did at the Cross addresses itself to every single problem that man may have, whether spiritual or emotional, etc. (I Cor. 1:17-18, 21, 23; 2:2, 5).

THE FAITH

The phrase, *"And exhort you that you should earnestly contend for the faith,"* gives the answer to the ills of man.

If man could solve his problems without the Cross, then Jesus died in vain. This means that He needlessly came down here and died on the Cross, thereby suffering unimaginably for that which was unnecessary. When we bypass the Cross, or else we look elsewhere, we are insulting Christ to a degree that is shameful to say the least.

Let's first of all look at the term *"the faith."*

"The Faith" of which Jude mentions here is not faith as exercised by the individual, but Christianity itself in its historic Doctrines and life-giving Salvation. To make it very simple, in the words of Paul, it is *"Jesus Christ and Him Crucified."* Through the Cross and by the Cross, comes Justification, Sanctification, Grace, Peace, Hope, Faith, Love, and Blessings of every description. In fact, and as stated,

the mighty Holy Spirit, the Third Person of the Godhead, to which He is sometimes alluded, brings about all His work within our hearts and lives, which includes all of these Graces we have mentioned, plus many we haven't mentioned, by and through the legal work of the Cross.

While every Believer should definitely avail himself of the knowledge of all of these Graces we have mentioned, still, it is not necessary that he fully understand everything in order to be a beneficiary of what Christ has done. The major function of the Believer should be according to the following. If he can first of all major in the following, which anyone can do, then the understanding of all of these other things will begin to fall into place.

THE CROSS OF CHRIST

Every Believer must understand that every single thing he receives from the Lord has all been made possible by what Jesus did at the Cross. The Cross holds the answer to every question, the solution to every problem, the benefit of every need. The Cross is the means by which God gives everything to Believers. It's where Jesus made everything possible.

The Believer must understand this and believe this. This means he must not look to anything else for help, only the Cross.

One might say I think, without fear of contradiction, that *"the Cross"* is *"the Faith."* That's why we constantly take the Lord's Supper, which exemplifies *"the Faith."* The broken bread represents His broken body, which took place on the Cross, and the cup represents His shed Blood, which as well took place on the Cross. That constitutes *"the Faith."*

FAITH

We have been speaking of *"the Faith,"* which refers to its historic doctrines and life-giving Salvation. Now we want to refer to *"faith"* as exercised by the individual.

Understanding that the Cross is the means by which God deals with humanity, our Faith as a Believer must rest in that great Sacrifice of Christ. In other words, and as we have repeatedly stated in this Volume, the Cross must ever be the object of our Faith. Now this is critically important! In fact, Satan will do everything within his power to shift your faith to something else, and he really doesn't care what the something else might be. Most of the time he shifts it to good things, and because these things are good, it fools most Christians. In other words, they think it is proper faith. But let the Reader understand this:

If it's not Faith in the Cross of Christ, then it's not Faith that God will recognize.

Due to the fact that most Christians understand very little about the Cross, and that their faith is in something else altogether, this means that basically such faith is wasted faith. Let me give you an example:

I can have faith all day long in my so-called good confession and boast about how correct and Biblical I am in my confession, but the faith of which I am speaking, God will not recognize. Pure and simple, and irrespective as to what we think, it is faith in *"self,"* which translates into *"the flesh."* And the Scripture plainly says: *"So then they that are in the flesh cannot please God"* (Rom. 8:8).

All of this fools us simply because we are quoting Scriptures, and we think by doing that this constitutes Faith.

While the quoting of Scriptures is always good, the doing of such must never be the object of our faith, but rather the Cross.

Every Promise in the Word of God is made possible by what Jesus did at the Cross, and by no other means. Now let those words sink in, because what we've stated is very, very important.

God cannot even look at man except through Christ and what Christ did at the Cross. So if you want the Promises of God to be made real in your heart and life, you must make the Cross of Christ the object of your faith, and the Cross of Christ alone as the object of your faith. Then the Word of God will become real to you, and to be sure, it will become real in no other way.

THE HOLY SPIRIT

Let us understand that every single thing done in our hearts and lives as it pertains to God, always and without exception, comes through the Power, Office, Ministry, Work, and Person of the Holy Spirit. This means that

every single thing the Holy Spirit does for us, and everything that is done is done by the Holy Spirit, is all carried out within the parameters of the Finished Work of Christ. What Jesus did at the Cross made it legally possible for the Holy Spirit to do all that He does.

However, He demands of us that we evidence Faith in the Finished Work of Christ, or else He will not function. In other words, if our faith is placed in other things, and no matter how good or even Scriptural in their own right these other things might be, if our faith is placed in those things, the Holy Spirit simply will not help us, and we are then left on our own, which guarantees defeat. This is derived from Paul's statement: *"For the Law of the Spirit of Life in Christ Jesus has made me free from the law of sin and death"* (Rom. 8:2).

Satan is going to come against the Child of God in every way possible, in order to get us to sin. That is his effort and the reason for all that he does. The idea that sin is no longer any bother as it regards the Christian is foolishness indeed! Or the idea that we can arrive at some certain place to where temptation will be no more problem is wrong as well. As long as we are in this body of clay, Satan is going to come against us. That need not cause any problem, however, if we function according to God's prescribed order of victory. That prescribed order is the understanding of the Cross, our faith in the Cross, which gives the Holy Spirit latitude to work within our lives (Rom. 6:3-14; 8:1-2, 11, 13).

EARNESTLY CONTEND

In essence, Jude is telling us that we should *"earnestly contend"* for these things which we have been telling you, which speaks of the Cross.

"Earnestly contend" in the Greek is *"epagonizomai,"* and is found only here in the New Testament. The word speaks of a vigorous, intense, determined struggle to defeat the opposition. In fact, our word *"agony"* is the English spelling of the noun form of this word. The simple verb was used of athletes contending in the athletic contests. The Greek athletes exerted themselves to the point of agony in an effort to win the contest. With such intense effort does Jude

say that Saints should defend the Doctrines of Christianity.

Peter, in his First Epistle (3:15), tells us how we are to do so. He says that we should *"be ready always to give an answer"* to the opposition. The words *"give an answer"* are in the Greek a technical term of the law courts, speaking of the attorney for the defense *"presenting a verbal defense"* for his client.

The intensity of the defense must be adjusted to the intensity of the opposition that comes from Satan through false doctrine.

I think we should surely understand from these statements just how important all of this actually is. We must remember that these words as given by Jude, are not merely his own thoughts, but are that which the Holy Spirit wants said and done. However, contending for the Faith means not only a presentation of the truth, but as well the pointing out of false ways. As should be understood, this is going to raise the anger of those who are guilty of propagating false doctrine, and those who have believed the false message. So, my statements regarding the error of the *"Word of Faith"* doctrine, and *"humanistic psychology,"* will not set well at all with those who propagate these particular doctrines and directions. But if in fact, these doctrines will lead Christians into spiritual declension, and even possibly the loss of their souls, then we're speaking here of something that is of extreme importance. In fact, it is so important that the Earth has literally been soaked with blood down through the centuries, in order that the True Gospel of Jesus Christ be proclaimed, rather than error. So what we're speaking of here is something that has been a problem from the very beginning.

The Lord gave to the first family the means by which they were to commune with Him and He with them, which would be through the sacrificial system. Abel believed what God said and offered up an innocent victim, a lamb. Cain rebelled against this particular way, substituting his own ways and methods, which God would not accept. It's all recorded in Genesis, Chapter 4.

Cain was not content to continue to offer up that which God wouldn't accept, but felt at the same time, that he must also stop the true sacrifice, which he attempted to do by

NOTES

the killing of his brother. These two problems have persisted from then until now.

Evil men within the Church, attempt to present a way other than the Cross of which the Sacrifices were a type. As well, they are not content with their erroneous message, but feel they must silence the one who is preaching the Cross. And they will use any method to do so, even up to murder.

So this struggle didn't begin yesterday, it has been with us from the very beginning. Unfortunately, most Preachers aren't willing to take the stand that Jude took, along with John, Peter, and Paul, etc. Most Preachers want to be accepted by the crowd, so they become hirelings. So what am I saying?

I'm saying that we must *"earnestly contend for the faith which was once delivered unto the Saints."*

ONCE DELIVERED

The phrase, *"Which was once delivered unto the Saints,"* refers to *"once for all."* In other words, no other faith will be given.

"Delivered" in the Greek is *"paradidomi,"* and means, *"to give over into one's power or use, to deliver to one something to keep, use, take care of, manage."* The idea is that God gave the Christian doctrines to the Saints as a deposit of truth to be guarded (Wuest).

All of this means that no change in it is possible.

The Christian Faith is complete in the Cross. It is a *"Finished Work,"* which means that nothing can be added, and nothing must be taken away.

All of this was done *"once"* in the sense that it is not to be done again, and, therefore, in the sense then that it is complete, and that means that nothing is to be added to it.

Everything that the Lord has revealed through the Cross, we are to defend as true. We are to surrender no part of it whatever, for every part of this system is of value to mankind. And if the Believer doesn't understand the Cross, then the Believer doesn't understand Christianity.

THE PENALTY OF SIN AND THE POWER OF SIN

This which I'm about to say has already been said in one form or the other; however, simply because it so very, very important, I feel I must address the subject every opportunity that presents itself.

In Romans, Chapters 4 and 5, Paul deals with Justification by Faith, which in essence, tells us how that we are saved. In other words, it tells us what Jesus did at the Cross in order that the *"penalty of sin"* may be addressed. And then in Romans, Chapters 6, 7, and 8, he deals with the *"power of sin,"* and how it is broken.

Most Christians have a smattering of knowledge as it regards Justification by Faith. At least they understand that they are saved because of what Jesus did at the Cross. Most have at least that much knowledge; however, when it comes to the *"power of sin"* being broken, which refers to our Sanctification, most Christians don't have the foggiest idea as to what Paul is saying in those three Chapters. So this means that the knowledge of the Christian Faith, which must include both aspects of the Cross, is not held by many Christians. As a result, most Christians walk in spiritual failure, despite trying to do otherwise.

QUESTIONS

This of which we say I know to be true. As well, the way to victory which we have proposed in this Volume, I know to be true as well, and simply because it is exactly that which was taught by the Apostle Paul. Paul was given the meaning of the New Covenant, which in effect, was and is the meaning of the Cross. He gave that to us in Romans, Chapters 4 through 8, and elaborated on it in his other Epistles as well.

This way of the Cross will lead one to unparalleled victory. It will open up the Word of God to an extent that most Believers have not previously known. The Lord Jesus Christ will become more real in one's life, with a greater understanding of the Cross, than one has ever known before.

This is the way, and in fact, the only way, that one can have victory over the world, the flesh, and the Devil. This means that every single bad habit that one has can be laid aside, with proper Faith in the Finished Work of Christ, which gives the Holy Spirit latitude to work within our lives.

NOTES

Even though it is so obvious that the Message is Scriptural, and in fact, totally Scriptural, and it will even bear witness with the spirits of individuals who hear it, many for the first time. But yet, only a tiny few will take advantage of this life-giving flow. Why?

I suppose the reasons are as varied as the number of people involved; however, the main reason is, Satan fights the Way of the Cross more so than anything else. In fact, Satan aids and abets much that goes under the guise of Christendom, with people thinking it's of the Lord, when in reality it isn't. As we have repeatedly stated, Satan doesn't really care too very much what a Christian does, just as long as he doesn't obey Christ in regard to denying himself and taking up the Cross daily (Lk. 9:23).

Millions of Christians refuse that which could save their very lives, and even their souls, simply because they don't like the messenger. In other words, their Denomination doesn't approve of this particular one, or whatever the reason. As stated, the reasons are probably as varied as the number of people involved. But in actuality, these really aren't reasons but rather excuses. If a person doesn't like the messenger, the Lord to satisfy their whims is not going to change messengers. If one didn't like Paul, that was just too bad. The Lord had given the meaning of the New Covenant to Paul, and Paul was to give it to the people, which he did.

The Apostle fought vigorously that the great message of Grace would remain unsullied. When those who were trying to project law into this Message made their appearance, Paul opposed them with all the strength he had, and rightly so! In fact, had he kept silent, we would not have the Gospel today. It would have been destroyed!

(4) "FOR THERE ARE CERTAIN MEN CREPT IN UNAWARES, WHO WERE BEFORE OF OLD ORDAINED TO THIS CONDEMNATION, UNGODLY MEN, TURNING THE GRACE OF OUR GOD INTO LASCIVIOUSNESS, AND DENYING THE ONLY LORD GOD, AND OUR LORD JESUS CHRIST."

The exegesis is:

1. False teachers had crept into the Church.

2. They had come in by stealth and dishonesty.

3. The words *"before of old"* refer to their methods, which are by no means new. They must assume an outward expression of light, exactly as Satan has always done in his methods of seduction.

4. *"Turning the Grace of our God into lasciviousness,"* refers to evangelical terms such as *"salvation, faith, regeneration, atonement, resurrection,"* etc., being changed to mean something else. In other words, the terminology is the same, but the meaning is different.

5. To deny God and our Lord Jesus Christ is to deny the Plan of Salvation.

FALSE TEACHERS

The phrase, *"For there are certain men crept in unawares,"* refers to false teachers.

"Crept in" in the Greek is *"pareisduno duno,"* and means *"to enter alongside, to get in by the side, to slip in a side-door."* The rest of the phrases in this Verse tell us how they do this.

The Apostle Peter, describing these same persons, says, *"Who privily shall bring in damnable heresies"* (II Pet. 2:1).

"Unawares" means that these *"certain men"* profess to teach the Christian Faith, when in fact they deny some of its fundamental doctrines.

There is a Greek word in II Corinthians 11:13-15 which admirably describes the methods of the false teachers, who take after their father, the Devil. It is *"metaschematizo,"* and is translated *"transformed."*

It refers to the act of an individual changing his outward expression by assuming an expression put on from the outside, an expression that does not come from nor is it representative of what he is in his inner character. Lucifer did that after he struck at God's Throne and became the fallen Angel, Satan. As a fallen Angel he gave expression to his sin-darkened heart. But he knew that he could not attract the human race that way. He must impersonate God if he expected to be worshipped as God. He, therefore, assumed an outward expression of light, put on from the outside, and not representative of his inner sinful being. He disguised himself as an Angel of light.

His ministers (II Cor. 11:14-15), have done the same.

NOTES

Using Evangelical terms such as *"salvation, faith, regeneration, atonement, resurrection,"* etc., they put their own private meanings upon them that negate the Biblical definition. So while they may use the same words, they mean something else (Wuest).

CONDEMNATION

The phrase, *"Who were before of old ordained to this condemnation, ungodly men,"* tells us two things:

1. They who would denigrate the Cross of Christ, or place it in a subservient position in any manner, are called by the Holy Spirit *"ungodly."*

2. The word *"condemnation"* actually means *"judgment,"* and speaks of their activities as being wrong. In other words, they will ultimately be judged by God for what they are doing. That is an ordained fact.

This Text is a favorite one with Calvinists; however, the word *"ordained"* in the Greek text has quite a different connotation. The idea is, those who attempt to compromise *"the faith,"* will be judged by God, and it is ordained that it will be so.

Jude is explaining why he was compelled to write. Ungodly men had *"secretly slipped in"* among the Believers, with their pernicious doctrine. Paul uses the related word *"paraeisaktos"* of the Judaizers who had *"infiltrated"* Christian congregations to spy on their freedom in Christ Jesus (Gal. 2:4). The Holy Spirit through Jude is letting us know here that any efforts to counteract *"the faith"* will ultimately be met with severe condemnation, i.e., *"judgment."* As stated, we must take this admonition very seriously. The very reason the Christian way is referred to as *"the faith,"* is because of the way and manner in which it is constructed. God operates strictly on a system of faith, which refers to Believers trusting in something that He has done. That *"something"* is what Jesus did at the Cross on behalf of lost humanity. If faith and trust is placed in anything else, irrespective as to how good these other things might be, *"the faith"* is nullified.

GRACE

The phrase, *"Turning the Grace of our God into lasciviousness,"* refers to the fact that *"Grace"* had been turned to license.

Paul dealt with this problem as well. Due to the fact that Grace abounded over sin, false teachers were claiming that it didn't really matter how much they sinned, because Grace would automatically cover it. Paul answered that by saying:

"What shall we say then? Shall we continue in sin that Grace may abound?"

His answer was instant: *"God forbid, how shall we, who are dead to sin, live any longer therein?"* (Rom. 5:20; 6:1-2).

The modern counterparts of those in Paul's day function in several different ways.

Many in the Baptist faith one might say, function in the same manner as those in Paul's time. They claim to have faith in Christ, so the Grace of God which accompanies such faith, covers all of their sins, so sin to them is not really a problem. In other words, there is no effort to rid themselves of sin, which means they completely ignore the Sixth Chapter of Romans. The truth is, most of these people have really never been Born-Again. Despite their claims, they aren't saved, and in fact, have never been saved. They have adopted a philosophy of Christianity, but they've never really known Christ in a heartfelt manner.

There are others who address the problem of sin, by claiming that the soul and the spirit are made pure and perfect at conversion, and whatever happens in the realm of their physical body, has no bearing on their soul and spirit. Paul addressed this as well. He said:

"Having therefore these Promises, dearly beloved, let us cleanse ourselves from all filthiness of the flesh and spirit, perfecting holiness in the Fear of God" (II Cor. 7:1).

This Passage plainly tells us that whatever sinful filthiness takes place in the flesh also is, at the same time, taking place in the spirit.

Man is made up of spirit, soul, and body (I Thess. 5:23). Whatever affects one, affects the other. In other words, it's not possible for one to sin in one's physical body without the soul and the spirit being affected. So the contention of those who claim that their spirit is unaffected by sin, is unscriptural.

Let us understand first of all that Jude is speaking of false teachers who aren't actually saved. While they may have once been

saved, meaning that they had originally accepted the Lord as their Saviour, but ceasing to believe in the Finished Work of Christ, they have gone deeper and deeper into error, and have to be judged as unsaved, i.e., *"ungodly men."* In their ungodly state, which Jude will further emphasize later on, they have no intention of living right, but seek only to draw others into their web.

But most true Believers when having a problem with sin do so because they do not understand the *"sin nature,"* or the Cross of Christ. Inasmuch as this is probably the greatest problem in the realm of Christianity, perhaps it would be helpful here to address this subject.

THE SIN NATURE

Despite the fact that some Preachers teach that Christians no longer have a sin nature, the truth is the opposite. In fact, Paul dealt with this extensively in Romans, Chapter 6. He uses the word *"sin"* some 17 times, and almost all of these times he is referring to the sin nature. Actually, the original Greek text uses the term *"the sin,"* which is the way Paul addresses himself to this subject. This means that he's not speaking of particular acts of sin, but rather the *"sin nature."*

In effect, the Christian has three natures:

1. A human nature: even Christ had a human nature. And it's the human nature that is swayed, one way or the other, by one of the natures we will now list.

2. The Divine nature: Peter said: *"Whereby are given unto us exceeding great and precious promises: that by these you might be partakers of the Divine Nature . . ."* (II Pet. 1:4). This nature comes into the Child of God at conversion.

3. The sin nature: as stated, this is what Paul was talking about in Romans, Chapter 6. As well, John the Beloved said, *"If we say that we have no sin* (no sin nature), *we deceive ourselves, and the truth is not in us"* (I Jn. 1:8). However, when we come to Christ, even though the sin nature remains with us, which simply means *"a propensity to sin,"* its power is broken. And Paul tells us how that power is broken. He says:

"For he that is dead is freed from sin" (Rom. 6:7). The actual Text reads: *"For he

that is dead is freed from the sin," i.e., *"the sin nature."*

He also said, *"Likewise reckon ye also yourselves to be dead indeed unto the sin"* (Rom. 6:11). While the sin nature is not dead, we are in fact, dead to the sin nature, and became that way through what Christ did at the Cross. In other words, we were crucified with Him, buried with Him, and raised with Him in newness of life. Consequently, what we once were, we no longer are, meaning that the *"old man"* is dead (Rom. 6:6).

As long as our Faith is in the Cross of Christ, meaning that we know and understand that all that we have from God, comes through that Finished Work, we will have no trouble with the sin nature. This doesn't mean that all temptation will stop, for that will not be the case until the Trump of God sounds, or we die. Satan is going to continue to try to master us in any way that he can; however, if we *"deny ourselves,"* which refers to the fact of our understanding that we cannot do this thing ourselves, and must depend totally upon Christ and what He did at the Cross, and then take up the Cross daily, which means to renew our Faith daily in that Finished Work, we then need have no fear of being dominated again by the sin nature (Lk. 9:23-24).

Looking to the Cross is the only way that victory can be assured on a constant basis over the sin nature. No, we are not teaching sinless perfection; however, we definitely are teaching that *"sin shall not have dominion over you"* (Rom. 6:14).

WHAT DOES IT MEAN TO BE DOMINATED BY THE SIN NATURE?

The very fact that Paul said, *"Sin shall not have dominion over you,"* at the same time, means that sin *can* definitely have dominion over us. What do we mean by that?

Every unsaved person in the world is dominated completely by the sin nature. In other words, everything they do is sin. They do not know God, and their little self-help efforts amount to little, in their attempting to live some type of moral life. As stated, they are dominated by sin, which means they do its bidding, and do so constantly!

But when the individual comes to Christ, as we've already stated, the power of the sin nature is broken, and was broken when we were *"baptized into His Death"* (Rom. 6:3). This speaks of the Crucifixion of Christ.

Of course, we were not there when Jesus died, and as I've previously stated, it would have done us no good if in fact we had been there. This is not speaking of a physical death on our part, but rather something else altogether.

When the believing sinner expresses Faith in Christ, which refers to the moment of his Salvation, in the Mind of God that person is literally placed in Christ, which means that Christ as our Substitute, in a sense becomes us. In the Mind of God we died with Christ, were buried with Him and raised with Him in newness of life. This is all done by faith, which means that we place our faith and trust in Christ and what He did at the Cross.

As the penalty of sin is then removed, which of course is spiritual death, as well, the power of sin is broken, which means that sin is no longer to dominate the Child of God.

As long as the Believer keeps looking to the Cross, depending on what Jesus did there, and doesn't allow his Faith to be moved to other things, the Holy Spirit will work mightily on his behalf, and sin will not dominate him. But if the Believer takes his eyes from the Cross, and starts to look elsewhere, thereby rebelling against God's prescribed order of victory, whether he realizes what he's doing or not, the Holy Spirit will not be a party to such, and the Believer is then doomed to fail, which he always does. In other words, his own personal strength is not enough to overcome sin.

As stated, in such a situation, he fails in some way. He then seeks to try to stop the failure from happening again, and tries to do so by his own ability and strength, which God looks at as *"the flesh."* As stated, the Holy Spirit will not be a party to such efforts.

Most of the time, the Believer not knowing or understanding God's way, which is the Cross, attempts to find victory in other ways. He always fails, with the problem not getting better, but rather getting worse (Rom. 7:15).

This is very confusing, especially considering that such a Believer is trying so very hard. He has the Divine Nature within him, and he doesn't want to fail. Actually, failing the Lord is abhorrent to him, and brings tremendous grief and pain; nevertheless, the failure continues, and even gets worse, with the sin nature now dominating that Christian. In fact, due to most Christians not understanding the Cross as it refers to the Sanctification process, they are actually dominated by the sin nature. To say the least, this doesn't make for a very healthy Christian experience. In fact, it is everything but *"joy unspeakable and full of glory."*

WHAT DOES SUCH A CHRISTIAN DO?

If the Christian doesn't understand the Cross, their problem will continue to get worse and worse. In other words, *"works of the flesh"* will dominate them, despite all of their efforts to overcome (Gal. 5:16-21).

Unless such a Christian is taught the meaning of Romans, Chapter 6, such a Christian is doomed to live a life of spiritual failure. While they are still saved, and while they love the Lord supremely, there is no victory in their lives.

Unfortunately, the modern Church has been taught to lie about the situation. In other words, they've been taught to claim victory when in reality there is no victory. But let me show you the way and the manner in which Satan has worked, to attempt to camouflage the situation.

The major effort of the Holy Spirit is to make us Christlike. In other words, He wants to develop Righteousness and Holiness within our hearts and lives. He wants to develop His *"Fruit"* (Gal. 5:22-23).

All of these ways and means proposed by the Church for this to be brought about, and of course I speak of ways and means other than the Cross, simply won't work. So what has Satan now done?

He has diverted the attention of the modern Church from Righteousness and Holiness to *"money."* In fact, this is the central theme of the *"Word of Faith"* doctrine — money. Christians are taught that if they have enough faith, they can be rich. So if you turn on what proposes to be *"Christian Television,"* far too often, the subject matter of the Preacher is not at all on Christlikeness,

NOTES

but rather on *"how to get rich."* So millions of Christians are attempting to use their faith to bring this about.

The truth is, the only ones who are going to get rich are the Preachers. And they will get rich not from honest ways of making money, but by seducing Christians into giving sums of money to them, under the pretense that they are going to get much more money in return.

Never mind that they get nothing, there is enough greed, it seems, in all of us, to keep coming back for more. In other words, as the great circus entrepreneur P. T. Barnum said, *"There is a sucker born every minute!"*

Before the Christian can climb out of this morass, they must turn away from false doctrine, which seems to abound, and turn to the Cross. Now this can only be done, as they hear the Word of God truly preached as it regards this subject. The Scripture plainly tells us: *"Faith cometh by hearing, and hearing by the Word of God"* (Rom. 10:17). So, there is no way that faith, at least the right kind of faith, can be generated in the hearts and lives of Believers, unless they hear the truth as it ought to be heard. That's why Jesus also said:

"You shall know the truth, and the truth shall make you free" (Jn. 8:32). That's one of the reasons I plead with people to give one of these Commentaries to a friend. Whether it's the spoken or the written word, it must be given to Believers, or they cannot know God's way of victory. The whole thing is tied up in *"the faith!"* That's why John the Beloved said:

"This is the victory that overcometh the world, even our faith" (I Jn. 5:4).

It's why Paul said: *"But God forbid that I should glory, save in the Cross of our Lord Jesus Christ, by Whom the world is crucified unto me, and I unto the world"* (Gal. 6:14).

In effect Paul is saying here that one cannot have victory over the world, the flesh, and the Devil, except by Faith and trust *"in the Cross of our Lord Jesus Christ."* How much clearer can it be!

DENIAL

The phrase, *"And denying the only Lord God, and our Lord Jesus Christ,"* presents God the Father and God the Son.

"Deny" in the Greek is *"arneomai,"* and means, *"to deny, disown."* It is used of professing followers of Christ who, for fear of death or persecution, or for whatever reason, deny that Jesus is their Master, and desert His cause; it also refers, and is basically the intent here, of those who have apostatized from God and Christ through and by false doctrine.

The name *"Lord"* before *"God,"* is normally in the Greek text *"kurios"*; however, here it is *"despotes,"* which speaks of one who is the absolute owner, and has uncontrolled power over another.

It is only in the Son that we have the full revelation of God as Father. In other words, God the Father can be Lord in our lives, which means He has absolute control of all things as it regards our person, only as we properly understand Christ and make Him the Lord of our lives. In making Christ our Lord, we at the same time, make God the Father our Lord.

AS THIS REFERS TO THE CROSS

All of this in one way or the other refers to the Cross. For instance, the Name *"Lord,"* as given to Christ, is done so because of what Jesus did at the Cross. The Scripture says:

"And being found in fashion as a man, He humbled Himself, and became obedient unto death, even the death of the Cross.

"Wherefore God also has highly exalted Him, and given Him a Name which is above every name."

That Name is given in Verse 11: *"And that every tongue should confess that Jesus Christ is Lord, to the glory of God the Father"* (Phil. 2:8-11).

As stated, the title *"Lord"* as used here, speaks of one who is the absolute owner and has absolute power.

Jesus was and is God. So, how could God the Father exalt Him any higher than He already was? I suppose the best way to say this is to ask the question, *"How can perfection be improved upon?"*

Perfection cannot be improved upon, but one can add to perfection. And this is what happened in the case of Christ.

He has always been Creator, but now added to that highly esteemed position, He is also the Saviour. But let it be understood that

Jesus carries the exalted name of *"Lord,"* simply because He was *"obedient unto death, even the death of the Cross."*

If one attempts to know Christ outside of the Cross, or apart from the Cross, the Jesus that one then knows, will be *"another Jesus"* (II Cor. 11:4).

During Jude's day, the Gnostics taught that a form of Deity descended upon the man Jesus at His Baptism and left Him before His passion. In other words, they teach that His dying on the Cross was no more than any other man. In fact, their teaching was very similar to the *"Word of Faith"* teaching presently given.

The Gnostics taught that all matter is evil, and inasmuch as the human body is matter, for Jesus to have to die on the Cross, meant that in some way evil became a part of Him. The modern *"Word of Faith"* teachers, also claim that Jesus became a sinner on the Cross, in effect, taking upon Himself the Satanic nature, and thereby died as a sinner dies, which means that He went to Hell, and we speak of the burning side of the pit, to where all sinners and unsaved go. As the teaching of the Gnostics was altogether wrong, which Jude is addressing here, likewise the teaching of the *"Word of Faith"* people is wrong as well.

The Scripture nowhere says that Jesus on the Cross became a sinner. To become a sinner one has to sin, and Jesus never sinned. The Scripture does say that *"He was made to be sin for us"* (II Cor. 5:21), which is much different than one being a sinner. It actually means that Jesus became a Sin-Offering (Isa. 53:10). This means that God treated Him as though He was a sinner, and we speak of the penalty, which was death. However, His dying was not like anyone else.

In the first place, the Romans or the Jews didn't actually kill him. In fact, no one killed Him in the sense as we normally think, He rather laid down His life as a Sacrifice. Of this He said:

"No man taketh it (My life) *from Me, but I lay it down of Myself. I have power to lay it down, and I have power to take it again. This Commandment have I received of My Father"* (Jn. 10:18).

Being the very Source of Life, and not having a sin nature, He could not have died, unless He purposely willed Himself to die, which He did. Also, His death was a perfect death as it regards a perfect body, soul, and spirit. Thereby, it was a perfect Sacrifice, which God could and in fact, did accept.

Now our Word of Faith friends teach that Jesus not only died physically, but as well, that He died spiritually, which means He died as a lost sinner. Peter completely refutes that by saying:

"For Christ also has once suffered for sins (the Cross), *the just for the unjust, that He might bring us to God, being put to death in the flesh, but quickened by the Spirit"* (I Pet. 3:18).

The Holy Spirit through Peter plainly says here that Jesus was *"put to death in the flesh"* only. In other words, He died physically but not spiritually.

Had He died spiritually, He would have had to have gone to the burning side of Hell, and remained there forever and forever, not just three days and nights, as our Word of Faith friends claim.

Why do we make so much of this?

We do so for two reasons:

1. We are dealing with the souls of men. And this means that if a person has an improper understanding of the Cross, i.e., *"the Atonement,"* they will be seriously weakened spiritually, and they could lose their soul. Understanding that in that light, it becomes very, very serious!

2. No sinner can get saved believing such a doctrine. The Scripture plainly says:

"For God so loved the world, that He gave His only Begotten Son (gave Him at the Cross), *that whosoever believeth in Him* (believes in Christ and what He did at the Cross), *should not perish, but have everlasting life"* (Jn. 3:16).

DEATHS?

Those who propose that Jesus died spiritually, use as one of their Scriptures, Isaiah 53:9. The Prophet there said:

"And He (Christ) *made His grave with the wicked, and with the rich in His death; because He had done no violence, neither was any deceit in His mouth."*

They claim that inasmuch as the word *"death"* in the Hebrew is actually *"deaths,"*

which speaks of the plural, that Jesus died not only physically, but as well, spiritually.

However, the oldest manuscript of Isaiah in existence, which is the Dead Sea Scrolls, translates the Hebrew word here used, as *"tomb,"* as, *"And He made His grave with the wicked, and with the rich in His tomb."* In fact, where He made His Grave is the subject matter of the Verse, hence the word *"tomb"* being correct.

And if the Hebrew Scholars insist upon the translation of the Hebrew word as *"deaths,"* it refers to Him fulfilling the five-fold Sacrifices, in His one physical death.

Scripture must interpret Scripture, and always will, if interpreted properly. In other words, it is Scripturally improper, to attempt to make a doctrine out of one Verse, whenever such a doctrine clashes with many other Scriptures on the same subject. The Word plainly tells us that what Christ did as it regards the Redemption of humanity, was all done at the Cross, and not in Hell itself, etc. (Rom. 6:1-14; I Cor. 1:17-18, 21, 23; 2:2; Gal. 6:14; Eph. 2:10-18; Col. 1:14; 2:14-15).

To deny the Cross in any way is to deny the *"Lord Jesus Christ."* Of this Paul said:

"For many walk, of whom I have told you often, and now tell you even weeping, that they are the enemies of the Cross of Christ."

He then said, *"Whose end is destruction, whose God is their belly, and whose glory is in their shame, who mind earthly things"* (Phil. 3:18-19).

(5) "I WILL THEREFORE PUT YOU IN REMEMBRANCE, THOUGH YOU ONCE KNEW THIS, HOW THAT THE LORD, HAVING SAVED THE PEOPLE OUT OF THE LAND OF EGYPT, AFTERWARD DESTROYED THEM THAT BELIEVED NOT."

The diagram is:

1. The tone of *"I will therefore put you in remembrance,"* suggests something of anxiety and upbraiding, which may be compared to the tone of Paul in writing Galatians.

2. A lack of faith destroyed the Israelites in the wilderness.

3. This statement in Verse 5, about the Lord saving the people out of the land of Egypt, and then afterward destroying them who believed not, refutes unconditional eternal security.

REMEMBRANCE

The phrase, *"I will therefore put you in remembrance,"* could be translated, *"I wish to remind you."* Jude's statement as he will give it, is taken directly from the Word of God.

As did Peter in II Peter 1:12, Jude states that his readers already know what he is about to say but that he will remind them of it. So he gives them three examples of the Lord's judgments:

1. On the unbelievers at the time of the Exodus.
2. On the fallen angels.
3. On Sodom and Gomorrah.

In each instance the objects of judgment are notable rebels against the Lord.

While Jude has three illustrations of judgment as given here (Israel, angels, Sodom and Gomorrah) and has two that are used by Peter (angels and Sodom and Gomorrah), we see at once that Jude does his own thinking and does it well. To what Peter wrote a few years ago to the same Readers he adds one striking, new example and an inner connection between the ones that are selected. The commentators, as a rule, do not stress this connection and thus do not point out why Jude uses Israel and properly places this illustration first.

UNBELIEF

The phrase, *"Though you once knew this, how that the Lord, having saved the people out of the land of Egypt, afterward destroyed them that believed not,"* tells us a whole lot as to how the Lord deals with people.

The first thing of which Jude reminds his readers is that the Lord, after having saved Israel out of Egypt, destroyed such as did not believe. The account is found in Numbers, Chapter 14.

Inasmuch as the Holy Spirit through Jude places *"unbelief"* first in the order of sin, and especially that it is Israel, God's chosen people, used as an example, we learn several things:

We learn just how bad that unbelief actually is, and we learn that even God's choice are not exempt from the demand of faith and the potential judgment of unbelief.

All of Israel was saved out of Egypt, which means they were now part of the Covenant, which means they were saved. But in the wilderness, all of the older generation, with the exception of Joshua and Caleb, were condemned to death, and because of unbelief. While it is certainly possible that some repented of this action, and if they did their souls were saved; however, the Scripture gives us no clue of such.

God doesn't demand much of the human race, only faith, and the faith that He demands, is Faith in Christ and Him Crucified. In fact, the faith of the Old Testament Saints was to be likewise. Actually, Israel always went astray, when their faith was changed from the Sacrifices and what the Sacrifices represented, Which and Who was Jesus Christ and His sacrificial death on the Cross, to something else. In fact it was the same here of which Jude spoke.

ISRAEL AND THE PROMISED LAND

Israel was delivered out of Egyptian bondage for a particular purpose. They were to occupy a particular land, which was Canaan, and were there to be the recipients of the Blessings of God, and above all, to ultimately bring the Redeemer into the world, for which purpose they had literally been raised up. Because of unbelief, they now refused to go into that land. In essence, they were saying *"no,"* to the Plan of God for their very existence. Without this Redeemer man was hopelessly lost, and as well, Israel was hopelessly lost! So their refusing to believe God, thereby going in to possess the land, which the younger generation would do nearly 40 years later, in effect, one might say, was rebellion against the Cross.

If chronological order here has any reference to the severity of the situation, then we know that unbelief is the worst sin of all. And the unbelief of which we speak, in some way pertains to the Person of Christ, and/or the Mission of Christ.

(6) "AND THE ANGELS WHICH KEPT NOT THEIR FIRST ESTATE, BUT LEFT THEIR OWN HABITATION, HE HAS RESERVED IN EVERLASTING CHAINS UNDER DARKNESS UNTO THE JUDGMENT OF THE GREAT DAY."

The structure is:

1. From the apostasy of Israel, Jude turns now to the sin of the angels.

2. These particular angels did not maintain their original position in which they were created, but transgressed those limits to invade territory that was foreign to them, namely, the human race.

3. They left Heaven and came to Earth, seeking to cohabit with women, which they did (Gen. 6:4).

4. As a result, God has imprisoned these rebellious angels for this particular sin, and they are now under a complete and careful guard.

5. They will be judged at the Great White Throne Judgment, and then placed in the *"lake of fire"* where they will remain forever and forever (Rev. 20:10).

FALLEN ANGELS

The phrase, *"And the angels which kept not their first estate,"* refers to the fact that they left their original status as angels. Angels are a separate creation from the human race, with human beings occupying a different category than that of angels. Angels are a host and were created that way. They do not reproduce themselves. There is the same number of angels today as there was when they were created. By contrast, the human race reproduces itself. From a beginning of two individuals the race has grown to the proportions it is today.

What they did is recorded in Genesis 6:4. They left their realm and native state and entered the human realm in order to marry the daughters of men in an attempt to do away with the pure strain of man, and thus keep the *"Seed of the woman"* from coming into the world to defeat them. These angels constitute a part of the one-third of the angels that rebelled with Lucifer (Rev. 12:4).

For this act, and we speak of committing fornication with women, they were locked away in a special confinement in the heart of the Earth. In fact, the Scripture tells us that during the three days and nights after Jesus was crucified, *"He went and preached unto the spirits in prison"* (I Pet. 3:19). These are the angels in question, and are referred to by Peter as *"spirits."*

Incidentally, the word *"preached"* as it regards what Christ then did, is not the normal word used for *"preached"* which is *"euaggelizo,"* and means, *"to announce good news."* The word that Peter used is *"kerusso,"* which means, *"to herald a Divine truth."* There was no good news for these fallen angels. There was rather a herald given by Christ, which probably stated that despite their efforts to foil the Incarnation, they had not succeeded. Christ had come, and furthermore, had died on the Cross, which opened up the way to God for believing sinners.

Going back to the manner in which Jude proclaims this example, to say that *"Angels"* should be named first means not to see why they are placed second. No Salvation preceded their Fall, as it did with Israel. When Jude looks at its inwardness, the case of Israel ranks first in the estimation of Jude and in view of the application which he desires to make to his readers: a whole people (Israel) was saved, then so many fell into unbelief and were *"destroyed."* So the Readers of Jude's Epistle were saved and are now God's people; they must not fall into unbelief and be destroyed, presents the greater thrust of what Jude is saying.

The case of the angels is different. From their creation onward they had their own principality, their own glorious habitation with God. They did not keep what they had, but rather left; they are doomed!

These angels came to Earth, took up with women and committed fornication with them, begat a race that was half-devil and half-man, which was so wicked that God sent the Flood lest all mankind be contaminated. This is what II Peter 2:4 and Jude, Verse 6 mean.

HABITATION

The phrase, *"But left their own habitation,"* refers to Heaven.

"Habitation" in the Greek is *"oiketerion,"* and means *"a dwelling-place,"* and in this instance, it refers to Heaven.

"Their own" in the Greek is *"idion,"* and means *"one's own private, personal, unique possession,"* indicating here that Heaven is the peculiar, private abode of the angels. Heaven was made for the angels, not for man. While it is the temporary abode of the departed Saints until the new Heavens and new Earth are brought into being, the eternal dwelling-place of man will be on this perfect Earth — the Earth made new (Rev. 21:1-3).

"Left" in the Greek is "apoleipo," and means, "to leave." The way this word is given in the Greek, it refers to a once-for-all act. This was apostasy with a vengeance. They had, so to speak, burned their bridges behind them, and had descended to a new sphere, the Earth, and into a foreign relationship, that with the human race, foreign, because the latter belongs to a different category of created intelligences than they. These angels left Heaven behind. That is, they had abandoned Heaven. They were done with it forever.

This all plays into the idea that Lucifer once ruled on this Earth, and we speak of the time before his Fall. At the time of his rebellion against God, every evidence is that the Lord destroyed whatever it was that was on this Earth at that time. This is the so-called gap between Genesis 1:1 and 1:2. God originally created this Earth, whenever that was, to be beautiful and perfect; however, something happened which caused it to go into the chaos of Genesis 1:2. Many Bible Scholars believe the rebellion of Lucifer occasioned this chaos.

At the time of Adam, when God brought the world back to a habitable condition, Satan by subterfuge, attempted to get control of the Earth, which he did. Paul refers to him as the "god of this world" (II Cor. 4:4).

Knowing that God has promised a Redeemer, and that the Redeemer would be the "Seed of the woman," which had to be a man, Satan would attempt to foil this Plan of God, by corrupting the bloodline of the human race. Some of his fellow angels (Satan is himself an angel) would cohabit with women, and if enough of this could be done, it would destroy the human race, making the Incarnation impossible.

EVERLASTING CHAINS

The phrase, "He has reserved in everlasting chains under darkness," refers to these particular angels now imprisoned in the underworld.

The question may well be asked, if God imprisoned these particular angels, why didn't He imprison all the fallen angels at the very beginning of their rebellion?

The only answer we can give is that He couldn't legally do so. The reason He could imprison these in question is because they

NOTES

broke the law of their creation. They "kept not their first estate, but left their own habitation." While the other fallen angels rebelled against God, they did not commit this terrible sin, so one might say, God could not legally imprison them at that time. To be sure, however, all the fallen angels will ultimately be imprisoned in the lake of fire (Rev. 20:10).

THE GREAT WHITE THRONE JUDGMENT

The phrase, "Unto the judgment of the great day," refers to the coming "Great White Throne Judgment," which will take place a thousand years after the Rapture of the Church (Rev. 20:5-15).

At the Great White Throne Judgment, Jesus Christ will be the Judge. He is today the Saviour of man, at least those who will believe, but tomorrow He will be the Judge. So we accept Him now as Saviour, or we will face Him on that day, as Judge.

At this particular Judgment, only the unredeemed will be present, and will include all unredeemed who have ever lived from the very beginning. Hell will deliver up all that is in it, with all unredeemed alive on Earth at that time, joining in this great crowd of eternal doom. As well, and as stated here, fallen angels will be judged there as well, which of course will include Satan, because he is an angel. This account is given in Revelation, Chapter 20.

At this Judgment all will be lost, because all are lost. That being the case, some might ask, why the Judgment?

A record being kept of all that is done (Rev. 20:12), no one will be able to claim they were treated unjustly.

The consignment for all will be "the lake of fire," from which there will be no reprieve, and which will exist forever and forever (Rev. 20:10, 15).

No redeemed will be at this Judgment, our sins having already been judged in Christ.

THE POWERS OF DARKNESS

Even though the general thrust of this Passage as given by Jude, doesn't lean toward this of which I desire to address, with the Brother of our Lord basically addressing himself to the sin of rebellion; still, the statement concerning fallen angels opens the door.

We learn from Jude's statement, however, just how powerful these beings actually are. Paul addressed himself to this, and concerning the opposition of spirit beings to the Saints, by saying: *"For we wrestle not against flesh and blood, but against principalities, against powers, against the rulers of the darkness of this world, against spiritual wickedness in high places"* (Eph. 6:12). The idea is this:

Considering what we as Christians are facing, it is imperative that we follow God's prescribed order of victory. If not, there is absolutely no way that we can come out victorious. Spiritual warfare is very real, and if it's not addressed properly, we will suffer defeat.

GOD'S PRESCRIBED ORDER

It is at the Cross where Jesus satisfied the demands of the broken law, and as well, defeated every power of darkness (Eph. 2:13-18; Col. 2:14-15).

Paul said: *"And having spoiled principalities and powers, He made a show of them openly, triumphing over them in it"* (Col. 2:15).

So, the answer to our dilemma is what Jesus did for us at the Cross, and to be sure, all that He did there was totally and completely for us, and not at all for Himself.

Understanding this, the second step is that our faith ever rests in that Finished Work. This is very, very important! The object of the faith of the Child of God must always be the Cross, and nothing but the Cross.

When this is done, the third thing, and that which will follow, will be the help of the Holy Spirit. Working strictly within the parameters of the great Sacrifice of Christ, the Holy Spirit demands faith of us, but more particularly, Faith in Christ and what Christ did at the Cross. Then the Holy Spirit will work mightily on our behalf (Rom. 8:1-2, 11).

This is God's prescribed order of victory: A. The Cross; B. Our Faith in the Cross; and, C. The Moving and Operation of the Holy Spirit, Who works according to our Faith in the Finished Work of Christ.

FALSE DIRECTIONS

If the Christian doesn't understand the Message of the Cross, and regrettably, most

NOTES

don't, and because it's seldom preached behind the pulpit, then they will resort to other things, mostly foolish things. I suppose the reason this is seldom preached, is because Satan fights the Cross as he fights nothing else. His greatest opposition is expended in this direction. But let us understand, for the Christian to not understand the Cross, is like a fish that doesn't understand water, or a human being that doesn't understand breathing. The first thing as a Believer that we should know and understand is the Cross and all that it affords. This is given to us in Romans, Chapter 6, with Paul taking us step by step through the single most important part of the Believer's life in Christ. As I've said already several times in this Volume, the Sixth Chapter of Romans tells us *"how"* the Holy Spirit works and functions, which is all by and through what Jesus did at the Cross, as is clearly obvious. Romans, Chapter 8, tells us *"what"* the Spirit will do, once we learn *"how"* He works. The *"how"* is by and through the Cross, while the *"what"* is by and through our Faith in the Cross, i.e., *"the Finished Work of Christ."*

As stated, if Preachers do not know God's way of victory, which is the Cross, they will always manufacture their own ways. Some of these *"ways"* run all the way from the sublime to the ridiculous. They run the gamut from the many methods of humanistic psychology, with new ways being added to that genre almost daily, to that which proposes to be Spiritual and thereby Scriptural. But let the Reader understand that if it's not Faith in the Cross, then it's not the true armor of God, and it simply will not work. The Church has come through many proposed solutions, such as demons, confession, the buddy system, slain in the Spirit, the family curse, territorial curses, being militant against Satan, fasting, etc. While some of these things are right in their proper use, others aren't right. For instance:

The family curse is a case in point. Christians are told, that is if they are having problems, that it's probably caused by a *"family curse,"* meaning, that the great, great grandfather did something terrible, and the Judgment of God was upon him, and has passed down to the particular individual in question.

This is derived from Exodus 20:5. The Scripture says:

"Thou shall not bow down thyself to them (idols), *nor serve them: for I the LORD your God am a jealous God, visiting the iniquity of the fathers upon the children unto the third and fourth generation of them who hate Me."*

This tells us that the *"family curse"* is definitely real; however, it is extended to *"the third and fourth generation"* only as it pertains to those who continue to hate the Lord, which means to refuse to serve Him.

The moment an individual gives his or her heart to Christ, the family curse is broken. The Scripture plainly tells us: *"Therefore if any man* (and that means all) *be in Christ, he is a new creature: old things are passed away; behold, all things are become new"* (II Cor. 5:17).

Therefore, Preachers telling Christians that their problems are caused by a *"family curse,"* is basely unscriptural. While the Believer definitely might be having problems, the so-called family curse is definitely not the problem. Consequently, laying hands on them and rebuking the family curse, is in effect, unscriptural.

The reason the individual is having problems, is because they do not know and understand the Cross. So, the Preacher should explain the Victory of the Cross to such a person, which will help them to understand their place and position in Christ, which will then give them the help of the Holy Spirit, which alone and Who alone will solve the problem.

Preachers telling Believers these type of things, and I continue to speak of the family curse, etc., they are *"making the Cross of Christ of none effect"* (I Cor. 1:17). In other words, if we emphasize anything other than the Cross, we are abrogating God's prescribed order of victory. And that is a serious sin! The Cross must ever be held up as the answer to man's dilemma, whether the unredeemed or the Redeemed (I Cor. 1:17-18, 21, 23; 2:2, 5).

(7) "EVEN AS SODOM AND GOMORRHA, AND THE CITIES ABOUT THEM IN LIKE MANNER, GIVING THEMSELVES OVER TO FORNICATION, AND GOING AFTER STRANGE FLESH, ARE SET FORTH FOR AN EXAMPLE, SUFFERING THE VENGEANCE OF ETERNAL FIRE."

NOTES

The composite is:

1. The Greek Text introduces a comparison showing a likeness between the angels of Verse 6 and the cities of Sodom and Gomorrha of this Verse. But the likeness between them lies deeper than the fact that both were guilty of committing sin. It extends to the fact that both were guilty of the same identical sin.

2. This Verse tells us that the sin of the fallen angels was fornication. It is described in the words, *"going after strange flesh."*

3. The sin of Sodom and Gomorrha, and the cities about them, was homosexuality, which Paul describes in Romans 1:27.

4. Those who engage in the sin of homosexuality, and refuse to repent, will suffer the vengeance of eternal fire.

SODOM AND GOMORRHA

The phrase, *"Even as Sodom and Gomorrha, and the cities about them in like manner,"* likens the sin as similar to the sin of the fallen angels. It extends to the fact that both were guilty, as stated, of the same identical sin. The translation should read, *"Just as Sodom and Gomorrha and the cities about them, in like manner do these angels, having given themselves over to fornication and having gone after strange flesh."*

In a simple past fact, the unbelieving Israelites are dead and gone. Concerning the fallen angels, the Lord is now keeping them under blackness. Neither of these two do we see. But Sodom and Gomorrha lie before our very eyes in the region of the Dead Sea, at least where they once were. At one time they were rich, verdant, a garden spot. Now they are salt, blasted forever, a terrible place.

Lot chose Sodom because it was *"as the garden of the LORD* (like a paradise), *like the land of Egypt* (so rich and fertile), *well watered everywhere before the twin cities were destroyed"* (Gen. 13:10).

I have personally been there. Not a thing grows; not a creature lives in the waters of the Dead Sea. It seems almost incredible that Genesis 13:10 could at one time have been true of this wasted land.

Two other cities besides Sodom and Gomorrha were destroyed, Admah and Zeboim (Deut. 29:23; Hos. 11:8). The fifth city, Zoar, was spared, but *"all the plain"* was destroyed (Gen. 19:21-25) (Lenski).

FORNICATION

The phrase, *"Giving themselves over to fornication,"* presents the type of sin committed by the fallen angels and the inhabitants of Sodom and Gomorrha.

Some claim that adultery is unlawful relationship between those who are married, while fornication pertains to those who are unmarried. That is basely incorrect.

The definition of adultery pertains to unlawful relationship between men and women, whether they are single or married. And yet, the term *"adultery"* is much more limited than the term *"fornication."* In other words, all fornication is adultery, but all adultery is not fornication.

Fornication covers a wide spectrum of unlawful acts — unlawful according to the Word of God. It encompasses all of the following:

1. Adultery, whether the people are married or single (Mat. 5:32; 19:9; I Cor. 7:2; 10:8; I Thess. 4:3; Rev. 9:21).

2. Incest (I Cor. 5:1; 10:8).

3. Idolatry and adultery respecting idol gods (II Chron. 21:11; Isa. 23:17; Ezek. 16:15, 26, 29; Acts 15:20, 29; 21:25; Rev. 2:14-21; 14:8; 17:2-4; 18:3-9; 19:2).

4. Harlotry (Jn. 8:41; I Cor. 6:13-18).

5. Spiritual harlotry (Ezek. 16:15, 26, 29; Rev. 17:2-4; 18:3-9; 19:2).

6. Homosexuality (Rom. 1:24-29; I Cor. 6:9-11; II Cor. 12:21; Gal. 5:19; Eph. 5:3; Col. 3:5; Heb. 12:16; Jude Vss. 6-7).

So we see that *"fornication"* covers a wide range of immorality, but as Jude speaks of it, he is referring to homosexuality.

STRANGE FLESH

The phrase, *"And going after strange flesh,"* refers to *"another of a different kind."*

That is, these angels transgressed the limits of their own natures to invade a realm of created beings of a different nature. This invasion took the form of fornication, a cohabitation with beings of a different nature from theirs, namely women. This takes us back to Genesis 6:1-4 where we have the account of the sons of God (here, fallen angels), cohabiting with women of the human race (Wuest).

The sin of the angels was against nature. In the case of the cities mentioned, this sin was also against nature, that which Paul mentions in Romans 1:27, men with men and women with women, a departure from the natural use and against nature.

HOMOSEXUALITY

Despite claims to the contrary, homosexuals are not born that way. While all human beings may definitely be born with certain proclivities toward certain directions, it is only a matter of degree. In other words, if every man has an approximate 10 percent proclivity toward femininity (the number is mine and not a biological fact), some might even be born with 15 or 20 percent. But as stated, it's all a matter of degree, which means that despite the degree, certain boundaries are not crossed. In other words, the boundaries are always *"after his kind"* (Gen. 1:21, 24-25).

Men become homosexuals, and women become lesbians, as a result of something happening to them as a child. Most are molested homosexually in some way, or else they are drawn into a relationship through *"lusts."* Once the line is crossed, the tendency in that particular direction becomes more exaggerated, with the problem steadily growing worse. Only the Power of God can break the thing. In addressing this issue Paul said:

"Know ye not that the unrighteous shall not inherit the Kingdom of God? Be not deceived: neither fornicators, nor idolaters, nor adulterers, nor effeminate, nor abusers of themselves with mankind."

And then he said: *"And such were some of you: but you are washed, but you are sanctified, but you are justified in the Name of the Lord Jesus, and by the Spirit of God"* (I Cor. 6:9-11).

"Abusers of themselves with mankind," refer to homosexuals. The Greek word for *"abusers"* is *"arsenokoites,"* and means *"one guilty of unnatural offenses; a sodomite; homosexual; sex pervert."*

CAN A HOMOSEXUAL BE SAVED?

Even as we just quoted you from I Corinthians, homosexuals, as well as anyone else, can definitely be saved; however, the practice of homosexuality must stop after conversion, and in fact will stop, if the person has truly come to the Lord. This doesn't mean that there will not be any more temptation, but it does mean that the person will ultimately have victory, if they continue to look to what Jesus did for them at the Cross.

There are many homosexuals who claim to be saved while continuing to practice their sin. But the Holy Spirit through Paul plainly tells the human race, *"be not deceived."* He then said, *"Know ye not that the unrighteous shall not inherit the Kingdom of God?"* He then went on to list some of the types of sin which fall into the category of the *"unrighteous."* Homosexuality definitely falls into that category.

WHY HOMOSEXUALITY IS AN ABOMINABLE SIN

Homosexuality is one of the ways that fallen man has departed from his Creator's intention. Homosexuality cuts across the individual's natural sexual orientation, which means that it flies in the face of God's creation scheme for human sexual expression. Consequently, it is unnatural, and no matter what type of laws may favor this sin, and so-called same sex marriages, it is still an abomination in the eyes of God.

Three sins have always become prominent in the society of nations or empires, which are on the verge of destruction. In other words, they rot from within. Those sins are: A. Homosexuality; B. Pedophilia — the sexual molestation of children; and, C. Murder. Abortion only adds to this crime. Unfortunately, these three sins (crimes) are pandemic in America at present, and getting worse.

We gloat that we are the only superpower on Earth; however, powerful armies, navies, and sophisticated weaponry do not at all address the problems we've just mentioned. These problems are spiritual and can only be addressed by spiritual means, which refer to an encounter with the Lord Jesus Christ, resulting in the change of one's heart. There is no other solution!

And we might quickly add, Revival cannot begin in the State House or the White House. It cannot even begin with searching souls. It can only begin with the Church.

The Holy Spirit through Simon Peter plainly said: *"For the time is come that judgment must begin at the House of God: and if it first begin at us, what shall the end be of them who obey not the Gospel of God?"* (I Pet. 4:17).

THE JUDGMENT OF ETERNAL FIRE

The phrase, *"Are set forth for an example, suffering the vengeance of eternal fire,"* proclaims the judgment of all homosexuals who refuse to repent, and as well, all who do not know the Lord.

Just as the incarceration of the fallen angels is an example of God's judgment upon sin, so the cities of Sodom and Gomorrha, *"are set forth as an example, suffering the vengeance of eternal fire."* *"Are set forth"* in the Greek is *"prokeimai,"* and means *"to lie exposed, as a corpse laid out for burial."* It refers to something that is held up to view as a warning.

"Suffering" in the Greek is *"hupecho,"* and means, *"to sustain, undergo."* Vincent says, *"The participle is present, indicating that they are suffering to this day the punishment which came upon them in Lot's time,"* and will continue to suffer forever. The reference to these cities is not, therefore, limited to the ruins of the literal cities, but to the inhabitants who right now are suffering in Hades. The rich man in Hades (Lk. 16:22-24) is another instance of the lost who are now in confinement, suffering, awaiting the Great White Throne Judgment and everlasting suffering in Hell (Wuest).

"Vengeance" in the Greek is *"dike,"* and speaks of *"a judicial decision, especially a sentence of condemnation, execution of sentence, punishment."* Vincent suggests *"punishment"* rather than *"vengeance"* as the most appropriate word.

Lumby says: *"A destruction so utter and so permanent as theirs has been, is the nearest approach that can be found in this world to the destruction which awaits those who are kept under darkness to the judgment of the great day."*

"Eternal" in the Greek is *"aionios,"* and should be rendered *"everlasting"* rather than *"eternal"* since the suffering has a beginning but no ending.

HELL

The knowledge of Hell comes almost exclusively from the teachings of Christ, Who spoke emphatically on the subject on a number of occasions:

1. Jesus states that *"whosoever says, 'you fool!' shall be liable to the hell of fire."* In the context Jesus is saying that whereas the Old Testament simply condemned murder, He has a higher demand and the result is that expressions of anger toward one's brother can lead to the most severe punishment (Mat. 5:22).

2. Jesus says that the punishment of Hell is so severe that it would be better for a person to lose an eye or a hand rather than that these members of the body should be instruments of sins that would lead to Hell. Twice He speaks about the whole body being thrown into Hell (Mat. 5:29-30).

3. Jesus is obviously speaking of the punishment of Hell when He says that the tree that does not bear good fruit will be cut down and *"thrown into the fire"* (Mat. 7:19). It is noteworthy that all the above references come from the Sermon on the Mount.

4. Part of the punishment pronounced upon the ungodly will be that they will be cast out from the Presence of Christ (Mat. 7:23).

5. The ultimate punishing resulting from apostasy will include being consigned to *"the outer darkness"* that will produce a reaction of extreme anguish on the part of those who suffer this punishment. *"There men will weep and gnash their teeth"* (Mat. 8:12).

6. Jesus states that God has the power to *"destroy both soul and body in Hell"* (Mat. 10:28).

7. At the conclusion of the parable of the tares, Jesus says that at the end of the world, sinners will be cast into *"the furnace of fire,"* which will produce anguish described in the same words as those of Matthew, Chapter 12. In the Parable of the Net (Mat. 13:49-50), the same punishment and the same reaction are again predicted.

8. The ultimate punishment inflicted upon sinners is described by Jesus as being much worse than death itself, for it would be better to be drowned than to be punished for causing another Christian to be led astray (Mat. 18:6). In the parallel Passage in Mark,

Jesus then adds that it would be better to lose a limb that was the source of sinfulness than to *"go to Hell, to the unquenchable fire"* (Mk. 9:42-43). Hell is further described as the place *"where their worm does not die, and the fire is not quenched"* (Mk. 9:48). Here Jesus is using the terminology of Isaiah 66:24. In the parallel Passage in Matthew 18:8-9, the threat is that of being thrown into *"the eternal fire"* or the *"hell of fire."*

9. In the Parable of the Wedding Feast, the punishment is again described as that of being cast into *"outer darkness"* with resulting anguish of *"weeping and gnashing of teeth"* (Mat. 22:13).

10. Jesus condemns the Pharisees for making their converts *"twice as much a child of Hell as yourselves"* (Mat. 23:15). A little later He warns that they will not be able to escape *"being sentenced to Hell"* (Mat. 23:33).

11. In the Parable of the Talents, Jesus again uses the phrases *"outer darkness"* and *"weeping and gnashing of teeth"* (Mat. 25:30). In the Parable of the Sheep and the Goats, Jesus says to those whom He condemns, *"Depart from Me, you cursed, into the eternal fire prepared for the Devil and his angels"* (Mat. 25:41). Later in the same parable, Jesus describes their fate as *"eternal punishment"* (Mat. 25:46).

DEGREES OF PUNISHMENT IN HELL

In several Passages, Jesus implies that there will be degrees of punishment in Hell. He speaks of hypocrites as those who will *"receive the greater condemnation"* (Mk. 12:40), and Jesus speaks of some who will receive *"many stripes,"* whereas others who have a lesser knowledge of the Master's Will, will receive *"few stripes"* (Lk. 12:47-48).

The certain conclusion from all of these Passages is that Jesus taught the Doctrine of Hell clearly and emphatically. Some may claim that these statements as given by Christ are not to be taken literally; however, about something so serious, to be sure, Jesus would teach nothing but that which is an actual fact. That of which He speaks presents a most terrible reality, and of that one can be certain!

WRITINGS OF THE APOSTLES

1. Paul speaks of the impending judgment

of God, which will result in eternal life for those who do good, but *"wrath and fury"* for those who do wickedness. For the evildoer, *"there will be tribulation and distress"* (Rom. 2:3-9).

2. Even appearance before the Judgment Seat of Christ, which pertains only to Believers, and where sins will not be judged, that already having been done in Christ, will result in receiving rewards according to one's motivation and consecration. Paul sees this as an impelling force in his ministry (II Cor. 5:10-11).

3. At the return of Christ, those dwelling in complacency will experience *"sudden destruction . . . and there will be no escape"* (I Thess. 5:3).

4. The fate of the ungodly at the Second Coming of Christ will be administered by the angels accompanying Christ who will come *"in flaming fire, inflicting vengeance upon those who do not know God and upon those who do not obey the Gospel of our Lord Jesus. They shall suffer the punishment of eternal destruction and exclusion from the Presence of the Lord"* (II Thess. 1:6-9).

5. In Hebrews, Paul speaks of *"eternal judgment"* as a fundamental of the faith (Heb. 6:1-2) and of the threat of punishment in these terms, *"a fearful prospect of judgment, and a fury of fire which will consume the adversaries"* (Heb. 10:27). He speaks of this as *"much worse punishment"* (vs. 29) than the death that was administered to those who broke the Law of Moses.

6. James 3:6 speaks of the tongue as *"set on fire of Hell."*

7. Peter in his Second Epistle deals with the subject of the angels who sinned and were cast *"into Hell,"* which is described as *"pits of nether gloom"* (II Pet. 2:4-9). Later in the Passage, God is described as knowing how *"to keep the unrighteous under punishment until the day of judgment."* The ungodly who revel in sin will *"be destroyed in the same destruction"* (vs. 12). *"For them the nether gloom of darkness has been reserved"* (vs. 17).

8. In the similar Passage in Jude, it is revealed that the fallen angels *"have been kept by Him* (God) *in eternal chains in the nether gloom until the judgment of the great day"* (vs. 6). The inhabitants of Sodom and Gomorrah, the Passage of our study, *"serve*

NOTES

as an example by undergoing a punishment of eternal fire" (vs. 7).

9. The Revelation of John says, *"the smoke of their torment goes up forever and ever; and they have no rest"* (Rev. 14:11); *"their lot shall be in the lake that burns with fire and brimstone, which is the second death"* (Rev. 21:8).

These Scriptural references demonstrate that the Apostles followed Christ in teaching that life issues in two possible destinies, eternal blessedness with the Lord, or the torment of Hell. While the New Testament writers are very reserved in their description of Hell, still, they are clear in teaching a judgment issuing in eternal punishment.

THE DOCTRINE OF HELL, A THOROUGHLY BIBLICAL DOCTRINE

If we are to properly interpret the Bible, we must come to the conclusion, that the Doctrine of Hell is a thoroughly Biblical Doctrine. Therefore, it is not surprising that in the history of theology, a denial of this Doctrine has often accompanied weak views of Biblical inspiration.

Possibly a cause of reaction against the Doctrine of Hell has been the exultant glee or other unloving attitudes held by some who have proclaimed it; however, this is not really a part of the Biblical Doctrine. In other words, God loves the sinner but He hates the sin, and that must be our attitude and spirit as well.

For an individual to die eternally lost, thereby, going to Hell, where they will burn in a lake of fire forever and forever, is the most horrible thing that one could ever begin to imagine. For any person who claims to be a Christian, and at the same time expresses delight at something of this nature, is beyond comprehension. The attitude and spirit of the true Christian is, exactly the same as the attitude of God, where it is said: *"For God so loved the world, that He gave His only begotten Son, that whosoever believeth in Him should not perish, but have everlasting life"* (Jn. 3:16).

God does not send people to Hell so much for what they are, as for their rejection of His solution to this terrible problem, Who is Jesus Christ. We learn from the great price that was paid in order that man might be redeemed, as to how much that God loves man. If man rejects this solution, there is nothing else that God can do except consign that soul to eternal Hell. The refusal to accept Christ is at the same time, a continued acceptance of sin that steals, kills, and destroys (Jn. 10:10). In the ultimate conclusion, if God continued to allow that, such an allowance would guarantee the continuance of death, suffering, and destruction. Jesus died that all of that may be put to an end. If men refuse His offer of Salvation, then they must be consigned to an eternal Hell. There is no other choice.

(8) "LIKEWISE ALSO THESE FILTHY DREAMERS DEFILE THE FLESH, DESPISE DOMINION, AND SPEAK EVIL OF DIGNITIES."

The exegesis is:

1. The word *"likewise"* proclaims the fact that even though man has these fearful examples before him, yet he persists in his sin.

2. *"Filthy dreamers"* refer to immoral images formed in the mind, which concludes in a course of conduct.

3. *"Defiling the flesh"* speaks of immorality in some manner, in this case, homosexuality.

4. *"Despising dominion,"* refers to the fact that such individuals despise the ways of God, thereby throwing off what they consider to be His restraints.

5. *"Speaking evil of dignities,"* refers to reviling the Word of God, and more particularly, Christ and the Cross.

FILTHY DREAMERS

The phrase, *"Likewise also these filthy dreamers,"* actually proclaims two things:

1. The sins they commit first appear as fantasies of the mind, and then are carried out in their conduct.

2. Jude is speaking of false teachers, with the words *"filthy dreamers"* also referring to their doctrines being the fruits of mere imagination and of fancies.

The true *"Testimony of God"* (I Cor. 2:1), is the Message, *"Jesus Christ and Him Crucified"* (I Cor. 2:2).

As we've said many times, the Message of the Cross is not a mere doctrine, but rather the foundation from which all Biblical

NOTES

Doctrine must flow. I am absolutely positive that Jesus considered His suffering on the Cross as far more than mere doctrine. So while we might correctly mention the *"doctrine of the Cross,"* we must understand such a statement in its proper sense. Doctrine simply means *"teaching,"* therefore, it is proper to use the word in that fashion as it regards the Cross. But at the same time, we must understand that the Cross while it certainly is to be taught, which we are doing here, and which refers to doctrine; still, the Message of the Cross is far more than a mere doctrine, but rather, as stated, the foundation on which all Biblical Doctrine is built.

The great sin of the Church is not preaching the Cross. Paul plainly said: *"We preach Christ crucified"* (I Cor. 1:23). It didn't matter that this was a *"stumblingblock"* to the Jews, and *"foolishness"* to the Greeks (Gentiles), this was the Message preached, and because it was the Message of Redemption, and in fact, the only Message of Redemption.

EMPHASIS

Lest the Reader think that we place too much emphasis on the Cross, please peruse carefully the following:

It is Simon Peter the great Apostle, who made the great confession to Christ, when Jesus asked: *"But whom say you that I am?"*

Peter answered: *"You are the Christ, the Son of the Living God."*

In answer to that, Jesus said: *"Blessed are you, Simon Bar-jona: for flesh and blood has not revealed it unto you, but My Father which is in Heaven."*

A short time later, Jesus said: *"I must go unto Jerusalem, and suffer many things of the Elders and Chief Priests and Scribes, and be killed, and be raised again the third day."*

The Scripture then says that *"Peter took Him, and began to rebuke Him, saying, be it far from You, Lord: this shall not be unto You."*

The response of Jesus to the statement as made by Peter was swift and to the point: *"Get behind Me, Satan: you are an offense unto Me: for you savor not the things that be of God, but those that be of men"* (Mat. 16:15-23).

Even though this was Peter who said this as it regards the Death and Resurrection of

NOTES

Christ, he was roundly rebuked by Christ. In other words, there must not be a wrong interpretation of the *"Purpose"* of Christ, which was the Cross, and which was necessary, in order for man to be redeemed.

As we've said over and over, all false doctrine begins with an incorrect interpretation of the *"Person"* of Christ and/or the *"Purpose"* of Christ. In this case, Peter was right about the *"Person of Christ,"* but totally wrong as it regards the *"Purpose of Christ,"* which was the Cross.

To be sure, the Holy Spirit is still rebuking all such false direction, irrespective as to whom the Preacher might be who proclaims such false doctrine. If the *"Person"* of Christ is misinterpreted, or the *"Purpose"* of Christ is misinterpreted, the misinterpretation then must be construed as of the Devil, just as Jesus proclaims here.

From this, we see how serious this matter is, and how the Word of God is to ever be the criteria for all things, and not Apostles or anyone else for that matter.

Concerning the Message of the Cross, Paul said: *"But though we* (Paul himself), *or an angel from Heaven, preach any other gospel unto you than that which we have preached unto you* (the Message of the Cross), *let him be accursed"* (let him be damned) (Gal. 1:8).

I think by now, we should understand just how important the Message of the Cross actually is, and that in fact, it is impossible to overstate the case. In fact, I think one can say without fear of Scriptural contradiction that those who propose another Message can be described as *"filthy dreamers."*

DEFILEMENT OF THE FLESH

The phrase, *"Defile the flesh,"* refers to sinning against our physical bodies, which are supposed to be temples of the Holy Spirit (I Cor. 3:16).

Any type of immorality, not only defiles the soul and the spirit of the individual, but it also defiles the physical body. Of course, some defilement would be worse than others, and inasmuch as Jude has just spoken of homosexuality, this is the worst defilement of all as it concerns the flesh. Let me explain:

Regarding the flesh, which has to do with the physical body and even the appearance of the individual, homosexuality has a tendency, to leave its aborting mark upon the mannerisms, demeanor, and very appearance of the individual. In other words, it becomes more and more repulsive. It affects the voice, the gestures, even with the very *"look"* of the individual becoming perverted and twisted.

DOMINION

The phrase, *"Despise Dominion,"* refers to rejecting and thereby despising the Word of the Lord that condemns these types of things. In other words, they claim that the Word of God will have no dominion over them, and they will do whatever it is they desire to do.

As an example, we have portrayed to us the contempt shown by the Israelites towards the Commandments of God. As well, the desertion of their appointed station and abode by the angels showed their disregard for the Divine Ordinance, and the behavior of the men of Sodom combined with the vilest lusts, showed an impious irreverence towards God's representatives, the righteous angels, who were sent to retrieve Lot and his family from this evil place (Gen. 19:5).

DIGNITIES

The phrase, *"And speak evil of dignities,"* presents the fact, that it's impossible to despise the dominion of the Lord, and not at the same time, speak evil of His Person.

To despise the Word of God, which means to ignore its precepts, is at the same time to despise the dominion of the Lord our Creator. To do that is to speak evil of Him. It cannot be any other way. If we ignore His Word, we ignore Him. If we blaspheme or disobey His Word, we have at the same time, insulted Him.

(9) "YET MICHAEL THE ARCHANGEL, WHEN CONTENDING WITH THE DEVIL HE DISPUTED ABOUT THE BODY OF MOSES, DOES NOT BRING AGAINST HIM A RAILING ACCUSATION, BUT SAID, THE LORD REBUKE YOU."

The diagram is:

1. No other angel bears the title of Archangel, as recorded, but there are others who are also chief angels, for Michael is only one of them (Dan. 10:13).

2. After the death of Moses, Satan demanded his body, which was denied him by

Michael the Archangel.

3. To Satan's contention, Michael simply said, *"The Lord rebuke you."*

MICHAEL THE ARCHANGEL

The phrase, *"Yet Michael the Archangel,"* refers to the only angel so named, consequently of this particular rank.

"Archangel" in the Greek is *"Archaggelos,"* and means *"first in rank, chief of the angels."* His name means, *"who is like God?"* He was regarded, and is still regarded, as the special protector of the Jewish nation (Dan. 10:13-14, 21). The word *"Archangel"* occurs only in one other place in the Scriptures, and no doubt refers to Michael there as well (I Thess. 4:16).

Some have contended that this account between Michael the Archangel and Satan as it regards the body of Moses is spurious, because it's not given as well in the Old Testament; however, there were untold numbers of things which happened in Old Testament Times which were not recorded in that account, but it doesn't mean they didn't happen.

Where Jude got this account we do not know. Perhaps he derived it from one of the Jewish Targums, which were a type of commentary on the Old Testament. But this we do know:

Wherever he derived this information, the Holy Spirit proclaimed it to him to be true. In fact, all prophecy is given by direct Revelation (Gal. 1:12); we do not know its extent and its boundary.

We do know that the holy writers of both the Old and New Testaments were inspired. Jesus says that they would be *"guided into all truth,"* kept in what is true, preserved from error, falsehood, legend, and the like. It is not the function of Inspiration to supply facts; that is the function of Revelation. Inspiration prevents error, assures us that what is written is true. No matter where or how an inspired writer obtained his information, the Holy Spirit enabled him to sift out and adequately to present only what is genuine, and true.

As with all time periods, wrong notions in Bible times concerning natural phenomena prevailed, but not one of them got into the Old or the New Testament, although we do not hesitate to say that the writers may very well have held some strange notions in their own minds. Ancient histories, documents, traditions contain some true things that were more or less admixed with fiction, legend, fancies. However, we always see that the inspired writers were protected; none of them adopted a single fiction.

Concerning the Word of God, Jesus said: *"Till heaven and earth pass, one jot or one tittle shall in no wise pass from the Law, till all be fulfilled"* (Mat. 5:18).

Furthermore, Jesus referred to the Bible as *"all truth."* He said: *"Howbeit when He, the Spirit of Truth, is come, He will guide you into all truth"* (Jn. 16:13).

He then said: *"Your Word is Truth"* (Jn. 17:17).

Concerning the writers of the Word of God, we know that some were educated men, and some were not. So the question must be asked, did the Holy Spirit keep His writers from *"imperfect grammar"*?

According to the Scholars, most definitely, *"Yes!"* While the writing of some is more polished than others, the grammar according to the usage of such in that particular time is correct. We must remember that the Bible has never been edited; translated yes, but edited, no!

To be sure, the account given here by Jude concerning Michael the Archangel and Satan, happened exactly as he said it did. The Holy Spirit says so! (II Pet. 1:21).

THE DEVIL

The phrase, *"When contending with the Devil he disputed about the body of Moses,"* concerns as is obvious, the death of the great Law-Giver.

Other than the account given here, what happened to the body of Moses after his death, we know only from Deuteronomy 34:6. From the account given there, it is obvious that something strange happened at that time.

First of all, the Scripture indicates the Lord Himself officiated at the funeral of Moses. According to the Scripture, no Israelites were present, because *"no man knows of his sepulchre unto this day."*

From the account by Jude, Michael the great Archangel was present and so was Satan. It seems that Satan demanded the body of the Law-Giver, but that his conversation was with Michael instead of the Lord. It is even possible that the phrase *"He buried him in the valley in the land of Moab,"* refers to the Lord seeing to the situation, but actually doing it through Michael the Archangel (Deut. 34:6).

Why did Satan want the body of Moses?

In the first place, the Devil had the power of death until Christ conquered Him on the Cross (Col. 2:14-17; Heb. 2:14-15; Rev. 1:18).

This means that whenever the Saints died who lived under the Old Testament system, their soul and spirit at that time did not go to Heaven, but rather down into Paradise, which was actually next door one might say to Hell, separated only by a great gulf (Lk. 16:26). But since the Cross, whenever the Saint of God dies, their soul and spirit instantly go to be with the Lord in Heaven.

This is because the blood of bulls and goats could not take away sin, which system prevailed before the Cross. At the Cross, Christ settled the sin debt, which meant that the price was paid, and all sin was taken away, past, present, and future, at least for those who will believe, which means, that believing man no longer owes God a sin debt, due to the fact that Jesus paid the price, i.e., *"the debt."*

As to why Satan wanted the physical body of Moses after his death, we are given some clue in Deuteronomy 34:6. Due to the fact that God did not allow anyone to attend the funeral of Moses, and that He buried him Himself, or at least had Michael the Archangel to perform the task, and buried him in a place which was not known, tells us that quite possibly, Satan wanted the body of Moses, which he in some way would have devised as an idol for the children of Israel to worship. They were prone to idolatry anyway, and had they known where the body of Moses was, they would have made a shrine out of his corpse, or at least would have worshipped his burial place. Satan of course would foster such a thing, as would be obvious! But Michael would not allow the Evil One to have his way in this matter, even though at that time, Satan did in fact, have the power of death. Due to the Cross, Satan no longer has that power.

NO RAILING ACCUSATION

The phrase, *"Does not bring against him*

NOTES

a railing accusation, but said, the Lord rebuke you," presents the same wording which the Lord said unto Satan as recorded in Zechariah 3:2.

The Holy Spirit through Jude is, I think, saying two things here:

1. He is saying that one who knows their ground doesn't have to bring a railing accusation, a simple rebuke being sufficient.

2. The manner in which Michael answered Satan and the Lord as well, showed that they greatly held the upper hand. Superior strength doesn't need to boast or rail!

A *"railing accusation"* would have placed Michael on the same level with the Devil, to which the great archangel would not stoop, and rightly so!

The particular word for *"rebuke"* here is *"epitimao,"* which means to rebuke another but without any affect upon the person rebuked, the latter not being convicted of any wrongdoing on his part nor brought to the place of conviction or confession, and for either one of two reasons; either the person is innocent, or he is incorrigible, that is, his heart is so hard that he refuses to be convicted of his sin or to confess it.

Satan is incorrigible, meaning there is no hope of Repentance. Jude knew this and, therefore, used that particular word.

There is another word for rebuke, *"elegcho,"* which speaks of a rebuke that brings out either conviction or confession of sin, but this would not have sufficed for Satan.

Regarding rank, there is some evidence that Lucifer, being a created angel himself, may have outranked Michael. Ezekiel, Chapter 28 lends some credence to this thought. However, coupling the statement made by Michael as recorded by Jude with the statement made by the Lord in Zechariah concerning Satan, we are led to believe that his former rank was now of no consequence. I think what we've said regarding Michael's answer, and the tone of his answer, is closer to what really happened possibly than other proposals.

(10) "BUT THESE SPEAK EVIL OF THOSE THINGS WHICH THEY KNOW NOT: BUT WHAT THEY KNOW NATURALLY, AS BRUTE BEASTS, IN THOSE THINGS THEY CORRUPT THEMSELVES."

The structure is:

1. The Holy Spirit through Jude characterizes false teachers as being mentally deficient.

2. These individuals, whomever they may have been, do the contrary of what we are told by the respect shown by the Angel even toward Satan; they speak evil of that spiritual world, though spiritual beings, of which they know nothing.

3. Jude refers to the false teachers as in a class with unreasoning animals.

4. These things are their ruin.

CHARACTERISTICS OF APOSTATES

The phrase, *"But these speak evil of those things which they know not,"* proclaims the truth of the adage, *"Fools rush in where angels fear to tread."*

By the pronoun *"these"* we know that Jude is speaking of Preachers and Teachers who were proclaiming false doctrine. Whatever it was they were teaching, was evidently strong enough that it was causing problems in the Early Church, which necessitated the writing by Jude of this Epistle. He calls them *"ungodly men"* (vs. 4), *"filthy dreamers"* (vs. 8), *"murmurers"* (vs. 16), *"sensual"* (vs. 19), etc.

Once we begin to understand that false doctrine will lead Christians to spiritual declension, and possibly even to the loss of their souls, we then begin to understand the terrible danger involved. The problem of the modern Church is not at all that it contends for the faith too much, but rather that it *"contends for the faith"* little, if at all! As we've said previously, we're not dealing here with mundane matters, but rather with the most serious and important thing on the face of the Earth, the souls of men.

KNOW NATURALLY

The phrase, *"But what they know naturally, as brute beasts,"* in effect completely puts these individuals in the same class as the unredeemed, who have absolutely no knowledge whatsoever of the things of God or the Word of God. This tells us that the unredeemed don't really know any more about the Lord than animals.

Considering that the Holy Spirit is the One who inspired this statement, even the very words, we are certainly able to get a general idea as to the spiritual plight of the unredeemed. And considering these false teachers were preaching and teaching something that was wholly unscriptural, which evidently impacted the very foundation of the faith, the Holy Spirit places them in the same category.

CORRUPTION

The phrase, *"In those things they corrupt themselves,"* could have been translated, *"By these things they are being brought to ruin."*

The two halves of the Verse are in emphatic contrast. What they do not know, and cannot know, they abuse by gross irreverence: what they know, and cannot help knowing, they abuse by gross licentiousness.

Going back to Verse 3 and *"the faith,"* we have to conclude that the gist of the false doctrine propagated by these false teachers, in some way, had to impact negatively the *"Person"* of Christ, and the *"Purpose"* of Christ. And generally, if the Person of Christ is misinterpreted, it is conclusive that the Purpose of Christ will be treated accordingly, and vice versa.

Then, and I speak of the time of Jude, the greater thrust of the Gospel was that which it should have been, or so it seems. Today it is the very opposite. The Gospel of Jesus Christ has been so compromised presently, that instead of the error standing out in its abnormality, the very opposite is happening. There is so little of the straight and True Gospel of Jesus Christ being proclaimed, when it is heard, it rather seems abnormal. For the most part, the Gospel has been reduced to a religious slot machine. Put in your $10 and get back $1,000. Or else it's been reduced to some psychological mishmash. And about the best that can be hoped for is a gospel of ethics.

It's pointless to ask most people if they are saved. In some form or the other, almost everyone claims some type of Salvation. Churches are filled with people who are religious, but unsaved! Even the Churches which were once known for preaching the Gospel, and because they once relied upon the Holy Spirit, have for the most part, given over to humanistic psychology. Far too often what they preach is psychological claptrap, or else they chase fads. The Cross of Christ is little preached, and in fact, it's not even understood. What is being preached, so closely coincides with this which Jude proclaims, that as well, most modern Churches are being brought to ruin, at least in the spiritual sense. The modern Church for all practical purposes, I personally believe, is in worse shape spiritually, than at any time since the Reformation, a time span of nearly 600 years. People are chasing *"spirits,"* thinking it's the Holy Spirit. Entertainment is labeled as the Power of God. And the sadness is, so much error is presently being preached, that any more, most Christians hardly know what is right or wrong.

While of course, there is an exception here and there, and thank God for that; however, the words of Paul are already coming to pass:

"Now the Spirit speaketh expressly, that in the latter times (the times in which we now live) *some shall depart from the faith, giving heed to seducing spirits, and doctrines of Devils"* (I Tim. 4:1).

However, despite the efforts of the Evil One, the Cross is once again beginning to be preached. And I have to believe that *"When the enemy shall come in like a flood, the Spirit of the LORD shall lift up a standard against him"* (Isa. 59:19).

(11) "WOE UNTO THEM! FOR THEY HAVE GONE IN THE WAY OF CAIN, AND RAN GREEDILY AFTER THE ERROR OF BALAAM FOR REWARD, AND PERISHED IN THE GAINSAYING OF CORE."

The exegesis is:

1. Concerning apostasy and apostates, the Holy Spirit says unto them, *"Woe!"*

2. Cain is the type of a religious man who believes in God and in *"religion,"* but after his own will, and who rejects redemption by blood.

3. The error of Balaam was that he was blind to the higher morality of the Cross, through which God maintains and enforces the authority and awful sanctions of His Law, so that He can be Just and the Justifier of a believing sinner.

4. The *"Gainsaying of Core"* (Korah), in effect was the contention that he could hold the High Priesthood of Israel as well as Aaron. In effect, he was saying that he did not need a Mediator, i.e., *"Christ."* He could be his own mediator.

WOE

The phrase, *"Woe unto them,"* is an interjection of the Holy Spirit of denunciation. Williams says: *"The imprecatory prayers of the New Testament, and their related praises, are much more terrible than those of the Old Testament. For example: Acts 8:20; Rom. 3:8; Gal. 1:8; I Cor. 16:22; Rev. 6:10; 8:13; 9:5-6; 16:5-7; 18:20; 19:1-5; 22:11, 18-19."* Jude here pronounces *"Woe"* on the false teachers as Jesus did on the Scribes and Pharisees (Mat. 23:13, 15-16, 23, 25, 27, 29).

THE WAY OF CAIN

The phrase, *"For they have gone in the way of Cain,"* refers to a course of conduct, a way, a manner of thinking, etc.

Cain was a very religious man. He offered up sacrifice the same as his brother Abel (Gen., Chpt. 4). The difference is, he rejected redemption by blood, which Abel's sacrifice proclaimed, and submitted a sacrifice of his own will.

The Church world is full of this type. The Cross, as far as they are concerned, is uncouth, ugly, or else they do not see its necessity at all. Of course, a rejection of the Cross in any form is a rejection of what God says that man actually is — a sinner in desperate need of a Redeemer, Who is Christ. As well, the Cross specifies that a terrible price had to be paid in order for man to be redeemed, with those in the *"way of Cain"* denying that their situation is that critical.

The Cross of Christ proclaims to the entirety of mankind, and for all time, how good, wonderful, and altogether loving that God actually is, and how sinful, wicked, and ungodly that man is. Man seeks to believe that even though something may be wrong, he can straighten it out himself. He can do it with education, money, or in some way. He is loathe to admit that his situation is so critical that it is terminal, and as such that he cannot solve his problem. The idea that it takes something so drastic as the Cross, he will not accept!

But let not the Reader think that Cain is not religious. In fact, he is very religious. His sacrifices are beautiful to behold. His *"way"* is readily acceptable to the world, and regrettably, to many, if not most, of the Church.

But however beautiful it might be, it effects no Salvation, and saves no one who is lost. It is a *"way that seems right unto a man, but the end thereof are the ways of death"* (Prov. 16:25).

THE ERROR OF BALAAM

The phrase, *"And ran greedily after the error of Balaam for reward,"* must be distinguished from his *"way,"* and his *"doctrine."*

The *"way of Balaam"* was, pure and simple, love of money. He coveted the gifts of Balak (Num. 22:7, 17, 37; 24:11; II Pet. 2:15).

The *"doctrine of Balaam"* was that of immorality. He taught Balak how to seduce the Israelite men with beautiful women, causing them to commit idolatry and adultery. Then God Himself would curse Israel (Num. 21:8, 16; 25:1-9; Rev. 2:14).

The *"error of Balaam"* was that, reasoning from natural morality, and seeing the evil in Israel, he supposed a righteous God must curse them. As stated, he was blind to the higher morality of the Cross, through which God maintains and enforces the authority and awful sanctions of His Law, which He did through Christ in the giving of His life, so that He can be Just and the Justifier of a believing sinner.

Mayor commenting on the *"error of Balaam"* says: *"Balaam went wrong because he allowed himself to hanker after gain and so lost communion with God. He not only went wrong himself, but he abused his great influence and his reputation as a Prophet, to lead astray the Israelites by drawing them away from the holy worship of Jehovah to the impure worship of Baal Peor.*

"So these false teachers used their prophetical gifts for the purpose of self-aggrandizement, and endeavor to make their services attractive by excluding from faith all that is strenuous and difficult, and thereby opening the door to every kind of indulgence."

The *"error of Balaam"* perfectly describes the present *"greed gospel."* As it was with Balaam, the Gospel is for sale. The sideshow hucksters hawk their healings for money, by openly saying, *"The more you give, the more likely you are to be healed,"* or words to that effect. *"Give $100 and get $1,000 back, or even $10,000."* As stated, the *"way of Balaam"* describes it perfectly. Balaam hired himself out as a Prophet, and scores of Charismatic Preachers are doing the same!

THE GAINSAYING OF CORE

The phrase, *"And perished in the gainsaying of Core,"* finds his experience in Numbers, Chapter 16.

The gainsaying of this man was his rebellion against Aaron as God's appointed Priest. This was, in principle, a denial of the High Priesthood of Christ. He was dissatisfied at his role, and laid claim to the position of being a sacrificing Priest.

In effect, he was denying his need for a Mediator, of which Aaron was a type. Christ is our Mediator, and in effect, Korah was saying that he could serve in this capacity, as could any one of his associates.

We learn from the Sixteenth Chapter of Numbers what God thought of this spectacle. The Scripture says:

"And the earth opened her mouth, and swallowed them up, and their houses, and all the men that appertained unto Korah, and all their goods" (Num. 16:32).

In effect, Korah was saying that he didn't need Christ, and that he didn't need the Cross.

If it is to be noticed, the rebellion of all three of these men was in effect, a rebellion against *"Jesus Christ and Him Crucified."* Even though other things entered into the spectacle of all three, the major sin, that which caused the Holy Spirit to catalog them forever, even using them as an example, was the rejection of the Cross. To me that seems to be painfully obvious! Consequently, it should be a tremendous lesson to us, for it is certain that the Holy Spirit means for us to learn from these examples. These men, Cain, Balaam, and Korah, are in Hell this very moment. They will be there forever and forever. Whatever sins they committed, that which put them there, was their rejection of the Cross.

(12) "THESE ARE SPOTS IN YOUR FEASTS OF CHARITY, WHEN THEY FEAST WITH YOU, FEEDING THEMSELVES WITHOUT FEAR: CLOUDS THEY ARE WITHOUT WATER, CARRIED ABOUT OF WINDS; TREES WHOSE FRUIT WITHERETH, WITHOUT FRUIT, TWICE DEAD, PLUCKED UP BY THE ROOTS;"

The composition is:

1. *"These are spots"* should have been translated *"these are rocks."*

2. These false teachers participated in the Lord's Supper, claiming to be Godly.

3. *"Feeding themselves without fear,"* refers to *"furthering their own schemes and lusts instead of tending the flock of God."*

4. As *"clouds without water,"* disappoint the ground that needs rain, likewise, these false teachers look good outwardly, but inwardly there is no substance.

5. *"Carried about of winds,"* refer to the fact that they seek Believers with itching ears. They have no true course of the Word of God.

6. *"Trees whose fruit withereth,"* refers to that which looks like fruit, but is all outward and, therefore, withers.

7. There is no proper fruit, simply because good fruit cannot come from a bad tree.

8. They are *"twice dead,"* meaning they were dead in trespasses and sins before they were initially saved, but they have now gone back on God, therefore, dead again, i.e., *"twice dead."*

9. They have no proper fruit, because they have no proper roots. They are not like the tree planted by the waters.

ROCKS

The phrase, *"These are spots in your feasts of charity, when they feast with you,"* proclaims the beginning statement of what and who these false teachers actually are.

The word *"spots"* should have been translated *"rocks,"* with its actual meaning being *"hidden rocks."* These men were no longer mere *"spots,"* but rather elements of danger and wreckage. The word is used of rocks covered with water and thus hidden. The idea is, to whoever follows their teaching, even though the waters at the outset may look excellent, good for sailing; however, there are sharp rocks immediately beneath the surface that will rip open the hull of any vessel. Likewise, those who follow false teachers, and we speak of those who do not rightly divide the Word of Truth, will not come away unsullied or unscathed. Spiritual wreckage will be the result. In fact, even as the Holy Spirit here tells us, it cannot be otherwise.

NOTES

The *"feasts of charity"* were called *"love feasts"* in the Early Church, which was a form of that which we refer to presently as the *"Lord's Supper."* The idea is, these false teachers were in the mainstream of the Church and, therefore, looked legitimate. But their teaching, in some way, repudiated the *"Person"* of Christ and/or the *"Purpose"* of Christ, which was the Cross.

Who is Christ?

He is God manifest in the flesh (Phil. 2:5-11). He is as well, *"The Living Word"* (Jn. 1:1). He is also the Creator of all things (Jn. 1:3). As well as being the Creator of all things, He is also the Saviour of mankind, which refers to redeeming man from man's sins (Eph. 2:13-18).

How did Christ redeem lost humanity?

He did it by *"Blotting out the handwriting of Ordinances that was against us, which was contrary to us, and took it out of the way, nailing it to His Cross;*

"And having spoiled principalities and powers, He made a show of them openly, triumphing over them in it" (Col. 2:14-15). Jesus redeemed mankind, which refers to the fact that He made it possible for man to be saved, and did so by the offering up of Himself on the Cross. It was there, as we have just quoted to you from Colossians, where Christ became a Sin-Offering, which satisfied the demands of the broken Law, which He did on behalf of fallen mankind, which atoned for all sin. The Sacrifice of Himself pertained to Him giving His Own life, which necessitated the pouring out of His Life's Blood, which was a Sacrifice that God could accept, and in fact, did accept (Eph. 2:13).

BLOOD

Paul uses the word *"Cross"* as a synonym, which refers to all that Christ did there; however, the actual price that was paid, was the pouring out of His Life's Blood. Paul said:

"Whom God has set forth (Jesus) *to be a propitiation* (an atoning Sacrifice) *through faith in His Blood"* (Rom. 3:25).

"Much more then, being now justified (made just) *by His Blood, we shall be saved from wrath through Him"* (Rom. 5:9).

"In Whom we have Redemption (to buy back) *through His Blood, the forgiveness of*

sins, according to the riches of His grace" (Eph. 1:7).

"But now in Christ Jesus (what He did at the Cross) you (Gentiles) who sometimes (before the Cross) were far off (had no access to God) are made near by the Blood of Christ" (Eph. 2:13).

"And, having made peace (with God) through the Blood of His Cross" (Col. 1:20).

"Neither by the blood of goats and calves, but by His Own Blood (which He shed at the Cross) He entered in once into the Holy Place (the Holy of Holies in Heaven), having obtained eternal redemption for us" (Heb. 9:12).

"How much more shall the Blood of Christ, Who through the eternal Spirit offered Himself without spot to God, purge your conscience from dead works to serve the Living God?" (Heb. 9:14).

"Now the God of peace, that brought again from the dead our Lord Jesus, that great Shepherd of the sheep, through the Blood (which He shed at the Cross) of the Everlasting Covenant" (Heb. 13:20).

"Elect (Born-Again Believers) according to the foreknowledge of God the Father, through Sanctification of the Spirit, unto obedience and sprinkling of the Blood of Jesus Christ: Grace unto you, and peace be multiplied" (I Pet. 1:2).

"Forasmuch as you know that you are not redeemed with corruptible things, as silver and gold . . . but with the Precious Blood of Christ, as of a lamb without blemish and without spot" (I Pet. 1:18-19).

"And the Blood of Jesus Christ His Son cleanses us from all sin" (I Jn. 1:7).

"And from Jesus Christ, Who is the faithful witness, and the first begotten of the dead, and the prince of the kings of the earth. Unto Him Who loved us, and washed us from our sins in His Own Blood" (Rev. 1:5).

When we read these Passages how can we claim, as some do who hold to the Word of Faith doctrine, that the Blood of Jesus Christ atones for nothing? But this is what many of them teach. That's the reason I say that their doctrine may seem good on the surface, but immediately under the surface there are rocks that will rip apart those who try to sail those waters. They may get by for awhile,

NOTES

but ultimately, spiritual wreckage will be the result. Let me say it again:

The "Person" of Christ must never be compromised in any fashion. And when the Word of Faith people claim that Jesus Christ became a sinner on the Cross, actually taking upon Himself the nature of Satan, thereby dying and going to the burning side of Hell as a sinner, they are blaspheming the "Person" of Christ. While we may soft-pedal the issue, the truth is, exactly as I have said, it is "blasphemy!"

Jesus Christ did not become a sinner on the Cross, He became a "Sin-Offering," which He had to do, in order to pay the penalty of sin. Becoming a sinner would not pay any penalty whatsoever. Becoming a "Sin-Offering" would definitely fulfill the type, and pay the penalty. In fact, Jesus Christ on the Cross became a "Sin-Offering," which means He atoned for all sin, "Trespass-Offering," which atoned for sinning against a fellow Believer, "Whole Burnt-Offering," which refers to giving His all for us in atoning for all sin, "Peace-Offering," which refers to peace made with God after the Sacrifice has been offered, "Thanks-Offering," which refers to an Offering of Thanksgiving in that God has accepted the Sacrifice. With the one Sacrifice of Himself, Christ fulfilled all five of the Levitical Offerings. Let us say it again:

Jesus did not become a sinner on the Cross, but rather a Sin-Offering.

As we must not violate the "Person" of Christ, likewise, we must not violate the "Purpose" of Christ. His Purpose was the Cross, and this we must never forget. This is "where" He redeemed humanity, and this is "How" He redeemed humanity!

WITHOUT FEAR

The phrase, "Feeding themselves without fear," refers to constant planning to further their own schemes and lusts instead of tending the flock of God.

"Feeding" in the Greek is "poimaino," and means, "to feed, tend a flock of sheep." It is used of shepherds pasturing their flocks.

In other words, they pretend to be proper Shepherds, but their intention is to "fleece" the flock, instead of "feed" the flock! And whatever the outward may seem to be, if we look deep enough, we will find that *"money"* is at the core of the problem. Perhaps we should say *"the love of money."* That's the reason that Paul said:

"Perverse disputings of men of corrupt minds, and destitute of the truth, supposing that gain is Godliness: from such withdraw thyself" (I Tim. 6:5).

Regrettably, as it regards most of the Preachers over Television of the Charismatic persuasion, their major topic is *"money."* In fact, it is money that drives the largest so-called Christian Television Network (T.B.N.). It's certainly not the Spirit of God, and it should be overly obvious to all Christians that it is money. But unfortunately, and as we've already stated, most of the modern Church is so led by the flesh that it little knows or understands the Moving and Operation of the Holy Spirit any more. Actually, that particular Network is the de facto leader of the apostate church. To be even more blunt, whoever supports the work of Satan has supported Satan. Let me ask a question:

Do you think the Christians who were supporting these false teachers which Jude holds up to ridicule, were supporting the Work of God? Of course not! To support their modern counterparts is not supporting the Work of God either.

I realize the things I say will make some folk angry. I regret that; however, as much as I want and need your support and well-wishes, that is not my first priority. My priority is to hear from Heaven, and then to deliver that which I believe the Lord has given unto me, and to do so without fear or favor, not adding to what the Lord has given me, or taking from what the Lord has given me.

Exactly as Jude portrays, Satan has always done his best work from inside the Church. He seeks to become a part of the Church, and then he slowly but surely (and sometimes not so slowly), erodes and corrodes it from within. The only way he can be stopped is for Godly men and women to proclaim the Truth, and as well, to point out the error, exactly as Jude is doing here, along with all of the other writers of the Word of God.

The tragedy is, these false leaders have absolutely no fear of leading people astray, of making mockery of the Word of God, while far too often, true Preachers fear to say the things they know they need to say!

CLOUDS WITHOUT WATER

The phrase, *"Clouds they are without water,"* refers to a parched Earth that desperately needs rain, but the clouds above it, although they look promising, will in fact give no moisture at all.

To be sure, Satan knows exactly how to dress up his wares. Outwardly they look good, but there is nothing within. In fact, they are designed for one purpose, and that is to deceive. That's exactly what these clouds without water do. They deceive people into thinking they will provide moisture, but when the day is done, they have given forth no rain whatsoever! So what is Jude saying?

He is saying that those who follow false doctrine are doing so, because of base motives within their hearts and lives. In many cases it is pure *"greed."* But let all hear, see, and understand. The greed will not be satisfied by listening to these false teachers. While they promise untold riches, the only ones who will get rich, are the Preachers themselves. It's identical to the gambling interests:

Gambling holds out the lure of instant and great riches; however, the only ones who get rich are the owners of the Casinos.

"The just shall live by faith," is not a gamble (Rom. 1:17).

Jesus Christ died on a Cross, not in order that we might trade our Neon for a Cadillac, but rather that we may be washed, cleansed, and forgiven of our sins. To make the primary interest of the Gospel that of money is to prostitute the Gospel, and to do so in a most ungodly way. Such is a sin of unimagined proportions.

The only way to satisfy the hunger and thirst of the soul is for one to properly be in Christ. Everything else leaves nothing but a bad taste. But it is worse yet, to pervert the Gospel, in order to pull it away from its true purpose of Redemption. *"Clouds they are without water."*

WINDS

The phrase, *"Carried about of winds,"* refers to the fact that these false teachers are mere wind, devoid of promise and performance, at least as the things of God are concerned, although they boast great and mighty things. In fact, the *"winds"* typify their great boasts. They are the people of faith, the *"Word people!"* In fact, this is the hallmark of these false teachers. They boast of stupendous things, claiming that if one has enough faith, one can be rich, drive the biggest cars, wear the finest of clothes, live in the biggest of houses, and stay in the Presidential Suite in the finest hotels. Oh yes! Their boasts are mighty.

But let the Reader understand that the Holy Spirit refers to all of these boasts as *"winds,"* referring to the fact, that it's all *"hot air"* and has no substance.

Once again, I refer to the fact of how strongly I speak. However, if one looks at my words closely, one will find that they are not nearly as strong as the words of Jude, or that of Peter or Paul for that matter. The trouble is, the Church has been fed pabulum preaching for so long, that any more, that which should be *"normal,"* is looked at as *"abnormal."*

As someone has well said, there was a time that along with our positive preaching we had as well some negative preaching, which produced positive living. Today we have all positive preaching, and nothing but positive preaching, which has produced a lot of negative living.

WITHERED FRUIT

The phrase, *"Trees whose fruit withereth, without fruit,"* presents fruit that is not edible.

The meaning is, *"autumn trees,"* which ought to be full of luscious fruit, but have rather the opposite. What little they do have is not edible, and so as far as being of service is concerned, they are *"without fruit."*

I suspect that Jude had in mind the Words of Christ, when He said:

"Beware of false prophets, which come to you in sheep's clothing, but inwardly they are ravening wolves.

"You shall know them by their fruits. Do men gather grapes of thorns, or figs of thistles?

"Even so every good tree brings forth good fruit; but a corrupt tree brings forth evil fruit.

"A good tree cannot bring forth evil fruit, neither can a corrupt tree bring forth good fruit.

"Every tree that brings not forth good fruit is cut down, and cast into the fire.

"Wherefore by their fruits you shall know them" (Mat. 7:15-20).

PLUCKED UP

The phrase, *"Twice dead, plucked up by the roots,"* tells us several things:

1. The short phrase *"twice dead,"* proclaims to us that these individuals had once truly known the Lord, but had turned their backs on Him, hence now being referred to as *"twice dead."* They were spiritually dead before they were initially saved, and now they are spiritually dead again, after turning their backs on the Lord by going into false doctrine, etc. These two words *"twice dead"* refute the unscriptural doctrine of unconditional eternal security.

2. To be *"plucked up by the roots,"* refers to the fact that they are of no more service whatsoever. They are dead even down to the roots, which means there is no chance of restoration.

Jude could have been thinking of this Parable as uttered by Christ:

"A certain man had a fig tree planted in his vineyard; and he came and sought fruit thereon, and found none.

"Then said he unto the dresser of his vineyard, behold, these three years I come seeking fruit on this fig tree, and find none: cut it down; why cumber it the ground?" (Lk. 13:6-7).

As Jude is using the terminology here, *"uprooted"* means that what these false teachers are bringing to the people is not in the firm soil of the Word of God. In other words, what they are proposing is unscriptural.

Let the Reader understand several things about all of this:

1. As we have previously stated, all false doctrine is fostered and nurtured by demon spirits, and in fact, *"seducing spirits"* (I Tim. 4:1). Consequently, it has what one might call a mesmerizing effect upon the listeners, hence the entrapment.

2. Due to this fact, along with the truth being proclaimed to the people, false doctrine must be pointed out as well, as well as those who proclaim the false doctrine, exactly as Jude is doing here.

3. Inasmuch as we are dealing here with the matters of life and death, in fact, the care

of the soul, which is the single most important thing there is, we must not be negligent in this task. Remember this:

No one will be lost by the Preacher calling attention to false doctrine, but many will be lost if he doesn't.

According to the Word of God, truth is always presented in two ways. It is presented by plainly, clearly, and simply proclaiming that which is the truth, and it is presented as well by pointing out error, which brings people back to truth, at least those who will believe.

(13) "RAGING WAVES OF THE SEA, FOAMING OUT THEIR OWN SHAME; WANDERING STARS, TO WHOM IS RESERVED THE BLACKNESS OF DARKNESS FOREVER."

The composition is:

1. *"Raging waves of the sea,"* refer to the destruction caused by false doctrine.

2. *"Foaming out their own shame,"* refers to debris cast out by the waves. False doctrine is like the foam or scum at the seashore.

3. *"Wandering stars,"* is an unpredictable star which provides no guidance for navigation. So false teachers are useless and untrustworthy.

4. *"The blackness of darkness forever,"* refers to their eternal doom (II Pet. 2:4).

RAGING WAVES

The phrase, *"Raging waves of the sea,"* refers to that which is destructive, which characterizes all false doctrine. Let the Reader understand the following:

To be submitted to false doctrine, and to believe its lie, does not leave the individual as it found him. *"Raging waves"* will ultimately destroy anything and everything they hit. The word *"raging"* implies destructive force, which Satan most definitely means as it regards the effect of false doctrine. He *"steals, kills, and destroys"* (Jn. 10:10).

Continuing to use the metaphor, the swimmer may look at these waves, and they may seem exciting; however, once he feels the brunt of their power, he can be drowned, and at the least, severely handled, as should be obvious.

SHAME

The phrase, *"Foaming out their own shame,"* refers to the fact of what they produce.

It is not sparkling, clear, clean water, but rather scum and debris.

It is amazing, thousands of Churches have been built upon the foundation of false doctrine. In fact, most of the Churches presently are built on this foundation. It is ironical, such Churches were few during the time of the Apostles, but now the Churches that truly proclaim the Gospel are rare. The normal is made to appear abnormal, and the abnormal is made to appear normal!

Looking at the Church world as a whole, we find it divided between those who do not believe in the Baptism with the Holy Spirit, with the evidence of speaking with other tongues, and those that do, or at least claim to do so.

Considering the light that has been given as it regards the Spirit Baptism in the last 100 years, and especially considering that this *"Latter Rain"* outpouring, even as predicted by the Prophet Joel (Joel, Chpt. 2), and quoted by Peter on the Day of Pentecost (Acts, Chpt. 2), those who have rejected this outpouring, are presently for all practical purposes, of no spiritual consequence. If light is rejected, light is withdrawn, which means that these particular Churches and Denominations, whatever their claims, are Spirit-directed not at all!

Regrettably, most of the Churches that claim the Baptism with the Holy Spirit are little more than hollow shells of what they once were. In fact, many, if not most, of these particular Churches and Denominations, are little different, if any at all, than those which do not even believe in the Moving and Operation of the Spirit. There are definitely exceptions in all of this, but not many!

In one sense of the word, their position, and I continue to speak of the latter group, is in worse condition than the others. It is bad enough to reject the light and thereby never have it, but worse yet, to have the light, and to walk in that light, but then to reject the light.

Such are like that described by Christ:

"When the unclean spirit is gone out of man, he (the unclean spirit) *walks through dry places, seeking rest, and finds none.*

"Then he says, I will return into my house from where I came out; and when he is come, he finds it empty, swept, and garnished.

"Then goes he, and takes with him seven other spirits more wicked than himself, and they enter in and dwell there: and the last state of that man is worse than the first. Even so shall it be unto this wicked generation" (Mat. 12:43-45).

There was a day you could look at the name on the door regarding a Church, and could tell at least to some degree what that particular Church believed. But no more! And the problem is, millions are attending Churches that provide no spiritual sustenance whatsoever, in other words there is no Moving and Operation of the Holy Spirit, and the people are satisfied to have it like that. They seek Churches which soothe their consciences, but which provide no true spiritual sustenance. They seek *"feel good"* Churches, or Churches which are not only *"feel good"* Churches, but also which claim to make people financially rich. In other words, if you give your money here, and give lots of it, the Lord will give back to you ten times or even a hundred times that amount.

People who attend such Churches, aren't seeking Christlikeness, but rather something else altogether. In fact, many, if not most, of the people attending such Churches aren't even saved. The same goes for the Churches that have rejected the Holy Spirit!

THE CROSS

It was to the Apostle Paul that the meaning of the New Covenant was given, which in reality was the meaning of the Cross. Consequently, his Epistles proclaim this great truth, in fact, the foundation of all truth. *"Jesus Christ and Him Crucified"* was his Message (I Cor. 1:17-18, 21, 23; 2:2, 5). All of this means that if the Cross isn't preached, then the Gospel is not being preached.

While some few Churches preach the Cross as it regards the initial Salvation experience, almost none preach the Cross as it regards the Sanctification of the Saint. They basically preach, Salvation by *"Grace,"* and Sanctification by *"self."* Consequently, we have Christians who are stunted in their Spiritual Growth, and who are at the same time, susceptible to false doctrine, which abounds at this particular time, and as a result, Christians who cannot live victoriously, no matter how hard they try.

In fact, the reason that false doctrine abounds is because the Cross is so little preached. If the Believer doesn't understand the Cross, at least as it regards his Sanctification experience (Rom. 6:3-5), then his foundation is destroyed, which means he is susceptible to whatever Satan is producing. Not understanding the Cross, the only avenue left open for such a Christian is law, with which the modern Church is plagued, and which produces self-righteousness only.

To understand the Cross, is to understand the *"in Christ"* experience, which is the very foundation of all that the true Christian actually is. The Believer doesn't have to be a theologian. All he has to do, is to understand that everything he receives from the Lord comes exclusively to him by the Holy Spirit, with everything made possible by what Jesus did at the Cross. His faith is to be totally and completely in the Finished Work of Christ, i.e., *"the Sacrifice of Christ,"* and then the Holy Spirit will work mightily on his behalf (Rom. 8:1-2, 11, 13).

Even though what we've just said is very simple, it carries, however, a far wider sweep than at first realized.

For the Believer to understand that everything he receives from the Lord comes by the means of the Cross, and that his faith must be placed there 100 percent, which gives the Holy Spirit latitude to work within his life, means as well, that certain other things drop off. What do we mean by that?

WHAT IT MEANS TO TRUST FULLY IN CHRIST AND WHAT HE DID AT THE CROSS

Most Christians presently think that whatever they are in Christ, is because of them belonging to a certain Church, or a certain Denomination, or following a certain Preacher, or even a particular doctrine. Others place their faith and confidence in the good works they perform such as being faithful to Church, paying their tithe, witnessing to the unsaved, etc.

To properly understand the Cross, which is to properly understand the Gospel, which is to properly understand Christ, faith, trust, and confidence must be moved from those things, whatever they might be, and however good they might be, exclusively to Christ and what He did at the Cross. Now that's not as easy as it seems!

Millions actually believe that a part of their Salvation or victory, or whatever terminology they would use, depend upon their belonging to a certain Church or Denomination. To break away from that, many are not willing to do.

What we're saying here is not that Christians should leave their respective Churches. That's not the idea at all! The idea is that not one particle of our faith and confidence be placed in these things, but wholly in Christ and His great Sacrifice.

Now almost all Christians would claim to do this. In other words, all Christians as far as I know, claim to be trusting Christ. But in reality, while some few of these people may definitely be trusting Christ, the far greater majority aren't. And how do I know that?

I know that by their attitudes, demeanor, lifestyle, and the fact that there is little or no victory in their lives. Without a proper understanding of the Cross, it is literally impossible for the Believer to walk in victory before the Lord. Listen to what John said:

"This is the victory that overcometh the world, even our faith" (I Jn. 5:4).

Faith in what?

John answered that by saying: *"This is He* (Christ) *Who came by water and blood, even Jesus Christ; not by water only, but by water and blood. And it is the Spirit Who bears witness, because the Spirit is truth"* (I Jn. 5:6).

The *"water"* typifies the Incarnation, in other words, Jesus being born of the Virgin Mary, and being born as a human being, etc. But then John said *"not by water only."* What did he mean by that?

He meant that God becoming man, which is the Incarnation, while totally necessary, was not sufficient within itself to redeem humanity.

For that to be accomplished, Jesus must die on the Cross, which resulted in the pouring out of His Precious Blood, which atoned for all sin, at least for all who will believe (Jn. 3:16).

So our Faith must rest exclusively in the Cross, and what Jesus did there, that is if we

NOTES

are to be what we ought to be in Christ. There is no other way, and because no other way is needed.

But Satan's greatest trickery is to move the Faith of the Christian from the Cross to other things. To be sure, most of the time these other things are good, even very good, and in fact, that which good Christians will definitely do; however, the only Faith which God will recognize, is that which is placed exclusively in Christ, which means what He did for us at the Cross.

Have you the Reader done that? If not, are you willing to do that?

WANDERING STARS

The short phrase, *"Wandering stars,"* provides no guidance for navigation, even as false doctrine provides no guidance for the Christian seeking to be Christlike.

"Stars" provide fixed points for navigation. But *"shooting stars,"* and this is what is meant here, as would be obvious, can provide no guidance whatsoever. In fact, while they may burn brightly for a short period of time, they are destined after a certain period to burn out. As well, they have no predictable course.

But yet, because they are attractive, at least for a short period of time, they draw attention to themselves, just as do false apostles and false doctrine.

As an example, in the early 1990's, the Pentecostal and Charismatic Church worlds experienced the *"laughing phenomenon."* In other words, thousands of Christians would gather together, with many of them going into fits of uncontrollable laughter, which would last for a period of time, possibly even several hours. This was touted as the road to victory, or at the least, a Moving and Operation of the Holy Spirit.

Was it?

While the Lord can definitely make people laugh, in the final analysis what was being done was not of God. Is it to be noticed that it is no longer with us! It was a passing phenomenon, a *"shooting star."* That which is truly of God, doesn't die.

But yet Preachers by the thousands, were exclaiming this phenomenon as a *"great move of God,"* the *"throughway to all victory,"* etc.

I think I can say without any fear of contradiction that all the Preachers promoting this particular phenomenon had little or no understanding of the Cross; consequently, they were and are susceptible to *"angels of light."* As well, sensing that something is not quite right, they are searching for that which will bring victory.

Let all know and understand that victory can be found in Christ only by faith in what He did for us at the Cross, and not in a passing fad or phenomenon. Let me be a little more blunt:

In the decade of the 90's, all types of fads were springing up. The greatest question was, *"Is it of the Lord?"*

While the question is definitely not improper, its constant use as it was addressed to one fad after the other, let's us know that something is wrong. I think I can say again without fear of contradiction that these fads spring up simply because the foundation is improper to begin with. Not looking to Christ and the Cross, something has to fill that void, and Satan is ever ready to do so as an angel of light (II Cor. 11:13-15).

Again I go back to the point that *"wandering stars"* provide no navigational aid. If one charts their course by these *"shooting stars"* one will come to the same end as the shooting star, a burn-out into *"the blackness of darkness forever."*

THE BLACKNESS OF DARKNESS

The phrase, *"To whom is reserved the blackness of darkness forever,"* tells us in no uncertain terms, the end result of false doctrine. It is *"the Faith which was once delivered unto the Saints,"* or else it is *"the way of Cain,"* or *"the error of Balaam,"* or *"the gainsaying of Core."*

Let the Reader understand that the Holy Spirit through Jude is saying here that the end result for most people who follow false doctrine will not be what they think, but rather to be eternally lost, and to be lost forever and forever. We're speaking here of the loss of the soul. That's the reason Jude gives such stern warnings. That's the reason he doesn't mince words, but calls it exactly as it is.

The kind of preaching that Jude is doing

here would not be tolerated in most Churches. It would be considered uncouth, out of step, and above all, a disturbing of the unity. He would be accused of *"touching the Lord's Anointed."* But let the Reader understand that those who propagate false doctrine aren't the Lord's Anointed. And the ones who are truly the Lord's Anointed are the ones who will be honest enough to tell you the Truth.

(14) "AND ENOCH ALSO, THE SEVENTH FROM ADAM, PROPHESIED OF THESE, SAYING, BEHOLD, THE LORD COMETH WITH TEN THOUSANDS OF HIS SAINTS,"

The exegesis is:

1. Enoch is the Old Testament person of that name, the man who *"walked with God"* (Gen. 5:18-24).

2. The quotation given is from the Book of Enoch. This Book, known to the Church Fathers of the Second Century, lost for some centuries with the exception of a few fragments, was found in its entirety in a copy of the Ethiopic Bible in 1773.

3. Enoch prophesied with respect to these false teachers of these last days. So the translation should read, *"prophesied with respect to these."*

4. The phrase, *"Behold, the Lord cometh,"* refers to the Second Advent of Christ with all the resurrected Saints who will have been raptured before this.

5. The phrase, *"With ten thousands of His Saints,"* is literally, *"His holy ten thousands,"* which literally means *"an unlimited number."*

ENOCH

The phrase, *"And Enoch also, the seventh from Adam,"* seems to be given in this fashion to identify the Enoch of Genesis, Chapter 5. The line of descent is Adam, Seth, Enos, Cainan, Mahalaleel, Jared, Enoch.

Enoch was a Prophet of God, actually one of the first, if not the first. He was translated in that he did not see death (Rom. 10:17; Heb. 11:5).

He lived during a time of the greatest of evil. Quite possibly, he was one of the few at that time who truly lived for God. He and Elijah both were translated, the only two men in history which did not see death.

All we know of Enoch is found in Genesis, Chapter 5, Luke 3:37, where he is mentioned in the genealogies, and Hebrews 11:5, and in Jude, Verse 14, the Passage of our study.

Concerning this man, whom we know to be one of the greatest of the pre-Flood era, at least with God, lived, the Scripture says *"60 and 5 years, and begat Methuselah."*

It then says, *"And Enoch walked with God after he begat Methuselah 300 years, and begat sons and daughters."*

And finally: *"And all the days of Enoch were 360 and 5 years:*

"And Enoch walked with God: and he was not (meaning he didn't die, but was rather translated)*; for God took him"* (Gen. 5:21-24).

The expression *"walked with God"* denotes a devout life, lived in close communion with God.

While he was a Prophet, even as Jude mentions, it was his faith that stands out. The Scripture says: *"By faith Enoch was translated that he should not see death . . . for before his translation he had this testimony, that he pleased God"* (Heb. 11:5).

His testimony was his faith, and this pleased God (Heb. 11:6).

THE BOOK OF ENOCH

Jude quotes from this Book that was well-known in his day. It is a lengthy composite work of 108 chapters seemingly compiled in five sections or *"Books."* It is called *"The Book of Enoch,"* simply because it begins with this man's history and goes forward.

Book 1, which consists of chapters 6 through 36 is concerned largely with angels and the universe. Chapters 6 through 11, which come from the Book of Noah, suggest that certain fallen angels increased their rebellion by marriage with the daughters of men (Gen. 6:1). The angels in turn taught mankind the various arts and skills of civilization and mankind became corrupted and Godless. God then pronounced judgment on mankind and on the angel Azazel who led them astray.

In chapters 12 through 16 Enoch had a vision and, while he intercedes passionately on behalf of the fallen angels, he is finally instructed to predict their utter doom.

In chapters 17 through 36 Enoch is escorted by the angels of light on various tours

NOTES

throughout the Earth, to the place of punishment of the fallen angels, to Sheol, to the tree of life, to Jerusalem with its mountains, rivers, and streams, and to the Garden of Righteousness.

Book 2 covers chapters 37 through 71 and is composed of three parables or similitudes. Each parable is quite lengthy compared to a parable of the Gospels, for example, and each is primarily concerned with the triumph of Righteousness over wickedness.

The first parable (chpts. 38-44) deals with the impending judgment of the wicked, the abode of the Righteous and Elect One, the four Archangels and certain astronomical and meteorological sequence.

The second parable (chpts. 45-57) is concerned mainly with the Elect One or Son of Man sitting in judgment. He is not pictured as a human being but rather as a Majestic Heavenly Being possessing absolute dominion over the world of men and of angels.

The third parable (chpts. 58-71) speaks of the blessedness of the Saints, the measuring of paradise, the judgment of the kings and mighty ones, and gives the names and functions of the fallen angels.

Book 3 is the so-called Book of the Heavenly Luminaries and covers chapters 72 through 82. It is an almost purely scientific treatise, showing virtually no interest in ethical questions. The author seeks to construct a uniform astronomical system from the data of the Old Testament and argues that the measurement of time should be solar rather than lunar. Interestingly, however, the author's solar year is 364 days though he is aware of the 365 ¼ day year. The interest in the last two or three chapters suddenly becomes ethical, however, and it is stated that in the last days the heavenly bodies as well as the Earth will suffer serious disorders.

Book 4, covering chapters 83 through 90, consists of two lengthy dream-visions predicting the future history of Israel. Chapters 83 and 84 give the first dream-vision that, in the view assumed by the author, predicts the Flood as a judgment upon the world. The second dream-vision encompasses chapters 85 through 90 and, after recounting the history from the beginning to the time of Enoch, goes on to predict the history of the world to the founding of the Messianic Kingdom. This history is given using a wide array of symbolism.

Thus, oxen appear to symbolize the Patriarchs; sheep the true house of Israel; preying beasts and birds to heathen; and a white bull with great horns the Messiah.

The dream-vision ends with the New Jerusalem, the conversion of the Gentiles, the Resurrection of the righteous, and the establishment of the Messianic reign. The fact that the history as understood from the symbols goes no further than the Maccabean period is an indication of the date of this part of the work (this period covered the time immediately preceding Christ).

Book 5 is a work that includes exhortations for the righteous and maledictions for the wicked and occupies chapters 91 through 105. The structure of this section is difficult, though the theme is much the same as the rest of the work.

A noble feature of this Book is the Apocalypse of Weeks found in chapter 93:1-10 and chapter 91:12-17. The history of the world from Enoch's time and on is divided into 10 weeks of unequal length, each seemingly marked by some special event. Thus, the first is marked by Enoch's birth, the third by Abraham's call, and the seventh by the publication of Enoch's writings. In the eighth week the righteous will gain the victory over their oppressors. In the ninth week the world will be made ready for destruction. In the tenth and endless week a new Heaven will be ushered in.

The conclusion of the work occupies chapters 106 through 108. Chapters 106 and 107 derive from the earlier Book of Noah and relate the increase of sin after the Flood until the Messianic reign. The final chapter again returns to the theme of rewards for the righteous and punishment for the wicked.

INFLUENCE

The Book of Enoch exerted a strong and widespread influence on both Jewish and Christian literature. Quite a few of the writers of the uninspired Books quote from it, along with Jude in Verses 14 and 15 of his short Epistle.

In addition to this apparent literary dependence, however, many of the concepts

familiar to us from the New Testament appeared either first or most prominently in the Book of Enoch, or as it is sometimes referred to as First Enoch. Thus, for example, the spiritual nature of the Messianic reign. Thus, also the titles used to refer to the Messiah, such as, *"Christ,"* or *"The Anointed One," "The Righteous One," "The Elect One,"* and *"The Son of Man."* The New Testament concepts of Hell, resurrection, and demonology also bear striking similarities to those of Enoch.

SECOND ENOCH

This is another work ascribed to Enoch and known to us only from two Slavonic texts that were translated and published near the end of the Nineteenth Century. While showing some similarities with the earlier Book of Enoch, this Book is by no means to be identified with it.

Second Enoch is basically an account of Enoch's travels through the seven heavens and includes certain revelations given to him and his exhortations to his children. The revelations are concerned with creation and the history of mankind.

In the beginning God, it states, created the world out of nothing. He also created seven heavens with all the angelic hosts and mankind as well. Just as God performed His created work in six days and rested the seventh, even so the history of the word would span 6,000 years and it would then rest for 1,000 years. After this, an eternal day of blessing would begin.

The souls of men, the Book states, were created before the world began and also a place either in Heaven or in Hell for the future habitation of each soul. The soul was created good, but because of free will and because of the soul's habitation in the body, sin appeared despite the instruction man had received regarding the Two Ways. Therefore, men will have to face judgment and only the righteous will escape the hell prepared for sinners.

The ethical teaching of the Book is in many respects noble. Man should work and be just, charitable, unavenging, and humble. Above all, he should fear God.

About all that can be said about these Books is that they are uninspired. This means that some things in them are true and some things aren't. Evidently and obvious, that which Jude quoted as it regards Enoch is true. And how do we know that?

The prophecy as given by Enoch was evidently knowledge in Jude's day, or else the Holy Spirit revealed to him the truthfulness of this statement.

PROPHECY

The phrase, *"Prophesied of these,"* refers to Enoch prophesying with respect to the false teachers of these lasts days.

In fact, and as should be obvious, there have always been false teachers; however, Paul, Peter, John, and Jude, along with Enoch, proclaimed the severity of the situation as to what will happen in these last days. When we consider that the Holy Spirit gave this information through Enoch over 5,000 years ago, we surely should understand how important this information is.

The striking thing about all of this is, these days of which Enoch prophesied, along with the great Apostles of the Early Church, pertain to the time we are living in presently. This means, as bad as the situation is now, it is going to get worse, and in fact, even as Paul describes in II Thessalonians, Chapter 2, will lead to the advent of the Antichrist. In other words, this great deception that has already begun, the false doctrine propagated by false teachers, the apostasy of the modern Church, are all driving toward the great deception of the Antichrist. Satan will make his greatest and final effort at this particular time, at least as it refers to the time before the Second Coming.

Of this we can be certain, the warnings of last day apostasy given not merely by one, but by several, not only guarantee the happening, but more than all, guarantees the severity of this which, as stated, has already begun.

DECEPTION

Jude told us to *"earnestly contend for the faith which was once delivered unto the Saints"* (vs. 3). Paul said that *"in the latter times some shall depart from the faith, giving heed to seducing spirits, and doctrines of Devils"* (I Tim. 4:1).

It is *"the Faith"* which is under attack, and it is under attack by a concentrated force

NOTES

especially designed by the powers of darkness for these last days. *"Seducing spirits"* are leading the attack.

When Jude made his statement in Verse 3, he was speaking of the day in which he lived; however, the Holy Spirit showed him, along with his Readers, that the greater thrust of what He (the Spirit) was saying, pertained to the last days, and in effect, the last of the last days.

As I've already stated, I personally feel that the state of the Church at this present time is worse, and I speak of the spiritual sense, than any other time since the Reformation, a period of several hundreds of years. And yet, very, very few would agree with what I've just said.

I remember in the early 1960's, preaching a Campmeeting with A. N. Trotter. This man was the prince of Preachers, and one of the Godliest men I've ever known. He had a touch of the Holy Spirit in his Ministry that was exceptional to say the least. In fact, in all of my years I've never seen anything quite like the moving of the Holy Spirit as it regards the Services that he conducted. I was privileged to have the opportunity of preaching several Campmeetings with him, as inadequate as I actually was.

After one of the morning Services, several of us Preachers and our wives were walking across the street to the Cafeteria. He said something that startled me then, but looking back now, I realize how right it was. Concerning the Denomination with which both of us at that time were associated, he said, *"It's too late, it's gone too far down the road to turn back."* He was speaking in the spiritual sense, and making the statement that spiritually, this particular Denomination had charted a course, which would lead to its spiritual ruin.

I was so startled by his statement that I asked him to repeat it, which he did. I'll be frank, that at that particular time, I didn't understand what he said, and in fact, didn't really believe what he said.

This particular Denomination was then on a roll so to speak. They were building several Churches a week all over the nation, and at that time, probably had the most effective Missions outreach in the world.

Having learned some things, and looking back, I realize that Brother Trotter knew exactly what he was talking about, and was exactly right in what he said. Today, that particular Denomination is only a shell of what it once was. And to be sure, the course for its present dilemma was charted at that particular time, or even before. And what was that course?

A LACK OF DEPENDENCE
ON THE HOLY SPIRIT

In the late 1950's and especially in the 1960's, the Denomination of which I have spoken, which is very similar to all the other Pentecostal Denominations, at least in the United States and Canada, had already opted for the psychological way. As we've already stated innumerable times in this Volume, there is no way that the Christian can trust in the Cross and the psychological way at the same time. Either one cancels out the other. They are so diametrically opposed to each other that for one to claim that an amalgamation can be undertaken proclaims the fact of a serious lack of knowledge of the Word of God. The uniting of the two simply cannot be done!

Psychology can probably be said to be the religion of humanism. I was reading after a Theologian a short time back, a man incidentally who did not even claim to be Spirit baptized, but who had enough spiritual insight to recognize the following:

He said, *"The Church and the world has become so psychologized, that it no longer believes in a coming judgment."*

He then said, *"How can it believe in a coming judgment, when psychology teaches that man is not responsible for his perversions, sins, and aberrations, but rather outside forces are responsible!"*

As well, I might quickly add that when one abandons the Cross, one has also abandoned the Holy Spirit. The two, the Holy Spirit and the Cross, are so closely intertwined (Rom. 8:2) that it's impossible to violate one without violating the other. Let me give you an example:

For a period of time, the non-Pentecostal Church world attempted to preach the Cross without the Holy Spirit. For the most part,

they now preach neither. The Pentecostals have tried to preach the Holy Spirit without the Cross, and for the most part they now preach neither!

Let it be quickly but sadly said that the Jesus now preached in most Churches is *"another Jesus,"* and the *"spirit"* now claimed is, pure and simple, *"another spirit,"* which means that the people are hearing *"another gospel"* (II Cor. 11:4).

Remember this: *"If it's not Jesus Christ and Him Crucified,"* then it's *"another Jesus."* And if it's not the Cross that is preached, then pure and simple, it's *"another spirit."* And if it's not Faith in the Cross of Christ, then again, it is *"another gospel."* Now let me ask this question:

How much Cross is the modern Church preaching?

THE PREACHING OF THE CROSS

Listen to what Paul said:

"But shun profane and vain babblings: for they will increase unto more ungodliness.

"And their word will eat as does a canker: of whom is Hymenaeus and Philetus;

"Who concerning the Truth have erred, saying that the Resurrection is past already; and overthrow the faith of some" (II Tim. 2:16-18).

I would certainly say that the *"Resurrection"* is very important; however, according to Paul, it's not nearly as important as the Cross (Rom. 6:3-14; 8:1-2, 11; I Cor. 1:17-18, 21, 23; 2:2, 5; Gal. 6:14; Col. 2:14-15).

And if an erroneous interpretation of the Resurrection would result in the overthrowing of the faith of some, even as the Holy Spirit through Paul said it would, well then how much more serious would it be to falsely teach the Cross, which is the very heartbeat of Christianity!

Incidentally, Paul did not draw back from naming these particular Preachers, because it was necessary to do so.

Not only is the modern Church little preaching the Cross presently, but the truth is, the modern Church knows almost nothing about the Cross, while at the same time, thinking it knows everything about the Cross.

The facts are, what little it does know, concerns the initial Salvation experience. In other words, *"Jesus died for me,"* is about the extent of what is known. Make no mistake about it, that little simple statement is probably the most important statement ever made; however, the Cross pertains not only to our initial Salvation, but also to our everyday living. In fact, it is impossible for any Saint, irrespective as to whom that Saint might be, to live a holy life, without understanding the Message of the Cross. It simply cannot be done, even as the Seventh Chapter of Romans bears out.

I personally feel that the apostasy of these last days, which will be the worst apostasy of all, will center up on the Cross. In other words, to oppose the Cross is to fall into the apostate church. To accept the Cross, is to be in the True Church. Actually, it has always been that way, but I personally believe, it's going to be more pronounced now than ever. In other words, the Holy Spirit is going to make the Cross the primary Message of this day and age, at least as it regards the True Church.

And as we've already stated, to properly understand the Cross, is to properly understand the Holy Spirit and how He works (Rom. 8:1-2, 11, 13).

THE SECOND COMING OF THE LORD

The phrase, *"Saying, behold, the Lord cometh with ten thousands of His Saints,"* refers to the Second Coming of the Lord, Who will be accompanied by every Saint who has ever lived, even from the very beginning, all the way through the Rapture of the Church.

"Ten thousands of His Saints" are literally, *"His holy ten thousands."* The word *"myriad"* is the English spelling of the Greek word here, which latter word means in the singular, *"ten thousand,"* and in the plural as it is here, *"an innumerable multitude, an unlimited number."* The translation could also read, *"His holy myriads."*

These would not be limited to Saints, but would also include Angels.

SAINTS

Among Protestants today, the word *"Saints"* has almost totally lost its original meaning, that is, of being set aside for the exclusive ownership and use of the Triune

NOTES

God. But yet the term is of course correct, as is used extensively in the New Testament (Mat. 27:52; Acts 9:13, 32, 41; 26:10; Rom. 1:7; 8:27; 12:13; 15:25-26, 31; 16:2, 15; I Cor. 1:2; 6:1-2; 14:33; 16:1, 15, etc.).

The word *"Saint"* or *"Saints"* has in its general meaning both in the Hebrew and the Greek, the meaning of consecration and Divine claim and ownership. It expresses a relation to God as being set apart for His Own.

While the word *"Saint"* or *"Saints"* occurs more frequently in the New Testament than in the Old, yet both are applied with practical uniformity to the company of God's people rather than to any particular individual.

Perhaps the rendering *"Saints"* cannot be improved, but it is necessary for the ordinary reader constantly to guard against the idea that New Testament Saintship was in any way a result of personal character, and consequently that it implied approval of moral attainment already made.

Such a rendering as *"consecrate ones,"* for example, would bring out more clearly the relation to God which is involved, but, besides the fact that it is not a simple statement, it might lead to other errors, for it is not easy to remember that consecration — the setting apart of the individual as one of the company whom God has in a peculiar way as His Own — springs not from man, but from God Himself, and that consequently it is in no way something optional, and admits of no degrees of progress, but, on the contrary, is from the beginning absolute duty.

It should also be noted that while, as has been said, to be a Saint is not directly and primarily to be good but rather to be set apart by God as His Own, yet the Godly and holy character ought inevitably and immediately to result. When God consecrates and claims moral beings for Himself and His service, He demands that we should go on to be fit for and worthy of the relation in which He has placed us, and so we read of certain actions being performed as *"worthily of the Saints"* (Rom. 16:2) and as such *"as becometh Saints"* (Eph. 5:3).

The thought of the holy character of the *"Saints,"* which is now so common as almost completely to obscure the real thought of the New Testament writers, already lay in their thinking very close to their conception of Saintship as consecration by God to be His Own.

The real thought of the Holy Spirit through the New Testament writers as it regards *"Saints,"* is that all Believers belong to God, and that we belong to Him by virtue of what Jesus Christ did at the Cross on our behalf, and our faith in that Finished Work. As also stated, it does not refer to the individual being good on a personal basis, but rather placing faith and trust in One Who is definitely good, namely, the Lord Jesus Christ. It is all *"in Christ,"* and it is only *"in Christ,"* which refers always to the Cross, that one can be understood to be a *"Saint."*

THE ERROR OF ROMAN CATHOLICISM REGARDING SAINTS

It is easy to see how the term *"Saints"* would inevitably take on an ethical and moral meaning. If a person belongs to Christ, and he showed his Christian character by an exemplary life, and if he made notable progress in Sanctification, so that his reputation as a good, moral, and spiritual person became widely spread among the Churches, people would begin to speak, not only of his belonging to God more than other people, but of his *"Saintly"* character more than ordinary Christians. In that way the term would gradually be used only of such persons who were outstanding in spirituality, or were thought to be so.

That is probably the origin of the Roman Catholic custom of restricting the usage of the term *"Saints"* to those notable persons like the Apostles and those whom the Church selected and honored officially as *"Saints."* The fact that most Christians still have sinful characteristics, even though they are genuine Christians, would cause the Church gradually to withhold the term *"Saints"* from ordinary Christians, and apply it only to such special, spiritual individuals.

Even the restriction of the use of the term to those whom the Catholic Church hierarchy selected can be explained by the difficulty of selecting the best individuals to whom the term *"Saint"* could be applied. There would have to be a final authority to decide such a selection, and during the lifetime of those

who knew the Saint personally, it would be difficult to cover up minor defects of character. That is probably the reason why people must be dead many years before they can even be considered by the Roman Church as suitable saintly material.

As someone has well said, the closer we get to the Godliest of individuals, the more we see their flaws. Conversely, the closer we get to Christ, the more we see His perfection. That's the reason that Sainthood, which is automatic with every Child of God, even a new convert, and the moment they are saved, is always totally and completely *"in Christ."*

ROMAN CATHOLIC THEOLOGY

According to Roman Catholic theology, individuals can store up a reservoir of merit, by good deeds and blameless lives. That reservoir of such merit becomes available to other humble Christians in answer to prayers offered to the Saint. Those who feel themselves particularly in need of merit would then pray to the Saint for help and merit.

The worship of the Saints would easily develop from such a doctrine. If a Saint could really give his or her merit to any person, would not that Saint be likely to give special favor to that person if he burned candles and brought special offerings to the Saint?

Would he or she not be more likely to give greater favors who brought better offerings? Gradually prayers and petitions would be offered almost exclusively to the Saint, and the honor and worship that belong to God Alone would be transferred almost exclusively to the alleged Saint. Because of the danger of such a situation arising, one can readily understand why God forbade all prayers and worship to anyone, but to God Himself. All so-called aids-to-worship have their danger intrinsic in them.

In fact, Roman Catholic theology as it regards *"Sainthood,"* has no Scripturality whatsoever, and is purely a fiction of the Catholic Church. In fact, *"Sainthood"* as practiced by the Roman Church, impugns the Grace of God, and as well makes less of the merit of Christ as it regards His great Sacrifice.

Every person who is truly saved, is such because of what Jesus did at the Cross on our behalf, and our Faith in that Finished Work.

The Scripture plainly says, and in no uncertain terms: *"For by Grace are you saved through Faith; and that not of yourselves, it is the Gift of God:*

"Not of works, lest any man should boast" (Eph. 2:8-9).

Paul also said:

"But God forbid that I should glory (boast), *save in the Cross of our Lord Jesus Christ, by Whom the world is crucified unto me, and I unto the world"* (Gal. 6:14).

The only *"boast"* the Christian has is the Cross of Christ. To boast in our so-called good works, thinking that such merits us something with God, is an insult to Christ and what He has done for us at the Cross. Once again we must say with Paul:

"God forbid that I should boast, save in the Cross of our Lord Jesus Christ."

THE SECOND COMING OF CHRIST TO THE EARTH

A prominent Doctrine of Christology, the predicted Second Advent of Christ, is implied in hundreds of Old Testament Prophecies of future judgment on the world and a coming Kingdom of Righteousness on Earth, and is explicitly detailed in major New Testament Passages. The last Book of the Bible, the Revelation of Jesus Christ, refers specifically to His Second Coming itself (Chpt. 19), the Millennium, and future state that follows (Chpts. 20-22).

GENERAL OLD TESTAMENT REFERENCES

The Old Testament presents a mingled prophecy of the First and Second Advents of Christ (I Pet. 1:10-12), often combining both Comings in the same context (Isa. 61:1-3; Lk. 4:17-20).

The first reference to the Second Coming is found in Deuteronomy 30:3 in the King James rendering where it is predicted, *"Then the LORD your God will turn your captivity, and have compassion on you, and will return and gather you from all the nations where the LORD your God has scattered you."*

The *"return"* results in Israel being regathered to their ancient land and their spiritual and physical restoration. This is typical

of Old Testament Prophecies of the Second Advent. The Old Testament seldom pictures the Second Coming per se, but often dwells upon the circumstances of the Second Coming, such as the preceding regathering of Israel to the land (Jer. 30:3; Amos 9:14-15), and the results of the Second Coming — the judgment of the nations (Isa. 2:4), deliverance of Israel (Jer. 31:28), and a kingdom of Righteousness and Peace on Earth (Ps. 72:7).

SECOND COMING IN THE PSALMS

The Second Coming of Christ is linked with the moral struggle between God and His creatures. Psalm 2 for instance, after picturing the world's rejection of the Sovereignty of God, declares God's purpose, *"I have set My king on Zion, My holy hill."* In the Verses that follow, the decree of God is stated concerning His purpose to place His Son over the nations, to subdue the nations with a rod of iron, and dash them in pieces like a potter's vessel (Ps. 2:9).

On the basis of God's intention to make His Son the King of the Earth, the exhortation to earthly kings is *"serve the LORD with fear and rejoice, with trembling. Kiss the Son* (Kiss His feet)*"* (Ps. 2:11). The conclusion is reached *"Blessed are all who take refuge in Him"* (Ps. 2:12). This Psalm is typical of the Old Testament Passages relating to the Second Coming. The event itself is assumed, but the results are detailed.

Psalm 24 is another great Passage dealing with Christ's coming as *"the King of glory."* The gates of Jerusalem are exhorted to open to this King when He comes. His rule on the Earth is based on the promise of Psalm 24:1, *"The earth is the LORD's and the fullness thereof, the world and those who dwell therein."*

Another complete presentation of the Second Coming of Christ and its result is found in Psalm 72, presented in the form of a prayer, but describing the certain results of Christ's return. His dominion is described as *"from sea to sea"* (Ps. 72:8). Kings and nations are described as serving Him (Ps. 72:11). Psalm 72 ends with the prayer, *"May His glory fill the whole earth!"* Although in the form of an inspired prayer, it clearly anticipates fulfillment.

Other Psalms are similar in character such as Psalm 96 that declares, *"The LORD reigns!"* (Ps. 96:10), and states, *"for He comes, for He comes to judge the earth"* (Ps. 96:13). The present position of Christ seated at the right hand of the Father in Psalms 110:1-2 is considered temporary, for the day will come when *"the Lord sends forth from Zion your mighty Scepter"* and *"will execute judgment among the nations"* (Ps. 110:2-6).

SECOND COMING AND THE PROPHETS

The major Prophets take up the same theme of the coming of the Lord to reign. A familiar text is Isaiah 9:6-7 where it declares: *"Of the increase of His Government and of Peace there will be no end, upon the throne of David, and over His Kingdom."* The rule of the Messiah on Earth is described in Isaiah, Chapter 11 as one of complete Righteousness and Justice, of tranquility in nature, with universal knowledge of the Lord. Isaiah prays for the coming of the Lord (Isa. 64:1), *"Oh that You would rend the heavens and come down, that the mountains might quake at Your presence."* Isaiah's great prophecy concludes in Chapters 65 and 66 with a description of the reign of Christ on Earth and the judgments that relate to it.

Jeremiah speaks of the results of the Lord's coming when the Son of David *"shall reign as King and deal wisely, and shall execute Justice and Righteousness in the land"* (Jer. 23:5). The judgments and tribulation that precede the Second Coming are followed by the deliverance of Israel according to Jeremiah, Chapters 30 and 31, and many other prophecies in Jeremiah deal with the ultimate triumph of God during the reign of Christ. The presentation of the right to rule over the Earth following His Second Coming is described in Daniel 7:13-14, where the Son of Man is given dominion over the entire Earth and an everlasting kingdom.

One of the most specific references to the Second Coming in the Old Testament is in Zechariah 14:3-5. The Lord is described as fighting in defense of Israel, and the statement is made, *"On that day His feet shall stand on the Mount of Olives, which lies before Jerusalem on the east; and the Mount of Olives shall be split in two from east to west by a very wide valley; so that one half of the Mount shall withdraw northward, and the other half southward."* The Revelation goes on to picture that *"the LORD will become King over all the earth; on that day the LORD will be one and His Name one"* (Zech. 14:9).

THE SECOND COMING
AND THE GOSPELS

One of the most explicit Passages relating to the Second Coming is found in the Olivet Discourse recorded in Matthew, Chapters 24 and 25; Mark, Chapter 13; and, Luke 21:5-38. Matthew, which gives the most complete account, like Old Testament Prophecies relating to the Second Coming, describes the preceding great Tribulation (Mat. 24:15-28). This will climax an age that includes war, famine, pestilence, earthquakes, and many persecutions.

Christ warned His Disciples not to be deceived by premature, false reports that the Lord has returned. He describes the event in such language as to make it unmistakable. The Second Advent is described as *"lightning that comes from the east and shines to the west"* (Mat. 24:27). It will occur *"immediately after the tribulation of those days"* (Mat. 24:15-26).

At the Second Advent *"the sun will be darkened, and the moon will not give its light, and the stars will fall from heaven, and the powers of the heavens shall be shaken"* (Mat. 24:29).

The world will then see *"the sign of the Son of Man in Heaven,"* that is, *"they will see the Son of Man coming in the clouds of Heaven with power and great glory"* (Mat. 24:30).

At this time there will be a loud trumpet call and the Angels will be commissioned to collect the Elect of God in Heaven and Earth. The Second Coming is described as the time of the doom of the wicked in the Earth. It is prophesied, *"then all the tribes of the earth will mourn"* (Mat. 24:30) as they see the Second Coming of Christ from Heaven to the Earth. The fact that the entire Earth sees the event presumes that it will take many hours during which the Earth turning on its axis will expose the entire globe to the Heavenly Glory. And as well, it is no doubt that

Television Cameras will record the event, portraying it over the entirety of the Earth.

The procession will end, however, in the Holy Land, as indicated in Zechariah 14:4 and many other Passages.

THE SECOND COMING IN JUDE

The Epistle of Jude, actually, the Epistle of our study, presents the Second Coming as a time of judgment, quoting Enoch, *"Behold, the Lord cometh with His holy myriads, to execute judgment on all, and to convict all the ungodly of all their deeds of ungodliness which they have committed in such an ungodly way, and of all the harsh things which ungodly sinners have spoken against Him"* (vss. 14-15).

As in Matthew, Chapter 24, the Second Coming in Jude is declared to be a distinct event, one in which the holy angels will participate and culminating in dramatic judgment upon the wicked.

Even before the Flood, actually, approximately a thousand years before that time, God gave the Revelation to Enoch concerning the Second Coming. This was approximately 600 years after Adam.

We learn from this several things:

1. God through foreknowledge knows exactly what is going to happen regarding the future of this world. Actually, it's all described in the Bible.

2. He not only knows what is going to happen, He has directed the happening of all major events, at least as it concerns what He will do.

3. As stated, it's all outlined in the Word of God. As such, we can be absolutely certain that what is predicted is going to come to pass.

About one-third of the Bible is history; about one-third is instruction; about one-third is prophecy. About half of the prophecies have already been fulfilled, and we are standing presently on the very eve of the fulfillment of many other Endtime events.

THE SECOND COMING IN THE BOOK OF REVELATION

The Book of Revelation provides the most comprehensive prophecy of the Second Advent. The title of the Book itself, the Revelation of Jesus Christ, refers to the Revelation of Christ to the Earth that will occur at the Second Advent. The first eighteen Chapters of this Book deal with that which precedes — the age of the Churches, which takes up Chapters 2 and 3, and scenes in Heaven and Earth leading up to the Second Advent in Chapters 4 through 18. Chapter 19 describes the Second Coming itself, Chapters 20 through 22 the epilogue, the Millennium in Chapter 20, and the new Heaven and the new Earth in Chapters 21 and 22. The obvious implication is that the Second Advent is the crowning event climaxing human history, paralleling in importance the First Advent, which pertains to the Incarnation, God becoming Man when Jesus was born.

John opens his presentation of the Second Coming with the words: *"Then I saw heaven opened, and behold, a white horse! He Who sat upon it is called Faithful and True, and in righteousness He judges and makes war"* (Rev. 19:11). That this is none other than Christ Himself is made clear from the title, *"The Word of God"* (Rev. 19:13) and *"King of kings and Lord of lords"* (Rev. 19:16).

His appearance is most awesome. *"His eyes are like a flame of fire, and on His head are many diadems"* (Rev. 19:12). His robe is dipped in blood (Rev. 19:13), signifying two things; the price He paid on the Cross of Calvary, and that much blood will be shed during the Battle of Armageddon, at which time the Second Coming will take place. He is followed by the hosts of Heaven, clad in white linen, mounted on white horses, which constitute all the Redeemed of the Lord (Rev. 19:14). Out of the mouth of Christ *"issues a sharp sword with which to smite the nations"* and it is predicted *"He will rule them with a rod of iron"* (Rev. 19:15). His coming signals His intention to *"tread the winepress of the fury and wrath of God the Almighty."*

THE BATTLE OF ARMAGEDDON

This awe-inspiring scene is attended by the invitation of the Angel to the birds of Heaven to eat the flesh of men and beasts slain in the great battle that follows. The armies of the world gathered in the Holy Land at that time in the final great world conflict are destroyed. The beast or world political leader, and the false prophet, the world religious leader, who had dominated the preceding period are thrown alive into the lake of fire (Rev. 19:19-20). The armies themselves are slain by the sword issuing from the mouth of the Rider (Rev. 19:21).

In what would naturally be considered subsequent action in Chapter 20, Satan is bound, the martyred dead of the Great Tribulation period are resurrected, judgment is given, and the thousand-year reign of Christ follows (Rev. 20:1-4).

If Scripture is taken in its normal sense, it yields a dramatic picture of this tremendous event that will judge wickedness and unbelief, deliver those trusting in the Lord, and inaugurate a kingdom of righteousness and peace on Earth. As well, Israel will now be restored to her rightful place and position as the leading nation on Earth, but only after she accepts Christ not only as Messiah, but also as Saviour and Lord (Zech., Chpts. 12-14).

THE RAPTURE OF THE CHURCH

In addition to major Passages dealing with the Second Advent are prophecies of a Rapture or catching up of Believers in Christ to meet the Lord in the air.

The Rapture is totally different from the Second Coming. In other words, it is not a part of the Second Coming. In fact, the two comings will be separated by at least seven years, and possibly longer.

At the Rapture Christ will come close to this Earth, but in fact will not come all the way to the Earth. At the Second Coming, the Lord will definitely come to this Earth, actually coming Personally to set up a Kingdom.

At the Rapture, Christ will come *"for"* the Saints (I Thess. 4:13-18), while at the Second Coming, the Lord will come *"with"* the Saints.

The Coming of Christ for His Own was mentioned by Christ in the Upper Room when He declared to His Disciples, *"In My Father's house are many mansions; if it were not so, would I have told you that I go to prepare a place for you? And when I go and prepare a place for you, I will come again and will take you to Myself, that where I am you may be also"* (Jn. 14:2-3).

This simple Revelation is later amplified by Paul (I Thess. 4:13-18). At the coming of Christ for His Church, it is declared that God will bring with Him the souls of Christians who had died, in order that their bodies might be resurrected from the grave. The dramatic event is described, *"For the Lord Himself will descend from heaven with a shout, with the Archangel's call, and with the sound of the Trumpet of God. And the dead in Christ will rise first, then we who are alive, who are left, shall be caught up together with them in the clouds to meet the Lord in the air; and so we shall always be with the Lord"* (I Thess. 4:16-18). In I Thessalonians, Chapter 5, this event is declared to be one that will come without warning to the unbelieving world, but one that Believers in Christ shall participate.

THE RESURRECTION

A parallel Revelation of this event is given in I Corinthians 15:51-58. Here it is plainly declared that all Christians will not die, but at the coming of the Lord all will be changed — the living translated and given new bodies, and the dead in Christ resurrected (I Cor. 15:51-52). The new bodies that Believers will receive are declared to be imperishable, immortal, or deathless. According to I John 3:2, they will be like the resurrection body of Christ and hence sinless. This hope of the coming of the Lord, or the Rapture of the Church as it is commonly called, was held out as an imminent possibility to early Christians.

In fact, the Early Church Fathers interpreted Scripture as teaching the Rapture as being possible at any moment, despite the fact that Paul in II Thessalonians, Chapter 2 had stated that certain things must happen before these things could take place.

Because some in the Early Church mistakenly identified their sufferings as those of the Great Tribulation, they did not distinguish the Rapture itself from the Second Advent to the Earth. However, a proper interpretation of II Thessalonians, Chapter 2 will put everything in its proper place.

Due to living in the very last of the last days, the Rapture of the Church, I believe, could take place at any moment (I Thess. 4:13-18). This will be followed by the Great Tribulation and the rise of the man of sin (II Thess., Chpt. 2; Rev., Chpts. 6-18). In fact, the Great Tribulation will conclude with the

Battle of Armageddon, when and where the Antichrist will seek to destroy Israel. This Battle will be halted by the Second Coming (Rev., Chpt. 19).

At the Second Coming, Christ will Personally introduce a Kingdom on this Earth, with Himself as King, with Righteousness as the prevailing spirit, which will last for a thousand years (Rev., Chpt. 20). At this time, Satan along with all fallen angels and demon spirits, will be locked away in the bottomless pit; consequently, the world at that time will know peace and security as it has never known in its history. The Prince of Peace, the Lord Jesus Christ will be present and, therefore, peace will reign. As well, it will be a time of prosperity as the world has never known, and a prosperity that is equally divided among all the people of the world (Isa. 11:1-10).

At the conclusion of the thousand year reign with Christ, Satan will be loosed out of the bottomless pit for a short period of time (Rev. 20:7-8).

The Scripture doesn't give us much information concerning this event, only to say that *"fire came down from God out of heaven, and devoured them,"* which speaks of those who at that time were throwing their lot with the Evil One. The Scripture then says:

"And the Devil that deceived them was cast into the lake of fire and brimstone, where the beast and the false prophet are, and shall be tormented day and night forever and ever" (Rev. 20:9-10).

Immediately after this event, or probably immediately before, the Great White Throne Judgment will commence, when all the unsaved of all time will stand before God, and will be judged. No Believers will be at this Judgment, this event reserved for those who do not know God. They will be shown from the Books their lives and opportunities in detail, which will conclude with them understanding that they are without excuse (Rev. 20:11-15).

After that, there will be *a new heaven and a new earth: for the first heaven and the first earth were passed away; and there was no more sea"* (Rev. 21:1).

At that time, the Lord will literally transfer His Headquarters from Heaven to Earth, actually bringing the entirety of the New

NOTES

Jerusalem down to this planet. The world will then be what God originally intended for it to be, and will last forever and forever (Rev., Chpts. 21-22).

THE CROSS

Incidentally, even though Satan and all of his cohorts along with sin and sinners will be forever done away, still, we are to be forever reminded that all of this came at great price, the price of the Lamb of God in the shedding of His Own Precious Blood. Seven times in the last two Chapters of Revelation, which portrays the perfect age, Jesus is referred to as the *"Lamb."* To be sure, He could have been referred to in many other ways; however, the Holy Spirit had this done for a purpose. We are to never forget that He is the One Who paid the price, and that He did so by the giving of Himself (Rev. 21:9, 14, 22-23, 27; 22:1, 3).

(15) "TO EXECUTE JUDGMENT UPON ALL, AND TO CONVINCE ALL THAT ARE UNGODLY AMONG THEM OF ALL THEIR UNGODLY DEEDS WHICH THEY HAVE UNGODLY COMMITTED, AND OF ALL THEIR HARD SPEECHES WHICH UNGODLY SINNERS HAVE SPOKEN AGAINST HIM."

The construction is:

1. *"To execute judgment upon all,"* refers to Christ judging the nations of the world, which will commence at the beginning of the Millennial Reign.

2. *"And to convince all that are ungodly among them,"* refers to Christ correcting the wrong direction of untold millions.

3. The stress is on two words, each used four times: *"all"* and *"ungodly."*

JUDGMENT

The phrase, *"To execute judgment upon all,"* refers to the judgment of the nations that will take place at Christ's Second Advent (Mat. 25:31-34).

The reason and basis of the judgment of the nations will pertain to Israel. God will curse or bless according to how men have dealt with Israel. He will forever respect and fulfill the Abrahamic Covenant (Gen. 12:1-3).

However, as the nations will be judged at that time, likewise, every human being that's ever lived will be judged, although at a different time. For all those who have accepted Christ, our judgment was satisfied in Him. In other words, He was judged for the sins of the whole world, and for all time, past, present, and future, meaning that He paid the price for our sins by the shedding of His Life's Blood, which suspends all judgment for those who will believe in Him (Jn. 3:16). So, the true Christian doesn't have to worry about a judgment for sin, that all having been addressed in Christ.

But for those who will not accept Christ, which means that they refuse the price that He paid, they will suffer the judgment of the Great White Throne, which to be sure, will be the most horrifying time of all (Rev. 20:11-15).

The world has been so psychologized that any more it denies judgment. The idea, according to this erroneous way of thinking, that man is responsible, and will have to be one day judged, is denied.

Psychology teaches that man is inherently good, and if he is bad, it is because of outward circumstances or situations not of his own making. Therefore, at least as they claim, there can be no judgment.

The Bible says the very opposite. It says that man, due to the Fall, is inherently evil (Rom., Chpt. 3). As well, it teaches that man is responsible for his actions, and will one day be judged for those actions. Such judgment can take place in Christ, as we've already explained, or it can take place at the Great White Throne, but take place it shall! Jesus Christ is the Saviour of the world. In Him every sin has been judged, but only for those who will believe. If men refuse Him as their Saviour, to be sure, they will tomorrow face Him as their Judge. One way or the other, in Christ or by Christ, judgment is inevitable!

TO CORRECT

The phrase, *"And to convince all that are ungodly among them of all their ungodly deeds which they have ungodly committed,"* proclaims in no uncertain terms, the ungodliness of men who have rejected Christ.

Inasmuch as the word *"ungodly"* is used four times in this Verse, this tells us that the ungodliness is total. As well, and as stated, the word *"all"* is used four times, which

NOTES

means that none will escape this judgment. *"All"* means *"all!"*

"All" will be judged; *"all"* will be corrected; *"all"* ungodly deeds will be addressed; and, *"all"* the hard words against Christ will be judged.

This one Scripture tells us that all who have rejected Christ are *"ungodly."* It also tells us that all the deeds they commit, whether claimed by them to be good or bad, in the eyes of God are *"ungodly."* As well, every deed was committed in an *"ungodly"* way, which means it originated in an evil heart. Being *"ungodly,"* they have *"spoken against Him."* Men are either for Christ or against Christ. There is no middle ground.

THE MANNER IN WHICH MEN WILL BE CORRECTED

"Convince" in the Greek is *"elencho,"* and means *"to convict, to refute."* It gradually took on additional meanings: *"to correct,"* often by accusing.

God's correcting is a powerful ministry; it confronts human beings in their sin (Jn. 16:8; Jude, vs. 15). The Holy Spirit is the active Agent in this ministry. John 16:8 gives us Jesus' promise that when the Spirit comes, *"He will convict the world of guilt in regard to sin and righteousness and judgment."*

This active ministry of the Spirit carried out since His *"coming"* at Pentecost does not guarantee conversion. A person may hear the Gospel, recognize his or her personal sin and need, and yet may choose not to believe. Even the brilliant light of God's Revelation, directed by His Spirit to reveal an individual's heart, does not release that individual from responsibility of personal choice.

The type of correction that Christ will administer in the coming day of the Millennial Reign, is proclaimed by the Prophet Isaiah:

"And there shall come forth a Rod out of the stem of Jesse, and a Branch shall grow out of His roots:

"And the Spirit of the LORD shall rest upon Him, the Spirit of wisdom and understanding, the Spirit of counsel and might, the Spirit of knowledge and of the fear of the LORD;

"And shall make Him (Christ) of quick understanding in the fear of the LORD: and He shall not judge after the sight of His

eyes, neither reprove after the hearing of His ears:

"But with righteousness shall He judge the poor, and reprove with equity for the meek of the earth: and He shall smite the earth with the rod of His mouth, and with the breath of His lips shall He slay the wicked.

"And righteousness shall be the girdle of His loins, and faithfulness the girdle of His reins" (Isa. 11:1-5).

SPOKEN AGAINST HIM

The phrase, *"And of all their hard speeches which ungodly sinners have spoken against Him,"* records the fact that everything that has been said against the Lord has been noted, and for those statements every single soul will give account. The word *"ungodly"* refers to the individuals in question, and as well refers to the fact that what is said against Christ is ungodly also.

The purpose of the Coming of the Lord will not be to convince men in that sense, though it is undoubtedly true that the wicked will see that their lives have been wrong; but it will be to pronounce a sentence on them as the result of the evidence of their guilt.

In regard to this Passage, thus quoted from an ancient prophecy, we may remark that the style bears the mark of it being a quotation, or of it being preserved by Jude in the language in which it had been handed down by tradition. It is not the style of Jude.

It has every mark of it having been actually delivered by Enoch. The age in which he lived was corrupt. The world was ripening for the deluge. He was himself a good man, and, as would seem perhaps, almost the only good man of his generation. Nothing would be more natural than that he should be reproached by hard words and speeches, and nothing more natural than that he should have pointed the men of his own age to the future judgment.

The Doctrine of the final judgment was an early doctrine in the world. It was held even in the first generations of the race. It was one of the great truths early communicated to man to restrain him from sin, and to lead him to prepare for the great events that are to occur on the Earth.

To be sure, it is coming closer day by day, and in fact, is even at the door.

NOTES

I think one can say without fear of contradiction that this prophecy regarding judgment is the oldest specimen in existence of Hebrew poetic parallelism. Lamech's poem was perhaps composed in mockery of Enoch (Gen. 4:23-24). The one announced coming judgment; the other denied there would be any judgment. All opposition to truth and its confessor is *"against Him."*

(16) "THESE ARE MURMURERS, COMPLAINERS, WALKING AFTER THEIR OWN LUSTS; AND THEIR MOUTH SPEAKETH GREAT SWELLING WORDS, HAVING MEN'S PERSONS IN ADMIRATION BECAUSE OF ADVANTAGE."

The structure is:

1. *"Murmurers"* are those who discontentedly complain.

2. Complainers are those who find fault.

3. *"Walking"* speaks of a planned course of conduct.

4. As the fear of God drives out the fear of man, so defiance of God tends to put man in His place.

MURMURERS

The phrase, *"These are murmurers,"* refers not to a loud, outspoken dissatisfaction, but to an undertone muttering.

The word used here does not elsewhere occur, though the word *"murmur"* is frequent (Mat. 20:11; Lk. 5:30; Jn. 6:41, 43, 61; 7:32; I Cor. 10:10). The sense is that of repining or complaining, finding fault with God's plans, and purposes, and doings.

COMPLAINERS

The phrase, *"Complainers, walking after their own lusts,"* is to be understood in the widest sense; with the *"proceeding according to their lusts,"* Jude has in mind men who cannot get enough to satisfy their lusts and thus complain.

Men who shape their course according to their own lusts can never be content, and for the following reasons:

1. The means of gratifying such lusts are not always available.

2. Lusts are insatiable, meaning that it's impossible to satisfy lusts, irrespective of what is done.

It must be remembered that Jude is speaking here of individuals who claim Salvation.

In other words, they claim Christ; however, their demeanor and comportment proclaim what they actually are.

ADVANTAGE

The phrase, *"And their mouth speaketh great swelling words, having men's persons in admiration because of advantage,"* refers to *"showing respect of persons."* They use *"flattering for the sake of profit."* It means flattering a person to his face with the object of wheedling something out of him.

The literal sense of the Greek Text is *"honoring faces for the sake of advantage."* It is a highly picturesque portrayal.

As should be overly obvious, such type people are not trusting God, but rather attempting to maneuver people into a position of exploitation. Unfortunately, the Ministry is full of that type.

I've been ministering through the media since 1969. Before we went on Television, we went on Radio, with a daily program, Monday through Friday, called *The Campmeeting Hour."* It was only 15 minutes in length, but God blessed it abundantly. Soon we were on some 600 Stations, and I suppose, had the largest audience at that time in Radio, at least as it regards a *"daily"* program.

The Lord at one particular juncture spoke to me, telling me that if I ever exploited the people, He would lift the anointing. Instead, I must develop those who tuned in to our program.

I've never forgotten that! To be sure, the Preacher is in a position to exploit those who follow him. To do such, is a terrible breach of confidence, and in fact, is a terrible sin.

The word *"advantage"* which of course means to take advantage of someone's confidence, presents itself as a sin against that person. To do such is definitely not overlooked by the Lord.

(17) "BUT, BELOVED, REMEMBER YOU THE WORDS WHICH WERE SPOKEN BEFORE OF THE APOSTLES OF OUR LORD JESUS CHRIST;"

The composite is:

1. The word *"beloved"* does not refer to Jude's love for those to whom he is writing, but to the fact that the Saints are beloved ones of God.

NOTES

2. When Jude entreats his readers to remember the words that were spoken by the Apostles, it is not necessarily to be inferred that he was not himself an Apostle. Even though he did not allude to himself as one, I think his Ministry proves that he was.

3. The highest calling is that of an Apostle of our Lord Jesus Christ.

BELOVED

The short phrase, *"But, beloved,"* does not merely represent a statement of endearment. The Greek word is *"agapao,"* the distinctive word for *"love"* as used in John 3:16, for instance. It refers to the fact that the Saints are beloved ones of God.

We are beloved of God because we are following the Lord Jesus Christ. Jude wants to make certain that we continue to follow Christ, and not be lured away by false teachers, which if brought about, would lead to spiritual wreckage.

"But, beloved," actually states in the Greek, *"But you, beloved."* *"You"* is emphatic in both cases: *"You,"* in contrast to these false teachers.

While taking the form of an exhortation, the Passage still remains virtually descriptive. *"Be not deceived by their impudent boasting and interested pandering, for these are the scoffing sensualists against whom the Apostles warned you."*

APOSTLES

The phrase, *"Remember you the words which were spoken before of the Apostles of our Lord Jesus Christ,"* actually refers to that given by Peter and others.

Peter said: *"This second Epistle, beloved, I now write unto you; in both which I stir up your pure minds by way of remembrance:*

"That you may be mindful of the words which were spoken before by the Holy Prophets, and of the Commandment of us the Apostles of the Lord and Saviour:

"Knowing this first, that there shall come in the last days scoffers, walking after their own lusts" (II Pet. 3:1-3).

Because he did not refer to himself as such, most have concluded that Jude was not an Apostle. The fact of him not stating his own case proves nothing. I personally feel he definitely was an Apostle.

In fact, most adhere to a wrong definition as it regards the Apostle. First of all, as should be obvious in the Scriptures, a person is an Apostle as it regards their Message. And Jude definitely had a Message!

And by the word *"Message,"* we're speaking of a particular direction of Ministry which the Church is to follow, and which Message will always be backed up 100 percent by the Word of God. Perhaps one might say that the word *"emphasis,"* would better explain the Message.

Without a doubt, Paul is the greatest example of all. His Message and emphasis were *"the Grace of God,"* and one might even say, *"the Cross of Christ."* This was a special Word for the Church, and in fact, the most special Word the Church has ever known. Actually, the Lord gave to Paul the meaning of the New Covenant, which in effect, was the meaning of the Cross.

Looking specifically at Jude, his Message and Emphasis, which the Holy Spirit inspired, which speaks volumes within itself, was a message of warning as it regarded false doctrine. In fact, I believe this particular emphasis is portrayed in the Ministry of all Apostles.

Some 24 Apostles are recorded in the New Testament, that is if we are to count our Lord and Saviour, Jesus Christ, Who is definitely referred to as an Apostle, which of course means that He had a special Message, as would be obvious (Heb. 3:1).

The very word *"Apostle"* refers to the fact of one sent with a full power of attorney to act in the place of another, the sender remaining behind to back up the one sent.

To be sure, the calling of the Apostle is just as appropriate now as it was then (Eph. 4:11). And yet, not many refer to themselves today as an *"Apostle."* Actually, the title is not that necessary. It becomes obvious as to who is really an Apostle, in other words, who has the call for such, by the Message they present to the Church, and the particular emphasis on that Message.

"Prophets" carried this responsibility in Old Testament Times. Prophets are still one of the fivefold callings; however, regarding leadership for the Church, Apostles now fill that role. As should be understood, Apostles aren't appointed by other men, and neither

NOTES

are they elected by popular ballot. This is a Call of God.

(18) "HOW THAT THEY TOLD YOU THERE SHOULD BE MOCKERS IN THE LAST TIME, WHO SHOULD WALK AFTER THEIR OWN UNGODLY LUSTS."

The structure is:

1. The word rendered *"mockers"* is the same which in the parallel place in II Peter 3:3 is rendered *"scoffers."*

2. The words *"last time,"* refer to the last days, in fact, the very time in which we now live.

3. *"Walk"* refers to the manner of life, or lifestyle.

4. *"After their own ungodly lusts,"* means they definitely aren't walking after the Will of God.

MOCKERS

The phrase, *"How that they told you there should be mockers in the last time,"* refers to the last of the last days. In fact, the time of which Jude speaks, is the very time in which we now live. The time will come, and actually has already begun, that men will be more religious than ever, but farther away from God. We are nearing the Rapture of the Church; however, the following should be noted:

The spiritual condition of the Church is so bad, and in fact getting worse, that were it not for the Rapture of the Church, there would basically be no one left living for God. The situation is that critical! As the Second Coming will in effect save the world, meaning were it not for the Second Coming, the world would be destroyed, likewise, were it not for the Rapture of the Church, there would be no Church remaining. That's how bad the situation will be spiritually speaking, and in fact, already well on its way.

As we've already stated some pages back, the Church presently is in worse condition spiritually than at any time previously since the Reformation. In fact, the Church desperately needs a Reformation, and without a Reformation, Revival is impossible.

Without going into a lot of theological jargon, Reformation refers to the Church *"coming back to the Cross."* When that happens, and only when that happens, can there be true

Revival. If one will look down through Church history, one will find that every single time a Move of God took place, the Holy Spirit first of all, brought the Church back to the Cross.

Martin Luther stated, that as one viewed the Cross, so they viewed the Reformation. In other words, if they opposed the Cross, they opposed the Reformation. If they gloried in the Cross, they were in favor of the Reformation.

It is impossible for the Church to have anything from God, unless the Church is squarely anchored in the Cross. The Cross is the instrument through which all things come to the Believer from God (I Cor. 1:17-18, 21, 23; 2:2, 5). As well, it is the Cross by and through which the Holy Spirit works. In other words, He works totally and completely within the parameters of the Finished Work of Christ (Rom. 8:1-2, 11, 13).

OF WHAT DO THEY MOCK?

I want to be as clear and as simple as I know how to be, in order that no one will misunderstand what I have to say. We are dealing here with the issues of life and death, so we must not confuse the issue.

There are several salient issues around which revolve the Moving and Operation of the Holy Spirit. Let's look at these issues:

MUSIC

The Holy Spirit I think we can say, works through music and singing more so than anything else as it regards praise and worship. Praise is what we do, while worship is what we are.

The Book of Psalms is the largest Book in the Bible, and its very size gives us information. *"Psalms"* are actually *"songs."* Considering that the Holy Spirit devoted more space to this form of praise and worship than anything else, we are given to understand how important that music and singing actually are. If Satan can pervert this means of praise and worship, he will greatly hinder the Church. And regrettably, he has been very successful in doing exactly that.

Most of the Christian Radio Stations major in that which is labeled *"Contemporary Christian Music."* Music is designed by the Lord with three distinct parts — melody,

NOTES

rhythm, and harmony. If any one of those three parts is hindered, then it becomes impossible for such to be used in the realm of praise and worship. And it is flat out impossible to worship the Lord by the means of so-called Christian Contemporary Music. It simply cannot be done, despite those who would claim otherwise. But that's what the majority of the Christian Radio Stations are playing, and I think I can say without fear of exaggeration, that's what is being sung in many Churches.

This type of music had its beginnings under the guise of *"winning the youth to Christ,"* which of course, is ludicrous to say the least! That claim is seldom ventured any more, with the name of the game now being *"money."* In other words, it's entertainment pure and simple, with one thought in mind, and that is to bring in as much cash as possible. So the Reader will have absolutely no doubt as to what I'm saying, please allow me to make the following statements:

Contemporary Christian Music is not of God, which means it is of the Devil. It is an effort by Satan to destroy the greatest means of worship designed by the Holy Spirit, which pertains to music and singing. Any Christian who participates in such, is participating in that which is nurtured and fostered by Satan himself. Any Preachers who promote such in their Churches, or among their young people, or over Radio Stations, pure and simple, are promoting the work of Satan. That's blunt, but it happens to be the truth.

Those who participate in such, which includes almost all, *"mock"* that which is truly of the Lord. Consequently, they fulfill exactly what Jude said would happen.

Music groups claiming to be Christian are brought into Churches, who in fact, are not even saved. The idols of these groups are the secular rock groups of the world, which means they know absolutely nothing about the Lord. And yet they are placed on the platforms of our Churches as examples to our youth. One can only describe it as a *"mockery."*

THE HOLY SPIRIT

The Holy Spirit doesn't borrow from the spirit of the world in order to carry out His work. In fact, to even suggest such, borders on the edge of blasphemy, if in fact, it isn't blasphemy! The truth is, the Holy Spirit not only doesn't borrow from the world, He cannot use anything that is of the world. Listen to what He said through Paul concerning the world:

"Wherein in time past you walked according to the course of this world, according to the prince of the power of the air, the spirit that now worketh in the children of disobedience" (Eph. 2:2).

He plainly tells us here that the *"course of this world,"* is after Satan, i.e., *"according to the prince of the power of the air."*

He also said through John: *"Love not the world, neither the things that are in the world. If any man love the world, the love of the Father is not in him.*

"For all that is in the world, the lust of the flesh, and the lust of the eyes, and the pride of life, is not of the Father, but is of the world" (I Jn. 2:15-16).

To insinuate that the Holy Spirit can work in that which is so obviously of the world, either shows a complete ignorance of the Holy Spirit, which I would pray is the case, or else it shows a complete disregard and disrespect for the Holy Spirit, which can be construed as none other than *"mockery."* While I pray the former is the case, I fear the latter is rather the case.

THE PSYCHOLOGICAL WAY

Whether it's understood or not, the psychological way which made its debut into the world about a hundred years ago, and into the Church about 50 years ago, is Satan's greatest attack against the Cross. Pure and simple, the Cross is the answer to the sins, perversions, aberrations, and wrong direction of man. The psychological way is the answer of the world to the Biblical claims of the Cross. That would be understandable if in fact, this particular *"way"* remained in the world. But considering that it has been adopted by the Church makes it the most dangerous thrust that the Church has ever experienced in its entire history. If anyone knows anything about the Biblical way, they know that it's impossible to wed the psychological way with the Bible. It simply cannot be done. One cancels out the other!

So to propose the psychological way as the answer to the human dilemma is at the same time, a vote of no confidence as it regards the Cross.

We believe the Bible teaches (Rom., Chpts. 6, 8; I Cor., Chpt. 1; Col. 2:14-15) that Jesus addressed every need of mankind, and in every capacity, irrespective as to what it might be, at the Cross. We teach that faith in what Christ did at the Cross, will give the Believer victory over the world, the flesh, and the Devil. As well, we teach that the Work of Christ is a Finished Work, which means that it is complete within itself, and doesn't need help, such as the psychological way, or any other way. In fact, to attempt to add something else is in effect saying, that what Christ did there, and we speak of the Cross, was insufficient. Such can only be construed as blasphemy. So this is what I'm saying:

The psychological way makes a mockery of the Cross. In fact, those who would proclaim that particular way are in effect mocking the Cross. One cannot have it any other way. To accept that which is of the Devil, and to be sure the psychological way is definitely of the Devil, is in effect to mock that which is truly of God (Rom. 6:3-14; 8:1-2, 11; I Cor. 1:17-18, 21, 23; 2:2, 5).

The way of the Spirit of God is the Way of the Cross (Rom. 8:2). To think or teach that the Holy Spirit will function in any other capacity shows a complete lack of knowledge regarding the Spirit, and the Word of God for that matter!

WALK

The phrase, *"Who should walk after their own ungodly lusts,"* refers to charting a course which is not of God, but rather after the flesh.

The word *"walk"* refers to *"manner of life"* or *"lifestyle."* It concerns the manner or way in which we conduct our lives.

The unsaved can only *"walk"* in one way, and that is, as previously stated, *"according to the course of this world, according to the prince of the power of the air, the spirit that now worketh in the children of disobedience"* (Eph. 2:2).

By contrast, and due to the Born-Again experience, the Believer can *"walk after the*

Spirit," which is the opposite of the course of this world (Rom. 8:1). However, the Believer can as well, *"walk after the flesh,"* which in effect, is the same way that the ungodly walk.

Keep it in mind, that these individuals of whom Jude speaks, are referred to as *"twice dead"* (vs. 12), which means they once knew the Lord, but have now gone in another direction, while at the same time continuing to profess the Lord. To *"walk after the flesh"* (Rom. 8:1), is at the same time to *"walk after one's own ungodly lusts."* To *"walk after the Spirit"* of course, is to do the very opposite, which means to walk in the Will of God, which means to walk according to the Word of God. Let me be a little more plain and clear in my observation:

If the Believer doesn't understand the Cross, doesn't understand that one's faith must be perpetually in the Cross, which gives the Holy Spirit latitude to work (Rom. 6:3-14; 8:1-2, 11), then without fail, such a Believer is going to *"walk after their own ungodly lusts."* There is no alternative. It is either the Cross, which is the Finished Work of Christ, or it is our own devised ways, which will always lead to works of the flesh. So what am I saying?

I'm saying that these false teachers are in their present spiritual condition, because of incorrectly interpreting the *"Person"* of Christ and/or the *"Purpose"* of Christ.

(19) "THESE BE THEY WHO SEPARATE THEMSELVES, SENSUAL, HAVING NOT THE SPIRIT."

The exegesis is:

1. These false teachers separate themselves from the Cross, one might say, which in effect, is to separate themselves from the Word of God.

2. *"Sensual"* refers to that which is not of the Spirit, but rather of the flesh.

3. If we are *"walking after the flesh,"* this means that we are not *"walking after the Spirit."*

SEPARATE

The phrase, *"These be they who separate themselves,"* should be translated, *"These be they who separate."* The scholars say *"themselves"* must be omitted, the evidence against it being overwhelming.

The idea is, they *"separate,"* which means they create a schism, like Korah and his company; claiming to be the chief and most enlightened members in the Church to which they still profess to belong, though they turn upside down its fundamental principles. They are no longer *"contending for the faith"* (vs. 3), but are rather proposing *"another Jesus, another spirit, and another gospel"* (II Cor. 11:4).

To make this easier to understand, I think one can say without fear of contradiction, that Preachers who separate us from the Cross, in other words, *"making the Cross of none effect,"* fall into the category mentioned here by Jude. I realize this covers a lot of territory, especially considering that the modern Church is almost Cross illiterate. But at the same time, I cannot read it any other way.

Whether intentional or through ignorance, if the Believer is not pointed toward the Cross, then the Believer is being separated from the Cross, which is the only means of his life and victory.

I do not say that all Preachers who do this through ignorance fall into this category, and I speak of the category of false teachers; however, even though the Cross may be ignored through ignorance, and much of the time is; still, the end result will be wreckage just the same. But I feel that presently the major problem is not ignorance, but rather unbelief. As a case in point, it is impossible, I think, to promote the psychological way, and to do so merely through ignorance. It is done through unbelief. Listen to the Prophet Hosea:

"My people are destroyed for lack of knowledge." This within itself speaks of ignorance; however, it's ignorance that must be qualified. Hosea continues:

"Because you have rejected knowledge, I will also reject you, that you shall be no priest to Me: seeing you have forgotten the law of your God, I will also forget your children" (Hos. 4:6).

While it was true that Israel as portrayed here was ignorant of what God wanted, the full truth was, it was a contrived ignorance. In other words, they didn't want the knowledge addressed here.

I am concerned that this is the same with many presently as it regards the Cross. They know nothing about the Cross, and they like it that way.

Why?

If leaders of Denominations embrace the Cross, most would not be able to continue on in their present fashion. Most Denominations function outside of the Grace of God, rather according to *"law."* While it's law they have made up themselves, it is still *"law"* in the eyes of God, which means it's not Grace. In fact, the constitution and bylaws of most Denominations would have to be completely rewritten, if these particular Denominations would decide to follow the way of the Cross. Most don't want to do that. In fact, in all of history, there's never been a religious Denomination that has turned around, as we are stating here. Almost, if not every time, the Holy Spirit has had to abandon such Denominations, going outside and beginning another move.

To prove that the Cross is to be the center point of all that we believe and teach, Paul said:

"For Christ sent me not to baptize, but to preach the Gospel: not with wisdom of words, lest the Cross of Christ should be made of none effect" (I Cor. 1:17).

This proves beyond the shadow of a doubt, that the Cross is to be the central focus of our Message. And anything that takes its place, in other words, that removes the emphasis from the Cross, is not the Gospel. The Apostle plainly says here that the Cross of Christ is in effect *"the Gospel."*

So anything that separates us from the Cross is roundly condemned here by the Holy Spirit through Jude.

SENSUAL

The Greek word used here is *"psychic,"* and has no English equivalent; *"sensuous"* would perhaps be best. It occurs several times in the New Testament. Three times it is translated *"natural"* (I Cor. 2:14; 15:44, 46). Twice it is translated *"sensual"* (James 3:15, where it has *"natural"* in the margin, and in Jude, Verse 19, the Verse of our study).

In I Corinthians 15:44, 46, the moral meaning is in the background; in the other three Passages the moral meaning is prominent and is distinctly bad.

"Psychic" is the middle term of a triplet of terms, *"carnal, psychic, spiritual."* *"Carnal"* and *"spiritual"* speak for themselves — the one bad, the other good. *"Psychic,"* which comes between, is much closer to *"carnal,"* and with it is opposed to *"spiritual."*

The carnal man is ruled by his passions, and rises little above the level of an animal. The psychic man is ruled by human reasoning, and human affections, and does not rise above the world of sense.

The spiritual man is ruled by his spirit — the noblest part of his nature — and this is ruled by the Spirit of God. He rises to and lives among those things that can only be *"spiritually discerned"* (I Cor. 2:10-15).

Our Christian terminology is seriously affected by the absence of any English word for *"psychic,"* which does not come across very good in our language, which is the part of man's nature which it represents, and is often lost sight of (Ellicott).

THE SPIRITUAL MAN

In the above, we have given you a brief dissertation on the natural man and the spiritual man. If you look in some Commentaries, they will go into great detail regarding the Greek language, and what it means respecting the spirit, the soul, and the body. Due to the extreme difficulty in understanding the terminology, most Christians simply ignore it, or else, they attempt to *"worship in spirit,"* with most of the time such efforts being of the flesh, etc.

To pull it down to the level to where all of us can understand what is being said, there is a *"natural man"* and there is a *"spiritual man."* Paul said:

"But the natural man receives not the things of the Spirit of God: for they are foolishness unto him, neither can he know them, because they are spiritually discerned" (I Cor. 2:14).

The *"natural man"* is the individual who is ruled by the five senses, and who knows nothing about the Spirit of God. In other words, he is unredeemed. But as well, Believers can function in this capacity also, and in fact, regrettably, most do. In their words, even though the Spirit of God is available to them, and in fact lives within their hearts;

JIMMY SWAGGART BIBLE COMMENTARY

nevertheless, they do not function at all in that realm, but only by natural means, which means they definitely aren't spiritually led.

The *"spiritual man"* is the one who is led by the Spirit of God, and functions in that capacity. Concerning this man, Paul said: *"But he that is spiritual judgeth all things"* (I Cor. 2:15).

One could say that the *"natural man"* is *"walking after the flesh,"* while the *"spiritual man"* is *"walking after the Spirit"* (Rom. 8:1).

If the Believer doesn't understand that which I'm about to say, even that which I've already said will be somewhat confusing. I think the following will clear it up:

THE CROSS OF CHRIST IS THE KEY

If the Believer understands that everything comes to him through the means of the Cross, and places his faith there, doing so on a constant basis, the Holy Spirit will then function grandly within his life. In fact, this is what constitutes *"walking after the Spirit."* This means that the person is a *"spiritual man"* (Rom. 8:2, 11, 13).

If the Cross is properly understood, the Believer doesn't have to try to differentiate between the spirit, the soul, and the body. In fact, if the Cross is properly understood, and faith is properly placed in the Cross, which guarantees the leading, guidance, and empowerment of the Holy Spirit, the entirety of our spiritual, mental, and physical makeup will be brought into line. Paul tells us this in Romans, Chapter 6. In fact, Romans, Chapter 6 tells us *"how"* the Holy Spirit works, which some have described as *"the mechanics of the Spirit,"* while Romans, Chapter 8 tells us *"what"* the Spirit does, once we know *"how"* He functions. Some refer to Romans, Chapter 8 as *"the dynamics of the Holy Spirit."*

For the Believer to *"walk after the flesh"* (Rom. 8:1), simply means, that he's functioning outside of the realm of the Holy Spirit, which means he's functioning outside of the Cross. As stated, that means he is functioning as a *"natural man,"* i.e., by his own strength and ability.

Everything is tied to the Cross, what Jesus did there, which constitutes *"the Finished Work of Christ."* That's why Paul said:

"But God forbid that I should glory (boast), *save in the Cross of our Lord Jesus Christ, by Whom the world is crucified unto me, and I unto the world"* (Gal. 6:14).

FAITH

The Believer doesn't have to worry about his spirit, soul, and body, as it regards the difference of each function, etc. The Believer only has to be concerned about his *"Faith."* And when we say *"Faith"* we are speaking of Faith in what Christ did at the Cross, and that exclusively. If there is a problem, that means that our faith is not right, or as one might say, not rightly placed. Paul also said:

"Likewise reckon ye also yourselves to be dead indeed unto sin, but alive unto God through Jesus Christ our Lord" (Rom. 6:11).

This Passage has to do with our Faith, and the faith reckoned, goes back to Romans 6:3-5. This speaks of the Crucifixion of Christ and our part in that crucifixion, in that we were literally, at least in the Mind of God, *"baptized into His death"* (Rom. 6:3). In fact, we not only died with Him, we also were buried with Him, and were raised with Him in newness of life, which speaks of His Resurrection (Rom. 6:4).

Without going into detail regarding the spirit, soul, and body, Paul then says: *"Let not sin therefore reign in your mortal body, that you should obey it in the lusts thereof"* (Rom. 6:12).

All of this tells us that the answer totally and completely is in the Cross. As stated, all that we have to be concerned about is our Faith. We must make certain, even doubly certain, that always, the object of our Faith is the Cross. That being the case, the Holy Spirit will then begin to work.

THE HOLY SPIRIT

The phrase, *"Having not the Spirit,"* refers to the fact that those who operate outside of the Cross of Christ *"have not the Spirit."* In other words, while such a person may in fact have the Spirit, and certainly does if that person is saved, the Spirit is not functioning as He desires to do so. One might say, that such a person doesn't have the help of the Spirit.

To be sure, these people of whom Jude speaks, do not have the Spirit at all, simply because they aren't saved; however, there are millions of Christians, and we speak of those who truly are saved, which means they definitely have the Spirit, simply because one cannot be saved otherwise, but who actually receive precious little of His help.

Anything and everything concerning the Christian as it pertains to the Lord, is always and without exception, carried out by the Holy Spirit. Nothing is going to be done for the Lord, and nothing for us which pertains to the Lord, except it be carried out by the Holy Spirit (Acts 1:4). Even though every Christian definitely has the Spirit, even as we've already stated, that doesn't mean that He is going to automatically work within our lives. The potential is there, but only the potential (Jn. 3:5-8).

The Holy Spirit doesn't require much of us, but He does require one thing, and He is definite about that one thing. Concerning that, Paul said:

"For the Law of the Spirit of Life in Christ Jesus has made me free from the law of sin and death" (Rom. 8:2).

The *"Law"* of which Paul speaks here, is not the Law of Moses, but rather a Law devised by the Godhead, within which the Spirit works. To be sure, He will not function outside of that Law.

We are told in this Verse that this *"Law"* is *"in Christ Jesus,"* which means that it is in what Jesus did at the Cross. Every time Paul uses the term *"in Christ Jesus,"* or *"in Christ,"* or one of its derivatives, which he does about 170 times in his 14 Epistles, without exception, he is speaking of what Jesus did at the Cross, and our faith in that.

So this means that the Holy Spirit functions entirely within the parameters of the great Sacrifice of Christ, i.e., *"the Finished Work of Christ."*

In fact, even as we've already stated elsewhere in this Volume, the Holy Spirit and Christ and Him Crucified are so intertwined that it's almost impossible to separate the two. Listen to what John said concerning his vision of the Throne of God:

"And I beheld, and, lo, in the midst of the Throne and of the four beasts, and in the midst of the Elders, stood a Lamb as it had been slain, having seven horns and seven eyes,

NOTES

which are the seven Spirits of God sent forth into all the earth" (Rev. 5:6). Now please understand, this of which John saw is before the Throne of God. This means that whatever it is that John saw, is that which God recognizes, and only that which God recognizes.

The *"four beasts"* signify the Holiness of God (Rev. 4:8). The *"Elders"* signify the Church.

The *"Lamb as it had been slain,"* of course, and as obvious, signifies Christ, but more importantly, *"the slain Lamb."* The Crucifixion of Christ, which of course proclaims the death of Christ on the Cross, is that which opened up the way to the very Throne of God. Let us quickly say, it is that and nothing else!

The *"seven horns"* speaks of dominion, with the number *"seven"* speaking of *"total dominion."* The *"seven eyes"* speaks of total illumination. All of this pertains to the Holy Spirit, Who is signified by the number *"seven,"* denoting His Perfect Work, which in fact, is portrayed in Isaiah 11:2.

As stated, the Two, the *"Lamb,"* and the *"Spirit"* are so closely connected that they seem to be one and the same. As well, the connection has to do with the crucified Christ. This tells us in no uncertain terms, how the Spirit of God functions and operates. It is by and through what Christ did at the Cross, and in no other way. In other words, the Cross made possible all that the Holy Spirit does. Therefore, the Believer is to understand, even as we have repeatedly stated, that everything comes to him through the means of the Cross, and that his faith is to ever be in that Sacrifice. Then the Holy Spirit will work mightily on his behalf.

(20) "BUT YOU, BELOVED, BUILDING UP YOURSELVES ON YOUR MOST HOLY FAITH, PRAYING IN THE HOLY SPIRIT,"

The diagram is:

1. *"But you, Beloved,"* contrasts the Saints with the false teachers.

2. *"Building up yourselves,"* is to build toward the finish of the structure of which the foundation has already been laid. Jude is speaking metaphorically. It refers to a constant increase in Christian knowledge, etc.

3. *"Faith"* as described here does not refer to faith as exercised by the Saint, for it is described as *"most holy,"* but to the Christian

Faith, Christianity, i.e., *"Jesus Christ and Him Crucified."*

4. Prayer is the vital factor in the Christian life that activates all the other departments of the Christian experience.

5. Our praying must be exercised in the sphere of the Holy Spirit, motivated and empowered by Him.

6. This means that if the Saint expects to really pray, he must be Spirit-filled, and as well, Spirit-controlled.

YOU

The phrase, *"But you, beloved,"* proclaims the change, from the false teachers, to those who are truly living for God, doing their very best, to abide by the Word of God. Whereas the previous instructions pertained entirely to the apostates, the balance of this Epistle pertains to the true Saints of God. As well, as this pertains to Jude's Readers, it pertains also to every single Believer who has lived since then. This is the Word of God; therefore, it is appropriate for all time, and for all Believers. It is very similar, if not identical, to the beginning of the 17th Verse.

CHRISTIAN GROWTH

The phrase, *"Building up yourselves,"* concerns building on the foundation they were given at conversion. The foundation being laid, God the Holy Spirit desires that a structure be built thereon. As stated, Jude is using the construction profession as a metaphor.

If it is to be noticed, the phrase is, *"building up yourselves,"* which means that we have a part to play in this process. While the part is small, it is very, very important. We are to furnish to the Lord a *"willing mind and obedient heart."* Both pertain to Faith.

As we've already stated, the Presence of the Holy Spirit, merely proclaims the potential. All that He wants to do, and in fact can do, is based on our cooperation.

HOW DO WE BUILD?

Spiritually, the word *"build"* or *"building"* is used of one's work in life, or of the formation of character and habits. The main thing here is the foundation. Those who build on Christ's Word build on rock; those who reject this Word build on sand (Mat. 7:24-27).

Christ is the sole True Foundation; the work that a man builds on this will be tried by fire (I Cor. 3:9-15).

The Church is compared to a building (I Cor. 3:9; I Pet. 2:4-6) reared on the foundation of Apostles and Prophets (their truths and teaching given to them by the Holy Spirit), Jesus Christ Himself being the Chief Cornerstone (Eph. 2:20-22).

Builders are *"builded up"* in Christ (Col. 2:7), and are exhorted to build ourselves up on our most holy faith.

In effect, Spiritual Growth is what we are addressing here. The Holy Spirit through Peter said:

"But grow in Grace, and in the knowledge of our Lord and Saviour Jesus Christ" (II Pet. 3:18).

Paul said, *"According to the Grace of God which is given unto me, as a wise masterbuilder, I have laid the foundation, and another builds thereon. But let every man take heed how he builds there upon.*

"For other foundation can no man lay than that is laid, which is Jesus Christ...."

"Every man's work shall be made manifest...."

"Know you not that you are the Temple of God, and that the spirit of God dwells in you?" (I Cor. 3:10-16).

WHAT DOES PAUL MEAN BY THE FOUNDATION BEING JESUS CHRIST?

In brief, it refers to Who Christ is, and What Christ has done.

The entirety of the Bible points to Christ. Immediately after the Fall, the Lord spoke to Satan through the serpent, telling him that the *"Seed of the woman"* Who is Christ, would bruise his head, which of course, speaks of Satan's head, even though Satan would bruise His heel, which latter phrase speaks of the crucifixion (Gen. 3:15). The Lord then gave to the first family the means by which Jesus Christ would redeem fallen humanity, symbolized by the Sacrifices. The Sacrifices portrayed what Christ would do as it regards the Cross, and is graphically outlined in Genesis, Chapter 4.

The Bible student will find the Word of God throughout the entirety of the Old Testament, pointing to the Sacrifices in one way or the other.

After the Flood had subsided, the Scripture says that *"Noah built an Altar unto the LORD; and took of every clean beast, and every clean foul, and offered Burnt-Offerings on the Altar."*

The Scripture then says, *"And the LORD smelled a sweet savour"* (Gen. 8:20-21).

This tells us that despite the terrible wickedness on the Earth, wickedness so great that it necessitated the destruction of all mankind with the exception of Noah and his family; still, by Noah offering up sacrifices, we find that some few during this some 1,600 years had kept alive their faith in God, and had engaged in the means by which man could commune with God after a fashion.

The *"sweet savor"* which God smelled as it regards the offering up of the clean animals, may seem strange to the carnal mind; however, the reason it was a sweet savor to God, despite the fact that animals had to give their lives, was that it represented the coming Redeemer and the means by which He would redeem fallen humanity.

About 400 years after Noah, we have the call of Abraham. He built so many Altars that he is referred to by some Bible Scholars, as *"the Altar builder."* All of this symbolized Christ and the means by which He would redeem humanity (Gen. 12:7-8; 13:4, 18). In fact, God gave to Abraham the greatest object lesson that possibly any man has ever had to undergo, in relating to him exactly how redemption would come. It concerned the proposed offering up of Isaac, Abraham's only son by Sarah. Even though the sacrifice was stopped at the last minute, even the last moment, it definitely served as a most powerful object lesson as to how God would carry out the great task of world redemption (Gen., Chpt. 22).

Isaac continued the practice of Altar building (Gen. 26:25), even as did Jacob (Gen. 33:20; 35:7).

One of the most graphic illustrations of all pertains to the deliverance of the Children of Israel out of Egypt. Even though God performed mighty miracles in Egypt, actually one after the other, Pharaoh still wouldn't let Israel go. It took the blood applied to the doorpost, which without it meant that every firstborn in every home in Egypt

NOTES

would die. Then the heathen monarch finally buckled. This was a most powerful illustration of the Cross!

And then some 50 days after Israel's deliverance, the Law was given on Mount Sinai, which included the sacrificial system, which was the very center of Israel's way with God (Lev., Chpts. 1-7).

After being in the land for about 500 years, God would give to David the blueprints for the magnificent Temple which would be built, wherein God would dwell between the Mercy Seat and the Cherubim as it regarded the Ark of the Covenant, housed in the Holy of Holies of the Temple. Solomon, David's son, would build the Temple, and at its dedication would *"offer in sacrifice 2,000 oxen and 120,000 sheep"* (II Chron. 7:5).

By this tremendous spectacle, which the Holy Spirit impressed upon Solomon to do, Israel was to ever understand that her prosperity, safety, protection, and above all, her Salvation, were all predicated on the Blood of the Lamb.

During all of this time, the Prophets predicted that One was coming Who would redeem lost humanity, with Isaiah, Chapter 53 being the most graphic example. This great Chapter along with Psalm 22, plus of course, many others in the Word, proclaimed in graphic detail as to how Redemption would be carried out as it regards the Lord Jesus Christ.

Even though the word *"Cross"* was not used, the word *"Altar,"* which symbolized the Cross, was used constantly. The Altar signified Sacrifice, which signified death, which graphically portrayed the manner in which Christ would redeem fallen humanity.

After Jesus came, and with His earthly ministry commencing, the Prophet said concerning Him, *"I gave My back to the smiters, and My cheeks to them who plucked off the hair: I hid not my face from shame and spitting.*

"For the Lord GOD will help Me; therefore shall I not be confounded: therefore have I set my face like a flint" (Isa. 50:6-7).

The phrase, *"I set My face like a flint,"* means that the Messiah was dedicated to one end in life — He came to die, not live. His death was not just an event that happened; He accomplished it; He steadfastly set His face like a flint to go to His death (Lk. 9:31,

51). He purposely laid down His life (Jn. 10:15-18).

So, the foundation of all that we are before God, is Jesus Christ, which pertains to Who He is, the Son of God, and What He did, which refers exclusively to the Cross. Everything we build must be built without fail on this foundation. As Paul aptly said, it is *"Jesus Christ, and Him Crucified"* (I Cor. 2:2). If the *"Person"* of Christ is diminished in any way, we sin! If the *"Purpose"* of Christ is diminished in any way, we as well sin.

This is the reason I have spoken at length as it regards the modern Faith movement, i.e., *"the Word of Faith."* I do not think it can be looked at in any manner except that of *"heresy."*

HERESY

D. R. McConnell in his book *"A Different Gospel,"* said:

"Historically, the term 'heresy' is best reserved for major departures from Christian orthodoxy, especially the doctrines of God, Christ, Revelation, and Salvation. There are many peculiar ideas and practices in the Faith theology, however, which merits it the label of heresy. They are the following:

"1. Its deistic view of God, Who must dance to men's attempts to manipulate the spiritual laws of the universe.

"2. Its demonic view of Christ, Who is filled with 'the Satanic nature' and must be 'born-again' in Hell.

"3. Its Gnostic view of Revelation, which demands denial of the physical senses and classifies Christians by their willingness to do so.

"4. Its metaphysical view of Salvation, which deifies man and spiritualizes the Atonement, locating it in Hell rather than on the Cross, thereby subverting the crucial Biblical belief that it is Christ's physical death and shed Blood, which alone atoned for sin. All four of these heresies may be accounted for by Kenyon's syncretism (the combination of different forms of belief or practice) of metaphysical thought (that which is subjective instead of objective) with traditional Biblical doctrine.

"(E.W. Kenyon is actually the father of the Faith movement. All the Faith teachers, whether they admit it or not, are the spiritual sons and grandsons of this man. It was Kenyon, who formulated every major doctrine of the modern Faith movement. The roots of Kenyon's theology may be traced to his personal background in the metaphysical cults, specifically New Thought and Christian Science. Kenyon's education exposed him to a wide variety of non-Christian ideologies. In 1891, he attended the Emerson School of Oratory, an institution that has been described by its own historians as permeated with New Thought metaphysics, and whose founder, Charles Emerson, died a member of the Christian Science mother church in Boston.*

"His friends also verify that Kenyon openly confessed the influence of metaphysical thought upon his own theology. John Kennington said that Kenyon was 'very conversant with Christian Science concepts' and that 'he admitted that he freely drew the water of his thinking from this well.')"

McConnell goes on to say: *"Many of the eccentric and dangerous practices of the Faith movement may also be accounted for by this association. These practices may not directly challenge Christian orthodoxy (right belief), but they do violate the Church's orthopraxy (right practice), and, thus, pose a serious threat to the spiritual, and even physical safety of God's people. The following cultic practices of the Faith theology are mentioned in this regard."*

POSITIVE CONFESSION

"Many regard this as a healthy practice, emphasizing the psychological benefits of positive thinking and speaking. What this fails to consider is the historical fact that those who first taught positive confession — the New Thought metaphysicians — attributed its power to cosmic principles and occultic deities. Though the Bible does emphasize the importance of a pure mind and holy speech, it no where states that a person can alter physical reality through mental means, and it certainly does not encourage verbal confession of the Divine Name and Word as means of manipulating God's will. In fact, the Scriptures strictly contradict both (Rom. 8:27-28)."

SENSORY DENIAL

"Like the metaphysical cults, the Faith movement teaches Believers to deny sensory reality, particularly when it indicates the physical symptoms of illness. This practice has led to numerous tragic deaths."

IMPLICIT REJECTION OF MEDICAL SCIENCE

"These deaths were all the more tragic because with prompt medical care, many could have been easily avoided. The Faith teachers do not, however, like Christian Science practitioners, explicitly forbid the use of medical science; like the less radical New Thought teachers, their rejection of medicine and doctors is implicit. By virtue of their own example, the Faith teachers insist that Believers can, and should, grow in their faith to the point where they no longer need medical science. Only those in the Faith movement who are immature in their faith guiltily seek medical care."

PROSPERITY

"This practice, and I speak of prosperity, which has become both the drawing card and the holy grail of the Faith movement, may also be traced to the metaphysical cults. The doctrine of prosperity instills greed for material things, it teaches the egocentric notion that one should give to get, and it has bankrolled the unbridled ambitions of more than a few Charismatic Ministers and Televangelists."

Irenaeus said many centuries ago: *"Error, indeed, is never set forth in its naked deformity, lest, being thus exposed, it should at once be detected. But it is craftily decked out in an attractive dress, so as, by its outward form, to make it appear to the inexperienced (ridiculous as the expression may seem) more true than truth itself."*

I continue to quote McConnell:

"Sadly, the struggle with false doctrine did not end with the writing of the New Testament. History attests to numerous 'different gospels,' and from the first century on these gospels have found a ready market in the Church. The true and orthodox Gospel of Jesus Christ has always had to compete with false doctrine for the hearts and minds of Believers. In fact, it has often been said that 'the history of theology is in large part a history of heresies.' In other words, the struggle between heresy and orthodoxy has taken place in every century of Church history.

"Each new generation of Church leadership has had 'to exhort in sound doctrine and refute those who contradict' (Titus 1:9). We can thank God that we have centuries of historical orthodoxy to fall back on in this struggle, but the struggle itself continues.

"This is no less true today. The 21st-century Christian is faced with a plethora, a virtual 'legion' of gospels. All of these are garbed in the most alluring of dress and call to the Believer in the most seductive of whispers. As quoted above, Irenaeus, the great 2nd-century defender of the faith against the heresy of Gnosticism, warned that error is never put forward in a manner that exposes its grotesque deformities. Instead, it is packaged in outward adornment so appealing that it appears 'more true than truth itself.' The tremendous appeal of heresy is that it looks and sounds like the real thing! Consequently, the demarcation between heresy and orthodoxy is rarely clear cut.

"The most dangerous heresies lie in the gray area, a shadowy place of both light and darkness. These 'different gospels' may vary in the particular doctrinal error they propagate but all heresies have one thing in common: their threat to the Church is directly proportionate to the degree in which they appear orthodox. The most dangerous of lies is not the bald-faced lie, for that is easily detected and rejected. A half-truth always does far more damage than a bald-faced lie."

MOST HOLY FAITH

The phrase, *"On your most holy faith,"* doesn't refer to the faith that we exercise on a day-to-day basis, but to the Christian faith in general, to Christianity as a whole.

Mayor says: *"The Faith here is called 'most holy' because it comes to us from God, and reveals God to us, and because it is by its means that man is made righteous, and enabled to overcome the world."*

How does it help us to overcome the world?

When Paul mentions *"Faith,"* almost always, he is referring to Faith in Christ and what Christ did for us at the Cross. In fact, *"Christ"* and *"The Cross"* must never be separated. To separate them, presents *"another Jesus, another spirit, and another gospel"* (II Cor. 11:4).

To give a very abbreviated portrayal of *"the Faith,"* it is *"Jesus Christ and Him Crucified"* (I Cor. 1:17-18, 21, 23; 2:2, 5). To make it even more abbreviated, that is if possible, the words *"in Christ,"* would be the most abbreviated of all. In fact, Paul uses this term or one of its derivatives, 170 times in his 14 Epistles.

The term *"your most holy faith,"* is the same as *"the faith"* of Verse 3.

This *"Faith"* is objective as it was in Verse 3, which means that this Truth or Doctrine will never change. This is the opposite of that which is metaphysical, which is that which refers to one's own experiences, which are changeable, etc. The Word of God does not change. It is the same today as it was 3,000 years ago, or any time for that matter. The problem with the Church, as we have attempted to explain, is the attempt to change this great Truth of *"Jesus Christ and Him Crucified,"* which is the Word of God, which is the Gospel. That's the reason we keep saying that the object of our Faith must always be Christ and Him Crucified. If it changes from that to something else, then we have gone into heresy, and will bring upon ourselves untold difficulties. Always remember this:

Any erroneous belief about any part of the Bible will always bring about negative results; however, to be in error as it regards *"the faith,"* which means the *"fundamentals,"* which translates into the Atonement, will not only fall out to negative results, but can lead to the loss of one's soul.

THE HOLY SPIRIT

The phrase, *"Praying in the Holy Spirit,"* shows how we Saints are to build up ourselves in our most holy faith. Wuest says:

"Prayer is the vital factor in the Christian life which activates all the other departments of the Christian experience."

He went on to say: *"All true prayer is exercised in the sphere of the Holy Spirit, motivated and empowered by Him. That means,"* he said *"that if the Saint expects to really*

pray, he must be Spirit-filled and Spirit-controlled. The fullness of the Holy Spirit is the prerequisite to effectual praying. The Spirit, when yielded to, leads in our petitions and generates within us the faith necessary to acceptable and answered prayer."*

Before the turn of the Twentieth Century, little was known about the Baptism with the Holy Spirit, which is always accompanied by speaking with other Tongues (Acts 2:4). But at approximately the turn of that time period, the great Prophecies of Joel concerning the *"Latter Rain"* began to be fulfilled (Joel 2:23). As the Light on the Baptism with the Holy Spirit began to be more and more given, God expected the entirety of the Church to walk in that Light.

I'm very appreciative to the Lord that He allowed the Ministry of this unworthy Evangelist to play a part, even though small, in this great outpouring. I will always thank the Lord for that privilege. We have seen literally tens of thousands Baptized with the Holy Spirit, and continue to do so unto this hour.

While hundreds of thousands of Believers from every known Church Denomination and affiliation, received this Light gladly, and were baptized with the Holy Spirit, with the evidence of speaking with other Tongues, which in fact, has greatly revolutionized the Work of God all over the world; still, the institutionalized Church, regarding the non-Pentecostal branch, for the most part, has rejected this outpouring of the Spirit. Light rejected, is always ultimately light withdrawn.

For those who have rejected the Spirit, and I continue to speak of the Spirit Baptism, for all practical purposes, their usefulness to the Work of God is pretty close to zero. While they may continue to have much religious machinery in motion, the truth is, what they are doing is man-devised and man-led, which means it's not Spirit-devised and led, and which means that very little is truly being done for God. Regrettably and sadly, due to apostasy, even the Denominations that claim to be Pentecostal are any more, little depending upon the Spirit. In other words, most of the Pentecostal Denominations, at least in the United States and Canada, are Pentecostal in name only. I take no delight in saying that, but regrettably, it is true!

Considering the great significance of the Spirit Baptism, please allow me to address myself to the following:

THE BAPTISM WITH THE HOLY SPIRIT

We believe the Holy Spirit Baptism is an experience apart from Salvation, which actually follows Salvation. In other words, we teach that one must first be saved before one can be baptized with the Holy Spirit. While it is certainly true that the Holy Spirit comes into the hearts and lives of all believing sinners at conversion, there is a vast difference in being *"born of the Spirit"* and being *"Baptized with the Spirit"* (Jn. 3:3-8; Acts 1:4). In fact, concerning this very thing, Jesus said:

"Even the Spirit of Truth; Whom the world cannot receive, because it sees Him not, neither knows Him (speaking of those who are unsaved): *but you know Him* (speaking of those who are saved); *for He dwells with you, and shall be in you"* (Jn. 14:17).

It is obvious that all those who were Baptized with the Spirit on the Day of Pentecost were already saved people. So what they were to receive would not make them more saved, but actually, was given to them as it regards power (Acts 1:4, 8).

Acts, Chapter 8 is another account of individuals being Baptized with the Spirit after they had been saved, which is always the case in one measure or the other. Philip had preached a revival in Samaria, with many saved; however, none had been Baptized with the Holy Spirit, possibly because Philip did not preach this particular Doctrine at that time.

But the Scripture says, *"When the Apostles which were at Jerusalem heard that Samaria had received the Word of God, they sent unto them Peter and John:*

"Who, when they were come down, prayed for them, that they might receive the Holy Spirit."

The Scripture continues to say: *"For as yet He was fallen upon none of them: only they were baptized in the Name of the Lord Jesus.*

"Then laid they their hands on them, and they received the Holy Spirit" (Acts 8:14-17).

Now if the new convert receives everything at conversion, as it regards the Holy Spirit, as some teach, then what were Peter and John doing?

NOTES

Acts, Chapter 9 records the case of Paul. He had been saved on the Road to Damascus as a result of the appearance of Christ to him. And then some three days later, Ananias was sent to him, in order to pray for him that *"thou mightest receive thy sight, and be filled with the Holy Spirit"* (Acts 9:17).

Again I ask the question, if we receive everything at conversion as many teach, what was Ananias doing?

Acts, Chapter 10 records the Salvation and Spirit Baptism of Cornelius, the first Gentile to receive.

Cornelius and those with him were saved and then Baptized with the Holy Spirit only seconds later (Acts 10:44-48).

Ideally this is the way it always ought to be; however, for many and varied reasons it doesn't happen this way often.

We have another account in Acts, Chapter 19. Paul in speaking with certain men in Ephesus said unto them: *"Have you received the Holy Spirit since you believed?"*

They had not, so the Scripture says: *"When Paul had laid his hands upon them, the Holy Spirit came on them; and they spoke with Tongues, and prophesied"* (Acts 19:1-7).

Some have tried to claim that these people were not really saved; however, every time in the Book of Acts that the word *"Disciples,"* is used, it always refers to a follower of Christ, one in effect, who has given is heart and life to Christ.

Yes, these particular individuals were already saved, but had not been Baptized with the Holy Spirit, simply because no one had preached this Message to them. Paul did and they were!

Regrettably, there are untold millions of Christians who presently fit into the same category as these men at Ephesus. They *"have not so much as heard whether there be any Holy Spirit"* (Acts 19:2).

So I think from the Scripture, we have settled the fact that the Baptism with the Holy Spirit is an experience that's always received subsequent to Salvation. In other words, one has to first be saved before one can be a candidate for the Spirit Baptism.

TONGUES

We also teach and believe that every recipient of the Holy Spirit Baptism speaks with other Tongues, and that there are no exceptions. Once again, we go back to the Word of God.

Acts 2:4 plainly tells us that all those on the Day of Pentecost who received, spoke with other Tongues. In fact, this should settle the case once and for all.

But then again, some may argue that these individuals also heard the *"sound from Heaven as of a rushing mighty wind,"* and that *"cloven Tongues like as of fire . . . sat upon each of them"* (Acts 2:1-3).

That is true; however, we do not read again of this phenomenon. In other words, in the accounts given in Acts, Chapters 8, 9, 10, and 19, with Believers being baptized with the Spirit, while there is a mention of *"Tongues"* there is no mention of the *"rushing mighty wind,"* or the *"cloven Tongues like as of fire."*

Why?

In the first place, the *"sound from Heaven as of a rushing mighty wind,"* was the Holy Spirit coming to this Earth in a new Dispensation, all made possible by the Cross. He has not left. If He came and went, this particular sound should be heard again; however, due to that not being the case, there is no record in the Scriptures of this phenomenon being heard again.

Also, the *"cloven Tongues like as of fire,"* was a fulfillment of the prophecy of John the Baptist, when he said, *"I indeed baptize you with water unto repentance: but He Who comes after me is mightier than I, Whose shoes I am not worthy to bear: He shall baptize you with the Holy Spirit, and with fire"* (Mat. 3:11).

As stated, we never see this phenomenon again in future accounts of Believers being baptized with the Holy Spirit, as recorded in Acts. So this tells us that it is not to be expected presently.

The account given in Acts, Chapter 8, doesn't say anything about the Samaritans speaking in Tongues; however, it does mention that Simon the Sorcerer, when he saw the Apostles lay hands on these people and that they received the Spirit, asked if he could buy the same power.

If as some teach, nothing happens at this particular time, and we continue to speak of

NOTES

Tongues, then why would the Sorcerer offer money for such?

In fact, the Scripture doesn't really mention about them speaking in Tongues or not speaking in Tongues. It just says, *"they received the Holy Spirit"* (Acts 8:17).

As well, whenever I speak of people being filled with the Spirit, I very seldom mention that they spoke with Tongues. I just simply say, exactly as Luke recorded this, that a certain number, or some people etc., *"received the Holy Spirit."* But because I don't mention Tongues, doesn't mean they didn't speak in Tongues. It is the same here with Luke.

Likewise in Acts, Chapter 9, it doesn't mention Tongues. It just says that Ananias told Paul that he wanted to pray for him that he might *"be filled with the Holy Spirit."* It mentions nothing about Tongues one way or the other.

Acts, Chapter 10 does graphically say: *"For they heard them speak with Tongues, and magnify God"* (Acts 10:46).

In fact, it says the same thing about the Ephesians when they were filled with the Spirit. It says: *"They spoke with Tongues, and prophesied"* (Acts 19:6).

So if anyone wants to look at Biblical proof, which should be the only proof that we will recognize, then we must come to the conclusion that all recipients when baptized with the Holy Spirit, will at the same time, speak with other Tongues.

WHAT ARE TONGUES?

Tongues are not incoherent babble or gibberish, as some have claimed. The Bible proclaims the fact that they are languages, known somewhere in the world, but not by the speaker. We are given this information in Acts, Chapter 2. The Scripture says:

"And there were dwelling at Jerusalem Jews, devout men, out of every nation under heaven.

"Now when this was noised abroad, the multitude came together, and were confounded, because that every man heard them speak in his own language.

"And they were all Amazed and marvelled, saying one to another, Behold, are not all these which speak Galilaeans?

"And how hear we every man in our own tongue, wherein we were born?

"Parthians, and Medes, and Elamites, and the dwellers in Mesopotamia, and in Judaea, and Cappadocia, in Pontus, and Asia,

"Phrygia, and Pamphylia, in Egypt, and in the parts of Libya about Cyrene, and strangers of Rome, Jews and proselytes,

"Cretes and Arabians, we do hear them speak in our Tongues the wonderful Works of God" (Acts 2:5-11).

Incidentally, the reaction of those who were there that day, and were not participants themselves, was pretty well the reaction of all presently. Some *"marvelled"* (Acts 2:7), while others *"mocked"* (Acts 2:13).

WHAT GOOD ARE TONGUES?

I suppose that millions have asked that question. But to even ask such a question, is at the same time, to insult the Lord. It is in effect saying that this which He has done is of no consequence. Does anyone seriously want to say such a thing?

I don't suppose any human being knows all the good that accompanies speaking with other Tongues, and of course I speak of those who have truly been Baptized with the Holy Spirit; however, we are given this information in Isaiah:

"For with stammering lips and another tongue will He speak to this people.

"To whom He said, 'This is the rest wherewith you may cause the weary to rest; and this is the refreshing: yet they would not hear" (Isa. 28:11-12).

Incidentally, Paul in the giving of his great dissertation on Tongues quoted a part of these two Verses (I Cor. 14:21).

We are told by Isaiah that speaking with other Tongues *"causes the weary to rest."* But it doesn't stop there; he also said: *"This is the refreshing,"* with both statements referring of course, to two things.

The cares of life are many, and we are told here that speaking with other Tongues provides a *"rest"* for the weary. But it doesn't stop there:

It also revitalizes or recharges our spiritual man, which flows over as well into the physical, hence *"the refreshing."*

Jude told us to *"pray in the Holy Spirit,"* meaning that we are to be Spirit directed in our praying.

As I dictate these notes, I have just come back from our morning Prayer Meeting. The Spirit of God moved upon me in a mighty way, bringing to my mind something that happened many years ago, which proved to be a tremendous strength. It was something incidentally, which He had given me years ago, but which yet in totality has not been completely fulfilled. I believe the Spirit of God was telling me that it definitely will be fulfilled.

As the Spirit of the Lord came upon me to pray, I prayed in English for awhile, and then began to worship in Tongues.

When I began to pray, I was very burdened in my spirit about several things; however, in that few minutes time, with some small part of my praying done in Tongues, which was mostly in worship, I experienced a *"rest"* and a *"refreshing"* which are so great within themselves, that it's even difficult to explain. In fact, I have had this happen untold numbers of times while in prayer.

Now if in fact what I've said is true, and I refer to this definition of the *"good"* brought about by *"Tongues,"* and it definitely is, then I would trust that the Reader can see the tremendous worth of this which God has done. As stated, I am certain that there are many other attributes, but the two I've just named, are what the Christian desperately needs. Instead of the Believer living in a state of stress, worry, anxiety, and fear, and even seeking the help of humanistic psychologists, why not try God's prescription! This one thing we can guarantee, whatever the Lord does, it always works.

HOW IS ONE BAPTIZED WITH THE HOLY SPIRIT?

First of all, the Baptism with the Holy Spirit is a *"Gift"* (Acts 2:38; 8:20; 10:45; 11:17). This means, as should be obvious, that it's not something that can be earned.

The following are seven steps regarding being baptized with the Holy Spirit, or in other words, how to receive. Now please understand, God is not limited to any particular formula. So I give these only to be of help. Actually, the following is given in our Commentary on I Corinthians, Chapter 14. But due to the manner in which most Commentaries are studied, I felt it would be helpful here for the information to be given again. The seven steps are as follows:

BORN-AGAIN

The first requirement for one to be Baptized with the Holy Spirit is to be *"born again"* (Jn. 3:3).

Regrettably, many people ignorantly try to add requirements and qualifications that are not given in the Word of God. Such manufactured qualifications pertain to about anything that one could think. However, the only real qualification, although other things may be mentioned, even as we are doing here, is, to be *"born again."*

Actually, even after people come to Christ, there are still problems at times in their lives that hinder their progress with the Lord. To be frank, that's at least one of the reasons we need the Holy Spirit. But to try to tell these people they've got to get rid of all these things before they receive the Spirit, whatever those things might be, is putting the cart before the horse.

For instance, my Grandmother was one of the Godliest women I ever knew. But yet, after she came to Christ, she had a real problem giving up cigarettes. In fact, she smoked cigarettes right up until the time the Lord filled her with the Spirit. After that, she never touched another one, with the reasons being obvious.

She now had the power she had not previously had, and due to the fact that my Grandmother understood the Message of the Cross, at least a great deal more than most, she now had the secret to victory.

But if she had been told that all of these problems had to be eliminated out of her life before she could be filled, this may have been a serious hindrance, even as it is with others. Let's not add to the Scriptures, and let's not take away from the Scriptures.

When one surveys the Book of Acts and the Epistles, we do not find the Apostles demanding anything of the people as it regards being Baptized with the Holy Spirit, other than being Born-Again.

SCRIPTURAL

Second, the one who is asking for the Holy Spirit must settle it in his spirit once and for all that this great Gift is for all Believers, and it is for all Believers at this particular time. He must get all doubt out of his heart, and every question that casts aspersions on the Word of God.

Jesus referred to the Holy Spirit as the *"Promise of the Father"* (Acts 1:4). He also said, *"But you shall be Baptized with the Holy Spirit . . ."* (Acts 1:5).

Satan will do everything within his power to bring doubt to the Believer, telling him this passed away with the Apostles, or that it was only for the Early Church, or that one gets everything when one is saved, etc. The list is endless, especially when one is making up their own doctrine and not following the Bible.

For the Believer to receive, he must understand that the Baptism with the Spirit is Scriptural, that it is for all, and that means every single, solitary Believer. Doubt has kept more from receiving than anything else. It is for you, and you must not allow Satan or any of Satan's tools (unbelieving Preachers) to talk you out of that which God has promised to you.

FAITH

Third, everything that everyone receives from the Lord is always by Faith. In other words, we are to believe what He has promised in His Word, and He has promised the Holy Spirit (Acts 1:4).

As I mentioned, if one is in a state of unbelief concerning the Baptism with the Holy Spirit, the Lord will not respond to that person favorably. The Scripture plainly says: *"But without Faith it is impossible to please Him: for he who comes to God must believe that He is, and that He is a rewarder of them who diligently seek Him"* (Heb. 11:6).

So, one must believe!

DO NOT FEAR

Some people have been erroneously taught that if they ask the Lord for the Spirit Baptism that they are opening themselves up to the spirit world, and can receive demon spirits, etc. That is patently untrue!

The Scripture plainly tells us:

"If a son shall ask bread of any of you who is a father, will he give him a stone? Or if he

asks a fish, will he for a fish give him a serpent? Or if he shall ask an egg, will he offer him a scorpion? If you then, being evil, know how to give good gifts unto your children: how much more shall your Heavenly Father give the Holy Spirit to them who ask Him?" (Lk. 11:11-13).

In other words, the Lord is telling us that if we ask for the Spirit Baptism, He will not allow us to receive anything else, except that for which we ask. In fact, and as is obvious, the Lord actually places a shield around those who ask for the Spirit Baptism, which Satan is not allowed to enter.

Once again, we are speaking of those who are *"born again"* asking for the Spirit Baptism, and not the unsaved. To be frank, if those who are unsaved would ask for such, it definitely is possible for them to receive that which is not of the Lord. It is a different thing entirely when the unredeemed ask for such, but if a person is a Child of God, he is not going to receive an evil spirit. The Scripture says so!

WHAT TO EXPECT

Fifth, most Believers don't know what to expect relative to asking the Lord to Baptize them with the Spirit. Consequently, they should be told what to expect. If we don't tell them, they won't know what is going on when the Spirit moves on them.

Tell the person that they are to expect the Holy Spirit to put supernatural words (Tongues) into their spirit, and then to move upon their vocal organs, etc.

Many Believers have the idea that the Lord will make them or force them to speak in Tongues, which He will not. He will give the Utterance, but that's all that He will do. It is left up to the Believer to speak out the words given to him by the Spirit within his heart — incidentally, words that aren't his mother tongue.

To be frank, the Holy Spirit will not take you over and make you do anything. He will move upon the person, but we have to work in cooperation with Him. It is the Believer who speaks with other Tongues, not the Holy Spirit. Nowhere in the Bible do we find that the Holy Spirit speaks in Tongues Himself. Every Scripture reference tells us that it is people who do the speaking.

The Scripture says: *"They (the people) began to speak with other Tongues, as the Spirit gave them utterance"* (Acts 2:4).

"For they heard them speak with Tongues, and magnify God" (Acts 10:46).

"And when Paul had laid his hands upon them, the Holy Spirit came on them; and they spake with Tongues, and Prophesied" (Acts 19:6).

Notice in the Scriptures we have given, and many more we could give, that it is always the individual who speaks in Tongues, while the Holy Spirit is the One Who gives the Utterance.

So, the Believer is to speak out the words that he hears down in his spirit, which are not English or any language he already knows. The words he speaks are those given by the Holy Spirit, but that is all the Spirit will do. It is up to the individual to go ahead and speak out what the Spirit is giving. If he doesn't do it, he cannot be filled.

Of course, this does not mean that one is to make up unintelligible words, etc. That is not the idea at all. However, whenever the person comes to receive the Spirit, and they are sincere, and they yield before the Lord, the Holy Spirit will then begin to give the Utterance, which will be obvious in the person's heart.

As well, one may speak in Tongues for quite a length of time after being filled, or one may only speak a few words.

At Family Worship Center some time ago, we were praying one particular night for people to be filled with the Spirit. A dear Baptist lady came forward to be filled, and when the Service was over she, along with several others, confessed that the Lord had filled her with the Spirit. However, what she said was a little bit different than usual.

She went on to relate to me how that she had only spoken one word in Tongues. Thank the Lord that I had a little more experience at that particular time, and I encouraged her and agreed with her that she was filled. On the way home that night with friends, the one word ceased to be enough, with the Holy Spirit all of a sudden right there in the automobile, beginning to flow through her as she began to speak out volumes, in fact, speaking in Tongues all the way home.

So, it is not how long one speaks, but just that there be some evidence even, as stated, just one word, which to be frank is rare, but sometimes does happen. Nevertheless, that person has genuinely been filled with the Spirit.

YIELD

Sixth, when the individual comes to be filled with the Spirit, they should be told to yield to the Spirit, which is absolutely necessary.

By yielding, I am meaning that in their heart they should say (not necessarily out loud), *"I am asking You Lord to fill me with the Spirit, and I now receive."*

In fact, I encourage people not to pray out loud and actually not even to themselves, when they are coming to be Baptized with the Spirit, other than what I have just said. The reason being is that they cannot speak two languages at one time. If they are speaking English (or another language that they've learned in school or somewhere), they can only speak that and nothing else. And as stated, the Lord will not break in upon them and force them to speak in Tongues.

So, the person should open his (her) mouth and breathe in as deeply as possible, in their heart telling the Lord that they receive. Then he (the person) will begin to sense the words given him by the Holy Spirit which is not a language that he knows. He is to then speak those words, and continue to do so. This is what I mean by yielding.

The Scripture says: *"Unto Me men give ear, and waited, and kept silence at My counsel. After My Words they spoke not again; and My speech dropped upon them."* As is obvious, the Scripture says they did not say anything but kept silent, and then the Lord said, *"My speech dropped upon them."*

It also says: *"And they waited for Me as for the rain; and they opened their mouth wide as for the Latter Rain"* (Job 29:21-23). The Latter Rain, as every Bible student knows, is the outpouring of the Holy Spirit as prophesied by Joel (Joel 2:23; Acts 2:16-18).

RECEIVED

The seventh and final step is for the candidate to understand that God has already given the Spirit and that it is up to that person to receive the Gift now. As previously stated, it is a *"Gift,"* and, consequently, the only thing one can do respecting a gift is to receive it.

Peter said in his Sermon on the Day of Pentecost, *"And you shall receive the Gift of the Holy Spirit"* (Acts 2:38).

So, the Believer does not come before the Lord to tarry, at least as it regards receiving the Holy Spirit. While tarrying is wonderful and something that every Christian should do before the Lord on a daily basis; still, we are not told in Scripture to do that in respect to receiving the Holy Spirit Baptism.

Many confuse the Scripture in Luke where Jesus said, *"And, behold, I send the Promise of My Father upon you: but you tarry in the city of Jerusalem, until you be endued with power from on high"* (Lk. 24:49).

While it is true that Jesus told His followers to *"tarry,"* as it refers to the Holy Spirit, it was only because the Holy Spirit had not yet come, as it regards the new Dimension. On the Day of Pentecost, He came. Consequently, every other time that one reads in the Book of Acts about people receiving the Holy Spirit, there was no tarrying involved, which means they received immediately. If that is the Scriptural case, and it definitely is, then it should be the same presently.

The Holy Spirit has already come as should be overly obvious, so there is no more need to tarry to receive Him.

To do so, constitutes works, and nullifies the *"Gift"* aspect of the Holy Spirit. So, even though tarrying is very good, it is good only for other particular types of things, not to be Baptized with the Holy Spirit.

So, the Believer must say: *"I am going to receive this Gift of God,"* which is all that the Lord expects one to do, other than having faith and believing, etc. It is yours, promised by the Lord (Acts 1:4-5).

PRAYER

As we've already stated, the way we build up ourselves in the most holy Faith, is to *"pray in the Spirit."*

Prayer is such a privilege, but yet one of which most Christians seldom take advantage. I think the reason is, they have never learned how to *"pray in the Spirit."* Unfortunately (or fortunately), there is much that goes along with *"praying in the Spirit."*

First of all, and again as we've previously stated, I personally believe that one has to be Baptized with the Holy Spirit, with the evidence of speaking with other tongues, before one can properly *"pray in the Spirit."* Now that statement needs qualification.

The Lord will definitely be patient with any and all of His Children; however, once Light is given, then He expects us to walk in that Light. If Believers reject the Baptism with the Holy Spirit, claiming that it is not for us today, or it passed away with the Apostles, or that it's of the Devil, as some have said, then I cannot see how the Spirit of God, can function at all in such a life. And regrettably, that is where the far greater majority of the modern Church presently are. It is not a case so much of ignorance, but rather of outright rejection. So I think it's hardly likely that such people will be able to *"pray in the Spirit,"* or that they would even try. To be frank, *"praying in the Spirit,"* is completely foreign to people who aren't Baptized with the Spirit, and regrettably, *"praying in the Spirit"* is foreign even to many, if not most, who are in fact baptized with the Spirit.

Along with being baptized with the Spirit, one needs to be Spirit-controlled, which regrettably, few are.

WHAT CONSTITUTES SPIRIT CONTROL?

Two things:

1. First of all, the Spirit-filled Believer must strongly desire to be controlled by the Spirit. The Holy Spirit is always a perfect gentleman. While He wants total control within our lives, He will never take such control, which means that we are to freely give to Him that of which we speak. In this desire, is the knowledge and understanding that self is to be totally hidden in Christ, with the Holy Spirit charting the course in our lives in everything. That's what I've said, everything! Everything must be Spirit-conceived, Spirit-born, and Spirit-led.

2. Many Christians want the Spirit to take over at a certain period or place. That He will not do! He will only lead that which He has conceived. Now this is very, very important. Let's say it another way:

There was no way that Abraham could turn Ishmael into a Spirit-led product, so to speak. Ishmael was conceived by the flesh, and thereby, could not be led by the Spirit. Only that which is conceived by the Spirit, which was Isaac, could then be led by the Spirit. In fact, all that pertained to the flesh had to be removed, which Ishmael eventually was.

It is the same with us presently. Things that we conceive cannot be ultimately turned over to the Spirit. They must be laid aside, with Him conceiving that which He desires, and then we can be assured of His leadership.

THE CROSS

I have placed a desire to be led by the Spirit first, because the *"will"* of the individual must be set in motion in that direction before the Lord will do anything (Rev. 22:17). However, all of this is predicated, and I speak of what the actual object of the desire should be, on the Cross of Christ, and our Faith in that Finished Work. This is absolutely imperative.

The Holy Spirit will not work, will not function, in fact, will do very little of anything, until our faith is properly placed (Rom. 8:1-2, 11, 13). The Holy Spirit through Paul plainly said: *"So then they who are in the flesh cannot please God"* (Rom. 8:8).

The Holy Spirit works totally and completely within the parameters of the great Sacrifice of Christ. He will not work outside of those parameters, which means He will work only within those parameters. The Cross and what Jesus did there is what gives Him the legal right to carry forth His great work. So He demands that our Faith ever be in the Cross of Christ. That's the reason that Paul said:

"For Christ sent me not to baptize, but to preach the Gospel: not with wisdom of words, lest the Cross of Christ should be made of none effect" (I Cor. 1:17).

In this one Passage, plus scores of others similar, the Holy Spirit Who inspired these words, is in effect, telling us that the Cross must be the central point of our Faith. That lacking, we nullify the benefits of the Cross, which guarantees failure on the part of the Christian, simply because it places the Christian in a position in which the Holy Spirit will not help him. And without the Holy Spirit, to use some street language, we are dead ducks!

A PERSONAL EXPERIENCE

I've always, by the help of the Lord, been able to pray in the Spirit; however, since the Lord began to give me the Revelation of the Cross, which actually began in 1996, I have noticed a distinct increase in this particular activity. Over and over again, in our prayer meetings, I will begin to pray, mostly beginning as the Scripture tells us to do, which is with Praise and thanksgiving (Ps. 100:4), and then at some point, the Holy Spirit will bring to mind something which He desires to make real in my heart. When that happens, and it's getting to the place that it happens more and more frequently, I will then begin to *"pray in the Spirit."* It is the most wonderful, the most joyous, the most fulfilling, the most strengthening, and the most informative, that one could ever experience. During these times, Promises are made by the Lord, with direction and instruction given.

Please allow me to go back to what we have originally said: I think the reason most Christians do not pray, is simply because they do not *"pray in the Spirit,"* without which there can be precious few benefits. But to *"pray in the Spirit,"* is beneficial beyond words or compare.

(21) "KEEP YOURSELVES IN THE LOVE OF GOD, LOOKING FOR THE MERCY OF OUR LORD JESUS CHRIST UNTO ETERNAL LIFE."

The diagram is:

1. One is to keep oneself in the Love of God by the means of the two things just mentioned, building up one's self, and to do so by praying in the Holy Spirit.

2. *"Keep"* means *"to attend to carefully, take care of, guard."* The exhortation is to the Saints, to keep ourselves within the sphere of the Love of God. We are to see to it that we stay within the circle of His love.

3. This is the love that God is, and the love with which He loves the Saints.

4. To live in this manner, will keep ourselves in the place of blessing.

5. There is no hint here that God will stop loving us; however, if we allow sin to remain

in our lives, it will make it impossible for God to give us blessings in the fullest sense.

6. *"Looking"* has respect to the coming Rapture of the Church, when we will then be glorified.

7. All of this is given by the *"Mercy"* of God, made possible by what Jesus did at the Cross on our behalf.

KEEP YOURSELVES

The short phrase, *"Keep yourselves,"* refers as should be obvious, to the part we must play.

The word doesn't imply that we can contribute anything toward our Salvation or our victory for that matter; however, it does refer to that which every Saint can do, and in fact, must do.

All we can really do is to *"furnish a willing mind, and have an obedient heart."* The *"willing mind"* refers to going God's Way and His Way entirely. The *"obedient heart"* refers to a desire to obey Him in all things, but more particularly in the realm of the Cross.

If we understand that everything comes to us from God through the Cross, which of course refers to what our Saviour did there, and our faith is properly placed in that Finished Work, which gives the Holy Spirit the latitude to work, everything else will then fall into place. Without proper Faith in the Cross, nothing will fall into place.

So we can properly *"keep ourselves"* by subscribing to God's order of victory, and only by subscribing to God's order of victory. That *"Order"* is the Cross, and what Jesus did there on our behalf, and our faith in that Finished Work (Rom. 6:3-14).

THE LOVE OF GOD

The phrase, *"In the Love of God,"* presents the Love of God for the Believer and not our love for God. To keep oneself in God's love is to stay where God can love us as His children and can shower upon us all the gifts of Love that He has for those who are His Children.

God, indeed, loves all men; but men are not urged *"to keep themselves"* in this universal love since it already extends to all of them without exception. God's love cannot bestow the saving gifts and the blessings upon those who spurn His love; He can and does bestow them upon true Believers who as His Children hunger for these gifts, pray for them, use His Word and Truth, and let the Holy Spirit lead and guide us in its proper use.

"In the love of God" is locative of sphere. In other words, it's where God is! Therefore, the exhortation to us is to keep ourselves within the sphere of the Love of God. That is, we are to see to it that we stay within the circle of His love.

In effect, we are exhorted to so build ourselves up on our Christian foundation of Faith, and so pray in the power of the Holy Spirit, that we as a result keep ourselves in the place where God is able to shower all of His love upon us. In other words, we are to so live that we will keep ourselves in the place of blessing. As we've already stated, there is no hint here that God will stop loving us; however, with sin in our lives, such makes it impossible for God to do for us and with us in the sense of blessings, which He so desires. In other words, living in that particular type of situation, which is outside the sphere of His love, we cut ourselves off from all the good things that God can do. The Reader should read these words very carefully:

Are we living in the place where the Lord can shower upon us all His blessings?

And what type of blessings are we speaking about?

BLESSINGS

The modern Church has been so inundated with the so-called *"faith teaching,"* which in reality is no faith at all, at least that which God will recognize, that almost altogether, when we think of *"blessings,"* we think of material things. What a loss! What a come down! What a travesty of the Word of God!

While the Lord definitely does bless as it regards material things, by all means, that is not the idea here of the Holy Spirit.

While these things certainly are important, Jesus told us clearly, *"Take no thought for your life, what you shall eat; neither for the body, what you shall put on."*

He then said: *"The life is more than meat, and the body is more than raiment"* (Lk. 12:22-23).

So it plainly tells us here, in the Words of Christ, that our *"Father knows that we have need of these things."* He then said:

"But rather seek you the Kingdom of God; and all these things shall be added unto you" (Lk. 12:30-31).

The true riches of life have to do with the things of the *"Kingdom of God,"* which pertains to that for which Jesus died. I speak of the *"Fruit of the Spirit"* (Gal. 5:22-23); the *"Gifts of the Spirit"* (I Cor. 12:1-11); and, *"Christlikeness"* (I Pet. 2:21). Of course, if there is proper Christlikeness, at the same time, there will be *"Righteousness"* and *"Holiness."*

All of these things are works of the Holy Spirit, and constitute the true Blessings of God. But sadly and regrettably, and as stated, the Church has slowly but surely, been turned away from these things we've just mentioned, to material objects. It is the result of the *"faith teaching."* It has almost destroyed the Church, and I exaggerate not!

Arnold Prater said: *"What you believe about faith tells me the kind of god in whom you believe. You cannot escape it: The kind of god on whom you have risked everything comes shining through when you tell me what you believe about faith. If you believe in a god who answers prayer only according to the 'amount' of faith a person has, you have to deal with my question: How much faith does it take? Does it take a pound? A gallon? An ounce? . . . Once more: what you believe about faith reveals the kind of god in whom you believe."*

Kenneth Hagin says: *"Did you ever stop to think about having faith in your own faith? Evidently God had faith in His faith, because He spoke words of faith and they came to pass . . . In other words, having faith in your words is having faith in your faith. That's what you've got to learn to do to get things from God: have faith in your faith."*

Since faith is the proud banner under which the Faith movement marches, we would have to agree with Kenneth Hagin that the god of the Faith movement must, indeed *"have faith in his own faith."* But Brother Hagin's statement begs the question: Why does God, as Kenneth Hagin portrays Him, need faith? How much and what kind of faith pleases Him? And ultimately, what kind of god is it that needs faith in his faith?

D. R. McConnell answers that question by saying, *"Any god who has to 'have faith in his own faith' is not the God and Father of our Lord Jesus Christ. He is really no god at all. He* (it?) *is the impersonal 'force' of the metaphysical cults. This force is the puppet of anybody who knows the 'formulas' and 'spiritual laws' of how to control him. These formulas and laws are called 'faith' in the Faith movement, but in reality, they are nothing more than recycled New Thought metaphysics"* (that which is supernatural, but which is subject to one's own experience, even though it may contradict the Word of God. Objective truth is that which is the Word of God and which does not change. Subjective truth is that which changes with one's experience, etc., of which is the metaphysical).

FAITH AS A FORMULA

Before I deal with this particular subject, let me say first of all, how distasteful it is to me to have to address, what I believe to be false doctrine. I take no delight in this whatsoever. As well, I hold no animosity whatsoever against any of these men whom I might name, or who might be involved in the teaching of this which I believe will cause great harm to its adherents.

But yet, I would like to believe that I love them enough to tell them the truth, and that I love you, the Reader enough, to do the same. We aren't dealing here with mundane matters, but rather the issues of life and death. In other words, there is absolutely nothing more important than a correct interpretation of the Word of God.

Satan has always done his best work inside the Church. In fact, some 30 to 35 years after the Ascension of Christ back to Heaven, the Gospel He had entrusted to the Church was being perverted. Paul warned of *"a different gospel."* He said:

"I marvel that you are so soon removed from Him Who called you into the Grace of Christ unto another gospel:

"Which is not another; but there be some that trouble you, and would pervert the Gospel of Christ" (Gal. 1:6-7).

That's the problem, *"the perversion of the Gospel of Christ."* He then gave the startling announcement that we had better heed:

"But though we, or an Angel from Heaven, preach any other gospel unto you than that which we have preached unto you, let him be accursed" (Gal. 1:8).

He expresses anger, and rightly so, that false teachers in the Church were *"hindering"* and *"disturbing"* it with false doctrine (Gal. 5:7-12). In fact, he went on to say that the Galatians were in danger of *"being severed from Christ"* and *"falling from grace"* as a result of listening to these *"teachers"* (Gal. 5:4).

If the Churches in Galatia were the only example of this problem, then perhaps it could be dismissed as an isolated incident. There are, however, numerous examples in the New Testament of this bitter conflict with false doctrine. Paul also warned the Church of Ephesus that soon after his departure, *"savage wolves will come in among you, not sparing the flock; and from among your own selves men will arise, speaking perverse things, to draw away the Disciples after them"* (Acts 20:29-30). These individuals were all the more dangerous because they had infiltrated the Christian community and were doing their damage from within.

We often think of the First Century Church in very idealistic terms. However, if it had not been for these *"different gospels,"* the New Testament as we know it today would never have been written, and simply because, much of it was written to refute that which was error. Consequently, whether I enjoy this task or not, it is my duty as a God-called Preacher of the Gospel, to not only preach the Truth, but as well, to point out error. And we must remember this about error:

TRUTH?

Almost all the time, error contains some truth. And because it contains some truth, which incidentally serves as bait, it then becomes all the more dangerous. The facts are, if some Preacher doesn't point out the error, most of the Saints, due to its clever cover, will never spot the wrong direction. Now back to our subject:

Kenneth Hagin claims that Jesus appeared to him in a vision and said, *"If anybody, anywhere, will take these four steps or put these four principles into operation, he will always receive whatever he wants from Me or God the Father."* With these *"steps,"* Jesus said to Hagin, *"You can write your own ticket with God."* The four steps that Jesus gave to Hagin were: *"A. Say it; B. Do it; C. Receive it; and, D. Tell it."*

This is the *"formula"* that our Brother claimed that Christ gave to him. This formula of Faith theology is based upon its world view.

The world, they claim, was created by God speaking the Word and calling into being everything that is. The Faith theology claims that *"God is a faith God"* because He had faith that His words would bring forth creation *"out of nothing."* As a result, the Word is woven into the very fabric of creation. Indeed, the Word is what holds the creation together and maintains its operation. Kenyon taught that *"faith-filled words brought the universe into being, and faith-filled words are ruling the universe today."* Following Kenyon's lead, Hagin claims that through the discovery of these *"spiritual laws"* established by God to run the universe, the Believer can put these laws to *"work"* for his own use. Hence they refer to themselves quite often as *"Word people."* In other words, they can take, they say, the Word of God, and *"put it to work for them."*

LAWS

Kenneth Hagin says: *"In the spiritual realm God has set into motion certain laws, just as He set laws in the natural realm. Those laws in the natural realm work, don't they? Just as you get into contact with those natural laws or put them into practice they work for you. Over in the spiritual realm the same thing is true. I have come to the conclusion that the Law of Faith is spiritual law, that God has put this law into motion, and that as surely as you come into contact with it it will work for you."*

Now as we've already stated, there is much truth in what the man has just said; however, the heresy is in the following:

These teachers claim that anybody, Christian or non-Christian, can plug into this universal law of faith and get *"results."* *"It used

to bother me,"* explains Hagin, *"when I'd see unsaved people getting results. Then it dawned on me what the sinners were doing: they were cooperating with the law of God — the Law of Faith."*

In effect, Hagin is teaching that since the Law of Faith is impersonal, just like the law of gravity, it works regardless of whom the person is or where he or she stands with Christ. To get these *"results,"* the Faith teachers often recommend *"formulas"* to follow for whatever a person needs from God.

Fred Price, for instance, teaches that Romans 10:10 is a *"formula"* and that anybody *"could put anything in there* (the formula) *you want — healing, your needs met, new job, car, home, whatever you need."* Formulas such as these will, for anybody who uses them, place the resources of the world, Heaven, and the universe at one's disposal.

POSITIVE CONFESSION

These Teachers claim that the way to set these laws into motion is by confessing them, i.e., *"confessing the Word of God over and over, etc."* Consequently, positive confession is, undoubtedly, the most distinctive doctrine of the Faith movement. However, it originated with E. W. Kenyon and not Kenneth Hagin, as many believe. The most popular saying about the nature of faith, though attributed to Hagin, actually was coined by Kenyon: *"What I confess, I possess."*

Confession is commonly defined in Faith theology as *"affirming something we believe . . . testifying to something we know . . . witnessing for a truth that we have embraced."*

The working presupposition of positive confession is that one's mental attitude determines what one believes and confesses, and what one believes and confesses determines what one gets from God. As Hagin puts it, *"What we believe is a result of our thinking. If we think wrong we will believe wrong . . . if we believe wrong, our confession will be wrong. In other words, what we say will be wrong and it will all hinge on our thinking."* So, a positive mental attitude (P.M.A.) is the fount from which all positive confession flows.

The concept of positive confession fits well into the world view of Faith theology.

Positive confession is the spiritual shove that sets into motion, as stated, the *"spiritual laws"* that govern the universe. *"A spiritual law that few of us realize,"* states Kenyon, *"is that our confession rules us."* A *"right"* or *"wrong"* confession is the determining factor in one's harmony with these universal spiritual laws. Confession is the catalyst that evokes their blessings, or their curses. A person will possess only to the extent he has faith to confess these spiritual laws: *"Sooner or later we become what we confess."* A Believer will only grow in faith to the degree, they state, which he practices positive confession.

Kenyon's emphasis, for that's where all of this came from, upon positive mental attitude (P.M.A.) and positive confession as the basis of *"faith"* also finds its roots in the metaphysical cults. Since all of these cults teach that reality is the sum total of whatever man thinks it to be, man possesses the innate ability to shape and reshape reality through the power of his mind and his words. As the founder of the Unity School of Christianity, Charles Fillmore, puts it, *"What we think, we usually express in words; and our words bring about in our life and affairs whatever we put into them."*

The Faith teachers, of course would deny that they teach *"the drawing power of the mind."* They would say that faith comes from the *"recreated human spirit,"* not the human mind. They would also say that their confession is based on the Word of God. Both of these objections, however, do not alleviate the charge of cultism.

In the first place, the cults refer to the spirit as often as they do the mind; second, like the Faith movement, these cults also use the Word of God as the basis of their positive confession. Third, both the cults and the Faith theology base their confession on a system of spiritual laws that work for anybody, independently of the specific Will of God. And this is at least one of the great sins of the Faith movement. They totally ignore the Will of God, as though they create the Will of God by their own actions. In fact, they believe and teach that whatever they say is in fact, the Will of God. It's as if God sits back, and lets the Faith people run His universe. In Faith theology, a personal loving

NOTES

God does not determine what comes into the Believer's life. A positive mental attitude and positive confession do. The Faith god can neither withhold the good, nor inhibit the bad from happening to those whose confessions invoke his spiritual laws. Now let the Reader understand that this is not the sovereign, personal God of the New Testament. This is the god of metaphysics.

FAITH AS CREATIVE POWER

Based on his view that the universe is *"ruled by words,"* Kenyon advocates *"creative faith"* by which the Believer can use God's formula for creation — *"Let there be"* — to create his own reality. Charles Capps expands Kenyon's concept of *"creative faith"* to the point that man, not God, is the only creator left in the universe. Capps claims to have received this revelation of man's role as creator from God Himself. He says:

"In August of 1973, the Word of the Lord came unto me saying, 'If men would believe Me, long prayers are not necessary. Just speaking the Word will bring what you desire. My creative power is given to man in Word form. I have ceased for a time from my creative work and have given man the book of My creative power. That power is still in my word."

Through *"creative faith,"* man, Capps says, becomes not only a god, he becomes a creator.

THE FORCE OF FAITH

As the result of his book *"The Force of Faith,"* Kenneth Copeland has made popular the term *"faith-force."* Copeland teaches that *"in the reborn human spirit there are four major forces"*: the force of faith, the force of righteousness, the force of wisdom, and the force of love. Although the basic formula that confession brings possession is the same, the unique aspect of faith-force is its definition, Copeland says, according to the following:

"Faith is a power force. It is a conductive force. It will move things. Faith will change things. Faith will change the human body. It will change the human heart. Faith will change circumstances . . . the force of faith is released by words. Faith-filled words put the law of the Spirit of life into operation."

Copeland teaches that since *"God is a faith Being"* and since man is *"a faith being,"* man has the faith *"to operate in the same way"* that God operates. As a Believer grows in his faith-force, he possesses more power and can move bigger obstacles in the spirit realm. With faith and patience, *"the power twins,"* a Believer can receive whatever his faith-force is powerful enough and patient enough to believe for.

(The above material on the doctrine of faith was derived from the book *"A Different Gospel"* by D. R. McConnell.)

THIS IS NOT FAITH IN THE WORD OF GOD

Despite the claims of the *"Word of Faith"* Teachers, the faith that they espouse is a faith of their own making, and not faith in the Word as they claim. While they may *"use"* the Word, their faith is really in their faith instead of the Word. In other words, it's *"Faith in Faith."* In their thinking and teaching, faith has become a power source of its own making, which God will never recognize.

Let the Reader understand that *"the Faith"* of which Paul spoke (Rom. 1:17; 3:25, 27-28, 30; 4:5; I Cor. 2:5; II Cor. 1:24; 5:7; Gal. 2:16, 20, etc.), and of which he spoke so abundantly, was always and without exception, Faith in the Finished Work of Christ, i.e., *"the Cross."* The great Apostle said:

"For Christ sent me not to baptize, but to preach the Gospel: not with wisdom of words, lest the Cross of Christ should be made of none effect" (I Cor. 1:17).

The *"Word of Faith"* people do not even believe in the Cross. Kenneth Copeland refers to it as *"past miseries."* Their Teachers claim that the Cross was the greatest defeat in human history. Copeland also states that *"the Blood of Jesus Christ did not atone for anything."*

Let the Reader come to the conclusion as to what is Scriptural, that which Copeland espouses, or that which Paul proclaimed?

Pure and simple, the *"Word of Faith"* doctrine, presents *"another Jesus, another spirit, and another gospel"* (II Cor. 11:4). Consequently, it will ultimately destroy anyone who adheres to its false direction.

To claim that Jesus died as a sinner on the Cross, actually taking upon Himself the

Satanic nature, which means that He became one with Satan, and then died and went to Hell, and we speak of the burning side of Hell, and suffered there for three days and nights in agony even as sinners suffer such punishment, with God at the end of that time period then saying *"it is enough,"* with Jesus then being *"born again,"* just as any sinner is Born-Again, is pure blasphemy. It is fiction from the word go, and let the Reader understand that to be in error about some things as it regards the Bible is bad enough, but to be that far off base as it regards the Atonement, is catastrophic!

THE RAPTURE OF THE CHURCH

The phrase, *"Looking for the Mercy of our Lord Jesus Christ unto Eternal Life,"* refers to the Rapture of the Church, when the physical bodies of all Saints will then be glorified. Incidentally, the Reader should not fail to observe the reference of Jude to the Three Persons of the Godhead in these two Verses.

"Looking" in the Greek is *"prosdechomai,"* and means *"to receive to one's self, to admit, give access to, to expect, wait for."* The idea is, every Saint of God should be earnestly looking for the imminent return of Christ to take away His Own. And yet, most of the modern Church does not even believe in a coming Rapture. I think that most of those who fall into that category, do not understand that the Rapture and the Resurrection are one and the same. In other words, to say that one doesn't believe in the Rapture is at the same time saying that one doesn't believe in the Resurrection.

To be frank, the Doctrine of the *"Resurrection"* is one of the cardinal stanchions of the Faith. To have an erroneous view of the coming Resurrection refers to the possibility of overthrowing the Faith of some, which the Holy Spirit through Paul greatly condemned (II Tim. 2:17-18). The Holy Spirit here through Jude, tells us that we should be earnestly and sincerely *"looking"* for this event.

MERCY

The Saint must never forget that every single thing we receive from God is not at all through any merit on our part, but always by and through the *"Mercy of God."* In fact, Mercy is a product of Grace.

Some time in eternity past, God chose Grace as the means by which He would deal with humanity. The Reader must understand that Grace must be a choice, or else it isn't Grace.

However, once Grace was chosen and selected, God literally had no choice but to extend Mercy, considering that Mercy is a by-product of Grace. If the Grace of God is freely flowing to the Christian, Mercy is being extended at the same time; however, if the flow of Grace stops, Mercy stops as well, and of necessity.

What can stop the flow of Grace to the Believer?

THE FRUSTRATION OF
THE GRACE OF GOD

Many Christians erroneously believe that due to the fact that this is the Dispensation of Grace, and it is, that being the case, Grace, they think, is an automatic blessing to the Christian. In other words, we are living in the Dispensation of Grace, so we automatically have Grace. That is basely incorrect!

The truth is, despite the fact that we definitely are living in the Dispensation of Grace, most Christians are little enjoying the Grace of God, but are rather living under Law. In other words, they are living somewhat as the Jews lived before Christ. While it's not the Law of Moses under which they are living, it is law nevertheless, and I speak of laws made up by themselves, or their Churches, etc. Listen to what Paul said:

"I am crucified with Christ: nevertheless I live; yet not I, but Christ lives in me: and the life which I now live in the flesh I live by the faith of the Son of God, Who loved me, and gave Himself for me" (Gal. 2:20).

In this one Verse of Scripture, Paul gives us the secret to victorious, overcoming, Christian living. Let's see what he says:

1. *"I am crucified with Christ"*: The Apostle is here taking us back to Romans 6:3-5. When Jesus died on the Cross as our Substitute, our identification with Him gives us all for which He died. The moment the believing sinner expresses Faith in Christ, in the Mind of God, the believing sinner is

literally *"crucified with Christ."* This means that when you were saved, you died to your old life, to your old nature, to what you were in totality before coming to Christ. This means that Christ didn't try to rehabilitate you, but rather gave you a brand-new beginning. That's why He called it *"born again"* (Jn. 3:3).

Let the Reader understand that these five words *"I am crucified with Christ,"* are the single most important words in any language. That is the key not only to your initial Salvation, but as well, to your victorious living.

The Crucifixion is where everything was done. It's where Jesus satisfied the demands of the broken Law, which satisfied the Justice and Righteousness of a thrice-Holy God, which atoned for all sin. When Jesus did that, in which He did by the pouring out of His Life's Blood, inasmuch as all sin was atoned, this destroyed Satan's legal right to hold man in bondage. Sin being that legal right, and sin being taken away (Jn. 1:29), Satan was defeated, and defeated totally (Col. 2:14-15). This is why Paul stressed the Cross so much, because it was there that the price was paid, and Redemption for the entirety of the human race was effected, at least for those who will believe (Jn. 3:16; I Cor. 1:17-18, 21, 23; 2:2, 5).

2. *"Nevertheless I live"*: We died with Christ, spiritually speaking, but as well, we were raised with Christ as it regards His Resurrection, and raised *"in newness of life."* This new life that we now have, all made possible by the Cross and our Faith in that Finished Work, stems totally from Christ. In other words, He is the Source. As Christ is in the Father, we are now in Him, and He in us (Jn. 14:20).

Christ now lives in me, through the Person, Work, Office, and Ministry of the Holy Spirit. Consequently, I now have a power source that helps me to live as I ought to live (Rom. 8:2).

3. *"And the life which I now live in the flesh"*: This speaks of our daily living, and thereby facing the vicissitudes of life. Paul is now going to tell us how to live this life.

4. *"I live by the faith of the Son of God"*: Please notice that he didn't say *"I live by faith in the Son of God,"* but rather *"I live by the faith of the Son of God."*

What did he mean by that? He tells us what he means in the last phrase.

5. *"Who loved me, and gave Himself for me"*: The Cross of Christ is *"the faith."* What He did at the Cross, and my Faith in that Finished Work, which enables the Holy Spirit to function grandly on my behalf, enables me to live the life I should live. By continuing to trust in what Christ did at the Cross, victory is mine, and *"sin shall not have dominion over me"* (Rom. 6:14).

THE CROSS OF CHRIST

The entire scenario is described in the following three abbreviated points. To be sure, we've already given them several times in this Volume, but because we are dealing with the very heart of the Gospel, I feel in my spirit I must make certain that you the Reader will have absolutely no misunderstanding as it regards this all-important aspect of our lives and living:

1. The Believer must understand that every single thing he receives from God, and that means everything, comes to him solely through the Sacrifice of Christ on the Cross. In other words, the Cross is the means by which God grants us His Grace (Rom. 6:3-14; I Cor. 1:17).

2. Understanding that the Cross is the means by which all things come to us, the Cross must ever be the object of our Faith. That's what Paul was talking about when he said, *"I live by the faith of the Son of God."* One can say and not be Scripturally wrong, that *"the Cross"* in effect is *"the Faith"* (Col. 2:14-15). Consequently, the Cross must ever be the object of our Faith. In fact, this is where Satan will fight the hardest. He will try his best to shift our Faith from the Cross to something else.

3. With Faith properly placed in the Cross, and remaining in the Cross, the Holy Spirit will then work mightily on our behalf. Everything the Holy Spirit does with us and for us is all predicated on the legal work of Calvary. In other words, it's the Cross which gives the Holy Spirit the latitude to do what He does for us; consequently, He demands that our Faith always be *"in Christ"* (Rom. 8:1-2, 11, 13), with the short phrase *"in Christ"* always referring to what Christ did at the Cross.

NOTES

THE SECRET OF ALL VICTORY

The secret to all victory is to have the Grace of God flowing to us at all times. The secret to seeing that this is brought about and continues on an unending basis, is for us to place our Faith in the Sacrifice of Christ, even as Paul has stated in Galatians 2:20-21. All victory is found in the Finished Work of Christ, and only in the Finished Work of Christ. That's the very reason that Jesus came. For us to obtain this victory, which incidentally, was carried out completely for you and me, all we have to do is evidence faith in that which Christ has done. This guarantees an uninterrupted flow of Grace; however, far too often, we attempt to bring about victory, or whatever it is we desire from the Lord, by *"works."* When this happens, we then shift our Faith from the Cross to these works, which *"frustrates the Grace of God"* (Gal. 2:21). This means that the Grace of God actually stops, or at the least perhaps it would be better said, that the Grace of God simply cannot function in our lives, if we are trying to make something else function at the same time. It's like trying to speak two languages at one time. It simply cannot be done.

Paul plainly tells us that Righteousness cannot come by the Law, i.e., *"works."* If it could, the great Apostle in essence said, *"Christ died in vain."* In other words, if we could get this task accomplished by our own machinations, then Christ would not have had to come down here and die on a Cross. But the very fact that He had to do that, tells us that under no circumstances can we carry out this work of Redemption, or the work of Victory, by our own efforts and ability. When will the Church ever learn this?

Notice what John said:

"This is the victory that overcometh the world, even our faith" (I Jn. 5:4).

While I'm on the subject, I might as well dig a little deeper:

WALKING AFTER THE FLESH

Paul said: *"There is therefore now no condemnation to them which are in Christ Jesus, who walk not after the flesh, but after the Spirit"* (Rom. 8:1).

First of all, we must understand that Paul is speaking here to Believers. In other words, folk who are already saved.

In this Passage he tells us that it is quite possible for Saints to *"walk after the flesh,"* and thereby, not *"walk after the Spirit."* In fact, one cannot do both at the same time.

What is walking after the flesh?

Most Christians think that it's watching too much television, being too interested in sports, being too taken up with hunting or fishing, or too interested in making money, etc. None of that is correct!

"Walking after the flesh" is the Believer attempting to live this life for Christ by his own efforts and ability, which means he is not looking to the Cross. In other words, anything the Believer does attempting to live for God, outside of Faith in the Cross, is *"walking after the flesh."*

Considering that almost none of the modern Church knows anything about the Cross, at least as it regards the Sanctification experience, this means that most modern Christians are in fact, *"walking after the flesh."*

What is the flesh?

Paul uses the word *"flesh,"* at least most of the time, as a symbolism that portrays one's own human ability and strength. It is not that such is wrong within itself, but simply that it's not sufficient for the task. As we said several paragraphs back, if we could do this thing ourselves, then Christ would not have had to have come down here and died on the Cross.

Incidentally, *"walking after the flesh"* is *"frustrating the Grace of God,"* simply because, it's attempting to do what only Christ can do, and in fact has already done.

WALKING AFTER THE SPIRIT

The Holy Spirit is the only One Who can bring about in our lives that which we need. Of course, I'm speaking of Righteousness, Holiness, Christlikeness, the Fruit of the Spirit, etc. It is not possible for the Saint of God to bring these things about. As we stated some pages back, we can only furnish a *"willing mind and obedient heart."* That's as far as we can go. The Holy Spirit must do the rest.

So how does the Believer walk after the Spirit?

Most Christians think that *"walking after the Spirit,"* is doing spiritual things such as reading one's Bible so much each day, having a select prayer time each day, witnessing to souls, giving money to the Work of the Lord, being faithful to Church, etc.

To be sure, any good Christian will definitely do these things we've mentioned; however, the doing of these things, is not *"walking after the Spirit."* As stated, because these things are *"spiritual,"* we automatically think that it constitutes *"walking after the Spirit."* It doesn't!

"Walking after the Spirit" is putting one's total faith and trust in what Christ has done at the Cross, and not allowing our Faith to be moved to other things. We are to understand that everything comes to us through the great Sacrifice of Christ; consequently, this must be at all times the object of our Faith.

The Holy Spirit will always lead the Believer to the Sacrifice of Christ. This is the legal boundaries in which the Spirit works.

Now how do I know this?

Paul said: *"For the Law of the Spirit of Life in Christ Jesus has made me free from the law of sin and death"* (Rom. 8:2).

I've already dissected this Scripture, so I will not go into detail now; however, the three words *"in Christ Jesus,"* tells us how *"the Law of the Spirit of Life"* works. Now please understand, the Holy Spirit through Paul told us here that this is a *"Law,"* which means that for sure the Spirit is going to abide thereby.

But He tells us that this great *"Law"* is *"in Christ Jesus,"* which refers to what Christ did at the Cross. As we've already stated several times in this Volume, every time that Paul uses the phrase *"in Christ Jesus,"* or one of its derivatives such as *"in Him,"* etc., without exception, he is always referring to what Christ did at the Cross (Rom. 6:3-14; Eph. 2:13-18; Col. 2:14-15).

Incidentally, the word *"walk"* refers to our lifestyle, in other words, how we live this life.

(22) "AND OF SOME HAVE COMPASSION, MAKING A DIFFERENCE:"

The diagram is:

1. In Verses 22 and 23, Jude is speaking to those who have been misled by the false doctrine of the false teachers.

2. By the use of the word *"compassion,"* he is stating that these particular individuals must be handled gently, showing them love.

3. *"Making a difference"* refers to the fact that some people have to be handled differently than others.

COMPASSION

The phrase, *"And of some have compassion,"* refers as stated, to those who have been lured away from True Doctrine to the false doctrine of the false teachers. The teaching and example of the false teachers have caused them to be uncertain about the Truth of the Gospel. They must be dealt with patiently and mercifully by showing them Christian love.

Some Scholars claim that three groups are referred to in Verses 22 and 23; however, I don't think so! There are only two groups, the first on which we should show compassion, and the other group that should be addressed more forcefully.

Pride enters into all of this. Whenever individuals place their confidence in something, and they come to feel that their confidence has been misled, their pride enters the picture. To be sure, such isn't right and always causes problems, nevertheless, that is the case with most! So I would think the Holy Spirit is telling us here that people fall into one of two categories. One group has to be dealt with gently, while the other group has to be dealt with more forcibly.

If it is to be noticed, Jude doesn't say anything here about the false teachers. He has, I think, in unmistakable terms described them as outcasts, and he does not need to say that the Readers are to treat them as such.

MAKING A DIFFERENCE

The phrase, *"Making a difference,"* refers to the manner in which this particular class should be addressed. To be able to do this is one of the highest qualifications to be sought by one who endeavors to carry out the Will of God, and in effect, to save souls. The young, the tender, the delicate, the refined, need a different kind of treatment from others. In fact, this wisdom was shown by the Saviour in all His preaching; it was imminent in the preaching of Paul as well.

So how is one to know?

NOTES

If one is led by the Spirit, one will quickly sense what is needed.

(23) "AND OTHERS SAVE WITH FEAR, PULLING THEM OUT OF THE FIRE; HATING EVEN THE GARMENT SPOTTED BY THE FLESH."

The construction is:

1. This particular group needs to be dealt with directly and vigorously.

2. The rescue concerns individuals who are slipping into the eternal fire, and are pulled out by the Grace and Truth of God.

3. We learn from this that Christians can lose their way and thereby lose their Faith, and then be eternally lost.

4. *"The garments spotted by the flesh,"* presents the terrible ravages of sin.

5. We also learn from this that no one, not even the most defiled sinner, is beyond Salvation through Faith in Christ's redeeming work.

FEAR

The phrase, *"And others save with fear,"* constitutes the second group. As stated, they are to be dealt with directly, which refers to straightforward, and vigorously. Salvation is God's work, and here Christians are portrayed as God's instruments for snatching brands out of the fire (Zech. 3:3). The picture is of a person slipping into the eternal fire but rescued from error by the Grace and Truth of God (Blum).

These statements completely debunk the erroneous doctrine of unconditional eternal security. In fact, the entirety of the Book of Hebrews does this same identical thing. It speaks to Christian Jews, which refer to those who have truly accepted Christ, thereby *"born again,"* who through discouragement, or fear of persecution, etc., turn their backs on Christ by going back into Judaism. While the Lord doesn't throw a Christian over because of sin, that is if such a Believer will earnestly seek Mercy and Grace, if in fact, the Believer loses his Faith in Christ, thereby ceasing to believe, such an individual definitely reverts to a *"lost condition"* (Heb. 6:4-6; 10:26-31).

THE FIRE

The phrase, *"Pulling them out of the fire,"* in effect states that the spiritual position of these who have believed the false doctrine has brought them to the very edge of hellfire. True Believers pulling them back to the right way are portrayed as literally snatching these individuals from the brink. This is the reason that a forceful approach is needed.

If a person is about to walk off the edge of a cliff that he doesn't know is there, one would treat such a situation with force, urgency, and haste. In other words, they would be vigorous in their efforts, which in fact are demanded.

That's the reason that Preachers, nor any Believer for that matter, should take false doctrine lightly. It has to be addressed, or else souls will be eternally lost. This is what Jude is saying. To be sure, it's distasteful to do so, simply because it incurs the wrath of those who are the propagators of such, however, we must ever realize that there is much more at stake than the mere feelings of individuals. As stated, we are speaking of the issues of life and death, in effect, the literal souls of men. False doctrine is designed by Satan, in effect by angels of light, and it is always superintended by *"seducing spirits"* (I Tim. 4:1).

Many Preachers boast that they preach the Truth, and that's all that is required. In other words, they never say anything about a false doctrine. Regrettably, their methods will not work. False doctrine thrives in such an atmosphere. For people to know the right way, somebody has got to point out that right way, which is the truth, plus they've got to point out the wrong way, so there will be no misunderstanding as it regards the erroneous direction.

To use a secular example, Adolph Hitler prospered at the beginning of his world conquest, simply because no one opposed him. The leaders of the free world buttoned themselves up in their countries, claiming to espouse democracy, but at the same time not opposing evil. That policy did not work, resulting in the deaths of some 50 million human beings, plus the most horrible atrocities the world has ever known. It is the same in the Gospel.

There are many things in the Word of God about which all of us disagree to one extent or the other; however, when it comes to the fundamentals of the Faith, and we primarily speak of the Atonement, there can be no deviation from *"Jesus Christ and Him Crucified"* (I Cor. 2:2). Error here will damn the souls of men!

THE SPOTTED GARMENT

The phrase, *"Hating even the garment spotted by the flesh,"* refers to hating the sin but loving the sinner.

This second group appears to be deep in the immorality and wrong direction of the false teachers. Their very clothing spiritually speaking, is *"stained by corrupted flesh,"* which means, that their erroneous direction has infected every part of their being, which sin always does. Christians are to show mercy as in the first case, but now they are to be fearful lest the infection spread to them. Yet even here God's wondrous grace can exchange the excrement-covered garments for festive garments of righteousness (Zech. 3:3). For no one, not even the most defiled sinner, is beyond Salvation through Faith in Christ and what Christ has done for us at the Cross. In other words, Jesus died even for the vilest of sinners!

All of this is beautifully and aptly proven by that which Jesus told as it regards the prodigal son. Filthy with the husks and mud of the swine pen, still, his father welcomed him with open arms.

The first thing he did was to give him *"the best robe,"* which took the place of the one that was filthy. The Scripture says, *"and put it on him"* (Lk. 15:22). He then *"put a ring on his hand,"* showing that he was now a member of the family once again. Then *"shoes were placed on his feet,"* giving him the dominion which he had lost. John says it beautifully:

"The Blood of Jesus Christ His Son cleanseth us from all sin" (I Jn. 1:7).

Going to the Old Testament, which gave example after example, we find that of course, the garment was necessary; however, if it had even one spot of leprosy upon it, it was to be hated and destroyed (Lev., Chpts. 13-15). Gold and brass are necessary and valuable metals, but Moses destroyed the gold of which the calf was made, and Hezekiah, the brass of the brazen serpent. Both metals were *"spotted by the flesh"* because connected with idolatry.

The brazen serpent, like the Paschal Supper, was of Divine appointment, but both having become idolatrous should alike be judged.

We learn here the horror and destructive power of sin. It is never to be taken lightly! But at the same time, we are to never forget that no matter how vile the sin may be, if the penitent seeker is earnest before God, as stated, the Blood of Jesus Christ can cleanse from any sin, from all sin, and as the song says, *"It will never lose its power."*

(24) "NOW UNTO HIM THAT IS ABLE TO KEEP YOU FROM FALLING, AND TO PRESENT YOU FAULTLESS BEFORE THE PRESENCE OF HIS GLORY WITH EXCEEDING JOY,"

The structure is:

1. To live this life, the Believer must have the Power of the Holy Spirit.

2. *"From falling"* means, *"surefooted as a horse that does not stumble."*

3. The Holy Spirit can bring it to pass that you stand blameless before the Judgment Seat.

4. As well, the presentation will be *"with exceeding joy."*

HE IS ABLE

The phrase, *"Now unto Him who is able,"* refers to the Holy Spirit; however, all three Members of the Godhead are involved in this great Salvation Plan, and as well, all that it entails, which refers to personal dealings with each Believer also.

"To the One able" to guard and place you does not mean that He will do this by means of His omnipotence but by means of His Grace, Mercy, Word, and Spirit. He is able to guard you in this life despite all dangers, despite the mockers, *"as non-stumbling,"* as not stumbling to a fatal fall. There is no lack in God; only by willfully turning from His enabling Grace can anyone be lost.

Let the Reader understand that the Power of God that is expended to the Believer by the Godhead, which is all channeled through the Holy Spirit, is not done, as stated, through omnipotence. Due to particulars, which I will not take the time to address, God must deal with mankind through the Cross. While

it is certainly true that the omnipotence of God is definitely present in all that He does, it is always, and without exception, filtered through the Sacrifice of Christ. It comes under the heading of *"Grace,"* and *"Mercy,"* all by His *"Love,"* with everything based on the *"Word."* As stated, it is all channeled through the Holy Spirit.

For a greater understanding of this of which we speak, the Book of Hebrews is a perfect example. It portrays the inadequacy of the High Priest of Israel, plus Angels or Prophets, to open up the way to the very Presence of God, but which was accomplished by the Lord Jesus Christ, through what He did at the Cross. Now the way is opened!

The point is, irrespective of what Satan may bring against the Believer, *"God is able!"*

FALLING

The phrase, *"To keep you from falling,"* could be translated, *"To keep you unfallen."*

From his own warnings, denunciations, and exhortations, which have been severe and somber throughout, Jude turns in joyous, exulting confidence to Him Who Alone can make them effectual. *"Keep you,"* or, *"guard you,"* means *"preserved"* in the Greek; however, it is not the more general word translated *"preserved"* in Verse 1, but another more in harmony with the present context, as indicating *"protection"* against the great perils just pointed out.

As well, the very nature of the phrase proclaims the fact that it definitely is possible for a Christian to *"fall."* Such a fall would refer to *"falling from Faith."* In other words, the person simply ceases to believe in Christ and what Christ did at the Cross.

And let the Reader understand that it is quite possible for a fallen individual to continue to believe in Christ, at least in a convoluted way, while no longer believing in the Cross. Actually, I think that the far greater majority of those who lose their way do so in this fashion: Their faith turns away from the Cross to other things, and they find themselves serving *"another Jesus"* (II Cor. 11:4). But let me say it again, and because it is so very, very important, the very nature of this phrase, proclaims the fact that it is definitely possible for a Believer to quit believing and to, therefore, fall from Grace. And let it be understood that if one stays in this condition, and I speak of the fallen condition, they will lose their souls, despite the fact that they once knew the Lord.

FAULTLESS

The phrase, *"And to present you faultless,"* represents what God can do.

Jude's message of warning and doom might have depressed and discouraged his Readers. Beset by so much false teaching and immorality, how can Christians ever reach Heaven?

The answer lies only in the Power of God. So this doxology, surely one of the greatest in the New Testament, reminds us of God's ability to bring every one of His Own safely to Himself. *"God is able to keep you from falling,"* and besides that, *"to present you faultless before the Presence of His Glory, and with exceeding joy."*

The word here rendered *"faultless"* is the same which is rendered *"unblameable"* in Colossians 1:22.

This doesn't mean that Believers at that time, will not be deserving of blame, or will not be unworthy, but that we will be purified from our sins, and done so by the Precious Blood of Jesus Christ. It is all in Christ.

In fact, left on our own, and irrespective as to whom we might be, we definitely would *"fall."* Also, left on our own, there is no sane person who would put the label of *"faultless"* on himself; however, the Holy Spirit through Jude doesn't say these things out of the merit of the Believer, but rather the merit of Christ. In Christ we are *"faultless,"* and because Christ is faultless. Our faith in Him, gives to us all that He purchased for us at the Cross of Calvary. This is what makes the Christian experience so beautiful. But yet, all of us, I think, keep trying to go in different directions than by the means of *"faith."* And please remember, every time we use the word *"faith,"* always and without exception, it is faith in Christ and what Christ has done at the Cross on our behalf. And let the Reader read these words once again:

To think of Christ, to look at Christ, to claim Christ, without attaching to Him the Cross, frankly presents *"another Jesus."* Always and without exception, we must

NOTES

understand that it is *"Jesus Christ and Him Crucified"* (I Cor. 1:25; 2:2). That is always the password. If we try to enter any other way, the following applies:

"Verily, verily, I say unto you, he who enters not by the door into the sheepfold, but climbs up some other way, the same is a thief and a robber" (Jn. 10:1).

First of all, Jesus is *"the Door of the sheep"* (Jn. 10:7). And He is *"the Door of the Sheep,"* by virtue of what He did for us at the Cross (Jn. 3:14).

Thus, this Epistle guides the Christian as to his conduct in the midst of the corruption of Christendom; reminds him of the infinite provision provided for him in the Scriptures as his Counsellor; and animates him with the promise and assurance that his Lord will never fail him but will guard him even from stumbling (Williams).

THE PRESENCE OF HIS GLORY

The phrase, *"Before the Presence of His Glory with exceeding joy,"* presents the Believer standing blameless before the Judgment Seat (Col. 1:22; I Thess. 3:13). The Saints are to be presented there as redeemed and sanctified, and as made worthy by Grace to dwell there forever. As well, one can readily understand how that such will be done *"with exceeding joy."* We have been rescued by the Lord Jesus Christ from sorrow, sin, and death, and on top of that, we will be privileged to dwell with the Lord forever and forever. Who now can form an adequate idea of the happiness of that hour?

This refers to the last great day when *"the Son of Man shall come in the Glory of His Father"* (Mat. 16:27). In Matthew 25:34, Jesus describes how God will so place us. All blemishes are removed by Justification.

In Verse 4 Jude has *"only"* with reference to Christ. In the absolute sense there is and can be no other. It is all of Jesus Christ, and that means it is all Jesus Christ. And again we state, when we use these terms, we are always and without exception, referring to what He did for us at the Cross. There the terrible sin debt was paid making it possible for the lost sons of Adam's race to be once again reconciled to God. There all sin was atoned, past, present, and future. There Satan was totally and completely defeated, along with all his cohorts of darkness (Col. 2:14-15). There Jesus made it possible for man to be washed, sanctified, and justified (I Cor. 6:11). There Christ opened up the way to Heaven's gate!

(25) "TO THE ONLY WISE GOD OUR SAVIOUR, BE GLORY AND MAJESTY, DO-MINION AND POWER, BOTH NOW AND EVER. AMEN."

The construction is:

1. *"To the only God our Saviour"* points to the monotheistic nature of the faith by showing that the Father is the Saviour as well as the Son.

2. Whatever the false teachers may say, there is only one God and Saviour, and He is Saviour by virtue of the Cross.

3. *"Glory and majesty"* refer to *"Who"* He is! *"Dominion and power"* refer to *"What"* He is!

4. The solemn time notation *"before all ages, now and forever more"* indicates that these attributes of God suffer no change and, therefore, that His Divine Plan will surely be carried out.

5. Salvation is completely secured because God's Own purpose stands and because He is able to do all that He wills (Isa. 46:9-10).

GOD OUR SAVIOUR

The phrase, *"To the only wise God our Saviour,"* tells us two things:

1. There is only one God, although manifest in three Persons, *"God the Father, God the Son, and God the Holy Spirit."*

2. The word *"Saviour"* may be appropriately applied to God the Father as such, because He is the great Author of Salvation, though it is commonly applied to the Lord Jesus Christ. Actually, in some manuscripts, after the word *"Saviour"* is the statement *"through Jesus Christ our Lord."* In other words, God is our Saviour, through what Christ has done at the Cross on our behalf.

The work of the Son is the work of the Father; and so in the Old Testament we have Jehovah spoken of as the Saviour and Redeemer of His people (Ps. 106:21; Isa. 41:15, 21; 49:26; 60:16). And this is the meaning of the phrase which textual criticism has restored to us in this Passage. God is our Saviour *"through Jesus Christ our Lord."* And

in essence, He is our Saviour through what Christ has done at the Cross. As I keep saying, we must never separate Christ from the Cross, as it refers to that which He did there.

GLORY AND MAJESTY

The phrase, *"Be glory and majesty,"* in effect tells us Who the Lord actually is. He is surrounded by Glory, in fact, a Glory that is beyond comprehension. This speaks of beauty, wonder, splendor, magnificence, greatness, grandeur, or whatever other superlatives or adjectives we may add.

The word *"majesty"* refers to His greatness in the sense of the *"glory"* which He possesses.

Most earthly potentates have majesty, that is if we would use this word in that regard, through a series or set of circumstances. But with God, His majesty does not at all depend on circumstances, but is derived from What and Who He is. As stated, the *"glory"* proclaims His *"Majesty."*

DOMINION AND POWER

The phrase, *"Dominion and power,"* tells us *"What"* He is. His *"Dominion"* covers all, and He has the *"Power"* to guarantee His Dominion.

All of this is what Satan wants, even as described in Isaiah, Chapter 14; however, this he will never have!

NOW AND FOREVER

The phrase, *"Both now and ever. Amen,"* refers to the fact that God has always been thus, and will always be thus. The word *"Amen,"* in effect proclaims the fact that this is *"truth,"* and it will not change.

The type of *"Glory, Majesty, Dominion, and Power"* which the Lord has, and in fact is, is beyond our comprehension. As creatures, we cannot really contemplate something that has no beginning or no ending. As human beings, we measure everything according to a beginning and an ending, which is constituted by time between those two points. But those things with God do not exist. He is unformed, unmade, uncreated, always has been, always is, and always shall be. As stated, this is terminology that does not fit our thinking. But yet, belonging to Christ, we have entered the realm of the eternal.

CONCLUDING REMARKS

It is May 10, 2001 as I conclude our efforts regarding commentary on I, II, and II John, along with Jude. As usual, each one of these Epistles, as short as they may be, hold their own place as far as *"Truth"* is concerned. Of course, they do not merely contain Truth, but in fact, are Truth. Again as usual, I have gained a much greater appreciation for the Beloved Apostle John, feeling that I know him a little better after minutely studying that which he wrote regarding his Epistles. I feel the same about Jude.

But as with all, I come away with my appetite only whetted, strongly desiring to know more. Of course, that desire cannot be satisfied, until we all stand before our Lord and Saviour, Jesus Christ, Who has redeemed us with His Own Precious Blood. The thousand questions I now desire to ask, I will then be allowed to ask. And I'm certain the answers which will be forthcoming, will be of even grander nature than I could even now begin to contemplate.

I have tried my best to open up these Passages in the light of the Cross, which I think the Holy Spirit has compelled me to do. How successful I have been can only be determined by you the Reader, playing out to the effect it may have on your hearts and lives. I pray the Lord has helped me to explain it succinctly, clearly, and plainly. If so, then it will be a blessing.

If in fact that is the case, the Lord be praised!

"There is never a day so dreary,
"There is never a night so long,
"But the soul that is trusting Jesus
"Will somewhere find a song."

"There is never a cross so heavy,
"There is never a weight of woe,
"But that Jesus will help to carry
"Because He loveth so."

"There is never a care or burden,
"There is never a grief or loss,
"But that Jesus in love will lighten
"When carried to the Cross."

NOTES

"There is never a guilty sinner,
"There is never a wandering one,
"But that God can in mercy pardon
"Through Jesus Christ, His Son."

BIBLIOGRAPHY:

The Student's Commentary, George Williams

Barnes Notes On the New Testament, Albert Barnes

The Expositor's Bible Commentary, A. Skevington Wood

The Word of God Revealed, Bernard Rossier

The New Bible Dictionary

Commentary on the Whole Bible, Charles John Ellicott

Vine's Expository Dictionary of New Testament Words, W. E. Vine

Wuest's Word Studies, I, II, II John, Jude, Kenneth Wuest

Young's Literal Translation of the Bible

A Different Gospel, D. R. McConnell

Expository Dictionary of Bible Words, Lawrence O. Richards

Word Studies from the Greek New Testament, Kenneth Wuest

The Expositor's Bible, G. G. Findlay, B.A.

The International Standard Bible Encyclopedia

The Zondervan Pictorial Encyclopedia of the Bible

INDEX

The index is listed according to subjects. The treatment may include a complete dissertation or no more than a paragraph. But hopefully it will provide some help.

As well, even though extended treatment of a subject may not be carried in this Commentary, one of the other Commentaries may well include the desired material.

For all information concerning the *Jimmy Swaggart Bible Commentary,* please request a Gift Catalog.

You may inquire by using Books of the Bible.

- Genesis (639 pages) (11-201)
- Exodus (639 pages) (11-202)
- Leviticus (435 pages) (11-203)
- Numbers
  Deuteronomy (493 pages) (11-204)
- Joshua
  Judges
  Ruth (329 pages) (11-205)
- I Samuel
  II Samuel (528 pages) (11-206)
- I Kings
  II Kings (560 pages) (11-207)
- I Chronicles
  II Chronicles (528 pages) (11-226)
- Ezra
  Nehemiah
  Esther *(will be ready Summer 2011)* (11-208)
- Job (320 pages) (11-225)
- Psalms (688 pages) (11-216)
- Isaiah (688 pages) (11-220)
- Jeremiah
  Lamentations (456 pages) (11-070)
- Ezekiel (508 pages) (11-223)
- Daniel (403 pages) (11-224)
- Matthew (625 pages) (11-073)
- Mark (606 pages) (11-074)

- Luke (626 pages) (11-075)
- John (532 pages) (11-076)
- Acts (697 pages) (11-077)
- Romans (536 pages) (11-078)
- I Corinthians (632 pages) (11-079)
- II Corinthians (589 pages) (11-080)
- Galatians (478 pages) (11-081)
- Ephesians (550 pages) (11-082)
- Philippians (476 pages) (11-083)
- Colossians (374 pages) (11-084)
- I Thessalonians
  II Thessalonians (498 pages) (11-085)
- I Timothy
  II Timothy
  Titus
  Philemon (687 pages) (11-086)
- Hebrews (831 pages) (11-087)
- James
  I Peter
  II Peter (730 pages) (11-088)
- I John
  II John
  III John
  Jude (377 pages) (11-089)
- Revelation (602 pages) (11-090)

For telephone orders you may call 1-800-288-8350 with bankcard information. All Baton Rouge residents please use (225) 768-7000. For mail orders send to:

Jimmy Swaggart Ministries
P.O. Box 262550
Baton Rouge, LA 70826-2550

Visit our website: www.jsm.org